Lecture Notes in Computer Science 5569

Marco Bernardo Luca Padovani
Gianluigi Zavattaro (Eds.)

Formal Methods for Web Services

9th International School on Formal Methods for the Design of Computer, Communication, and Software Systems, SFM 2009
Bertinoro, Italy, June 1-6, 2009
Advanced Lectures

Springer

Volume Editors

Marco Bernardo
Università di Urbino "Carlo Bo"
Istituto di Scienze e Tecnologie dell'Informazione
Piazza della Repubblica 13, 61029 Urbino, Italy
E-mail: bernardo@sti.uniurb.it

Luca Padovani
Università di Urbino "Carlo Bo"
Istituto di Scienze e Tecnologie dell'Informazione
Piazza della Repubblica 13, 61029 Urbino, Italy
E-mail: padovani@sti.uniurb.it

Gianluigi Zavattaro
Università di Bologna
Dipartimento di Scienze dell'Informazione
Mura Anteo Zamboni 7, 40127 Bologna, Italy
E-mail: zavattar@cs.unibo.it

Library of Congress Control Number: Applied for

CR Subject Classification (1998): D.2.4, H.3.5, D.3.1, F.4, H.3.5

LNCS Sublibrary: SL 2 – Programming and Software Engineering

ISSN 0302-9743
ISBN-10 3-642-01917-X Springer Berlin Heidelberg New York
ISBN-13 978-3-642-01917-3 Springer Berlin Heidelberg New York

springer.com

Typesetting: Camera-ready by author, data conversion by Scientific Publishing Services, Chennai, India
Printed on acid-free paper SPIN: 12676064 06/3180 5 4 3 2 1 0

Preface

This volume presents the set of papers accompanying the lectures of the 9th International School on Formal Methods for the Design of Computer, Communication and Software Systems (SFM).

This series of schools addresses the use of formal methods in computer science as a prominent approach to the rigorous design of computer, communication, and software systems. The main aim of the SFM series is to offer a good spectrum of current research in foundations as well as applications of formal methods, which can be of help for graduate students and young researchers who intend to approach the field.

SFM 2009 was devoted to formal methods for Web services and covered several aspects including choreography, orchestration, description techniques, interaction, synthesis, composition, session types, contracts, verification, security, and performance.

This volume comprises eight articles. Bruni's paper overviews some of the most recently proposed abstractions in the setting of process calculi tailored to the well-disciplined handling of issues such as long-running interactions, orchestration, and unexpected events. Van der Aalst, Mooij, Stahl, and Wolf provide some foundational notions related to service interaction and address in a Petri net setting challenges like how to expose a service, how to replace and refine services, and how to generate service adapters. The paper by Marconi and Pistore presents a survey of existing approaches to the synthesis of Web service compositions, a difficult and error-prone task that requires automated solutions. Vasconcelos's paper illustrates a reconstruction of session types in a linear π-calculus where types are qualified as linear or unrestricted, together with an algorithmic type-checking system. Carbone, Yoshida, and Honda explore two extensions of session types to interactional exceptions and multiparty sessions in the presence of asynchronous communications. Padovani's paper discusses a set-theoretic semantics of contracts, which is employed for defining a family of equivalence relations that can be effectively used for discovering and adapting Web services implementing specific contracts. The paper by Bravetti and Zavattaro also focusses on contracts by following the idea of designing a service system through the description of the behavior of each of its participants and then instantiating such participants by retrieving services exposing contracts that conform to the given behaviors. Clark, Gilmore, and Tribastone introduce quantitative methods for analyzing Web services with the goal of understanding how they will perform under increased demand or when asked to serve a larger pool of service subscribers.

We believe that this book offers a comprehensive view of what has been done and what is going on worldwide in the field of formal methods for Web services. We wish to thank all the speakers and all the participants for a lively and fruitful school. We also wish to thank the entire staff of the University Residential Center of Bertinoro for the organizational and administrative support. Finally, we are very grateful to the University of Bologna, which kindly provided sponsorship for this event under the International Summer School Program.

June 2009

Marco Bernardo
Luca Padovani
Gianluigi Zavattaro

Table of Contents

Calculi for Service-Oriented Computing*

Roberto Bruni

Dipartimento di Informatica, Università di Pisa
bruni@di.unipi.it

Abstract. It is widely recognised that process calculi stay to concurrent computing as lambda-calculus stays to sequential computing; in fact, they lay abstract, rigorous foundations for the analysis of interactive, communicating systems. Nowadays, the increasing popularity of Service-Oriented Computing (SOC) challenges the quest for novel abstractions tailored to the well-disciplined handling of specific issues, like long running interactions, orchestration, and unexpected events. In fact, these features emerge neatly in most SOC applications and need to be studied as first-class aspects, whereas they would be obfuscated if dealt with by sophisticated encoding in traditional process calculi. This paper overviews some of the most recent proposals emerged in the literature, pointing out their main characteristics and presents in more detail one such proposal, called CaSPiS, by providing several examples to give evidence of its flexibility. No prior acquaintance with process calculi is assumed, indeed a gentle introduction to their basics is provided before the more advanced material be presented.

1 Introduction

Service-oriented computing has been one of the latest trend in the IT community, finding in Web Services (WS) technology its major realisation. Services are autonomous computational entities, that are developed separately, loosely coupled, globally available over a widely distributed network in a platform-independent way, and not fully reliable. Service computing consists of assembling services in well-engineered ways to form complex open-ended applications, and this must be done in a highly dynamic way, possibly on demand. To this aim, it is essential to find suitable abstractions to describe services, the so-called *service descriptors*, to be published in public registries. Such registries can be queried by other services and applications to locate those services that best match certain requirements, yielding a brokering architecture. When satisfactory matches are found, then the located services can be dynamically linked and invoked. Therefore, service engineering has to do with the development of methodologies, techniques, formal methods and tools able to guarantee a safe service composition, in the sense of being able to provide some strong guarantees on such dynamic, open-ended applications by applying some static or semi-static analysis.

WS technology has established *de facto* standards for naming schemes and service access (URI, URL), service descriptors (WSDL and BPEL in UDDI registries), communication protocols (SOAP over HTTP, TCP/IP and SMTP) and message format (XML)

* Research supported by the Project FET-GC II IST-2005-16004 Sensoria and by the Italian FIRB Project Tocai.it.

M. Bernardo, L. Padovani, and G. Zavattaro (Eds.): SFM 2009, LNCS 5569, pp. 1–41, 2009.

over the web. Existing infrastructures already enable providers to describe web services in terms of their interfaces, access policies and behaviour, and to combine simpler services into more structured and complex ones. However, some research and solid foundations are still needed to move WS technology from skilled handcrafting to an engineered practice, a step where formal methods must play a fundamental role. For example, it has been shown that the lack of unambiguous semantics of BPEL has led different BPEL engines to exhibit different behaviours under the same circumstances [43].

Research on formal methods for SOC can be roughly separated in two main strands, both equally worth the effort: one dedicated to establishing the missing theoretical foundations of state-of-the-art technologies, so to fix rigorous semantic and logic frameworks for the analysis and verification of SOC and WS systems; another one aimed to rethink the design and development of next generation technology, by understanding the key distinguishing features of SOC, assessing the necessary bits of theory for them in technology agnostic terms, and paving the way to their well-disciplined engineering. In both cases, the mathematical models and tools from the literature that seem to be particularly suited are those coming from concurrency theory, ranging from workflow like models like Petri nets, to Graph Transformation systems and process calculi.

As suggested by the title of this contribution, we shall focus on the use of process calculi for modelling SOC systems. This choice is motivated by the more natural way in which process calculi can accommodate for SOC features such as open-endedness, dynamicity, compositionality, interaction and event handling w.r.t. the other afore mentioned models. Moreover, we shall favour the second strand of research outlined above, trying to distill some key aspects of SOC together with a small set of primitives associated with them and to expose some of the main causes (motivation) and consequences (benefits) of our approach.

Due to the particular nature of this volume, which contains the proceedings of a summer school, and the audience to which this paper is oriented, which for the most we assume to consist of young computer science researchers, we have decided to structure this paper as a tutorial, so that no prior acquaintance with process calculi is assumed on the reader. Being worried that the more expert readers can find some arguments of our survey not dealt with at the sufficient levels of details for their taste, we added, whenever necessary, suitable links to the more advanced papers and texts where the technicalities are exposed in their full glory. Furthermore, we have put some efforts in trying to accompany each calculus by original examples and modelling puzzles in the hope they will provide an enjoyable reading experience by themselves, possibly reusable as course material.

1.1 What You Will Not Find Here

The level of abstraction at which we intend to model SOC systems disregards the technologies and the implementation details, hence we are to some extent disconnected from current WS standards. More precisely, we disregards those aspects related to the so-called semantic web, like ontologies for classifying services, XML coding and standardisation issues. In fact these aspects can be superimposed later, on the concrete realisation of our techniques.

For analogous reasons, we are not concerned with the exact ways in which services and their descriptors are made public available, queried and located, even if some of these issues can be reasonably encoded in the same formalisms we shall present. Instead we handle service publication, discovery and linking in terms of name-handling á la pi-calculus, i.e. the scope of certain service names can be restricted, new services can be dynamically deployed and updated, their names can be communicated and extruded to enlarge their scope, etc.

Moreover, we abstract away from non-functional aspects (like Quality of Service and Service Level Agreement) and quantitative analysis, which also constitute themselves an active area of research. On the other hand, some preliminary ideas in this field have already led to process calculi extensions that are compatible with the proposals discussed here and we give relevant pointers to the related literature.

We also deliberately omit the exact formulation of many useful theorems (and any proof sketch) from the literature, which we try to replace by more intuitive descriptions of their underlying properties and consequences, at the informal level.

1.2 Aspects of Interest

The common trait of all issues we aim to encompass here is the handy, disciplined composition of services. This includes: the possibility to extract service descriptors that carry some behavioural information rather than mere syntactic information as those found in WSDL documents; the possibility to carry long-running conversation between the service caller and its callee, which are far more general than limited one-way and request-response patterns of WS; suitable techniques for checking the behavioural conformance of the service to be invoked w.r.t. the application requirements; the way in which service invocations and their outcomes can be orchestrated; the way in which the system can foresee at the design time the actions to undergo in case some unexpected event will happen during a conversation, like a peer abandoning a business transaction. More precisely, we briefly discuss below different alternatives proposed in the literature on the above topics, and outline our preferred design choices.

Orchestration and choreography: The terms *orchestration* and *choreography* were coined to describe two different flavours of service compositions: orchestration is about describing and executing a single view point model, while choreography is about specifying and guiding a global model. Though the difference between the two terms can be sometimes abused or blurred, substantially orchestration is usually associated with an executable flavour, for which a centralised orchestration engine is responsible (although distributed engines can be also considered), as opposed to the fully distributed vision of choreography, usually associated with some sort of protocol narration. Roughly, from a formal modelling viewpoint, orchestration is mainly concerned with governing the control and data flow between services, while choreography is concerned with interaction protocols between single and composite autonomous services. Our presentation shall privilege orchestration, but out approach is compatible with the choreography perspective, as the type systems defined to check the conformance of services w.r.t. the requirements of the invoker share some similarities with the use of so-called *contracts* to express choreographies.

Interaction: Process calculi can exploit different forms of interactions, ranging from shared data-space, to event-based (subscribe-notify), and message passing. We shall rely on synchronous message passing, that is best suited for the level of abstraction of this tutorial.

Sessions and correlation sets: When long-running conversation with services are established, different instances of the same service can be running concurrently to serve different requests. Therefore it is important to route interaction between the correct pairs, avoiding any interference. Web service standards exploit the idea of *correlation sets*, i.e., pre-defined subsets of the invocation parameters that are used each time to choose the corresponding service instance (e.g., requests are routed according to usernames). Though correlation sets offer a good expressiveness, we argue that they might complicate static analysis, because all interactions rely on data values. For example, applications can interfere with each other if they know (or use by chance) the right values. A different school of thought advocates the notion of a *session* as a more convenient abstraction mechanism for enclosing arbitrarily complex interactions between peers. Session keys are data-independent and can be created implicitly when the service is first invoked. This way, type systems can be more easily developed to check properties like the presence of exactly one peer. Session can come in different flavours: nested, interleaved, with delegation, used recursively, dyadic, multy-party, mergeable, closeable, permeable, etc. We shall focus on primitives for a well-disciplined use of nested, dyadic and closeable sessions.

Compensations and session handlers: Each service has full autonomy in denying a request or abandoning a pending interaction. It is then important to rely on standard mechanisms for programming such decisions and to handle their consequences in a *safe* way. For example, the classical travel agency scenario may involve a complex interaction between the customer and the travel agent, to let the service learn the customer preferences, let the customer select one among available packages, confirm or cancel the choice, and the service may need to invoke third-party services to get, say, up-to-date flight or hotel information. By *safe*, we mean that, in principle, the involved parties should always be able either to complete the interaction or to recover from errors that prevent its completion, like when a time-out expires or when one of the third-party services unexpectedly abandon the conversation because its server is overloaded. In the area of transactions, compensation mechanisms have to do with the programming of suitable counter-actions that are installed after a certain activity has been executed to compensate for its effects in case the rest of the interaction cannot be completed successfully. Of course, it is often the case that the previous actions cannot be simply undone (e.g., a sent message cannot disappear, booking cancellation can require some fees) hence full recovery is simply not possible. In the case of sessions, we shall consider a simple built-in mechanism for the graceful closure of nested sessions upon the abandon of a peer.

The outcome of the above consideration language was a new calculus, called CaSPiS (*Calculus of Sessions and Pipelines*) [8], which is the main objective of this tutorial.

1.3 Related Work

CaSPiS has been developed inside the SENSORIA project [57], as part of a larger research effort aimed to develop *core calculi for SOC* at three different levels of abstraction: (i) the service middleware level (close to current networking technologies to be directly implementable, but sufficiently expressive to support service oriented applications), (ii) the service description level (favouring more abstract formalisation of basic concepts such as service definition, invocation, instantiation, and communication), and (iii) the service composition level (with mechanisms for the modelling and analysis of qualitative and quantitative aspects of multiparty service compositions).

At the middleware level we find, e.g., the *signal calculus* (SC) [28]: it is based on a flexible and dynamical reconfigurable network of components communicating via the publish-subscribe message delivery paradigm. Sessions and message correlation are supported through a type system [29]. This calculus revealed easily implementable (in terms of a Java library) as well as expressive enough to support a high-level graphical programming environment.

At the service composition level we find, e.g., λreq [3] and *concurrent constraint pi-calculus* (cc-pi) [16]. The former has been exploited to support the development of techniques for the analysis of service compositions (such as statical analysis of the access to protected resources) within the so-called "call-by-contract" paradigm, while the latter integrates name handling features with constraint semirings to deal more effectively with quantitative aspects of negotiations (such as the so-called service level agreement).

CaSPiS lies at the service description level, where several other interesting proposals are also present, which can roughly be divided in two families: correlation-based and session-based.

The first group comprises COWS [42] (based on message-passing and stateless components) and SOCK [17] (based on shared data spaces and stateful components). The former can be seen as an extension of the pi-calculus with correlation-based communication mechanism and primitives for activity cancellation and preservation, while the latter is closer to WS standards like BPEL and it includes an explicit modelling of processes obtained as service instantiations, process memory, etc..

The second group comprises the so-called SCC-family of calculi [7, 8, 12, 20, 39], spawned by a first proposal of a basic calculus with nested session, the *Service Centred Calculus* SCC, later enriched and refined with different mechanisms for inter-session communication, like *data streaming* [39], *context-sensitive message passing* [20], *locations* and *dynamic multiparty sessions* [12], and *pipelines* [8].

While the above calculi are closer to the orchestration perspective, the *global calculus* [21] is closer to the choreography perspective and allows for static multiparty sessions, where session identifiers are modelled just as pi-calculus channel names (freshly created and distributed to participants during the initialisation phase of the service protocol). In [6] multiparty sessions are considered, but they are required to include one master endpoint and one or more slave endpoints, and direct communication is allowed only between the master and any slave.

It is important to remark that communication mechanisms are somehow orthogonal to sessions. In fact, while CCS-like communication [46] is the obvious choice when only two-party sessions are considered, in the presence of multiparty sessions a more natural and more sophisticated alternative would be some variant of multicast (like broadcast [27] or CSP-like interaction [33], or even some combination of different policies [11]).

Behavioural type systems can also play a crucial measure for evaluating the various proposals, because they offer a mean to establish the compatibility of peers [1, 6, 15, 21, 26, 30, 34, 35, 36, 39, 44]. In this sense, it is interesting to relate behavioural types and the language independent approach based on contracts [9, 22] along the ideas in [40]. More generally, there are some interesting analogies between the way in which behavioural types resemble orchestration mechanisms and contracts resemble choreography descriptions.

1.4 Structure of the Paper

Section 2 gives some background on the basics mathematical ingredients of process calculi, like labelled transition systems, operational semantics, structural congruence, reduction systems, bisimilarity equivalences. We illustrate such concepts by simple and detailed presentation of the main sources of inspiration for CaSPiS. Step by step, we go from the basic interaction primitives of CCS, to the more advanced name handling features of the pi-calculus, to the use of explicit sessions and to the orchestration primitives of Orc. Section 3 introduces the main principles of CaSPiS, its syntax and reduction semantics and some modelling examples. Section 4 relates CaSPiS with other well-known formalisms by presenting several intuitive encoding. Some concluding remarks are in Section 5.

2 Setting the Context on Interactive and Orchestrated Systems

2.1 CCS, Labelled Transition Systems and SOS Rules

An elementary *action* of a system represents the atomic (i.e., that cannot be interrupted at the given level of granularity) abstract step of a computation that is performed by a system to move from one state to the other.

Ordinary computational models like Turing machines, register machines, several kinds of automata, the lambda-calculus and many imperative programming languages all rely on basic activities like reading from or writing on some kind of (passive) storage device or invoking a procedure with actual parameters.

Milner's *Calculus of Communicating Systems* [46] (CCS) introduced a model whose basic activities rely on some sort of handshake between two autonomous *processes*. Hence, in the case of concurrent systems, actions represent activities such as sending a message and receiving a message, exposing some alternatives and picking one alternative, producing a resource and consuming a resource, etc. On the one hand, when studying one process in separation from the others it is important to observe the kind of handshake it is willing to perform with other processes. On the other hand, when an handshake is performed between two entities, it constitutes a special *silent* action that has no further interaction capability.

To convince yourself about the ease of CCS in modelling concurrent systems and communication protocols, try writing down the solution to the puzzle below, adapted from [54], using first your favourite formalism, and then, after having learnt CCS basics, using CCS processes for modelling the various interacting entities (the light, the special room, and the strategies followed by humans). We shall show later some bits of the solution for the case where the light is initially on.

Exercise 1. 50 young, bright computer scientists are kept in Bertinoro until all exams will be completed, each locked in her/his own room. Their chance to be released is as follows: from time to time, one of them will be carried in a special room (in no particular order, possibly multiple times consecutively, but with a fair schedule to avoid infinite wait) and then back to her/his room. The special room is completely empty except for a switch that can turn the light either on or off (the light is not visible from outside and cannot be broken). At any time, if one of them truthfully asserts that all of them have already entered the special room at least once, then they all pass the exam and are released, but if she/he is wrong, then the chance ends and they will never pass the exam. Before the challenge starts, they have the possibility to discuss together some "protocol" to follow. Can you find a winning strategy when the initial state of the light in the room is known? And if it is not?

In CCS, we assume given a set A of activities, ranged by a, and let $\overline{A} \triangleq \{ \overline{a} \mid a \in A \}$ be the set of co-activities (disjoint from A), with $\overline{\overline{a}} = a$. The set of CCS *labels* is $\mathcal{L} \triangleq A \cup \overline{A}$, ranged by λ, and the set of CCS *actions* is $\mathrm{Act} \triangleq \mathcal{L} \cup \{ \tau \}$, ranged by α, where τ is the special *silent action*. Then, a CCS *processes* P is composed via a number of primitives, that we sketch below in an incremental way. Though the syntax may slightly vary in the literature, we let CCS processes generated by the grammar:

$$P \quad ::= \quad \textstyle\sum_{i \in I} \alpha_i.P_i \quad | \quad P[\phi] \quad | \quad P_1 | P_2 \quad | \quad (\nu a)P \quad | \quad X \quad | \quad \mathrm{rec}X.P$$

The meaning of each such process is given by a suitable *Labelled Transition System* (LTS) defined by structural induction on the syntax of the process, following Plotkin's *Structural Operational Semantics* (SOS) scheme [51, 52, 53].

We recall that an LTS $T = (S, L, \rightarrow)$ consists of: a set S of *states*, a set L of *labels*, and a *transition relation* $\rightarrow \subseteq S \times L \times S$. Sometimes a distinguished initial state $s_0 \in S$ is also considered. As usual, we shall write $s \xrightarrow{\lambda} s'$ instead of $(s, \lambda, s') \in \rightarrow$, with the meaning that there is a transition leading from state s to state s' and exposing label λ. The label gives some abstract information about the nature of the evolution. For a given label λ we denote by $\xrightarrow{\lambda}$ the binary relation $\{ (s, s') \mid s \xrightarrow{\lambda} s' \} \subseteq S \times S$.

Formally, in the case of CCS, the states of the LTS are CCS processes, the set of labels is Act, and the transition relation is the least one satisfying all SOS inference rules. When a particular process P is considered, then the initial state s_0 of its LTS is P itself and the LTS can be restricted just to the states reachable from P (after any number of transitions). The elegance of SOS relies on the fact that few inference rules define the LTS of any process that can ever be specified. Moreover, SOS rules allow for proofs by structural induction, where the interaction of complex systems is defined in terms of (the behaviour of) their components and proofs by rule induction, where a property can be proved to hold true for the whole LTS if whenever it holds for the premises of each rule, it holds also for the conclusions.

The simplest process is the *inactive* process, written $\mathbf{0}$ and called *nil*: it is not capable of performing any action. Trailing $\mathbf{0}$s are often omitted. No inference rule is needed for $\mathbf{0}$. *Action prefix*, written $\alpha.P$, prefixes a process P by an action α: the process $\alpha.P$ can perform α and then behave as P. The inference rule for action prefix is the axiom:

$$(\text{ACT})\ \frac{}{\alpha.P \xrightarrow{\alpha} P}$$

Non-deterministic choice, written $P_1 + P_2$, composes two processes in mutual exclusion: process $P_1 + P_2$ can behave as either P_1 or P_2. The inference rules for choice are:

$$(\text{LSUM})\ \frac{P_1 \xrightarrow{\alpha} P_1'}{P_1 + P_2 \xrightarrow{\alpha} P_1'} \qquad (\text{RSUM})\ \frac{P_2 \xrightarrow{\alpha} P_2'}{P_1 + P_2 \xrightarrow{\alpha} P_2'}$$

Sometimes *guarded summation* $\sum_{i\in I} \alpha_i.P_i$ is preferred to choice, prefix (single sum) and nil (empty sum). The corresponding inference rule is:

$$(\text{ACT})\ \frac{j \in I}{\sum_{i\in I} \alpha_i.P_i \xrightarrow{\alpha_j} P_j}$$

Renaming, written $P[\phi]$, renames any action α performed by P to $\phi(\alpha)$, where $\phi : \text{Act} \to \text{Act}$ is any renaming function such that $\phi(\overline{\lambda}) = \overline{\phi(\lambda)}$ and $\phi(\tau) = \tau$. The corresponding inference rule is:

$$(\text{REN})\ \frac{P \xrightarrow{a} P'}{P[\phi] \xrightarrow{\phi(a)} P'[\phi]}$$

Parallel composition, written $P_1 | P_2$, composes two processes in parallel: P_1 and P_2 evolve autonomously by interleaving their actions, but with the possibility to handshake on complementary actions, in which case $P_1 | P_2$ performs a τ action. The corresponding inference rules are:

$$(\text{LPAR})\ \frac{P_1 \xrightarrow{\alpha} P_1'}{P_1 | P_2 \xrightarrow{\alpha} P_1' | P_2} \qquad (\text{RPAR})\ \frac{P_2 \xrightarrow{\alpha} P_2'}{P_1 | P_2 \xrightarrow{\alpha} P_1 | P_2'} \qquad (\text{COMM})\ \frac{P_1 \xrightarrow{\lambda} P_1' \quad P_2 \xrightarrow{\overline{\lambda}} P_2'}{P_1 | P_2 \xrightarrow{\tau} P_1' | P_2'}$$

Restriction, usually written $P\backslash a$, but here written in pi-calculus style as $(\nu a)P$, restricts the scope of activity a to process P: the process $(\nu a)P$ is allowed to perform neither action a nor $\overline{a}$; however, if P comprises two parallel processes P_1 and P_2 that can perform a and $\overline{a}$, respectively, then they can still handshake on a "under" the restriction. As usual, we abbreviate $(\nu a_1)(\nu a_2)P$ by $(\nu a_1, a_2)P$ (and similarly for three or more consecutive restrictions). The corresponding inference rule is:

$$(\text{RES})\ \frac{P \xrightarrow{\alpha} P' \quad \alpha \notin \{a, \overline{a}\}}{(\nu a)P \xrightarrow{\alpha} (\nu a)P'}$$

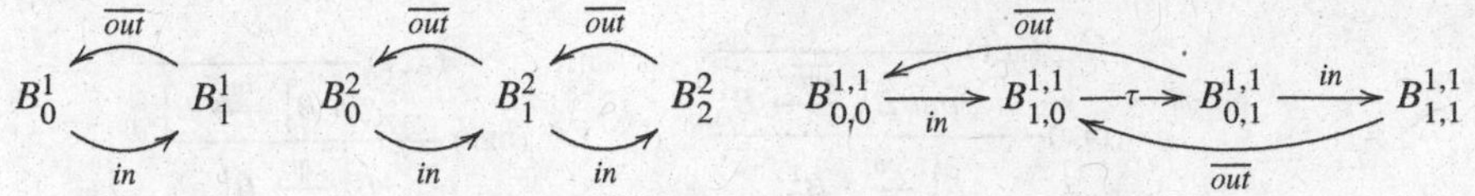

(a) LTS for B^1_0 (b) LTS for B^2_0 (c) LTS for $B^{1,1}_{0,0}$

Fig. 1. Labelled transition systems associated with some simple buffers

It should be obvious that the above operators can define only finite behaviours. There are several ways to introduce some form of interation and recursion. *Replication*, written $!P$ or also $*P$ accounts for making an unlimited number of copies of P available. Sometimes it is restricted to some guarded form, like $!\alpha.P$ or $!\sum_{i\in I}\alpha_i.P_i$. The usual inference rule for replication is:

$$(\textsc{Rep})\ \frac{P\,|\,!P \xrightarrow{\alpha} P'}{!P \xrightarrow{\alpha} P'}$$

However, (Rep) has a couple of drawbacks: 1) it makes the transition relation not *image-finite*, i.e. there are processes P that can reach infinitely many syntactically different processes by performing the same action α, 2) it disallows proofs by structural induction, which is maybe a minor issue. If needed, rule (Rep) can be safely replaced by the following two rules, that account for the possibility of one copy of P to evolve alone, or for two copies of P to handshake:

$$(\textsc{Rep}1)\ \frac{P \xrightarrow{\alpha} P'}{!P \xrightarrow{\alpha} P'\,|\,!P} \qquad (\textsc{Rep}2)\ \frac{P \xrightarrow{\lambda} P_1 \quad P \xrightarrow{\overline{\lambda}} P_2}{!P \xrightarrow{\alpha} P_1|P_2|\,!P}$$

A more flexible alternative to replication is given by the *recursion operator* $\mathrm{rec}\,X.P$, where X can appear as a process variable in P. The corresponding rule is:

$$(\textsc{Rec})\ \frac{P\{^{\mathrm{rec}\,X.P}/_X\} \xrightarrow{\alpha} P'}{\mathrm{rec}\,X.P \xrightarrow{\alpha} P'}$$

where $\{^t/_x\}$ stands for the substitution of x by t. Alternatively, one can assume a set of *mutually recursive definitions* $\Delta = \{\, A_i \triangleq P_i \,\}_i$ is available, that defines suitable constants A_i. The corresponding rule is:

$$(\textsc{Def})\ \frac{A_i \triangleq P_i \in \Delta \quad P_i \xrightarrow{\alpha} P'}{A_i \xrightarrow{\alpha} P'}$$

To acquire some confidence with the notation, let us consider a classical and simple example from CCS textbooks, namely the modelling of buffers with limited capacities.

Example 1. A process B^n modelling an initially empty buffer of capacity n can be defined by letting:

$$\begin{aligned}
B^n_0 &\triangleq in.B^n_1 \\
B^n_i &\triangleq in.B^n_{i+1} + \overline{out}.B^n_{i-1} \qquad (0 < i < n) \\
B^n_n &\triangleq \overline{out}.B^n_{n-1}
\end{aligned}$$

$$
\dfrac{\dfrac{\dfrac{\dfrac{}{\overline{out}.B^1_0 \xrightarrow{\overline{out}} B^1_0}\,(\text{ACT})}{B^1_1 \xrightarrow{\overline{out}} B^1_0}\,(\text{DEF})}{B^1_1[\phi_1] \xrightarrow{\overline{a}} B^1_0[\phi_1]}\,(\text{REN}) \quad \dfrac{\dfrac{\dfrac{}{in.B^1_1 \xrightarrow{in} B^1_1}\,(\text{ACT})}{B^1_0 \xrightarrow{in} B^1_1}\,(\text{DEF})}{B^1_0[\phi_2] \xrightarrow{a} B^1_1[\phi_2]}\,(\text{REN})}{\dfrac{B^1_1[\phi_1]|B^1_0[\phi_2] \xrightarrow{\tau} B^1_0[\phi_1]|B^1_1[\phi_2]}{(\nu a)\big(\,B^1_1[\phi_1]|B^1_0[\phi_2]\,\big) \xrightarrow{\tau} (\nu a)\big(\,B^1_0[\phi_1]|B^1_1[\phi_2]\,\big)}\,(\text{RES})}\,(\text{COMM})
$$

Fig. 2. Proof of transition $B^{1,1}_{1,0} \xrightarrow{\tau} B^{1,1}_{0,1}$

taking $B^n \triangleq B^n_0$. The LTS for B^1 is in Fig. 1(a) and for B^2 in Fig. 1(b). A process P put in parallel with B^n can handshake by performing actions in and $\overline{out}$. If renaming ϕ_1 maps out to a and renaming ϕ_2 maps in to a, then two buffers B^1_0 could be composed in series by writing the process $(\nu a)\big(\,B^1[\phi_1]|B^1[\phi_2]\,\big)$. The corresponding LTS is illustrated in Fig. 1(c), where we write $B^{n,k}_{i,j} = (\nu a)\big(\,B^n_i[\phi_1]|B^k_j[\phi_2]\,\big)$ for brevity. Figure 2 shows the proof of transition $B^{1,1}_{1,0} \xrightarrow{\tau} B^{1,1}_{0,1}$.

Exercise 2. Draw the LTS for the processes $B^1\,|\,B^1$ and $B^{2,2}_{0,0}$.

Coming back to the puzzle from Exercise 1, the light could be modelled as a buffer of capacity one, where action *in* corresponds to "switch the light off" (it is initially on) and action *out* to "switch the light off". Then the scientists could agree to use the light as a counter: 49 of them will switch the light on only the first time they enter the room and find it off, while one distinguished scientist will count the number of times that she/he finds the light on (and will switch it off). Since the light is initially on, the count can start only after the distinguished scientist has switched the light off for the first time. A first solution is therefore:

$$
\begin{aligned}
Bertinoro &\triangleq (\nu\, swOff, swOn)(\, LightON|C_0|S|\cdots|S\,)\\
LightON &\triangleq swOff.LightOFF\\
LightOFF &\triangleq swOn.LightON\\
C_i &\triangleq \overline{swOff}.C_{i+1} + \overline{swOn}.\overline{swOff}.C_i \quad (0 \le i < 50)\\
C_{50} &\triangleq \overline{freeAll}.\mathbf{0}\\
S &\triangleq \overline{swOn}.\mathbf{0} + \overline{swOff}.\overline{swOn}.S
\end{aligned}
$$

where C_0 models the counting scientist and S any other scientist. Note that a scientist can wish to perform two consecutive interactions with the light just to leave its state unchanged. Unfortunately, this way there is no guarantee that consecutive interactions like $\overline{swOff}.\overline{swOn}$ are executed atomically, therefore it is better to modify the protocols in order to constrain the scientists to access the light in mutual exclusion. This can be done by modelling the special room as a one-capacity buffer, where action *in* corresponds to "enter the room" and action *out* to "leave the room": only after the room has been entered it is possible to interact with the light. To make the model more faithful, we also introduce the process for representing a "waiting scientist", i.e. a scientist who does not need to interact any more with the light but can keep entering and leaving the room.

$$
\begin{aligned}
\mathit{Bertinoro} &\triangleq (\nu\, in, out, swOff, swOn)(\,\mathit{Room} \,|\, \mathit{LightON} \,|\, C_0 \,|\, S \,|\, \cdots \,|\, S\,) \\
\mathit{Room} &\triangleq B^1 \\
\mathit{LightON} &\triangleq swOff.\mathit{LightOFF} \\
\mathit{LightOFF} &\triangleq swOn.\mathit{LightON} \\
C_i &\triangleq \overline{in}.\big(\overline{swOff}.out.C_{i+1} + \overline{swOn}.\overline{swOff}.out.C_i\big) \quad (0 \le i < 50) \\
C_{50} &\triangleq \overline{freeAll}.\mathbf{0} \\
S &\triangleq \overline{in}.\big(\overline{swOn}.out.WS + \overline{swOff}.\overline{swOn}.out.S\,\big) \\
WS &\triangleq \overline{in}.\tau.out.WS
\end{aligned}
$$

We leave to the reader finding a solution for the case where the initial state of the light is not known in advance, e.g. when the light is modelled as the process $\tau.\mathit{LightON} + \tau.\mathit{LightOFF}$.

A vast literature on CCS has established different criteria for when two processes should be considered as "equivalent". Without entering into the details, we mention two of the most widely used notion of equivalence, namely *strong bisimilarity* and *weak bisimilarity*. Contrary to trace equivalence, bisimilarities can take into account the branching structure of the transition systems, i.e. the points where choices are made. We refer the interested reader to [31, 32] for a wider range of options.

Definition 1 (Strong Bisimilarity). *A binary relation $\mathcal{R}$ over processes is a* strong bisimulation *iff whenever $(P,Q) \in \mathcal{R}$ then for each $\alpha \in$* Act*:*

- *if $P \xrightarrow{\alpha} P'$ then $Q \xrightarrow{\alpha} Q'$ for some Q' such that $(P',Q') \in \mathcal{R}$*
- *if $Q \xrightarrow{\alpha} Q'$ then $P \xrightarrow{\alpha} P'$ for some P' such that $(P',Q') \in \mathcal{R}$.*

Two processes P and Q are strongly bisimilar, *written $P \sim Q$, iff there exists a strong bisimulation $\mathcal{R}$ such that $(P,Q) \in \mathcal{R}$, i.e. $\sim \triangleq \bigcup\{\,\mathcal{R} \mid \mathcal{R}$ is a strong bisimulation$\,\}$.*

Strong bisimilarity is an equivalence relation and it is a congruence w.r.t. all CCS operators, meaning that if we replace any subterm $P'$of P with a strongly bisimilar term Q' then the result is guaranteed to be strongly bisimilar to P. Notably, $\sim$ admits a logical characterisation in terms of Hennessy-Milner logic, a modal logic of actions for the analysis and verification of reactive systems [2].

Exercise 3. Prove that $B^2 \sim B^1 \,|\, B^1$ and $B^2 \nsim B^{1,1}_{0,0}$.

Strong bisimilarity is coarser than LTS isomorphism, but it still distinguishes too many processes that have essentially the same behaviour. In particular, it is often the case that some additional silent transitions may arise or not depending on different attitudes to modelling the same system. Weak bisimilarity, denoted by $\approx$, relaxes the notion of strong equivalence by allowing to simulate a move also performing additional silent transitions beforehand and afterwards: roughly, letting $\rightarrow^*$ denote the reflexive and transitive closure of $\xrightarrow{\tau}$ (i.e. $\rightarrow^*$ is the relation such that $P \rightarrow^* P'$ iff P' is reachable from P via any number of consecutive silent transitions, possibly none), in the weak case a step $P \xrightarrow{\lambda} P'$ can be simulated via a sequence of steps $Q \rightarrow^* \xrightarrow{\lambda} \rightarrow^* Q'$ and silent transitions $P \xrightarrow{\tau} P'$ can be simulated via a possible empty sequence of silent steps $Q \rightarrow^* Q'$. For example, $B^2 \approx B^{1,1}_{0,0}$. Weak bisimilarity is an equivalence relation that includes strong bisimilarity (in the sense that $P \sim Q$ implies $P \approx Q$ for any processes P and Q), but it is not a congruence (because it is not preserved by the choice operator).

2.2 Pi-Calculus, Structural Congruence and Reduction Semantics

CCS is Turing powerful, and it can be used at several level of analysis, as a specification language, as a programming language, as a description language, as a type language, etc. However, when one wants to model interactive systems with dynamic changes in connectivity, or networks where processes can move between physical or virtual locations, then the representation distance is quite increased and the modelling activity can become cumbersome.

Milner, Parrow and Walker's *Calculus of Mobile Processes* [48, 49, 56] (i.e., the π-calculus or also pi-calculus) introduces a key ingredient: the possibility to communicate channel names. This way, a process can acquire new communication links, pass its own private channels to other processes, create fresh channels, and much more. Even if the required extension to CCS syntax is to some extent minimal, it opened a still flourishing research thread. Nowadays, there are many variants of π-calculus (monadic, polyadic, synchronous, asynchronous, with mixed choice, higher-order, to name a few) each with a consolidated theory on its own. To appreciate the key difference w.r.t. CCS, let us consider the following puzzle, adapted from [24].

Exercise 4. 100 young, bright computer scientists are kept awake in Bertinoro until all exams will be completed. Their chance to have some sleep is as follows: first each of them is assigned a different id from 1 to 100 and a different room (assume rooms are also numbered from 1 to 100); then the ids are randomly distributed one per room; each scientist is given the possibility to open 50 rooms of her/his choice and look at the ids contained there; if all scientists are able to find their own id, then they are all given access to the rooms, otherwise (even if only one of them is not able to find her/his own id) they will not be able to sleep until all exams have been given. Each scientist is not allowed to look at the ids found in the rooms by her/his colleagues, and they are not allowed to speak to each other once the procedure is started. Before the challenge starts, they have the possibility to discuss together some "protocol" to follow. Can you find an optimal strategy to let them have some sleep with highest probability?

The best possible strategy leaves almost 1/3 of probability to get some sleep. It is based on a simple protocol, equal for all participants: the first room opened by scientist with id i must be room i; at each stage, if an id k different from her/his own is found in a room, then the next room to be opened is room k. The idea is that rooms and the id they contain define a set of permutation cycles: the strategy is "winning" iff all such cycles have length less than or equal to 50. As there can be at most one cycle of length greater than 50, the probability to win coincides with the probability that such a long cycle is not present. If modelled in CCS, the protocol should consider 100 different continuations for each room, one for each possible id contained therein. Using pi-calculus instead, the next room to open can be just communicated.

From the point of view of the syntax, the only primitives to be changed are action prefixes. In the following we assume an infinite set of names $\mathcal{N}$, ranged by x, y, z, is available. The action prefixes of the pi-calculus represents either the sending $\overline{x}\langle y \rangle$ of a name y along x, or the receiving $x(y)$ of a name y along x, or the silent action τ. Sometimes the matching prefixes $[x = y]$ and mismatching $[x \neq y]$ are also considered: they represent ordinary test for equality and inequality of names, and can be used to follow different alternatives depending on the received names. The use of mismatch prefixes is discouraged because their presence can violate useful monotonicity properties of processes, like the fact that name-substitution does not decrease action capabilities of a process.

Unfortunately, the inference rules of CCS cannot be smoothly extended to pi-calculus and some additional care and machinery is needed. To see why, consider the straight extensions of inference rules for action prefixes, where in the case of input one simply guesses the name z that will be received:

$$(\text{INP})\ \frac{}{x(y).P \xrightarrow{xz} P\{^z/_y\}} \qquad (\text{OUT})\ \frac{}{\overline{x}\langle z \rangle.P \xrightarrow{\overline{xz}} P}$$

Now we should decide which actions should be forbidden under restriction. Take the process $(\nu n)P$ and suppose $P \xrightarrow{xz} P'$:

- if $n \notin \{ x, z \}$ then we can let $(\nu n)P \xrightarrow{xz} (\nu n)P'$;
- if $n = x$ then we must forbid the move;
- if $n = z \neq x$ then we must forbid the move, because n is a private name that cannot be received from the outside.

Now suppose $P \xrightarrow{\overline{xz}} P'$:

- if $n \notin \{ x, z \}$ then we can let $(\nu n)P \xrightarrow{\overline{xz}} (\nu n)P'$;
- if $n = x$ then we must forbid the move;
- if $n = z \neq x$ then what? If we forbid the move, then private names cannot be extruded to other processes, which would be a severe limitation. If we allow the move, then we would like to extrude the scope of n only to the processes that handshake on $\overline{xn}$, hence we should have $(\nu n)P \xrightarrow{\overline{xz}} P'$, where the restriction disappears from the target. On the other hand, when handshake is accomplished, we would like to restore the restriction.

The so-called *early operational semantics* solves the problem by introducing different labels for the free output $\overline{x}z$ and the bound output $\overline{x}(z)$ (where the name z is extruded). This in turn have several consequences on the rules for parallel composition: some side conditions are needed in order to avoid that an extruded name captures a free name of a process running in parallel, and two kinds of handshakes are possible, depending on the kind of output that is considered: the handshake between actions xz and

$$\begin{array}{llll} S+\mathbf{0}\equiv S & S_1+S_2\equiv S_2+S_1 & S_1+(S_2+S_3)\equiv(S_1+S_2)+S_3 & [a=a]\pi.P\equiv\pi.P \\ P|\mathbf{0}\equiv P & P_1|P_2\equiv P_2|P_1 & P_1|(P_2|P_3)\equiv(P_1|P_2)|P_3 & P\equiv P\,|\,!P \\ (\nu a)\mathbf{0}\equiv\mathbf{0} & (\nu a)(\nu b)P\equiv(\nu b)(\nu a)P & P\,|\,(\nu a)Q\equiv(\nu a)(P\,|\,Q)\ \text{ if } a\notin \mathrm{fn}(P) & \end{array}$$

Fig. 3. Structural congruence laws for the pi-calculus

$\overline{x}z$ is the ordinary one (as in CCS); the handshake between actions xz and $\overline{x}(z)$ move the restriction (νz) on top of the parallel composition. In general, it emerges the necessity to take into account which are the free names of a process (denoted by fn(P)) and which are its bound names (denoted by bn(P)). In the case of pi-calculus, the only binders are input prefix and restriction, i.e. in both $x(y).P$ and $(\nu y)P$ the name y is bound and its scope is restricted to P. There are further consequences also on the definition of strong bisimilarity, when the actions to be simulated depend on the free names of a process. These caveats make the formal presentation of pi-calculus semantics more complicated and less intuitive than CCS one, when encountered for the first time.

For the above reasons, a different style of presentation is sometimes preferred for pi-calculus (and for many other calculi with name-handling features). It has two main ingredients: a *structural congruence* relation, used to write processes in some canonical form, easier to manipulate; a *reduction* relation that represents only completed interactions, roughly the τ moves.

Let us consider the following syntax for pi-calculus processes:

$$\begin{array}{rlll} \text{(Processes)} & P & ::= & S \;\mid\; P_1|P_2 \;\mid\; (\nu x)P \;\mid\; !P \\ \text{(Sums)} & S & ::= & \mathbf{0} \;\mid\; \pi.P \;\mid\; S_1+S_2 \\ \text{(Prefixes)} & \pi & ::= & \overline{x}\langle y\rangle \;\mid\; x(y) \;\mid\; \tau \;\mid\; [x=y]\pi \end{array}$$

The structural congruence $\equiv$ of pi-calculus is the least congruence relation that satisfies the equalities in Fig. 3 plus alpha-conversion of bound names.[1] The structural congruence allows one to rearrange the syntax of processes so that any two possible interacting entities can be put side by side (in parallel composition). Note in particular that: the order in which we compose processes in sums should not matter; the order in which we compose processes in parallel should not matter; the order in which we restrict names should not matter. Moreover, the scope extrusion law (the rightmost equality in the bottom row of Fig. 3) can broaden the scope of a restricted name before it is communicated. It is not difficult to see that each π-calculus process P can be put in a canonical form like $P \equiv (\nu x_1)...(\nu x_k)(S_1|...|S_n|!P_1|...|!P_m)$ for some suitable names $x_1,...,x_k$, sums $S_1,...,S_n$, and processes $P_1,...,P_m$ in canonical forms. Thus, all interactions can now be expressed by considering only a small number of reductions over canonical forms. Essentially there are two rules for basic reductions:

$$\text{(RTAU)}\ \frac{}{\tau.P+S \xrightarrow{\tau} P} \qquad \text{(RCOM)}\ \frac{}{(x(y).P_1+S_1)|(\overline{x}\langle z\rangle.P_2+S_2) \xrightarrow{\tau} P_1\{^z/_y\}|P_2}$$

[1] The laws for alpha-conversion allow for the arbitrary renaming of bound names, but avoiding clashes with free names. In the case of pi-calculus, alpha-conversion means that for any process P and any names x,y,z with $z \notin \mathrm{fn}(P)$ we have $x(y).P \equiv x(z).(P\{^z/_y\})$ and $(\nu y).P \equiv (\nu z)(P\{^z/_y\})$.

plus two rules for the so-called reactive contexts (restriction and parallel composition):

$$(\text{RPAR})\ \frac{P_1 \xrightarrow{\tau} P_1'}{P_1 \,|\, P_2 \xrightarrow{\tau} P_1' \,|\, P_2} \qquad (\text{RRES})\ \frac{P \xrightarrow{\tau} P'}{(\nu x)P \xrightarrow{\tau} (\nu x)P'}$$

together with the (often implicit) rule for structural congruence:

$$(\text{RSTR})\ \frac{P \equiv Q \quad Q \xrightarrow{\tau} Q' \quad Q' \equiv P'}{P \xrightarrow{\tau} P'}$$

The version we have presented is the so-called (synchronous) monadic pi-calculus. In the polyadic case, messages can consist of (possibly empty) name tuples $\vec{y}$ and communication requires the number of transmitted values to match exactly the number of received ones. In the case of empty tuples, input and output prefixes $x()$ and $\overline{x}\langle\rangle$ are sometimes written more concisely in CCS-like notation as x and $\overline{x}$.

Coming back to the puzzle (Exercise 4), we consider names $x_1,...,x_{100}$, and model the fact that room k contains id n by writing the process $R_k \triangleq !\overline{x_k}\langle x_n\rangle$. Then the strategy S_i of player i is defined as follows, where we use parametrised constants for simplicity:

$$S_i \triangleq S_i^{50}(x_i) \quad (1 \le i \le 100)$$
$$S_i^t(x) \triangleq x(y).\big([y = x_i]\overline{ok_i} \,|\, S_i^{t-1}(y)\big) \quad (1 \le i \le 100, 1 < t \le 50)$$
$$S_i^1(x) \triangleq x(y).[y = x_i]\overline{ok_i} \quad (1 \le i \le 100)$$

The guard for success can be written as $G \triangleq ok_1.ok_2 \ldots ok_{100}.\overline{ok}$, and the whole system as $(\nu x_1,...,x_{100}, ok_1,...,ok_{100})(S_1 | \cdots | S_{100} | R_1 | \cdots | R_{100} | G)$: after finitely many silent transitions the system will either be ready to handshake on $\overline{ok}$, or it will deadlock because some scientists have not been able to find their ids.

From the operational point of view, reduction semantics can be tightly reconciled with LTS semantics, by the so-called *Harmony Lemma* [56]. From the observational point of view, the situation is more complicated, because reduction semantics provides no meaningful "observables". Then, a meaningful abstract equivalence can be defined in terms of some simple predicates, called *barbs*, which express the capabilities to emit and receive on a given channel (but notably, neither the sent / received message nor the target state are observed). By combining barbs and reductions (and closing under contexts), we obtain *strong* and *weak barbed congruences* that can be shown to coincide with the analogous congruences originated from the LTS semantics.

Example 2. We now provide evidence of the expressiveness of pi-calculus by showing that functional programming can be recovered as a special flavour of interactive system. This is done by encoding λ-calculus in pi-calculus [47].

We recall that *λ-expressions* $M, N, ...$ can be either a variable x, the *λ-abstraction* $\lambda x.M$ or the *application* $M\,N$, with obvious notions of free and bound variables. The reduction rules (for the lazy semantics) are:

$$(\beta)\frac{}{(\lambda x.M)N \rightarrow M\{^N/_x\}} \qquad (\mu)\frac{M \rightarrow M'}{M\,N \rightarrow M'\,N}$$

Roughly, processes can represent both "functions" and "arguments" which are composed in parallel and interact to β-reduce. However, they interact by transmitting *access points* to terms instead of terms themselves. The pi-calculus process that encodes a λ-expression M is parametric w.r.t. the access point a for retrieving arguments, and it is written $[\![M]\!]_a^{\lambda 2\pi}$. The encoding is shown in Fig. 4.

$$
\begin{aligned}
[\![x]\!]_a^{\lambda 2\pi} &\triangleq \overline{x}\langle a\rangle \\
[\![\lambda x.M]\!]_a^{\lambda 2\pi} &\triangleq a(x,m).[\![M]\!]_m^{\lambda 2\pi} \\
[\![MN]\!]_a^{\lambda 2\pi} &\triangleq (\nu m)\Big(\,[\![M]\!]_m^{\lambda 2\pi}\,|\,(\nu b)(\;!b(n).[\![N]\!]_n^{\lambda 2\pi}\,|\,\overline{m}\langle b,a\rangle\,)\Big) \quad \text{for } b \notin \mathrm{fv}(N)
\end{aligned}
$$

Fig. 4. Encoding of λ-calculus in pi-calculus

In the case of a variable x, the corresponding processes sends the access point a to the function available at x. In the case of a λ-abstraction, the process is waiting to receive on a the argument x and the name of a further access point m for further arguments, needed when evaluating M. In the case of application, a fresh server b is installed for handling the requests to the argument N, together with a new access point m for the argument of M, to which b and a are sent. The correspondence can be formalised by showing that $[\![(\lambda x.M)N]\!]^{\lambda 2\pi}$ and $[\![M\{^x/_N\}]\!]^{\lambda 2\pi}$ are related by the weak equivalence $\approx$.

Exercise 5. Write the pi-calculus processes $[\![\lambda x.x]\!]_a^{\lambda 2\pi}$ and $[\![(\lambda x.x)N]\!]_a^{\lambda 2\pi}$. Then shows that $[\![(\lambda x.x)N]\!]_a^{\lambda 2\pi}$ reduces after some steps to $[\![N]\!]_a^{\lambda 2\pi}\,|\,(\nu b)!b(n).[\![N]\!]_n^{\lambda 2\pi}$ (which can be shown strongly bisimilar to $[\![N]\!]_a^{\lambda 2\pi}$, as $(\nu b)!b(n).P$ is clearly inert).

It is evident that pi-calculus provides a rather sophisticated framework for the study of interaction. For example, Sangiorgi proved in his PhD thesis [55] that name mobility can encode some sort of higher-order communication, in the sense of process mobility. Nevertheless, the considered primitives and the overall framework are rather low-level. As a main consequence, when the size of processes increases, it becomes harder to acquire confidence in the correctness of the modelling. This fact opened a major research strand on type systems for process calculi, where different kinds of types and annotations are devised to offer static guarantees about the validity of certain properties, ranging from the absence of communication errors (e.g. receiving a message of mismatched arity or type) to termination and deadlock avoidance. In particular, there is now a renewed interest in the area of service oriented calculi around the notion of *session types*, introduced about a decade ago by Honda, Kubo and Vasconcelos [35].

2.3 A Session Calculus

One of the problem with pi-calculus is that names are used to encode many different behavioural aspects all in terms of communication. In principle, one should at least distinguish between two different usages: the first one is concerned with some sort of static sorting discipline, like establishing that all names transmitted on x must be integers, or that all names transmitted on y must be names of channels where integers can be sent, or that z can only be used for input; the second one has to do with dynamic prescriptions, like protocol narrations for the peers of a session, establishing e.g. that on channel z must first be sent an integer, then be received a name of a channel where integers can be sent and finally be received another integer.

The idea in [35] is to structure the language so to guarantee that, at any time, each session-like channel is shared between two peers only. This way, the protocol run on one side can be more conveniently checked for compatibility w.r.t. the protocol on the other side, as the two must be related by some form of duality. The key idea is to impose a symmetric form of communication for opening a session.

Example 3. To see how it works, consider the specification of a server that repeatedly receives values, computes some heavy scientific calculation f on it and then returns the result to the caller. If it is written as $S \triangleq !in(x).\overline{out}\langle f(x)\rangle$, then there is a big problem: if two or more clients are around, they could intercept the result of other calculations. For example:

$$\begin{aligned}
& S \,|\, \overline{in}\langle 1\rangle.out(y_1).P_1 \,|\, \overline{in}\langle 2\rangle.out(y_2).P_2 \\
& \xrightarrow{\tau} S \,|\, \overline{out}\langle f(1)\rangle \,|\, out(y_1).P_1 \,|\, \overline{in}\langle 2\rangle.out(y_2).P_2 \\
& \xrightarrow{\tau} S \,|\, \overline{out}\langle f(1)\rangle \,|\, \overline{out}\langle f(2)\rangle \,|\, out(y_1).P_1 \,|\, out(y_2).P_2 \\
& \xrightarrow{\tau} S \,|\, \overline{out}\langle f(1)\rangle \,|\, P_1\{^{f(2)}/_{y_1}\} \,|\, out(y_2).P_2 \\
& \xrightarrow{\tau} S \,|\, P_1\{^{f(2)}/_{y_1}\} \,|\, P_2\{^{f(1)}/_{y_2}\}
\end{aligned}$$

The typical way to solve this problem consists of receiving the result on a private channel, freshly established at the moment of the call. The server is thus written like $S \triangleq !in(x,k).\overline{k}\langle f(x)\rangle$, so that each time the result will be sent to a channel specified by the caller, which can, e.g., employ a fresh name for the goal, like in $(\nu k)\overline{in}\langle 1,k\rangle.k(y_1).P_1$. In the monadic case, k can be used both for sending the value and for receiving the result: the server would become $S \triangleq !in(k).k(x).\overline{k}\langle f(x)\rangle$ and the client would become $(\nu k)\overline{in}\langle k\rangle.\overline{k}\langle 1\rangle.k(y_1).P_1$. It can be seen that k plays the role of a session key, with dual usages on the server and on the client. When the pattern $(\nu k)\overline{in}\langle k\rangle.P$ is frequent, it can be more conveniently written as a macro $\overline{in}(k).P$, which is reminiscent of bound output and is symmetric to ordinary input.

Conceptually, the calculus proposed in [35] exposes three different communication pairs. The first consists of prefixes for session acceptance $a(k)$ and session request $\overline{a}(k)$. The corresponding reduction rule is:

$$(\text{LINK})\ \frac{}{a(k).P \,|\, \overline{a}(k).Q \xrightarrow{\tau} P \,|\, Q}$$

(note that alpha-conversion is exploited to choose the same name k on both sides before applying the reduction).

Then there are ordinary input $k?(x)$ and output $k!\langle x\rangle$ on a session k (only the former is a binder for x). The corresponding reduction rule is:

$$(\text{COMM})\ \frac{}{k?(x).P \,|\, k!\langle y\rangle.Q \xrightarrow{\tau} P\{^{y}/_{x}\} \,|\, Q}$$

Finally there are primitives for delegation of a session key to a different process: session receiving $k?((k'))$ and session sending $k!\langle\langle k'\rangle\rangle$ (only the former is a binder for k'). The corresponding reduction rule is:

$$(\textsc{pass})\ \frac{}{k?((x)).P \mid k!\langle\langle k'\rangle\rangle.Q \xrightarrow{\tau} P\{^{k'}/_{x}\} \mid Q}$$

Note that after having sent k' on k, process Q is no longer allowed to mention k'.

Sometimes a fourth communication pair is considered that involves label branching over a finite set of predefined labels $\sum_i k?l_i.P_i$ on one side and label selection $k!l.P$ on the opposite side. The corresponding reduction rule is:

$$(\textsc{lab})\ \frac{j \in I}{\sum_{i\in I} k?l_i.P_i \mid k!l_j.Q \xrightarrow{\tau} P_j \mid Q}$$

The remaining rules are the ordinary ones for parallel composition, restriction, structural congruence and recursion (considered in place of replication). Note that the same sequential process can open different sessions and interleave activities within them.

Exercise 6. One young, bright computer scientists is given the possibility to pass the exam if she is able to play chess twice against the state-of-the-art computer player available on the web, without loosing both games. She has never played chess before. Which strategy can she take?

The idea is essentially to let the computer AI play against itself. We can model the web site as follows:

$$\begin{aligned} \mathit{Chess} &\triangleq \mathit{start}(k).(\,\mathit{Chess} \mid k?\mathsf{black}.B(k) + k?\mathsf{white}.W(k)) \\ B(k) &\triangleq \mathrm{rec}\,X.k?(m).k!\langle m :: \mathit{next}(m)\rangle.X \\ W(k) &\triangleq \mathrm{rec}\,X.k!\langle \mathit{next}(\epsilon)\rangle.k?(m).X \end{aligned}$$

Thus, the web site let the human player choose the colour and then, depending on such choice, either it waits for the first move of the human or it starts the game by sending its first move. For simplicity we assume the game protocol consists of sending and receiving the list of moves made so far. The AI will compute its best move by exploiting some function *next* applied on the history of moves. Note that each game runs in its own session k, to avoid mixing the games of different players.

The best strategy would be to open two gaming sessions, choosing to play holding black pieces in one and white pieces in the other, and then always send on one game the latest move performed by the computer player in the other game.

$$\begin{aligned} \mathit{Human} &\triangleq \overline{\mathit{start}}(k_1).k_1!\mathsf{black}.\overline{\mathit{start}}(k_2).k_2!\mathsf{white}.P(k_1,k_2) \\ P(k_1,k_2) &\triangleq \mathrm{rec}\,X.k_1?(m).k_2!\langle m\rangle.k_2?(n).k_1!\langle n\rangle.X \end{aligned}$$

The main advantage w.r.t. pi-calculus is that sophisticated typing disciplines can now be defined by exploiting the different syntactic categories and primitives. To know more on this topic see Vasconcelos's contribution in this volume [58].

2.4 Orc

Quite independently from traditional process calculi as CCS and pi-calculus, where control and data flow is always encoded in terms of interaction, Cook and Misra have proposed a basic programming language for structured orchestration, called Orc [23, 37, 50], whose primitives meet simplicity with yet great generality. Orc neatly separates orchestration from computation: Orc expressions e should be considered as scripts to be invoked, e.g., within imperative programming languages using assignments such as $z :\in e$, where z is a variable and the Orc expression e can involve wide-area computation over multiple servers. The assignment symbol $:\in$ (due to Hoare) makes it explicit that e can return zero or more results, one of which is assigned to z. Even if Orc looks quite different from ordinary process calculi, it relies on hidden mechanisms for name handling (creation and passing) and for atomic distributed termination. We recaps Orc basics, borrowing definitions from [50]. Apart from minor differences w.r.t. the literature, we let Orc expressions be defined by the following grammar:

$$\begin{array}{llll} \text{(Expressions)} & e & ::= & \mathbf{0} \quad | \quad b \quad | \quad e_1 | e_2 \quad | \quad e_1 > x > e_2 \quad | \quad e_2 \textbf{ where } x :\in e_1 \\ \text{(Basic expr.)} & b & ::= & \langle p \rangle \quad | \quad x\langle \vec{p} \rangle \quad | \quad s\langle \vec{p} \rangle \quad | \quad E\langle \vec{p} \rangle \quad | \quad ?k \end{array}$$

where we assume given the following (pairwise disjoint) sets: a set $\mathcal{V}$ of *values*, ranged by v, a set X of *variables*, ranged by x, a set $\mathcal{S}$ of *sites*, ranged by s, a set $\mathcal{E} \triangleq \{ E_i(\vec{x}) \triangleq e_i \}_i$ of *defined expressions*, ranged by E, and a set $\mathcal{K}$ of *invocation keys*, ranged by k. Moreover, we let the set of *parameters* $\mathcal{P} \triangleq \mathcal{V} \cup \mathcal{S} \cup X$, ranged by p. The expressions $e_1 > x > e_2$ and e_2 **where** $x :\in e_1$ bind the occurrences of x in e_2. The occurrences of non-bound variables are free and the set of free variables of an expression e is denoted by $\mathrm{fv}(e)$. All defined expressions $E(\vec{x}) \triangleq e$ are well-formed, in the sense that $\mathrm{fv}(e) \subseteq \vec{x}$.

Orc semantics is defined in the LTS style, via SOS rules. The basic expressions $?k$ must be considered as run-time syntax: they denote response handlers for site invocations. The set of labels include action $\overline{s}\langle \vec{v} \rangle @k$ for a site invocation to s with parameters $\vec{v}$ and invocation key k, action $v@k$ for the receipt of the value v in response to a site invocation handled by k, action $\langle v \rangle$ for the local publication of value v, and the silent action τ. We let o range over labels.

The basic computational entities orchestrated by Orc expressions are *sites*: a site call can be thought of as an RMI, a call to a monitor procedure, to a function or to a (web) service. Each invocation to site s elicits at most one value published by s. (Note instead that, in principle, an Orc expression can publish any number of values.) Values are published locally using the primitive *let*(v), here rendered just as $\langle v \rangle$ for brevity.

$$(\text{CALL})\ \frac{k \text{ globally fresh}}{s\langle \vec{v} \rangle \xrightarrow{\overline{s}\langle \vec{v} \rangle @k} ?k} \qquad (\text{RESP})\ \frac{}{?k \xrightarrow{v@k} \langle v \rangle} \qquad (\text{LET})\ \frac{}{\langle v \rangle \xrightarrow{\langle v \rangle} \mathbf{0}}$$

While site call is strict, in the sense that actual parameters are evaluated before the call, the evaluation of defined expressions is non-strict. The corresponding inference rule is:

$$(\text{DEF})\ \frac{E_i(\vec{x}) \triangleq e_i \in \mathcal{E}}{E_i\langle \vec{p} \rangle \xrightarrow{\tau} e_i\{\vec{p}/\vec{x}\}}$$

Orc has three composition principles. The first one is the ordinary parallel composition $e_1 \mid e_2$, here called *symmetric parallel* (e.g., the parallel composition of two site calls can produce zero, one or many values). We remark that there is no interaction between e_1 and e_2. The corresponding inference rules are:

$$(\text{LSYM})\ \frac{e_1 \xrightarrow{o} e_1'}{e_1 \mid e_2 \xrightarrow{o} e_1' \mid e_2} \qquad (\text{RSYM})\ \frac{e_2 \xrightarrow{o} e_2'}{e_1 \mid e_2 \xrightarrow{o} e_1 \mid e_2'}$$

The second composition principle is called *sequencing* and it takes inspiration from universal quantification: in the sequential expression $e_1 > x > e_2$, a fresh copy $e_2\{^v/_x\}$ of e_2 is spawned for *any* value v published by e_1, i.e., a sort of pipeline is established between e_1 and e_2. When $x \notin \text{fv}(e_2)$, then we write $e_1 >> e_2$ as a shorthand for $e_1 > x > e_2$ (because x is inessential). The corresponding inference rules are:

$$(\text{SEQ})\ \frac{e_1 \xrightarrow{o} e_1' \quad o \neq \langle v \rangle}{e_1 > x > e_2 \xrightarrow{o} e_1' > x > e_2} \qquad (\text{PIPE})\ \frac{e_1 \xrightarrow{\langle v \rangle} e_1'}{e_1 > x > e_2 \xrightarrow{\tau} (e_1' > x > e_2) \mid e_2\{^v/_x\}}$$

The third and last composition principle is called *asymmetric parallel composition* and takes inspiration from existential quantification. The evaluation of the asymmetric parallel expression e_2 **where** $x :\in e_1$ (written as $e_2 < x < e_1$ in the latest papers on Orc) is lazy: e_1 and e_2 start in parallel, but all sub-expressions of e_2 that depend on the value of x must wait for e_1 to publish *one* value. When e_1 produces a value it is assigned to x and that side of the orchestration is cancelled. The corresponding inference rules are:

$$(\text{LASYM})\ \frac{e_2 \xrightarrow{o} e_2'}{e_2 \textbf{ where } x :\in e_1 \xrightarrow{o} e_2' \textbf{ where } x :\in e_1}$$

$$(\text{RASYM})\ \frac{e_1 \xrightarrow{o} e_1' \quad o \neq \langle v \rangle}{e_2 \textbf{ where } x :\in e_1 \xrightarrow{o} e_2 \textbf{ where } x :\in e_1'} \qquad (\text{PICK})\ \frac{e_1 \xrightarrow{\langle v \rangle} e_1'}{e_2 \textbf{ where } x :\in e_1 \xrightarrow{\tau} e_2\{^v/_x\}}$$

Although not evident from the operational semantics, the running implementation of Orc assumes that all concurrent invocations are executed instantaneously and that the asymmetric parallel operator picks the first value available, i.e. rules (CALL) and (PICK) have higher priorities than the remaining ones). We refer the interested reader to [59] for more details.

Example 4. We borrow from [50] some simple examples of Orc declarations. In the following we assume the existence of a site *timer* that receives an integer t and return a void datum $\langle\rangle$ after t units of time, of two sites *cnn* and *bbc* to be invoked with a date d as argument and that return selected news from date d, and of a site *email* that requires two arguments m and a and sends an email containing message m to the address a without returning any value. Moreover, we write $v_1 :: v_2$ to denote the concatenation of two messages.

- Declaration $MailTwice(a,d) \triangleq (cnn\langle d\rangle | bbc\langle d\rangle) > x > email\langle x,a\rangle$ specifies a service for notifying all news from *cnn and bbc* in two different emails.

$$e_1 \mid (e_2 \mid e_3) \sim (e_1 \mid e_2) \mid e_3 \qquad e_1 > x > (e_2 > y > e_3) \sim (e_1 > x > e_2) > y > e_3 \text{ if } x \notin \text{fv}(e_3)$$
$$e_1 \mid e_2 \sim e_2 \mid e_1 \qquad \mathbf{0} > x > e \sim \mathbf{0} \qquad (e_1 \mid e_2) > x > e \sim (e_1 > x > e) \mid (e_2 > x > e)$$
$$e \mid \mathbf{0} \sim e \qquad \mathbf{0} \text{ **where** } x :\in \mathbf{0} \sim \mathbf{0} \qquad (e_2 \mid e_3) \text{ **where** } x :\in e_1 \sim (e_2 \text{ **where** } x :\in e_1) \mid e_3 \text{ if } x \notin \text{fv}(e_3)$$
$$(e_3 \text{ **where** } y :\in e_2) \text{ **where** } x :\in e_1 \sim (e_3 \text{ **where** } x :\in e_1) \text{ **where** } y :\in e_2 \text{ if } x \notin \text{fv}(e_2) \text{ and } y \notin \text{fv}(e_1)$$
$$(e_2 > y > e_3) \text{ **where** } x :\in e_1 \sim (e_2 \text{ **where** } x :\in e_1) > y > e_3 \text{ if } x \notin \text{fv}(e_3)$$

Fig. 5. Some strongly bisimilar Orc expressions

- Declaration $MailOnce(a,d) \triangleq email\langle x,a\rangle$ **where** $x :\in (cnn\langle d\rangle | bbc\langle d\rangle)$ specifies a service that notifies address a with only one of the news selected either from *cnn* or from *bbc*.
- Declaration

$$MailBoth(a,d) \triangleq ((\langle x_1 :: x_2\rangle > x > email\langle x,a\rangle) \textbf{ where } x_1 :\in cnn\langle d\rangle \textbf{ where } x_2 :\in bbc\langle d\rangle$$

  specifies a service that notifies address a with both news selected from *cnn* and from *bbc* in a unique message.
- Declaration $Delay(s,d,t) \triangleq timer\langle t\rangle >> \langle x\rangle$ **where** $x :\in s\langle d\rangle$ specifies a service that contact site s with argument d but delays the response up to t time units, in the sense that even if the response is available before t time units then it will be published only after the timer expires, while if it is available after the timer already expired, then it is readily published. Note that the timer invocation does not depend on x and therefore it is activated concurrently with the invocation to s.
- Declaration $UnfairPick(s_1,s_2,d,t) \triangleq \langle x\rangle$ **where** $x :\in (s_1\langle d\rangle | Delay\langle s_2,d,t\rangle)$ specifies a service that contact both sites s_1 and s_2 with argument d but privileges the response from site s_1, in the sense that if it arrives before t time units then the response of s_2, if any, is ignored. For example

$$UnfairMail(a,d) \triangleq UnfairPick\langle cnn,bbc,d,20\rangle > x > email\langle x,a\rangle$$

  specifies a service that notifies address a with only one of the news selected either from *cnn* or from *bbc*, but preferably from *cnn* (that has 20 time units of advantage).

Exercise 7. A classic problem in non-strict evaluation is the so-called *parallel-or*. Suppose there are two sites s_1 and s_2 that publish some booleans. Write an Orc expression *POR* that publishes the value *false* only if both sites return *false*, the value *true* as soon as either site returns *true*, and otherwise it never publishes a value. In the solution it can be assumed: (1) the existence of a site $ift(b)$ that receives a boolean value and returns *true* if b is *true*, and otherwise it does not respond; (2) the existence of a site $or(b_1,b_2)$ that return the inclusive logical or of the two booleans received as arguments. Note that *POR* must publish one result at most.

The abstract semantics of Orc can be defined in terms of strong and weak bisimilarities and gives rise to interesting equivalences, some of which are in Fig. 5.

3 A Calculus of Sessions and Pipelines

In the previous section we have seen different frameworks for the modelling of interaction, sessions, orchestration and cancellation of activities, each offering elegant and flexible solutions to tackle specific issues. Starting from these premises, the objective of a coordinated effort within the EU funded project SENSORIA [57] was to synthesise so-called *core calculi for SOC*, where all the above aspects are dealt with in a uniform and structured way. One of the outcomes of the project is CaSPiS [8], a *Calculus of Sessions and Pipelines*, which evolved as an improved refinement of SCC [7] (*Service Centred Calculus*). CaSPiS exploits *nested sessions* and *pipelines* as natural tools for structuring client-service communication and orchestration, respectively. Activity cancellation is built around the ability of peers to leave sessions and to program suitable handlers for such cases. We discuss below the essential guidelines around the design of CaSPiS, emphasising the differences w.r.t. the calculi in Section 2:

Interaction: Contrary to CCS and pi-calculus where the same form of communication is used for different purposes, in CaSPiS a few forms of basic interactions are distinguished and regulated on their own. For example, services are globally available and can be invoked independently from the surrounding context, while ordinary input-output communication is context sensitive and implicitly driven.

Sessions: When CaSPiS is viewed as a programmable abstraction of SOC, the idea is to relieve programmers from the burden of dealing with session keys. Therefore the choice made in CaSPiS is to handle sessions as an implicit mechanism for enclosing the communications between a caller and its callee, avoiding external interferences. Like in Section 2.3, a name-scoping mechanism is used to handle sessions, but contrary to the calculus in [35], each CaSPiS process has its own implicit current session and it is possible neither to program interleaved communications in different sessions, nor session delegation. However, sessions can be nested (e.g. when calling a service within a session, the interaction will take place in a dedicated subsession) and it is allowed to pass values from nested sessions up.

Orchestration: As in Orc, orchestration is kept separate from interaction and pipelines are seen as a convenient mechanism for modelling the flow of data between local processes: it is more general than sequential composition, better suited w.r.t. concurrency and does not require the explicit and improper use of channels for orchestration tasks. Here a more sophisticated form of pipeline is introduced, which is well-integrated with the other features of CaSPiS, not considered in Orc.

Cancellation: Orc's asymmetric parallel operator provides a convenient form of cancellation for pending activities, but whose effect is purely local: the operational semantics is designed in such a way that if a site has been invoked, but the local handler for its response is cancelled, then the response cannot show up. This is maybe fine if only one-way or request-response interactions are considered, but not in CaSPiS, where the cancellation of activities could leave some pending peers in the middle of long-running interactions. Likewise signing a contract implies some obligations, opening a session implies notifying the peer when leaving the session before its conclusion. Also inspired by some recent work on process calculi for modelling transactions [13, 14, 18, 19, 41], CaSPiS comprises a novel mechanism for ensuring the notification of any activity cancellation, for which we are not aware of any similar counterpart in the literature on process calculi.

Readability and typeability: To tackle the complexity of SOC systems, it should be possible to structure complex processes in smaller parts tailored to specific issues and it should be possible to guarantee the compliance of the whole process by checking the compliance of its parts. Moreover, type checking and type inference systems should be available that automatically detect protocol inconsistencies and communication errors. For type systems to be effective, it is important that the abstraction distance w.r.t. the concrete formalism is not too large, so that any detected type problem can be immediately explained, tracked and understood over the underlying processes. Some preliminary investigation has shown that quite simple type systems can be developed for CaSPiS that guarantee nice properties (communication safety, client progress and deadlock freedom). A prototype tool, called TypeSes[2] for type inference is also available (see [45]).

3.1 A CaSPiS Walk-through

We introduce CaSPiS primitives in an incremental way. Let $\mathcal{N}_{\text{srv}}$ and $\mathcal{N}_{\text{sess}}$ be two disjoint countable sets, respectively of *service* names, ranged by s and of *session* names, ranged by r. We assume $\mathcal{N}_{\text{srv}}$ and $\mathcal{N}_{\text{sess}}$ are included in a larger set of *names* $\mathcal{N}$, ranged by n, and let $x, y, ..., u, v...$ range over $\mathcal{N} \setminus \mathcal{N}_{\text{sess}}$.

In the following we shall exploit the notion of a *context*, written $\mathbb{C}[\![\cdot]\!]$, i.e. a process term with one hole $[\![\cdot]\!]$. We write $\mathbb{C}[\![P]\!]$ for the process where the hole is textually replaced by process P. The contexts we are interested in are called *static*, and characterised by the fact that the hole occurs in an actively running position and it is ready to interact (e.g. it is not under a prefix). See Section 3.2 for the exact definition.

Service definition and invocation. Service definitions and invocations resemble CCS prefixes. Thus $s.P$ defines a service s and we write $\overline{s}.Q$ for invoking s. The similarity with CCS is merely syntactical, because after the handshake P and Q are not quite separate continuations, but rather protocols that will interact in a fresh, private session. The name of the session is not to be mentioned in P and Q, and therefore it is handled implicitly by the operational semantics rules. Each protocol can contain other service definitions and invocations, which in turn can establish nested sessions with other peers. Services are typically one-shot, in the sense that when invoked, a new instance serving the request is created, but the service in no longer available. This choice facilitates service updates. Replication (or recursion) can be used to specify persistent services, like $!s.P$. Moreover, it is possible to have different definitions $s.P_1$ and $s.P_2$ available at the same time for the same service name s.

Session sides. The handshake between $s.P$ and $\overline{s}.Q$ leads to the creation of a fresh session name r that can be viewed as a private, synchronous channel binding caller and callee. Since client and service may be far apart, a session naturally comes with two sides, written $r \triangleright P$ and $r \triangleright Q$, with r bound somewhere above them. For example,

[2] `http://www.di.unipi.it/~mezzina`

starting from $R|\mathbb{C}_1[\![s.P]\!]|\mathbb{C}_2[\![\bar{s}.Q]\!]$ we can arrive to $R|(\nu r)(\mathbb{C}_1[\![r \rhd P]\!]|\mathbb{C}_2[\![r \rhd Q]\!])$. Similarly, starting from $\mathbb{C}_1[\![s_1.(P_1|\bar{s}_2.P_2)]\!]|\mathbb{C}_2[\![\bar{s}_1.Q]\!]|\mathbb{C}_3[\![s_2.R]\!]$ we can arrive in two steps to $(\nu r_1,r_2)(\mathbb{C}_1[\![r_1 \rhd (P_1|r_2 \rhd P_2)]\!]|\mathbb{C}_2[\![r_1 \rhd Q]\!]|\mathbb{C}_3[\![r_2 \rhd R]\!])$, where P_1 interacts with Q and P_2 interacts with R. Sometimes, especially when type systems are considered, *polarities* $+$ and $-$ are attached to session sides in order to mark the caller and the callee. In the example above, we should have written, e.g., $(\nu r_1,r_2)(\mathbb{C}_1[\![r_1^+ \rhd (P_1|r_2^- \rhd P_2)]\!]|\mathbb{C}_2[\![r_1^- \rhd Q]\!]|\mathbb{C}_3[\![r_2^+ \rhd R]\!])$

Intra-session communication. Two peers P and Q running on opposite session sides of r can exchange messages. Since the peer is uniquely determined, input and output primitives are, respectively, abstraction prefixes $(?\vec{x})P$ or concretion prefixes $\langle\vec{v}\rangle Q$. For example, $\mathbb{C}_1[\![r \rhd \langle 5\rangle P]\!]|\mathbb{C}_2[\![r \rhd (?x)Q]\!]$ can evolve to $\mathbb{C}_1[\![r \rhd P]\!]|\mathbb{C}_2[\![r \rhd Q\{^5/_x\}]\!]$.

If we now reconsider the service for scientific calculations from Example 3, then we can write it just as $S \triangleq !in.(?x)\langle f(x)\rangle$. Then if two clients $\overline{in}.\langle 1\rangle(?y_1)P_1$ and $\overline{in}.\langle 2\rangle(?y_2)P_2$ are present, there is no risk of interference, because the two interactions are served separately.

$$
\begin{aligned}
&S\,|\,\overline{in}.\langle 1\rangle(?y_1)P_1\,|\,\overline{in}.\langle 2\rangle(?y_2)P_2\\
&\quad\xrightarrow{\tau} (\nu r_1)(S\,|\,r_1 \rhd (?x)\langle f(x)\rangle\,|\,r_1 \rhd \langle 1\rangle(?y_1)P_1\,|\,\overline{in}.\langle 2\rangle(?y_2)P_2)\\
&\quad\xrightarrow{\tau} (\nu r_1,r_2)(S\,|\,r_1 \rhd (?x)\langle f(x)\rangle\,|\,r_2 \rhd (?x)\langle f(x)\rangle\,|\,r_1 \rhd \langle 1\rangle(?y_1)P_1\,|\,r_2 \rhd \langle 2\rangle(?y_2)P_2)\\
&\quad\xrightarrow{\tau} (\nu r_1,r_2)(S\,|\,r_1 \rhd \langle f(1)\rangle\,|\,r_2 \rhd (?x)\langle f(x)\rangle\,|\,r_1 \rhd (?y_1)P_1\,|\,r_2 \rhd \langle 2\rangle(?y_2)P_2)\\
&\quad\xrightarrow{\tau} (\nu r_1,r_2)(S\,|\,r_1 \rhd \langle f(1)\rangle\,|\,r_2 \rhd \langle f(2)\rangle\,|\,r_1 \rhd (?y_1)P_1\,|\,r_2 \rhd (?y_2)P_2)\\
&\quad\xrightarrow{\tau} (\nu r_1,r_2)(S\,|\,r_1 \rhd \mathbf{0}\,|\,r_2 \rhd \langle f(2)\rangle\,|\,r_1 \rhd P_1\{^{f(1)}/_{y_1}\}\,|\,r_2 \rhd (?y_2)P_2)\\
&\quad\xrightarrow{\tau} (\nu r_1,r_2)(S\,|\,r_1 \rhd \mathbf{0}\,|\,r_2 \rhd \mathbf{0}\,|\,r_1 \rhd P_1\{^{f(1)}/_{y_1}\}\,|\,r_2 \rhd P_2\{^{f(2)}/_{y_2}\})
\end{aligned}
$$

Note that the initial processes are much simpler than those considered in Example 3, where session identifiers k should appear explicitly. Moreover, the session side construct must be considered as run-time syntax, as all the more complex processes traversed by the above computation.

Inter-session communication. It is quite useful to have the possibility to make the responses obtained upon some service invocation available to the parent session, e.g. to collect the fares offered from different providers and compare them to choose the best one. To this purpose, another prefix is available in CaSPiS, called *return prefix*, written $\langle\vec{v}\rangle^{\uparrow}P$, which can be seen as a concretion at the level of the parent session, i.e. $r \rhd \langle\vec{v}\rangle^{\uparrow}P$ can be read as $\langle\vec{v}\rangle|r \rhd P$, except for the fact that P cannot execute until $\vec{v}$ has been consumed.

Pipelining. CaSPiS exploits a generalised form of Orc sequencing operator, called *pipeline* and written $P > Q$, which allows to feed Q with all values produced by P: for each value, a fresh instance of Q will be activated, running in parallel with $P > Q$. A pipeline can be seen as some sort of redirection for the concretions available in P: instead of being available to the peer of the current session, they are given in input to Q, which is typically guarded by some abstraction prefix. For example, Orc sequencing operator can be written as $P > (?x)Q$.

Note that in a term like $(r \rhd (P > Q)) | r \rhd R$, process P can input from R and output to Q. This is clearly different from $((r \rhd P) > Q) | r \rhd R$, where P can input from R and output to R, but can pass values to Q using return prefixes. In combination with the return operator, pipeline allows to make the responses obtained upon some service invocation available locally, to some suitable continuation. In the example of the service for scientific calculations, a client such as $\overline{in}.\langle 1 \rangle (?y_1)P_1$ would run P_1 in the session established with S, i.e. it will reduce after some steps to $r_1 \rhd P_1\{f(1)/y_1\}$. Instead the client $(\overline{in}.\langle 1 \rangle (?y_1) \langle y_1 \rangle^{\uparrow}) > (?y_1)P_1$ will reduce, after some further steps, to $(r_1 \rhd \mathbf{0} > (?y_1)P_1) | P_1\{f(1)/y_1\}$, which can be read as $P_1\{f(1)/y_1\}$, because $(r_1 \rhd \mathbf{0} > (?y_1)P_1)$ is a terminated process.

Cancellation. Processes must be able to abandon their current sessions in full autonomy. The command close is used to terminate the enclosing session side. A terminated session enters the special state $\blacktriangleright P$ that recursively terminates any other session side nested in P. Note that the execution of a close can depend on some local choice as well as be guarded by the input of some data from the opposite session side.

Closure notification. The distinguishing feature of CaSPiS is the presence of novel primitives to handle (unexpected or programmed) session termination. In fact, even if processes can abandon their current sessions, we would like sessions units to represent a controlled and safe form interaction, and therefore their peers should be somehow notified. The idea is that upon termination of a session side, the opposite session side will be informed and take some proper counteraction, if needed. To this purpose, the more general syntax for invocation is $\overline{s}_k.Q$: it mentions a name k at which the handler of the client-side is listening. Symmetrically, the more general syntax for service definition is $s_k.P$, which mentions a name k at which the handler of the service-side is listening. Upon creation of a session, a pair of names (k_1, k_2) is thus associated with the fresh session r, identifying a pair of *termination handlers*, one for each side. The more general syntax for sessions is thus $r \rhd_k P$ where the subscript k refers to the termination handler of the opposite side.

Then, after a close is executed, a notification $\dagger(k)$ is sent to the termination-handler service k listening at the *opposite* side of the session to manage the appropriate actions.

The final ingredient is the possibility to define suitable *termination listeners* $k \cdot P$ that are used to handle termination signals $\dagger(k)$.

To sum up the above discussion: $s_{k_1}.P | \overline{s}_{k_2}.Q$ can evolve to $(\nu r)(r \rhd_{k_2} P | r \rhd_{k_1} Q)$. (Note that the handlers have been exchanged between the peers.) Then, if say P executes close, the termination handler k_2 of the caller will be activated, and vice versa, if Q terminates, then k_1 will be activated. For example: $r \rhd_{k_2} (\mathsf{close} | P) | r \rhd_{k_1} (Q | k_2 \cdot \mathsf{close})$ can evolve to $\blacktriangleright P | \dagger(k_2) | r \rhd_{k_1} (Q | k_2 \cdot \mathsf{close})$, then to $\blacktriangleright P | r \rhd_{k_1} (Q | \mathsf{close})$ and finally to $\blacktriangleright P | \blacktriangleright Q | \dagger(k_1)$. Note that the emitted notification $\dagger(k)$ is essentially *asynchronous*, i.e., we have no guarantee as to when the listener at the opposite side will catch $\dagger(k)$. For example, before $\dagger(k)$ reaches its destination, the other side might in turn have entered a closing state $\blacktriangleright Q$ on its own, or be closed right away, as a result of the closing of a parent session. While dangling $\dagger(k)$ cannot be avoided in general, simple patterns can avoid the even worst situation of dangling session sides pending forever.

Pattern matching and guarded choice. Last but not least, CaSPiS interactions is empowered by pattern-matching facilities that can be suited, e.g., to deal with XML-like data typical of web service scenarios. Roughly, this is obtained by allowing: 1) output and return prefixes whose values are structured, exploiting a signature Σ of *constructors*, ranged by f (each coming with a fixed arity); 2) input prefixes where plain input variables $?x$ are generalised by *patterns* that exploit the constructors in Σ. Together with ordinary prefix-guarded choices, the presence of patterns makes it possible to manage and route messages on the basis of their contents. For example, a pipeline like $P > (\mathsf{pdf}(?x))Q + (\mathsf{ps}(?x))R$ can be used to handle in different ways the documents produced by P depending on whether they are in PDF (Portable Document Format) or PS (PostScript) format.

3.2 Close-Free Fragment

We start presenting the fragment of CaSPiS without cancellation and closure notification, whose syntax is in Fig. 6. The operators are listed in decreasing order of precedence. Service definition $s.[\![\cdot]\!]$ and invocation $\overline{s}.[\![\cdot]\!]$, prefix $\pi_i[\![\cdot]\!]$, left-sided pipeline $P > [\![\cdot]\!]$ and replication $![\![\cdot]\!]$ are called *dynamic* operators, while the remaining operators are *static*.

As expected, in $(\nu n)P$, the restriction (νn) binds free occurrences of n in P, while in $(F)P$ any $?x$ in the pattern F binds the free occurrences of name x in P. We denote by $\mathrm{bn}(F)$ the set of names x such that $?x$ occurs in F. The empty sum is denoted $\mathbf{0}$. Trailing $\mathbf{0}$'s will often be omitted. When the arguments of prefixes are void or inessential, we abbreviate them as $()P$, $\langle\rangle P$ and $\langle\rangle^{\uparrow} P$.

The structural congruence relation $\equiv$ is defined as the least congruence that includes alpha-equivalence and the laws in Fig. 7. This set of laws comprises the structural rules for parallel composition and restriction, plus the obvious extension of restriction's scope extrusion law to pipelines and sessions.

$P,Q ::= \sum_{i\in I}\pi_i P_i$	Guarded Sum	$\pi ::= (F)$	Abstraction
$\mid u.P$	Service Definition	$\mid \langle V\rangle$	Concretion
$\mid \overline{u}.P$	Service Invocation	$\mid \langle V\rangle^{\uparrow}$	Return
$\mid r \rhd P$	Session		
$\mid P > Q$	Pipeline	$V ::= u \mid f(\tilde{V})$	Value ($f \in \Sigma$)
$\mid P \mid Q$	Parallel Composition		
$\mid (\nu n)P$	Restriction	$F ::= u \mid ?x \mid f(\tilde{F})$	Pattern ($f \in \Sigma$)
$\mid !P$	Replication		

Fig. 6. Syntax of close-free CaSPiS

$$
\begin{array}{rclrclrcl}
P|\mathbf{0} & \equiv & P & (\nu n)\mathbf{0} & \equiv & \mathbf{0} & ((\nu n)P) > Q & \equiv & (\nu n)(P > Q) \text{ if } n \notin \mathrm{fn}(Q) \\
P|Q & \equiv & Q|P & (\nu n)(\nu m)P & \equiv & (\nu m)(\nu n)P & ((\nu n)P)|Q & \equiv & (\nu n)(P|Q) \text{ if } n \notin \mathrm{fn}(Q) \\
(P|Q)|R & \equiv & P|(Q|R) & !P & \equiv & P|!P & r \rhd (\nu n)P & \equiv & (\nu n)(r \rhd P) \text{ if } r \neq n
\end{array}
$$

Fig. 7. Structural congruence laws

The reduction semantics is given by exploiting suitable contexts surrounding the active redexes. A context is *static* if its hole does not occur under a dynamic operator. Moreover, we say that a context is *session-immune* if its hole does not occur under a session operator, and *pipeline-immune* if its hole does not occur under a right-sided pipeline operator. In the following we let $\mathbb{C}[\![\cdot]\!]$ range over static contexts, $\mathbb{S}[\![\cdot]\!]$ over static session-immune contexts, and $\mathbb{P}[\![\cdot]\!]$ over contexts that are static, session-immune and pipeline-immune. Roughly, a static session-immune context $\mathbb{S}[\![\cdot]\!]$ cannot "intercept" abstraction and return prefixes, while a static, session-immune and pipeline-immune context $\mathbb{P}[\![\cdot]\!]$ cannot "intercept" concretion prefixes. Analogous definitions apply to the case of two-holes contexts $\mathbb{C}[\![\cdot,\cdot]\!]$.

The first reduction regards the handshake between a service definition and a service invocation.

$$(\text{SYNC})\frac{r \text{ fresh for } \mathbb{C}[\![\cdot,\cdot]\!], P, Q}{\mathbb{C}[\![\, s.P, \overline{s}.Q \,]\!] \xrightarrow{\tau} (\nu r)\mathbb{C}[\![\, r \rhd P, r \rhd Q \,]\!]}$$

The second reduction regards intra-session communication. Below we let $\mathbb{C}_r[\![\cdot,\cdot]\!]$ be a context of the form $\mathbb{C}[\![\, r \rhd \mathbb{P}[\![\cdot]\!], r \rhd \mathbb{S}[\![\cdot]\!] \,]\!]$ (for some $\mathbb{P}[\![\cdot]\!]$ and $\mathbb{S}[\![\cdot]\!]$), which captures the most general situation in which intra-session communication can happen. Pattern-matching is accounted for by a substitution $\sigma = \text{match}(F,V)$, defined as the (only) substitution such that $\text{dom}(\sigma) = \text{bn}(F)$ and $F\sigma = V$. Moreover, we implicitly require that names in F and V are not bound by $\mathbb{C}_r[\![\cdot,\cdot]\!]$

$$(\text{SSYNC})\frac{\sigma = \text{match}(F,V)}{\mathbb{C}_r[\![\, \langle V\rangle P + \sum_i \pi_i P_i, (F)Q + \sum_j \pi_j Q_i \,]\!] \xrightarrow{\tau} \mathbb{C}_r[\![\, P, Q\sigma \,]\!]}$$

Intra-session communication can be triggered also by a return prefix in a subsession of r. The corresponding rule is:

$$(\text{SRSYNC})\frac{\sigma = \text{match}(F,V)}{\mathbb{C}_r[\![\, r_1 \rhd \mathbb{S}_1[\![\, \langle V\rangle^{\uparrow} P + \sum_i \pi_i P_i \,]\!], (F)Q + \sum_j \pi_j Q_i \,]\!] \xrightarrow{\tau} \mathbb{C}_r[\![\, r_1 \rhd \mathbb{S}_1[\![\, P \,]\!], Q\sigma \,]\!]}$$

Finally, there are two more rules for pipeline orchestration, handling the "redirection" of concretions and returns.

$$(\text{PSYNC})\frac{Q \equiv \mathbb{S}[\![\, (F)Q' + \sum_j \pi_j Q_i \,]\!] \quad \sigma = \text{match}(F,V)}{\mathbb{C}[\![\, \mathbb{P}[\![\, \langle V\rangle P + \sum_i \pi_i P_i \,]\!] > Q \,]\!] \xrightarrow{\tau} \mathbb{C}[\![\, \mathbb{S}[\![\, Q'\sigma \,]\!] | (\mathbb{P}[\![\, P \,]\!] > Q) \,]\!]}$$

$$(\text{PRSYNC})\frac{Q \equiv \mathbb{S}[\![\, (F)Q' + \sum_j \pi_j Q_i \,]\!] \quad \sigma = \text{match}(F,V)}{\mathbb{C}[\![\, \mathbb{P}[\![\, r \rhd \mathbb{S}_1[\![\, \langle V\rangle^{\uparrow} P + \sum_i \pi_i P_i \,]\!] \,]\!] > Q \,]\!] \xrightarrow{\tau} \mathbb{C}[\![\, \mathbb{S}[\![\, Q'\sigma \,]\!] | (\mathbb{P}[\![\, r \rhd \mathbb{S}_1[\![\, P \,]\!] \,]\!] > Q) \,]\!]}$$

The presence of contexts in the reduction rules accounts for the execution of silent transitions under restriction, parallel composition, etc, while we omit deliberately the obvious rule for structural congruence, which is the same as the rule (RSTR) of pi-calculus (see Section 2.2). The LTS semantics and the Lemma that reconciles the silent transitions of the two semantics can be found in [8].

Example 5. The one-way and request-response invocation patterns from web services (to service s with argument V) can be easily encoded as $\overline{s}.\langle V\rangle\langle\rangle^{\uparrow}$ and $\overline{s}.\langle V\rangle(?x)\langle x\rangle^{\uparrow}$, respectively. Note that in both cases a value is returned (possibly void) that can be used to activate a suitable continuation, if any. The one-way pattern can also be rendered in a fully asynchronous fashion by writing $\overline{s}.(\langle V\rangle | \langle\rangle^{\uparrow})$.

The following e-shop example is adapted from [5], where it is used to illustrate a static analysis machinery for the detection of logic flaws in service applications, i.e. to prevent the so-called *application logic attacks* that exploit the vulnerabilities of the specific functionality of the application (e.g., by violating the business logic) rather than the ones of the underlying platform.

Example 6. We model a simple e-shop application S that exchanges information with customers C and the data base D that stores item prices. The service *price* to retrieve item prices is private to S and D. Essentially, a honest customer invokes service *buy*, chooses an item, receives its price inside an order form and if interested in finalising the order, must fill in a payment form with personal data and credit card information. In the same form are reported: the transaction code, the chosen item, and the received price of the purchase.

$$HC \triangleq \overline{buy}.\langle \mathsf{item}_k\rangle(\mathsf{orderForm}(?x_{code}, \mathsf{item}_k, ?x_{price_k}))\langle \mathsf{payForm}(x_{code}, \mathsf{item}_k, x_{price_k}, \mathsf{name}, \mathsf{cc})\rangle$$

However, a malicious user may try to finalise the transaction sending a forged copy of the payment form, where the price field has been abusively discounted (like when downloading a web order form associated with an e-shopping cart, editing some hidden field outside the browser and resubmitting it in place of the original one).

$$MC \triangleq \overline{buy}.\langle \mathsf{item}_k\rangle(\mathsf{orderForm}(?x_{code}, \mathsf{item}_k, ?x_{price_k}))\langle \mathsf{payForm}(x_{code}, \mathsf{item}_k, \mathsf{5cents}, \mathsf{name}, \mathsf{cc})\rangle$$

In the specification shown below, the application S exploits, for each item, two concurrent processes OF_i and PF_i, respectively for sending the order form to the customer and for receiving the cancellation or the payment of the order. This way it cannot check if the form sent by the costumer contains the right price.

$$\begin{aligned}
ESHOP &\triangleq (\nu price)(D\,|\,S)\\
D &\triangleq\ !price.\textstyle\sum_i(\mathsf{item}_i)\langle \mathsf{price}_i\rangle)\\
S &\triangleq\ !buy.\textstyle\sum_i(\mathsf{item}_i)(\nu code)(OF_i\,|\,PF_i)\\
OF_i &\triangleq \overline{price}.\langle \mathsf{item}_i\rangle\ (?x_{price_i})\langle \mathsf{orderForm}(code, \mathsf{item}_i, x_{price_i})\rangle^{\uparrow}\\
PF_i &\triangleq (\mathsf{cancel})\mathbf{0} + (\mathsf{payForm}(code, \mathsf{item}_i, ?y_{price_i}, ?y_{name}, ?y_{cc}))PAY
\end{aligned}$$

Then both the honest customer HC and the malicious customer MC shown above are capable to interact with the application, each fulfilling their purposes.

Exercise 8. Redesign the e-shop application S in such a way that the price indicated by the customer in the payment form is matched against the one provided by the data base.

We conclude by hinting at two important properties of CaSPiS processes P that do not contain the session operator $r \rhd [\![\cdot]\!]$. Let Q be any process reachable from P via any

$P,Q ::= \sum_{i\in I}\pi_i P_i$	Guarded Sum	$\mid \dagger(k)$	Signal
$\mid s_k.P$	Service Definition	$\mid r \rhd_k P$	Session
$\mid \overline{s}_k.P$	Service Invocation	$\mid \blacktriangleright P$	Terminated Session
$\mid P > Q$	Pipeline	$\mid P\|Q$	Parallel Composition
$\mid \mathsf{close}$	Close	$\mid (\nu n)P$	Restriction
$\mid k \cdot P$	Listener	$\mid !P$	Replication

Fig. 8. Syntax of full CaSPiS

$$
\begin{array}{rclrclrcl}
r \rhd_{k'} (\dagger(k)|P) & \equiv & \dagger(k)|r \rhd_{k'} P & (\dagger(k)|P) > Q & \equiv & \dagger(k)|(P > Q) & \blacktriangleright \dagger(k) & \equiv & \dagger(k) \\
\blacktriangleright r \rhd_k P & \equiv & \blacktriangleright r \rhd_k \blacktriangleright P & \blacktriangleright (P > Q) & \equiv & (\blacktriangleright P) > Q & \blacktriangleright\blacktriangleright P & \equiv & \blacktriangleright P \\
\blacktriangleright P|Q & \equiv & \blacktriangleright P| \blacktriangleright Q & \blacktriangleright (\nu x)P & \equiv & (\nu x) \blacktriangleright P & \blacktriangleright \mathbf{0} & \equiv & \mathbf{0}
\end{array}
$$

Fig. 9. Structural congruence rules for $\dagger(k)$ and $\blacktriangleright$

number of reductions and let r any session in Q, then: 1) there are exactly two session sides for r in Q (*dyadic session*), 2) it is never the case that one of the session side for r is nested into the other (*session acyclicity*). We refer to [8] for the formal presentation of such properties.

3.3 Full Calculus

We can now present the full syntax and semantics of CaSPiS. In what follows, we assume a new countable set $\mathcal{K}$ of *signal names*, ranged by k, disjoint from session and service names. The syntax of full CaSPiS is reported in Fig. 8. The difference w.r.t. Fig. 6 is given by the extended primitives $s_k.P$, $\overline{s}_k.P$ and $r \rhd_k P$ and the new primitives close, $\dagger(k)$, $\blacktriangleright P$ and $k \cdot P$. Like in the case of $r \rhd P$, we reserve $r \rhd_k P$ and $\blacktriangleright P$ as run-time syntax. When the handler k in $s_k.P$ is vacuous or inessential then we can safely omit it, and the same for $\overline{s}_k.P$ and $r \rhd_k P$.

The structural rules listed in Fig. 9 enrich the set of rules already introduced for the close-free fragment. The law $\blacktriangleright \dagger(k) \equiv \dagger(k)$ is motivated by subtle race conditions on the order of closings due to the nesting of sessions (see [8] for an example). The remaining rules serve the purpose of letting signals $\dagger(k)$ freely move within a term to reach the corresponding listeners, and distributing the terminated session $\blacktriangleright$ over static operators. Note that, as usual, structural congruence can be exploited to move to top level all restrictions that are not in the scope of a dynamic operator.

The reductions must be updated to take into account termination handlers. The only significant change regards the handshake between a service definition and a service invocation, where termination handlers must be annotated in the freshly created session sides.

$$
(\textsc{sync})\ \frac{r \text{ fresh for } \mathbb{C}[\![\cdot,\cdot]\!],P,Q}{\mathbb{C}[\![s_{k_1}.P,\overline{s}_{k_2}.Q]\!] \xrightarrow{\tau} (\nu r)\mathbb{C}[\![r \rhd_{k_2} P, r \rhd_{k_1} Q]\!]}
$$

Rule (PSYNC) is left unchanged, while we need to annotate the sessions appearing in rules (SSYNC), (SRSYNC) and (PRSYNC) (and in the notation $\mathbb{C}_r[\![\cdot,\cdot]\!]$) with suitable termination handlers k and k_1.

Three new rules are needed to handle session cancellation. Two of them regards the generation of notifications to be delivered on the opposite side, which may be due to the execution of the close primitive

$$\text{(SEND)}\quad \mathbb{C}[\![r \rhd_k \mathbb{S}[\![\mathsf{close}]\!]]\!] \xrightarrow{\tau} \mathbb{C}[\![\dagger(k) \mid \blacktriangleright \mathbb{S}[\![\mathbf{0}]\!]]\!]$$

or to the termination of an enclosing session:

$$\text{(TEND)}\frac{}{\mathbb{C}[\![\blacktriangleright (r \rhd_k P)]\!] \xrightarrow{\tau} \mathbb{C}[\![\blacktriangleright P \mid \dagger(k)]\!]}$$

The last rule models the handshake between a notification signal and its handler:

$$\text{(TSYNC)}\frac{}{\mathbb{C}[\![\dagger(k) \mid k \cdot P]\!] \xrightarrow{\tau} \mathbb{C}[\![P]\!]}$$

The session closing primitives do not guarantee *per se* that forever-dangling, one-sided sessions never arise, in the same way as deadlock can arise in pi-calculus processes or sequential programs may diverge. However, many situations can be handled satisfactorily just by installing suitable termination handlers of the form $k \cdot \mathbb{C}[\![\mathsf{close}]\!]$ in the bodies of client invocations and service definitions. Moreover, we can allow rather liberal choices of $\mathbb{C}[\![\cdot]\!]$, that may contain extra actions the termination handler may wish to take upon invocation, e.g., further signalling to other listeners (a sort of compensation, in the language of long-running transactions).

Again, the full technical details can be found in [8], here we just mention the main constraints over CaSPiS processes that can guarantee the so-called *graceful termination property*. Informally, the key concept is that of a *balanced* term, roughly, a term with only pairs of session-sides that balance with each other. Termination of one side may lead to unbalanced terms. The graceful property guarantees that *any possibly unbalanced term reachable from a balanced term can get balanced in a finite number of reductions.*

For a process P that contains no session constructs, we require e.g. that for any $Q \equiv P$ and for each s and k: (a) $s_k.$ may only occur in Q in subterms of the form $s_k.\mathbb{S}_1[\![k \cdot \mathbb{S}_2[\![\mathsf{close}]\!]]\!]$ and analogously for $\overline{s}_k.$; (b) in Q there is at most one occurrence of the listener for k.

For example, obvious "graceful" usages for service invocation and service definition are $(\nu k_1)\overline{s}_{k_1}.(P_1|k_1 \cdot \mathsf{close})$ and $(\nu k_2)s_{k_2}.(P_2|k_2 \cdot \mathsf{close})$, respectively. The process *News* from next example (adapted from [8]) also fits the requirements for the graceful property.

Example 7. Let *BBC* and *CNN* be services that, upon invocation, return a possibly infinite sequence of values representing pieces of news (disregarding the identity of these news, these services resemble $!BBC.!(\nu n)\langle n\rangle$, etc.). Let us consider the process *News* below that exposes a *news collector* service *collect*:

$$\begin{aligned} News \triangleq\ !(\nu k)collect_k.(\ k\cdot \mathsf{close}\ |\ (\nu k_1)\overline{BBC}_{k_1}.(!(?x)\langle x\rangle^{\uparrow}\ |\ k_1\cdot(\mathsf{close}\,|\,\dagger(k)))\\ |\ (\nu k_2)\overline{CNN}_{k_2}.(!(?x)\langle x\rangle^{\uparrow}\ |\ k_2\cdot(\mathsf{close}\,|\,\dagger(k)))\ ) \end{aligned}$$

The established session can be closed: either (i) by the client-side, when an action close on the client's side is performed, as this will yield a signal $\dagger(k)$ able to activate the corresponding service-side listener $k\cdot\mathsf{close}$; or, (ii) when any of the three nested sessions used for interacting with the news services is closed by peer, yielding the signal $\dagger(k_i)$ and hence $\dagger(k)$. The termination of the topmost session will in turn cause the termination of all (not yet terminated) nested news clients.

For example, after invoking *collect*, the client below receives all the news produced by *BBC* and *CNN* (in some interleaved order):

$$HeavyReader \triangleq (\nu k')\overline{collect}_{k'}.(!(?y)\langle y\rangle^{\uparrow}\,|\,k'\cdot\mathsf{close})$$

Instead the client below receives only the first news produced either by *BBC* or *CNN* and then abandons the session:

$$EasyReader \triangleq (\nu k')\overline{collect}_{k'}.((?y)\langle y\rangle^{\uparrow}\mathsf{close}\,|\,k'\cdot\mathsf{close})$$

It is worth mentioning that there are at least two obvious alternatives to the mechanism we have chosen. One would be to use close as a primitive for terminating instantaneously *both* the client-side and service-side sessions. But this strategy violates the principle that each party is in charge for the closing of its own session side. A second alternative would be to use close as a synchronisation primitive, so that the client-side and service-side sessions are terminated when close is encountered on one side and $\overline{\mathsf{close}}$ on the other side. This strategy conflicts with parties being able to decide autonomously when to end their own sessions. The use of termination handlers looks a reasonable compromise: each party can exit a session autonomously but it is obliged to inform the other party.

3.4 Other Variants

Some variants of CaSPiS have been recently considered in recent literature, that introduce suitable restrictions to favour analysis and verification of processes. We mention a few significant works.

In [15], it is assumed that: (1) service definitions can only be present at the top level and cannot dynamically deployed, (2) label-guarded sums and label-choice are considered instead of guarded sums and pattern-matching, (3) the pipeline is restricted to the form $P > (?\vec{x})Q$, i.e. to Orc sequencing, (4) conditional statements are introduced, (5) session sides are polarised, (6) services are persistent and can be invoked recursively, but general replication is not allowed. Under these requirements, a type system is developed that guarantees that all session protocols are deadlock free, in the sense that well-typed processes either reach a normal form or diverge by opening new nested sessions. In [1], under similar restrictions, it is shown that session names can be disregarded and a type system is provided that guarantees client-progress property (i.e., client-side protocols will not deadlock). The above results have then been extended in [45] by introducing general recursion at the level of session protocols and using the type system to prevent communication errors.

In [38] a security-oriented extension of the work in [15] is presented, where security levels can be assigned to service definitions, clients and data. In order to invoke a service, a client must be endowed with an appropriate clearance, and once the service and client agree on the security level, the data exchanged in the initiated session will not exceed this level. The main result is a type system that guarantees these security properties.

Besides qualitative aspects, in SOC it is also important to consider phenomena related to performance and dependability to deal with issues related to Quality of Service. They are particularly relevant for services running over congestioned networks, where unpredictable delays and failures are more likely. In [25] a Markovian extension of CaSPiS, called MarCaSPiS, has been studied, where: output activities are enriched with rates (characterising random variables with exponential distributions) and input activities are equipped with weights (characterising the relative selection probability). Then continuous time Markov chains can be obtained from MarCaSPiS specifications to perform quantitative analysis.

Some prototype implementations of CaSPiS have been proposed in [4, 10].

4 Application Examples

In this section we show a few intuitive encoding of paradigmatic calculi in CaSPiS and of a simple fragment of CaSPiS in pi-calculus, but without proving any strong formal correspondence.

4.1 From Lambda-Calculus to CaSPiS

We start by showing that the close-free fragment of CaSPiS is expressive enough to encode λ-calculus, in a similar way as done, e.g., in pi-calculus (see Example 2).

The encoding is summarised in Fig. 10, where $[\![M]\!]_a^{\lambda 2c}$ denotes the CaSPiS process modelling the λ-expression M with arguments retrieved through the service a. Notably the encoding uses just monadic messaging without exploiting pipelines, choices, return prefixes and pattern matching.

From the point of view of syntax, the main differences w.r.t. the pi-calculus encoding are: (i) service definitions replace input prefixes; (ii) service invocations replace output

$$
\begin{aligned}
[\![x]\!]_a^{\lambda 2c} &\triangleq \overline{x}.\langle a\rangle \\
[\![\lambda x.M]\!]_a^{\lambda 2c} &\triangleq a.(?x)(?m)[\![M]\!]_m^{\lambda 2c} \\
[\![MN]\!]_a^{\lambda 2c} &\triangleq (\nu m)\Big([\![M]\!]_m^{\lambda 2c} \,|\, (\nu b)(\; !b.(?n)[\![N]\!]_n^{\lambda 2c} \,|\, \overline{m}.\langle b\rangle\langle a\rangle\,)\Big) \quad \text{for } b \notin \mathrm{fv}(N)
\end{aligned}
$$

Fig. 10. Encoding of λ-calculus in CaSPiS

prefixes. From the point of view of semantics, the more important differences are: (i) each service invocation opens a new session where the computation can progress; (ii) the session can be nested at different levels of depth and are never closed.

Exercise 9. Write the CaSPiS processes $[\![\lambda x.x]\!]_a^{\lambda 2c}$ and $[\![(\lambda x.x)N]\!]_a^{\lambda 2c}$. Then write all reduction steps of $[\![(\lambda x.x)N]\!]_a^{\lambda 2c}$.

4.2 From Pi-Calculus to CaSPiS

Quite interestingly, choice-free pi-calculus can be encoded in the close-free fragment of CaSPiS. In fact, pi-calculus communication primitives can be seen as services with minimal protocols. Note however that encoding the pi-calculus process $a(x).P$ as the CaSPiS process $a.(?x)C$ (for C the encoding of P) would unnecessarily run C in a nested session. To avoid this problem, and to make the encoding more elegant, it suffices to exploit pipelines and pattern-matching. For simplicity we focus on the monadic pi-calculus without sum. The problem with choices is due to the fact that CaSPiS sums can be applied only to abstraction, concretion and return prefixes, but not to service definition and invocations.

The encoding of pi-calculus processes is defined rather straightforwardly in Fig. 11.

$$
\begin{aligned}
[\![\mathbf{0}]\!]^{\pi 2c} &\triangleq \mathbf{0} \\
[\![x(y).P]\!]^{\pi 2c} &\triangleq x.(?y)\langle y\rangle^{\uparrow} > (?y)[\![P]\!]^{\pi 2c} \\
[\![\overline{x}\langle y\rangle.P]\!]^{\pi 2c} &\triangleq \overline{x}.\langle y\rangle\langle\rangle^{\uparrow} > ()[\![P]\!]^{\pi 2c} \\
[\![\tau.P]\!]^{\pi 2c} &\triangleq \langle\rangle > ()[\![P]\!]^{\pi 2c} \\
[\![[x=y]\pi.P]\!]^{\pi 2c} &\triangleq \langle x\rangle > (y)[\![\pi.P]\!]^{\pi 2c} \\
[\![P_1 \,|\, P_2]\!]^{\pi 2c} &\triangleq [\![P_1]\!]^{\pi 2c} \,|\, [\![P_2]\!]^{\pi 2c} \\
[\![(\nu x)P]\!]^{\pi 2c} &\triangleq (\nu x)[\![P]\!]^{\pi 2c} \\
[\![!P]\!]^{\pi 2c} &\triangleq ![\![P]\!]^{\pi 2c}
\end{aligned}
$$

Fig. 11. Encoding of π-calculus in CaSPiS

Exercise 10. The encoding of λ-calculus in pi-calculus $[\![M]\!]_a^{\lambda 2\pi}$ can be combined with the above encoding of pi-calculus in CaSPiS to obtain an encoding $[\![M]\!]_a^{\lambda 2\pi 2c}$ of λ-calculus in CaSPiS. After giving the explicit definition of $[\![x]\!]_a^{\lambda 2\pi 2c}$, $[\![\lambda x.M]\!]_a^{\lambda 2\pi 2c}$ and $[\![MN]\!]_a^{\lambda 2\pi 2c}$, compare the encoding with the one defined in Fig. 10 and explain the main differences, if any.

Then, write the CaSPiS processes $[\![\lambda x.x]\!]_a^{\lambda 2\pi 2c}$ and $[\![(\lambda x.x)N]\!]_a^{\lambda 2\pi 2c}$, together with all reduction steps of $[\![(\lambda x.x)N]\!]_a^{\lambda 2\pi 2c}$.

4.3 From Orc to CaSPiS

In [7] it was shown how to encode Orc in CaSPiS. Here we essentially rephrase (and simplify) the translation using CaSPiS syntax. An Orc expression may depend on a

$$
\begin{aligned}
[\![E(x) \triangleq e]\!]^{o2c} &\triangleq E.(?x)[\![e]\!]^{o2c} \\
[\![\mathbf{0}]\!]^{o2c} &\triangleq \mathbf{0} \\
[\![\langle p\rangle]\!]^{o2c} &\triangleq [\![p]\!]_{\mathrm{v}} \\
[\![E(p)]\!]^{o2c} &\triangleq \overline{E}.\langle p\rangle!(?x_r)\langle x_r\rangle^{\uparrow} \\
[\![s(p)]\!]^{o2c} &\triangleq [\![p]\!]_{\mathrm{v}} > (?x_p)\overline{s}.\langle x_p\rangle(?x_r)\langle x_r\rangle^{\uparrow} \\
[\![x(p)]\!]^{o2c} &\triangleq [\![x]\!]_{\mathrm{v}} > (?s)[\![s(p)]\!]^{o2c} \\
[\![e_1 \,|\, e_2]\!]^{o2c} &\triangleq [\![e_1]\!]^{o2c} \,|\, [\![e_2]\!]^{o2c} \\
[\![e_1 > x > e_2]\!]^{o2c} &\triangleq [\![e_1]\!]^{o2c} > (?x)[\![e_2]\!]^{o2c} \\
[\![e_2 \;\mathbf{where}\; x :\in e_1]\!]^{o2c} &\triangleq (\nu wh, re, k)(\, \overline{wh}_k.([\![e_1]\!]^{o2c} > (?x_1)\overline{re}.\langle x_1\rangle\langle\rangle^{\uparrow} \,|\, k\cdot\mathsf{close}\,)\,| \\
&\qquad wh.()\mathsf{close} \,|\, (\nu x)([\![e_2]\!]^{o2c} \,|\, re.(?x_1)!x.\langle x_1\rangle)\,)
\end{aligned}
$$

Fig. 12. Encoding of Orc in CaSPiS

set of expression definitions, hence the encoding of an Orc expression comprises the encoding of all expression definitions (as processes composed in parallel).

The encoding of Orc expressions is detailed in Fig. 12. A few points are worth some comments. While the call of a site is strict (and thus the actual parameters must have been evaluated), the evaluation of defined expressions is non-strict (and thus parameters can be passed by name). Correspondingly, we define the call by value by letting:

$$
[\![s]\!]_{\mathrm{v}} \triangleq \langle s\rangle \qquad [\![v]\!]_{\mathrm{v}} \triangleq \langle v\rangle \qquad [\![x]\!]_{\mathrm{v}} \triangleq \overline{x}.(?x_r)\langle x_r\rangle^{\uparrow}
$$

Note that the evaluation of a variable x is encoded as a request for the current value to the variable manager of x. Variable managers are created by both sequential composition and asymmetric parallel composition.

The most interesting part of the encoding regards the asymmetric parallel composition. Two fresh services *wh* and *re* are used, respectively, to enclose the evaluation of e_1 in a session that can be terminated and to receive the first value provided by e_1 and install the manager for variable x with that value. This is exemplified below, where we omit all restriction to improve readability and write P_1 and P_2 in place of $[\![e_1]\!]^{o2c}$ and $[\![e_2]\!]^{o2c}$, respectively.

$$
\begin{aligned}
&\overline{wh}_k.(P_1 > (?x_1)\overline{re}.\langle x_1\rangle\langle\rangle^{\uparrow} \,|\, k\cdot\mathsf{close})\,|\, wh.()\mathsf{close} \,|\, P_2 \,|\, re.(?x_1)!x.\langle x_1\rangle \\
&\xrightarrow{\tau} r_w \rhd (P_1 > (?x_1)\overline{re}.\langle x_1\rangle\langle\rangle^{\uparrow} \,|\, k\cdot\mathsf{close})\,|\, r_w \rhd_k ()\mathsf{close} \,|\, P_2 \,|\, re.(?x_1)!x.\langle x_1\rangle
\end{aligned}
$$

Note that $[\![e_2]\!]^{o2c}$ is executed concurrently, but may rely on value requests to the manager for x. When $[\![e_1]\!]^{o2c}$ produces a concretion, it flows through the pipeline and activates the invocation to *re*.

$$
\begin{aligned}
&r_w \rhd (P_1 > (?x_1)\overline{re}.\langle x_1\rangle\langle\rangle^{\uparrow} \,|\, k\cdot\mathsf{close})\,|\, r_w \rhd_k ()\mathsf{close} \,|\, P_2 \,|\, re.(?x_1)!x.\langle x_1\rangle \\
&\xrightarrow{\tau} r_w \rhd (\overline{re}.\langle 8\rangle\langle\rangle^{\uparrow} \,|\, (P_1' > (?x_1)\overline{re}.\langle x_1\rangle\langle\rangle^{\uparrow} \,|\, k\cdot\mathsf{close}))\,|\, r_w \rhd_k ()\mathsf{close} \,|\, P_2 \,|\, re.(?x_1)!x.\langle x_1\rangle \\
&\xrightarrow{\tau} r_w \rhd (r \rhd \langle 8\rangle\langle\rangle^{\uparrow} \,|\, (P_1' > (?x_1)\overline{re}.\langle x_1\rangle\langle\rangle^{\uparrow} \,|\, k\cdot\mathsf{close}))\,|\, r_w \rhd_k ()\mathsf{close} \,|\, P_2 \,|\, r \rhd (?x_1)!x.\langle x_1\rangle
\end{aligned}
$$

Note that the service definition for *re* is not replicated and thus only one request may be issued. The value produced by $[\![e_1]\!]^{o2c}$ is communicated by the client session side of *re* to its peer session side, which in turn can install a persistent service definition for variable x (its manager w.r.t. requests in $[\![e_2]\!]^{o2c}$). The void return prefix on the client side instance or *re* is now available and can handshake with the void abstraction on the service side instance of *wh*, enabling the execution of close.

$$
\begin{array}{l}
r_w \rhd (r \rhd \langle 8\rangle\langle\rangle^{\uparrow} \,|\, (P_1' > (?x_1)\overline{re}.\langle x_1\rangle\langle\rangle^{\uparrow} \,|\, k \cdot \mathsf{close})) \,|\, r_w \rhd_k ()\mathsf{close} \,|\, P_2 \,|\, r \rhd (?x_1)!x.\langle x_1\rangle \\
\xrightarrow{\tau} r_w \rhd (r \rhd \langle\rangle^{\uparrow} \,|\, (P_1' > (?x_1)\overline{re}.\langle x_1\rangle\langle\rangle^{\uparrow} \,|\, k \cdot \mathsf{close})) \,|\, r_w \rhd_k ()\mathsf{close} \,|\, P_2 \,|\, r \rhd !x.\langle 8\rangle \\
\xrightarrow{\tau} r_w \rhd (r \rhd \mathbf{0} \,|\, (P_1' > (?x_1)\overline{re}.\langle x_1\rangle\langle\rangle^{\uparrow} \,|\, k \cdot \mathsf{close})) \,|\, r_w \rhd_k \mathsf{close} \,|\, P_2 \,|\, r \rhd !x.\langle 8\rangle
\end{array}
$$

The effect of close is to terminate the enclosing session side and to notify the listener k (within the client side instance of *wh*), which in turn will terminate the enclosing session side.

$$
\begin{array}{rl}
& r_w \rhd (r \rhd \mathbf{0} \,|\, (P_1' > (?x_1)\overline{re}.\langle x_1\rangle\langle\rangle^{\uparrow} \,|\, k \cdot \mathsf{close})) \,|\, r_w \rhd_k \mathsf{close} \,|\, P_2 \,|\, r \rhd !x.\langle 8\rangle \\
\xrightarrow{\tau} & r_w \rhd (r \rhd \mathbf{0} \,|\, (P_1' > (?x_1)\overline{re}.\langle x_1\rangle\langle\rangle^{\uparrow} \,|\, k \cdot \mathsf{close})) \,|\, \dagger(k) \,|\, \blacktriangleright \mathbf{0} \,|\, P_2 \,|\, r \rhd !x.\langle 8\rangle \\
\equiv & r_w \rhd (r \rhd \mathbf{0} \,|\, (P_1' > (?x_1)\overline{re}.\langle x_1\rangle\langle\rangle^{\uparrow} \,|\, \dagger(k) \,|\, k \cdot \mathsf{close})) \,|\, P_2 \,|\, r \rhd !x.\langle 8\rangle \\
\xrightarrow{\tau} & r_w \rhd (r \rhd \mathbf{0} \,|\, (P_1' > (?x_1)\overline{re}.\langle x_1\rangle\langle\rangle^{\uparrow} \,|\, \mathsf{close})) \,|\, P_2 \,|\, r \rhd !x.\langle 8\rangle \\
\xrightarrow{\tau} & \blacktriangleright (r \rhd \mathbf{0} \,|\, (P_1' > (?x_1)\overline{re}.\langle x_1\rangle\langle\rangle^{\uparrow})) \,|\, P_2 \,|\, r \rhd !x.\langle 8\rangle
\end{array}
$$

Consequently, the nested session side of *re* is also terminated, but not its peer (because no termination handler was exchanged when the session was created). In fact the manager for x is running inside that peer and we cannot terminate it.

$$
\begin{array}{rl}
& \blacktriangleright (r \rhd \mathbf{0} \,|\, (P_1' > (?x_1)\overline{re}.\langle x_1\rangle\langle\rangle^{\uparrow})) \,|\, P_2 \,|\, r \rhd !x.\langle 8\rangle \\
\equiv & (\blacktriangleright P_1' > (?x_1)\overline{re}.\langle x_1\rangle\langle\rangle^{\uparrow}) \,|\, P_2 \,|\, r \rhd !x.\langle 8\rangle \\
\to^* & (\blacktriangleright \mathbf{0} > (?x_1)\overline{re}.\langle x_1\rangle\langle\rangle^{\uparrow}) \,|\, P_2 \,|\, r \rhd !x.\langle 8\rangle \\
\equiv & (\mathbf{0} > (?x_1)\overline{re}.\langle x_1\rangle\langle\rangle^{\uparrow}) \,|\, P_2 \,|\, r \rhd !x.\langle 8\rangle
\end{array}
$$

Note that this makes the process not well-balanced, as it contains a dangling session side that cannot terminate, i.e., the encoding we have provided does not satisfy the graceful closure property.

Exercise 11. Write the CaSPiS processes that encodes the Orc expressions $\langle 1\rangle|\langle 2\rangle > x > \langle x\rangle$ and $\langle x\rangle$ **where** $x :\in \langle 1\rangle|\langle 2\rangle$. Then write all the CaSPiS processes that can be reached from them via any number of reductions.

Exercise 12. Write the CaSPiS processes that encodes the Orc expression *POR* for the parallel-or (see Exercise 7).

Exercise 13. Modify the encoding shown in Fig. 12 to guarantee the graceful termination property. Start by changing the way in which the manager of x is installed in the encoding of asymmetric parallel composition. Then, remind that $[\![e_1]\!]^{o2c}$ could have opened many other session sides before cancellation occurs and hence find suitable policies for invoking sites, expression definitions and local services.

4.4 From Close-Free CaSPiS to Pi-Calculus

We conclude by sketching an encoding of a fragment of CaSPiS in pi-calculus. In particular we restrict to consider the close-free fragment, without pattern matching and with a limited form of pipeline (which essentially coincides with Orc sequencing operator). Moreover we assume session sides are polarised $r^+ \rhd P$ and $r^- \rhd Q$.

The encoding of a CaSPiS process is dependent on its context. In particular, one can imagine that each CaSPiS process has three dedicated channels: one for the input associated with abstraction prefixes, one for output associated with concretion prefixes and one for output associated with return prefixes. Correspondingly, our encoding $[\![P]\!]^{c2\pi}_{in,out,ret}$ is parametric w.r.t. three names *in*, *out* and *ret*. The encoding is shown in Fig. 13, where we write $r^{\overline{p}}$ to denote the dual session of r^p.

$$
\begin{aligned}
[\![\textstyle\sum_i \pi_i P_i]\!]^{c2\pi}_{in,out,ret} &\triangleq \textstyle\sum_i [\![\pi_i P_i]\!]^{c2\pi}_{in,out,ret}\\
[\![(?x)P]\!]^{c2\pi}_{in,out,ret} &\triangleq in(x).[\![P]\!]^{c2\pi}_{in,out,ret}\\
[\![\langle v\rangle P]\!]^{c2\pi}_{in,out,ret} &\triangleq \overline{out}\langle v\rangle.[\![P]\!]^{c2\pi}_{in,out,ret}\\
[\![\langle v\rangle^{\uparrow} P]\!]^{c2\pi}_{in,out,ret} &\triangleq \overline{ret}\langle v\rangle.[\![P]\!]^{c2\pi}_{in,out,ret}\\
[\![u.P]\!]^{c2\pi}_{in,out,ret} &\triangleq u(r^p, r^q).[\![P]\!]^{c2\pi}_{r^p,r^q,out}\\
[\![\overline{u}.P]\!]^{c2\pi}_{in,out,ret} &\triangleq (\nu r^+, r^-)\overline{u}\langle r^+, r^-\rangle.[\![P]\!]^{c2\pi}_{r^-,r^+,out}\\
[\![r^p \rhd P]\!]^{c2\pi}_{in,out,ret} &\triangleq [\![P]\!]^{c2\pi}_{r^p,r^{\overline{p}},out}\\
[\![P > (?x)Q]\!]^{c2\pi}_{in,out,ret} &\triangleq (\nu p)(\,[\![P]\!]^{c2\pi}_{in,p,ret} \,|\, !p(x).[\![Q]\!]^{c2\pi}_{in,out,ret}\,) \ \text{ for } p \notin \mathrm{fn}(P|Q)\\
[\![P_1 | P_2]\!]^{c2\pi}_{in,out,ret} &\triangleq [\![P_1]\!]^{c2\pi}_{in,out,ret} \,|\, [\![P_2]\!]^{c2\pi}_{in,out,ret}\\
[\![(\nu n)P]\!]^{c2\pi}_{in,out,ret} &\triangleq (\nu n)[\![P]\!]^{c2\pi}_{in,out,ret}\\
[\![!P]\!]^{c2\pi}_{in,out,ret} &\triangleq ![\![P]\!]^{c2\pi}_{in,out,ret}
\end{aligned}
$$

Fig. 13. Encoding of CaSPiS in pi-calculus

The most interesting part of the encoding is concerned with service definition, service invocation, session siding and pipeline. A service invocation is encoded by creating two fresh names r^+ and r^- that will be used for intra-session communication: the service side will use them for input and output, respectively; vice versa the client side will use them for output and input, respectively. The presence of two names instead of just one guarantees that two concurrent processes running on the same session side cannot interact. Consequently, a session side r^p uses the name r^p for input and $r^{\overline{p}}$ for output. Note also the name for return in the nested session coincides with the name used for output by its parent. Finally, a pipeline $P > (?x)Q$ must intercept the output of P and use it to spawn fresh copies of Q. This is achieved by creating a fresh name p that is used for output by the encoding of P and that is used as input guard of a replicated process that spawns the copies of (the encoding of) Q.

Exercise 14. The encoding of λ-calculus in CaSPiS $[\![M]\!]_a^{\lambda 2c}$ can be combined with the above encoding of CaSPiS in pi-calculus to obtain an encoding $[\![M]\!]_a^{\lambda 2c2\pi}$ of λ-calculus in pi-calculus. After giving the explicit definition of $[\![x]\!]_a^{\lambda 2c2\pi}$, $[\![\lambda x.M]\!]_a^{\lambda 2c2\pi}$ and $[\![MN]\!]_a^{\lambda 2c2\pi}$, compare the encoding with the one defined in Fig. 4 and explain the main differences, if any.

Then, write the pi-calculus processes $[\![\lambda x.x]\!]_a^{\lambda 2c2\pi}$ and $[\![(\lambda x.x)N]\!]_a^{\lambda 2c2\pi}$, together with all reduction steps of $[\![(\lambda x.x)N]\!]_a^{\lambda 2c2\pi}$.

A type preserving encoding of (a variant of) CaSPiS in (a variant of) Honda, Vasconcelos and Kubo's session calculus has been recently defined in Leonardo Mezzina's PhD thesis [45].

5 Conclusion and Future Perspectives

In this tutorial we have tried to contribute along the following directions: (1) to outline several key characteristics of Service-Oriented Computing systems, (2) to sketch the basic principles, techniques and formal tools offered by the theory of process calculi, (3) to show that process calculi can likely offer a convenient formalism for representing SOC systems, but they need to be empowered by novel modelling approaches, developed at the right level of abstraction, (4) to overview some existing proposals and the different guidelines they are driven by, (5) to present in detail one such proposal, namely CaSPiS, and explain the rationale around its design choices, (6) to show how CaSPiS can be related w.r.t. other well-established formalisms, so that readers more familiar with them can catch similarities and get a better understand of CaSPiS semantics, (7) to show that CaSPiS mechanism of termination handlers is very expressive, disciplined and flexible: even if it may look overcomplicated to use, we emphasise that, up to our knowledge, this is the only proposal able to guarantee a disciplined termination of nested sessions. We conjecture that any mechanism of this kind would be very complicated to handle in say pi-calculus.

We hope the quite informal level of presentation has been appreciated by readers not familiar with process calculi and may serve as a valid basis to learn more, possibly with the help of the many simple exercises populating the technical sections.

Regarding future work, there is still quite a lot of research to be done for refining and consolidating the different process calculi proposed for SOC, for integrating them with other more advanced aspects, like transactions and quality of service, for comparing them and relating them in a formal way. In particular, for CaSPiS, the overall objective is to have a rigorous theoretical framework, with some automatic tools available for type checking, type inference, quantitative analysis and rapid prototyping. We would like also to integrate other techniques, like those based on choreography, contracts, correlation sets, and multiparty sessions, within CaSPiS, possibly finding seamless ways to support such concepts on the existing machinery. Current work is also concerned with graphical encoding and concurrent semantics for SOC calculi, using models based on hierarchical graphs (that best reflect the nesting of sessions and the possibility to operate on the nested session sides as a whole, like when terminating atomically a session side and all its descendants).

References

1. Acciai, L., Boreale, M.: A type system for client progress in a service-oriented calculus. In: Degano, P., De Nicola, R., Meseguer, J. (eds.) Concurrency, Graphs and Models. LNCS, vol. 5065, pp. 642–658. Springer, Heidelberg (2008)
2. Aceto, L., Ingólfsdóttir, A., Larsen, K., Srba, J.: Reactive Systems: Modelling, Specification and Verification. Cambridge University Press, Cambridge (2007)
3. Bartoletti, M., Degano, P., Ferrari, G., Zunino, R.: Types and effects for Resource Usage Analysis. In: Seidl, H. (ed.) FOSSACS 2007. LNCS, vol. 4423, pp. 32–47. Springer, Heidelberg (2007)
4. Bettini, L., De Nicola, R., Loreti, M.: Implementing Session Centered Calculi. In: Lea, D., Zavattaro, G. (eds.) COORDINATION 2008. LNCS, vol. 5052, pp. 17–32. Springer, Heidelberg (2008)
5. Bodei, C., Brodo, L., Bruni, R.: Static detection of logic flaws in service applications. In: Proceedings of ARSPA-WITS 2009, Joint Workshop on Automated Reasoning for Security Protocol Analysis and Issues in the Theory of Security. LNCS. Springer, Heidelberg (2009) (to appear)
6. Bonelli, E., Compagnoni, A.: Multisession session types for a distributed calculus. In: Barthe, G., Fournet, C. (eds.) TGC 2007. LNCS, vol. 4912, pp. 240–256. Springer, Heidelberg (2008)
7. Boreale, M., Bruni, R., Caires, L., De Nicola, R., Lanese, I., Loreti, M., Martins, F., Montanari, U., Ravara, A., Sangiorgi, D., Vasconcelos, V., Zavattaro, G.: SCC: a service centered calculus. In: Bravetti, M., Núñez, M., Zavattaro, G. (eds.) WS-FM 2006. LNCS, vol. 4184, pp. 38–57. Springer, Heidelberg (2006)
8. Boreale, M., Bruni, R., De Nicola, R., Loreti, M.: Sessions and pipelines for structured service programming. In: Barthe, G., de Boer, F.S. (eds.) FMOODS 2008. LNCS, vol. 5051, pp. 19–38. Springer, Heidelberg (2008)
9. Bravetti, M., Zavattaro, G.: A Foundational Theory of Contracts for Multi-party Service Composition. Fundam. Inform. 89(4), 451–478 (2008)
10. Bruni, R., De Nicola, R., Loreti, M., Mezzina, L.: Provably correct implementations of services. In: Kaklamanis, C., Nielson, F. (eds.) TGC 2008. LNCS, vol. 5474, pp. 69–86. Springer, Heidelberg (2009)
11. Bruni, R., Lanese, I.: Parametric synchronizations in mobile nominal calculi. Theoretical Computer Science 402(2-3), 102–119 (2008)
12. Bruni, R., Lanese, I., Melgratti, H., Tuosto, E.: Multiparty sessions in SOC. In: Lea, D., Zavattaro, G. (eds.) COORDINATION 2008. LNCS, vol. 5052, pp. 67–82. Springer, Heidelberg (2008)
13. Bruni, R., Melgratti, H., Montanari, U.: Nested commits for mobile calculi: extending Join. In: Lévy, J.-J., Mayr, E., Mitchell, J. (eds.) Proceedings of the 3rd IFIP-TCS 2004, 3rd IFIP Intl. Conference on Theoretical Computer Science, pp. 569–582. Kluwer Academic Publishers, Dordrecht (2004)
14. Bruni, R., Melgratti, H., Montanari, U.: Theoretical foundations for compensations in flow composition languages. In: POPL 2005: Proceedings of the 32nd ACM SIGPLAN-SIGACT sysposium on Principles of programming languages, pp. 209–220. ACM Press, New York (2005)

15. Bruni, R., Mezzina, L.: Types and deadlock freedom in a calculus of services, sessions and pipelines. In: Rosu, G., Meseguer, J. (eds.) AMAST 2008. LNCS, vol. 5140, pp. 100–115. Springer, Heidelberg (2008)
16. Buscemi, M., Montanari, U.: CC-Pi: A Constraint-Based Language for Specifying Service Level Agreements. In: Nicola, R.D. (ed.) ESOP 2007. LNCS, vol. 4421, pp. 18–32. Springer, Heidelberg (2007)
17. Busi, N., Gorrieri, R., Guidi, C., Lucchi, R., Zavattaro, G.: Choreography and orchestration conformance for system design. In: Ciancarini, P., Wiklicky, H. (eds.) COORDINATION 2006. LNCS, vol. 4038, pp. 63–81. Springer, Heidelberg (2006)
18. Butler, M., Bruni, R., Ferreira, C., Hoare, T., Melgratti, H., Montanari, U.: Comparing two approaches to compensable flow composition. In: Abadi, M., de Alfaro, L. (eds.) CONCUR 2005. LNCS, vol. 3653, pp. 383–397. Springer, Heidelberg (2005)
19. Butler, M., Hoare, T., Ferreira, C.: A trace semantics for long-running transactions. In: Abdallah, A., Sanders, J. (eds.) 25 Years Communicating Sequential Processes. LNCS, vol. 3525, pp. 133–150. Springer, Heidelberg (2005)
20. Caires, L., Vieira, H.T., Seco, J.C.: The conversation calculus: A model of service oriented computation. In: Drossopoulou, S. (ed.) ESOP 2008. LNCS, vol. 4960, pp. 269–283. Springer, Heidelberg (2008)
21. Carbone, M., Honda, K., Yoshida, N.: Structured communication-centred programming for web services. In: De Nicola, R. (ed.) ESOP 2007. LNCS, vol. 4421, pp. 2–17. Springer, Heidelberg (2007)
22. Castagna, G., Gesbert, N., Padovani, L.: A theory of contracts for web services. In: Proceedings of POPL 2008, pp. 261–272. ACM, New York (2008)
23. Cook, W.R., Patwardhan, S., Misra, J.: Workflow patterns in Orc. In: Ciancarini, P., Wiklicky, H. (eds.) COORDINATION 2006. LNCS, vol. 4038, pp. 82–96. Springer, Heidelberg (2006)
24. Curtin, E., Warshauer, M.: The locker puzzle. The Mathematical Intelligencer 28(1), 28–31 (2006)
25. De Nicola, R., Latella, D., Loreti, M., Massink, M.: MarCaSPiS: a markovian extension of a calculus for services. In: Proceedings of SOS 2008. Elect. Notes in Th. Comput. Sci. (2008) (to appear)
26. Dezani-Ciancaglini, M., Yoshida, N., Ahern, A., Drossopoulou, S.: A distributed object-oriented language with session types. In: De Nicola, R., Sangiorgi, D. (eds.) TGC 2005. LNCS, vol. 3705, pp. 299–318. Springer, Heidelberg (2005)
27. Ene, C., Muntean, T.: A broadcast-based calculus for communicating systems. In: Proc. of IPDPS 2001. IEEE Computer Society, Los Alamitos (2001)
28. Ferrari, G., Guanciale, R., Strollo, D.: JSCL: A Middleware for Service Coordination. In: Najm, E., Pradat-Peyre, J.-F., Donzeau-Gouge, V.V. (eds.) FORTE 2006. LNCS, vol. 4229, pp. 46–60. Springer, Heidelberg (2006)
29. Ferrari, G., Guanciale, R., Strollo, D., Tuosto, E.: Coordination via types in an event-based framework. In: Derrick, J., Vain, J. (eds.) FORTE 2007. LNCS, vol. 4574, pp. 66–80. Springer, Heidelberg (2007)
30. Gay, S., Hole, M.: Types and subtypes for client-server interactions. In: Swierstra, S.D. (ed.) ESOP 1999. LNCS, vol. 1576, pp. 74–90. Springer, Heidelberg (1999)
31. van Glabbeek, R.: The linear time – branching time spectrum II; the semantics of sequential systems with silent moves (extended abstract). In: Best, E. (ed.) CONCUR 1993. LNCS, vol. 715, pp. 66–81. Springer, Heidelberg (1993)
32. van Glabbeek, R.: The linear time – branching time spectrum I; the semantics of concrete, sequential processes. In: Bergstra, J., Ponse, A., Smolka, S. (eds.) Handbook of Process Algebra, ch. 1, pp. 3–99. Elsevier, Amsterdam (2001)
33. Hoare, C.: A model for communicating sequential processes. In: On the Construction of Programs. Cambridge University Press, Cambridge (1980)

34. Honda, K.: Types for dyadic interaction. In: Best, E. (ed.) CONCUR 1993. LNCS, vol. 715, pp. 509–523. Springer, Heidelberg (1993)
35. Honda, K., Vasconcelos, V., Kubo, M.: Language primitives and type disciplines for structured communication-based programming. In: Hankin, C. (ed.) ESOP 1998. LNCS, vol. 1381, pp. 122–138. Springer, Heidelberg (1998)
36. Honda, K., Yoshida, N., Carbone, M.: Multiparty asynchronous session types. In: POPL 2008, Proceedings of the 35th ACM SIGPLAN-SIGACT Symposium on Priniciples of Programming Languages, pp. 273–284. ACM Press, New York (2008)
37. Kitchin, D., Cook, W.R., Misra, J.: A language for task orchestration and its semantic properties. In: Baier, C., Hermanns, H. (eds.) CONCUR 2006. LNCS, vol. 4137, pp. 477–491. Springer, Heidelberg (2006)
38. Kolundzija, M.: Security types for sessions and pipelines. In: Bruni, R., Wolf, K. (eds.) WS-FM 2008. LNCS, vol. 5387, pp. 176–190. Springer, Heidelberg (2009)
39. Lanese, I., Vasconcelos, V., Martins, F., Ravara, A.: Disciplining orchestration and conversation in service-oriented computing. In: Proc. of SEFM 2007, Fifth IEEE International Conference on Software Engineering and Formal Methods, pp. 305–314. IEEE Computer Society Press, Los Alamitos (2007)
40. Laneve, C., Padovani, L.: The pairing of contracts and session types. In: Degano, P., De Nicola, R., Meseguer, J. (eds.) Concurrency, Graphs and Models. LNCS, vol. 5065, pp. 681–700. Springer, Heidelberg (2008)
41. Laneve, C., Zavattaro, G.: Foundations of web transactions. In: Sassone, V. (ed.) FOSSACS 2005. LNCS, vol. 3441, pp. 282–298. Springer, Heidelberg (2005)
42. Lapadula, A., Pugliese, R., Tiezzi, F.: A calculus for orchestration of web services. In: De Nicola, R. (ed.) ESOP 2007. LNCS, vol. 4421, pp. 33–47. Springer, Heidelberg (2007)
43. Lapadula, A., Pugliese, R., Tiezzi, F.: A formal account of WS-BPEL. In: Lea, D., Zavattaro, G. (eds.) COORDINATION 2008. LNCS, vol. 5052, pp. 199–215. Springer, Heidelberg (2008)
44. Mezzina, L.: How to infer finite session types in a calculus of services and sessions. In: Lea, D., Zavattaro, G. (eds.) COORDINATION 2008. LNCS, vol. 5052, pp. 216–231. Springer, Heidelberg (2008)
45. Mezzina, L.: Typing Services. Ph.D in Computer Science and Engineering, IMT Institute for Advanced Studies, Lucca (2009)
46. Milner, R. (ed.): A Calculus of Communication Systems. LNCS, vol. 92. Springer, Heidelberg (1980)
47. Milner, R.: Functions as processes. Math. Struct. in Comput. Sci. 2(2), 119–141 (1992)
48. Milner, R.: Communicating and Mobile Systems: The pi-calculus. Cambridge University Press, Cambridge (1997)
49. Milner, R., Parrow, J., Walker, J.: A calculus of mobile processes, I and II. Inform. and Comput. 100(1), 1–77 (1992)
50. Misra, J., Cook, W.R.: Computation orchestration: A basis for wide-area computing. Journal of Software and Systems Modeling 6(1), 83–110 (2007); A preliminary version of this paper appeared in the Lecture Notes for NATO summer school, held at Marktoberdorf in August 2004
51. Plotkin, G.: A structural approach to operational semantics. Technical Report DAIMI FN-19, Aarhus University, Computer Science Department (1981)
52. Plotkin, G.D.: The origins of structural operational semantics. Journal of Logic and Algebraic Programming 60-61, 3–15 (2004)
53. Plotkin, G.D.: A structural approach to operational semantics. Journal of Logic and Algebraic Programming 60-61, 17–139 (2004)
54. Rosaz, L.: Puzzle corner #70: The 50 prisoners. Bulletin of the European Association for Theoretical Computer Science (EATCS) 86, 229 (2005)

55. Sangiorgi, D.: Expressing Mobility in Process Algebras: First-Order and Higher-Order Paradigms. Ph.D thesis, LFCS, University of Edinburgh, CST-99-93 (also published as ECS-LFCS-93-266) (1993)
56. Sangiorgi, D., Walker, D.: The pi-calculus: a theory of mobile processes. Cambridge University Press, Cambridge (2001)
57. Sensoria Project. Software Engineering for Service-Oriented Overlay Computers. Public Web Site, `http://sensoria.fast.de/`
58. Vasconcelos, V.: Fundamentals of session types. In: Bernardo, M., Padovani, L., Zavattaro, G. (eds.) SFM 2009. LNCS, vol. 5569, pp. 158–186. Springer, Heidelberg (2009)
59. Wehrman, I., Kitchin, D., Cook, W.R., Misra, J.: A timed semantics of Orc. Theoretical Computer Science 402(2-3), 234–248 (2008)

Service Interaction: Patterns, Formalization, and Analysis

Wil M.P. van der Aalst[1], Arjan J. Mooij[1], Christian Stahl[1], and Karsten Wolf[2]

[1] Department of Mathematics and Computer Science
Technische Universiteit Eindhoven
P.O. Box 513, 5600 MB Eindhoven, The Netherlands
{W.M.P.v.d.Aalst,A.J.Mooij,C.Stahl}@tue.nl
[2] Universität Rostock, Institut für Informatik
18051 Rostock, Germany
Karsten.Wolf@uni-rostock.de

Abstract. As systems become more service oriented and processes increasingly cross organizational boundaries, interaction becomes more important. New technologies support the development of such systems. However, the paradigm shift towards service orientation, requires a fundamentally different way of looking at processes. This survey aims to provide some foundational notions related to service interaction. A set of service interaction patterns is given to illustrate the challenges in this domain. Moreover, key results are given for three of these challenges: (1) How to expose a service?, (2) How to replace and refine services?, and (3) How to generate service adapters? These challenges will be addressed in a Petri net setting. However, the results extend to other languages used in this domain.

Keywords: Service Orientation, Service Choreography, Open Nets, Verification, Service Interaction Patterns.

1 Introduction

Information technology has changed business processes within and between enterprises. Traditionally, information technology was mainly used to support individual tasks ("type a letter") and to store information. However, today's business processes and their information systems are intertwined. Processes heavily depend on information systems and information systems are driven by the processes they support [1]. In the last decade, information systems have become *"process aware"*, i.e., processes are taken as the starting point [1].

At the same time, there is an increasing acceptance of *Service-Oriented Architectures* (SOA) as a paradigm for integrating software applications within and across organizational boundaries [2]. XML-based standards like SOAP and WSDL facilitate the realization of such loosely coupled architectures. Interestingly, SOA and associated technologies have blurred the classical distinction between intra-organizational processes and inter-organizational processes. Whether

M. Bernardo, L. Padovani, and G. Zavattaro (Eds.): SFM 2009, LNCS 5569, pp. 42–88, 2009.

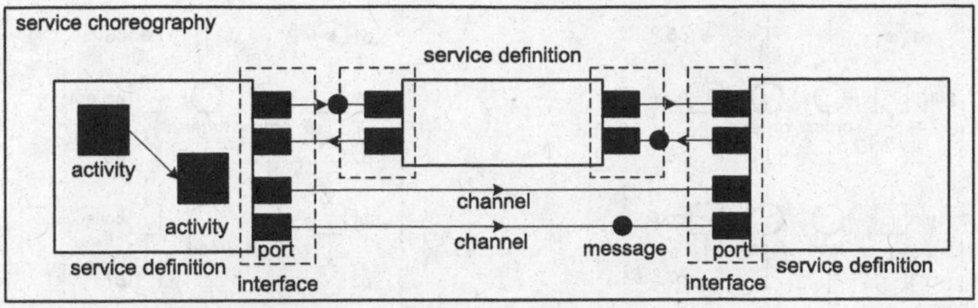

Fig. 1. An illustration showing the main terms used to describe services

work is subcontracted to an internal service or an external service, is no longer relevant from a technological point of view.

However, the *importance of interaction is increasing as more and more monolithic systems are broken down into smaller services.* The importance of interaction has been stressed by many authors [3,4,5,6,7,8]. Moreover, interaction is also considered a first-class citizen in various industry standards. For example, the *Web Services Business Process Execution Language* (BPEL) has primitive activities such as *invoke* (invoking an operation on a web service), *receive* (waiting for a message from an external source), and *reply* (replying to an external source) [9]. Moreover, the *pick* construct that can be used for race conditions based on external triggers is clearly inspired by the needs of service interaction.

Foundations. In this paper, we focus on the *foundations of service interaction.* We will not review the industry standards and associated tools. Instead we focus on fundamental concepts that are independent of a particular implementation language.

We first present some of the terms we will be using. A service has a *definition.* This definition describes the behavior and the interface of the service. A service can be *instantiated.* An instance corresponds to an execution of a service, and hence it can execute *activities*, and receive and send *messages.* Activities are the atomic units of work in a service and are specified in the service definition. The interface of a service consists of a set of *ports.* A pair of ports can be connected using a *channel*, thus enabling the exchange of *messages.* Services can be *composed* by connecting the interfaces. We use the term *service choreography* to refer to a set of fully-connected service definitions. Figure 1 illustrates these terms.

In Sect. 2 we categorize some recurring service interactions in terms of a set of *service interaction patterns.* Inspired by the Workflow Patterns Initiative (cf. `www.workflowpatterns.com`), in particular the control-flow patterns [10] and the set of interaction patterns [3] presented by Barros et al., we use a patterns-based approach [10,3] to introduce the foundational concepts and challenges of service interaction in a language and tool independent manner.

In Sect. 3 we introduce *open nets* [11] as a basic tool to explain and formalize services. Open nets are a refinement of Petri nets [12,13,14] with interface places for communication and designated initial and final markings. Open nets can

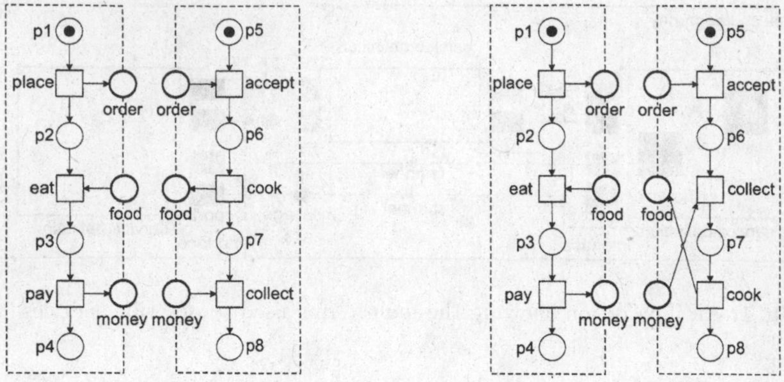

(a) Two services: a guest service GS_1 and a friendly restaurant service RS_1

(b) Two services: a guest service GS_1 and an unfriendly restaurant service RS_2

Fig. 2. Two pairs of services: $GS_1 \oplus RS_1$ and $GS_1 \oplus RS_2$

be seen as a generalization of workflow nets [15], extended with communication and a more relaxed net structure. A service definition is modeled as an open net. Ports are modeled as interface places. Service definitions can be composed by merging interface places into channel places. These channel places are internal to the composed service. Messages correspond to tokens passed from one service to another via interface places. A service choreography is the result of composing a set of open nets such that all interface places become internal.

We define service composition in terms of open nets. The composition of services may lead to all kinds of (behavioral) problems, e.g., deadlocks, livelocks, inability to terminate, etc. Two or more services are *compatible* if their composition "behaves well", but there exist several notions of compatibility in the literature. Based on a particular compatibility notion, one can define *controllability*, i.e., "Does a service have a compatible service?".

Examples. Let us look at some examples of open nets representing very simple "toy services". Figure 2(a) shows two service definitions. The composition of these two service definitions can be achieved by merging equally labeled interface places (depicted on the frame). Each of the service definitions corresponds to an open net and in the composition the interface places are fused. The open net on the left (GS_1) represents a guest that first places an order, eats the food, and finally pays. The three activities of this service, i.e., place, eat, and pay, are modeled in terms of transitions. These activities are connected to the other service via ports and channels. In our open-net representation these have been mapped onto the places order, food, and money. In this toy example, real objects are passed via the connecting places (e.g., food). In the context of web services, of course only messages are exchanged via such places. The open net on the right-hand side of Fig. 2(a) (RS_1) models the other service that consist of activities

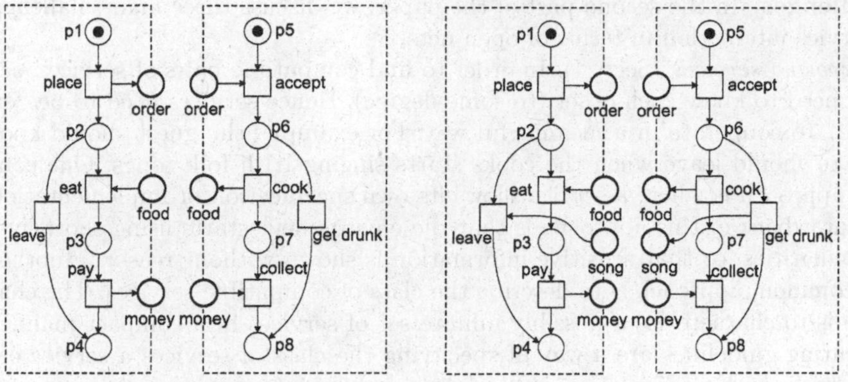

(a) Two incompatible services GS_2 and RS_3

(b) Two compatible services GS_3 and RS_4

Fig. 3. Another two pairs of services: $GS_2 \oplus RS_3$ and $GS_3 \oplus RS_4$

accept, cook, and collect. This is the "friendly restaurant service" RS_1, which can be seen as the obvious counterpart of GS_1. The composition of GS_1 and RS_1, denoted by $GS_1 \oplus RS_1$, has only one possible execution trace: place, accept, cook, eat, pay, and collect. It seems obvious that the two services are compatible, even without having a precise definition of compatibility in mind.

Consider Fig. 2(b) modeling two similar services consisting of the same activities. However, the restaurant service now is less friendly and requires the guest to pay before preparing the food (i.e., collect should occur before cook). This "unfriendly restaurant service" is named RS_2. The composition $GS_1 \oplus RS_2$ always runs into a deadlock, i.e., after executing place and accept both services are blocked waiting for one another. Clearly these two services are not compatible.

To illustrate the complexity and intricate subtleties of service interaction, consider Fig. 3(a). This time the guest may leave without eating and paying for the food. Moreover, the cook is an alcoholic and may get drunk instead of cooking the food. The resulting service composition $GS_2 \oplus RS_3$ clearly has problems. It may be the case that the customer leaves while the food has been or will be delivered. One may wonder which service would be compatible with RS_3, as it is unclear for the outside whether the food will be delivered or not. We will come back to this question in Sect. 3.

Figure 3(b) shows improved versions of the "potentially leaving guest service" and the "drunk cook restaurant service": GS_3 and RS_4. In the new service choreography the cook starts singing Irish folk songs when he gets drunk. As a result, the customer knows when to leave. The composition $GS_3 \oplus RS_4$ has only two possible execution traces: (1) the original scenario: place, accept, cook, eat, pay, and collect, and (2) an added scenario: place, accept, get drunk, and leave. Hence these two services are compatible.

Challenges. In the second part of the paper, we discuss three main challenges of service interaction in terms of open nets.

Exposing services (Sect. 4). In order to find compatible pairs of services, services need to know each other (to some degree). Hence services need to be "exposed" to cooperate in a meaningful way. For example, the guest should know that he should leave when the cooks starts singing Irish folk songs. One common approach is where a service shows its own specification or implementation. The drawback of this approach is that the environment starts using short-lived particularities, or that sensitive information is shown without reason. Another, less common, approach is to describe the class of compatible services. The challenge is to characterize a possibly infinite set of services in a compact manner. Operating guidelines are a way of specifying the class of services a service can work with, without exposing irrelevant or sensitive information.

Replacing and refining services (Sect. 5). One of the advantages of using an SOA is that things can be changed more easily, i.e., one service may be replaced by another service, or an unavailable service is replaced by several simpler services. However, all of these changes may cause various errors that break the service choreography. The challenge is to provide rules for replacing and refining services while guaranteeing forward/backward compatibility. Note for example that RS_3 in Fig. 3(a) can be replaced by RS_1 in Fig. 2(a), but not the other way around. How to capture this in a generic rule?

Integrating services using adapters (Sect. 6). In reality, existing services need to be composed to achieve a specific goal. However, services are often not compatible. This triggers many questions, e.g., how to repair a service, how to diagnose problems, etc. In Sect. 6 we focus on the challenge of adapter synthesis, i.e., the (semi-)automatic generation of "glue logic" that makes incompatible services compatible while achieving a given goal. For example, suppose that GS_4 is an anorexic guest that just wants to order and pay without actually eating. It is easy to make an adapter service AS that throws away the food such that the service choreography $GS_4 \oplus AS \oplus RS_1$ functions without any problems.

After discussing these challenges and providing an overview of the known results for these problems, we present tool support for these methods in Sect. 7. Finally, Sect. 8 concludes the paper.

2 Service Interaction Patterns

Before formalizing service definitions and addressing the various challenges in this domain, we provide some examples of service interaction patterns. The goal is not to summarize the existing patterns or to present new ones. Instead various service interaction patterns are presented informally using a notation close to open nets. Since we do not aim to describe the patterns in any detail, we do not use the typical patterns format describing various aspects of a pattern (e.g., description, examples, forces, motivation, overview, context, implementation, issues, and solutions) like in [3,10,16,17,18,19]. Instead, we just show a figure and provide a brief description for each pattern.

2.1 Workflow Patterns Initiative

The use of patterns is very appealing for identifying functionality in a system/language independent manner. The most well-known patterns collection in the IT domain is the set of design patterns documented by Gamma, Helm, Johnson, and Vlissides [16]. This collection describes a set of problems and solutions frequently encountered in object-oriented software design. This triggered many patterns initiatives in the IT field, including the Workflow Patterns Initiative. However, the idea to use a patterns-based approach originates from the work of the architect Christopher Alexander. In [20], he provides rules and diagrams describing methods for constructing buildings. The goal of the patterns documented by Alexander was to provide generic solutions for recurrent problems in architectural design.

The work described in this section is part of the *Workflow Patterns Initiative* (cf. `www.workflowpatterns.com`). This initiative is a joint effort of Eindhoven University of Technology and Queensland University of Technology which started in the late nineties. The aim of this initiative is to provide a conceptual basis for process technology. In particular, the research provides a thorough examination of the various perspectives (control flow, data, resource, and exception handling) that need to be supported by a workflow language or a business process modeling language. The results can be used for examining the suitability of a particular process language or process-aware information system, assessing relative strengths and weaknesses of various approaches to process specification, implementing certain business requirements in a particular system, and as a basis for language and tool development.

Originally the workflow patterns focussed exclusively on the control-flow perspective [10]. The initial set of 20 patterns was later extended to a set of more than 40 control-flow patterns [21]. In parallel, patterns were identified for the resource perspective [18], for the data perspective [19], and for exception handling [22]. Especially the control-flow patterns have had a huge impact on the selection of systems in practice and the definition of new standards. For example standardization efforts related to BPEL, XPDL, BPMN, etc. have been influenced by these patterns.

In the context of the Workflow Patterns Initiative, several collections for service interaction patterns have been collected. In [3], Barros, Dumas, and Ter Hofstede document such patterns and divide them into several groups: single-transmission bilateral interaction patterns (elementary interactions where a party sends/receives a message, and as a result expects/sends a reply), single-transmission non-routed patterns (also dealing with multi-lateral interactions), multi-transmission interaction patterns (a party sends/receives more than one message to/from the same logical party), and routed interaction patterns (involving complex routing of messages through the network). These patterns were described in an informal manner. In [4] some of these patterns are formalized using both π-calculus and Petri nets. A more systematic approach for the identification of service interaction patterns was conducted in the PhD thesis of Mulyar [17]. She identified five pattern families: multi-party multi-message request-reply

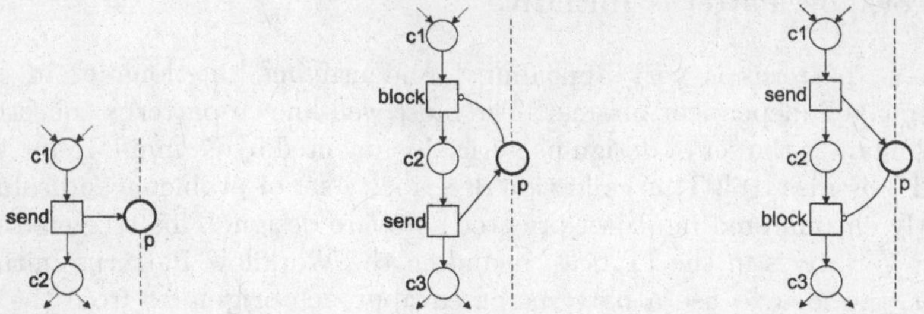

(a) SIP-1 Send pattern (b) SIP-2 Pre-Blocking Send pattern (c) SIP-3 Post-Blocking Send pattern

Fig. 4. Patterns related to sending a message

conversation [6], renewable subscription, message correlation, message mediation, and bipartite conversation correlation. Using a generative approach, more than 1,500 service interaction patterns are documented in [17]. While the above service interaction patterns have been developed in the context of the Workflow Patterns Initiative, other relevant patterns have been identified in related domains. A notable example is the collection of enterprise integration patterns by Hophe and Woolf [5].

2.2 Basic Service Interaction Patterns

First, we describe the basic service interaction patterns. These patterns abstract from correlation, i.e., at this stage we do not worry about routing a message to a specific service or service instance.

The first pattern is the SIP-1 *Send* pattern. The basic idea is shown in Fig. 4(a). Note that in this open net fragment, transition send represents an activity with precondition c1 and postcondition c2, both modeled by a place. Place p represents an output port. The dashed line separates the interface from the rest of the service definition. In Fig. 2(a) and the other examples in the introduction, this pattern was used multiple times, e.g., to place an order or to pay money. Pattern SIP-2 *Pre-Blocking Send* shown in Fig. 4(b) is a variant of the same idea. However, now the sender blocks if the previously sent message was not yet consumed. This is modeled by a so-called inhibitor arc between block and p, i.e., block can only be executed if p is empty. Pattern SIP-3 *Post-Blocking Send* is another variant. Now the thread in the sender service blocks until the message sent is consumed, cf. Fig. 4(c). After sending the message, transition block waits until the message is removed from output port p. Note that SIP-2 and SIP-3 can be combined, i.e., the sender blocks before and after sending (if necessary).

Figure 5 shows two basic patterns to receive messages. Pattern SIP-4 *Receive* is the straightforward receipt of messages. The receiver blocks until the message arrives. However, the message may arrive when the receiving service is not expecting it. In this scenario, the message waits until the receiver is ready, i.e., the

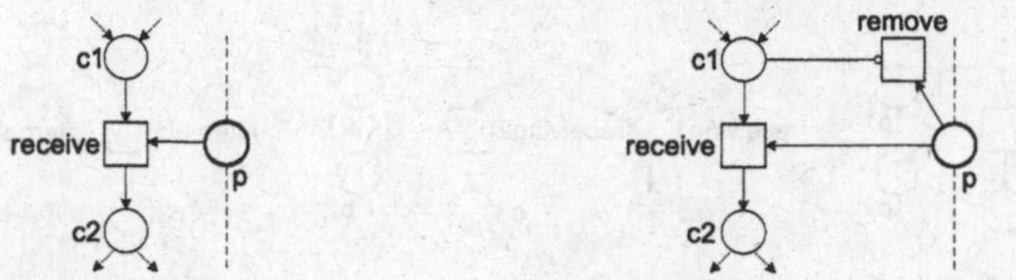

(a) SIP-4 Receive pattern (b) SIP-5 Lossy Receive pattern

Fig. 5. Patterns related to receiving a message

message is queued in the channel connected to place p. If this is not possible, the message may get lost as shown in Fig. 5(b). This is pattern SIP-5 *Lossy Receive*. Note that transition remove has an inhibitor arc connected to the input place c1 of receive. Hence, it can only be executed if receive is not enabled. If receive has multiple places, more remove transitions are needed (one for every input place). These transitions may be considered as part of the channel.

Figure 6(a) shows pattern SIP-6 *Concurrent Send* and Fig. 6(b) shows pattern SIP-7 *Concurrent Receive*. SIP-6 describes the pattern where a service can send two messages in any order: one via p1 and one via p2. SIP-7 is the logical counterpart and here the receiver can receive two messages in any order. Note that SIP-6 and SIP-7 can be combined with services that receive and send sequentially, i.e., from an interaction point these are quite "robust" unlike the choice patterns described next.

Figure 7 shows three choice patterns: SIP-8 *Sending Choice*, SIP-9 *Receiving Choice*, and SIP-10 *Internal Choice*. SIP-8 describes the situation where the choice is made within the service and communicated to the environment. Note that other services may be able to see which internal path is taken, e.g., a message via p1 reveals that send1 is executed. This pattern is used in Fig. 3(b) where the restaurant service communicates the choice to "cook" or "get drunk" by sending the food or singing Irish folk songs. SIP-9 shown in Fig. 7(b) models the pattern where the choice is influenced by the environment, i.e., the environment forces the service to take one path or another. This pattern is used in Fig. 3(b) by the

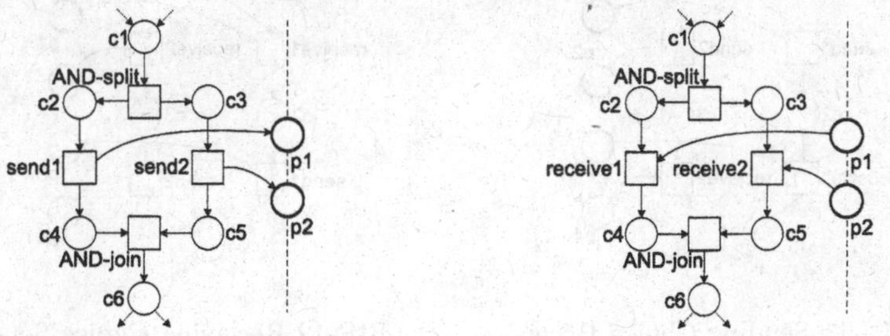

(a) SIP-6 Concurrent Send pattern (b) SIP-7 Concurrent Receive pattern

Fig. 6. Patterns related to the concurrent sending or receiving of messages

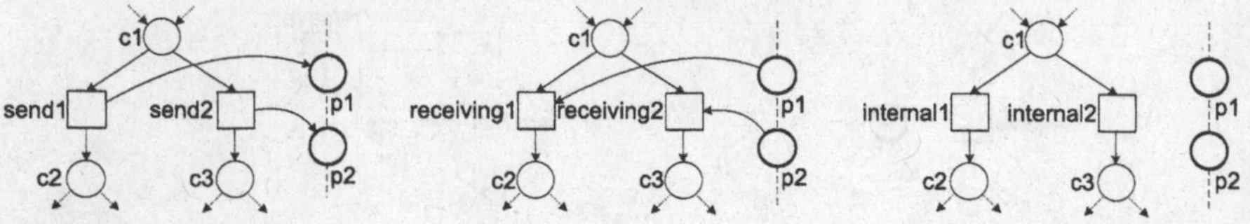

(a) SIP-8 Sending Choice pattern

(b) SIP-9 Receiving Choice pattern

(c) SIP-10 Internal Choice pattern

Fig. 7. Patterns related to choices in the presence or absence of communication

guest service. Pattern SIP-10 describes a third variant where the choice is not enforced by the environment nor communicated (cf. Fig. 7(c)).

Figure 8 shows two patterns where a choice is followed by a subsequent message exchange depending on the choice. SIP-11 *Sending Choice Receiving Follow-Up* shown in Fig. 8(a) corresponds to the scenario where the service makes a choice (SIP-8) followed by the receipt of a particular message depending on the initial choice. Hence, the environment is expected to send a message via p3 if it received a message via p1 and it is expected to send a message via p4 if it received a message via p2. This is indicated by the dotted curves in Fig. 8(a). Figure 8(b) shows the symmetrical case, i.e., pattern SIP-12 *Receiving Choice Sending Follow-Up*. In this pattern the environment takes the lead and the service follows, e.g., when receiving a message via p1, the service responds by sending a message via p3. Not shown are the patterns SIP-13 *Sending Choice Sending Follow-Up*, SIP-14 *Receiving Choice Receiving Follow-Up*, and SIP-15 *Internal Choice Sending Follow-Up*. However, given their names and the two earlier examples, their meaning is obvious. We do not consider situations where the follow-up is an internal step, because this would not really be a follow-up related to the choice.

Figure 9(a) shows a so-called *anti-pattern*: AP-1 *Internal Choice Receiving Follow-Up*. Anti-patterns describe undesirable constructs that may introduce errors or inefficiencies. In AP-1 an internal choice is followed by a receive which

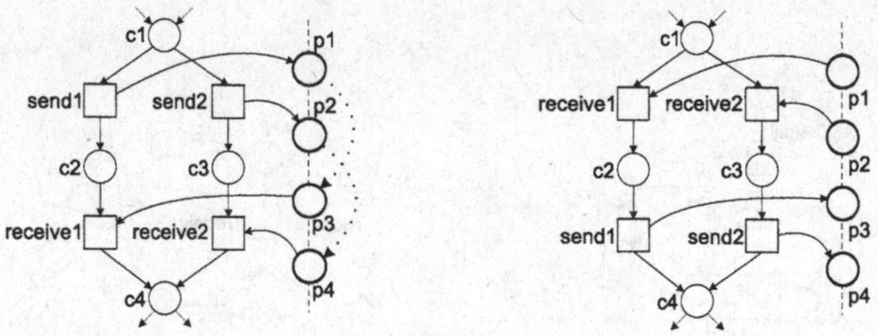

(a) SIP-11 Sending Choice Receiving Follow-Up pattern

(b) SIP-12 Receiving Choice Sending Follow-Up pattern

Fig. 8. Choice with a follow-up patterns

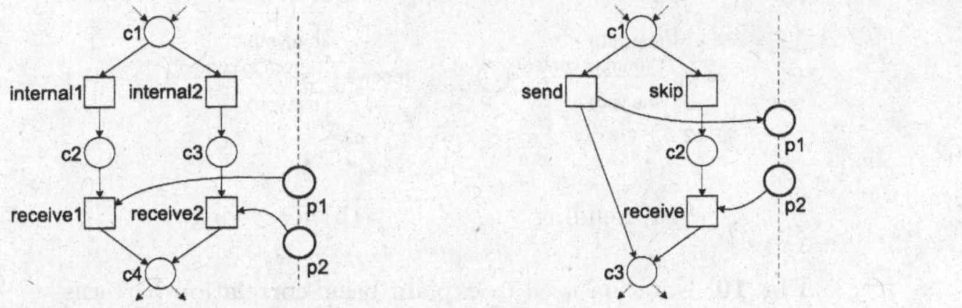

(a) AP-1 Internal Choice Receiving Follow-Up anti-pattern

(b) Another variant of the anti-pattern

Fig. 9. Two examples showing that "choices that matter" need to be communicated

should depend on the internal choice. Sometimes the service expects a message via p1 and sometimes via p2. However, the environment has no way of telling what to do, because the choice was never communicated. If one compares this with the two patterns shown in Fig. 8, it is good to see that the essential difference is that in AP-1 the environment has no way of determining an adequate strategy. By not sending a message via p1 the receiving service may deadlock and by sending a message via p1 the message may get stuck in the channel. Figure 9(b) shows a variant of the same anti-pattern. The choice to execute skip is not communicated, so the environment does not know whether it should send a message via p2 or wait forever for a message to arrive via p1.

Note that the problem in Fig. 3(a) is similar to AP-1. The restaurant service never communicates that the cook decided to get drunk, so the guest does not know whether to leave or not.

2.3 Correlation Patterns

The patterns presented thus far abstract from *correlation*, i.e., when sending a message via a channel it is assumed that it is routed to the appropriate service instance. For example, in Fig. 2(a) it is assumed that the "food message" is routed to the right instance of the guest service. If there are multiple guests, there will be multiple instances of GS_1 and RS_1. The "food message" needs to the related to the "order message" (i.e., the right dish is cooked), and the "money message" needs to be related to the two previous messages, because the price probably depends on the dish that was ordered. In this paper we define correlation as *establishing a relationship between a service instance and a message.*

Correlation is a neglected topic in service interaction. Yet correlation is omnipresent. Consider for example the booking of a trip, ordering a book, reviewing papers, requesting a lab test, etc. In each of these examples multiple parties are involved while there may be many concurrent instances. To be able to link messages to service instances, so-called *correlation identifiers* are used. For example,

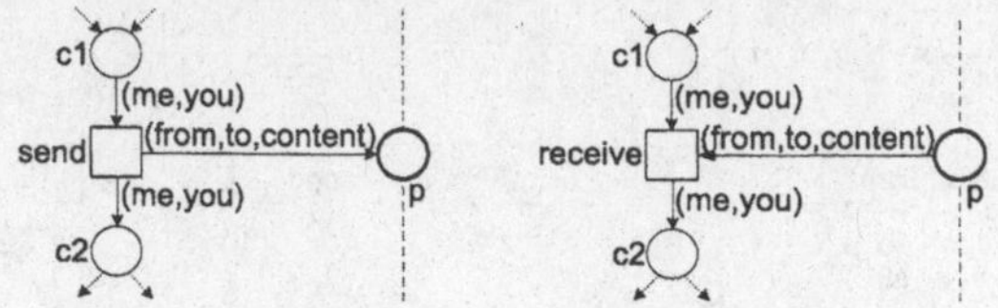

(a) Sending (b) Receiving

Fig. 10. Notation used to explain basic correlation patterns

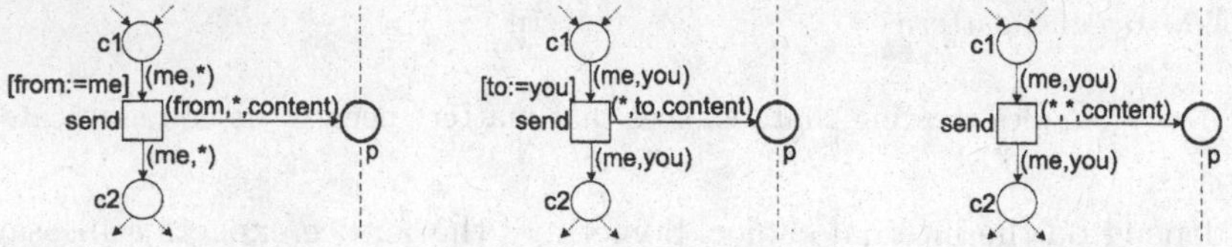

(a) SIP-16 Leading Correlated Send pattern (b) SIP-17 Following Correlated Send pattern (c) AP-2 Uncorrelated Send anti-pattern

Fig. 11. Correlation patterns related to sending a message

when booking a trip a booking reference is given by the travel agency. In a hospital the patient identifier is used to route lab tests to the right department. Therefore, languages such as BPEL provide explicit mechanisms for correlation. For example, BPEL supports the concept of "correlation sets" [9]. When a message arrives for a web service which has been implemented using BPEL, the message must be delivered somewhere: either to a new or an existing instance of the BPEL process. The task of determining to which conversation (i.e., service instance) a message belongs, is supported by correlation sets. To use a correlation set, a BPEL program defines the set by enumerating the properties which comprise it, and then refers to that set from receive, reply, invoke, or pick activities (i.e., all BPEL activities involving interaction).

To illustrate the basics of correlation, consider Fig. 10. In this figure me refers to the identity of the service instance and you refers to the identity of some other service instance. Messages are described by the triplet (from,to,content). from refers to the sender of the message, to refers to the intended recipient of the message, and content refers to the message body. The variables me, you, from, and to refer to service instances and may be used for correlation. We replace me, you, from, and to by the symbol * when the variable has no value or the value does not matter. Figure 10(a) shows the notation for sending a message (from,to,content) by a service instance described by (me,you). Figure 10(b) shows the receiving counterpart. These notations will be used to illustrate correlation patterns.

Figure 11 shows two correlation patterns and one anti-pattern. All refer to sending a message. Pattern SIP-16 *Leading Correlated Send* depicted in Fig. 11(a) describes the situation where a message (from,*,content) is sent. This implies that the sender expects the other party to use the sender's identification (i.e., from = me). Therefore, we say that the sender is "leading" in SIP-16. Note that the you and to variables shown in Fig. 10(a) are all replaced by * to denote that they are irrelevant or missing. The assignment [from:=me] attached to transition send makes sure that the sender instance reveals itself appropriately. Pattern SIP-17 *Following Correlated Send* shown in Fig. 11(b) assumes that the sender is "following" and uses a correlation id set by the other party. Here the tuple (*,to,content) is sent. Therefore, the sender needs to know the identity of the receiver instance (i.e., to:=you). Figure 11(c) shows the anti-pattern AP-2 *Uncorrelated Send.* This anti-pattern refers to the situation where no explicit correlation information is given when sending the message. Other than the content of the message, there is no way in which the environment can correlate the message (*,*,content) to the instance me.

Figure 12 shows four correlation patterns and one anti-pattern. Pattern SIP-18 *Leading Correlated Receive* is the logical counterpart of SIP-17, i.e., the sender uses the correlation id of the receiver. Figure 12(a) shows the type of message (*,to,content) received and the guard [me=to] making sure that the message is routed to the right instance. Pattern SIP-19 *Following Correlated Receive* depicted in Fig. 12(b) shows the situation where the receiver "follows" the sender and needs to know its identity you. Pattern SIP-20 *Learning Correlated Receive* depicted in Fig. 12(c) shows yet another variant. Here the receiver does not know the identity of the sender, but learns this from the incoming message. Note that the service instance is denoted by (me,you) after receiving the message while before it was denoted by (me,*). Pattern SIP-21 *Creating Correlated Receive*

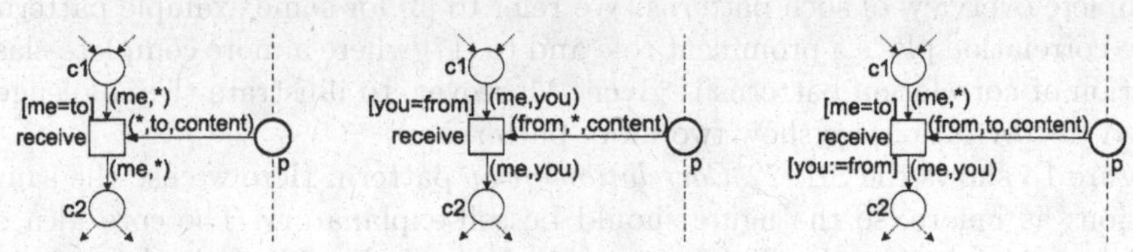

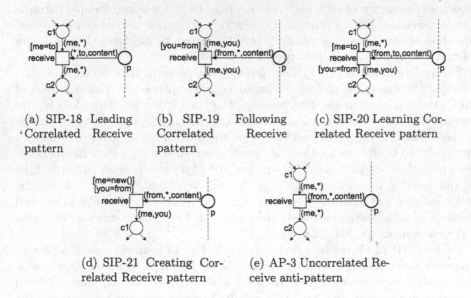

(a) SIP-18 Leading Correlated Receive pattern

(b) SIP-19 Following Correlated Receive pattern

(c) SIP-20 Learning Correlated Receive pattern

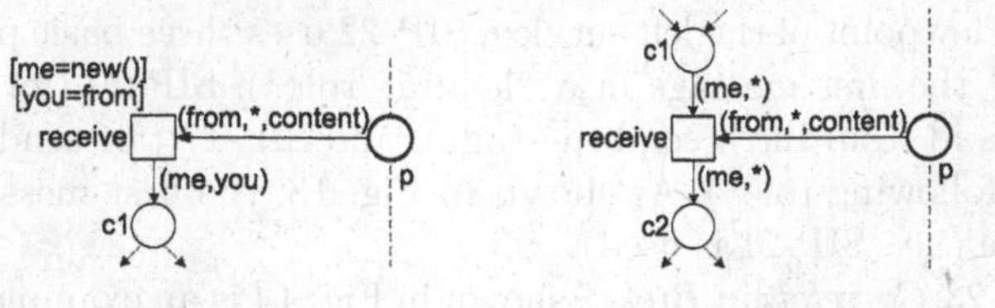

(d) SIP-21 Creating Correlated Receive pattern

(e) AP-3 Uncorrelated Receive anti-pattern

Fig. 12. Correlation patterns related to receiving a message

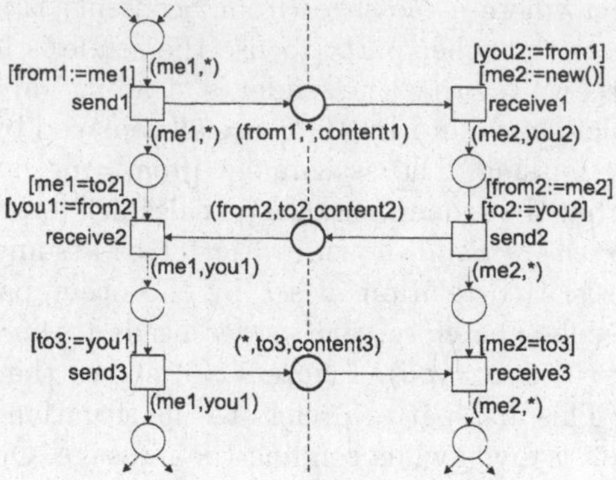

Fig. 13. SIP-22 Correlation Swap pattern

shown in Fig. 12(d) is similar to SIP-19 but now a new instance is created. Note that some languages provide a combination of SIP-19 and SIP-21, i.e., if the message can be correlated to an existing instance, then this is done, otherwise a new instance is created. Figure 12(e) shows the anti-pattern AP-3 *Uncorrelated Receive*. Although the sender reveals its identity, the receiver has no possibility to correlate properly (without analyzing the content of the message for "clues"). In the example of the restaurant this would correspond to preparing a dish without knowing which guest has ordered it.

Figures 11 and 12 show some of the basic correlation patterns. Clearly these can be combined to identify more complex patterns. We do not aim at providing a complete overview of such patterns. We refer to [3] for some example patterns where correlation plays a prominent role and to [17] where a more complete classification of correlation patterns is given. Moreover, to illustrate the challenges related to correlation, we show two more patterns.

Figure 13 shows the SIP-22 *Correlation Swap* pattern. Here we use the same notations as before, so the figure should be self-explanatory. The core idea of the pattern is that in the first message the correlation id of the left service instance is used while in the last message the correlation id of the right service is used. The message in the middle helps the left service instance to build up knowledge to be able to use the other party's correlation id in later interactions. Seen from the viewpoint of the left service, SIP-22 uses three basic patterns: SIP-16 (for sending the first message in a "leading role"), SIP-20 (for learning the other instance's id from the second message), and SIP-17 (for sending the third message in a "following role"). As shown in Fig. 13, the first message creates a service instance (i.e., SIP-21 is used).

Pattern SIP-23 *Correlation Broker* shown in Fig. 14 is an example of a pattern involving three services. The service in the middle acts as a mediator and is instantiated for any connection between a service instance on the right and a service instance on the left. As a result, two services can interact without knowing each other's identity. Note that place db holds a token for each pair of

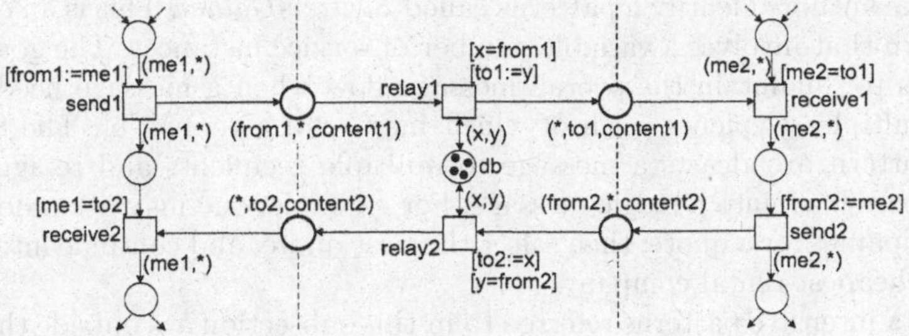

Fig. 14. SIP-23 Correlation Broker pattern

service instances (we assume that there is a one-to-one correspondence). The first message is relayed to the appropriate service instance using this information. The return message is relayed in a similar way without exposing the sending service.

2.4 More Advanced Correlation Patterns

As indicated before, correlation is of the utmost importance and the patterns shown thus far only scratch the surface. For example, the patterns shown in this paper use the identity of the sending or receiving instance as a correlation id. Of course, both parties can also agree on a more neutral correlation id. Also note that languages like BPEL support multiple correlation sets [9]. The topic of correlation has many aspects and based on [3,5,17] we mention two dimensions showing the broad scope of this problem.

SIP-23 is the only correlation pattern considering *multilateral interaction*. All other correlation patterns consider just bilateral interactions. In realistic service choreographies multilateral correlation is needed. Consider for example the booking of a trip involving two flights, three hotels nights, two train trips, and a rental car. This requires a network of service instances involving non-binary dependencies (e.g., the hotel should be canceled if the flight is not possible and the pick-up time of the car depends on the flight data).

Another dimension is related to *multiple instances* inside a service instance or message. Thus far we assumed activities and messages to be atomic. This is often not the case. For example, consider a service handling customer orders that may consist of multiple order lines. This service needs to deal with messages and activities at the level of a customer order and at the level of individual order lines. For example, a customer places one order that is decomposed in smaller orders for specific suppliers. Moreover, for a single order line there may be multiple potential suppliers. Another example, is the organization of a conference. One instance of a conference involves multiple authors, PC members, and reviewers. There may be many papers, each paper requires multiple reviews, and papers are ranked and compared based on their reviews. One reviewer may submit multiple reviews and each paper has multiple reviews, authors, etc. This example, shows that various types of instances interact in a complex manner.

In [5] the authors identify a patterns called *Scatter-Gather*. This is an example of a pattern that involves a variable number of service instances. The goal of the patterns is to "maintain the overall message flow when a message needs to be sent to multiple recipients, each of which may send a reply" [5]. The Scatter-Gather pattern broadcasts a message to multiple recipients and re-aggregates the responses back into a single message. For example, one may ask a dozen car rental companies for a quote, then select the best quote, and continue interacting with the cheapest rental company.

The data intensive patterns referred to in this subsection are outside the scope of this paper. In the remainder, we abstract from correlation and restrict the scope to the patterns presented in Sect. 2.2. For analysis purposes we typically look at one instance or conversation in isolation. We will show that this is often a valid abstraction. Nevertheless, we presented several correlation patterns to stress the importance of correlation.

3 Specifying Services

Petri nets have proven to be successful for the modeling of business processes and workflows (see the work of Van der Aalst [15,23], for instance). In this section we introduce our modeling formalism for services, viz., *open nets*, which is a refinement of Petri nets. In terms of the patterns we introduced in the previous section the focus is on the basic patterns (cf. Sect. 2.2), i.e., we only consider a single instance of each service and no correlation. We focus on service interaction, and abstract from non-functional properties, semantical information and data. We introduce the concept of open net composition and also formalize the notion of compatibility. As the formalism of open nets refines classical place/transition Petri nets, we first provide the basic definitions on Petri nets.

3.1 Basic Definitions on Petri Nets

Petri nets [12,13,14] consists of two kinds of nodes, *places* and *transitions*, and a *flow relation* on nodes. Graphically, a place is represented by a circle, a transition by a box, and the flow relation by directed arcs between them. Whilst transitions represent dynamic elements, for example an activity in a service, places represent static elements, such as causality between activities or an interface port. A *state* of the Petri net is represented by a marking, which is a distribution of tokens over the places. Graphically, a token is depicted by a black dot.

Definition 1 (Petri net). *A* Petri net $N = [P, T, F, m_0]$ *consists of*

- *two finite and disjoint sets* P *and* T *of* places *and* transitions,
- *a* flow relation $F \subseteq (P \times T) \cup (T \times P)$*, and*
- *an* initial marking m_0*, where a marking is a mapping* $m : P \to \mathbb{N}$.

When referring to several Petri nets we use indices, to distinguish the constituents of different Petri nets, for example, P_N refers to the set of places of Petri net N.

For the flow relation of a Petri net N we introduce the following notation to denote the pre-set and the post-set of places and transitions. Let $x \in P \cup T$ be a node of N. Then, ${}^\bullet x = \{y \mid [y, x] \in F\}$ denotes the *pre-set* of x (i.e. all nodes y that have an arc to x) and $x^\bullet = \{y \mid [x, y] \in F\}$ denotes the *post-set* of x (i.e. all nodes y with an arc from x to y).

Consider the Petri net of the guest service GS_1 in Fig. 2(a) and ignore for the moment the interface places and its adjacent arcs. This Petri net consists of the four places $\mathsf{p1}, \ldots, \mathsf{p4}$ and the three transitions place, eat, pay. Its initial marking is $m_0 = [\mathsf{p1}]$. For example, we have ${}^\bullet\mathsf{p2} = \{\mathsf{place}\}$ and $\mathsf{p2}^\bullet = \{\mathsf{eat}\}$.

The dynamics of a Petri net N is defined by the *firing rule*. The firing rule defines *enabledness* of Petri net transitions and their effects. A transition t is enabled at a marking m if there is a token on every place in its pre-set. The firing of an enabled transition t yields a new marking m', which is derived from its predecessor marking m by consuming (i.e. removing) a token from each place of t's pre-set and producing (i.e. adding) a token on each place of t's post-set. The described firing relation is denoted $m \xrightarrow{t} m'$. Thereby $m \xrightarrow{t} m'$ is a *step of* N.

The behavior of a Petri net N can be enhanced from single steps to potentially infinite transition sequences, called runs. A finite or infinite sequence $m_0 \xrightarrow{t_1} m_1 \xrightarrow{t_2} m_2 \xrightarrow{t_3} \ldots$ is a *run of* N if and only if, for all i, $m_i \xrightarrow{t_i} m_{i+1}$ is a step of N. Let m and m' be markings of N. Then, m' is *reachable* from m if and only if there exists a finite run $m_0 \xrightarrow{t_0} m_1 \xrightarrow{t_1} \ldots \xrightarrow{t_{k-2}} m_{k-1} \xrightarrow{t_{k-1}} m_k$ with $m = m_0$ and $m_k = m'$. We denote this reflexive transitive closure of the firing rule by $m \xrightarrow{*} m'$. With $R_N(m) = \{m' \mid m \xrightarrow{*} m'\}$ we denote the set of all markings that can be reached from m by firing any number of transitions.

The set $R_N(m_0)$ of reachable markings of a Petri net N contains all markings that are reachable from the initial marking m_0. That way, $R_N(m_0)$ spans a graph that has the set of reachable markings as its states and the transitions between these markings as its edges. This graph is known as the *reachability graph*, which can be represented by a *transition system*.

Consider again GS_1 in Fig. 2(a) without the interface places and their adjacent arcs. In its initial marking, [p1], only transition place is enabled. Firing of transition place yields marking [p2]. There is only one firing sequence and four reachable markings: $[\mathsf{p1}] \xrightarrow{\mathsf{place}} [\mathsf{p2}] \xrightarrow{\mathsf{eat}} [\mathsf{p3}] \xrightarrow{\mathsf{pay}} [\mathsf{p4}]$.

3.2 Open Nets

A service consists of a control structure describing its behavior and an interface to communicate asynchronously with other services. Thereby an interface consists of a set of (input and output) *ports*. In order that two services can interact with each other, an input port of the one service has to be connected with an output port of the other service. These connected ports then form a *channel*. Asynchronous message passing means that communication is non-blocking, i.e., after a service has sent a message it can continue its execution and does not have to wait until this message is received. Furthermore, messages can 'overtake' each other, i.e., the order in which the messages are sent is not necessarily the order in which they are received.

We model services as open nets which have been introduced as 'open workflow nets' in [24]. An open net is a Petri net as defined in the previous section and thus it can adequately model the control structure of a service. The set of final states of a service, i.e., the states in which it may successfully terminate, is modeled by a set of final markings. The service interface is reflected by two disjoint sets of input and output places. Thereby, each interface place corresponds to a port. An input place has an empty pre-set and is used for receiving messages from a distinguished channel whereas an output place has an empty post-set and is used for sending messages via a distinguished channel.

Definition 2 (Open net). *An* open net $N = [P, T, F, I, O, m_0, \Omega]$ *consists of a Petri net* $[P, T, F, m_0]$ *together with*

- *an* interface $(I \cup O) \subseteq P$ *defined as two disjoint sets* I *of* input places *and* O *of* output places *such that* $^\bullet p = \emptyset$ *for any* $p \in I$ *and* $p^\bullet = \emptyset$ *for any* $p \in O$, *and*
- *a set* Ω *of* final markings.

We further require that in the initial and the final markings the interface places are not marked, i.e., for all $m \in \Omega \cup \{m_0\}$ *we have* $m(p) = 0$, *for all* $p \in I \cup O$.

Graphically, we represent an open net like a Petri net with a dashed frame around it. The interface places are depicted on the frame. Final markings have to be described separately.

We refer to an open net with an empty interface as a *closed net.* A closed net can be used to model a *service choreography,* for instance.

Definition 3 (Closed net). *An open net* N *with an empty interface, i.e.,* $I_N = \emptyset$ *and* $O_N = \emptyset$, *is a* closed-net.

The seven nets in Figs. 2 and 3 are open nets. For example, the open net GS_1 in Fig. 2(a) has $I = \{\mathsf{food}\}$ and $O = \{\mathsf{order}, \mathsf{money}\}$. We define the final marking $\Omega = \{[\mathsf{p4}]\}$.

A closed net has finitely many states if it is *bounded,* i.e., no place can contain infinitely many tokens in any reachable marking.

Definition 4 (Boundedness). *A closed net* N *is* k-bounded *if there exists a* $k \in \mathbb{N}$ *such that for each reachable marking* $m \in R_{(N)}(m_0)$, $m(p) \leq k$, *for all* $p \in P_N$.

3.3 Composing Open Nets

The general idea of SOA is to use services as building blocks for designing complex services. To this end, services have to be composed, i.e., pairs of input and output ports of these services are connected using a channel. Communication between these services takes place by exchanging messages via these channels. Composing two open nets is modeled by fusing pairwise equally labeled input and output places. Such a fused interface place models a channel and a token on such a place corresponds to a pending message in the respective channel.

For the composition of open nets, we assume that all constituents (except for the interfaces) are pairwise disjoint. This can be achieved easily by renaming. In contrast, the interfaces intentionally overlap. For a reasonable concept of composition of open nets, however, it is convenient to require that all communication is bilateral and directed, i.e., every interface place $p \in I \cup O$ has only one open net that sends into p and one open net that receives from p. Thereby the sending open net has the output place and the receiving open net has the corresponding equally labeled input place. We refer to open nets that fulfill these properties as *interface compatible*.

Definition 5 (Interface compatible open nets). *Let N_1, N_2 be two open nets with pairwise disjoint constituents except for the interfaces. If only input places of one open net overlap with output places of the other open net, i.e., $I_1 \cap I_2 = \emptyset$ and $O_1 \cap O_2 = \emptyset$, then N_1 and N_2 are* interface compatible.

As an example, each of the four pairs of open nets depicted in Figs. 2 and 3 are interface compatible open nets.

Composing two open nets means to merge their respective shared constituents. As we only define composition for interface compatible open nets, the only shared constituents are the interface places. In other words, composition corresponds to *place fusion* which is well-known in the theory of Petri nets.

Definition 6 (Composition of open nets). *Let N_1 and N_2 be two interface compatible open nets. The* composition *$N = N_1 \oplus N_2$ is the open net with the following constituents:*

- $P = P_1 \cup P_2$,
- $T = T_1 \cup T_2$,
- $F = F_1 \cup F_2$,
- $I = (I_1 \cup I_2) \setminus (O_1 \cup O_2)$,
- $O = (O_1 \cup O_2) \setminus (I_1 \cup I_2)$,
- $m_0 = m_{01} \oplus m_{02}$, *and*
- $\Omega = \{m_1 \oplus m_2 \mid m_1 \in \Omega_1, m_2 \in \Omega_2\}$.

For markings m_1 of N_1 and m_2 of N_2 which do not mark the interface places, their composition $m = m_1 \oplus m_2$ is defined by $m(p) = m_i(p)$ if $p \in P_i$, for $i = 1, 2$.

Composition of two open nets M and N results in an open net again. Composing M and N means merging input places of M with equally labeled output places of N (and vice versa). Therein, bilateral and directed communication between the components is guaranteed. The initial marking of the composition is the sum of the initial markings of M and N, and the set of final markings of the composition is the Cartesian product of the sets of final markings of M

and N. This is reasonable, because Definition 2 ensures that the only shared constituents of M and N, the interface places, are not marked in the initial or final markings.

As an example, all pairs of open nets in Sect. 1 are interface compatible. Thus we can compose them by merging equally labeled interface places. Each resulting composition is a closed net.

To apply composition to an arbitrary number of open nets, we require these open nets to be pairwise interface compatible. This ensures bilateral communication as for a third open net N_3, a communication taking place inside the composition of open nets N_1 and N_2 is internal matter.

Open net composition is commutative and associative, i.e., for interface compatible open nets N_1, N_2 and N_3 holds $N_1 \oplus N_2 = N_2 \oplus N_1$ and $(N_1 \oplus N_2) \oplus N_3 = N_1 \oplus (N_2 \oplus N_3)$. Thus, composition of a set of open nets can be broken into recursive pairwise composition.

3.4 Behavioral Properties

We want the composition of a set of services to be *compatible*. Obviously, there is no unique definition of compatibility. A minimal requirement is, however, the absence of deadlocks in a service. A stronger criterion is the possibility of a service to terminate from every reachable state. This criterion excludes deadlocks and in addition livelocks, where a livelock is a set of reachable states of a service from which neither a deadlock nor a final state is reachable. Besides deadlocks and livelocks one may also want to exclude the existence of dead activities in a service. This criterion of compatibility coincides with the soundness notion for workflows [15]. Obviously, compatibility is only of interest for a service choreography which is modeled by a closed net, i.e., an open net with an empty interface.

In this paper we say that a closed net is compatible if it is deadlock-free, but most of the techniques can also be used for other notions of compatibility. Thereby a *deadlock* is a reachable, non-final marking m in N in which the open net N gets stuck, i.e., no transition is enabled in m.

Definition 7 (Deadlock). *Let $N = [P, T, F, I, O, m_0, \Omega]$ be a closed net. A reachable marking $m \in R_N(m_0)$ is a* deadlock *in N iff $m \notin \Omega$ and no transition $t \in T$ is enabled in m. If no such m exists in N, then N is* deadlock-free.

This definition of a deadlock differs from the standard definition in the literature, as we discriminate between terminating (final) states and non-terminating states (i.e., deadlocks).

If we assume $\Omega = \{[\mathsf{p4}, \mathsf{p8}]\}$ for all compositions in Figs. 2 and 3, then $GS_1 \oplus RS_2$ has a deadlock ($[\mathsf{p2}, \mathsf{p6}]$) and $GS_2 \oplus RS_3$ has also a deadlock ($[\mathsf{p4}, \mathsf{food}, \mathsf{p7}]$). The other two compositions, $GS_1 \oplus RS_1$ and $GS_3 \oplus RS_4$, are deadlock-free.

Given an open net N we are interested in those open nets M such that their composition $M \oplus N$ is a deadlock-free closed net.

Definition 8 (Strategy, controllability). *Let M, N be two open nets such that $I_M = O_N$ and $O_M = I_N$. Then, M is a* strategy *for N iff $M \oplus N$ is deadlock-free. With $Strat(N)$ we denote the set of all strategies for N. N is* controllable *iff its set of strategies is nonempty.*

If N is not controllable, then it is fundamentally ill-designed, because it cannot properly interact with any other open net.

In our examples, GS_1 is a strategy for RS_1 and vice versa, for instance. Hence, both open nets are controllable. Moreover, each of the seven open nets in Figs. 2 and 3 is controllable. For GS_2 and RS_3 this might be surprising at first sight. However, a restaurant service that only receives the order and then terminates is a strategy for GS_2, thus forcing the customer to leave. A strategy for RS_3 must be aware that after having ordered the cook may get drunk, in which case no food will be served. Nevertheless, the guest cannot be sure, and hence he must stay in the restaurant in order to eat the food in case it is served. This can be modeled by open net GS_1 with final markings $\Omega = \{[\mathsf{p2}], [\mathsf{p4}]\}$, i.e., after having ordered, the guest does not need to eat, but if food is served, he will eat and pay.

4 Exposing Services

For automatically selecting and composing services in a well-behaved manner, information about the services has to be exposed. In particular, this information must be sufficient to decide whether the composition of any service R with any service S is compatible. Usually, the information about some services S is stored in a repository. Selecting a service means to find for a given service R (whose behavior is given) a compatible service S in the repository. There are two ways of exposing services.

In the first approach, the *behavior of* S is exposed. Well-behavior of the composition of R and S can be verified using standard state space verification techniques [25]. However, organizations usually want to hide the trade secrets of their services and thus need to find a proper abstraction of S which is published instead of S.

The second approach does not expose the behavior of S, but a *class of services* R that is compatible with S, e.g., the set $Strat(S)$. Then the composition of R and S is compatible if $Strat(S)$ contains R. From the set of strategies it is in general not possible to derive the original service.

However, $Strat(S)$ is in general an *infinite* set of services. Hence, the challenge is to find a compact representation of this set. To this end, *operating guidelines* can be used.

In this section we only consider the latter approach of exposing services and thus recapitulate the concept of an operating guidelines [26,27]. The operating guidelines $OG(N)$ of an open net N is a (finite) automaton enhanced with some annotations. It represents the set $Strat(N)$ of all strategies for N.

Strictly speaking, $OG(N)$ does not characterize a set of open nets, but the *behavior* of these nets, because two (structurally) different open nets may have the same behavior. So we continue by first defining the behavior of an open net, which is a labeled transition system, and then introducing operating guidelines.

4.1 Behavior of Open Nets

The behavior of an open net N is basically the reachability graph of the inner subnet *inner*(N) of N, which defines the Petri net that results from removing the interface places and the adjacent arcs from N. Obviously, *inner*(N) and N coincide if N is a closed net.

Definition 9 (Inner subnet). *Let* $N = [P, T, F, I, O, m_0, \Omega]$ *be an open net and let* $P' = P \setminus (I \cup O)$ *be the set of* internal places *of* N. *Then,* $inner(N) = [P', T, F \cap ((P' \times T) \cup (T \times P')), \emptyset, \emptyset, m_0, \Omega]$ *is the* inner subnet *of* N.

Often we restrict ourselves to open nets where every transition is connected to at most one interface place. We refer to such open nets as *elementary communicating open nets.* This restriction is not significant, as every open net can be transformed to an equivalent elementary communicating open net [27]. All examples shown in Sect. 1 are elementary communicating open nets.

For elementary communicating open nets we define a mapping that assigns a label to each transition. We use these labels to represent the transition system of an open net N.

Definition 10 (Transition label of open nets). *Let* $N = [P, T, F, I, O, m_0, \Omega]$ *be an elementary communicating open net. The* transition labels *for* N *are defined by the mapping* $l : T \rightarrow I \cup O \cup \{\tau\}$ $(\tau \notin I \cup O)$ *such that* $l(t)$ *is the unique interface place adjacent to* $t \in T$ *if one exists, and* $l(t) = \tau$ *if* t *is not adjacent to any interface place.*

In the examples we add a preceding question mark, '?', to each label of a transition connected to an input place and a preceding exclamation mark, '!', to each label of a transition connected to an output place. For example, the inner subnet of GS_2 has the labels l(place) = !order, l(eat) = ?food, l(pay) = !money, l(leave) = τ.

The behavior of an open net N can now be defined by the reachability graph of the inner structure of N, where the transitions are labeled using the mapping l defined in Definition 10. Notice, the transition labels represent actions on an asynchronous channel.

Definition 11 (Behavior of open nets). *The* behavior of an open net $N = [P, T, F, I, O, m_0, \Omega]$ *is defined by the transition system* $TS(N) = [Q, l, \delta, q_0, Q_F]$, *where*

- $Q = R_{inner(N)}(m_0)$ *is the (nonempty) set of reachable markings of* $inner(N)$,
- l *is the labeling function,*
- $[m, l(t), m'] \in \delta$ *iff* $m \xrightarrow{t} m'$, *for* $t \in T$, *is the transition relation,*
- $q_0 = m_0$ *is the initial state, and*
- $Q_F = \Omega$ *is the set of final states.*

Figures 15(a) and 15(b) show the behavior of open nets GS_1 and GS_2, respectively. States r4 and r8 denote final states. In Fig. 15(a) the states r1, r2, r3 and r4 correspond to the markings [p1], [p2], [p3], and [p4] in GS_1, respectively.

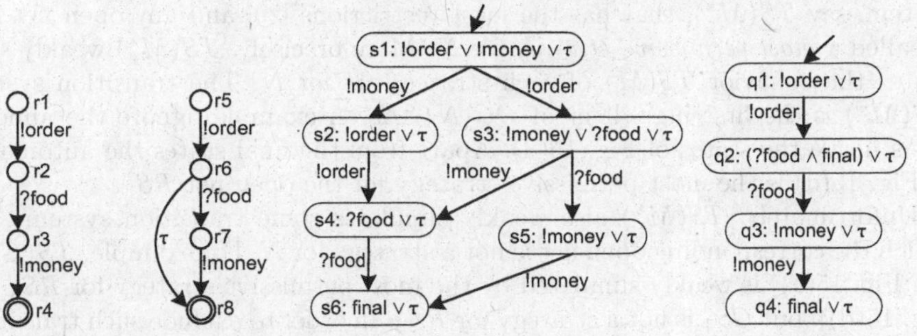

(a) $TS(GS_1)$ (b) $TS(GS_2)$ (c) $OG(RS_1)$ (d) $OG(RS_3)$

Fig. 15. Behavior of open nets GS_1 and GS_2 and operating guidelines (guaranteeing 1-boundedness) of open nets RS_1 and RS_3

To relate different service behaviors, we introduce the well-known weak simulation relation [28]. Weak simulation is defined for (labeled) transition systems. Since we can compute the behavior of any open net in terms of a transition system, weak simulation is also well-defined for open nets. Let τ^* denote a (possible empty) sequence of τ transitions.

Definition 12 (Weak simulation relation). *Let P and R be transition systems and let $\hat{a}$ stand for τ^* if transition label a is τ, and a otherwise. A binary relation $\varrho_{P,R} \subseteq Q_P \times Q_R$ is a* weak simulation relation of P by R *iff for every $[q_P, q_R] \in \varrho_{P,R}$, such that there is a transition $[q_P, a, q'_P] \in \delta_P$ in P, there is a transition $[q_R, \hat{a}, q'_R] \in \delta_R$ in R and $[q'_P, q'_R] \in \varrho_{P,R}$.* R weakly simulates P *iff there is a weak simulation relation $\varrho_{P,R}$ of P by R such that $[q_{0_P}, q_{0_R}] \in \varrho_{P,R}$.*

Consider again Figs. 15(a) and 15(b). $TS(GS_2)$ weakly simulates $TS(GS_1)$ using the relation $\varrho_{TS(GS_2),TS(GS_1)} = \{[\text{r1, r5}], [\text{r2, r6}], [\text{r3, r7}], [\text{r4, r8}]\}$. $TS(GS_1)$ also weakly simulates $TS(GS_2)$ using the relation $\varrho_{TS(GS_1),TS(GS_2)} = \{[\text{r5, r1}], [\text{r6, r2}], [\text{r7, r3}], [\text{r8, r4}], [\text{r8, r2}]\}$. So the final states do not matter for weak simulation.

4.2 Operating Guidelines

For an open net N we have the set *Strat*(N) of all strategies for N. Since the set *Strat*(N) is in general infinite, we need to construct a compact characterization of this set. To this end, we introduce *operating guidelines*, a (automaton-based) representation of *Strat*(N).

An operating guidelines $OG(N)$ of an open net N characterizes the set $Match(OG(N)) = \{TS(M) \mid M \in Strat(N)\}$, i.e., the behaviors of all strategies for N and thus the set *Strat*(N). The set $Match(OG(N))$ contains a transition system, say $TS(M^*)$, that has the least restrictions [29] and any open net M^* is called a *most permissive strategy* for N. More precisely, $TS(M^*)$ weakly simulates the behavior $TS(M)$ of each strategy M for N. The transition system $TS(M^*)$ is the first ingredient of $OG(N)$. As an example, ignore the annotations inside the states of Fig. 15(d). Apart from the final states the automaton of Fig. 15(d) is the most permissive strategy for the open net RS_3.

Unfortunately, $TS(M^*)$ also weakly simulates some transition systems, for which the corresponding open net is not a strategy for N. For example, $TS(GS_1)$ (cf. Fig. 15(a)) is weakly simulated by the most permissive strategy for RS_3 (cf. Fig. 15(d)), but GS_1 is not a strategy for RS_3. In order to exclude such transition systems, we need to specify which restrictions of the structure of $TS(M^*)$ are behaviors of strategies for N. This can be achieved by specifying which edges of $TS(M^*)$ have to be present in the weak simulation between $TS(M^*)$ and any $TS(M)$, for any strategy M for N. To this end, every state q of $TS(M^*)$ is annotated with a Boolean formula $\Phi(q)$, the second ingredient of $OG(N)$.

A *literal* of our Boolean formulae Φ is an element of the set MP of transition labels of M^* (MP stands for message ports) or one of the special literals τ and *final* (representing an internal transition and a final state, respectively). With MP^+ we denote the set $MP \cup \{final, \tau\}$. As Boolean connectors, we only need $\vee$ (Boolean *or*) and $\wedge$ (Boolean *and*). Let $\mathcal{BF}$ be the set of all such Boolean formulae over MP^+.

Thus, an operating guidelines $OG(N) = B^\Phi$ is a Boolean annotated service automaton that consists of a deterministic automaton B and a Boolean annotation Φ. Thereby B is the behavior $TS(M^*)$ of the most permissive strategy for N.

Definition 13 (Boolean annotated service automaton). *A* Boolean annotated service automaton *(BSA)* $B^\Phi = [Q, MP, \delta, q_0, \Phi]$ *consists of*

- *a nonempty set* Q *of states,*
- *a set* MP *of transition labels such that* $final, \tau \notin MP$*,*
- *a deterministic transition relation* $\delta \subseteq Q \times MP \times Q$*,*
- *an initial state* q_0*, and*
- *a Boolean* annotation *function* $\Phi : Q \to \mathcal{BF}$*.*

Figures 15(c) and 15(d) show two *BSA*s. For example, the *BSA* in Fig. 15(d) has four states q1, ..., q4. The initial state is q1. The annotations are !order $\vee\ \tau$ in state q1, (!food $\wedge$ final) $\vee\ \tau$ in state q2, etc.

We use Boolean annotated service automata to represent the behavior of a set of *open nets*. Therefore, we take a *BSA* B^Φ and define when a service described in terms of an open net M matches with B^Φ. A (Boolean) *assignment* is a mapping $\beta : MP^+ \to \{true, false\}$ assigning to each literal a truth value. Furthermore, an assignment β *satisfies* a Boolean formula $\phi \in \mathcal{BF}$, denoted by $\beta \models \phi$, if ϕ evaluates to *true* using standard propositional logic semantics. Open net M matches with B^Φ if

1. its *behavior* $TS(M)$ is weakly simulated by B^{Φ} and
2. for every state q_m of $TS(M)$ that is weakly simulated by a state q of B^{Φ}, the transitions leaving q_m and the fact whether q_m is a final state of $TS(M)$ constitute a satisfying assignment for $\Phi(q)$.

Definition 14 (Assignment). *Let MP be a set of message ports. An* assignment *of the behavior* $TS(M) = [Q, l, \delta, q_0, Q_F]$ *of an open net M assigns to each state* $q \in Q$ *a Boolean assignment* $\beta_{TS(M)}(q) : MP^{+} \to \{\text{true}, \text{false}\}$ *defined by:*

$$\beta_{TS(M)}(q)(x) = \begin{cases} \text{true}, & \text{if } x \neq \textit{final} \text{ and there is a state } q' \text{ with } [q, x, q'] \in \delta, \\ \text{true}, & \text{if } x = \textit{final} \text{ and } q \in Q_F, \\ \text{false}, & \text{otherwise.} \end{cases}$$

As an example, $TS(GS_2)$ (see Fig. 15(b)) assigns in state r5 *true* to !order, in state r6 *true* to ?food and τ, in state r7 *true* to !money and in state r8 *true* to final. To all other literals in each state *false* is assigned.

With the help of the Boolean assignment β matching of an open net with a *BSA* can be defined as follows.

Definition 15 (Matching). *Let* $TS(M)$ *be the behavior of an open net M and let* B^{Φ} *be a BSA such that* $TS(M)$ *and B have the same transition labels. Then M* matches *with* B^{Φ} *iff B weakly simulates* $TS(M)$ *using a relation* $\varrho \subseteq Q_{TS(M)} \times Q_B$ *such that for each* $[q_M, q_B] \in \varrho$*:* $\beta_{TS(M)}(q_M) \models \Phi(q_B)$*. Let* $Match(B^{\Phi})$ *denote the set of all open nets that match with* B^{Φ}*.*

Consider again Fig. 15. $TS(GS_1)$ matches with the *BSA* in Fig. 15(c), i.e., Fig. 15(c) weakly simulates $TS(GS_1)$ and in each pair of states of the weak simulation relation the assignment β assigns true to sufficiently many literals such that the formula holds. As a counterexample, $TS(GS_1)$ does not match with the *BSA* in Fig. 15(d). Observe the existence of a weak simulation relation. But being in related states [r2, q2], r2 assigns only *true* to ?food yielding (*true* ∧ *false*) ∨ *false* which is *false*. $TS(GS_2)$ matches with none of these *BSA*s. In case of Fig. 15(c), being in related states [r6, s3], a τ transition is possible in r6 yielding related states [r8, s3] in the weak simulation (note that by Definition 12 the *BSA* may execute the empty τ sequence). However, in this pair of states the annotation of s3 is violated, because r8 only assigns *true* to final. For the same reason $TS(GS_2)$ does not match with the *BSA* in Fig. 15(d). There is a pair of states [r8, q2] in the weak simulation relation, where the annotation of q2 is violated ($TS(GS_2)$ can neither receive a message food being in its final marking nor perform a τ-labeled transition).

An operating guidelines of an open net N is a *BSA* such that every matching service M is a strategy for N and every strategy for N matches with B^{Φ}. In other words, the sets $Match(B^{\phi})$ and $Strat(N)$ must be equal.

Definition 16 (Operating guidelines, *OG*). *The* operating guidelines $OG(N)$ *of an open net N is a BSA such that* $Match(OG(N)) = Strat(N)$*.*

For uncontrollable open nets N (i.e., $Strat(N) = \emptyset$) the OG consists of a single state that is annotated with *false*, assuring that *no* open net matches with this OG.

Figures 15(c) and 15(d) depict the operating guidelines of RS_1 and RS_3. Since $TS(GS_1)$ matches with $OG(RS_1)$, we conclude that GS_1 is a strategy for RS_1. $TS(GS_1)$ does not match with $OG(RS_3)$, and thus GS_1 is not a strategy for RS_3. For the same reason GS_2 is not a strategy for RS_1 nor for RS_3.

For every controllable open net N, there exists a *most permissive strategy*, i.e., a strategy M that has the least restrictions of all strategies [29]. Thus, the behavior $TS(M)$ of M corresponds exactly to the transition system of the underlying automaton of $OG(N)$. The final states of $TS(M)$ are the states of $OG(N)$ with *final* in their annotation.

Definition 17 (Most permissive strategy). *Let $OG(N) = [Q, MP, \delta, q_0, \Phi]$ be the operating guidelines for a controllable open net N. Then, an open net M is the most permissive strategy for N iff $TS(M) = [Q, MP, \delta, q_0, \Omega]$, where $\Omega = \{q \mid \mathit{final} \text{ occurs in } \Phi(q)\}$.*

So removing the annotations in the states of $OG(RS_1)$ and $OG(RS_3)$ and adding all states that contain a literal *final* to the set of final states yields the most permissive strategy for RS_1 and RS_3, respectively.

It is worthwhile mentioning that for each open net there exists an operating guidelines that only requires negation-free annotations and a deterministic structure [27]. This eases the implementation of the matching procedure. In spite of these restrictions, an operating guidelines is able to characterize even nondeterministic service models. To this end, each Boolean annotation has a disjunct τ (see Fig. 15, for instance) as otherwise a state of a transition system that can only perform a τ transition cannot satisfy the annotation of the respective state in the operating guidelines.

5 Replacing and Refining Services

In this section we consider another important application in an SOA: service replacement and service refinement. We define an accordance relation on any two services S and S' that ensures that every compatible service for S is also compatible with S', and hence S can be replaced by S. To decide accordance we present a sufficient criterion based on projection inheritance and a precise criterion based on operating guidelines. Finally, we show how to derive a service S' from a service S by using accordance-preserving transformation rules.

5.1 A Notion of Accordance

Given an open net N, it might be necessary to change or add some functionality of N by replacing it by a new version N'. Because we assume that N does not know each service that uses N, N' must support each *compatible* service for N, i.e., all elements in $Strat(N)$. With accordance we demand that every compatible service for N is compatible with N' as well. An application for accordance is the upgrade of a web shop which should not affect any client. This motivates the following notion of accordance between open nets N and N'. To this end, N and N' must be interface equivalent open nets.

Definition 18 (Interface equivalent open nets). *Two open nets M and N are* interface equivalent *iff $I_M = I_N$ and $O_M = O_N$.*

Definition 19 (Accordance). *Let N and N' be two interface equivalent open nets. N'* can replace N under accordance *(N' accords with N, for short) iff $Strat(N) \subseteq Strat(N')$.*

Accordance guarantees that every strategy for N is a strategy for N' as well. In addition, accordance allows N' to have more compatible services. Accordance is a pre-order, i.e., it is reflexive and transitive.

As an example, the open nets RS_1 and RS_3 in Figs. 2(b) and 3(a) are interface equivalent and RS_1 accords with RS_3. In the next subsection we present a method to prove this.

Many different accordance notions—often called conformance—exists in the literature, but there are always some differences to accordance. Vogler [30] presents a deadlock-preserving equivalence for Petri nets with an interface, but he does not distinguish between deadlocks and final markings. Fournet et al. [31] also formalize the absence of deadlocks, but their pre-order is coarser than accordance (see [32]). The approaches of [33,34] formalize a stronger termination criterion, namely the absence of deadlocks and livelocks. In addition, [34] demands only the environment to terminate, but not the service itself.

5.2 Deciding Accordance

Deciding accordance of two open nets N and N' is a nontrivial problem, because we have to compare the two possible infinite sets of strategies $Strat(N)$ and $Strat(N')$. We introduce two approaches for deciding accordance. One approach, projection inheritance, decides accordance on the net structure of N and N'. The second approach uses the operating guidelines $OG(N)$ and $OG(N')$, i.e., the compact characterizations of $Strat(N)$ and $Strat(N')$, to decide accordance.

Projection Inheritance. Inheritance is one of the key concepts of object-orientation. In object-oriented design, inheritance is typically restricted to the static aspects (e.g., data and methods) of an object class. In many cases, however, the dynamics is of prime importance. Therefore, *projection inheritance* [35] focuses on the dynamics. Projection inheritance compares process models by establishing a subclass-superclass relationship. The subclass process is indeed a subclass if it inherits particular dynamic properties of its superclass.

Projection inheritance is based on *branching bisimulation* [36] (to compare the processes) and *abstraction* (to hide tasks). The assumption is that the subclass adds tasks to the superclass such that after hiding the additional tasks both are equivalent. The basic idea of projection inheritance can be characterized as follows:

> "If it is not possible to distinguish the behaviors of x and y when arbitrary methods of x are executed, but when only the effects of methods that are also present in y are considered, then x is a subclass of y" [35].

Projection inheritance was defined for workflow nets in [35], but in this definition projection inheritance refers to "methods" rather than the "sending and receiving of messages". In [37] projection inheritance has been reformulated for open nets by the following mapping: A transition that is connected to an interface place presents a method present in both the superclass and the subclass.

We continue by defining branching bisimulation for transition systems (and hence also for open nets). In order to apply this equivalence notion in our setting, branching bisimulation should guarantee that, for each final state of TS, there exists a final state in TS' and both states are related by branching bisimulation.

Definition 20 (Branching bisimulation). *Two labeled transition systems TS and TS' are* branching bisimular *iff there exists a symmetric relation ϱ_{bb} such that $[q_0, q_0'] \in \varrho_{bb}$ and, for all q_1, q_1' holds: If $[q_1, q_1'] \in \varrho_{bb}$ and $q_1 \xrightarrow{\alpha} q_2$, then either*

- *$\alpha = \tau$ and $[q_2, q_1'] \in \varrho_{bb}$ or*
- *there are q_2', q_3' such that $q_1' \xrightarrow{\tau^*} q_2' \xrightarrow{\alpha} q_3'$, $[q_1, q_2'] \in \varrho_{bb}$, and $[q_2, q_3'] \in \varrho_{bb}$.*

Furthermore, for each final marking $q \in Q_F$ holds: if $[q, q'] \in \varrho_{bb}$, then either $q' \in Q_F'$ or there exists a transition sequence τ^* starting from q' that contains a state $q_1' \in Q_F'$ with $[q, q_1'] \in \varrho_{bb}$.

To decide whether two open nets are related by projection inheritance, it is sufficient to check if their behaviors are branching bisimular. In contrast to [35], we do not need to define an abstraction operator. In our mapping, the comparison of the two open nets is restricted to the transitions that are connected to an interface place. We abstract from all other transitions by labeling them with τ. The labeling, however, is fixed in Definition 10 (transition label) and thus no additional definition of an abstraction is necessary. Consequently, we can define projection inheritance of two open nets as follows.

Definition 21 (Projection inheritance). *Two open nets N and N' are related by* projection inheritance *iff their behaviors are branching bisimular.*

Note that projection inheritance is an equivalence.

As an example, consider $TS(GS_1)$ and $TS(GS_2)$ in Figs. 15(a) and 15(b), respectively. Although $TS(GS_2)$ simulates $TS(GS_1)$ they are not branching bisimular. The reason is that the τ transition in state r6 yields a relation between states r2 and r8 which obviously violates branching bisimulation. Thus, GS_1 and GS_2 are not related under projection inheritance.

In [37] we have proven that the accordance notion is more liberal than projection inheritance, i.e., projection inheritance implies accordance (in both directions). This gives a sufficient criterion for deciding accordance.

Theorem 1 (Projection inheritance implies accordance [37]). *Let N and N' be two open nets. If N and N' are related by projection inheritance, then N' accords with N and N accords with N'.*

Although the notion of projection inheritance preserves all strategies, it turns out that in practice it is too restrictive. In other words, N accords with N' and N' accords with N does in general not imply that N and N' are related by projection inheritance. This is mainly caused by the fact that projection inheritance looks at the structure of the nets rather than the exchange of messages. For example, when messages are sent, their order does not really matter. This is caused by the fact that we consider asynchronous message passing, i.e., messages may be consumed in a different order than they were produced. Nevertheless, projection inheritance will differentiate between different orderings of sending messages. As another example, open nets RS_1 and RS_3 are not branching bisimular, but RS_1 accords with RS_3.

Checking Accordance with Operating Guidelines. We consider now a more liberal refinement notion that is necessary *and* sufficient.

Remember that we need to compare the sets *Strat*(N) and *Strat*(N') in order to decide accordance of N and N'. The problem is that the set *Strat* may correspond to an infinite set of open nets. With the operating guidelines of N and N' we have, however, a compact representation of *Strat*(N) and *Strat*(N') which can be used to decide accordance. To this end, we define a refinement relation $\sqsubseteq$ for operating guidelines. Informally, $OG(N) \sqsubseteq OG(N')$, i.e., $OG(N')$ refines $OG(N)$, if and only if there is a simulation relation between the states of $OG(N)$ and $OG(N')$ such that the annotations in $OG(N)$ imply the annotations in $OG(N')$. Here we need a (strong) simulation relation. However, operating guidelines are deterministic (see Definition 13) and for deterministic transition systems the notions of (strong) and weak simulation are equivalent.

Definition 22 (Refinement of OGs). *Let N and N' be interface equivalent open nets and let $OG(N) = [Q, MP, \delta, q_0, \Phi]$ and $OG(N') = [Q', MP', \delta', q_0', \Phi']$ be the corresponding operating guidelines. Then, $OG(N) \sqsubseteq OG(N')$ (i.e., $OG(N')$ refines $OG(N)$) iff there is a simulation relation $\xi \subseteq Q \times Q'$ such that for all $[q, q'] \in \xi$, the formula $\Phi(q) \Rightarrow \Phi'(q')$ is a tautology.*

As an example, consider the two operating guidelines $OG(RS_1)$ and $OG(RS_3)$ in Fig. 15. RS_1 and RS_3 are interface equivalent and $OG(RS_1)$ simulates $OG(RS_3)$, i.e., each step in $OG(RS_3)$ can be mimicked in $OG(RS_1)$. Furthermore, the annotations of $OG(RS_3)$ imply the annotations in $OG(RS_1)$. For example, $\mathsf{!order} \vee \tau$ implies $\mathsf{!order} \vee \mathsf{!money} \vee \tau$ in $[\mathsf{q1}, \mathsf{s1}] \in \xi$, $(\mathsf{?food} \wedge \mathsf{final}) \vee \tau$ implies $\mathsf{!money} \vee \mathsf{?food} \vee \tau$ in $[\mathsf{q2}, \mathsf{s3}] \in \xi$, etc. Consequently, we have $OG(RS_3) \sqsubseteq OG(RS_1)$. It is easy to observe that $OG(RS_1) \sqsubseteq OG(RS_3)$ does not hold, because $OG(RS_3)$ does not simulate $OG(RS_1)$.

The relation $\sqsubseteq$ is a pre-order. With the help of the next theorem we show that $OG(N')$ refines $OG(N)$ iff N' accords with N and thus it can be used to decide accordance of N and N'. This result has been first introduced in [37] for acyclic open nets and has been extended to cyclic open nets in [32].

Theorem 2 (Checking accordance [32]). *Let N and N' be two open nets and let $OG(N)$ and $OG(N')$ be the corresponding operating guidelines. Then, $OG(N) \sqsubseteq OG(N')$ iff $Strat(N) \subseteq Strat(N')$.*

Based on the above consideration we conclude that $Strat(RS_3) \subseteq Strat(RS_1)$, and hence RS_1 accords with RS_3.

The value of Theorem 1 and Theorem 2 is that accordance can be checked independently of the services that use N, and only N and N' have to be known to decide accordance.

5.3 Refining Services

In the previous section we have presented an algorithm to decide for two given open nets N and N' whether N' accords with N and thus can replace N without violating any strategy for N. However, designing N' is a nontrivial and error-prone task even for experienced service designers. In order to support service designers, we introduce an approach to refine open nets. Given an open net N we want to incrementally transform N to an open net N' such that every transformation step preserves accordance. To this end, fragments of N are incrementally replaced by other fragments. In this approach, a fragment M of N is replaced by another fragment M' yielding the open net N'. We prove that if M' accords with M, then N' accords with N. The results we are going to present in this section have been published in [37].

An open net M is a fragment of an open net N if there is an open net N_{rest} and the composition of M and N_{rest} is the open net N. The set of interface places of M is divided into two sets: some interface places of N and some internal places $R \cup S$ of N. We use R to denote these input places and S to denote these output places. For technical reasons we require that the initial marking of M is the empty marking and the set of final markings is the singleton set with the empty marking.

Definition 23 (Fragment). *Let M be an open net with $m_0 = \underline{0}$ and $\Omega = \{\underline{0}\}$. Open net M is a* fragment *of an open net N iff there exists an open net N_{rest} such that $N = M \oplus N_{rest}$.*

As an example, consider the open net GS_1 in Fig. 2(a). A possible fragment M would be the open net with $P_M = \{\mathsf{p2}, \mathsf{p3}, \mathsf{food}\}$, $T_M = \{\mathsf{eat}\}$ and the adjacent arcs. In this case $R_M = \{\mathsf{p2}\}$ and $S_M = \{\mathsf{p3}\}$.

The next theorem states that if an open net N has a fragment M and there is another fragment M' that accords with M, then we can replace M by M' without affecting any strategy for N. Such transformations can be applied incrementally and thus refine a service specification to an implementation by applying transformation steps. The resulting implementation is correct by construction, i.e., it preserves all strategies of the specification.

Theorem 3 (Justification of transformation rules [37]). *Let $N_1 \oplus N_2$ be a deadlock-free open net composition. Let M be a fragment of N_1, and let N_{rest} be an open net such that $N_1 = M \oplus N_{rest}$. For any open net M' that accords with M, the composition $(M' \oplus N_{rest}) \oplus N_2$ is deadlock-free.*

Inheritance-preserving Transformation Rules. Based on the notion of projection inheritance, three *inheritance-preserving transformation rules* have been defined in [35]. These rules correspond to design patterns for extending a superclass to incorporate new behavior: (1) adding an internal loop (2) put a new internal transition in parallel with existing transitions, and (3) insert an internal transition in-between existing transitions.

We exemplify these rules in Fig. 16. Figure 16(a) represents a fragment M_0 of an open net N. M_0 contains transitions a, b and c. By Definition 23, there are no other connections of a, b, c, p1 and p2 than those shown in Fig. 16(a). Each transition is connected to an input and an output place. However, as indicated by the capital letters, each interface place may correspond to a set of places. Note that A_i, A_o, B_i, B_o, C_i, C_o do not need to be disjoint. Places R and S denote the input and output places to N. Again, R and S may be sets of places. Similar remarks hold for the other three fragments M_1, M_2 and M_3. For example, M_1 is obtained by adding transition d to M_0.

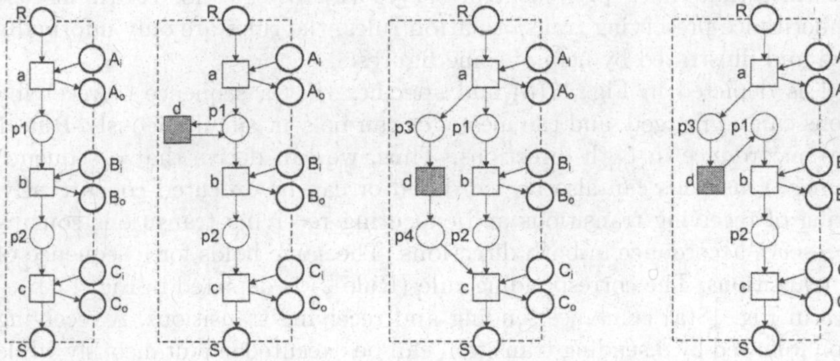

(a) M_0. (b) M_1: Adding a loop to M_0. (c) M_2: Putting transition d in parallel to b. (d) M_3: Inserting transition d in-between a and b.

Fig. 16. Accordance-preserving transformation rules based on projection inheritance

If one considers the behavior of these open nets, then M_0, M_1, M_2 and M_3 are branching bisimular. Hence each pair of these four fragments is related by projection inheritance. From Theorem 1 we conclude that the three transformation rules depicted in Fig. 16 preserve accordance in both directions.

Inheritance-preserving transformation rules only change internal transitions of an open net. Next we present transformation rules that affect transitions that are adjacent to an interface place.

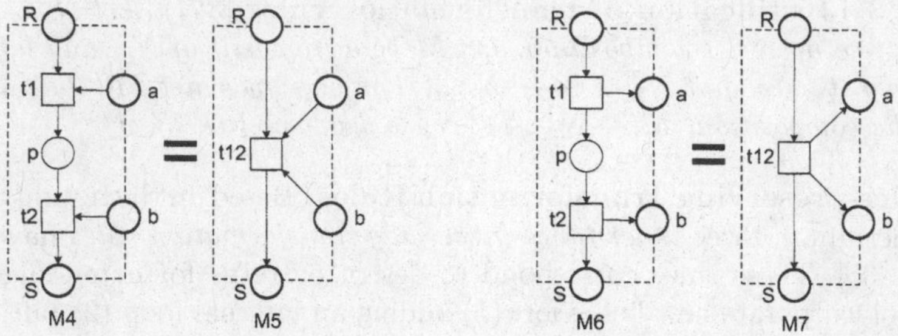

(a) Rule 1: $\mathit{Strat}(M_4) = \mathit{Strat}(M_5)$ (b) Rule 2: $\mathit{Strat}(M_6) = \mathit{Strat}(M_7)$

Fig. 17. Rule 1 and Rule 2

Accordance-preserving Transformation Rules. We present five accordance-preserving transformation rules. Four of these rules preserve accordance in both directions and one rule preserves accordance only in one direction. Although these transformation rules are sufficient, they are not complete, meaning they do not cover all possible service implementations. Given an open net N, each transformation rule specifies a fragment M of N (see Definition 23) which can be replaced by another open net M' yielding an implementation of N. Theorem 3 justifies that this replacement preserves all strategies for N. As in case of the inheritance-preserving transformation rules, the rules are only informally described and illustrated by help of some figures.

Rule 1 is depicted in Fig. 17(a) and specifies that a sequence of receiving transitions can be merged, and the messages can be sent simultaneously. Rule 1 preserves accordance in both directions. Thus, we can derive that a sequence of receiving transitions can also be reordered or can be executed concurrently. Reordering of receiving transitions and executing receiving transitions concurrently preserve accordance in both directions. The same holds for a sequence of sending transitions. The corresponding rule (Rule 2) is depicted in Fig. 17(b).

Rule 3 in Fig. 18(a) combines sending and receiving transitions. A receiving transition followed by a sending transition can be executed simultaneously while preserving accordance in both directions. Due to Rules 1 and 2, Rule 3 can be generalized to a sequence of receiving transitions followed by a sequence of sending transitions.

So far, we excluded the possibility that a sending transitions is followed by a receiving transitions. Rule 4, depicted in Fig. 18(b), specifies that first sending and then receiving a message can also be executed concurrently and vice versa. Rule 4 preserves accordance in both directions, too.

Figure 19(a) shows that first sending and then receiving cannot be reordered in general: M_{10} does not accord with M_8 and M_8 does not accord with M_{10}. Suppose the final markings to be equivalent to the singleton set with the empty marking. Then, the open net depicted in Fig. 19(b) is a strategy for M_{10}, but no strategy for M_8, and the open net depicted in Fig. 19(c) is a strategy for M_8 but not for M_{10}.

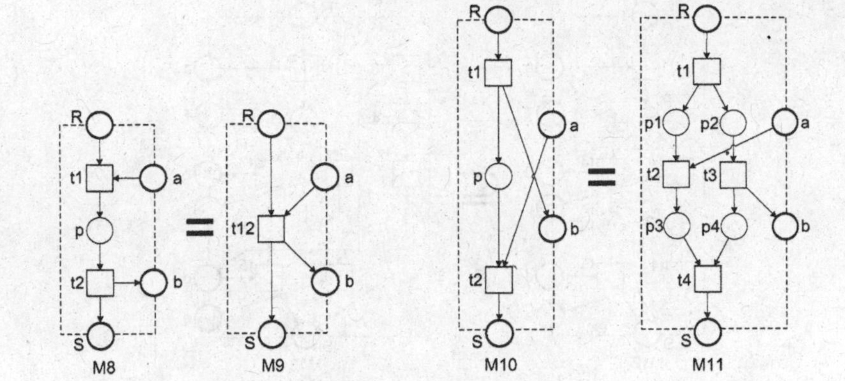

(a) Rule 3: $\mathit{Strat}(M_8) = \mathit{Strat}(M_9)$ (b) Rule 4: $\mathit{Strat}(M_{10}) = \mathit{Strat}(M_{11})$

Fig. 18. Rule 3 and Rule 4

Figure 19(a) can be seen as an anti-pattern, however, not in the sense of the anti-patterns mentioned in Sect. 2. The main difference is that Fig. 19(a) refers to a problematic modification while the earlier anti-patterns refer to problematic service definitions.

From the anti-pattern shown in Figure 19(a) it follows that first receiving and then sending (cf. M_8) cannot be transformed to a fragment that sends and receives concurrently (M_{11}), because we could transform the latter net to M_{10} by applying Rule 4. Consequently, first receiving then sending does not accord to sending and receiving concurrently and vice versa. Analogously, first

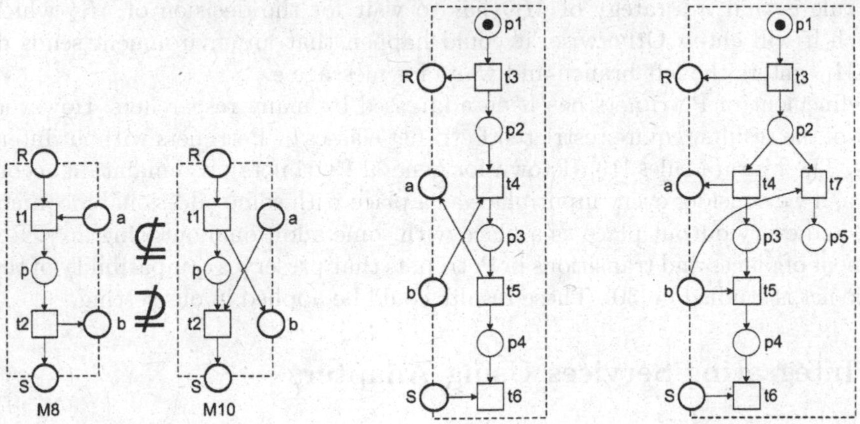

(a) Anti-pattern: $\mathit{Strat}(M_8) \neq \mathit{Strat}(M_{10})$ (b) Strategy for M_{10} but not for M_8. (c) Strategy for M_8 but not for M_{10}.

Fig. 19. Counterexamples

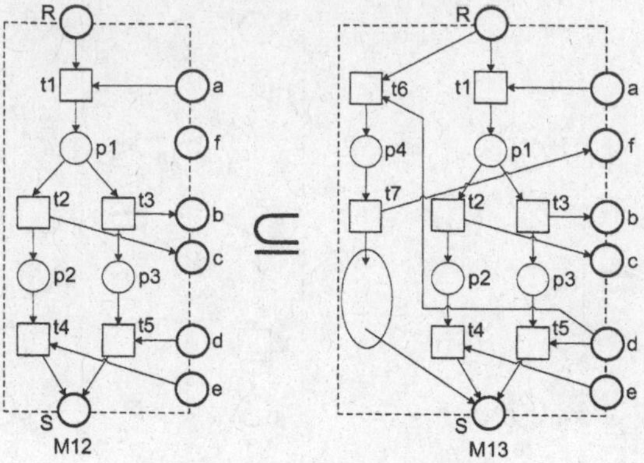

Fig. 20. Rule 5 (adding an alternative branch): $Strat(M_{12}) \subseteq Strat(M_{13})$

sending then receiving (M_{10}) cannot be transformed to sending and receiving simultaneously (M_9), because the latter can be transformed to M_8 by applying Rule 3. Thus, first sending then receiving does not accord with sending and receiving simultaneously and vice versa.

Rule 5 specifies a way to add an alternative branch to a fragment M_{12} depicted on the left hand side of Fig. 20. The fragment M_{12} first receives a and then enters either the left or the right branch. In the left (right) branch, message b (c) is sent, and then message d (e) is received. The fragment M_{12} can be transformed to M_{13} by adding an alternative branch. In this branch, d is received, and then a message f is sent. Afterwards, this branch can be arbitrary, i.e., there can be any continuation (including direct continuation in S) of this net as illustrated by the ellipse. Rule 5 preserves accordance in one direction only. The intuition behind this rule is that a strategy of M_{12} has to wait for the decision of M_{12} which branch it will enter. Otherwise, it could happen that an environment sends d, but M_{12} enters the left branch and waits for message e.

Refinement of Petri nets has been addressed by many researchers. However, most of the results require restricted Petri net classes or Petri nets without interfaces. The Murata rules [13] (known for general Petri nets) also maintain accordance, if we consider every input place as a place with some additional incoming arcs, and every output place as a place with some additional outgoing arcs. Refinement of places and transitions in Petri nets that preserves compatibility of the whole net is studied in [30]. These results could be applied in our setting.

6 Integrating Services Using Adapters

Service-oriented computing aims to create complex services by composing less-complex services. As services are often developed independently, upon composition they may turn out to be incompatible. In this section we discuss some sources of incompatibility and some ways to resolve them. This section is primarily based on [38].

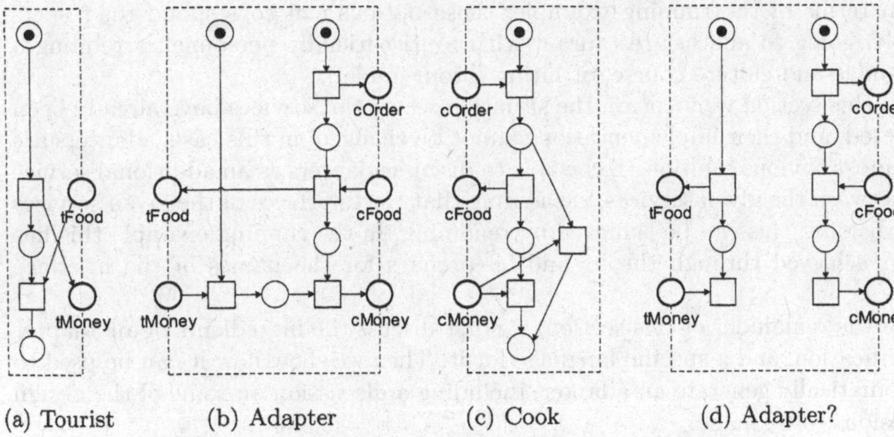

Fig. 21. Running example for adapter generation

Figure 21 contains the running example for this section. The tourist modeled in Fig. 21(a) enters a restaurant in a foreign country. The tourist noticed something like a special offer on the door, but he does not understand the local language. So he just places the required fee on the table and waits for food. The local cook modeled in Fig. 21(c), however, insists on an order before preparing any meal. Moreover, if the cook already gets some money before serving the food, he may immediately stop cooking.

When integrating some services that have been developed independently, some typical kinds of incompatibilities are:

- names of the message types;
- encoding of similar message types;
- semantics of similar message types;
- order in which messages are expected or transmitted.

It is clear that the open nets in Fig. 21(a) and Fig. 21(c) have different sets of interface places, even if we ignore the 't' and 'c' prefixes. Moreover, if we try to compose them by fusing the obvious combinations of interface places, and hide (i.e., make them internal) the other interface places, then the result contains a deadlock: the cook waits for an order, while the tourist gives some money and waits for food.

In this section we focus on the last kind of incompatibility, which we call *behavioral incompatibility*; however, we will not ignore the other ones. For simplicity reasons, we assume that the name of each message port coincides with the name of the message type that can be transmitted over the channel.

If the services to be composed are incompatible, there are a few options:

- replace some of the services by similar services that are compatible;
- change the implementation of some of the services;
- introduce an *adapter service* that bridges the incompatibilities.

In terms of the running example, these options can correspond to, respectively, going to another restaurant with tourist-friendly personnel, attending a language-and-culture course, or hiring a tour guide.

In this section we focus on the situation where the services have already been selected, and their implementation cannot be changed; in this case, adapters are the most obvious solution. To be able to discuss adapters as an additional service in between the given services, we assume that the interfaces of the given services are disjoint; this can be achieved by renaming. In the running example this has been achieved through the 't' and 'c' prefixes for the names of the interface places.

In the remainder of this section, we first discuss the ingredients of an adapter specification, and a specific language for it. Then we show how it can be used to automatically generate an adapter, including a discussion on some of the design decisions to be made.

6.1 Adapter Specification

In this section we discuss the contents of an adapter specification. Behavioral incompatibilities typically manifest itself in deadlocks of the composed system. Therefore the first ingredient of the adapter specification is a behavioral property, in our case deadlock freedom, on the composed system (which, by definition, guarantees that the composed system is closed). To be able to check whether an adapter establishes deadlock freedom, the adapter specification should also include models of the given services, say, open nets N_1 and N_2. For simplicity reasons, we only discuss the integration of two given services, although it can easily be scaled up to any number of services.

For the running example, an adapter service that establishes deadlock freedom is modeled in Fig. 21(b). It gives a default order to the cook, and then passes on the food when it arrives. In the mean time it accepts the money from the tourist, but it only forwards the money once the cook has actually served the food. The composition of Fig. 21(a), Fig. 21(b) and Fig. 21(c) is indeed a closed net and it is deadlock-free.

On the other hand, the service from Fig. 21(d) also establishes this property, but is this a proper adapter? Such an example illustrates that the specification so far admits adapters that are the composition of two unconnected components A_1 and A_2 such that both $N_1 \oplus A_1$ and $N_2 \oplus A_2$ are deadlock-free, but independently of each other. Hence it admits adapters that can arbitrarily create and delete messages, including real goods like food and money, which is not very realistic.

Apart from the requirement on the composed system, a requirement on the internals of the adapter is needed such that it can actually be implemented. To this end, we extend the adapter specification with the set of elementary activities (from a semantical perspective) that can be used in the adapter.

Thus the adapter specification consist of the following three parts:

- models of the services to be composed;
- behavioral property to be established by the composed system;
- elementary activities for the adapter.

6.2 Elementary Adapter Activities

In this section we explore the typical elementary activities for an adapter, and we describe a way to specify them. As the given services have an asynchronous communication interface, the basic activities of an adapter are receiving a message from an interface port, and sending a message to an interface port. As these are separate tasks, it also possible to delay the forwarding of messages.

Internally, the activities of an adapter include ways to deal with messages; thus reflecting semantic dependencies between certain message types. Most approaches [39,40,41,42,43,44] agree that the activities of an adapter should include the following activities:

- **Create a message:** This is possible for simple control messages, and messages with a default value. However, it is impossible for messages containing important data such as passwords, and personal data of a user.
- **Copy a message:** This is possible for most electronic messages, although it could be inappropriate for single-use data such as transaction numbers. It is also inappropriate for messages that represent real goods.
- **Delete a message:** This is possible for most electronic data, while it is inappropriate for real goods.
- **Transform/Split/Merge some messages:** This is possible if the underlying transformation routine is provided, e.g., calculating a metric measure from an imperial one, or deriving a city name from a zip code.

Based on these example activities, it becomes clear that the applicability of an activity to particular message types strongly depends on semantic considerations that depend on the message types. As a result, we conclude that the possible activities of an adapter must be specified per message type.

We specify the capabilities of an adapter using a *Specification of the Elementary Activities* (SEA). Given a set of message types MT, an SEA is a set of transformation rules on these message types. The set MT contains at least the names of the interface ports of the given services, but it may also contain auxiliary message types.

Definition 24 (Specification of the Elementary Activities (SEA)). *Given a set of message types MT. An SEA over the message types MT is a set of transformation rules of the shape*

$$X \overset{Z}{\mapsto} Y$$

where X and Y are bags (multi sets) over the set MT, and where Z is a total function from messages of the types X to messages of the types Y.

Such a rule denotes that, using the transformation Z, a message of each type in X is consumed, and a message of each type in Y is produced. After receiving some messages, the adapter can apply several transformations to the internally available messages before sending any messages. Synthesizing an adapter then boils down to applying these rules in a right order, and sending and receiving messages to and from the interface at a right moment.

Table 1. Examples of elementary activities in terms of transformation rules

Elementary activity	Possible transformation rule
Create a	$\mapsto a$
Copy a	$a \mapsto a, a$
Delete a	$a \mapsto$
Transform a, b, c into d, e	$a, b, c \mapsto d, e$ or $a, b, c \mapsto a, b, c, d, e$
Split a into b, c, d	$a \mapsto b, c, d$ or $a \mapsto a, b, c, d$
Merge a, b, c into d	$a, b, c \mapsto d$ or $a, b, c \mapsto a, b, c, d$

For the synthesis of an adapter, we can largely abstract from the actual data transformations Z. Therefore we often omit Z in the transformation rules, but in Sect. 7 we will discuss how Z can be integrated in the synthesized adapters.

Table 1 shows some examples of activities in terms of transformation rules. For some rules, we give two versions: one for real items and one for electronic items. Some more-complicated patterns would require multiple rules: a typical "collapse" pattern, where an arbitrary series of a messages has to be merged into one message b, could be modeled using the two rules $\mapsto b$ (create an empty 'b') and $a, b \mapsto b$ (add a single 'a' to an existing 'b').

Many languages have been proposed that are similar to the SEA rules, but there are subtle but essential differences. Languages like in [43,44] do not support multiple alternative rules, like two SEA rules $A \mapsto B$ and $A \mapsto C$ that specify that at any time the adapter can choose which rule to apply. The rules in languages like in [39,40,41] have no direction [45], while the SEA rules are asymmetric.

As an SEA represents semantical dependencies, it may be possible to use techniques related to semantic web and ontologies to construct an SEA. As these are research areas on their own, we only focus on using a given SEA. The approach of [44] is interesting as it presents an interactive approach to find and refine SEA-like specifications for adapters using mismatch trees.

For the running example, a possible SEA is the one in Table 2. Note that the adapter from Fig. 21(d) can violate the last two transformation rules. The adapter in Fig. 21(b) obeys the rules; moreover, it uses each rule exactly once, but this is a coincidence (see, e.g., the running example from [38]).

Table 2. Running example: SEA

	$\mapsto$ cOrder
cFood	$\mapsto$ tFood
tMoney	$\mapsto$ cMoney

6.3 Adapter Generation

In this section we discuss how to generate an adapter. The adapter specification consists of the given open nets N_1 and N_2, the deadlock-freedom property, and

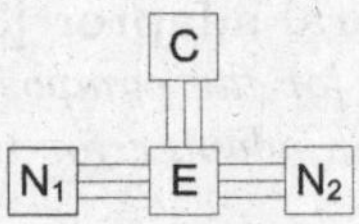

Fig. 22. Conceptual structure

an SEA. An adapter is an open net such that its composition with the given open nets N_1 and N_2 is closed and deadlock-free. Furthermore, to ensure implementability, an adapter may only be constructed from the elementary activities described by the SEA.

Adapter generation without SEA. Let us first ignore the SEA, and explore the basic construction of an adapter. Such an adapter is defined as an open net A such that $(N_1 \oplus N_2) \oplus A$ is deadlock-free. That is, A is a strategy for the composition $N_1 \oplus N_2$. Such an adapter can be computed as a witness for controllability of $N_1 \oplus N_2$.

Adapter generation with an SEA. The SEA imposes additional restrictions on the adapter. Most approaches to adapter generation modify the computation of a strategy with (on-the-fly) removal of the branches that violate this requirement. The result is typically a complex custom algorithm [39,40,41]. In [46,47] it is shown that there exists a dual approach that first integrates the SEA restrictions with the given open nets, such that afterwards every computed strategy is an adapter.

A conceptually simpler approach [38] is to immediately translate the SEA rules into a new open net that is part of the adapter. We call this part of the adapter the engine, and the remainder of the adapter the controller. This results in a two-piece adapter that separates *data* (implementability) and *control* (behavioral property).

The *engine* E is an open net that encodes all the elementary activities from the SEA. It has an interface with the given open nets N_1 and N_2, and hence it can ensure that all outgoing messages are obtained from the incoming messages using the SEA rules only. The engine E has an additional interface to a *controller* C. This interface allows the controller to decide in which order the elementary activities are performed. Figure 22 shows a schematic representation of this structure.

Before showing an example encoding of an SEA in terms of an engine, we first determine how it can be used to generate an adapter. Formally, given an engine E for the SEA, we want to construct a controller C such that $(N_1 \oplus N_2) \oplus (E \oplus C)$ is deadlock-free. Such a controller can be computed as a witness for controllability of $(N_1 \oplus N_2) \oplus E$. As every C yields an SEA-based open net $E \oplus C$, every witness C for controllability of the open net $(N_1 \oplus N_2) \oplus E$, yields an SEA-based adapter $E \oplus C$. So deadlock freedom is guaranteed independently of any specifics of the used engine.

Lemma 1 (Two-piece behavioral adapter [38]). *Given any open nets* N_1, N_2, *and* E. *For every strategy* C *for the composed open net* $(N_1 \oplus N_2) \oplus E$, *the composed open net* $E \oplus C$ *is an adapter for the open nets* N_1 *and* N_2.

So, at a conceptual level, this adapter-synthesis approach consists of the following steps, given the open nets N_1 and N_2 and an SEA:

1. generate an engine E from the SEA and the interface of the open net $N_1 \oplus N_2$;
2. synthesize a controller C as a strategy for the open net $(N_1 \oplus N_2) \oplus E$;
3. compose engine E and controller C to obtain the final adapter $A = E \oplus C$.

Note that the engine is used twice: for generating a controller, and as part of the final adapter. The constraint-oriented approach from [48,49] uses a "Store" that contains part of the functionality of an engine, but it is not part of the final adapter.

Regarding the running example, the adapter from Fig. 21(b) has been generated in this way. In what follows we first discuss the encoding of an engine and then the selection of a controller.

6.4 Encoding an SEA as an Engine

In this section we show how an SEA can be encoded as an engine E modeled by an open net. For simplicity of presentation, we assume that for each SEA rule, the bags before and after the $\mapsto$ are sets; the general case follows analogously using open nets with arc multiplicities.

Let N be the composition $N_1 \oplus N_2$. Let I_N and O_N denote the (disjoint sets of) input and output places, respectively, of N. Let K be a set such that the SEA consists of the rules $X_k \mapsto Y_k$, for any $k \in K$. Let MT be a set of message types, containing (the types of) the sets of places I_N and O_N, and the set of message types used in K. The SEA may contain auxiliary message types (ones that do not occur in the given open nets), and hence we have $I_N \cup O_N \subseteq MT$.

For defining the open net E, we use names from the space $(MT \cup K) \times \{e, n, c, r, s\}$, where e, n, c, r, and s denote fresh names that do not occur in the given open nets. Moreover, we assume that the sets MT and K are disjoint.

The interface of open net E consists of output places I_N, input places O_N (i.e., the interfaces of the given open nets in opposite orientation), and an interface (defined later on) for interaction with the controller (cf. Fig. 22). For each message type $m \in MT$, we introduce in the open net E an internal place (m, c), where c refers to "conceptual". In the initial and final markings, the internal places are empty.

The open net E has three kinds of transitions. For every input place $o \in O_N$, there is a transition (o, r), where r refers to "receive", to move arriving messages from interface place o to their internal place (o, c). For every transformation rule $X_k \mapsto Y_k$, where $k \in K$, there is a transition (k, c) to perform the actual transformation in terms of the internal places. Finally, for every output place $i \in I_N$, there is a transition (i, s), where s refers to "send", to move messages from their internal place (i, c) to interface place i.

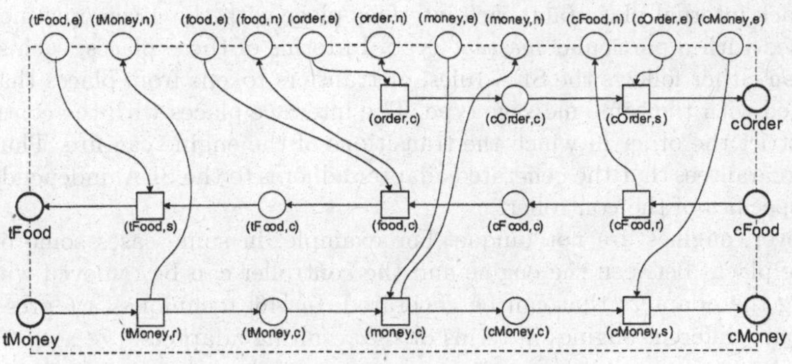

Fig. 23. Running example: engine

What remains is to describe the interface of the engine E with the controller C. For every transition (o, r), where $o \in O_N$, there is an output place (o, n) that notifies an arrived message o. For every transition (k, c), where $k \in K$, there is an input place (k, e) that enables transformation rule k, and an output place (k, n) that notifies an execution of transformation rule k. Finally, for every transition (i, s), where $i \in I_N$, there is an input place (i, e) that enables the delivery of a message i. Thus this engine is formally defined as:

Definition 25 (Engine). *Let I, O, MT, K be as introduced before. The engine E is defined as an open net with the following constituents:*

$$P = (MT \times \{c\}) \cup I \cup O; \quad m_0 = \underline{0}; \quad \Omega = \{\underline{0}\};$$
$$I = O_N \cup (K \times \{e\}) \cup (I_N \times \{e\}); \quad O = I_N \cup (K \times \{n\}) \cup (O_N \times \{n\});$$
$$T = (O_N \times \{r\}) \cup (K \times \{c\}) \cup (I_N \times \{s\});$$

$$F = F_r \cup F_c \cup F_s;$$
$$F_r = \bigcup_{o \in O_N} \{ [o, (o,r)], [(o,r),(o,n)], [(o,r),(o,c)] \};$$
$$F_c = \bigcup_{k \in K} (\{[(m,c),(k,c)] \mid m : m \in X_k\} \cup \{[(k,e),(k,c)]\} \cup \{[(k,c),(k,n)]\} \cup \{[(k,c),(m,c)] \mid m : m \in Y_k\});$$
$$F_s = \bigcup_{i \in I_N} \{ [(i,c),(i,s)], [(i,e),(i,s)], [(i,s),i] \}.$$

Figure 23 models the engine for the running example. The left and the right interfaces are for the tourist and the cook, respectively, while the top interface is for a controller; in this figure we use simplified names for the interface with the controller. As far as the transfer of money is concerned, the engine looks as follows. When there is a token on the interface place tMoney, transition (tMoney,r) transfers it to the internal place (tMoney,c) and sends a notification to the controller. Afterwards, transition (money,c) can transform a token from place (tMoney,c) into a token in place (cMoney,c); this is only possible if the controller has enabled this transition, and then the controller is notified. Finally, transition (cMoney,s) transfers a token from internal place (cMoney,c) to interface place cMoney, but only if the controller has enabled this transition.

So, each internal place (and each interface place with the given open nets) is associated with a particular message type. In terms of these places, each single transition either follows the SEA rules, or transfers tokens from places that are associated with the same message type. The interface places with the controller only restrict the order in which the transitions of the engine can fire. Thus the engine guarantees that the generated adapter adheres to the SEA, independently of any specifics of the controller.

However, engines are not unique. For example, in some cases some of the interface places between the engine and the controller can be removed without changing the adapters that can be generated. In [46] techniques are presented to compare different engines in terms of the resulting adapters.

6.5 Selecting a Controller

In this section we consider the selection of a controller for a two-piece adapter. In general, the open net $(N_1 \oplus N_2) \oplus E$ has several strategies, and every strategy can be used as a controller for an adapter (see Lemma 1).

A particularly interesting strategy is the most-permissive strategy (see Definition 17), as it represents somehow the largest behavior that can enforce the behavioral property to be established. In this way, it causes the smallest constraints on the interface of the controller. A potential drawback of a most-permissive strategy is its size, but it exhibits a tremendous amount of non-determinism, which, in many cases, results in nice concurrency in terms of open nets.

On the other hand, there are usually many strategies that are smaller than the most-permissive one. Such strategies often restrict the interaction with the given open nets, and, in particular, reduce concurrency.

To sum up, both most-permissive strategies and arbitrary small strategies have specific advantages and disadvantages which more or less complement each other. This gives an opportunity to make a trade-off between the complexity of adapter synthesis and the quality of the resulting adapter (in terms of its size and run-time behavior).

This is also related to two kinds of application scenario's for adapters. In the first one, a set of services is carefully selected, and then as a final engineering step an adapter is calculated. In the second one, a user at run-time selects some services, and an adapter is required to make these services work together. In the first scenario's larger run-times are permissable than in the second scenario, but also a higher quality is expected.

7 Tool Support

In this section we sketch how the techniques from the previous sections have been implemented in research tools. All described tools are available at

`http://www.service-technology.org/tools/`

7.1 Translating Services to Open Nets

In practice, services are not modeled by formalisms such as Petri nets. Instead, a number of service description languages have been proposed by several industrial consortiums. The most-prominent language is BPEL.

For BPEL, there exists a feature-complete open net semantics [50] and a compiler, BPEL2oWFN, to translate a BPEL process to an open net. This semantics is feature-complete in the sense that it supports all concepts of BPEL including control flow, data flow, message flow, exception handling, and compensation handling.

Since there is also a tool, oWFN2BPEL, to translate open nets to BPEL (using abstract processes) [51], a complete tool chain for translations between BPEL and open nets is available. Hence, all analysis methods for open nets can be used for BPEL processes.

7.2 Operating Guidelines

In Sect. 4 we have introduced the notion of operating guidelines as a compact characterization of all strategies for an open net N. Since the algorithm to compute operating guidelines explores all reachable states of N, in an implementation we have to restrict ourselves to *finite state services.* Such services can still have infinitely many strategies.

On the modeling level an open net has finitely many states if its inner structure $inner(N)$ is bounded. The composition of two bounded open nets may, however, result in an unbounded open net, because tokens may accumulate on the former interface places. To achieve a bounded open net composition, we have to restrict the number of tokens at those interface places. To this end, we need a notion of boundedness for interface places, which has been introduced in [27] as *k-limited communication.*

For unbounded open nets, controllability has been proven to be undecidable [52]. For the implementation of our algorithms we require open nets to be bounded and to satisfy k-limited communication, for some k. Since services in practice are finite-state services, this restriction does not harm our approach.

In [27] an algorithm has been presented to compute an operating guidelines of a bounded open net. The *OG* construction algorithm first computes the most permissive strategy. Therefore, it starts with an over-approximation of compatible behavior of any strategy and then iteratively removes all states which cause violations of the deadlock-freedom property. Finally, the annotations are derived from information collected during the computation. If the service is uncontrollable, the algorithm eventually removes all states. The algorithm is implemented in the service analysis tool Fiona [50].

Besides computing the operating guidelines of an open net, Fiona can also be used to

- decide matching of an open net with an operating guidelines;
- decide accordance of two open nets using Theorem 2;
- compute some strategy of an open net.

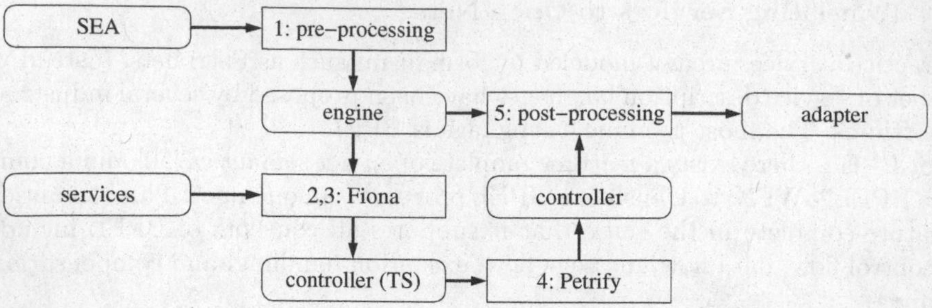

Fig. 24. Tool chain for adapter generation

7.3 Adapter Generation

In this section we discuss a Fiona-based implementation [38] of the adapter generation approach described in Sect. 6. It turns out that in the engine, the activities for message creation can easily lead to unbounded places, including interface places. To be able to compute an operating guidelines, we impose artificial bounds on these places. Using the techniques in [46], it can be shown that the resulting adapter is also an adapter for the given services without the artificial bounds. Moreover, every finite-state adapter can be synthesized if the bounds are chosen sufficiently large.

We use the tool-chain described in Fig. 24. The inputs are an open net model of each given service, and an SEA; the output is an open net model of the adapter. In what follows we briefly describe the various steps:

1. **Create an engine model from the SEA.** The procedure as described in Sect. 6.4, including the required bounds, has been implemented in Fiona. By construction, all outputs to the given services have been obtained from the inputs of these services using the SEA transformation rules only.
2. **Compose the service models and the engine model.** The composition of service models is supported by Fiona. Afterwards we apply structural Petri-net reduction, which consists of local graph-transformations in an open net. It preserves the interface behavior of the transformed net, but it may significantly reduce the number of reachable internal states. It is inspired by classical Petri-net reduction (like [13]). We apply it for the purpose of reducing complexity in subsequent steps.
3. **Synthesize a controller as a transition system.** A controller is a strategy, and strategy synthesis is the core functionality of Fiona. The resulting controller is represented as a transition system rather than an open net.
4. **Transform this transition system into an open net.** Petrify [53] is an external tool that translates a transition system into an equivalent Petri net. The resulting Petri net tends to exhibit a large degree of concurrency, and tends to be significantly more compact than the original transition system.
5. **Compose the engine and the controller into an adapter.** Like before, the composition is supported by Fiona, and we apply structural Petri-net

reduction afterwards. However, this time the reduction aims at simplifying the resulting structures, thus leading to a more compact Petri-net. In particular, the reduction may iron-out dead parts in the adapter (like SEA transitions that are not used) or collapse a sequence of transitions into a single transition. As such a sequence may consist of a transition that stems from the controller and another one that stems from the engine, the interface between them may become invisible in the resulting adapter.

An optional last step is to translate the open net for the adapter into an executable language. The tool oWFN2BPEL can generate an abstract BPEL process that includes an opaque activity for each transition of the open net. Remembering that SEA rules can be annotated with actual transformations (for instance in XSL), and SEA rules correspond to transitions in the engine, we can fill the opaque activities with actual code and turn them into executable activities.

Currently, we are developing engines with a synchronous interface to the controller, for which the first results show that these are more efficient. A most-permissive strategy as controller for a synchronous engine turns out to perform better than an arbitrary strategy (or a most-permissive strategy) as controller for an asynchronous engine. This applies to both the run-time of the adapter generator, and the size of the generated adapter in terms of open nets. The example adapter in Fig. 21(b) was actually generated in this way.

8 Conclusions

The shift towards service orientation was initially intended to mainly support cross-organizational processes. However, the wide adoption of service-oriented architectures shows that this paradigm shift is also important for intra-organizational processes. Monolithic information systems can now be decomposed into several smaller services. Service orientation leads to systems that can be viewed as *interacting services*. Therefore, it is vital to understand service interaction in all its aspects.

This paper studies service interaction from various angles. First of all, the paper provides a collection of *service interaction patterns*. This provides an overview of the challenges in this domain and aids in a better understanding of the important concepts. Moreover, by presenting a few anti-patterns we reveal typical pitfalls in the design of services.

Secondly, the paper *formalizes essential concepts* such as strategies, controllability, and accordance. This is done in the setting of open nets. Finally, the core of the paper focusses on three important challenges: *Exposing services* (Sect. 4), *Replacing and refining services* (Sect. 5), and *Integrating services using adapters* (Sect. 6). These challenges are non-trivial. However, the body of work centering around open nets provides a solid basis for addressing these challenges. This is illustrated by the availability of analysis tools that support all three challenges and that can also work with industrial languages such as BPEL.

Acknowledgements

Van der Aalst and Mooij participate in the Poseidon project at Thales under the responsibilities of the Embedded Systems Institute (ESI). This project is partially supported by the Dutch Ministry of Economic Affairs under the BSIK program.

References

1. Dumas, M., van der Aalst, W., ter Hofstede, A.: Process-Aware Information Systems: Bridging People and Software through Process Technology. Wiley & Sons, Chichester (2005)
2. Alonso, G., Casati, F., Kuno, H., Machiraju, V.: Web Services Concepts, Architectures and Applications. Springer, Berlin (2004)
3. Barros, A., Dumas, M., ter Hofstede, A.: Service Interaction Patterns. In: van der Aalst, W., Benatallah, B., Casati, F., Curbera, F. (eds.) BPM 2005. LNCS, vol. 3649, pp. 302–318. Springer, Heidelberg (2005)
4. Decker, G., Puhlmann, F., Weske, M.: Formalizing Service Interactions. In: Dustdar, S., Fiadeiro, J.L., Sheth, A.P. (eds.) BPM 2006. LNCS, vol. 4102, pp. 414–419. Springer, Heidelberg (2006)
5. Hohpe, G., Woolf, B.: Enterprise Integration Patterns. Addison-Wesley Professional, Reading (2003)
6. Mulyar, N., Aldred, L., van der Aalst, W.: The Conceptualization of a Configurable Multi-party Multi-message Request-Reply Conversation. In: Meersman, R., Tari, Z. (eds.) OTM 2007, Part I. LNCS, vol. 4803, pp. 735–753. Springer, Heidelberg (2007)
7. Wegner, P.: Why interaction is more powerful than algorithms. Communications of the ACM 40(5), 80–91 (1997)
8. Zaha, J., Dumas, M., ter Hofstede, A., Barros, A., Decker, G.: Service Interaction Modeling: Bridging Global and Local Views. In: International Enterprise Distributed Object Computing Conference (EDOC 2006), pp. 45–55. IEEE Computer Society Press, Los Alamitos (2006)
9. Alves, A., Arkin, A., Askary, S., Barreto, C., Bloch, B., Curbera, F., Ford, M., Goland, Y., Guízar, A., Kartha, N., Liu, C., Khalaf, R., Koenig, D., Marin, M., Mehta, V., Thatte, S., Rijn, D., Yendluri, P., Yiu, A.: Web Services Business Process Execution Language Version 2.0 (OASIS Standard). WS-BPEL TC OASIS (2007), `http://docs.oasis-open.org/wsbpel/2.0/wsbpel-v2.0.html`
10. van der Aalst, W., ter Hofstede, A., Kiepuszewski, B., Barros, A.: Workflow Patterns. Distributed and Parallel Databases 14(1), 5–51 (2003)
11. Massuthe, P., Reisig, W., Schmidt, K.: An Operating Guideline Approach to the SOA. Annals of Mathematics, Computing & Teleinformatics 1(3), 35–43 (2005)
12. Desel, J., Esparza, J.: Free Choice Petri Nets. Cambridge Tracts in Theoretical Computer Science, vol. 40. Cambridge University Press, Cambridge (1995)
13. Murata, T.: Petri Nets: Properties, Analysis and Applications. Proceedings of the IEEE 77(4), 541–580 (1989)
14. Reisig, W.: Petri Nets: An Introduction. EATCS Monographs in Theoretical Computer Science, vol. 4. Springer, Berlin (1985)
15. van der Aalst, W.: The Application of Petri Nets to Workflow Management. The Journal of Circuits, Systems and Computers 8(1), 21–66 (1998)

16. Gamma, E., Helm, R., Johnson, R., Vlissides, J.: Design Patterns: Elements of Reusable Object-Oriented Software. Professional Computing Series. Addison Wesley, Reading (1995)
17. Mulyar, N.: Patterns for Process-Aware Information Systems: An Approach Based on Colored Petri Nets. Ph.D thesis, Eindhoven University of Technology, Eindhoven (2009)
18. Russell, N., van der Aalst, W., ter Hofstede, A., Edmond, D.: Workflow Resource Patterns: Identification, Representation and Tool Support. In: Pastor, Ó., Falcão e Cunha, J. (eds.) CAiSE 2005. LNCS, vol. 3520, pp. 216–232. Springer, Heidelberg (2005)
19. Russell, N., ter Hofstede, A., Edmond, D., van der Aalst, W.: Workflow Data Patterns: Identification, Representation and Tool Support. In: Delcambre, L.M.L., Kop, C., Mayr, H.C., Mylopoulos, J., Pastor, Ó. (eds.) ER 2005. LNCS, vol. 3716, pp. 353–368. Springer, Heidelberg (2005)
20. Alexander, C.: A Pattern Language: Towns, Building and Construction. Oxford University Press, Oxford (1977)
21. Russell, N., ter Hofstede, A., van der Aalst, W., Mulyar, N.: Workflow Control-Flow Patterns: A Revised View. BPM Center Report BPM-06-22, BPMcenter.org (2006)
22. Russell, N., van der Aalst, W., ter Hofstede, A.: Workflow Exception Patterns. In: Dubois, E., Pohl, K. (eds.) CAiSE 2006. LNCS, vol. 4001, pp. 288–302. Springer, Heidelberg (2006)
23. van der Aalst, W., van Hee, K.: Workflow Management: Models, Methods, and Systems. MIT Press, Cambridge (2004)
24. Massuthe, P., Reisig, W., Schmidt, K.: An Operating Guideline Approach to the SOA. In: Proceedings of the 2nd South-East European Workshop on Formal Methods 2005 (SEEFM 2005), Ohrid, Republic of Macedonia (2005)
25. Clarke, E., Grumberg, O., Peled, D.: Model Checking. The MIT Press, Cambridge (1999)
26. Massuthe, P., Schmidt, K.: Operating Guidelines - an Automata-Theoretic Foundation for the Service-Oriented Architecture. In: Cai, K.Y., Ohnishi, A., Lau, M.F. (eds.) Proceedings of the Fifth International Conference on Quality Software (QSIC 2005), Melbourne, Australia, pp. 452–457. IEEE Computer Society, Los Alamitos (2005)
27. Lohmann, N., Massuthe, P., Wolf, K.: Operating guidelines for finite-state services. In: Kleijn, J., Yakovlev, A. (eds.) ICATPN 2007. LNCS, vol. 4546, pp. 321–341. Springer, Heidelberg (2007)
28. Milner, R.: Communication and Concurrency. Prentice-Hall, Inc., Englewood Cliffs (1989)
29. Wolf, K.: Does my service have partners? In: Jensen, K., van der Aalst, W.M.P. (eds.) ToPNoC II 2008. LNCS, vol. 5460, pp. 152–171. Springer, Heidelberg (2008)
30. Vogler, W.: Modular Construction and Partial Order Semantics of Petri Nets. LNCS, vol. 625. Springer, Heidelberg (1992)
31. Fournet, C., Hoare, C.A.R., Rajamani, S.K., Rehof, J.: Stuck-Free Conformance. In: Alur, R., Peled, D.A. (eds.) CAV 2004. LNCS, vol. 3114, pp. 242–254. Springer, Heidelberg (2004)
32. Stahl, C., Massuthe, P., Bretschneider, J.: Deciding substitutability of services with operating guidelines. In: Jensen, K., van der Aalst, W.M.P. (eds.) ToPNoC II 2008. LNCS, vol. 5460, pp. 172–191. Springer, Heidelberg (2008)
33. Bravetti, M., Zavattaro, G.: Contract Based Multi-party Service Composition. In: Arbab, F., Sirjani, M. (eds.) FSEN 2007. LNCS, vol. 4767, pp. 207–222. Springer, Heidelberg (2007)

34. Castagna, G., Gesbert, N., Padovani, L.: A Theory of Contracts for Web Services. SIGPLAN Not. 43(1), 261–272 (2008)
35. Basten, T., van der Aalst, W.: Inheritance of Behavior. Journal of Logic and Algebraic Programming 47(2), 47–145 (2001)
36. van Glabbeek, R., Weijland, W.: Branching Time and Abstraction in Bisimulation Semantics. Journal of the ACM 43(3), 555–600 (1996)
37. van der Aalst, W., Lohmann, N., Massuthe, P., Stahl, C., Wolf, K.: From Public Views to Private Views: Correctness-by-Design for Services. In: Dumas, M., Heckel, H. (eds.) WS-FM 2007. LNCS, vol. 4937, pp. 139–153. Springer, Heidelberg (2008)
38. Gierds, C., Mooij, A., Wolf, K.: Specifying and generating behavioral service adapters based on transformation rules. Preprints CS-02-08, Institut fur Informatik, Universitat Rostock (2008)
39. Benatallah, B., Casati, F., Grigori, D., Motahari Nezhad, H.R., Toumani, F.: Developing Adapters for Web Services Integration. In: Pastor, Ó., Falcão e Cunha, J. (eds.) CAiSE 2005. LNCS, vol. 3520, pp. 415–429. Springer, Heidelberg (2005)
40. Bracciali, A., Brogi, A., Canal, C.: A formal approach to component adaptation. Journal of Systems and Software 74(1), 45–54 (2005)
41. Brogi, A., Canal, C., Pimentel, E., Vallecillo, A.: Formalizing Web Service Choreographies. Electr. Notes Theor. Comput. Sci. 105, 73–94 (2004)
42. Brogi, A., Popescu, R.: Automated Generation of BPEL Adapters. In: Dan, A., Lamersdorf, W. (eds.) ICSOC 2006. LNCS, vol. 4294, pp. 27–39. Springer, Heidelberg (2006)
43. Dumas, M., Spork, M., Wang, K.: Adapt or Perish: Algebra and Visual Notation for Service Interface Adaptation. In: Dustdar, S., Fiadeiro, J.L., Sheth, A.P. (eds.) BPM 2006. LNCS, vol. 4102, pp. 65–80. Springer, Heidelberg (2006)
44. Motahari Nezhad, H., Benatallah, B., Martens, A., Curbera, F., Casati, F.: Semi-automated adaptation of service interactions. In: Proc. WWW, pp. 993–1002 (2007)
45. Brogi, A., Canal, C., Pimentel, E.: On the semantics of software adaptation. Science of Computer Programming 61, 136–151 (2006)
46. Mooij, A., Voorhoeve, M.: Proof techniques for adapter generation. In: Proc. WS-FM (2008)
47. Lohmann, N., Massuthe, P., Wolf, K.: Behavioral constraints for services. In: Alonso, G., Dadam, P., Rosemann, M. (eds.) BPM 2007. LNCS, vol. 4714, pp. 271–287. Springer, Heidelberg (2007)
48. Canal, C., Poizat, P., Salaün, G.: Model-based adaptation of behavioral mismatching components. IEEE Transactions on Software Engineering 34(4), 546–563 (2008)
49. Mateescu, R., Poizat, P., Salaün, G.: Adaptation of service protocols using process algebra and on-the-fly reduction techniques. In: Proc. ICSOC, pp. 84–99 (2008)
50. Lohmann, N., Massuthe, P., Stahl, C., Weinberg, D.: Analyzing interacting WS-BPEL processes using flexible model generation. Data & Knowledge Engineering 64(1), 38–54 (2008)
51. Lohmann, N., Kleine, J.: Fully-automatic Translation of Open Workflow Net Models into Human-readable Abstract BPEL Processes. In: Proc. Modellierung. Lecture Notes in Informatics (LNI), vol. P-127, pp. 57–72 (2008)
52. Massuthe, P., Serebrenik, A., Sidorova, N., Wolf, K.: Can I find a partner? Undecidablity of partner existence for open nets. Information Processing Letters 108(6), 374–378 (2008)
53. Cortadella, J., Kishinevsky, M., Kondratyev, A., Lavagno, L., Yakovlev, A.: Logic synthesis of asynchronous controllers and interfaces. In: Advanced Microelectronics. Springer, Heidelberg (2002)

Synthesis and Composition of Web Services

Annapaola Marconi and Marco Pistore

Fondazione Bruno Kessler
Service Oriented Applications Group
Via Sommarive 18
38100 Trento – Italy
{marconi,pistore}@fbk.eu

Abstract. One of the key ideas underlying Web services is that of allowing the combination of existing services published on the Web into a new service that achieves some higher-level functionality and satisfies some business goals. As the manual development of the new composite service is recognized as a difficult and error-prone task, the automated synthesis of the composition is considered one of the key challenges in the field of Web services.

In this paper, we will present a survey of existing approaches for the synthesis of Web service compositions. We will then focus on a specific approach, the ASTRO approach, which has been shown to support complex composition requirements and to be applicable in real domains. In the paper, we will present the formal framework behind the ASTRO approach; we will present the implementation of the framework and its integration within a commercial toolkit for developing Web services; we will finally evaluate the approach on a real-world composition domain.

1 Introduction

One of the key ideas underlying Web services is that of allowing the combination of existing services published on the Web into a new service that achieves some higher-level functionality and satisfies some business goals. The manual development of the new composite service is a difficult and error-prone task, because human domain experts have to take care about all possible situations during the service execution process. The ability to automatically compose Web services is an essential step to cut development time and costs.

With *automated synthesis of the Web service composition* — or automated composition for short — we mean the generation of an executable implementation of the new composite service. This implementation satisfies the composition requirements by invoking in a suitable way the set of existing Web services. It is widely recognised that solving this problem in practice is far from trivial. The component services are usually stateful processes whose interactions are long-running and asynchronous, and which exhibit complex, nondeterministic behaviours that are only partially controllable by the service consumer. Moreover, in order to cope with real world scenarios, there is the need to specify complex composition requirements constraining both the behaviour (control flow) and the data manipulation and exchange (data flow) for the new composite service.

M. Bernardo, L. Padovani, and G. Zavattaro (Eds.): SFM 2009, LNCS 5569, pp. 89–157, 2009.

A wide variety of approach has been proposed in the scientific literature for addressing the problem of Web service composition — we will provide a survey in this paper. Here we will focus on a specific approach to Web service composition, namely the ASTRO approach (see `http://www.astroproject.org`). This approach starts from the observation that, in most real-life scenarios, services are stateful and realize complex protocols (e.g., a multi-phase booking procedure includes search, selection, and checkout tasks); their behaviour may be non-deterministic (the search may provide no result, checkout may fail), and they may exchange messages asynchronously. The synthesis of a Web service composition in this setting consists in understanding how to orchestrate the interactions among the component services, so that their protocols are respected, all non-deterministic outcomes are covered, and the composition requirement is achieved.

More precisely, in this paper we present a formal framework for the automated composition of Web services that is able to cope with complex control and data flows, i.e., with Web services exposing complex protocols and exchanging structured data, and with composition requirements expressing constraints not only on the service interactions but also on the exchanged data. The framework is based on a model for Web services that is able to overcome the limitations of the existing approaches and to capture the complex protocols and data structures of services in real domains. For what concerns the specification of composition requirements, the framework provides advanced formal languages for specifying constraints both on the control flow and on the data flow. The framework is implemented and integrated in a toolkit that allows for automatically composing Web services. In the paper, we will also describe the toolkit and its application on a on real-world composition domains.

The structure of the paper is as follows. Section 2 provides a survey of the existing approaches for the composition of Web services. Section 3 illustrates the problem of synthesising the composition of stateful Web services through a simple example based on a Virtual Travel Agency. Section 4 introduces the formal model for Web service compositions; this model allows for specifying stateful component services, as well as composition requirements on the control-flow and on the data-flow. Section 5 shows how the synthesis of the service composition can be achieved by exploiting an existing approach for planning in asynchronous domains. Section 6 introduces a tool for Web service composition which implements the model and the automated synthesis approach described in the previous sections. Section 7 evaluates the approach on a real problem of service composition, which is based on the Amazon shopping services and the payment services of an Italian bank. Finally, Section 8 ends the paper with some concluding remarks.

2 Composing Web Services

Service composition [44] is one of the most promising ideas underlying Web services: composite Web services perform new functionalities by interacting with pre-existing services, called component Web services. Service composition has the potential to reduce development time and effort for new applications by re-using published services, thus allowing reusabilty and extensibility. In general, "service composition" can be defined as creating a composite service, obtained by combining available component services. It is used in situations where a client request cannot be satisfied by any single available service, but by a combination thereof [15].

The manual implementation of a service composition is a very difficult, time consuming, and error prone task; efficient automated support is needed to achieve cost effective, practically exploitable Web service composition. With automated synthesis of a composition of Web services — or automated composition for short — we mean automatically compose a set of existing services in order to satisfy some given composition requirements.

It is widely recognized that solving this problem in practice, by scaling up to realistic descriptions of Web services, is far from trivial [42,45,56,68]. As defined in [11] service composition concern the specification of both the control and data flow based on the elementary services or other composite services. This means that (1) since component services can be themselves composite, there is the need to handle complex workflows as components, (2) the data flow is a central aspect of composition that must be handled properly.

Web services cannot be simply modeled as atomic components, but as stateful processes whose interactions are intrinsically asynchronous. Moreover, this problem require to deal with nondeterminism (since the behavior of external services cannot be foreseen a priori), partial observability (since their status is opaque to the composed service), and complex composition requirements (since realistic requirements specify complex expected behaviors). Finally, in order to achieve correct coordination among component services, the composite service should handle the flow of data (values) and control.

Several methods and techniques have been proposed to solve this problem (e.g. [16,42,56,68,70]) and a comprehensive and fair comparison is quite difficult since they address different flavors of the same composition problem.

One of the main distinction to be done is between *centralized* (or mediated, orchestrated) composition methods and *distributed* (or peer-to-peer) methods. The difference lies in the automated composition result: the former aim at synthesizing a new service (*mediator*) that orchestrates the component services by properly exchanging messages, while in the latter the execution of the composition is distributed among all the component services. However, there exists several approaches, mostly based on program partitioning techniques, that allow to obtain a peer to peer composition from a centralized orchestrator. In [10] the approach consists in analyzing the service mediator through graph transformation techniques on the basis of a set of predefined transformation rules. This approach focuses on the problem of synchronizing the execution of the components while it doesn't address the problem of distributing data among the peers. In [60] the authors exploit program decentralization techniques to automatically distribute the execution of a WS-BPEL process. This method requires a deep analysis on the dependencies and precedences among the activities of the centralized process, involving both synchronization aspects and data management aspects. In [73] the dependency and precedence analysis is performed in a structural way on the graph resulting from the encoding of the process code, and the output is a set of synchronized graphs modeling the distributed execution of the composition. Anther approach, based on similar techniques, is the one proposed in [84,85]. The advantage of this approach is that it can deal with executable WS-BPEL processes and it clearly identifies points of choices where different approaches can be considered for the distribution of data and it allows to eliminate portions of the centralized program that can be excluded from the distribution without affecting the overall composition (Dead Path Elimination).

Another important aspect concerns the *specification of the requirements* that the composed services must satisfy. Since these requirements model the characteristics of the composition, as for the description of the components there is the need to specify constraints on the execution of the composition (e.g. termination conditions, handling failures, transactional issues), as well as to rule the flow and manipulation of messages within the composition and to specify other quality of service constraints (e.g. security, reliability).

Moreover, we can distinguish between automated techniques addressing a *static* composition problem, where the services to be composed are decided at design time, from those addressing a *dynamic* composition problem, where components are selected at run time. Similarly we can distinguish *design-time* and *run-time* automated composition methods. The latter allow to monitor the execution and to re-compose and adapt the composition at run-time as a reaction to unforeseen events.

In the rest of this section we will give an overview of most relevant works addressing the automated composition problem, focusing in particular on the kind of composition (mediated, peer to peer, data-aware), the modeling of component services (atomic, structured, semantically annotated), and the kind of composition requirements (termination conditions, data flow requirements, preferences, QoS).

2.1 Logic-Based Approaches

In [15,16,13] **Berardi et al.** describe all available component services as well as the request as finite state machines. Their goal is to find a composition of offered services that permits the requested interaction protocol. In particular, when approaching a composition problem through this approach, one has to specify the desired service, i.e., as a tree of actions, finitely represented as finite state machine. Given a set of available services and the requested protocol (all of them represented as finite state machine), the algorithm finds a labeling of the tree associated to the client request, such that each action is labeled with (i.e., delegated to) available services and each possible sequence of actions on the labeled tree corresponds to possible sequences of actions of the available services, suitably interleaved. By using DPDL (Deterministic Propositional Dynamic Logic) the problem of service composition is reduced to the problem of satisfiability of a constructed formula.

In [14] the approach has been extended to handle data. In particular, the authors present Colombo, a framework that models Web services in terms of the operations they offer and their impact on the 'real world' (a relational database).

A similar approach is presented in [26,42] where **Hull et al.** propose a formal framework for composing e-services from behavioral descriptions given in terms of automata. This work focuses on the theoretical foundations, without providing practical implementations. Moreover, the considered e-composition problem it is seen as the problem of coordinating the executions of a given set of available services. No concrete and executable processes can be generated with this approach.

2.2 Rule-Based Approaches

In the approach proposed in [70], by **Ponnekanti et al.**, component services are defined in terms of their inputs and outputs; given the inputs and outputs of the service, a rule is then defined which indicates which outputs can be obtained by the service given which inputs. When a developer wishes to create and deploy a new composite service, he specifies the inputs and outputs of the composite service and submits it to the system, which determines if the composite service can be realized using the existing services. This rule based approach can be adopted exclusively for modeling simple composition problems, where component services are atomic and deterministic.

2.3 AI Planning-Based Approaches

Planning is one of the most promising techniques for the automated composition of Web services. Several approaches (e.g. [61,74,45,83,68]) have investigated the potentials and boundaries of applying AI planning techniques to the problem of automated Web service composition. In these works, automated composition is described as a planning problem: existing services can be used to construct the planning domain, composition requirements can be formalized as planning goals, and planning algorithms can be used to generate plans that compose the published services.

The semantic Web community has used automated planning techniques to address the problem of the automated discovery and composition of semantic Web services, e.g., based on OWL-S descriptions of input/outputs and of preconditions/postconditions (see, e.g, [57]).

Mc Ilraith et al. in [57,61] developed a markup and automated reasoning technique to describe, simulate, compose, test, and verify the compositions of Web services. The starting point was the DARBA Agent Markup Language-Services (DAML-S) ([7]) ontology to provide a semantic markup of the content and capabilities of Web services. The approach in [61] is based on a translation of DAML-S to situation calculus and Golog. The Golog (alGOL in LOGic) ([48]) language is a high-level programming language particularly designed for the specification and execution of complex actions in dynamic domains. Golog is based on the situation calculus ([55]) which is often used as a means for providing a formal account of dynamic systems. ConGolog is a variant of Golog capable of dealing with concurrency (Concurrent Golog) ([40]). In [57] the ConGolog interpreter is extended with the ability to include customized user constraints. The Web service composition problem, according to this approach, would then be to find an execution of a Golog program that does satisfy the properties defined in the goal. These results are based on the idea of sequentially composing the available Web services, which are considered as black boxes, and hence atomically executed.

Hierarchical Task Network (HTN) planning (see [72,36,37]) provides hierarchical abstraction, a powerful strategy to deal with the complexity of large and complicated real world planning domains. A variant of HTN planning which received much attention recently is ordered task decomposition planning. Planners based on that principle, like SHOP (Simple Hierarchical Ordered Planner) ([63]) recursively decomposes the desired task into a set of sub-tasks until the resulting set of tasks consists only of primitive tasks, which can be executed directly by invoking atomic operations. During each round of task decomposition, it is tested whether certain given conditions are violated. The planning problem is successfully solved if the desired complex task is decomposed into a set of primitive tasks without violating any of the given conditions. An approach of using HTN planning in the realm of Web services is proposed in [74,83] by **Wu, Sirin, et al.** exploiting the SHOP2 system ([62]). This work present a transformation method of OWL-S processes into a hierarchical task network. OWL-S processes are, like HTN task networks, pre-defined descriptions of actions to be carried out to get a certain task done, which makes the transformation rather natural. The advantage of the approach is its ability to deal with very large problem domains; however, the need to explicitly provide the planner with a task it needs to accomplish may be seen as a disadvantage.

In [68] **Pistore et al.** present a formal framework for the automated composition of Web services which is based on planning as model checking. The planning as model checking approach was first proposed in [29,30]. In planning as model checking, the planning domain is formalized as a nondeterministic state-transition system, where an action is a transition that may bring the system from one state to a set of possible successor states. As in other planning approaches, planning goals may be expressed as constraints about a desired goal state (reachability goal); additionally, goals may be extended by statements about properties about the plan itself, e.g. by CTL (Computational Tree Logic) temporal formulas ([35]) or using the Eagle ([32]) language. Since real-world problems involve models that may contain very large numbers of states, practical implementations of these algorithm ([31]) usually adopt Symbolic Model Checking techniques ([27]). In Symbolic Model Checking the sets of possible states of a Kripke-structure and the transition relations between states are represented symbolically, usually using vectors of variables that represent the truth value of propositions in states, allowing for a more concise representation of states and for an efficient application of set-theoretic and logical operations. Planning is performed by searching through sets of states, rather then individual states. The practical implementation of the representation and the reasoning techniques of Symbolic Model Checking is often carried out using Binary Decision Diagrams (BDDs) ([25]). Systems like MBP (Model Based Planner) ([20]) have been designed to leverage a key advantage of model checking, which is to deal with nondeterministic environments: MBP can deal with uncertainty on the initial situation, on the action effects and on the state in which the actions are executed.

In [68,69] the authors extend the planning as model checking approach in order to handle asynchronous, message-based interaction between the domain (encoding the component services) and the plan (encoding the composite service). The resulting automated composition approach can deal with composition problems where the component services are non deterministic complex processes and where control flow composition requirements are complex conditions on the behavior of the process.

2.4 Other Approaches

In [24] **Brogi et al.** propose a methodology which, given a set of component services, tries to construct an aggregation of such services. Service protocols include a description of the service behaviour expressed by a YAWL ([81]) workflow, as well as an (ontology-annotated) signature. YAWL is a workflow/business processing system, which supports a workflow language and handles complex data, transformations and Web service integration. YAWL extends Petri Nets by introducing some workflow patterns (for multiple instances, complex synchronizations, and cancellation) that are not easy to express using (high-level) Petri Nets. A thorough analysis of how to transform WS-BPEL specifications into workflow patterns can be found in [82]. The core aggregation process basically performs a control-flow and an (ontology-aware) data-flow analysis of a set of YAWL workflows to build the contract of an aggregated service. Technically, this approach exploits ontology-matching mechanisms to derive data-flow information linking operations of (possibly) different services (matching requested inputs with offered outputs).

A semantic-based Web service composition system supporting both the modeling of components as well as service composition is proposed in [39] by **Fujii and Suda**. The system comprises three sub-systems: Component Service Model with Semantic (CoSMoS), Component Runtime Environment (CoRE), and Semantic Graph based Service Composition (SeGSeC). CoSMoS allows to model both the semantic and functional information of a component with a single semantic graph representation. CoRE is responsible of converting different component implementations into the CoSMoS representation. SeGSeC is a semantic-based service composition mechanism that allows users to request a service using a natural language sentence and generate the execution path of the requested service. The major disadvantage of this approach is that the set of queries that can be used as composition requirements is quite restricted and due to this the approach can be used to solve very limited scenarios.

In [77,78,79] **Ambite, Knoblock and Takkar** propose data integration techniques to dynamically compose atomic services. The composition algorithm takes in input the set of available services modeled as data-sources, and a user query, expressed in terms of inputs provided by the user and requested outputs. The output is a new, composite service that can execute an integration plan for a template query, so that all the user queries that differ only for intensional input values can be answered by the same (composite) service. They adopt a mediator based framework. First, the specific user query is generalized, associating each specific user input (parameter) with its class: this is done by exploiting attribute level ontologies. In order to reformulate the generalized user query into the source queries, the mediator constructs an integration plan consisting of a sequence of source queries and taking binding pattern into account. In [79] the integration plan is generated with a forward chaining algorithm; in [78] the authors implement an extension of the Inverse Rule Algorithm and map the produced datalog program into the integration plan. Then, the mediator optimizes the integration plan using a data flow analysis algorithm, to remove unnecessary source queries from the generated plan. Finally, the mediator utilizes source constraints and other services providing sensing functionalities to filter out the data at the tuple level, that do not meet the source constraints.

Benatallah et al. in [12] present SELF-SERV: a framework for dynamic and peer-to-peer provisioning of Web services. In SELF-SERV, Web services are declaratively composed, and the resulting composite services are executed in a decentralized way within a dynamic environment. The framework uses and adapts the state-charts as a visual declarative language. The significant advantage of SELF-SERV is the peer-to-peer service execution model, whereby the responsibility of coordinating the execution of a composite service is distributed across several peer software components called coordinators. Nevertheless, this system supports the manual development of service compositions but it does not provide a method to automatically synthesize a composition.

2.5 Comparison of Existing Approaches

In this section we compare those composition approaches that are closer to the one presented in this paper.

Comparing automated composition techniques is far from trivial. An exhaustive complete comparison should take into account several aspects: from the specific kind of composition problem tackled, to the techniques used, and the applicability of the approaches both in terms of scalability and usability.

A number of surveys on service composition exist ([11,34,46,58,66,71]). Surprisingly none of these covers all the aspects presented above.

Rao et al. [71] provide a quite comprehensive overview categorized according to the technique used, i.e. workflow techniques and various AI planning methods. Another survey solely centered around AI planning is [66]. In a more general overview Benatallah et al. [11] focus on workflow-based approaches for Web service integration. Some of the considered approaches are abstracted in the form of software design patterns. Another survey on Web service composition platforms is [34]. Milanovic et al. [58] provide an overview of different approaches for modelling composite services that are evaluated against a number of requirements to service composition modelling. The comparison in [46] is really interesting since it is structured around a classification of different applications of service composition and furthermore specifically focuses on automatic service composition.

The comparison presented here, without any claim to be thorough, focuses on the characteristics of the composition problems that the different approaches can deal with.

Most of the approaches presented in previous section (e.g. [57,61,70,75]) can handle composition problems where the component services are atomic (with atomic we mean that a service is described in terms of its input/output activities and, possibly, preconditions and effects). This is the case of the works in [70,75], which support forms of compositions starting from WSDL-like specifications of Web services. Other approaches that do not take into account behavioral descriptions of the component services are those proposed by the semantic Web community: in [57,56] the authors use automated planning techniques to address the problem of the automated discovery and composition of atomic semantic Web services, e.g., based on OWL-S; in [61], the authors propose an approach to the simulation, verification, and automated composition of Web services based on a translation of DAML-S to situation calculus and Petri Nets. More interesting are automated composition approaches where the component services can be stateful and complex business processes (see e.g. [15,42,67,68,69]).

Within the process-based methods, we should distinguish those addressing an orchestration problem from those addressing a real automated composition one. The former requires to fully specify the process model of the composite service (usually a set of tasks and data dependencies) and then automatically selects the component services that can fulfill the different requested tasks. The latter (sometimes referred to as dynamic composition) requires the specification of the requirements that the new composite process should satisfy and then both automatically synthesizes the composite process model and selects the components to be invoked. The work in [42] presents a formal framework for coordinating the execution of available services in such a way that their interaction satisfies a fully specified behavioral description (given in terms of automata). This work addresses an orchestration problem, rather then a composition one. The same considerations can be made also for the work described in [15,16]. The framework proposed in [68,69] addresses a dynamic composition problem since it automatically synthesizes an executable composite service that, interacting with a set of existing services, satisfies the given composition requirements. Moreover, it differs from other planning approaches since Web services are modeled with nondeterministic and partially observable behaviors and it assumes an asynchronous, message-based interaction between the domain (encoding the component services) and the plan (encoding the composite service).

For what concerns the formal specification of the requirements that the new composite service should satisfy, most of the existing approaches specify them as reachability conditions (e.g. [61]). In fact, when dealing with real world composition scenarios, there is the need to specify complex conditions on the behavior of the new process, and not only on its final state. A remarkable exception is the work described in [68,69] where they formalize the composition requirements using EAGLE [32], a language for extended goals. EAGLE operators are similar to Computational Tree Logic (CTL [35]) operators, but their semantics, formally defined in [32], take into account the notion of preference among subgoals and the handling of failure when subgoals cannot be achieved.

Most of the works that address the problem of the automated synthesis of process-level compositions do not take into account data flow specifications. This is the case of the work that address the problem of the automated synthesis of compositions with techniques based on automata theory [15,42], and this is also the case of extensions that model data in exchanges of messages [16]. The same can be said for work within the semantic Web community, see, e.g., [57]. An exception is the work described in [24], which proposes an approach to service aggregation that takes into account data flow requirements. However, data flow requirements express direct identity routings of data among processes, and do not allow for manipulations of data.

Finally, all existing composition approaches either fully specify the workflow of the composite process (e.g. [15,42]), or completely specify the interface (control and data flow) that the new composite service exports to its client. This is the case of the work presented in [68,69], where they expect the client interface of the new service to be completely specified and then consider it as another component service in the composition problem. The exhaustive specification of the client communication protocol requires a deep analysis of the component service behaviors to take into account all their possible evolutions (e.g. cancellation, exceptions); in realistic composition domains, such a description can be as time-consuming and error prone as the specification of the new composite process itself. A more convenient approach would require the specification of the static client interface (WSDL-like operations and messages) and of the relevant data flow, control flow and termination requirements presented before. Moreover, Web services composition can not be seen as a one-shot plan synthesis problem but rather as a continual process of manipulating complex workflows, which requires to solve synthesis, execution, optimization, and maintenance problems [76]; in such a dynamic scenario, a fundamental quality is the ability to easily modify, refine and adapt the composition requirements.

3 Automated Composition: Example Scenario

With automated synthesis of a composition of Web Services we mean the generation of a new composite service that interacts with a set of existing component services in order to achieve given composition requirements. Consider for instance the following composition scenario (see also Figure 1), which we will use as a reference example throughout this paper.

Example 1 (Virtual Travel Agency). Our reference example consists in providing a virtual travel agency service, say the VTA service, which offers holiday packages to potential customers, by combining three separate existing services: a flight booking service Flight, a hotel booking service Hotel, and a service that provides maps AllMaps. The idea is that of combining these three services so that the customer may directly interact with the composed service VTA to organize and possibly book his holiday package.

When addressing a Web service composition problem, the (manual or automatic) development of the new composite Web service must be driven by the analysis of published process specifications of component services (i.e. the Hotel, Flight and AllMaps services in the VTA example) and by requirements and constraints the composite service has to satisfy.

We assume that the interaction protocols of the component services are described as WS-BPEL [6] processes, even if the described approach does not depend on the specific

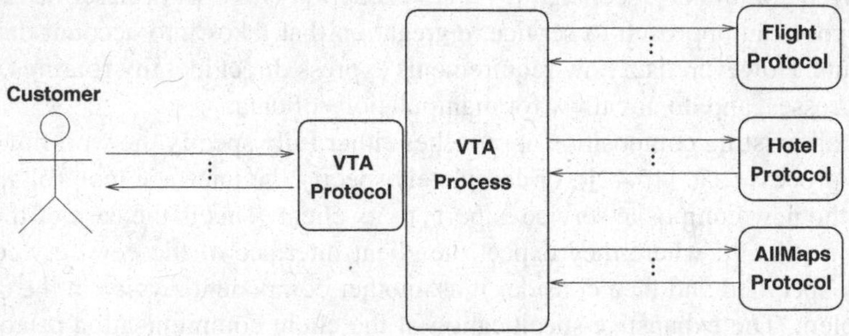

Fig. 1. The VTA Scenario

aspects of the WS-BPEL language. WS-BPEL is an industrial language for the specification and execution of business processes made available through Web services. WS-BPEL provides an operational description of the (stateful) behavior of Web services on top of the service interfaces defined in their Web Services Description Language (WSDL) specifications [28].

There are two flavors of WS-BPEL, namely *abstract* WS-BPEL specifications, which allow to publish the interaction protocol with external Web services without revealing internal implementation details, and *executable* WS-BPEL processes, that are used to implement the process defining a service. Executable WS-BPEL programs can be executed by standard engines, such as the Active BPEL Open Engine or the Oracle BPEL Process Manager [1,64].

The automated composition problem can therefore be described as follows: given a set of *abstract* WS-BPEL specifications describing the (interactions with) the component services, and given some composition requirements that describes the desired functionalities of a composed service, automatically synthesize the *executable* WS-BPEL that implements an orchestrator service that, when executed, satisfies the requirements.

Component Service Protocols. WSDL is used to define the functional description of a Web Service. A WSDL file describes the set of operations offered by the service, in-going and out-going messages, and data types used by the service (defined in terms of XML Schemas). Concrete protocol bindings and physical address port specifications complete a service description, supplying a mechanism to locate the Web Service. WSDL defines what the service does, not how it does it: it characterizes the service only in terms of its interface, without providing any behavioral description.

A WS-BPEL document describes a particular business process. The process definition consists of several parts describing partner links, process variables, correlation sets, main process workflow, the fault and compensation handling activities. The partner link declarations are used to define the relation between the process and its partners. In particular, it defines the role of the process in this relation (consumer or provider of an interface), and the interfaces used/provided by that role. The interfaces, operations, as well as their parameters and types, are those specified in the corresponding WSDL documents. The process variables are used to represent the state of the business process, they contain the information received from or sent to the partners of the process. The variables may be of primitive data types (e.g., strings, boolean, integers) or of some complex types defined in a WSDL document. The correlation sets define the parts of message data that are used to associate and route a particular message to a particular instance of the business process. Such information tokens uniquely identify the instance of the business process. The process flow is defined by a set of process activities. They specify the operations to be performed, their ordering, conditional logic, reactive rules, etc. We distinguish the following groups of activities: basic activities, structured activities, and the specific operational blocks, namely fault, exception and compensation handlers.

Basic activities represent primitive operations performed by the process, such as message emission/reception (`invoke`, `receive`, and `reply` activities), data modification (`assign`), process termination (`terminate`), waiting for a certain period of time (`wait`), or doing nothing (`empty`).

Structured activities define the order in which a collection of activities occurs. They compose the basic activities into structures that express the control flow patterns. The structured WS-BPEL activities include `sequence`, `switch`, and `while` that model traditional control constructs; `pick` that models nondeterministic choice based on external events (i.e., message reception or timeout); `flow` activity that models parallel execution of the nested activities. Structured activities can be recursively nested and combined. Fault handling in WS-BPEL is thought of as a mode switch from the normal processing. It is interpreted as "reverse work", since it aims at undoing the unsuccessful work. The fault may arise on reception of the fault message, or on explicit invocation of the `throw` activity. The `fault handler` declaration specify the activities to be performed when a fault arises. The compensation handlers are used to reverse the effect of some unit of work that has completed with a fault. The compensation is always initiated within a fault handler, and it is used to compensate some nested, previously successful, and completed, activities. A compensation handler is always associated with a work unit (WS-BPEL scope), and is invoked (explicitly or implicitly) using the WS-BPEL`compensate` activity. Event handlers are used to deal with events (reception of messages or timeouts) that happen independent of, and asynchronously to, the execution of the program.

Example 2 (Flight Booking WS Protocol). Let us consider a WS-BPEL process that describes the Flight Booking Service, a component of the Virtual Travel Agency case

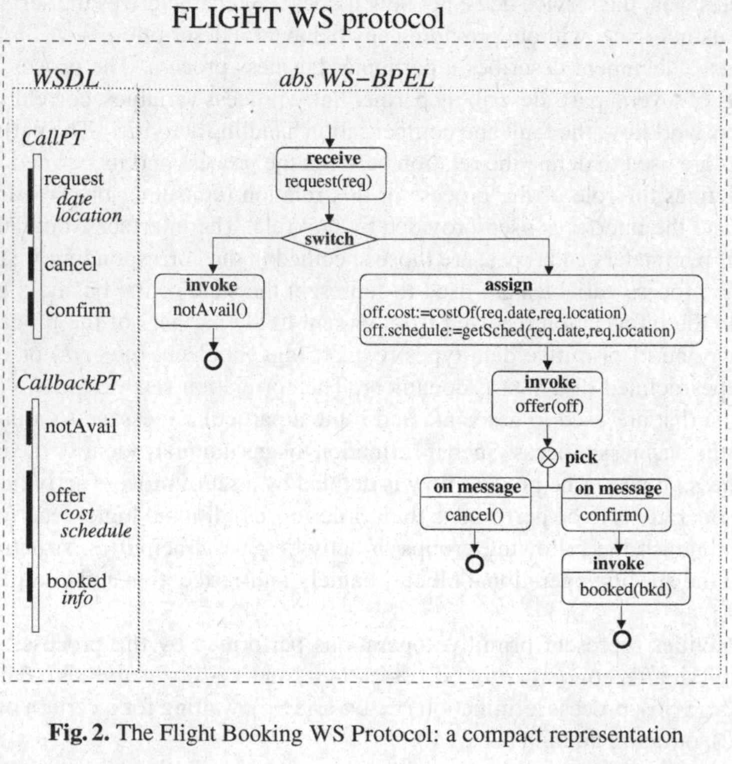

Fig. 2. The Flight Booking WS Protocol: a compact representation

```
types
 element name="dateT" type="xsd:date"
 element name="locationT" type="xsd:string"
 element name="costT" type="xsd:int"
 element name="scheduleT" type="tns:schedType"
 element name="infoT" type="tns:InfoType"
 ...
 complexType name="schedType"
  sequence
   element name="dep_date" type="xsd:date"
   element name="dep_airport" type="xsd:string"
   element name="arr_date" type="xsd:date"
   element name="arr_airport" type="xsd:string"

message name="requestMsg"
 part name="date" element="tns:dateT"
 part name="location" element="tns:locationT"
 part name="corrKey" type="xsd:string"
message name="cancelMsg"
 part name="corrKey" type="xsd:string"
message name="confirmMsg"
 part name="corrKey" type="xsd:string"
message name="notAvailMsg"
  part name="corrKey" type="xsd:string"
message name="offerMsg"
 part name="cost" element="tns:costT"
 part name="schedule" element="tns:scheduleT"
 part name="corrKey" type="xsd:string"
message name="bookedMsg"
 part name="info" element="tns:infoT"
 part name="corrKey" type="xsd:string"
message name="cancelMsg"
 part name="corrKey" type="xsd:string"
```

```
portType name="CallPT"
 operation name="request"
  input message="tns:requestMsg"
 operation name="cancel"
  input message="tns:cancelMsg"
 operation name="confirm"
  input message="tns:confirmMsg"
portType name="CallbackPT"
 operation name="notAvail"
  input message="tns:notAvailMsg"
 operation name="offer"
  input message="tns:offerMsg"
 operation name="booked"
  input message="tns:bookedMsg"

partnerLinkType name="FlightPLT"
 role name="provider"
  portType name="tns:CallPT"
 role name="client"
  portType name="tns:CallbackPT"

property name="key" type="xsd:string"
propertyAlias propertyname="tns:key"
     messageType="tns:requestMsg"
     part="corrKey"
...
propertyAlias propertyname="tns:key"
     messageType="tns:cancel"
     part="corrKey"
```

Fig. 3. The Flight Booking WS Protocol: WSDL file

study. A compact representation of the process, describing both its interface and its workflow, is represented in Figure 2. The Flight service receives requests for booking flights for a given date and location. If there are available flights, it sends an offer with a cost and a flight schedule. The client can either accept or refuse the offer. If he decides to accept, the Flight will book the flight and provide additional information such as an electronic ticket.

The complete WSDL and WS-BPEL specification of the Flight service is presented in Figure 3 and Figure 4 respectively.

In the following example we briefly describe the protocols of the other component services of which we give a compact representation in Figure 5 and in Figure 6.

Example 3 (VTA Component Protocols). In the following, we describe informally the Hotel Booking Service and the All Maps Service available services, whose interaction protocols are depicted respectively in Figure 5 and in Figure 6.

Hotel accepts requests for providing information on available hotels for a given date and a given location. If there are hotels available, it chooses a particular hotel and return an offer with a cost and other hotel information. This offer can be accepted or refused by the external service that has invoked the Hotel. In case of acceptance, the Hotel proceeds with the booking and sends a confirmation message to the client.

The AllMaps service receives requests with two locations and provides a digital map depicting distance information.

```
process name="F"

partnerLinks
 partnerLink name="FlightPL" partnerLinkType="FlightPLT"
     myRole="provider" partnerRole="client"

variables
 variable name="req" messageType="requestMsg"
 variable name="canc" messageType="cancelMsg"
 variable name="conf" messageType="confirmMsg"
 variable name="navail" messageType="notAvailMsg"
 variable name="off" messageType="offerMsg"
 variable name="book" messageType="bookedMsg"
 variable name="available" type="xsd:boolean"

correlationSet name="CS" properties="key"

sequence
 receive partnerLink="FlightPL" portType="CallPT" operation="request" variable="req"
   correlation set="CS" initiate="yes"
 assign
   copy
   from opaque="yes" to variable="available"
 switch
  case condition="available"
   sequence
    assign
     copy
      from opaque="yes" to variable="off" part="corrKey"
     copy
      from expression="CostOf(req.date,req.location)" to variable="off" part="cost"
     copy
      from expression="getSched(req.date,req.location)"
      to variable="off" part="schedule"
    invoke partnerLink="FlightPL" portType="CallbackPT"
           operation="offer" variable="off"
     correlation set="CS" initiate="no"
    pick
     onMessage partnerLink="FlightPL" portType="CallPT"
               operation="confirm" variable="conf"
     correlation set="CS" initiate="no"
      ...
     onMessage partnerLink="FlightPL" portType="CallPT"
               operation="cancel" variable="canc"
     correlation set="CS" initiate="no"
      ...

  otherwise
   sequence
    assign
     copy
      from opaque="yes" to variable="navail" part="corrKey"
    invoke partnerLink="FlightPL" portType="CallbackPT"
           operation="notAvail" variable="nav"
     correlation set="CS" initiate="no"
```

Fig. 4. The Flight Booking WS Protocol: abstract WS-BPEL file

The aim of the composition task is the development of a new process that will offer new functionalities and publish them through a Web Service interface. Due to this another important task of the composition is the specification of the protocol that the new composite service will expose to its clients. The protocol, as for the other components, is described through WSDL and abstract WS-BPEL.

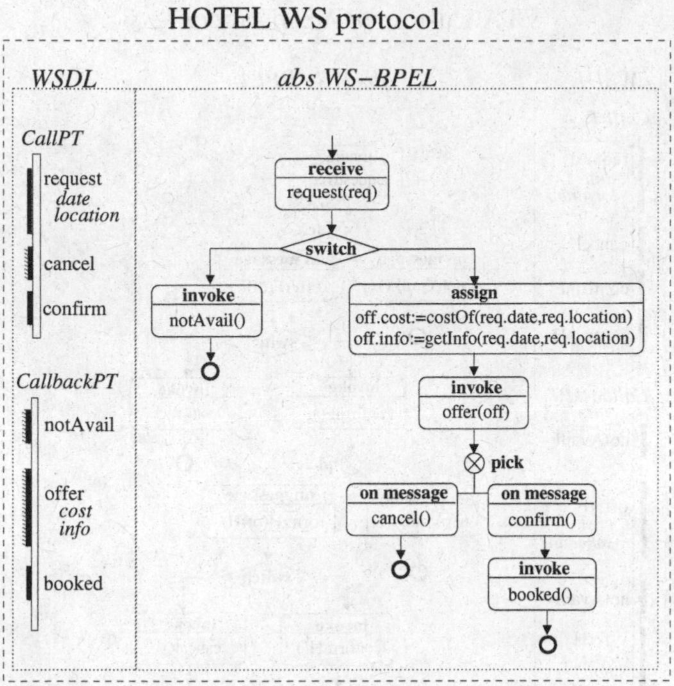

Fig. 5. The Hotel Booking WS Protocol

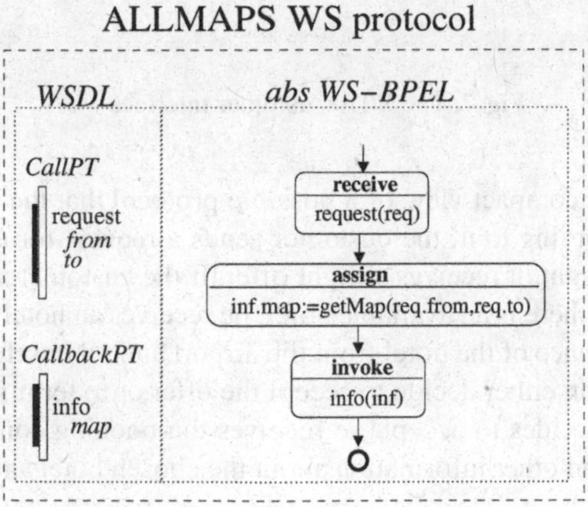

Fig. 6. The All Maps WS Protocols

Example 4 (VTA Customer Interaction Protocol). Intuitively, the VTA service should try to satisfy a given customer request by providing information on available flights and hotels (e.g., holiday cost, flight schedule, hotel description and a map showing distance from the airport) and book the holiday according to customer final decision.

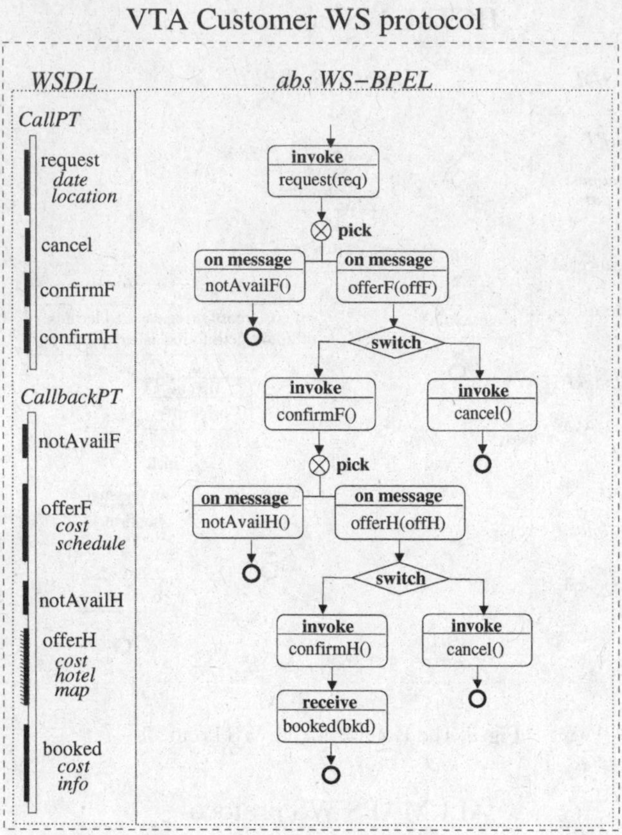

Fig. 7. The VTA Customer Interface

Figure 7 presents a compact view of a possible protocol that the VTA could expose to the customer. According to it, the customer sends a request for an holiday, then, if there is an available flight, it receives a flight offer. If the customer agrees on the flight schedule and cost and there is an available hotel, he receives an hotel offer consisting of the hotel cost, the distance of the hotel from the airport and other information about the hotel. The customer can either decide to accept the offer or to terminate the interaction with the VTA. If he decides to accept, he receives the booking confirmation with the overall holiday cost and other information about the chosen hotel and flight.

Composition Requirements. Given the description of the component services and of the customer interaction protocol, the next step towards the definition of the automated composition domain is the formal specification of the composition requirements. As we will see from the examples presented in the rest of this section, even for simple case studies we need a way to express requirements that define complex conditions, both for what concerns the control flow and for the data exchanged among the component services.

Example 5 (Control-flow requirements). The VTA service main goal is to "sell holiday packages". This means we want the VTA to reach a situation where the customer has accepted the offer and a flight and a hotel have been booked.

However, it may be the case that there are no available flights (or no available hotels) satisfying the customer request, or that the customer doesn't like the flight or the hotel offer and thus cancels the booking. We cannot avoid these situations, therefore we cannot ask the composite service to guarantee this requirement.

In case this requirement cannot be satisfied, we do not want the VTA to book a flight (nor a hotel) without being sure that our customer accepted the offer, as well as we do not want displeased customers that have booked holidays for which there are no available flights or hotels. Our control flow requirements would therefore be something like:

if it is possible "sell holiday packages";
upon failure,
do "never a single commitment".

Notice that the secondary requirement ("never a single commit") has a different strength w.r.t. the primary one ("sell holiday packages"). We write "do" satisfy, rather than "try" to satisfy. Indeed, in the case the primary requirement is not satisfied, we want the secondary requirement to be guaranteed.

Intuitively, we need a way to take into account the transactional aspects of the component services and of the composite one. In particular, as shown in Example 5, these conditions will talk about the final outcomes of the component services.

This termination requirement is only a partial specification of the constraints that the composition should satisfy. In particular, control requirements abstract completely from the relationship between the different data exchanged between the component services and the composite service.

This crucial aspect is taken in charge by data requirements. In particular, data requirements concern the specification of how incoming messages must be used by the composite service to obtain outgoing messages.

Example 6 (Data-flow requirements). In order to provide consistent information, the VTA service needs to exchange data with the components and its customer in an appropriate way. For instance, when invoking the Flight service, the information about the location and date of the flight must be the same ones that the VTA received in the customer request; similarly, the information sent to the customer about the distance between the proposed hotel and the airport must be those obtained from the interaction with the AllMaps service; and such a service must receive the information on the airport and hotel location according to the offer proposed by the Flight and Hotel service. In particular, the VTA must obtain the airport location from the flight schedule offered by the Flight service and must obtain the hotel location from the information received in the Hotel offer. Moreover, the cost proposed to the customer for the holiday package must be the sum of the hotel and flight cost plus some additional fee for the travel agency service; thus the cost offered to the customer must be computed by means of a function internal to the VTA service. And so on.

The example shows that, even for apparently simple composition problems, we need a way to express complex data flow requirements: from simple data links between incoming and outgoing message parts (e.g., forwarding the information received by the customer about the location to the Flight service) to the specification of complex data manipulation (e.g., when computing the holiday package cost or obtaining the airport and hotel locations).

4 Formal Model of Web Service Composition

In this section we describe a formal model that allows for the representation of Web service compositions. In particular, we define a single service as a *service graph* that properly describes the service both in terms of behavior and of data flow. A formal model for the composition, the *orchestrated transition system*, models the evolution of the component services when controlled by an orchestrator service.

4.1 Modeling Web Services

The formal model we use as a basis for the automated composition techniques consists of two parts, namely the data model and the behavioral model. The data model provides a formalization of the data manipulated by the services and is used to reason on the data flow of the compositions. The control flow is defined by the behavioral model, used to represent the behavior of the services.

Data Model. We represent data, operations on data, and data flow of the system execution using a ground model.

Definition 1 (Ground Context)
A ground context $\mathcal{C}$ *is a tuple* $\langle \mathcal{T}, \mathcal{V}, \mathcal{F} \rangle$ *where:*

- $\mathcal{T}$ *is a set of infinite or enumerative types;*
- $\mathcal{V}$ *is a set of typed variables;*
- $\mathcal{F}$ *is a set of typed functions.*

We denote the type of the variable x as $\mathrm{T}(x)$. Similarly, given that $\mathrm{A}(f)$ denotes the arity of function f, we denote the type of the i-th parameter of f as $\mathrm{T}(f)[i]$, where $\mathrm{T}(f)[0]$ is the type of the return parameter.

A ground state is characterized by a complete assignment over the set of typed variables $\mathcal{V}$ and by the function interpreter $\mathcal{I}_f$.

Definition 2 (Ground State)
Given a ground context $\langle \mathcal{T}, \mathcal{V}, \mathcal{F} \rangle$*, we define a* ground state *g as a pair* $\langle \mathcal{I}_v, \mathcal{I}_f \rangle$ *where:*

- $\mathcal{I}_v$ *is a set of pairs* $\langle x, v \rangle$ *such that for all* $x \in \mathcal{V}$ *there exists a unique* $\langle x, v \rangle \in \mathcal{I}_v$ *where* $v \in \mathrm{T}(x)$*;*

- *$\mathcal{I}_f$ is the function that given a typed function $f \in \mathcal{F}$ and a set of values $v_1, \ldots, v_n$, with $n \geq 0$, returns the result of the computation of $f(v_1, \ldots, v_n)$.*

We distinguish functions with fixed interpretation $\mathcal{F}^{\mathcal{S}} \subseteq \mathcal{F}$, i.e.

$$\forall f \in \mathcal{F}^{\mathcal{S}}, \forall \mathcal{I}_f, \mathcal{I}'_f \forall v_1, \ldots, v_n, \mathcal{I}_f(f, v_1, \ldots, v_n) = \mathcal{I}'_f(f, v_1, \ldots, v_n);$$

(typed) constants $\mathcal{F}^{\mathcal{C}} \subseteq \mathcal{F}$ as functions with zero parameters, and functions with arbitrary interpretation $\mathcal{F}^{\mathcal{U}} \subseteq \mathcal{F}$. Notice that two different applications of some function $f \in \mathcal{F}^{\mathcal{U}}$ may produce different values even for the same input in different ground states. These functions are used for the non-deterministic modelling of internal service calculations that depend on some "hidden" information.

Let e denote an expression and E a set of expressions. Let t denote a term and let T denote a set of terms. We use x to denote a variable in Var. The syntax of expression is as follows:

- $E \equiv (t_1 = t_2) \mid \neg e \mid (e_1 \vee e_2)$, that is equality between terms, negation or disjunction of expressions;
- $T \equiv x \mid f(t_1, \ldots, t_n)$, that is a variable or a function call.

An *atomic term* is a variable or a non-nested function call. An *atomic expression* is an equality between atomic terms. A *literal* is an atomic expression or its negation.

A *condition* ϕ is an expression of the form presented above. We denote with $\Phi_{\mathcal{C}}$ the set of all conditions of context $\mathcal{C}$. An assignment ω has the form $(x := t)$. The set of assignments defined on context $\mathcal{C}$ is denoted with $\Omega_{\mathcal{C}}$, moreover we denote with $\bar{\omega}$ an ordered sequence $(\omega_1, \ldots, \omega_n)$ of assignments.

Definition 3 (Evaluation Function)
We define the evaluation function Γ_g as the function that given a term t or an expression e returns the result of its computation with respect to a ground state $g = \langle \mathcal{I}_v, \mathcal{I}_f \rangle$:

- $\Gamma_g(x) = v$, *where* $x \in \mathcal{V}$ *and* $\langle x, v \rangle \in \mathcal{I}_v$;
- $\Gamma_g(f(t_1, \ldots, t_n)) = v$, *where* $v = \mathcal{I}_f(f, \Gamma_g(t_1), \ldots, \Gamma_g(t_n))$;
- $\Gamma_g(t_1 = t_2) = true$ *if* $\Gamma_g(t_1) = \Gamma_g(t_2)$;
- $\Gamma_g(\neg e) = \neg \Gamma_g(e)$;
- $\Gamma_g(e_1 \vee e_2) = \Gamma_g(e_1) \vee \Gamma_g(e_2)$.

We say that a ground state g satisfies a condition ϕ, written as $g \models \phi$, if $\Gamma_g(\phi) = true$.

Definition 4 (Ground Update)
The update of a ground state g with an assignment $\omega = (x := t)$, denoted as $update(g, \omega)$, is the state g' s.t.

$$\forall x' \in \mathcal{V}, \Gamma_{g'}(x) = \begin{cases} \Gamma_g(x'), \text{ if } x' \neq x \\ \Gamma_g(t), \text{ if } x' = x \end{cases}$$

We denote with $update(g, \bar{\omega})$ the update of a ground state g with an ordered sequence of assignments $\bar{\omega}$.

Behavioral Model. We encode the behavior of a Web service as a *service graph*. A service graph describes a dynamic system that can be in one of its possible locations (some of which are marked as initial) and can evolve to new locations as a result of performing some actions. This evolution is defined by the transition relation. The relation defines also the condition under which the action can be performed and the effects of its execution.

We distinguish external actions representing service interactions, and internal actions, which are used to represent evolutions of the system that do not involve interactions with the external services. We denote an internal action as τ. External actions are distinguished in input actions $\mathcal{I}$, which represent the reception of messages, and output actions $\mathcal{O}$, which represent the sending of messages to external services. The send action is denoted as $\overrightarrow{\mu}(\bar{x})$, where μ is a service operation, or message type, and $\bar{x}$ is a vector of service variables from which the message content is populated. The receive operation is denoted as $\overleftarrow{\mu}(\bar{x})$, where the message content is assigned to the variables in $\bar{x}$. We chose to model input and output actions instantiated on service variables since this encoding perfectly reflects the modeling choice in most service behavior description languages (e.g. WS-BPEL [6], OWL-S [65]).

We denote with $\mathcal{A}$ the set of all the internal and external actions of the service, formally $\mathcal{A} = \mathcal{I} \cup \mathcal{O} \cup \{\tau\}$.

Definition 5 (Service Graph)
A service graph *is a tuple* $\langle L, L_0, \mathcal{C}, \mathcal{A}, T \rangle$ *where*

- L *is a set of locations and* $L_0 \subseteq L$ *is the set of initial locations;*
- $\mathcal{C}$ *is a ground context;*
- $\mathcal{A}$ *is a set of actions;*
- $T \subseteq L \times \Phi_{\mathcal{C}} \times \mathcal{A} \times \Omega^*_{\mathcal{C}} \times L$ *is the transition relation.*

A transition $t = (l, \phi, \alpha, \bar{\omega}, l') \in T$ changes the location from l to l', fires action $\alpha \in \mathcal{A}$, and makes an ordered sequence of assignments $\bar{\omega} = (\omega_1, \ldots, \omega_n)$ where each $\omega_i \in \Omega_{\mathcal{C}}$. The transition guard has the form $\phi \in \Phi_{\mathcal{C}}$. Due to the nature of Web services, where input and output actions are not ruled by conditions and consists in the sending/receiving of messages, input and output transitions of a service graph do not have conditions nor assignments.

4.2 WS-BPEL Processes as Service Graphs

We have implemented a translation that associates a service graph to each component service, starting from its WSDL and abstract WS-BPEL specification.

For the moment, the translation is restricted to a significant subset of the WS-BPEL languages. More precisely, we support all WS-BPEL *basic* and *structured activities*, like invoke, receive, sequence, switch, while, pick (without timeouts), and flow (without links). Moreover we support restricted forms of assignments (specifically, we restrict the expressions that can appear in the `from` part of the copy statements) and of correlations. The translation does not deal at the moment with WS-BPEL constructs like scopes, fault, event and compensation handlers. However, we found the considered subset expressive enough for describing services as business processes in several applications in different domains.

The WSDL document and the declarative part of the WS-BPEL document is used to define the context of the process, i.e., the data types, functions, and data variables, and the input/output actions.

In particular, in the WS-BPEL document we distinguish variables associated to message types (those used by the process to store input/output messages) from those used to store internal information. We define a service graph variable for each internal WS-BPEL variable and for each message part of 'input/output' variables.

The types of the message parts and variables, obtained from the WSDL file, are used to define the data types of the service graph. In particular, enumerative and boolean types in the WS-BPEL process are mapped to enumerative types in the service graph, while all the other (complex or simple) WS-BPEL types are mapped to abstract types with infinite domains[1]. Similarly, from the functions used in the assignments within the WS-BPEL document, we obtain the service graph functions.

From the input/output actions in the WSDL document and their calls in the WS-BPEL file, we define the input/output actions of the service graph.

The translation of the process workflow (see also [43]) consists of the recursive translation of the process activities. In the rest of this Section we give an intuitive and informal description of the translation of WS-BPEL basic and structured activities.

We use the following notations to represent this translation. We denote the service graph location, where the activity starts, as l_b, and the location, where the activity (normally) ends, as l_e. Note that an activity may have several final locations. We write $l_b \xrightarrow{\alpha} l_e$ to denote the (recursive) mapping of the (structured or basic) activity α with l_e and l_b being an initial and final locations of the activity. In the description of the mapping we specify the explored locations, transitions, actions, and their parameters.

The examples of the basic activities and the corresponding STS transitions are represented in Table 1.

The interaction activities are described with the receive/reply/invoke activities. We handle both synchronous and asynchronous interactions.

The receive activity defines the reception of the message. It specifies an operation, an interface, and a variable to be populated from the message content. The reply activity defines the message being sent to the partner in response in a synchronous invocation. It also specifies an operation, an interface, while the variable is used to specify the value of the message to be sent. The invoke activity defines a one-way or a synchronous request-response invocation. In the first form the activity defines a message emission without waiting for a response (used in asynchronous interactions or in one-way interactions). The following information is specified: an operation and an interface of the invoked partner, variable used to specify the transmitted value. The second form of the invoke activity is used to define an invocation followed by the reply from the partner (two-way synchronous invocation). In this case, also the output variable is specified to store the value of the received message. The message emission part is mapped to the corresponding output transition, followed by the reception transitions.

[1] We adopt this simple translation for service variables and types to make the formalization more understandable, extending the model to more sophisticated data translation, e.g. handling complex types, it is straightforward.

Table 1. Mapping basic WS-BPEL activities to Service Graph transitions

WS-BPEL activity	Service Graph transitions

`receive`
`operation="op"`
`variable="x"`
	$(l_b, true, \overleftarrow{op}(x\_p_1, \ldots, x\_p_n), \emptyset, l_e)$

`reply`
`operation="op"`
`variable="x"`
	$(l_b, true, \overrightarrow{rep\_op}(x\_p1, \ldots, x\_pn), \emptyset, l_e)$

`invoke`
`operation="op"`
`inputVariable="x"`
	$(l_b, true, \overrightarrow{op}(x\_p1, \ldots, x\_pn), \emptyset, l_e)$

`invoke`
`operation="op"`
`inputVariable="x1"`
`outputVariable="x2"`
	$(l_b, true, \overleftarrow{op}(x1\_p1, \ldots, x1\_pn), \emptyset, l')$
	$(l', true, \overrightarrow{reply\_op}(x2\_p1, \ldots, x2\_pm)), \emptyset, l_e)$

`assign`
`copy from variable="x1"`
`part="p1"`
`to variable="x2"`
`part="p2"`
	$(l_b, true, \tau, x2\_p2 := x1\_p1, l_e)$

`assign`
`copy from`
`expression="term"`
`to variable="x" part="p"`
	$(l_b, true, \tau, x\_p := term, l_e)$

`empty`	$(l_b, true, \tau, \emptyset, l_e)$
`terminate`	$(l_b, true, \tau, \emptyset, l_e)$

There are three basic activity types that are mapped to the internal service graph transitions, namely copy in assign activities, empty, and terminate.

Each copy in an assign reads a value from a source data element and writes it to another data element. The source may be any term, i.e., a literal value, a variable, or a function call. Due to the simplified approach adopted for variables and types translation, we require copy source elements to be variable parts or (nested or simple) functions on variable parts, and restrict target elements to variable parts. For each of this copy activities we define an internal τ transition performing the corresponding assignment ω. All opaque assignments in copy activities are modeled as internal τ transitions without any associated assignment.

The empty is used to model a no-op activity of the process. terminate activity can be used to immediately terminate the behavior of a business process instance within which the terminate activity is performed. Both activities are modeled as internal τ transitions. By construction, the terminate activity ends in a location from which there are no outgoing transitions.

Table 2. Mapping structured WS-BPEL activities to Service Graph transitions .

WS-BPEL activity	Service Graph transitions

`sequence`
`activity a1`
`activity a2`
`activity a3`
	$l_b \xrightarrow{a_1} l_1, l_1 \xrightarrow{a_2} l_2, l_2 \xrightarrow{a_3} l_e$

`switch`
`case condition="c1"`
`activity a1`
`case condition="c2"`
`activity a2`
`otherwise`
`activity a3`
	$(l_b, c1, \tau, \emptyset, l_1)$
	$(l_b, \neg c1 \wedge c2, \tau, \emptyset, l_2)$
	$(l_b, \neg c1 \wedge \neg c2, \tau, \emptyset, l_3)$
	$l_1 \xrightarrow{a_1} l_e, l_2 \xrightarrow{a_2} l_e, l_3 \xrightarrow{a_3} l_e$

`while condition="c"` `activity a`	$(l_b, c, \tau, \emptyset, l')$ $(l_b, \neg c, \tau, \emptyset, l_e)$ $l' \xrightarrow{a} l_b$

`pick`
`onMessage`
`operation="op1"`
`variable="var1"`
`activity a1`
`onMessage`
`operation="op2"`
`variable="var2"`
`activity a2`
	$(l_b, true, \overleftarrow{op1}(x1\_p1, \ldots, x1\_pn), \emptyset, l_1)$
	$(l_b, true, \overleftarrow{op2}(x2\_p1, \ldots, x2\_pm), \emptyset, l_2)$
	$l_1 \xrightarrow{a1} l_e, l_2 \xrightarrow{a2} l_e$

`flow`
`activity a1`
`activity a2`
	$l_b \xrightarrow{a1} l_1, l_1 \xrightarrow{a2} l_e$
	$l_b \xrightarrow{a2} l_1, l_1 \xrightarrow{a1} l_e$

The mapping of the structured activities is presented in Table 2.

The sequence activity defines an ordered list of activities that must be executed in the order in which they appear.

The switch activity defines the conditional choice. It consists of an ordered list of branches, defined by case elements, followed optionally by an otherwise branch. The branches are considered in the order in which they appear: the first branch whose condition holds true is taken. If no branch with a condition is taken, then the otherwise branch is taken.

The while activity supports repeated performance of a specified iterative activity. The loop terminates when the condition evaluates to false.

The pick activity awaits the occurrence of one of a set of events and then performs the associated activity. If more than one of the events occurs simultaneously then the choice is nondeterministic. The form of pick is a set of branches of the form event/activity, and exactly one of the branches will be selected based on the occurrence of the associated event. We restrict the possible events to the arrival of some message (we do not handle timeout events).

In order to specify that the activities are to be executed in parallel, the flow activity is used. The activity completes when all the nested activities complete. The parallel execution is represented as a structure where all the activities are interleaved.

Figure 8 shows the service graph for the abstract WS-BPEL process of the Flight (see Figure 4), represented in the internal language that is used by the WS-BPEL to service graph translator.

Similarly, we have defined a translation from service graphs to executable WS-BPEL. This translation is used to obtain the new WS-BPEL process which implements the required composition starting from the orchestrator service graph. The translation is conceptually simple. Intuitively, the declarative part of the process is already defined in its WSDL description, that, together with the abstract WS-BPEL, is part of the inputs to the composition problem. Input/output actions in the service graph model an interaction of the composite service with one of the component services, while internal actions in the service graph correspond to manipulations of data by means of XPath expressions and assignments.

4.3 Formal Model of Web Service Orchestration

We now give a formal model and semantics of a Web service orchestration. In this model the composition is represented as a set of service graphs corresponding to the participating services that interact with a service graph corresponding to the orchestrator. The role of the orchestrator, also referenced as controller, is to rule the execution of the components through the exchange of messages.

The composition model is built from the set of n service graphs $W^i = \langle L^i, L^i_0, C^i, \mathcal{A}^i, T^i \rangle$ representing the abstract description of the component Web services and a service graph $W^c = \langle L^c, L^c_0, C^c, \mathcal{A}^c, T^c \rangle$ representing the composite Web service (orchestrator).

We require that the inputs of a controller coincide with the outputs of the component services, and vice versa.

Moreover, our definition requires that the actions of the component services are disjoint. This means that the component services may not communicate directly with each other. While an extension to the case where such component services may directly communicate is possible, we will not consider it, since in our scenario, we intend to compose independent existing services, which we assume not to be aware of each other.

```
SERVICE Flight

TYPES
 dateT: ABSTRACT
 locationT: ABSTRACT
 costT: ABSTRACT
 scheduleT: ABSTRACT
 ...
 boolean: {T,F}

VARIABLES
 req_date: dateT
 req_location: locationT
 off_cost: costT
 off_schedule: scheduleT
 ...
 available: boolean

FUNCTIONS
 costOf: (dateT,locationT): costT
 getSched: (dateT,locationT): scheduleT

INPUTS
 request(req_date,req_location)
 cancel()
 confirm()
 ...

OUTPUTS
 offer(off_cost,off_schedule)
 ...

LOCATIONS
 pc: {l1,l2,l3,....}

TRANSITIONS
 pc=l1 -[INPUT request(req_date,req_location)]-> pc:=l2
 pc=l2 -[TAU]-> pc:=l3
 pc=l3 & available=T -[TAU]-> pc:=l4
 ...
 pc=l7 -[OUTPUT offer(off_cost,off_schedule)]-> pc:=l8
 pc=l8 -[INPUT cancel()]-> pc:=l9
 ...
 pc=l8 -[INPUT confirm()]-> pc:=l10
 ...
```

Fig. 8. The Service Graph modeling the Flight Booking Service

A global state of the composition at a particular execution point is defined by the locations of all the participants, i.e. component services and orchestrator, and by the values of their variables. We call such a description a *configuration* of the composition.

More formally, a configuration γ of the composition is a tuple $\langle \bar{l}, \bar{g} \rangle$, where $\bar{l}$ is a *global location*, i.e. a combination of the locations of all the participants, and $\bar{g}$ is a *global ground state* that represents the values of all the local variables of the participants $\mathcal{V} = \bigcup_i \mathcal{V}^i \cup \mathcal{V}^c$. A *global location* is a vector $\bar{l} = \langle l_c, l_1, \ldots, l_n \rangle$ where l_c is the location of the orchestrator and l_i is the location of the ith service graph. We denote with $\bar{l}[l'_i/l_i]$ a vector with location l_i updated to l'_i. We denote with $\bar{l}(W^i)$ the location of the service graph W^i in global location $\bar{l}$.

The formal model of a Web service orchestration is defined as an *orchestrated transition system* that defines how a set of component services evolve when controlled by an orchestrator.

Definition 6 (Orchestrated Transition System)
An Orchestrated Transition System *(*OTS*)* $W^c \triangleright W^1, \ldots, W^n$*, that represents the execution of* n *service graphs* $W^1, \ldots, W^n$ *controlled by a service graph* W^c*, is a tuple* $\langle \Gamma, \Gamma_0, \mathcal{A}, \underset{c}{\rightarrow} \rangle$ *where* Γ *is a set of configurations,* $\Gamma_0 \subseteq \Gamma$ *is a set of initial configurations,* $\mathcal{A} = \mathcal{A}_c$ *is a set of actions, and* $\underset{c}{\rightarrow} \subseteq \Gamma \times \mathcal{A} \times \Gamma$ *is a transition relation such that:*

- $(\langle \bar{l}, \bar{g} \rangle, \overrightarrow{\mu}(\bar{x}), \langle \bar{l}[l'_i/l_i][l'_c/l_c], \bar{g}' \rangle) \in \underset{c}{\rightarrow}$ *if*
  - *for some* i*,* $(l_i, true, \overleftarrow{\mu}(\bar{y}), \emptyset, l'_i) \in T^i$*;*
  - $(l_c, true, \overrightarrow{\mu}(\bar{x}), \emptyset, l'_c) \in T^c$*;*
  - $\bar{g}' = update(\bar{g}, \bar{\omega})$ *where* $\bar{\omega} = (y_0 := x_0, \ldots, y_n := x_n)$*.*
- $(\langle \bar{l}, \bar{g} \rangle, \overleftarrow{\mu}(\bar{x}), \langle \bar{l}[l'_i/l_i][l'_c/l_c], \bar{g}' \rangle) \in \underset{c}{\rightarrow}$ *if*
  - *for some* i*,* $(l_i, true, \overrightarrow{\mu}(\bar{y}), \emptyset, l'_i) \in T^i$*;*
  - $(l_c, true, \overleftarrow{\mu}(\bar{x}), \emptyset, l'_c) \in T^c$*;*
  - $\bar{g}' = update(\bar{g}, \bar{\omega})$ *where* $\bar{\omega} = (x_0 := y_0, \ldots, x_n := y_n)$*.*
- $(\langle \bar{l}, \bar{g} \rangle, \tau, \langle \bar{l}[l'_c/l_c], \bar{g}' \rangle) \in \underset{c}{\rightarrow}$ *if*
  - $(l_c, \phi_c, \tau, \bar{\omega}_c, l'_c) \in T^c$*;*
  - $\bar{g} \models \phi_c$*;*
  - $\bar{g}' = update(\bar{g}, \bar{\omega}_c)$*.*
- $(\langle \bar{l}, \bar{g} \rangle, \tau, \langle \bar{l}[l'_i/l_i], \bar{g}' \rangle) \in \underset{c}{\rightarrow}$ *if*
  - *for some* i*,* $(l_i, \phi, \tau, \bar{\omega}, l'_i) \in T^i$*;*
  - $\bar{g} \models \phi$*;*
  - $\bar{g}' = update(\bar{g}, \bar{\omega})$*;*
- *no other transition belongs to* $\underset{c}{\rightarrow}$*.*

Intuitively, the evolution of each component service is synchronized on input and output actions with the orchestrator, while each service evolves autonomously when it performs internal actions. The global ground state, modeling the content of all the local variables, evolves according to the performed operations.

Composition Behavior. A *run* ω of an OTS is a sequence $\gamma_0, \alpha_0, \gamma_1, \alpha_1, \ldots$ such that $\gamma_0 \in \Gamma_0$ and $(\gamma_i, \alpha_i, \gamma_{i+1}) \in \underset{c}{\rightarrow}$. A configuration $\gamma \in \Gamma$ is said to be *reachable* if there exists a run $\omega = \gamma_0, \alpha_0, \ldots, \gamma_n, \alpha_n, \ldots$ such that for some i, $\gamma_i = \gamma$. We will denote with $Reachable(W^c \triangleright W^1, \ldots, W^n) \subseteq \Gamma$ the set of reachable configurations of the OTS $W^c \triangleright W^1, \ldots, W^n$.

A configuration $\gamma \in \Gamma$ is *final* if it is reachable and there is no transition leaving γ (formally, for each $(\gamma_i, \alpha, \gamma_{i+1}) \in \underset{c}{\rightarrow}$, $\gamma_i \neq \gamma$).

A *ground event* models a change in a ground state. In particular, we define a ground event e as a couple $\langle x, v \rangle$, where x is a variable and v a value belonging to x type. A *ground execution*, denoted with ε, is a sequence of ground events.

Given a run $\omega = \gamma_0, \alpha_0, \gamma_1, \alpha_1, \ldots$ of an OTS $W^c \triangleright W^1, \ldots, W^n$, with $\gamma_i = \langle \bar{l}_i, \bar{g}_i \rangle$, the corresponding ground execution ε is a sequence $\varepsilon_0, \varepsilon_1, \ldots$ where each ε_i is the sequence of events $\langle x_{i0}, v_{i0} \rangle, \ldots, \langle x_{ik}, v_{ik} \rangle$ modeling the changes of the variable values from ground state $\bar{g}_i$ to state $\bar{g}_{i+1}$ (formally, $\langle x_{ij}, v_{ij} \rangle \in \varepsilon_i$ if $\Gamma_{\bar{g}_{i+1}}(x_{ij}) = v_{ij}$ and $\Gamma_{\bar{g}_i}(x_{ij}) \neq v_{ij}$).

The *ground behavior* of an OTS $W^c \triangleright W^1, \ldots, W^n$ is defined by the set of its ground executions.

Deadlock-free Orchestrator. A controller W^c may not be adequate to control a set of component services. In particular, in order to avoid deadlocks, we need to guarantee that whenever W^c performs an output transition then the component service exporting the corresponding input action is able to accept it, and vice versa. Moreover, for sake of generality, we need to do so in a way which is independent from low-level engine-dependent implementation details, and in particular from the way I/O queuing mechanisms are realized. This requires a careful, conservative approach: we need to rule out any cases where the presence of a queuing mechanism is essential to the avoidance of deadlock situations, and where critical runs exist that affect the outcomes of the control. We define a *deadlock-freedom* condition that relies on the assumption that messages are associated to a buffer, but does not rely on the existence of any message queuing/buffering mechanism. This corresponds to the minimal requirement that allows for *asynchronous* execution of WS-BPEL services, and as such is guaranteed to be supported by any Web-service execution engine.

In particular, we assume that a service in a location l can accept a message $\overrightarrow{\mu}(\bar{y})$ if there is some successor $l' \in L$ of l, reachable from l through a chain of internal (τ) transitions, and the service from location l' can perform an input transition labelled with $\overleftarrow{\mu}(\bar{x})$. Vice versa, if location l has no such successor l', and message $\overrightarrow{\mu}(\bar{y})$ is sent, then a deadlock situation is reached.

In the following definition, and in the rest of the paper, we denote by τ-closure$_W(l)$ the set of locations reachable from l through a sequence of τ transitions.

Definition 7 **(τ-closure$_W$)**
Let $W = \langle L, L_0, \mathcal{C}, \mathcal{A}, T\rangle$ be a service graph, and $l \in L$. Then τ-closure$_W(l) = \{l'$: there exist $l_0, l_1, \ldots, l_n$ s.t. $l = l_0, l' = l_n$, and $(l_i, \phi, \tau, \bar{\omega}, l_{i+1}) \in T\}$.

Definition 8 **(Deadlock-Free Orchestrator)**
Let $W^c = \langle L^c, L_0^c, \mathcal{C}^c, \mathcal{A}^c, T^c\rangle$ be an orchestrator for service graphs $W^1, \ldots, W^n$, where each $W^i = \langle L^i, L_0^i, \mathcal{C}^i, \mathcal{A}^i, T^i\rangle$. W^c is deadlock free *for $W^1, \ldots, W^n$ if each configuration $\gamma = \langle\langle l_c, l_1, \ldots, l_n\rangle, \bar{g}\rangle \in Reachable(W^c \triangleright W^1, \ldots, W^n)$ satisfies the following conditions:*

1. *if, for some i, $(l_i, true, \overrightarrow{\mu}(\bar{x}), \emptyset, l_i') \in T^i$ then there is some $l_c' \in \tau$-closure$_W(l_c)$ such that $(l_c', true, \overleftarrow{\mu}(\bar{y}), \emptyset, l_c'') \in T^c$ for some $l_c'' \in L^c$;*
2. *if $(l_c, true, \overrightarrow{\mu}(\bar{x}), \emptyset, l_c') \in T^c$ then, for some i, there is some $l_i' \in \tau$-closure$_W(l_i)$ such that $(l_i', true, \overleftarrow{\mu}(\bar{y}), \emptyset, l_i'') \in T^i$ for some $l_i'' \in L^i$;*

We can now formally characterize a Web service composition problem.

Definition 9 **(Web Service Composition Problem)**
Let $W^1, \ldots, W^n$ be a set of service graphs, and let r be a composition requirement. The composition problem for $W^1, \ldots, W^n$ and r is the problem of finding a deadlock-free service graph W^c such that $W^c \triangleright W^1, \ldots, W^n$ satisfies r.

What needs to be done in the following is to define the requirements. We start from control flow requirements.

4.4 Control Flow Requirements

As shown in Example 5, in the control flow requirements we need to express conditions on the termination of the component services.

In particular, we must specify that, in case all services are available and the final user accepts, they should all terminate in a 'successful' state, i.e. a state where the final agreement to book or sell has been achieved with the VTA. Otherwise, each service must either remain inactive, or terminate in a 'failure' state where the service is aware of the impossibility to agree on the book/sell and any commitment to buy or sell has been withdrawn. In other words, our global termination requirement must take into account the transactionality of each component service within the overall composition.

In the specification of each service abstract WS-BPEL protocol we require (see Figure 9) to mark some states as successful (symbol ✓) and others as failing (symbol ×).

Example 7. Consider for instance the Flight service. When it receives an acknowledge message confirming the acceptance of the offer these means that a booking has been defined and the protocol terminates with success. While it terminates with failure in the case of unavailability of a flight or of refusal of the flight offer.

As shown by the following example, these annotations are used to specify the transactional requirements of the composition problem.

Example 8. If we consider the VTA scenario, the control flow requirements specification is the following.

	Flight	Hotel	VTA
Primary	✓	✓	✓
Secondary	×	×	×

The specification distinguishes two different requirements: a primary and a secondary one. The primary requirement is to reach a situation where all the services are in a successful state (in our case it models the condition "sell holiday packages"). The secondary requirement (modeling the condition "no single commitments") is to reach a situation where all the services are in a failing state.

We do not need this kind of semantic annotations for the AllMaps service since its protocol doesn't present any possibility of failure.

Notice that, while specifying control flow requirements, the developer models also the transactional nature of the new composite service. In particular, in the VTA example we are saying that the composite service is in a successful state if the customer has accepted the offer and the holiday package has been booked, while the VTA is in a failing state when either some service is not available or the customer has refused the offer.

If we consider real-world composition scenarios, we can have more complex transactional requirements. For instance it can be the case that the failure of a component service doesn't affect the success of the overall composition: the other components and the composite service can still be in a successful state.

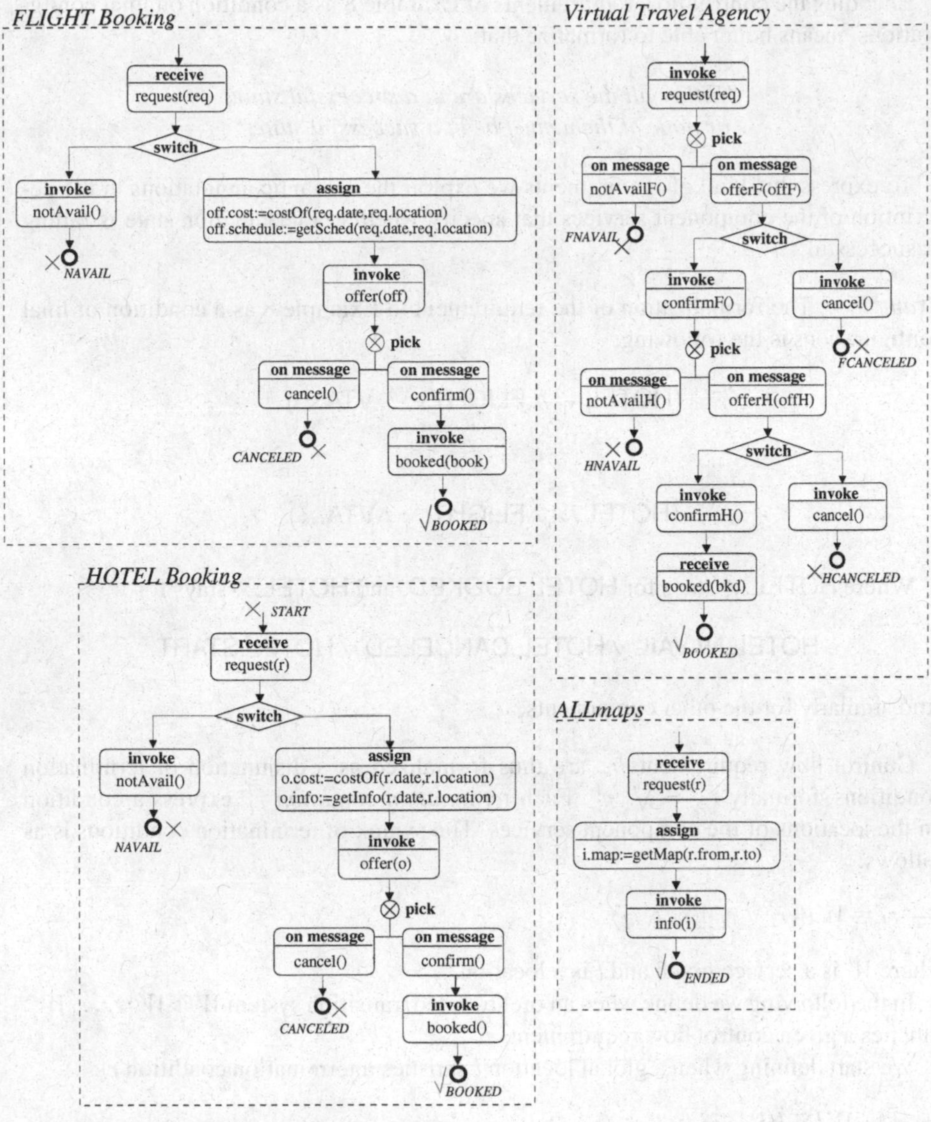

Fig. 9. VTA Composition Scenario: semantically annotated WS-BPEL protocols

Our approach thus provides the developer with the ability to specify with a simple tabular notation control-flow requirements that are then automatically translated into a formal internal notation that is hidden to the developer.

This kind of requirements can be formally expressed in several ways. In the following, we present a well-known approach, which consists in expressing control flow requirements as conditions on the final execution configurations.

Encoding the control flow requirements of Example 8 as a condition on final configurations, means being able to formalize that:

"Either all the services are in a successful state,
or none of them must be in a successful state."

To express this kind of requirements we exploit the semantic annotations in the description of the component services that specify whether a termination state is failing or successful.

Example 9. The formalization of the requirement in Example 8 as a condition of final configurations is the following.

$$(\mathsf{HOTEL}.\checkmark \wedge \mathsf{FLIGHT}.\checkmark \wedge \mathsf{VTA}.\checkmark)$$

$$\vee$$

$$(\mathsf{HOTEL}.\times \wedge \mathsf{FLIGHT}.\times \wedge \mathsf{VTA}.\times)$$

Where $\mathsf{HOTEL}.\checkmark$ stays for HOTEL.BOOKED, and $\mathsf{HOTEL}.\times$ stays for

$$\mathsf{HOTEL.NAVAIL} \vee \mathsf{HOTEL.CANCELED} \vee \mathsf{HOTEL.START}.$$

And similarly for the other components.

Control flow requirements r_c are thus formalized as a disjunction of termination conditions, formally $r_c = \bigvee_k r_l^k$. Each *termination condition* r_l^k express a condition on the locations of the component services. The syntax of termination conditions is as follows:

– $r_l \equiv W.l|(r_l \vee r_l)|(r_l \wedge r_l)$

where W is a service graph and l is a location.

In the following we define when an orchestrated transition system $W^c \triangleright W^1, \ldots, W^n$ satisfies a given control flow requirements r_c.

We start defining when a global location $\bar{l}$ satisfies a termination condition r_l:

– $\bar{l} \models W.l$ if $\bar{l}(W) = l$;
– $\bar{l} \models r_l^1 \vee r_l^2$ if $\bar{l} \models r_l^1$ or $\bar{l} \models r_l^2$;
– $\bar{l} \models r_l^1 \wedge r_l^2$ if $\bar{l} \models r_l^1$ and $\bar{l} \models r_l^2$.

A configuration $\gamma = \langle \bar{l}, \bar{g} \rangle$ satisfies $r_c = \bigvee_k r_l^k$, denoted with $\gamma \models r_c$, if for some k, $\bar{l} \models r_l^k$.

Definition 10 (Control Flow Requirements Satisfiability)
Let r_c be a control flow requirements and $W^c \triangleright W^1, \ldots, W^n$ an orchestrated transition system. We say that $W^c \triangleright W^1, \ldots, W^n$ satisfies r_c, denoted with $W^c \triangleright W^1, \ldots, W^n \models r_c$, if every final configuration γ_f of $W^c \triangleright W^1, \ldots, W^n$ is such that $\gamma_f \models r_c$.

4.5 Data Flow Requirements

The exchange and management of business data in service compositions using XML-based standards is one of the most important capabilities of the Web service technology. In data-intensive applications the data flow is as critical for the composition problem as the control flow, since the service execution is driven by the manipulated information. In this section, we describe a technique to deal with data requirements in Web service composition.

We propose to separate the specification of data-flow requirements from that of control-flow requirements, and to specify requirements on the data flow through a set of constraints that explicitly define the valid routings and manipulations of messages that the composed service can perform. These constraints can be described in a graphical way, as a *data net*, i.e., as a graph where the input/output ports of the existing services are modeled as nodes, the paths in the graph define the possible routes of the messages, and the arcs define basic manipulations of these messages performed by the composed service.

We now provide a formal definition of data flow requirements as data nets and describe its graphical representation.

Data Net Formal Model. Data flow requirements specify explicitly how output messages (messages sent to component services) must be obtained from input messages (messages received from component services). All these requirements are collected in a hypergraph called *data net*, whose nodes represent variables used to store data and whose hyperarcs represent flow and manipulation of data.

Hypergraphs, a generalization of graphs, have been widely and deeply studied (see [17,18]), and quite often have proved to be a successful tool to represent and model concepts and structures in various areas of Computer Science and Discrete Mathematics. Here we deal with directed hypergraphs. Sometimes with different names such as "labelled graphs" and "And-Or graphs", directed hypergraphs have been introduced in the literature as a way to deal with particular problems arising in Computer Science and in Combinatorial Optimization (see, for example, [23], [41], [49], [54]). In the following we recall some basic definitions concerning hypergraphs.

Definition 11 (Directed Hypergraph)
A hypergraph $\mathcal{H}$ is a pair $\langle N, E \rangle$ where:

- *N is the set of nodes;*
- *$E \subseteq \mathcal{P}(N) \times \mathcal{P}(N)$ is the set of* hyperarcs.

Given an hyperarc $e = \langle X, Y \rangle$, the set X of nodes is the *tail* of e, while the set Y of nodes is its *head*; in the following we denote them with $head(e)$ and $tail(e)$ respectively. A *backward* hyperarc, or simply *B-arc*, is a hyperarc e with $|head(e)| = 1$. A *forward* hyperarc, or simply *F-arc*, is a hyperarc e with $|tail(e)| = 1$. An *arc* is a hyperarc e with $|head(e)| = |tail(e)| = 1$. Given a node n, we denote with $FS(n)$ its *Forward Star*, that is the set of all its outgoing hyperarcs (formally $FS(n) = \{e \in E : n \in tail(e)\}$). Similarly, we denote with $BS(n)$ the *Backward Star* of a node n, that is the set of all its incoming hyperarcs (formally, $BS(n) = \{e \in E : n \in head(e)\}$).

A data net is characterized by a set of typed nodes N, a set of hyperarcs E, also called *data-flow arcs*, where each arc corresponds to a specific type of data net operator, and a set of typed functions $\mathcal{F}$.

There are three different kinds of nodes:

- *input nodes*, external connection nodes associated to input ports, that represent sources of data to the data net and thus can have only outgoing data-flow arcs. Given a set of nodes N we denote with N^I_{ext} its subset of input nodes.
- *output nodes*, external connection nodes associated to output actions, that represent target of data for the data net and thus can have only incoming data-flow arcs. Given a set of nodes N we denote with N^O_{ext} its subset of output nodes.
- and *internal nodes*, that represent internal storage of data used to hold data manipulation results, and that can have both incoming and outgoing data-flow arcs. Given a set of nodes N we denote with N_{int} its subset of internal nodes.

We denote with N_{ext} the set of all external connection nodes (formally, $N_{ext} = N^I_{ext} \cup N^O_{ext}$).

In the following we describe the data-flow arcs provided by the language, show how they can be composed to obtain complex expressions, and provide an intuitive semantics.

- *Identity* data-flow arc
  It is connected to one node in input and one node in output. The requirement states that data received from the tail node should be forwarded to the head node. The graphical notation for the data-flow identity arc $id(a)(b)$, with head node a and tail node b, is the following:

- *Operation* data-flow arc
  It is related to a function definition; its tail has as many nodes as the number of function parameters and its head has only one node corresponding to the function result. The requirement states that, when data is received from all the nodes in the tail, the result of the operation should be forwarded to the head node. The graphical notation for the data-flow operation arc $oper[f](a,b)(c)$ characterizing function f, with tail nodes a and b and head node c, is the following:

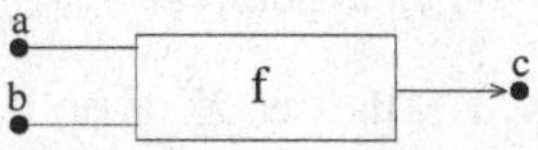

- *Fork* data-flow arc

  Its tail has a single node and its head can have as many nodes as needed. It forwards data received on the tail node to all the nodes in the head. The graphical notation for the data-flow fork arc $fork(a)(b,c)$, with tail node a and head nodes b and c, is the following:

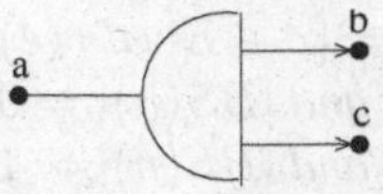

- *Merge* data-flow arc
  It can have as many nodes an needed in the tail and can have only one node as head. It forwards data received on some node in the tail to the head node. It preserves the temporal order of data arriving on tail nodes (if it receives data on two or more tail nodes at the same time, the order is nondeterministic). We represent the data-flow merge arc $merge(a, b)(c)$, with tail nodes a and b and head node c as:

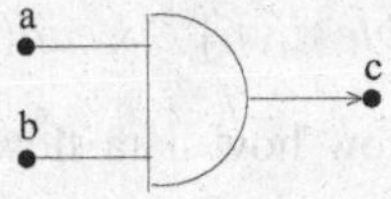

- *Cloner* data-flow arc
  Its tail and its head can have only one node each. It forwards, as many times as needed (min 1), to the head node the data received from the tail node. The data-flow cloner arc $clone(a)(b)$, with tail node a and head node b is represented as:

- *Filter* data-flow arc
  It has only one node in the tail and only one node in the head. When it receives data on the tail node, it either forwards it to the head node or discards it. We represent the data-flow filter arc $filt(a)(b)$, having tail node a and head node b as:

- *Last* data-flow arc
  It has only one node in the tail and only one node in the head. It requires that at most one data is forwarded to the head node: the last data received on the tail node. All other previously received data are discarded. The graphical notation for the data-flow last arc $last(a)(b)$, with tail node a and head node b, is the following:

Definition 12 (Data Net)
A data net $\mathcal{D}$ is a tuple $\langle \mathcal{H}, T, \mathcal{F}, \mathcal{L}_T, \mathcal{L}_F \rangle$ where:

- *$\mathcal{H} = \langle N, E \rangle$ is a directed hypergraph;*
- *$\mathcal{L}_T : E \to T$ is a function associating to each hyperarc its type, where $T = \{identity, operation, fork, merge, cloner, filter, last\}$;*

– $\mathcal{L}_F : E_F \rightarrow \mathcal{F}$ *is a function associating to each operation hyperarc the corresponding function, where* $E_F = \{e \in E : \mathcal{L}_T(e) = operation\}$;
– *for all* $n \in N^I_{ext}$, $|FS(n)| = 1$ *and* $|BS(n)| = 0$;
– *for all* $n \in N^O_{ext}$, $|FS(n)| = 0$ *and* $|BS(n)| = 1$;
– *for all* $n \in N_{int}$, $|FS(n)| = |BS(n)| = 1$;
– *for all* $e \in E$
  • *if* $\mathcal{L}_T(e) \in \{identity, cloner, filter, last\}$ *then e is an arc;*
  • *if* $\mathcal{L}_T(e) = fork$ *then e is a F-arc;*
  • *if* $\mathcal{L}_T(e) \in \{operation, merge\}$ *then e is a B-arc;*
– *for all* $e \in E$
  • *if* $\mathcal{L}_T(e) = operation$, $e = oper[f](n_1, \ldots, n_k)(n)$, *then* $\mathrm{T}(n) = \mathrm{T}(f)[0]$, $\mathrm{A}(f) = k$, *and* $\mathrm{T}(n_i) = \mathrm{T}(f)[i]$, *where* $1 \leq i \leq \mathrm{A}(\mathcal{L}_F(e))$;
  • *otherwise, for each possible* $n_i, n_j \in head(e) \cup tail(e)$, $\mathrm{T}(n_i) = \mathrm{T}(n_j)$.

In the following examples we show how data flow arcs can be composed to obtain complex data flow requirements.

Example 10. Let's consider the VTA composition scenario. Suppose we want to model that the new composite process must use the information on the cost of the Hotel both to obtain the hotel offer for the Customer, and, combining it with the cost offered by the Flight, to prepare the final cost for the Customer.

The following picture shows how we can specify this data flow requirements by composing $fork$ and *operation* data flow arcs, and appropriately linking them to external nodes.

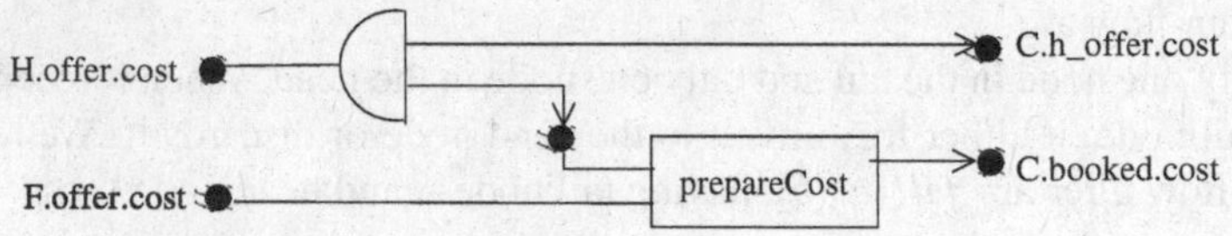

Example 11. In Figure 10 we represent the data-net requirements for the VTA scenario presented in Section 3 (see also [50]): they describe the constraints on the data exchanged among a Customer, a Flight booking service, a Hotel booking service and a AllMap service in the set-up of a vacation package.

When the VTA receives a request from the Customer, it must forward the date information to the Flight and the loc information both to the Flight and to the Hotel.

The VTA must forward the cost received in the offer from the Hotel to the Customer through the hOffer.cost message. Similarly, the VTA must forward the cost received in the offer from the Flight to the Customer through the fOffer.cost message. Moreover, the new composite service must combine both costs offered by the Flight and by the Hotel, by means of its internal function prepareCost, to obtain the cost to be sent in the booked message to the Customer.

The VTA must obtain the date information that it sends in the request to the Hotel by computing its internal function getDate on the schedule received in the offer of the Flight. The schedule received in the offer of the Flight is also forwarded to the

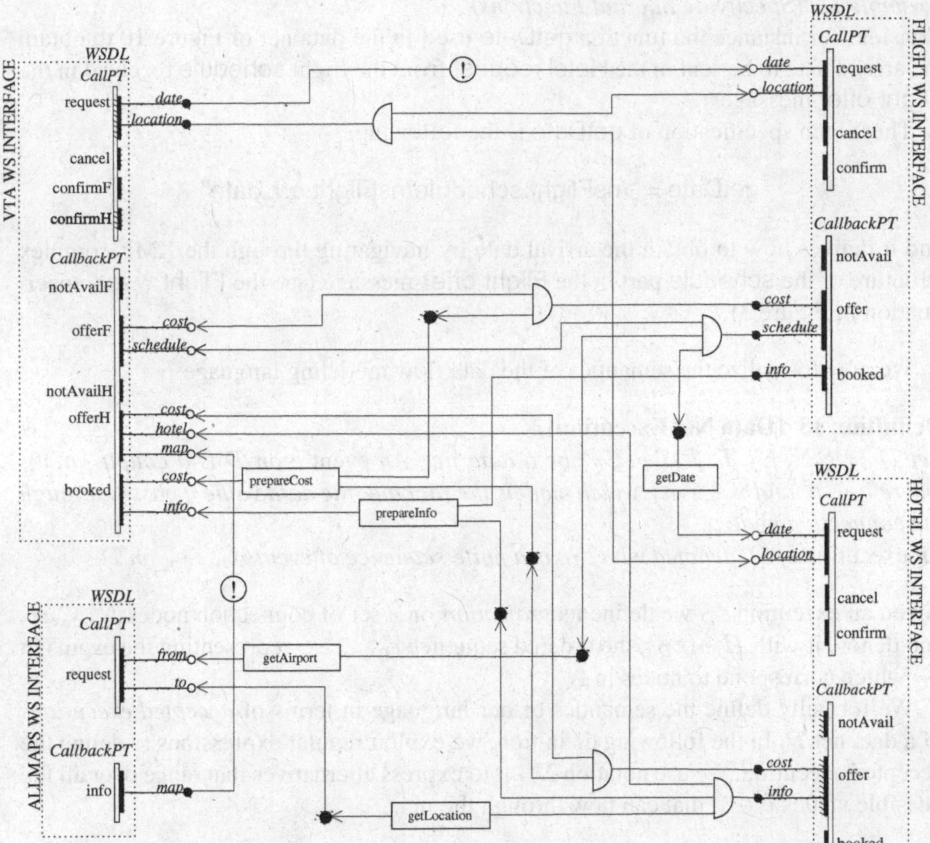

Fig. 10. The data net for a Travel Agency scenario

client, as part of the f_offer message. Moreover, the VTA exploits the internal function getAirport on the flight schedule to obtain the from information to be sent to the AllMaps service.

Similarly, all outgoing message parts are obtained by properly aggregating, manipulating, or simply forwarding incoming message parts by means of data flow arcs.

Each operation data flow arc in the data net (e.g. getDate in the VTA example) refers to an internal function that the new composite service uses to manipulate data. Since our aim is to automatically generate the executable WS-BPEL code implementing the composite service, the specification of each internal function is given as an *XML Path Language* [19] (XPath from now on) expression, which is the standard language used in WS-BPEL assignments. XPath is an expression language for addressing portions of an XML document, or for computing values (strings, numbers, or boolean values) based on the content of an XML document.

Example 12 (Specifying Internal Functions)
Consider for instance the function getDate used in the data net of Figure 10 to obtain the arrival date to be sent in the Hotel request from the flight schedule received in the Flight offer message.

The XPath specification of getDate is the following:

getDate = "/nsFlight:schedule/nsFlight:arr_date"

and it defines how to obtain the arrival date by navigating through the XML complex structure of the schedule part in the Flight offer message (see the Flight WSDL specification in Figure 3).

We now formalize the semantics of the data flow modeling language.

Definition 13 (Data Net Execution)
Let $\mathcal{D} = \langle\langle N, E\rangle, \mathcal{T}, \mathcal{F}, \mathcal{L}_T, \mathcal{L}_F\rangle$ be a data net. An event *e on $\mathcal{D}$ is a couple $\langle n, v\rangle$, where $n \in N$ and $v \in \mathrm{T}(n)$, which models the fact that the data value v passes through the connection node n.*
An execution *of $\mathcal{D}$, denoted with $\varepsilon_\mathcal{D}$, is a finite sequence of events $e_0, ..e_n$ on $\mathcal{D}$.*

Given an execution $\varepsilon_\mathcal{D}$ we define its *projection* on a set of connection nodes $N' \subseteq N$, and denote it with $\Pi_{N'}(\varepsilon_\mathcal{D})$, the ordered sequence $e'_0, ..., e'_m$ representing the events in $\varepsilon_\mathcal{D}$ which correspond to nodes in N'.

We formally define the semantics of our language in terms of *accepted executions* of a data net $\mathcal{D}$. In the following definition, we exploit regular expressions to define the accepted execution. We use notation $\Sigma_{v\in\mathcal{V}}$ to express alternatives that range over all the possible values $v \in \mathcal{V}$ that can flow through the net.

Definition 14 (Data Net Accepting Execution)
An execution $\varepsilon_\mathcal{D}$ is accepted by a data net $\mathcal{D} = \langle\langle N, E\rangle, \mathcal{T}, \mathcal{F}, \mathcal{L}_T, \mathcal{L}_F\rangle$ if it satisfies all the following properties:

- *for each identity arc $id(a)(b)$ in $\mathcal{D}$:*

$$\Pi_{\{a,b\}}(\varepsilon_\mathcal{D}) = \left(\sum_{v\in\mathrm{T}(a)} \langle a, v\rangle \cdot \langle b, v\rangle\right)^*$$

- *for each operation arc $oper[f](a,b)(c)$ in $\mathcal{D}$:*

$$\Pi_{\{a,b,c\}}(\varepsilon_\mathcal{D}) =$$

$$\left(\sum_{v\in\mathrm{T}(a), w\in\mathrm{T}(b)} (\langle a, v\rangle \cdot \langle b, w\rangle + \langle b, w\rangle \cdot \langle a, v\rangle) \cdot \langle c, f(v,w)\rangle\right)^*$$

– *for each fork arc $fork(a)(b,c)$ in $\mathcal{D}$:*

$$\Pi_{\{a,b,c\}}(\varepsilon_{\mathcal{D}}) = \left(\sum_{v \in \mathrm{T}(a)} \langle a,v \rangle \cdot (\langle b,v \rangle \cdot \langle c,v \rangle + \langle c,v \rangle \cdot \langle b,v \rangle) \right)^*$$

– *for each merge arc $merge(a,b)(c)$ in $\mathcal{D}$:*

$$\Pi_{\{a,b,c\}}(\varepsilon_{\mathcal{D}}) = \left(\sum_{v \in \mathrm{T}(a)} (\langle a,v \rangle \cdot \langle c,v \rangle + \langle b,v \rangle \cdot \langle c,v \rangle) \right)^*$$

– *for each cloner arc $clone(a)(b)$ in $\mathcal{D}$:*

$$\Pi_{\{a,b\}}(\varepsilon_{\mathcal{D}}) = \left(\sum_{v \in \mathrm{T}(a)} \langle a,v \rangle \cdot \langle b,v \rangle \cdot \langle b,v \rangle^* \right)^*$$

– *for each filter arc $filt(a)(b)$ in $\mathcal{D}$:*

$$\Pi_{\{a,b\}}(\varepsilon_{\mathcal{D}}) = \left(\sum_{v \in \mathrm{T}(a)} \langle a,v \rangle \cdot (\langle b,v \rangle + \epsilon) \right)^*$$

– *for each last arc $last(a)(b)$ in $\mathcal{D}$:*

$$\Pi_{\{a,b\}}(\varepsilon_{\mathcal{D}}) = \left(\sum_{v \in \mathrm{T}(a)} \langle a,v \rangle \right)^* \cdot \left(\sum_{v \in \mathrm{T}(a)} \langle a,v \rangle \cdot \langle b,v \rangle \right) + \epsilon$$

Given a data net $\mathcal{D}$, we denote with $\mathcal{E}_{\mathcal{D}}$ the set of all the executions accepted by $\mathcal{D}$.

Notice that this definition considers data net arcs connecting at most two input/output nodes, however it can easily be extended to handle arcs of the data net connecting more input/output nodes.

As defined in Section 4.3, the ground behavior of a service composition can be defined as a set of executions $\mathcal{E}$ on the set of all variables. The composition satisfies the requirements in the data net $\mathcal{D}$ if all the executions of the composition are accepted by $\mathcal{D}$.

Definition 15 (Data Net Satisfiability)
An orchestrated transition system $W^c \triangleright W^1, \ldots, W^n$ satisfies a data net $\mathcal{D}$, written as $W^c \triangleright W^1, \ldots, W^n \overset{DN}{\models} \mathcal{D}$, if each execution ε of $W^c \triangleright W^1, \ldots, W^n$ is such that $\varepsilon \in \mathcal{E}_{\mathcal{D}}$.

Given this definition and Definition 9, we have that an orchestrator service graph W^c is a solution for a data net composition problem with component services $W^1, \ldots, W^n$, control flow requirements r_c, and data flow requirements $r_d = \mathcal{D}$, if W^c is deadlock free, $W^c \triangleright W^1, \ldots, W^n \models r_c$, and each execution ε of $W^c \triangleright W^1, \ldots, W^n$ is an accepted execution of $\mathcal{D}$.

5 Automated Synthesis of a Web Service Composition

In this section we describe the approach for solving the composition problem described in the previous section. The approach is based on state-of-the-art techniques for planning in asynchronous domains [68], which we will now introduce.

5.1 Planning in Asynchronous Domains

The work in [68] presents a formal framework for the automated synthesis of a composition of Web services which is based on planning techniques: component services define the planning domain, composition requirements are formalized as planning goal, and planning algorithms are used to generate the composite service.

Due to the nature of Web services, the resulting planning domain is nondeterministic and partially observable. It differs from other planning frameworks since it assumes an asynchronous, message-based interaction between the domain (encoding the component services) and the plan (encoding the composite service).

More precisely, the planning domain is modeled as a *state transition system* (STS from now on) that can be in one of its possible states (a subset of which are *initial*) and can evolve to new states as a result of performing some actions.

In particular, *input* actions represent messages sent to the component services, while *output* actions are messages received from the component services. *Private* actions are actions that the composite service can perform internally, without interacting with the services.[2] Conversely, the special action τ is used to model internal evolutions of the component services which are not visible to the composite service. Finally, a labeling function associates to each state the set of properties $\mathcal{P}rop$ holding in that state.

Definition 16 (state transition system (STS))
A state transition system Σ *is a tuple* $\langle \mathcal{S}, \mathcal{S}^0, \mathcal{I}, \mathcal{O}, \mathcal{A}, \mathcal{R}, \mathcal{L} \rangle$ *where:*

- $\mathcal{S}$ *is the finite set of states;*
- $\mathcal{S}^0 \subseteq \mathcal{S}$ *is the set of initial states;*
- $\mathcal{I}$ *is a finite set of input actions;*
- $\mathcal{O}$ *is a finite set of output actions;*
- $\mathcal{A}$ *is a finite set of private actions;*
- $\mathcal{R} \subseteq \mathcal{S} \times (\mathcal{I} \cup \mathcal{O} \cup \mathcal{A} \cup \{\tau\}) \times \mathcal{S}$ *is the transition relation;*
- $\mathcal{L} : \mathcal{S} \rightarrow 2^{\mathcal{P}rop}$ *is the labeling function.*

[2] Private actions do not appear in [68], as they are specific of the approaches presented here. The extension of the theory of [68] to private actions is straightforward.

Some standard definitions on STS are now in order. We denote with A the set of all actions of the STS, formally $A = \mathcal{I} \cup \mathcal{O} \cup \mathcal{A} \cup \{\tau\}$

We say that an action $a \in A$ is *applicable* on a state $s \in \mathcal{S}$, denoted with Appl(a, s), if there exists a state $s' \in \mathcal{S}$ s.t. $(s, a, s') \in \mathcal{R}$. A state of an STS is *final* if no action $a \in A$ is applicable in s, i.e., if there is no transition leaving s.

The *behavior* of an STS is represented by its set of possible *runs*, i.e., of sequences $s_0, a_0, s_1, a_1, \ldots$ such that $s_0 \in \mathcal{S}^0$ and $(s_i, a_i, s_{i+1}) \in \mathcal{R}$. In general, such runs may be finite or infinite. A run σ is said to be *completed* if it is finite, and if its last state is final. A state $s \in \mathcal{S}$ will be said *reachable* if there exists a run $\sigma = s_0, a_0, \ldots, a_{n-1}, s_n, \ldots$ such that $s_n = s$. We will denote with $Reachable(\Sigma) \subseteq \mathcal{S}$ the set of reachable states of Σ.

Given a run $\sigma = s_0, a_0, s_1, a_1, \ldots$, we define its *projection* on a set of actions $A' \subseteq A$, and denote it with $\Pi_{A'}(\sigma)$, the ordered sequence $a'_0, ..., a'_m$ representing the actions in σ which are in A'.

In a composition problem, the composite service is defined as a "controller" Σ_c (also described as a STS), which interacts with the domain Σ, orchestrating the component services. We now recall the formal definition of the behavior of a STS Σ when controlled by Σ_c.

Definition 17 (controlled system)
Let $\Sigma = \langle \mathcal{S}, \mathcal{S}^0, \mathcal{I}, \mathcal{O}, \mathcal{A}, \mathcal{R}, \mathcal{L} \rangle$ *and* $\Sigma_c = \langle \mathcal{S}_c, \mathcal{S}^0_c, \mathcal{O}, \mathcal{I}, \mathcal{A}, \mathcal{R}_c, \mathcal{L}_\emptyset \rangle$ *be two state transition systems, where* $\mathcal{L}_\emptyset(s_c) = \emptyset$ *for all* $s_c \in \mathcal{S}_c$. *The STS* $\Sigma_c \triangleright \Sigma$, *describing the behaviors of system* Σ *when controlled by* Σ_c, *is defined as:*
$\Sigma_c \triangleright \Sigma = \langle \mathcal{S}_c \times \mathcal{S}, \mathcal{S}^0_c \times \mathcal{S}^0, \mathcal{I}, \mathcal{O}, \mathcal{A}, \mathcal{R}_c \triangleright \mathcal{R}, \mathcal{L} \rangle$
where:

- $\langle (s_c, s), \tau, (s'_c, s) \rangle \in (\mathcal{R}_c \triangleright \mathcal{R})$ *if* $\langle s_c, \tau, s'_c \rangle \in \mathcal{R}_c$;
- $\langle (s_c, s), \tau, (s_c, s') \rangle \in (\mathcal{R}_c \triangleright \mathcal{R})$ *if* $\langle s, \tau, s' \rangle \in \mathcal{R}$;
- $\langle (s_c, s), a, (s'_c, s') \rangle \in (\mathcal{R}_c \triangleright \mathcal{R})$, *with* $a \neq \tau$, *if* $\langle s_c, a, s'_c \rangle \in \mathcal{R}_c$ *and* $\langle s, a, s' \rangle \in \mathcal{R}$.

Due to the asynchronous nature of Web service interactions, and in order to guarantee a correct behavior of the composite service, we need to rule out explicitly the cases where the sender is ready to send a message that the receiver is not able to accept. According to [68], a state s is able to accept a message a if there exists some successor s' of s, reachable from s through a (possibly empty) sequence of τ transitions, such that an input transition labeled with a can be performed in s'. This intuition is captured in the following definition, where we denote by τ-closure$_\Sigma(s)$ the set of states reachable from s through a chain of τ transitions.

Definition 18 (deadlock-free controller)
Let $\Sigma = \langle \mathcal{S}, \mathcal{S}^0, \mathcal{I}, \mathcal{O}, \mathcal{A}, \mathcal{R}, \mathcal{L} \rangle$ *be a STS and* $\Sigma_c = \langle \mathcal{S}_c, \mathcal{S}^0_c, \mathcal{O}, \mathcal{I}, \mathcal{A}, \mathcal{R}_c, \mathcal{L}_\emptyset \rangle$ *be a controller for* Σ. Σ_c *is said to be* deadlock free *for* Σ *if all states* $(s_c, s) \in \mathcal{S}_c \times \mathcal{S}$ *that are reachable from the initial states of* $\Sigma_c \triangleright \Sigma$ *satisfy the following conditions:*

- *if* $\langle s, a, s' \rangle \in \mathcal{R}$ *with* $a \in \mathcal{O}$ *then there is some* $s'_c \in \tau$*-closure*$_\Sigma(s_c)$ *such that* $\langle s'_c, a, s''_c \rangle \in \mathcal{R}_c$ *for some* $s''_c \in \mathcal{S}_c$;

– *if* $\langle s_c, a, s'_c\rangle \in \mathcal{R}_c$ *with* $a \in \mathcal{I}$ *then there is some* $s' \in \tau\text{-}closure_\Sigma(s)$ *such that* $\langle s', a, s''\rangle \in \mathcal{R}$ *for some* $s'' \in \mathcal{S}$*;*
– *if* $\langle s_c, a, s'_c\rangle \in \mathcal{R}_c$ *with* $a \in \mathcal{A}$ *then there is some* $s' \in \tau\text{-}closure_\Sigma(s)$ *such that* $\langle s', a, s''\rangle \in \mathcal{R}$ *for some* $s'' \in \mathcal{S}$*.*

In [68], the composition problem for domain Σ and composition goal ρ consists in generating a STS Σ_c that controls Σ so that its behavior satisfy the requirement ρ (according to a formal notion of requirement satisfaction).

Intuitively, a controller is a *solution* for a requirement ρ if it guarantees that ρ is achieved. We can formally express this by requiring that every run σ of the controlled system $\Sigma_c \triangleright \Sigma_{||}$ ends up in a state where ρ holds.

Definition 19 (Satisfiability)
Let ρ *be a propositional formula and* Σ *a STS. We say that* Σ *satisfies* ρ*, denoted with* $\Sigma \models_f \rho$*, if*

– *every final state* s_f *of* Σ *satisfies* ρ *according to the standard notion of satisfaction of a propositional formula on a state.*

Definition 20 (Solution controller)
A controller Σ_c *is a solution for goal* ρ *and planning domain* Σ *if* $\Sigma_c \triangleright \Sigma \models \rho$ *and* Σ_c *is deadlock free for* Σ*.*

To solve this problem, in [68] they show how to adapt the "Planning as Model Checking" approach of [21,22,31], which can deal with the fact that the component services model nondeterministic, partially observable behaviors. In [68], they exploit the MBP platform (see [20]) that implements such approach.

Even if here we are assuming that planning goal are expressed as reachability goals, this planning framework is able to deal with more complex requirements. In particular, it can deal with planning goals expressed in EAGLE, a requirement language whose operators are similar to CTL operators, but their semantics, formally defined in [32], take into account the notion of preference and the handling of failure when subgoals cannot be achieved.

5.2 Automated Synthesis through Planning in Asynchronous Domains

In this Section we give an overview of the proposed automated synthesis approach. The main idea is to exploit and extend the planning techniques presented in Section 5.1 in order to define a comprehensive Web service automated composition framework that covers all the phases of the composition process, from requirements specification to composite process run. An overview of the framework is given in Figure 11.

The composition domain is characterized by the description of the protocols of the component services and by some composition requirements. As already mentioned, we assume that the component service protocols are specified as abstract WS-BPEL processes. For what concerns the composition requirements, they consist of control flow requirements r_c and of data flow requirements r_d; the latter are described as data nets. The output of the synthesis is an executable WS-BPEL process that implements the Web service composition.

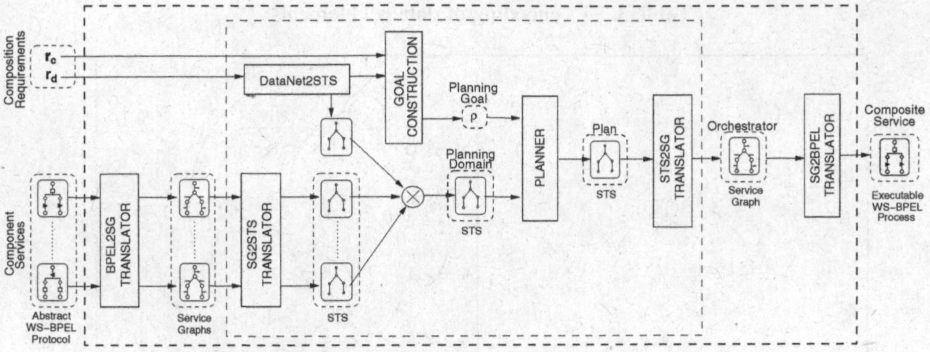

Fig. 11. The general automated composition framework

The first step in the framework is to model WS-BPEL specification using the service graph formalism presented in Section 4.1. The behaviour of the translation which associates a service graph to each WS-BPEL component service protocol (module "BPEL2SG Translator" of Figure 11) has been already presented in details in Section 4.2.

The second step is to transform a composition problem in a planning problem that can be solved by applying the techniques for planning in asynchronous domains proposed in Section 5.1. From each of the service graphs modeling the component services, an STS is then extracted (module "SG2STS Translator"), as described in Section 5.3. Also the data net requirements are transformed into an STS (module "DataNet2STS"), see Section 5.4. All the STS are then combined in a single STS through a synchronized product; this STS defines the domain for the planner. The goal of the planner is obtained by extending the control flow part of the composition requirements with additional constraints on the data net (module "Goal Construction"), as we will see in Section 5.5.

Once the composition problem has been encoded as a planning problem, we apply the techniques in Section 5.1 to obtain a deadlock free controller STS that interacts with the planning domain in such a way to satisfy the planning goal.

Then, from the controller STS, we obtain the service graph modeling the orchestrator (module "STS2SG Translator"), which is then translated into executable WS-BPEL to obtain the new composite process that implements the required composition.

5.3 Service Graphs as STS

The following definition describes the encoding of a service graph W, modeling a component service, with an STS Σ.

Definition 21 (Service Graph as STS)
Let $W = \langle L, L_0, \mathcal{C}, \mathcal{A}, T\rangle$ *be a component service graph and let* $\mathcal{C}^c = \langle \mathcal{T}^c, \mathcal{V}^c, \mathcal{F}^c\rangle$ *be the ground context of the controller. The corresponding STS* $\Sigma = \langle \mathcal{S}, \mathcal{S}^0, \mathcal{I}, \mathcal{O}, \emptyset, \mathcal{R}, \mathcal{L}_\emptyset\rangle$ *is obtained as follows:*

- *the set of states* $\mathcal{S}$ *are all the possible service locations* L*;*
- $\mathcal{S}^0 \subseteq \mathcal{S}$ *is the set of initial locations* L_0*;*

Table 3. STS encoding of data net elements

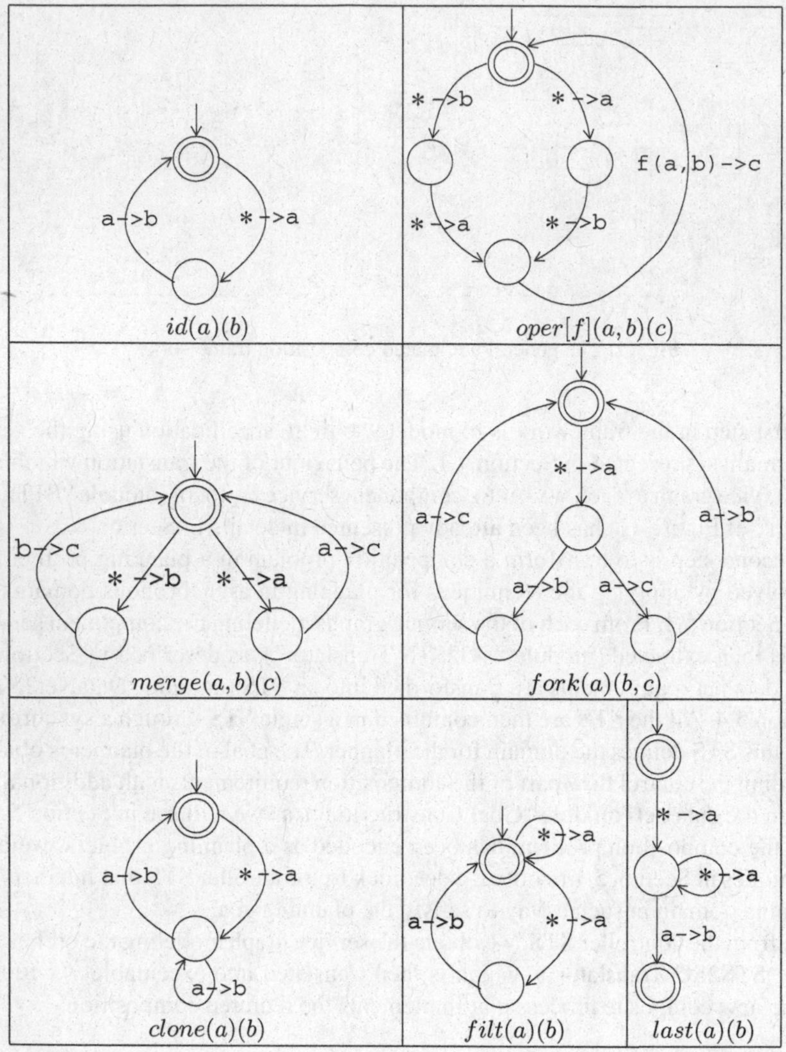

– *$\mathcal{I}$ is the set of input actions $\overleftarrow{\mu}(\bar{x})$ s. t. $\overleftarrow{\mu}(\bar{y}) \in \mathcal{A}$ and $x_1, \ldots, x_n \in \mathcal{V}^c$;*
– *$\mathcal{O}$ is the set of output actions $\overrightarrow{\mu}(\bar{x})$ s. t. $\overrightarrow{\mu}(\bar{y}) \in \mathcal{A}$ and $x_1, \ldots, x_n \in \mathcal{V}^c$;*
– *$\mathcal{R}$ is the transition relation defined as follows:*
  - $(l, \overrightarrow{\mu}(\bar{x}), l') \in \mathcal{R}$ *if* $(l, true, \overrightarrow{\mu}(\bar{y}), \emptyset, l') \in T$;
  - $(l, \overleftarrow{\mu}(\bar{x}), l') \in \mathcal{R}$ *if* $(l, true, \overleftarrow{\mu}(\bar{y}), \emptyset, l') \in T$;
  - $(l, \tau, l') \in \mathcal{R}$ *if* $(l, \phi, \tau, \bar{\omega}, l') \in T$;
  - *no other transition belong to* $\mathcal{R}$.

Intuitively, input actions of the STS represent messages received by the component service, output actions are messages sent by the component service, internal τ actions model non-observable evolutions of the component service, and the transition relation models the internal evolution of the service.

5.4 Data Nets as STS

As we have seen in previous sections, a data net $\mathcal{D}$ of a particular composition problem specifies how messages received from the component services can be used by the new composite process to obtain outgoing messages. Therefore, the idea of representing $\mathcal{D}$ as an STS $\Sigma_{\mathcal{D}}$, which models the allowed data flow actions (constraining the possible operations that the composite process can perform on its variables), is quite intuitive.

In particular, input actions in this STS represent messages received by the component services, output actions represent messages sent by the component services and internal actions represent assignments that the composite process performs on its internal variables. Variables associated to external connection nodes are those used by the new composite process to store received messages and to prepare the messages to be sent, while variables associated to internal connection nodes are those used to manipulate messages by means of internal functions and assignments.

A nice feature of our approach is that the encoding of the data net $\mathcal{D}$ can be done compositionally, i.e., a "small" automaton can be associated to each hyperarc of the data net, and the STS $\Sigma_{\mathcal{D}}$ is obtained as the synchronized product of all these small automata.

Table 3 shows the STS defined for each data-flow element of the data net. We use `* -> a` to denote all the operations that affect the value of variable a. So for instance, if a is an input node modeling the variable used to store a part of message $\overrightarrow{\mu}(\bar{x})$, then `* -> a` is instantied with action $\overrightarrow{\mu}(\bar{x})$; if a is an internal node, then `* -> a` denotes all internal actions copying any variable/expression x to variable a. Finally, accepting states are marked with an internal circle.

Example 13. Consider for instance the identity arc of the data net in Figure 10 connecting the input node C.request.date to the output node F.request.date. Its resulting STS encoding is the following:

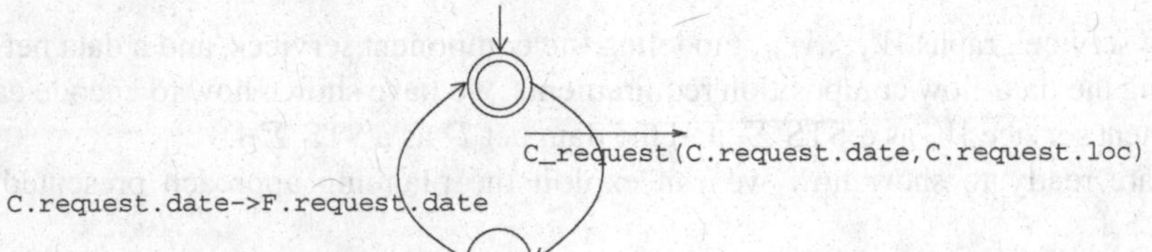

Moreover, for each output node of the data net connected to some data net element, we define a STS modeling the fact that the corresponding message can be sent only if the message part has been properly assigned.

Example 14. For the external output node F.request.date of the data net in Figure 10 we define the following STS:

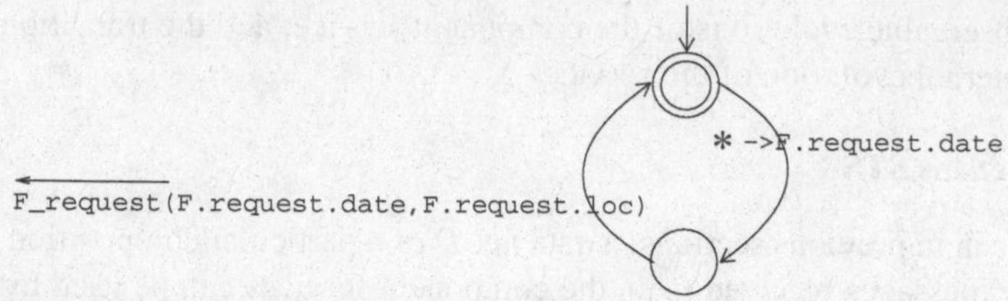

The STS $\Sigma_{\mathcal{D}}$, modeling the data net $\mathcal{D}$, is the synchronized product of all the STSs corresponding to connected output nodes and to data-flow elements of $\mathcal{D}$. As formally stated by the following definition, the synchronized product $\Sigma_1 \parallel \Sigma_2$ models the fact that the systems Σ_1 and Σ_2 evolve simultaneously on common actions and independently on actions belonging to a single system.

Definition 22 (STS Synchronized Product)
Let $\Sigma_1 = \langle \mathcal{S}_1, \mathcal{S}_1^0, \mathcal{I}_1, \mathcal{O}_1, \mathcal{A}_1, \mathcal{R}_1, \mathcal{L}_1 \rangle$ *and* $\Sigma_2 = \langle \mathcal{S}_2, \mathcal{S}_2^0, \mathcal{I}_2, \mathcal{O}_2, \mathcal{A}_2, \mathcal{R}_2, \mathcal{L}_1 \rangle$ *be two state transition systems s.t.* $(\mathcal{I}_1 \cup \mathcal{I}_2) \cap (\mathcal{O}_1 \cup \mathcal{O}_2) \cap (\mathcal{A}_1 \cup \mathcal{A}_2) = \emptyset$.
Their synchronized product $\Sigma_1 \parallel \Sigma_2$ *is defined as:*

$$\Sigma_1 \parallel \Sigma_2 = \langle \mathcal{S}_1 \times \mathcal{S}_2, \mathcal{S}_1^0 \times \mathcal{S}_2^0, \mathcal{I}_1 \cup \mathcal{I}_2, \mathcal{O}_1 \cup \mathcal{O}_2, \mathcal{A}_1 \cup \mathcal{A}_2, \mathcal{R}_1 \parallel \mathcal{R}_2, \mathcal{L}_1 \parallel \mathcal{L}_2 \rangle$$

where:

- $\langle (s_1, s_2), a, (s_1', s_2') \rangle \in \mathcal{R}_1 \parallel \mathcal{R}_2$ *iff* $\langle s_1, a, s_1' \rangle \in \mathcal{R}_1$ *and* $\langle s_2, a, s_2' \rangle \in \mathcal{R}_2$;
- $\langle (s_1, s_2), a, (s_1', s_2) \rangle \in \mathcal{R}_1 \parallel \mathcal{R}_2$ *iff* $\langle s_1, a, s_1' \rangle \in \mathcal{R}_1$ *and* $a \notin A_2$;
- $\langle (s_1, s_2), a, (s_1, s_2') \rangle \in \mathcal{R}_1 \parallel \mathcal{R}_2$ *iff* $\langle s_2, a, s_2' \rangle \in \mathcal{R}_2$ *and* $a \notin A_1$;
- $\mathcal{L}_1 \parallel \mathcal{L}_2$ *is the labeling function associating to each state* (s_1, s_2) *the corresponding set of propositions* $\mathcal{L}_1(s_1) \cup \mathcal{L}_2(s_2)$.

Let $s = (s_1, \ldots, s_n)$ be a state of the STS $\Sigma = \Sigma_1 \parallel \ldots \parallel \Sigma_n$, we denote with $s[\Sigma_i]$ the function returning the state s_i of Σ_i in s. A state $s = (s_1, \ldots, s_n)$ of the STS $\Sigma_{\mathcal{D}}$ is an *accepting state* of $\Sigma_{\mathcal{D}}$ if each state $s[\Sigma_i]$ is an accepting state of the STS Σ_i.

5.5 Generating the Composite Service

Given n service graphs $W_1, ..W_n$, modeling the component services, and a data net $\mathcal{D}$, modeling the data-flow composition requirements, we have shown how to encode each component service W_i as a STS Σ_i and the data net $\mathcal{D}$ as a STS $\Sigma_{\mathcal{D}}$.

We are ready to show how we can exploit the planning approach presented in Section 5.1.

The planning domain Σ for the automated composition problem is the synchronized product of all these STSs. Formally, $\Sigma = \Sigma_{\mathcal{D}} \parallel \Sigma_1 \parallel .. \parallel \Sigma_n$. The planning goal ρ is the formalization of the composition termination requirements as a reachability goal (see Section 4.4). We enrich ρ by requiring that the STS $\Sigma_{\mathcal{D}}$ encoding the data net is in an accepting state.

Given the domain Σ and the planning goal ρ we can apply the approach recalled in Section 5.1, to generate a controller Σ_c, which is such that $\Sigma_c \triangleright \Sigma \models \rho$.

The final step is to extract a service graph W^c corresponding to the controller of the composition.

From the data net $\mathcal{D} = \langle\langle N, E\rangle, \mathcal{T}, \mathcal{F}, \mathcal{L}_T, \mathcal{L}_F\rangle$ we directly obtain the ground context of the controller $\mathcal{C}^c = \langle\mathcal{T}^c, \mathcal{V}^c, \mathcal{F}^c\rangle$, where $\mathcal{T}^c = \mathcal{T}$, $\mathcal{V}^c = N$, and $\mathcal{F}^c = \mathcal{F}$. The other elements of the service graph are obtained from Σ_c. The behavior of the synthesized controller Σ_c is structured and complex, but its elementary actions model communication with the component services (sending and receiving of messages) and manipulation of goal variables through assignments; given this, it is straightforward to obtain the service graph W^c.

Definition 23 (Obtaining the data net controller service graph)
Let $\Sigma_c = \langle\mathcal{S}_c, \mathcal{S}_c^0, \mathcal{I}, \mathcal{O}, \mathcal{A}, \mathcal{R}_c, \mathcal{L}_\emptyset\rangle$ be a solution for a planning domain Σ and a planning goal ρ, and let $\mathcal{C}^c = \langle\mathcal{T}^c, \mathcal{V}^c, \mathcal{F}^c\rangle$ be the ground context of the controller. The corresponding orchestrator service graph $W^c = \langle L^c, L_0^c, \mathcal{C}^c, \mathcal{A}^c, T^c\rangle$ is obtained as follows:

- *L^c is the set of all controller states ($L^c = \mathcal{S}_c$) and L_0^c is the set of initial states ($L_0^c = \mathcal{S}_c^0$);*
- *$\mathcal{A}^c = \mathcal{I} \cup \mathcal{O} \cup \{\tau\}$*
- *T^c is the transition relation defined as follows:*
  - $(s, true, \overleftarrow{\mu}(\bar{x}), \emptyset, s') \in T^c$ *if* $(s, \overleftarrow{\mu}(\bar{x}), s') \in \mathcal{R}_c$
  - $(s, true, \overrightarrow{\mu}(\bar{x}), \emptyset, s') \in T^c$ *if* $(s, \overrightarrow{\mu}(\bar{x}), s') \in \mathcal{R}_c$
  - $(s, true, \tau, (x := t), s') \in T^c$ *if* $(s, t \texttt{->} x, s') \in \mathcal{R}_c$
  - $(s, true, \tau, \emptyset, s') \in T^c$ *if* $(s, \tau, s') \in \mathcal{R}_c$
  - *no other transition belongs to T^c.*

In the following we state the correctness of the proposed approach. In particular, we will show that the controller service graph W^c, modeling the new executable composite service, satisfies the data flow requirements in $\mathcal{D}$. To do so, according to Definition 15, we have to prove that each execution of $W^c \triangleright W^1, \ldots, W^n$ is an accepting executions of $\mathcal{D}$.

Theorem 1 (Correctness of the Data Net Approach)
Let W^c be the solution for the composition problem with set of service graphs $W^1, \ldots, W^n$, control requirements r_c and datanet $\mathcal{D} = \langle\langle N, E\rangle, \mathcal{T}, \mathcal{F}, \mathcal{L}_T, \mathcal{L}_F\rangle$. Then:

1. *W^c is deadlock free for $W^1, \ldots, W^n$;*
2. *$W^c \triangleright W^1, \ldots, W^n \models r_c$; and*
3. *$W^c \triangleright W^1, \ldots, W^n \overset{DN}{\models} \mathcal{D}$.*

The proof of this theorem can be found in [53].

6 The ASTRO WS-Compose Tool

The automated composition techniques and approaches presented in previous section were implemented as a prototype toolkit, namely WS-Compose. The toolkit was realized within the project ASTRO [9] and is available as part of the ASTRO Toolset.

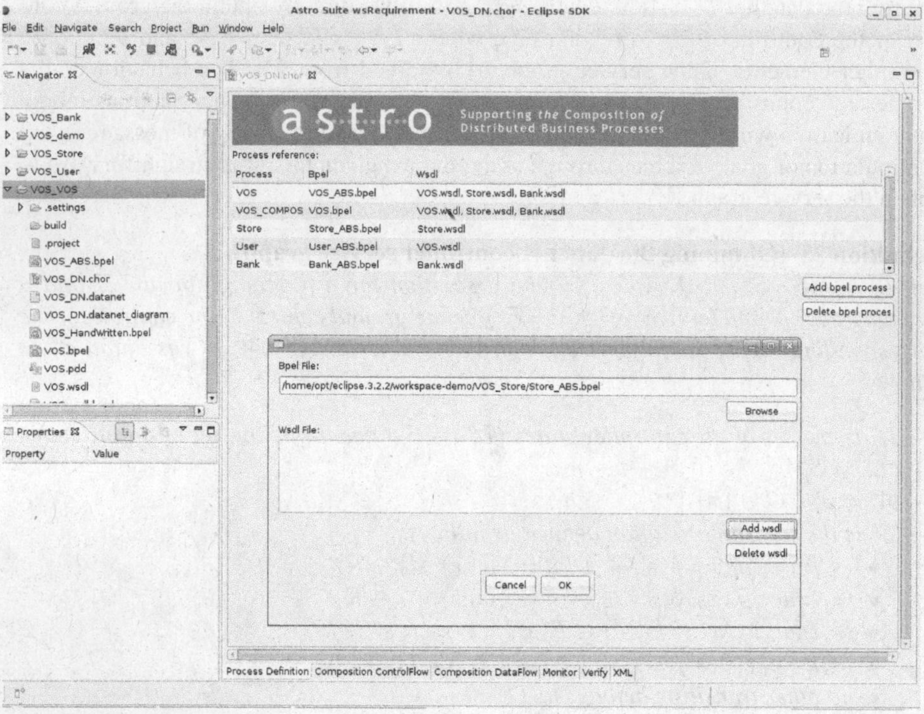

Fig. 12. WS-Req: Selection of the Component Services

The toolset has been designed as an extension of ActiveBPEL WebFlow Designer [33], a commercial software for designing and developing WS-BPEL processes which is based on the Eclipse platform. ActiveBPEL Designer also provides an open-source WS-BPEL execution engine, called ActiveBPEL [1]. Thanks to its integration within Active WebFlow, the advanced functionalities of the ASTRO Toolset can be combined with the "standard" functionalities provided by Active WebFlow; thus it is possible to inspect WS-BPEL code, write or modify business processes, deploy them and execute them. This way, the ASTRO Toolset is an integral part of the life cycle of business process design and execution.

The ASTRO Toolset covers several aspects of the Web service composition process by providing tools and techniques supporting the analyst in the different phases: tools that allow for detecting problems at design time (WS-Verify), tools supporting the automated synthesis of new services (WS-Compose), and tools that allow to detect conditions or violation of properties at run-time (WS-Mon).

For what concerns the automated synthesis of new services, WS-Compose supports all the phases of Web service automated composition: from the specification of control-flow and data-flow requirements by means of graphical tools for drawing data net diagrams and specifying control-flow requirements (WS-Req), to the automatic synthesis of the desired service (WS-Synth), to the deployment, simulation (WS-Animator), and execution of the new composite service.

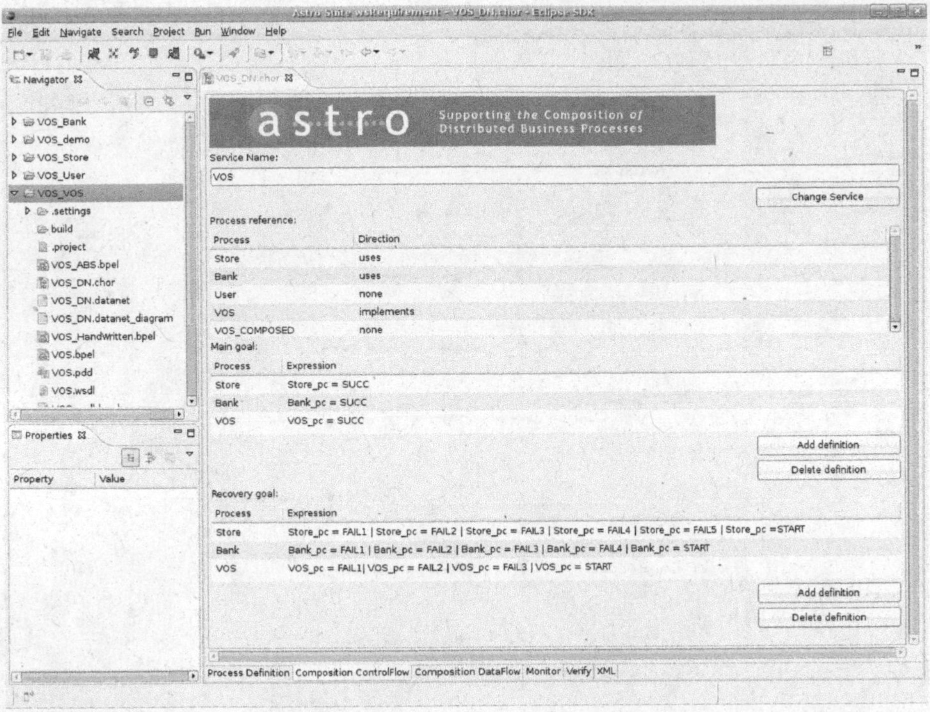

Fig. 13. WS-Req: Specification of Control Flow Requirements

In the rest of this Section we describe a nominal execution of WS-Compose and then explain in details the WS-Synth tool. For further details on the other tools of the ASTRO Toolset, please refer to the project official Web site [9].

6.1 WS-Compose: A Nominal Execution

In the following we describe the phases of a typical execution of the WS-Compose tool:

1. The user, through the WS-Req front-end integrated within Active WebFlow, selects the projects that participate to the composition (see Figure 12). These projects contain the WSDL and abstract WS-BPEL files describing the interfaces of the component Web services. The information necessary to retrieve these WSDL and WS-BPEL description is added to a file defining the composition problem (choreography file).
2. The developer defines the control flow composition requirements (termination conditions and transactional issues) through an intuitive tabular notation provided by the WS-Req front-end (see Figure 13).
3. Then the data net diagram is drawn through the data net editor provided by WS-Req (see Figure 14). The editor shows the input/output ports (message parts) of

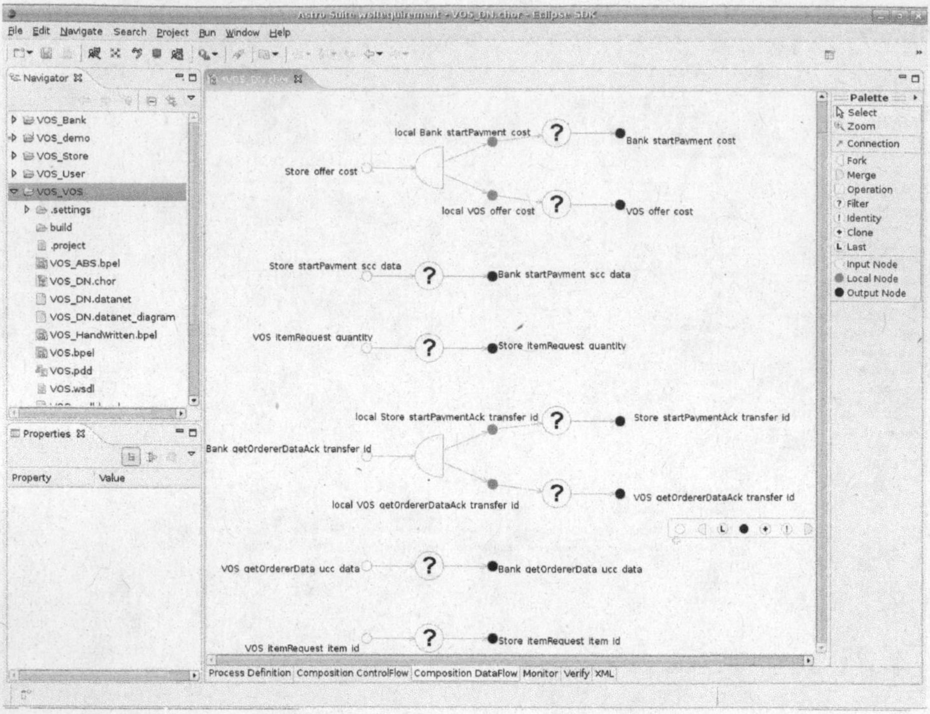

Fig. 14. WS-Req: Specification of Data Flow Requirements

the existing services and allows to connect them through data net arcs in order to define the routes ad manipulation of data within the composition.

4. WS-Synth is invoked and the front-end presents some information about the generation procedure (see Figure 15). The composed process has already been deployed on the ActiveBPEL engine.
5. To test the generated service it is possible to use WS-Animator (see Figure 16). This tool simulates the execution of the component services, while the composite process is executed on the engine. This configuration gives the possibility to test all the execution paths (failures, exceptions, ..) of the generated service controlling the execution of the partner processes.
6. The developer, on the basis of the test results and of the inspection of the new process code, can modify and gradually refine composition requirements (WS-Req) and automatically re-generate the composite service (WS-Synth).

As can be noticed from the presented execution scenario, although solving an automated composition problem involves several different modules and tools, thanks to the integration of the ASTRO Toolset within Active WebFlow, this is completely hidden to the developer, that perceives the whole process as a continuous and natural sequence of steps.

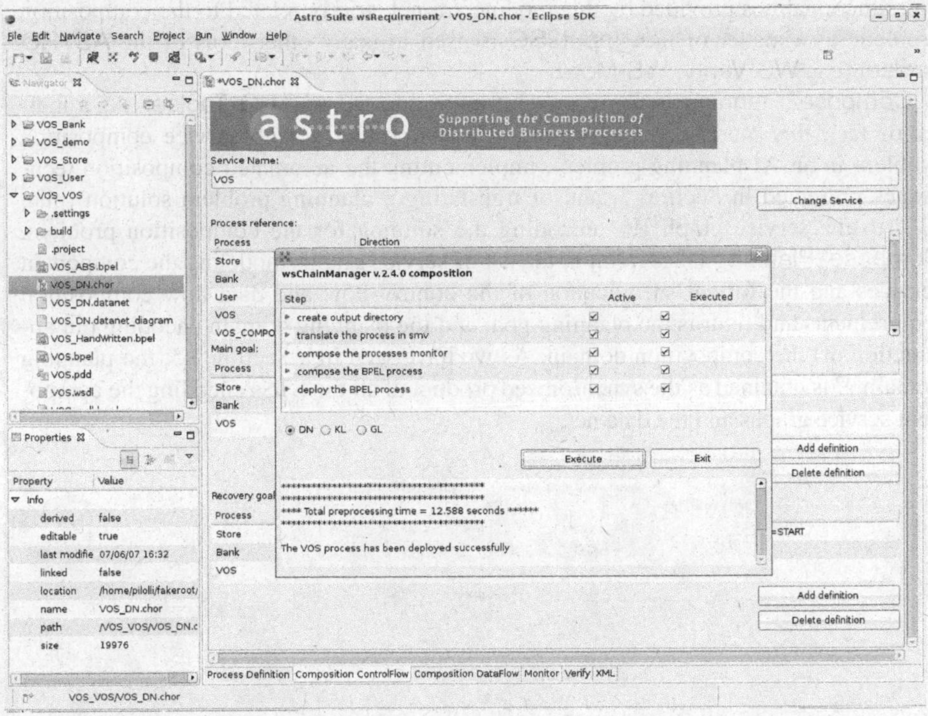

Fig. 15. WS-Synth: Generating the Composite Service

6.2 WS-Synth: An Overview of the Tool

WS-Synth is implemented as a Java API and extends the facilities of the ASTRO Toolset with the automated synthesis techniques presented in this paper.

WS-Synth takes in input a set of files describing the component Web services, and the files specifying control flow and data flow requirements and return as output the implementation of the composite service that is a solution of the composition problem.

As can be seen from Figure 17, the WS-Synth tool consists of four modules: a module responsible of the translation from WSDL and WS-BPEL specifications to service graph specifications (Input2SG), a module whose aim is to obtain the planning problem from the composition problem (Compose2Planning), a module responsible of solving planning problems in asynchronous domains (Planner), and a module (Controller) that coordinates the execution of the other modules according to the kind of composition problem to be solved.

Input2SG provides functionalities for translating service descriptions in standard languages to the service graphs internal notation, and vice-versa. The module supports different input languages, among which the standard WSDL and WS-BPEL description languages that we use in the Web service automated composition problem. The description of the translation that associates a service graph to each component service, starting from its WSDL and abstract WS-BPEL specification can be found in Section 4.2.

The functionalities provided by this module are not strictly related to the composition problem, as a matter of fact, Input2SG is used in many other tools of the ASTRO Toolset (e.g. WS-Verify, WS-Mon).

Compose2Planning is the main contribution to the ASTRO Toolset. As a matter of fact, this module is responsible of transforming a Web service composition problem in an AI planning problem, implementing the automated composition techniques presented in Section 5, and of translating a planning problem solution (plan Σ_C) to the service graph W_C encoding the solution for the composition problem. Compose2Planning takes in input the set of service graphs modeling the component services and the formal specification of the control flow and data flow composition requirements and returns the planning goal and the planning domain encoding (an abstraction of) the composition domain. As we have seen in a Section 5.5, the planning domain Σ is obtained as the synchronized product of all the STSs encoding the component service graphs and the data net.

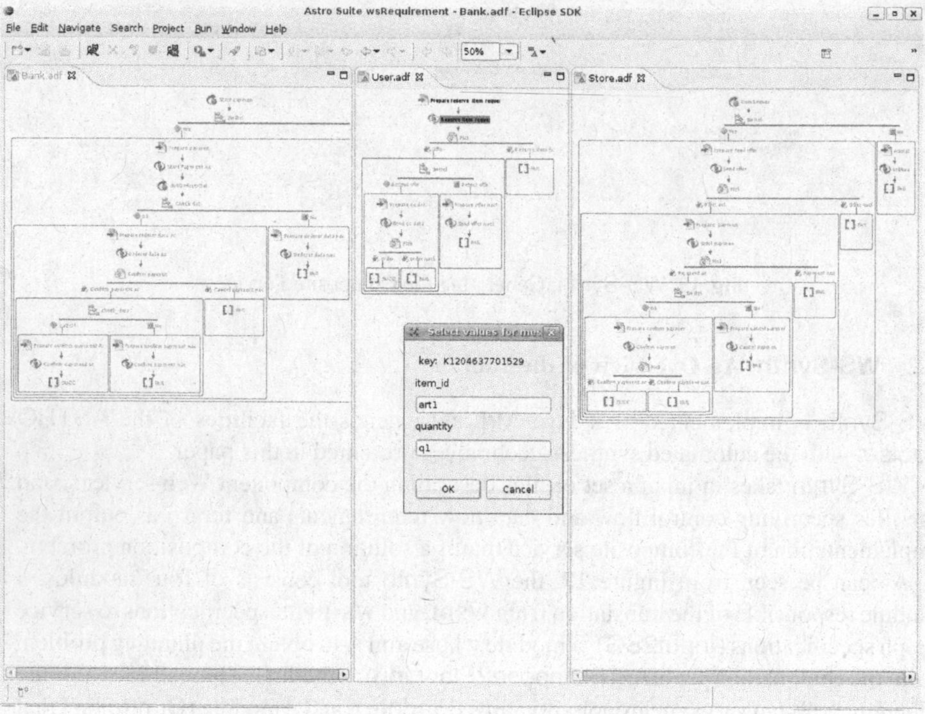

Fig. 16. WS-Animator: Simulating and Testing the Composition

Finally, the Planner module implements the AI planning algorithms described in [68] that are able to work in non-deterministic, partially observable, asynchronous domains by properly extending MBP (Model Based Planner) ([20]), an efficient planner based on planning as symbolic model checking techniques.

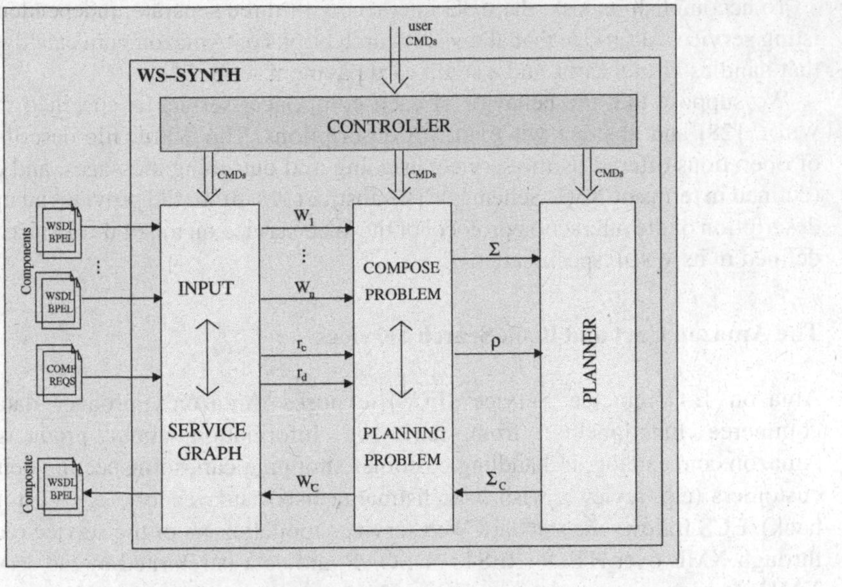

Fig. 17. The logical architecture of the WS-Synth tool

7 The Amazon-MPS Case Study

In this section we evaluate the feasibility and efficiency of the proposed approach to automating the composition task on a real scenario that entails a high level of complexity (see also [51,52]).

The considered scenario requires the composition of two real services, namely the Amazon E-Commerce Services [4] and the e-payment service offered by Banks of Monte dei Paschi di Siena Group (MPS), an important Italian financial Group (`http://www.mps.it/`). The goal of the composition is to generate an e-Bookstore application that allows to order books and buy them via a secure credit card payment transaction. This composition scenario is particularly challenging since all component services export complex interaction protocols and handle structured data in messages. As a consequence, developing by hand the composite service that orchestrates the components, e.g., in terms of a WS-BPEL process, is a complex, time consuming and error prone task.

7.1 The Amazon-MPS Composition Domain

In this section we analyze in depth the e-Bookstore (eBS) case study. The idea is to automatically synthesize a composite process that allows potential customers to search for books, add them to a virtual cart, checkout the order and monitor the credit card payment process.

To accomplish its task, the eBS interacts with three separate, independent, and existing services: a service that allows to search books on Amazon.com catalog, a service that handles virtual carts, and a credit card payment service [3].

We suppose that the behavior of each component service is specified through its WSDL [28] and abstract WS-BPEL [6] descriptions. The WSDL file describes the set of operations offered by the service, in-going and out-going messages, and data types (defined in terms of XML Schemas). The abstract WS-BPEL file provides an operational description of the interaction protocol of the Web service on top of the service interfaces defined in its WSDL specifications.

The Amazon Cart and Book Search Services

Amazon E-Commerce Service (ECS) exposes Amazon's product data and e-commerce functionality: from retrieving information about products in the Amazon.com catalog, to handling customer shopping cart, to inspecting content from customers (e.g. reviews, wish lists, listmania lists) and vendors (e.g. customer feedback). ECS follows the standard Web services model: users of the service request data through XML over HTTP (REST) or SOAP and data is returned by the service as an XML- formatted stream of text. ECS publishes a WSDL document [3] that defines all the available ECS operations, their messages, and the data structure of each message. Together with the WSDL description, Amazon provides several documents (see e.g. [4]) describing in details how to submit requests to ECS and the data that is returned by the service, as well as how to handle errors.

As one can see from its WSDL description, all ECS operations are synchronous atomic (request-response) Web service invocations. However, in order to actually work, these operations must be invoked in a precise sequence of steps. In practice, they belong to specific business workflows. In the Amazon ECS Developer Guide [4] these workflows are described informally.

For instance, the shopping cart flow, as well as other workflows, is described using natural language and flow charts. If we consider the description of the shopping cart workflow (see Figure 18), we have that first of all the cart must be created, then other items can be added to the cart, and finally the shopping cart can be checked out. The informal picture in Figure 18 describes only the workflow in its nominal case, while other operations are provided to modify the cart and get or clear its content.

In order to make the workflow explicit and formally defined, we modeled the abstract WS-BPEL specification of the Amazon Book-Search (ABS) and the Amazon Virtual-Cart (AVC) services starting from the descriptions in [4]. Both component services are specified on top of the original Amazon ECS WSDL specification. In order to precisely model the workflows we introduced asynchronicity in the operations: our component services implement for each ECS operation two callback operations modeling the sending of the

---

[3] Amazon allows on-line vendors to expose Amazon products and manage shopping carts. When the customer checkout the order, the vendor simply transfer the shopping cart to Amazon to complete the sale transaction. We decided to introduce an external bank handling the payment procedure to make the scenario more flexible (e.g. by providing alternative payment methods such as bank transfers with safe completion).

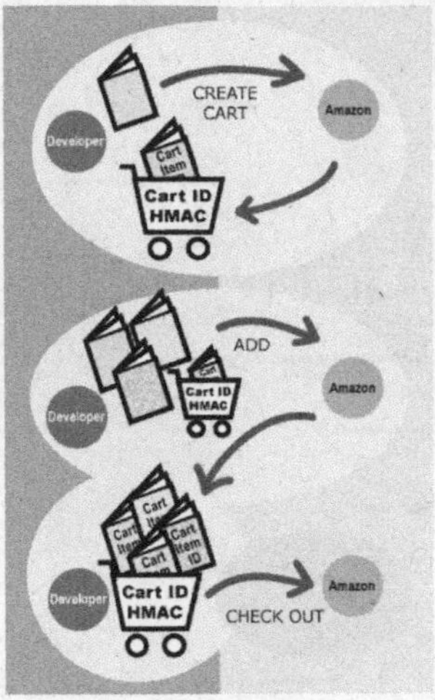

Fig. 18. The workflow of the Amazon Virtual Cart service (taken from [4])

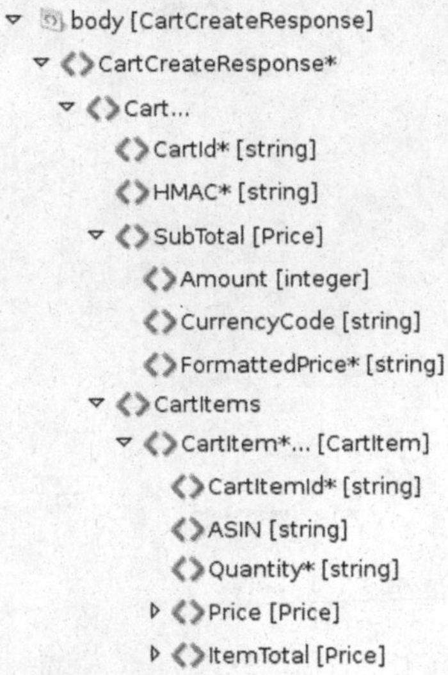

Fig. 19. The internal data structure of message cartCreateResp in the Amazon Virtual Cart service

operation result (in case of a successful interaction with ECS) or the sending of an error message. The structure of the messages and their complexity are preserved.

In the following examples we show in details the obtained abstract WS-BPEL specifications of the AVC and ABS services.

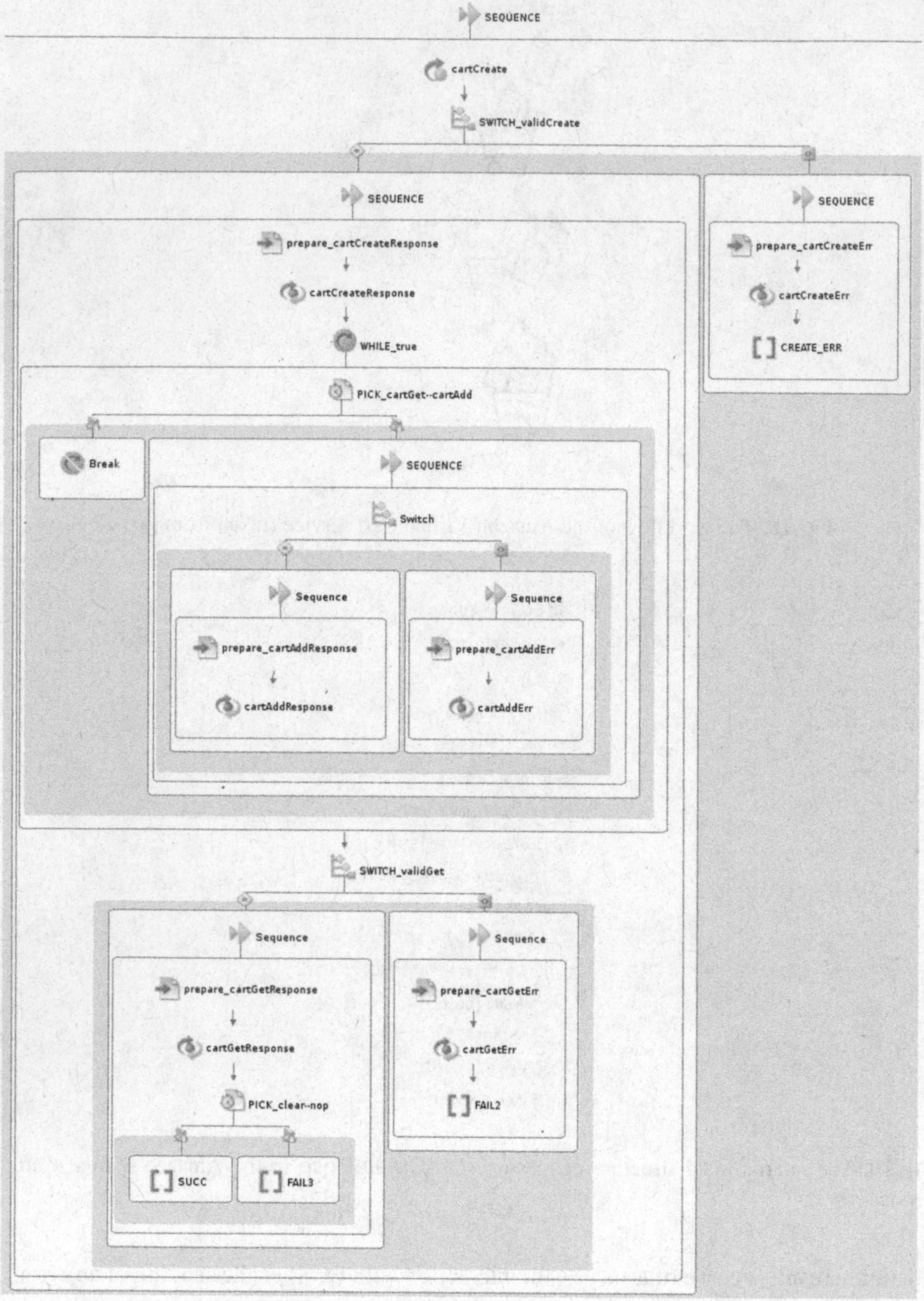

Fig. 20. The Amazon Virtual Cart abstract WS-BPEL description

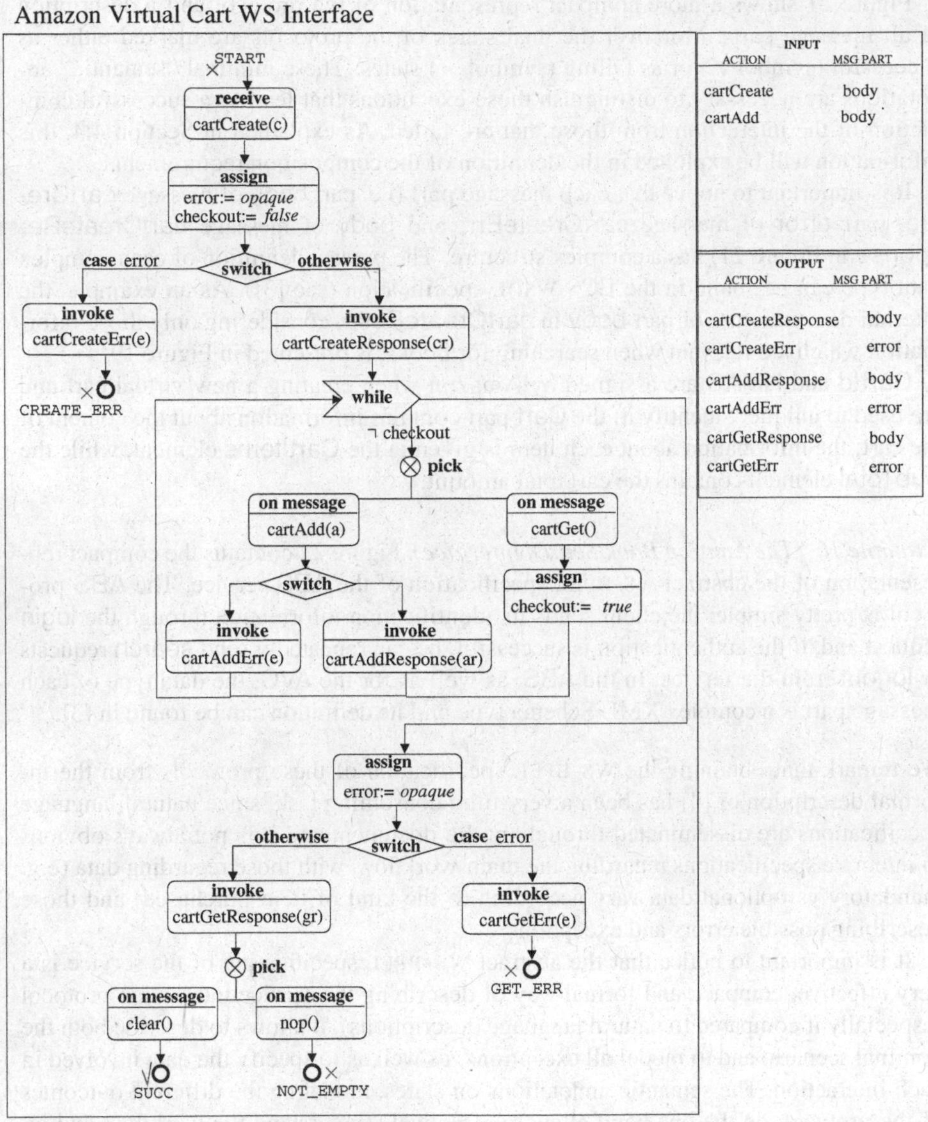

Fig. 21. The Amazon Virtual Cart service

Example 15 (The Amazon Virtual Cart interface). Figure 20 represents the graphical view in ActiveBPEL Designer [33] of the abstract WS-BPEL protocol of the AVC. According to this process, once the AVC receives a request to create a new cart and the operation is successful, the client can start to add items and eventually checkout its shopping cart. If the checkout is successful, the client can either clear the cart or keep its content for future use. In all these interactions if something goes wrong the AVC sends an error message describing the reason of the fault.

Figure 21 shows a more compact representation of the protocol and a description of all message parts. Moreover the final states of the protocols are marked either as successful (symbol ✓) or as failing (symbol ×) states. These minimal "semantic" annotations are necessary to distinguish those executions that lead to a successful completion of the interaction from those that are failed. As explained in Section 4.4, this information will be exploited in the definition of the composition requirements.

It is important to notice that each message part (i.e. part body of message cartCreate, part error of message cartCreateErr, and body of message cartCreateResponse in Figure 21) has a complex structure. The precise definition of each complex data type can be found in the ECS WSDL specification (see [3]). As an example, the internal data structure of part body in cartCreateResp, considering only those information which are relevant when searching for books, is presented in Figure 19.

CartId and HMAC are assigned by Amazon when creating a new virtual cart and are used to uniquely identify it; the Cart part contains information about the content of the cart: the information about each item is given in the CartItems element, while the SubTotal element contains the cart total amount.

Example 16 (The Amazon Book Search interface). Figure 22 contains the compact representation of the abstract WS-BPEL specification of the ABS service. The ABS protocol is pretty simple: the client sends its identification information through the login request and, if the authentication is successful, he can repeatedly send search requests or logout from the service. In the ABS, as well as for the AVC, the data type of each message part is a complex XML Schema type and its definition can be found in [3].

We remark that obtaining the WS-BPEL specification of these protocols from the informal description of [4] has been a very time consuming task, since natural language specifications are disseminated throughout the document and it is not always obvious to integrate specifications regarding the main workflow, with those regarding data (e.g. mandatory vs optional data vary according to the kind of item purchased) and those describing possible errors and exceptions.

It is important to notice that the abstract WS-BPEL specification of the service is a very effective, compact, and formal way of describing the service interaction protocol (especially if compared to natural language descriptions). It allows to describe both the nominal scenario and to model all exceptions, as well as to specify the data involved in each interaction. The semantic annotations on states, modeling the different outcomes of the protocol, on the one hand allow to effectively understand the workflow and on the other hand to apply automated techniques.

The MPS Virtual POS Service

The Virtual Point of Sale service (VPOS) models a real on-line payment procedure offered by an Italian bank (Monte dei Paschi di Siena). Such a process handles several possible failures: it checks both the validity of the target bank account (the e-Bookstore's one in our case), the validity of the credit card on international circuits, the credit capacity and limits, and so on. The next example describes the interaction protocol that the VPOS expects online shops to follow when using the service.

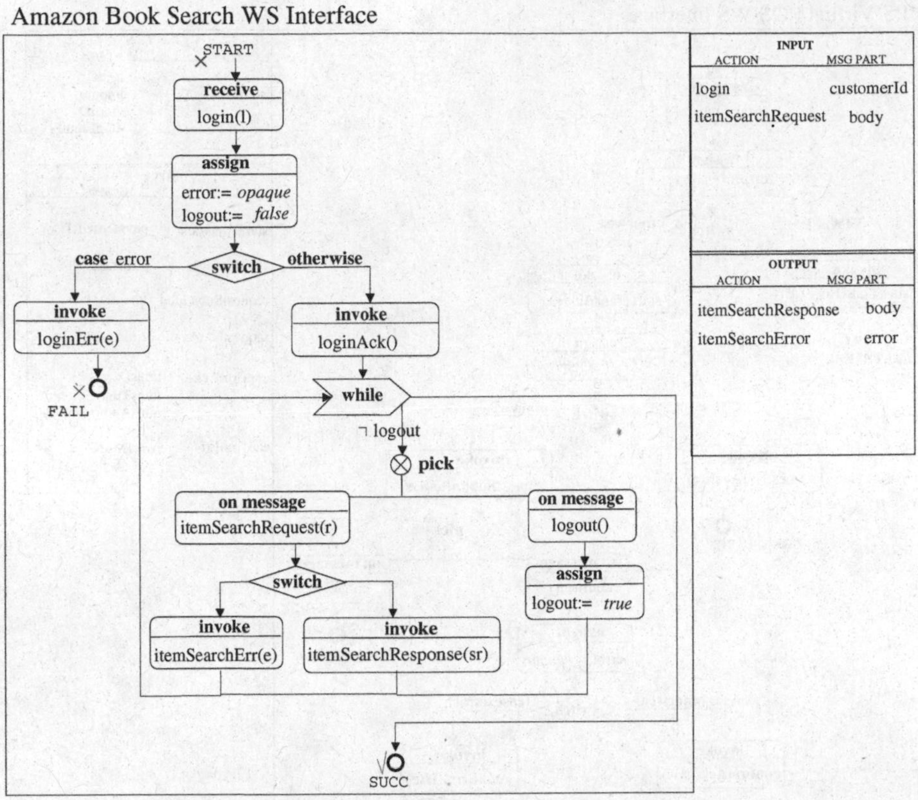

Fig. 22. The Amazon Book Search service

Example 17 (The Virtual POS interface) When the VPOS receives the request to start a new payment procedure, it checks the correctness of the request (identity of the online shop) and either sends an error message or a message carrying the information about the URL (part paymentURL of message startTransactionAck) that the shop must communicate to its customer. This information will be used by the customer to communicate its payment data (identification information and credit card number) directly to the bank. Notice that this protocol is such that the online shop never has direct information on the customer sensitive data.

Once the interaction between the bank and the customer has occurred, the VPOS notifies the online shop the outcome. At this point, the online shop can either confirm or cancel the payment transaction. If confirmed, the transaction is executed by the bank and the outcome (carrying all transaction details if successful) is sent to the online shop.

The e-Bookstore Customer Interface

In addition to the descriptions of the two Amazon services and of the MPS service, we need to define as input to the composition problem the interaction protocol that the eBS exposes to its customers.

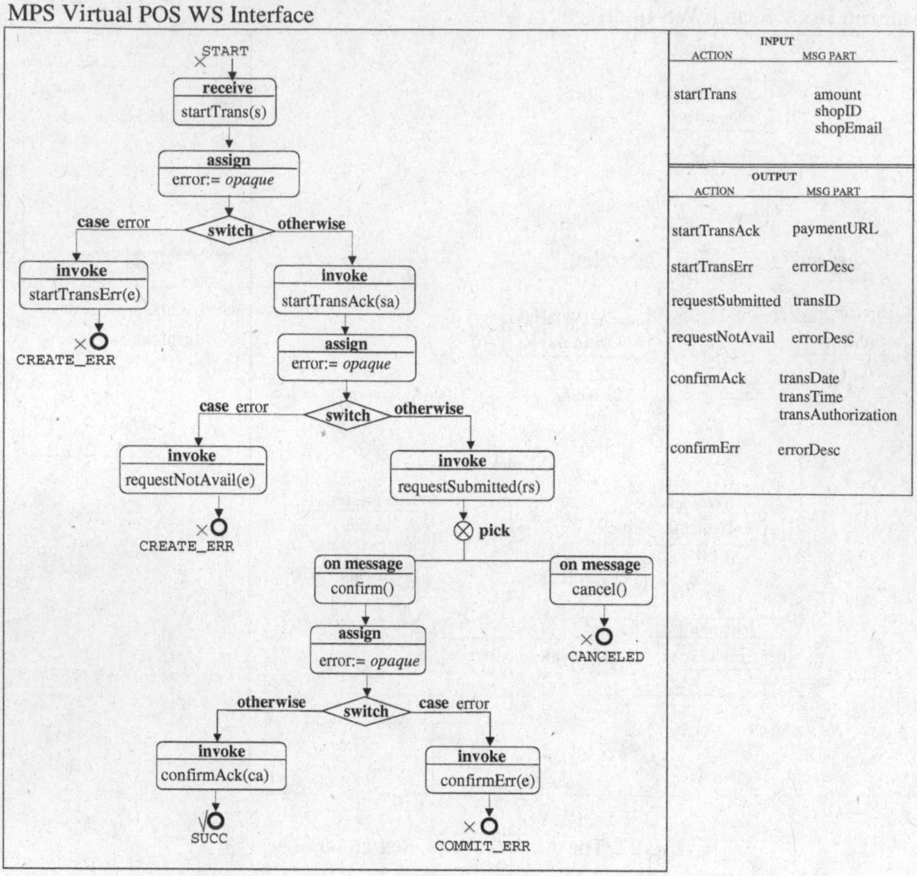

Fig. 23. The Virtual POS service

Example 18 (The e-Bookstore customer interface). As a first step (see Figure 24), the customer is required to login using its unique identification code. Once his identity has been verified, he can start interacting with the eBS searching for book offers and adding them to his virtual cart. The search can be done using a combination of different parameters: the book title, author, publisher, and/or some keywords. If the search is successful, the customer gets a message carrying all the information about the offer (e.g. book title, author, publisher, ISBN, offer price, the offer identification code ASIN, the detailPageURL where he can see further details, etc.), otherwise he receives an error message describing the fault (e.g. no results matching his search, unavailability of the book in the warehouse, etc.). The operations the customer can perform with his virtual cart are pretty limited: he can add new items to the cart, specifying the item ASIN and the quantity, or checkout the shopping cart to conclude the order. After sending an add request, the customer either gets a message carrying the information about the total price of the items in the cart (subTotal) or an error message. Similarly, when he sends a checkout request he can either receive the information about the total amount of

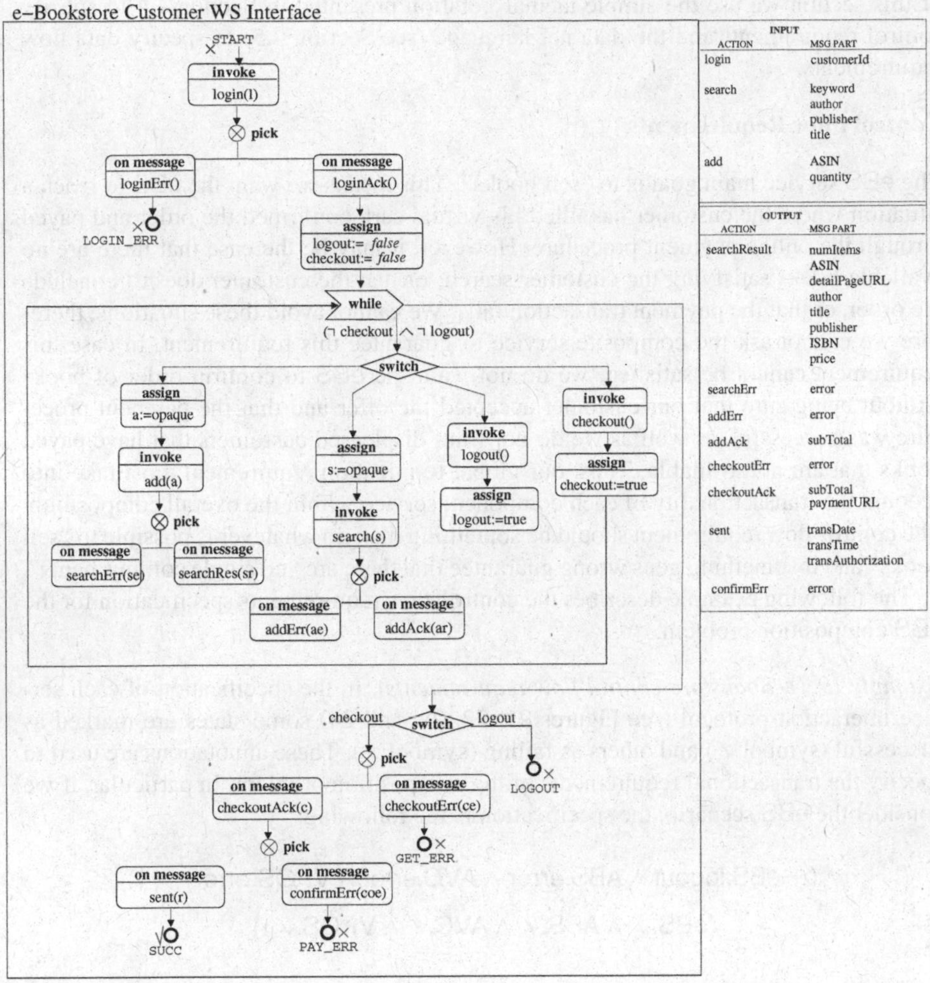

Fig. 24. The e-Bookstore customer interface

the order (subTotal) and an URL to visit to conclude the payment (paymentURL), or a message describing the error. Finally, when the customer attests the payment by sending the transaction information (transID), the e-Bookstore can either send a confirmation of the order, carrying all the details of the payment transaction, or an error message.

7.2 The Amazon-MPS Composition Requirements

Given the description (i.e. the WSDL and abstract WS-BPEL) of the component services (ABS, AVC, and VPOS) and of the customer interface (eBS), the next step is the formal specification of the composition requirements. As we will see in the rest of this section we use the simple tabular notation presented in Section 4.4 to specify control requirements and the data net language (see Section 4.5) to specify data flow requirements.

Control Flow Requirements

The eBS service main goal is to "sell books". This means we want the eBS to reach a situation where the customer has filled his virtual cart, confirmed the order and payed through the online payment procedure. However, it may be the case that there are no available books satisfying the customer search, or that the customer doesn't conclude the order, or that the payment transaction fails. We cannot avoid these situations, therefore we cannot ask the composite service to guarantee this requirement. In case this requirement cannot be satisfied, we do not want the eBS to confirm order of books without being sure that our customer accepted the offer and that the payment procedure was successful, as well as we do not want displeased customers that have payed books that are not available. Thus, our global termination requirement must take into account the transactionality of each component service within the overall composition. The control-flow requirement should be something like: do whatever is possible to "sell books" and if something goes wrong guarantee that there are "no single commitments".

The following example describes the control-flow requirements specification for the eBS composition problem.

Example 19 (e-Bookstore control-flow requirements). In the specification of each service interaction protocol (see Figures 21, 22, 23, and 24) some states are marked as successful (symbol ✓) and others as failing (symbol $\times$). These annotations are used to specify the transactional requirements of the composition problem. In particular, if we consider the eBS scenario, the specification is the following:

$$((\neg \text{eBS.logout} \wedge \text{ABS.error} \wedge \text{AVC.error} \wedge \text{VPOS.error}) \rightarrow$$
$$(\text{eBS.}\checkmark \wedge \text{ABS.}\checkmark \wedge \text{AVC.}\checkmark \wedge \text{VPOS.}\checkmark))$$
$$\wedge$$
$$(NOT(\neg \text{eBS.logout} \wedge \text{ABS.error} \wedge \text{AVC.error} \wedge \text{VPOS.error}) \rightarrow$$
$$(\text{eBS.}\times \wedge (\text{ABS.}\checkmark \vee \text{ABS.}\times) \wedge \text{AVC.}\times \wedge \text{VPOS.}\times))$$

Where eBS.✓ stays for eBS.SUCC, and eBS.$\times$ stays for

$$\text{eBS.LOGIN\_ERR} \vee \text{eBS.LOGOUT} \vee \text{eBS.GET\_ERR} \vee \text{eBS.PAY\_ERR}.$$

And similarly for the other components.

Notice that in case of failure of some service the ABS service can either be in a successful or failing state, this depends on the fact that such a service, unlike credit card payment or cart handling, doesn't need transactionality: we do not care whether the search is successful in case of failure of the other services.

Data Flow Requirements

In order to provide consistent information, the eBS service needs to exchange data with the components and its customer in an appropriate way. For instance, when invoking the ABS service, the information about the customer login must be the same ones that the eBS received in the customer login request; similarly, every time the customer sends a search request, the eBS must use the book search information to prepare the itemSearchRequest message for the ABS service. When the customer sends an add request to the eBS, the composite service can either use this information to prepare a cartCreate message (if the a cart hasn't been created yet) or a cartAdd message to be sent to the AVC service. And so on.

The specification of the data net for the e-Bookstore example is presented in Figure 25, which we will (partially) explain in the following example.

Example 20 (e-Bookstore data-flow requirements). When the eBS receives a login request from the customer, it must forward the customerId information to the ABS service. To obtain the body to be sent in the itemSearchRequest to the ABS, the eBS must apply its internal function createItemSearch to manipulate the data received in the search message from the customer. The eBS must obtain the error information that it sends in the searchError message to the customer by computing its internal function getError on the body of the itemSearchError message received from the ABS. The quantity and ASIN information received in the add message from the customer can either be used to prepare the cartCreate message (through the createCartCreate operation) or to prepare the cartAdd message (through the createCartAdd operation) to be sent to the AVC. The eBS exploits the internal functions getShopId to obtain the shopId information in the startTransaction message to be sent to the VPOS (and similarly for the shopEmail data).

Each operation arc in the datanet in Figure 25 refers to an internal function that the new composite service uses to manipulate data. Since our aim is to automatically generate the executable WS-BPEL code implementing the composite service, we require that the specification of each internal function is given as an XPath [19] expression, which is the standard language used in WS-BPEL assignments.

Example 21 (Specifying Internal Functions). Consider for instance the function getSubTotal used in the datanet of Figure 25 to obtain the C.addAck.subTotal message part from the AVC.cartCreateResponse.body part received from the AVC service. The XPath specification of getSubTotal, defining how to obtain the total cost navigating the XML tree structure of part body, is the following:

```
getSubTotal=
  /nsAVC:CartCreateResponse/nsAVC:Cart/
  nsAVC:SubTotal/nsAVC:FormattedPrice
```

Similarly, the function getError, used to obtain the C.searchError.error message part from the ABS.searchErr.body part received from the ABS service, has the following XPath specification:

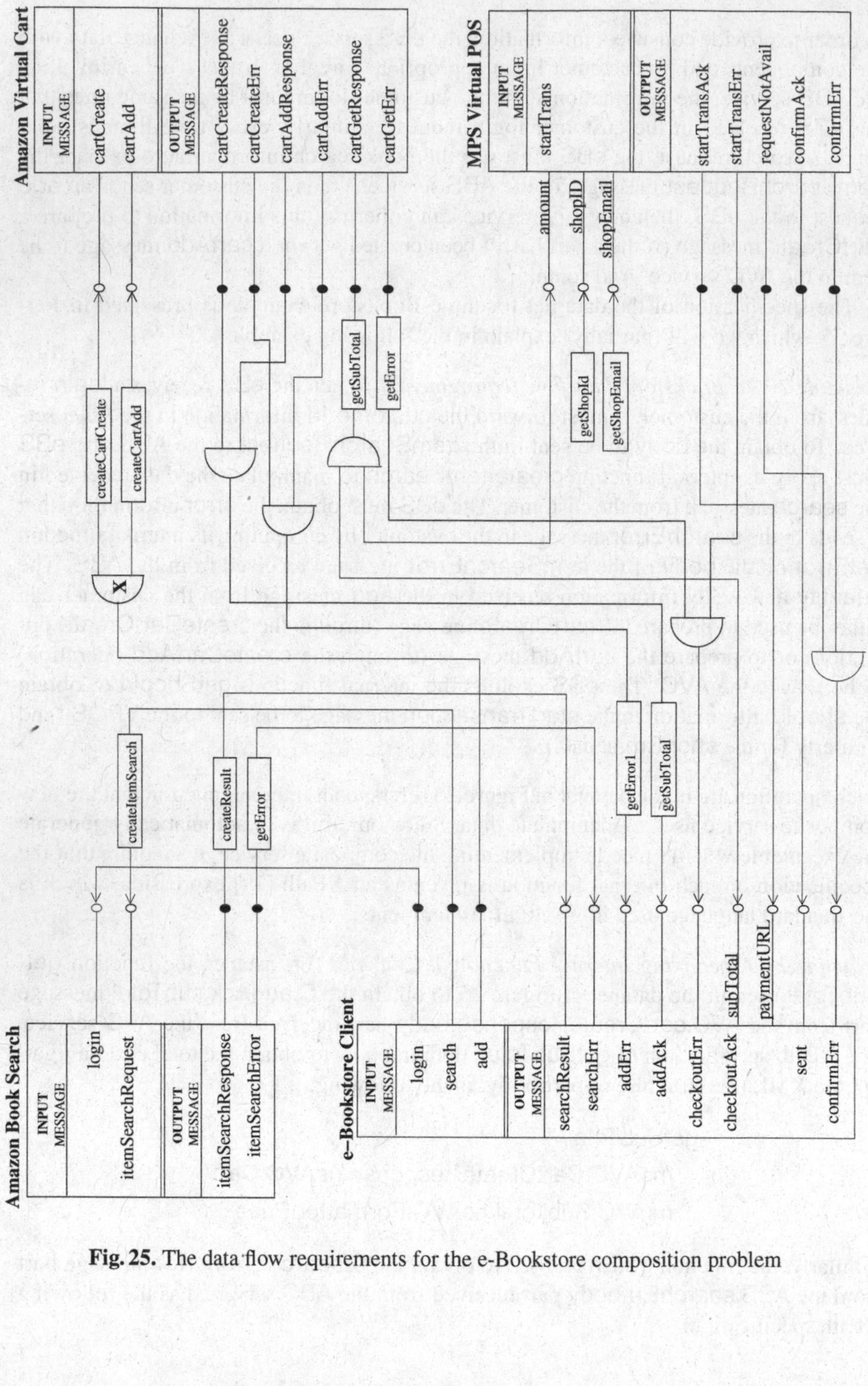

Fig. 25. The data flow requirements for the e-Bookstore composition problem

getError=
/nsABS:ItemSearchResponse/nsABS:Items/
nsABS:Request/nsABS:Errors/nsABS:Error/nsABS:Message

We remark that the data net of Figure 25 has been specified by hand, starting from the input and output messages of the component services. However, if the specifications of these messages and of the data types contain semantic information (e.g., if the WSDL specifications are extended to SA-WSDL [38] specification), then it is possible to derive (part of) the data net diagram automatically, using standard semantic matching techniques.

7.3 Generating the e-Bookstore Executable Process

The following table shows the results of the e-Bookstore automated composition problem, whose resulting executable WS-BPEL can be found at http://astroproject.org/e-Bookstore.zip.

	Time (Sec.)		WS-BPEL
	model construction	composition & emission	complex activities
e-Bookstore	2.7	605.2	177

The composition times have been obtained on a Pentium Centrino 1.6 GHz with 512 Mb RAM of memory running Linux. We distinguish between model construction time and composition time. The former is the time required to obtain the composition domain, i.e., to translate the WS-BPEL component services into STS and to encode the composition goal. The latter is the time required to synthesize the controller and to emit the corresponding eBS executable WS-BPEL process.

We have asked one of our experienced programmers to develop manually the WS-BPEL program for the e-Bookstore case. The task of manually encoding and testing the composition required several hours of work (more or less 20 hours). While, assuming to have the abstract WS-BPEL specification of the component services, the specification of the control-flow and data-flow requirements took no more than one hour.

The complexity of the composition problem derives from several aspects. First of all this scenario requires a high degree of interleaving between components: in order to satisfy the transactional requirements it is necessary to carry out interactions with all component services in an interleaved way (e.g. implementing the checkout of the cart is really complex since it requires to interact with the AVC, the VPOS and the eBS customer in such a way to guarantee a transactionally correct evolution of all these services). Moreover, when developing the composite service, the developer must take into account both the control-flow requirements and the requirements on data manipulation and exchange, which in this case are really elaborate. Thus, another advantage of our approach is a clear separation between the data-flow and control-flow aspects.

The complexity of the composition task can also be deduced from the size of the new composite WS-BPEL process, which in the e-Bookstore scenario consists of 177 activities. We remark that we report the number of WS-BPEL basic activities (e.g. `invoke`, `receive`, `reply`, `assign`, `onMessage`) and do not count the WS-BPEL structured activities that are used to aggregate basic activities (e.g. `sequence`, `switch`, `while`). Indeed, the former activities are a better measure of the complexity of the generated process, while the latter are more dependent on the coding style used in the composite WS-BPEL process.

Another important aspect is the quality of the generated WS-BPEL processes. To evaluate this aspect, we compared the automatically generated and the hand-written solutions. As a result, we discovered that the two solutions implement the same strategy and have a similar structure.

Finally, the separation of control and data flow requirements, and of technical details (e.g. XPath functions) from high level requirements, allows us to easily adapt the composition to changes in the component services specifications (e.g. if something changes in the data structure, it is sufficient to modify the data net diagram, or the XPath specification, and re-perform the automated composition). Manually modifying the executable WS-BPEL, expecially when dealing with complex processes as the e-Bookstore, is difficult and error prone, since it requires to take into account all the possible consequences of the update.

8 Concluding Remarks

Several works address the problem of the composition of stateful services, see, e.g., [15,16,24,42,69,68,67,80]. However, the key problem of the practical applicability of these approaches in real composition scenarios is still open. Addressing this problem requires to answer questions such as how to specify the stateful behavior of the component services, how to specify the requirements that define the goal of the composition, and whether the composition techniques are powerful enough to scale to scenarios of realistic size.

In this paper, we provided a solution towards addressing this problem by defining a framework for service composition that — besides being based on powerful automated synthesis techniques, and besides providing the possibility of expressing complex composition requirements — is integrated within a commercial platform for developing WS-BPEL services. Moreover, we have been evaluating the feasibility and efficiency of our proposed approach and prototype tool to automating the composition task on a real scenario that entails a high level of complexity, such as the generation of an e-Bookstore composite service interacting with Amazon E-Commerce Services and the e-payment service offered by Banks of Monte dei Paschi di Siena.

In particular, we show that the features offered by our composition framework — in terms of expressiveness of requirements and of automated synthesis techniques — are adequate for this composition scenario, providing a first positive answer to the question of the practical applicability of automated composition techniques. We show that the approach reduces dramatically the effort for the composition task by automatically generating a complex executable WS-BPEL process in few minutes starting from composition requirements that can be easily specified thanks to their intuitive graphical notation and the user friendly-editors provided by the ASTRO Toolset.

There is a wide range of future research directions to be investigated in order to extend the approach presented in the paper. Here, we just discuss two of them.

In this paper we concentrate on the centralized approach to the Web service composition and discuss the corresponding automated techniques and methods. An interesting feature to be investigated in the future would be to extend the approach in order to handle *peer-to-peer* automated composition problems. The main difference with respect to the proposed centralized approach reside in the automated composition outcome. Mediated methods aim at synthesizing a new centralized service (mediator) that orchestrates the component services by properly exchanging messages, while in peer-to-peer composition methods the execution of the composition is distributed among all the component services. The approach we are following is to obtain a peer to peer composition from a centralized orchestrator by exploiting program partitioning techniques, similarly to what is proposed in [84,85].

With respect to the specification of data flow requirements, future work will consider the possibility to automatically derive (part of) the data net specification. The idea, similarly to what is done in [5,2,47], is to add semantic annotations to the data used in the component services (e.g. through SAWSDL [38]) and then apply semantic matching and reasoning techniques to automatically derive the data links between message parts in order to obtain a first version of the data net diagram that can then be refined by hand. Moreover, one could think about applying semantic data mediation techniques as those in [59] to automatically derive the data net operation arcs that can be used to solve data heterogeneity problems between the messages exchanged by Web services. Moreover, adding semantic annotations concerning both control (e.g. OWL-S [65]) and data (e.g. SAWSDL [38]), to the description of the component services, would allow to extend our approach with existing methods to dynamically select, among a set of existing services, those that best match composition requirements (see [86,8,74]). This would allow us to evolve from *static* to *dynamic* composition, where the set of component services is automatically derived.

References

1. ActiveBPEL. The Open Source BPEL Engine, `http://www.activebpel.org`
2. Akkiraju, R., Srivastava, B., Ivan, A., Goodwin, R., Syeda-Mahmood, T.: Semaplan: Combining planning with semantic matching to achieve web service composition. In: Proc. of IEEE International Conference on Web Services, ICWS 2006 (2006)
3. Amazon Services. AWSECommerceService WSDL Specification (2006), `http://aws.amazon.com/`
4. Amazon Services. Amazon E-Commerce Service - Developer Guide (2007), `http://developer.amazonwebservices.com/`
5. Ambite, J.L., Kapoor, D.: Argos: a framework for automatically generating data processing workflows. In: Proc. of the 8th annual international conference on Digital government research, dg.o 2007 (2007)
6. Andrews, T., Curbera, F., Dolakia, H., Goland, J., Klein, J., Leymann, F., Liu, K., Roller, D., Smith, D., Thatte, S., Trickovic, I., Weeravarana, S.: Business Process Execution Language for Web Services, version 1.1 (2003)

7. Ankolekar, A., Burstein, M., Hobbs, J., Lassila, O., Martin, D., McIlraith, S., Narayanan, S.: DAML-S: semantic markup for web services. In: Horrocks, I., Hendler, J. (eds.) ISWC 2002. LNCS, vol. 2342, p. 348. Springer, Heidelberg (2002)
8. Ardagna, D., Pernici, B.: Dynamic web service composition with QoS constraints. International Journal of Business Process Integration and Management 1(4), 233–243 (2006)
9. ASTRO. Project ASTRO: Supporting the Composition of Distributed Business Processes, `http://astroproject.org`
10. Baresi, L., Maurino, A., Modalfieri, S.: Workflow partitioning in mobile information systems. In: Proc. of IFIP TC8 Working Conference on Mobile Systems (2004)
11. Benatallah, B., Dumas, M., Fauvet, M., Rabhi, F.: Towards patterns of web services composition (2002)
12. Benatallah, B., Dumas, M., Sheng, Q., Ngu, A.: Declarative composition and peer-to-peer provisioning of dynamic web services. In: Proc. of the International Conference on Data Engineering, ICDE 2002 (2002)
13. Berardi, D.: Automatic Service Composition: Models, Techniques and Tools. Ph.D Thesis (2005)
14. Berardi, D., Calvanese, D., De Giacomo, G., Hull, R., Mecella, M.: Automatic Composition of Transition-based Semantic Web Services with Messaging. In: Proc. of the 31st VLDB Conference, VLDB 2005 (2005)
15. Berardi, D., Calvanese, D., De Giacomo, G., Lenzerini, M., Mecella, M.: Automatic composition of E-Services that export their behaviour. In: Orlowska, M.E., Weerawarana, S., Papazoglou, M.P., Yang, J. (eds.) ICSOC 2003. LNCS, vol. 2910, pp. 43–58. Springer, Heidelberg (2003)
16. Berardi, D., Calvanese, D., De Giacomo, G., Mecella, M.: Composition of Services with Nondeterministic Observable Behaviour. In: Benatallah, B., Casati, F., Traverso, P. (eds.) ICSOC 2005. LNCS, vol. 3826, pp. 520–526. Springer, Heidelberg (2005)
17. Berge, C.: Graphs and Hypergraphs. North-Holland, Amsterdam (1973)
18. Berge, C.: Hypergraphs: Combinatorics of Finite Sets. North-Holland, Amsterdam (1989)
19. Berglund, A., Boag, S., Chamberlin, D., Ferndez, M.F., Kay, M., Robie, J., Siméon, J.: XML Path Language, XPath 2.0 (2007), `http://www.w3.org/TR/xpath20/`
20. Bertoli, P., Cimatti, A., Pistore, M., Roveri, M., Traverso, P.: MBP: a Model Based Planner. In: Proc. of IJCAI 2001 workshop on Planning under Uncertainty and Incomplete Information (2001)
21. Bertoli, P., Cimatti, A., Pistore, M., Traverso, P.: A Framework for Planning with Extended Goals under Partial Observability. In: Proc. ICAPS 2003 (2003)
22. Bertoli, P., Cimatti, A., Roveri, M., Traverso, P.: Planning in Nondeterministic Domains under Partial Observability via Symbolic Model Checking. In: Proc. IJCAI 2001 (2001)
23. Boley, H.: Directed recursive labelnode hypergraphs: a new representation language. Artificial Intelligence 9, 49–85 (1977)
24. Brogi, A., Popescu, R.: Towards Semi-automated Workflow-Based Aggregation of Web Services. In: Benatallah, B., Casati, F., Traverso, P. (eds.) ICSOC 2005. LNCS, vol. 3826, pp. 214–227. Springer, Heidelberg (2005)
25. Bryant, R.E.: Graph-based algorithms for Boolean function manipulation. IEEE Transactions on Computers 8(C-35), 677–691 (1986)
26. Bultan, T., Fu, X., Hull, R., Su, J.: Conversation specification: a new approach to design and analysis of e-service composition. In: In Proc. of the 12th international conference on World Wide Web (WWW 2003), pp. 403–410 (2003)
27. Burch, J.R., Clarke, E.M., McMillan, K.L., Dill, D.L., Hwang, L.J.: Symbolic model checking: 10^{20} states and beyond. In: Proc. of Symp. Logic in Computer Science, pp. 428–439 (1990)

28. Christensen, E., Curbera, F., Meredith, G., Weerawarana, S.: Web Service Description Language (WSDL), version 1.1 (2001)
29. Cimatti, A., Giunchiglia, F., Giunchiglia, E., Traverso, P.: Planning via model checking: A decision procedure for ar. In: Steel, S. (ed.) ECP 1997. LNCS, vol. 1348, pp. 130–142. Springer, Heidelberg (1997)
30. Cimatti, A., Giunchiglia, F., Giunchiglia, E., Traverso, P.: Planning as model checking. In: Proc. of ECP, pp. 1–20 (1999)
31. Cimatti, A., Pistore, M., Roveri, M., Traverso, P.: Weak, Strong, and Strong Cyclic Planning via Symbolic Model Checking. Artificial Intelligence 147(1-2), 35–84 (2003)
32. Dal Lago, U., Pistore, M., Traverso, P.: Planning with a Language for Extended Goals. In: Proc. AAAI 2002 (2002)
33. ActiveBPEL Designer. The Active Endpoints BPEL Designer, `http://www.active-endpoints.com`
34. Dustdar, S., Schreiner, W.: A survey on web services composition.. Int. J. Web and Grid Services 1, 1–30 (2005)
35. Emerson, E.A.: Temporal and modal logic. In: van Leeuwen, J. (ed.) Handbook of Theoretical Computer Science. Formal Models and Semantics, vol. B. Elsevier, Amsterdam (1990)
36. Erol, K., Hendler, J., Nau, D.: Semantics for HTN planning (1994)
37. Erol, K., Hendler, J., Nau, D.: UMCP: A sound and complete procedure for hierarchical task-network planning. In: Proc. Artificial Intelligence Planning Systems Symposium, pp. 249–254 (1994)
38. W3C Semantic Annotations for Web Service Description Language Working Group. Semantic Annotations for WSDL and XML Schema, SAWSDL (2007), `http://www.w3.org/TR/sawsdl/`
39. Fujii, K., Suda, T.: Dynamic service composition using semantic information. In: Proc. of International Conference on Service Oriented Computing, ICSOC 2004 (2004)
40. De Giacomo, G., Lesperance, Y., Levesque, H.J.: Congolog, a concurrent programming language based on the situation calculus. Artificial Intelligence 121(1-2), 109–169 (2000)
41. Gnesi, S., Montanari, U., Martelli, A.: Dynamic programming as graph searching: an algebraic approach. J. Assoc. Comp. Mach. 28, 737–751 (1981)
42. Hull, R., Benedikt, M., Christophides, V., Su, J.: E-Services: A Look Behind the Curtain. In: Proc. PODS 2003 (2003)
43. Kazhamiakin, R.: Formal Analysis of Web Service Compositions. Ph.D Thesis (2007)
44. Khalaf, R., Mukhi, N., Weerawarana, S.: Service Oriented Composition in BPEL4WS. In: Proc. WWW 2003 (2003)
45. Koehler, J., Srivastava, B.: Web Service Composition: Current Solutions and Open Problems. In: Proc. of ICAPS 2003 Workshop on Planning for Web Services (2003)
46. Kuster, U., Stern, M., Konig-Ries, B.: A classification of issures and approaches in service composition. In: Workshop Proc. First International Workshop on Engineering Service Compositions, WESC 2005 (2005)
47. Lecue, F., Delteil, A., Leger, A.: Applying abduction in semantic web service composition. In: Proc. of IEEE International Conference on Web Services, ICWS 2007 (2007)
48. Levesque, H.J., Reiter, R., Lesperance, Y., Lin, F., Scherl, R.B.: GOLOG: A logic programming language for dynamic domains. Journal of Logic Programming 31, 59–83 (1997)
49. Levi, G., Sirovich, F.: Generalized And/Or graphs. Artificial Intelligence 7, 243–259 (1976)
50. Marconi, A., Pistore, M., Traverso, P.: Specifying Data-Flow Requirements for the Automated Composition of Web Services. In: Proc. of Fourth IEEE International Conference on Software Engineering and Formal Methods, SEFM 2006 (2006)
51. Marconi, A., Pistore, M., Traverso, P.: Automated Web Service Composition at Work: the Amazon/MPS Case Study. In: Proc. of IEEE International Conference on Web Services, ICWS 2007 (2007)

52. Marconi, A., Pistore, M., Traverso, P.: Automated Web Service Composition in Practice: from Composition Requirements Specification to Process Run. In: Proc. of 2nd European Young Researchers Workshop on Service Oriented Computing, YRSOC 2007 (2007)
53. Marconi, A.: Automated Process-level Composition of Web Services: from Requirements Specification to Process Run. Ph.D thesis, Univerity of Trento (2008)
54. Martelli, A., Montanari, U.: Additive AND/OR graphs. In: Proc. IJCAI, vol. 3 (1973)
55. McCarthy, J.: Situations, actions and causal laws (1968)
56. McIlraith, S., Fadel, R.: Planning with Complex Actions. In: Proc. NMR 2002 (2002)
57. McIlraith, S., Son, S.: Adapting Golog for Composition of Semantic Web Services. In: Proc. of the Eighth International Conference on Knowledge Representation and Reasoning, KR 2002 (2002)
58. Milanovic, N., Malek, M.: Current solutions for web service composition. IEEE Internet Computing 8(6), 51–59 (2004)
59. Nagarajan, M., Verma, K., Sheth, A.P., Miller, J.A., Lathem, J.: Semantic interoperability of web services - challenges and experiences. In: Proc. of IEEE International Conference on Web Services, ICWS 2006 (2006)
60. Nanda, M.G., Chandra, S., Sarkar, V.: Decentralizing execution of composite web services. In: Proc. of 19th ACM SIGPLAN Conference on Object-Oriented Programming, Systems, Languages, and Applications, OOPSLA (2004)
61. Narayanan, S., McIlraith, S.: Simulation, Verification and Automated Composition of Web Services. In: Proc. of the Eleventh International Conference on World Wide Web, WWW 2002 (2002)
62. Nau, D., Au, T., Ilghami, O., Kuter, U., Murdock, W., Wu, D., Yaman, F.: SHOP2: An HTN planning system. Journal of Artificial Intelligence Research 20, 379–404 (2003)
63. Nau, D., Cao, Y., Lotem, A., Muroz-Avila, H.: Shop: Simple hierarchical ordered planner. In: Proc. of the Sixteenth International Joint Conference on Artificial Intelligence, IJCAI 1999 (1999)
64. Oracle. Oracle BPEL Process Manager, `http://www.oracle.com/appserver/bpel_home.html`
65. OWL-S. OWL-S: Semantic Markup for Web Services (OWL-S version 1.0) (2003)
66. Peer, J.: Web service composition as AI planning - a survey (2005)
67. Pistore, M., Marconi, A., Traverso, P., Bertoli, P.: Automated Composition of Web Services by Planning at the Knowledge Level. In: Proc. IJCAI 2005 (2005)
68. Pistore, M., Traverso, P., Bertoli, P.: Automated Composition of Web Services by Planning in Asynchronous Domains. In: Proc. ICAPS 2005 (2005)
69. Pistore, M., Traverso, P., Bertoli, P., Marconi, A.: Automated Synthesis of Composite BPEL4WS Web Services. In: Proc. of IEEE International Conference on Web Services, ICWS 2005 (2005)
70. Ponnekanti, S., Fox, A.: SWORD: A Developer Toolkit for Web Service Composition. In: Proc. WWW 2002 (2002)
71. Rao, J., Su, X.: A survey of automated web service composition methods. In: Cardoso, J., Sheth, A.P. (eds.) SWSWPC 2004. LNCS, vol. 3387, pp. 43–54. Springer, Heidelberg (2005)
72. Sacerdoti, E.D.: Planning in a hierarchy of abstraction spaces. In: Proc. of the Third International Joint Conference on Artificial Intelligence, IJCAI 1973 (1973)
73. Sadiq, W., Sadiq, S., Schulz, K.: Model-driven distribution of collaborative business processes. In: Proc. of IEEE International Conference on Services Computing, SCC (2006)
74. Sirin, E., Hendler, J., Parsia, B.: Semi automatic composition of web services using semantic descriptions. In: Proc. ICEIS 2003 Workshop on Web Services: Modeling, Architecture and Infrastructure (2003)
75. Skogan, D., Gronmo, R., Solheim, I.: Web Service Composition in UML. In: Proc. EDOC 2004 (2004)

76. Srivastava, B., Koehler, J.: Planning with Workflows - An Emerging Paradigm for Web Service Composition. In: Proc. of ICAPS 2004 Workshop on Planning and Scheduling for Web and Grid Services (2004)
77. Thakkar, S., Ambite, J.L., Knoblock, C.A.: A view integration approach to dynamic composition of web services. In: Proc. of the 1st ICAPS International Workshop on Planning for Web Services, P4WS 2003 (2003)
78. Thakkar, S., Ambite, J.L., Knoblock, C.A.: A data integration approach to automatically composing and optimizing web services. In: Proc. of the 2nd ICAPS International Workshop on Planning and Scheduling for Web and Grid Services (2004)
79. Thakkar, S., Ambite, J.L., Knoblock, C.A., Shahabi, C.: Dynamically composing web services from on-line sources. In: Proc. of 2002 AAAI Workshop on Intelligent Service Integration (2002)
80. Trainotti, M., Pistore, M., Calabrese, G., Zacco, G., Lucchese, G., Barbon, F., Bertoli, P., Traverso, P.: ASTRO: supporting the Composition and Execution of Web Services. In: Benatallah, B., Casati, F., Traverso, P. (eds.) ICSOC 2005. LNCS, vol. 3826, pp. 495–501. Springer, Heidelberg (2005)
81. van der Aalst, W.M.P., ter Hofstede, A.H.M.: YAWL: Yet Another Workflow Language (2003)
82. Wohed, P., van der Aalst, W.M.P., Dumas, M., ter Hofstede, A.H.M.: Analysis of Web Services Composition Languages: The Case of BPEL4WS. In: Proc. of the 22nd International Conference on Conceptual Modeling (2003)
83. Wu, D., Parsia, B., Sirin, E., Hendler, J., Nau, D.: Automating DAML-S Web Services Composition using SHOP2. In: Fensel, D., Sycara, K.P., Mylopoulos, J. (eds.) ISWC 2003. LNCS, vol. 2870, pp. 195–210. Springer, Heidelberg (2003)
84. Yildiz, U., Godart, C.: Centralized versus decentralized conversation-based orchestrations. In: Proc. of 4th IEEE International Conference on Enterprise Computing, E-Commerce and E-Services, CEC-EEE 2007 (2007)
85. Yildiz, U., Godart, C.: Information flow control with decentralized service composition. In: Proc. of IEEE International Conference on Web Services, ICWS 2007 (2007)
86. Zeng, L.: Dynamic web services composition. Ph.D Thesis (2003)

Fundamentals of Session Types

Vasco T. Vasconcelos

University of Lisbon

Abstract. We present a reconstruction of session types in a linear pi calculus where types are qualified as linear or unrestricted. Linearly qualified communication channels are guaranteed to occur in exactly one thread, possibly multiple times. In our language each channel is characterised by two distinct variables, one used for reading, the other for writing; scope restriction binds together two variables, thus establishing the correspondence between the two ends of a same channel. This mechanism allows a precise control of resources via a linear type system. We build the language gradually, starting from simple input/output, then adding choice, recursive types, replication and finally subtyping. We also present an algorithmic type checking system.

1 Introduction

In complex concurrent interactions partners often exchange a large number of messages as part of a pre-established protocol. The nature and order of this messages are a natural candidate for structuring interactions themselves. It is in this context that session types make their contribute by allowing a concise description of the continuous interactions among partners in a concurrent computation.

For example, consider a simplified distributed auction system with three kinds of players: sellers that want to sell items, auctioneers that sell items on their behalf, and bidders that bid for an item being auctioned. The protocol for sellers is simple: there is only one operation that sellers may invoke on an auctioneer—selling—where they provide the auctioneer with a description of the item to be sold (a string), and the minimum price they are willing to sell the item for. The protocol starts as follows, where $\oplus$ introduces the choices available to the seller, and ! the output of a value.

$$\oplus\{\mathit{selling}\colon !\mathrm{String}.!\mathrm{Price}\ldots\}$$

Sellers then wait on the outcome of their request. Two things can happen: either the item was sold (in which case the seller gets the price the item was sold for), or the item was not sold. The protocol then continues as below, where & denotes the range of alternatives offered by the seller at this point, and ? represents input.

$$\&\{\mathit{sold}\colon ?\mathrm{Price}\ldots, \mathit{notSold}\colon \ldots\}$$

In either case the protocols halts; we indicate that with the end mark. The complete protocol as seen by the seller can be concisely described.

$$\oplus\{\mathit{selling}\colon !\mathrm{String}.!\mathrm{Price}.\&\{\mathit{sold}\colon ?\mathrm{Price}.\mathsf{end}, \mathit{notSold}\colon \mathsf{end}\}\}$$

M. Bernardo, L. Padovani, and G. Zavattaro (Eds.): SFM 2009, LNCS 5569, pp. 158–186, 2009.

The protocol for auctioneers is slightly more complex, for they must interact not only with sellers but with bidders as well. Starting with the interaction with sellers, we know that auctioneers must offer a *selling* alternative, and if such alternative is taken, then they must accept a string (the item be sold) followed by the price the seller is asking.

$$\&\{\mathit{selling}\colon ?\mathrm{String}.?\mathrm{Price}\ldots\}$$

The auctioneer then puts the item on sale, and gets back to the seller with one of the possible outcomes: *sold* or *notSold*.

$$\oplus\{\mathit{sold}\colon !\mathrm{Price}\ldots, \mathit{notSold}\colon \ldots\}$$

Putting everything together we have two session types, the first for the seller, the second for the auctioneer.

$$\oplus\{\mathit{selling}\colon !\mathrm{String}.!\mathrm{Price}.\&\{\mathit{sold}\colon ?\mathrm{Price}.\mathsf{end}, \mathit{notSold}\colon \mathsf{end}\}\}$$
$$\&\{\mathit{selling}\colon ?\mathrm{String}.?\mathrm{Price}.\oplus\{\mathit{sold}\colon !\mathrm{Price}.\mathsf{end}, \mathit{notSold}\colon \mathsf{end}\}\}$$

The description implies that sellers should be able to safely interact with auctioneers; the session types for the two partners make this clear: when the seller selects the *selling* choice, the auctioneer offers that exact choice, and conversely for choices *sold* and *notSold*. Furthermore, when the seller outputs a value, the auctioneer inputs a value of the same type, and when the seller ends the protocol, so does the auctioneer. We say that the two types are *dual*, a notion central to session types.

But the auctioneer should also interact with bidders. Bidders start by registering themselves, then enter an interactive bidding session, and eventually unregister, thus leaving the protocol. The auctioneer offers a second option—register—to be used by bidders.

$$\&\{\mathit{selling}\ldots, \mathit{register}\colon \ldots\}$$

Bidders on the other hand must follow a protocol of the form $\oplus\{\mathit{register}\colon \ldots\}$, dual to that of the corresponding branch in the auctioneer. In summary we have the following situation

$$\mathrm{auctioneer}\colon \&\{\mathit{selling}\ldots, \mathit{register}\colon \ldots\}$$
$$\mathrm{seller}\colon \oplus\{\mathit{selling}\colon \ldots\}$$
$$\mathrm{bidder}\colon \oplus\{\mathit{register}\colon \ldots\}$$

but now the protocol of the auctioneer is not dual to neither that of seller nor that of the bidder. *Subtyping* allows to specialize the type of the auctioneer to that of the seller, as in $\&\{\mathit{selling}\ldots\}$, or to that of the bidder, $\&\{\mathit{register}\ldots\}$, as required by duality.

This chapter introduces a reconstruction of session types based on the ideas of linear type systems. Session types describe communication channels in the pi calculus, both linear and shared (or unrestricted). The various concepts usually associated to session types are introduced piecewise. We start by studying a language with input, output, parallel composition, and scope restriction. We then incorporate choice in the form of branching (external choice) and selection (internal choice). Even though the required machinery is in place, the particular form of types does not allow to type useful unrestricted channels—recursive types provide such a facility. Up to this point the language does not allow describing unbounded computations—we introduce replication for the effect. The next step is to introduce subtyping, thus enlarging the class of typable programs. The last step in the development of our language introduces an algorithmic type checking system. The closing section includes references to the sources of this chapter and discusses related work.

2 Syntax

Figure 1 presents the syntax of our language. There is one base set only: variables. When writing processes, any lower case roman-letter except u and v represents a variable. Depending on the context we also use the word channel to denote a variable.

In interactive behavior variables come in pairs, called *co-variables*. The best way to understand co-variables is to think of them as representing the two ends of a communication channel—one party writes on one end, others read from the other end. Interacting threads do not share variables for communication; since a channel is represented as a pair of co-variables, each thread owns its variable. This mechanism allows a precise control of resources via a linear type system.

The constructors of the language are those of the pi calculus with boolean values, except for a small difference in scope restriction. The output process $\overline{x}\,v.P$ writes value v on variable x and continues as P. Conversely, the input process $y(z).P$ receives on variable y a value it uses to substitute the bound variable z before continuing with the execution of process P. The parallel composition

P ::=		Processes:
	$\overline{x}\,v.P$	output
	$x(x).P$	input
	$P \mid P$	parallel composition
	$\mathsf{if}\ v\ \mathsf{then}\ P\ \mathsf{else}\ P$	conditional
	$\mathbf{0}$	inaction
	$(\nu xx)P$	scope restriction
v ::=		Values:
	x	variable
	$\mathsf{true} \mid \mathsf{false}$	boolean values

Fig. 1. The syntax of processes

$P \mid Q$ allows processes P and Q to proceed concurrently. The conditional process executes P or Q depending on the boolean value v. The terminated process, or inaction, is denoted by $\mathbf{0}$. The particular form of scope restriction $(\nu xy)P$ is the novelty with respect to the pi calculus—not only it hides two variables, but it also establishes x and y as two co-variables, allowing communication to happen in process P, between a thread writing on x and another thread reading from y. It should be stressed that $(\nu xy)P$ is not a short form for $(\nu x)(\nu y)P$; instead it binds two co-variables together.

3 Typing

The syntax of types is described in Figure 2. Type qualifiers annotate pretypes. For pretypes we have bool, the type of the boolean values. Pretype end may be used to represent a co-variable on which no further interaction is possible. Pretypes $!T.U$ and $?T.U$ describe channels ready to send or to receive a value of type T and then continuing its interaction as prescribed by type U.

Linearly qualified types describe variables that occur in exactly *one thread*, a thread being any process not comprising parallel composition. The unrestricted qualifier indicates that the value can occur in multiple threads. A type $\mathsf{lin\ bool}$ represents a boolean value that can be tested exactly once, whereas $\mathsf{un\ bool}$ describes a boolean value that can be tested a variable number of times. Similarly a type $\mathsf{lin}\ !T.U$ represents a channel that can be used once for sending a value of type T before becoming a channel that behaves as U. A channel $\mathsf{un}\ !T.U$ can be used multiple types to send values of type T. Typing contexts, also introduced in Figure 2, gather type information on variables.

$q ::=$		Qualifiers:
	lin	linear
	un	unrestricted
$p ::=$		Pretypes:
	bool	booleans
	end	termination
	$?T.T$	receive
	$!T.T$	send
$T ::=$		Types:
	$q\ p$	qualified pretype
$\Gamma ::=$		Contexts:
	$\emptyset$	empty context
	$\Gamma, x\colon T$	assumption

Fig. 2. The syntax of types

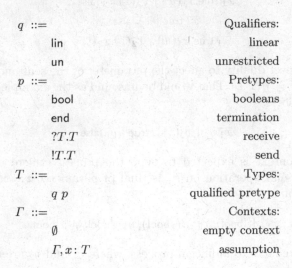

$$\overline{q\,?T.U} = q\,!T.\overline{U} \qquad \overline{q\,!T.U} = q\,?T.\overline{U} \qquad \overline{q\,\mathsf{end}} = q\,\mathsf{end}$$

Fig. 3. The dual function

To lighten the syntax in examples, we adopt a few abbreviations. First, we omit all unrestricted qualifiers and only annotate linear types. Second we omit the trailing **0** in processes. Third, we omit the trailing un end in types. In examples involving communication we also assume that co-variables are annotated with subscripts 1 and 2, for example (x_1, x_2) and (y_1, y_2).

If x is a variable of an arbitrarily qualified type, a is a variable of an unrestricted type and c a variable of a linear type, then the first two processes are well formed, whereas the last one is not.

$$\overline{x}\,\mathsf{true}.x(y) \qquad \text{:-)}$$
$$\overline{a}\,\mathsf{true} \mid \overline{a}\,\mathsf{true} \mid \overline{a}\,\mathsf{false} \qquad \text{:-)}$$
$$\overline{c}\,\mathsf{true} \mid \overline{c}\,\mathsf{false} \qquad \text{:-(}$$

Type duality plays a central role in the theory, ensuring that communication on co-variables proceeds smoothly. Intuitively, the dual of output is input and the dual of input is output. In particular if U is dual of T, then $q?S.U$ is dual of $q!S.T$. Pretype end is dual of itself; duality is not defined for the bool type. The definition is in Figure 3.

Based on duality, we would like to accept the first two processes, but not the last two.

$$\overline{x_1}\,\mathsf{true} \mid x_2(z) \qquad \text{:-)}$$
$$\overline{x_1}\,\mathsf{true}.x_1(w) \mid x_2(z).\overline{x_2}\,\mathsf{false} \qquad \text{:-)}$$
$$\overline{x_1}\,\mathsf{true} \mid \overline{x_2}\,\mathsf{false} \qquad \text{:-(}$$
$$\overline{x_1}\,\mathsf{true}.x_1(w) \mid x_2(z).x_2(t) \qquad \text{:-(}$$

One might expect duality to affect the parameter of the sent and the received type, e.g., $\overline{q\,?T.U} = q\,!\overline{T}.\overline{U}$. That would be unsound as the example below shows. Consider the process:

$$\overline{x_1}\,y_2 \mid x_2(z).\overline{z}\,\mathsf{true} \mid \overline{y_1}\,\mathsf{false} \qquad \text{:-(}$$

The following context is expected to type the process, where the argument $y_2 \colon !\mathsf{bool}$ of the send operation on x_1 is dual of parameter $z \colon ?\mathsf{bool}$ in the receive operation on x_2.

$$x_1 \colon !(!\mathsf{bool}), x_2 \colon ?(?\mathsf{bool}), y_1 \colon !\mathsf{bool}, y_2 \colon !\mathsf{bool}$$

Yet the process reduces to an illegal process, where y_1 and y_2 are not dual.

$$\overline{y_2}\,\mathsf{true} \mid \overline{y_1}\,\mathsf{false} \qquad \text{:-(}$$

$$\emptyset \cdot \emptyset = \emptyset \qquad \frac{\Gamma = \Gamma_1 \cdot \Gamma_2 \qquad \mathsf{un}(T)}{\Gamma, x\colon T = (\Gamma_1, x\colon T) \cdot (\Gamma_2, x\colon T)}$$

$$\frac{\Gamma = \Gamma_1 \cdot \Gamma_2 \qquad \mathsf{lin}(T)}{\Gamma, x\colon T = (\Gamma_1, x\colon T) \cdot \Gamma_2} \qquad \frac{\Gamma = \Gamma_1 \cdot \Gamma_2 \qquad \mathsf{lin}(T)}{\Gamma, x\colon T = \Gamma_1 \cdot (\Gamma_2, x\colon T)}$$

Fig. 4. Context splitting

Typing rules for values

$$\frac{\mathsf{un}(\Gamma)}{\Gamma \vdash \mathsf{false}, \mathsf{true}\colon \mathsf{bool}} \qquad \frac{\mathsf{un}(\Gamma_1, \Gamma_2)}{\Gamma_1, x\colon T, \Gamma_2 \vdash x\colon T} \qquad \text{[T-Bool] [T-Var]}$$

Typing rules for processes

$$\frac{\mathsf{un}(\Gamma)}{\Gamma \vdash \mathbf{0}} \qquad \frac{\Gamma_1 \vdash P \qquad \Gamma_2 \vdash Q}{\Gamma_1 \cdot \Gamma_2 \vdash P \mid Q} \qquad \text{[T-Inact] [T-Par]}$$

$$\frac{\Gamma_1 \vdash v\colon q\,\mathsf{bool} \qquad \Gamma_2 \vdash P \qquad \Gamma_2 \vdash Q}{\Gamma_1 \cdot \Gamma_2 \vdash \mathsf{if}\ v\ \mathsf{then}\ P\ \mathsf{else}\ Q} \qquad \frac{\Gamma, x_1\colon T, x_2\colon \overline{T} \vdash P}{\Gamma \vdash (\nu x_1 x_2)P} \qquad \text{[T-If] [T-Res]}$$

$$\frac{\Gamma_1 \vdash x\colon q\,?T.U \qquad (\Gamma_2, y\colon T) \cdot x\colon U \vdash P}{\Gamma_1 \cdot \Gamma_2 \vdash x(y).P} \qquad \text{[T-In]}$$

$$\frac{\Gamma_1 \vdash x\colon q\,!T.U \qquad \Gamma_2 \vdash v\colon T \qquad \Gamma_3 \cdot x\colon U \vdash P}{\Gamma_1 \cdot \Gamma_2 \cdot \Gamma_3 \vdash \overline{x}\,v.P} \qquad \text{[T-Out]}$$

Fig. 5. Typing rules

We maintain the linearity invariant through the standard linear context split operation. When type checking processes with two sub-processes we pass the unrestricted part of the context to both processes, while splitting the linear part in two and passing a different part to each process. In this way, if x is a linear variable then the process $\overline{x}\,\mathsf{true} \mid \overline{x}\,\mathsf{true}$ is not typable, since x can only occur in one of the parts, allowing to type one but not both processes. Figure 4 defines the context splitting relation $\Gamma = \Gamma_1 \cdot \Gamma_2$. Notice that in the third rule, x is not in Γ_2 since it is not in $\Gamma = \Gamma_1 \cdot \Gamma_2$, and similarly for the last rule and Γ_1.

For each qualifier q we define a predicate also named q which is true of types qp and also of contexts $x_1\colon qp_1, \ldots, x_n\colon qp_n$. Equipped with the notions of context splitting and type duality we are ready to introduce the typing rules. We distinguish typing rules for values with judgments of the form $\Gamma \vdash v\colon T$, from those for processes with judgments $\Gamma \vdash P$. The rules are in Figure 5.

Our type system maintains the following invariants.

- Linear channels occur in exactly one thread;
- Co-variables have dual types.

We want to make sure that linear variables are not discarded without being used; the base cases of the type system check that there is no linear variable in the context. In particular, in rules [T-Var] and [T-Bool] for values and [T-Inact] for processes, we check that Γ is unrestricted. Notice that this does not preclude type T itself from being linear in rule [T-VAR]. The typing rules for values are those one finds in the linear lambda calculus—boolean values have type bool, variables have the type prescribed by the context. Rule [T-VAR] allows variable x to occur anywhere in the context, as opposed to just at the beginning or at the end.

Rule [T-PAR] uses context splitting to partition linear variables between the two processes: the incoming context is split into Γ_1 and Γ_2, and we use the former to type check process P and the latter to type check process Q. Rule [T-IF] for the conditional process splits the incoming context in two parts: one used to check the condition, the other to check both branches. The same context for the two branches is justified by the fact that only one of P or Q will be executed. The qualifier of the boolean value is unimportant.

For rule [T-RES] we add to the context two extra hypotheses for the newly introduced variables, at dual types. The rule captures the essence of co-variables: they must have dual types.

Similarly to the rule for parallel composition, rule [T-IN] splits the context into two parts: one to type check variable x, the other to type check continuation P. If x is of type $?T.U$, we know that the bound variable y is of type T, and we type check P under the extra assumption $y\colon T$. Equally important is the fact that the continuation uses variable x at continuation type U, that is, process $x(y).P$ uses variable x at type $?T.U$ whereas P may use the *same* variable this time at type U. If x is a linear variable then it is certainly not in Γ_2 because it is in Γ_1. If, on the other hand, x is unrestricted then context splitting is only defined when U is equal to $q?T.U$, which will become possible in Section 6.

The rule for sending a value, [T-OUT], splits the context in three parts, one to check x, another to check v and the last to check continuation P. Similarly to the rule for reception, the continuation process uses variable x at the continuation type, that is, $\overline{x}\,v.P$ uses x at type $q!T.U$, whereas P uses the same variable at type U.

The dual function is not total: it is not defined on bool, nor on any type "terminating" in bool, such as ?bool.bool. Had we incorporated other base types in our language (integers for example), duality would not be defined on them as well. Duality is a function defined on session types only: input, output, and the terminated session end. Imagine that we set $\overline{\mathsf{bool}} = \mathsf{bool}$; we would be able to type process

$$(\nu xy)\mathsf{if}\ x\ \mathsf{then}\ \mathbf{0}\ \mathsf{else}\ \mathbf{0}$$

or any process reducing to it.

There are many interesting pi calculus processes that our type system fails to check, including $\overline{x}\,\mathsf{true} \mid \overline{x}\,\mathsf{true}$. In order to type this process we seek a context associating an unrestricted type to x, as in $x\colon !\mathsf{bool}.T$. Then the third premise of rule [T-OUT] reads $(x\colon !\mathsf{bool}.T)\cdot(x\colon T)$ which cannot be fulfilled by any type T built from the syntax in Figure 2. Clearly, so far, we are dealing with a language of linear channels only.

The following structural property of the type system is useful in the proof of preservation (Theorem 1).

Lemma 1 (Unrestricted weakening). *If* $\Gamma \vdash P$ *then* $\Gamma, x\colon \mathsf{lin}\, p \vdash P$.

Proof. The proof follows by induction on the structure of the derivation. We need to establish a similar result for values, whose proof is a simple case analysis on the two applicable typing rules. The hypothesis $\mathsf{un}(\Gamma)$ in rule [T-Inact] establishes the base case. □

4 Operational Semantics

In our language parenthesis represent bindings—variable y occurs *bound* in $x(y).P$ and in $(\nu xy)P$; variable x occurs bound in $(\nu xy)P$. A variable that occurs in a non-bound position within a process is said to be *free*. The set of free variables in a process P, denoted by $\mathrm{fv}(P)$, is defined accordingly, and so is alpha-conversion, as well as the capture-free substitution of variable x by value v in process P, denoted by $P[v/x]$. We work up to alpha-conversion and follow Barendregt's variable convention, whereby all variables in binding occurrences in any mathematical context are pairwise distinct and distinct from the free variables.

To evaluate processes we use a small step operational semantics. As usual in the pi calculus, we factor out a structural congruence relation on processes allowing the syntactic rearrangement of these, thus contributing for a more concise presentation of the reduction relation.

Structural congruence, $\equiv$, is the smallest congruence relation on processes that satisfies the axioms in Figure 6. The axioms are standard in pi calculus. The first three say that parallel composition is commutative, associative and contains the terminated process $\mathbf{0}$ for neutral. The first rule on the second line is called scope extrusion, and allows the scope of a ν-binder to extend to a new process Q or to retract from this, as needed. Notice that the proviso "x, y not free in Q" is redundant in face of the variable convention, for x occurring bound in $(\nu xy)P$ cannot occur free in Q. The last two rules allow to collect unused restrictions and to exchange the order of bindings.

The operational semantics is defined in Figure 7. In rule [R-Com], a process willing to send a value v on variable x, in parallel with another process ready to receive on variable y, engages in communication only if x, y are two co-channels, that is if the two processes are underneath a restriction (νxy). In that case, both prefixes are consumed and v replaces the bound variable z in the receiving party. The binding (νxy) persists, in order to potentiate further interactions in the resulting process. Process R witnesses reduction on unrestricted channels; it may represent the terminated process $\mathbf{0}$ on reduction on linear channels. A direct

$$P \mid Q \equiv Q \mid P \qquad (P \mid Q) \mid R \equiv P \mid (Q \mid R) \qquad P \mid \mathbf{0} \equiv P$$
$$(\nu xy)P \mid Q \equiv (\nu xy)(P \mid Q) \qquad (\nu xy)\mathbf{0} \equiv \mathbf{0} \qquad (\nu wz)(\nu xy)P \equiv (\nu xy)(\nu wz)P$$

Fig. 6. Structural congruence

$$(\nu xy)(\overline{x}\,v.P \mid y(z).Q \mid R) \to (\nu xy)(P \mid Q[v/z] \mid R) \qquad \text{[R-Com]}$$

$$\textsf{if true then } P \textsf{ else } Q \to P \qquad \text{[R-IfT]}$$

$$\textsf{if false then } P \textsf{ else } Q \to Q \qquad \text{[R-IfF]}$$

$$\frac{P \to Q}{(\nu xy)P \to (\nu xy)Q} \qquad \text{[R-Res]}$$

$$\frac{P \to Q}{P \mid R \to Q \mid R} \qquad \text{[R-Par]}$$

$$\frac{P \equiv P' \qquad P' \to Q' \qquad Q' \equiv Q}{P \to Q} \qquad \text{[R-Struct]}$$

Fig. 7. Operational semantics

consequence of this rule is that communication cannot happen on free variables for there is no way to tell what the co-variables are.

Rules [R-IfT] and [R-IfF] replace a conditional process with the then branch or with the else branch, depending on the value of the condition. Rules [R-Res] and [R-Par] allow reduction to happen underneath scope restriction and parallel composition, respectively. Finally, rule [R-Struct] incorporates structural congruence in the reduction relation.

Unlike the linear lambda calculus, our type system offers no guarantee of progress. If fact processes can deadlock quite easily, it suffices to create two sessions that read and write in the "wrong" order.

$$\overline{x_1}\,\textsf{true}.\overline{y_1}\,\textsf{false} \mid y_2(x).x_2(w) \qquad \text{:-)}$$

Even though one finds processes prefixed at any of the four linear variables, and the types are dual, the order by which the two threads order these prefixes is not conducting to reduction. An even more crafty process, uses channel passing to end up with a cycle including a single thread.

$$\overline{x_1}\,y_1 \mid x_2(z).\overline{z}\,\textsf{true}.y_2(w) \qquad \text{:-)}$$

The rest of this section is dedicated to the proof of the main results of our language.

Equipped with the notion of free variables and substitution we can prove two important results of our type system. Strengthening allows to remove extraneous entries from the context, but only when the variable does not occur free in the process. Clearly we have $x\colon ?\textsf{bool} \vdash x(y)$, but not $\vdash x(y)$. Also, linear variables occur in the context only if free in the process, e.g., $x\colon \textsf{lin}?\textsf{bool} \vdash \mathbf{0}$ is not a valid judgement.

Lemma 2 (Strengthening). *If $\Gamma, x\colon T \vdash P$ and $x \notin \text{fv}(P)$ then $\Gamma \vdash P$ and* $\textsf{un}(T)$.

Proof. The proof is by induction on the structure of the derivation. The hypothesis $\textsf{un}(\Gamma)$ in rule [T-Inact] establishes the base case. □

The following result related judgments $\Gamma \vdash P$ and the free variables of P.

Lemma 3 (Free variables)

- *If* $\Gamma \vdash P$ *and* $x \in \mathrm{fv}(P)$ *then* $x \in \Gamma$.
- *If* $\Gamma, x\colon \mathsf{lin}\, p \vdash P$ *then* $x \in \mathrm{fv}(P)$.

Proof The proofs are by induction on the derivations. □

The Substitution Lemma plays a central role in proof of type preservation (Theorem 1).

Lemma 4 (Substitution). *If* $\Gamma_1 \vdash v\colon T$ *and* $\Gamma_2, x\colon T \vdash P$ *and* $\Gamma_1 \cdot \Gamma_2$ *is defined then* $\Gamma_1 \cdot \Gamma_2 \vdash P[v/x]$.

Proof. The proof is by induction on the typing derivation and uses Strengthening and Weakening and Free variables (Lemmas 1, 2, and 3). This is the most elaborate proof in this section. We start with the simple observation that if $\Gamma_1 \vdash v\colon T$ then *either* $v = \mathsf{true}$ and $\mathsf{un}(\Gamma)$ *or* v is a variable and $\Gamma = \Gamma_1, v\colon T, \Gamma_2$ and $\mathsf{un}(\Gamma_1, \Gamma_2)$. For the base case (rule [T-INACT]), we know that $\mathsf{un}(\Gamma_2)$ and $\mathsf{un}(T)$. The result follows by Strengthening and Weakening. For each inductive case we prove two situations separately: $\mathsf{lin}(T)$ and $\mathsf{un}(T)$. □

The next lemma states that structural equivalent processes can be typed under the same contexts, and is used in the [R-STRUCT] case of the proof of preservation.

Lemma 5 (Preservation for $\equiv$). *If* $\Gamma \vdash P$ *and* $P \equiv Q$ *then* $\Gamma \vdash Q$.

Proof. The proof is by a simple analysis of derivations for each member of each axiom. We use Weakening, Strengthening, and Free variables (Lemmas 1, 2, and 3), and must not forget to check the two directions of each axiom.

A representative case is scope restriction. To show that, if $\Gamma \vdash (\nu xy)P \mid Q$ then $\Gamma \vdash (\nu xy)(P \mid Q)$, we start by building a derivation for $\Gamma \vdash (\nu xy)P \mid Q$, to conclude that Γ must be of the form $\Gamma_1 \cdot \Gamma_2$, that $\Gamma_1, x\colon T, y\colon \overline{T} \vdash P$, and that $\Gamma_2 \vdash Q$. To build a derivation for the conclusion we start with $\Gamma_2 \vdash Q$ and distinguish two cases. If T is linear, then $(\Gamma_1, x\colon T, y\colon \overline{T}) \cdot \Gamma_2 = \Gamma_1 \cdot \Gamma_2, x\colon T, y\colon \overline{T}$; otherwise use Weakening to conclude that $\Gamma_2, x\colon T, y\colon \overline{T} \vdash Q$ and $(\Gamma_1, x\colon T, y\colon \overline{T}) \cdot (\Gamma_2, x\colon T, y\colon \overline{T}) = \Gamma_1 \cdot \Gamma_2, x\colon T, y\colon \overline{T}$. In either case complete the proof with rules [T-RES] and [T-PAR].

In the reverse direction, to show that if $\Gamma \vdash (\nu xy)(P \mid Q)$ then $\Gamma \vdash (\nu xy)P \mid Q$, we consider two cases, depending on whether rule [T-RES] introduces an unrestricted or a linear type. For the former, applying rules [T-RES] and [T-PAR] from the conclusion $\Gamma \vdash (\nu xy)(P \mid Q)$, we know that $\Gamma = \Gamma_1 \cdot \Gamma_2$, that $\Gamma_1, x\colon T, y\colon \overline{T} \vdash P$ and that $\Gamma_2, x\colon T, y\colon \overline{T} \vdash Q$. To build a derivation for the conclusion, we apply Strengthening to the hypothesis on Q to obtain $\Gamma_2 \vdash Q$, and then apply [T-RES] and [T-PAR] as required.

If on the other hand T is linear, by Free variables there is one only way to split $\Gamma_1 \cdot \Gamma_2, x\colon T, y\colon \overline{T}$; we have $\Gamma_1, x\colon T, y\colon \overline{T} \vdash P$ and $\Gamma_2 \vdash Q$ and we conclude the proof using rules [T-RES] and [T-PAR]. □

Theorem 1 (Preservation). *If $\Gamma \vdash P$ and $P \rightarrow Q$ then $\Gamma \vdash Q$.*

Proof. The proof is by induction on the reduction derivation, and uses Weakening and Substitution (Lemmas 1 and 4). The inductive cases are straightforward; we use Lemma 5 in case [R-STRUCT].

The most interesting case is when the derivation of the reduction step ends with rule [R-COM]. Suppose that [T-RES] introduces $x\colon q!T.U, y\colon q?T.\overline{U}$. Building the tree for the hypothesis, we know that $\Gamma = \Gamma_1 \cdot \Gamma_2 \cdot \Gamma_3 \cdot \Gamma_4$ where $\Gamma_3 \vdash R$. At this point we distinguish two cases depending on nature of qualifier q. If linear then we have $\Gamma_1, x\colon U \vdash P$ and $\Gamma_2, z\colon T, x\colon \overline{U} \vdash Q$ and $\Gamma_4 \vdash v\colon T$. From $\Gamma_4 \vdash v\colon T$ and $\Gamma_2, z\colon T, x\colon \overline{U} \vdash Q$ we use Substitution to obtain $\Gamma_4 \cdot \Gamma_2, x\colon \overline{U} \vdash Q[v/z]$. We then conclude the proof with rules [T-PAR], [T-PAR], [T-RES].

If q is unrestricted, we have $(\Gamma_1, x\colon q!T.U)\cdot x\colon U \vdash P$, and $(\Gamma_2, y\colon q?T.\overline{U}, z\colon T)\cdot y\colon \overline{U} \vdash Q$ and $\Gamma_4, x\colon q!T.U \vdash v\colon T$. The first context splitting operation is defined only when $q!T.U$ is U, and the second when $q?T.\overline{U}$ is $\overline{U}$. Then we use Weakening four times: to go from $\Gamma_1, x\colon U \vdash P$ to $\Gamma_1, x\colon U, y\colon \overline{U} \vdash P$, from $\Gamma_2, z\colon T, y\colon \overline{U} \vdash Q$ to $\Gamma_2, z\colon T, x\colon U, y\colon \overline{U} \vdash Q$, from $\Gamma_3 \vdash R$ to $\Gamma_3, x\colon U, y\colon \overline{U} \vdash R$, and from $\Gamma_4, x\colon U \vdash v\colon T$ to $\Gamma_4, x\colon U, y\colon \overline{U} \vdash v\colon T$. Using Substitution, we conclude the proof as in the case of q linear. □

We now look at the guarantees offered by typable processes. To study what can go wrong with our machine, we look at the syntax of processes (Figure 1) and the reduction relation (Figure 7), and try to figure out in which cases can the machine get stuck, that is, not able to proceed because of ill-formed processes. There is an obvious case: the value in the condition is neither true nor false in rules [R-IFT] and [R-IFF].

But there are other processes that even though do not prevent the machine from advancing, we would like to dismiss as badly formed. These include processes with two threads sharing a variable, but using it with distinct interaction patterns, and two threads each possessing a co-variable, but using them in non-dual patterns.

$$\overline{a}\,\mathsf{true} \mid a(z) \qquad \text{:-(}$$
$$(\nu x_1 x_2)(\overline{x_1}\,\mathsf{true} \mid \overline{x_2}\,\mathsf{true}) \qquad \text{:-(}$$
$$(\nu x_1 x_2)(x_1(z) \mid x_2(w)) \qquad \text{:-(}$$

In order to define what we mean by a non well-formed process, we need two notions. An *x-prefixed process* is a process of the form $\overline{x}\,v.P$ or $x(y).P$. Given two variables x and y, a *xy-redex* is a process of the form $\overline{x}\,v.P \mid y(z).Q$. We say that a process is *non well-formed* if it can be written as $(\nu\tilde{x}\tilde{y})(P \mid Q \mid R)$ up to structural congruence, and one of the following happens.

1. P is of the form $\mathsf{if}\ v\ \mathsf{then}\ P'\ \mathsf{else}\ P''$ and $v \neq \mathsf{true}, \mathsf{false}$; or
2. P is of the from $\overline{x}\,v.P'$ and Q is $x(z).Q'$, or conversely; or
3. P is a x_i-prefixed process and Q is a y_i-prefixed process, but $P \mid Q$ is not a $x_i y_i$-redex.

Typable processes are in general not well-formed. The process if x then $\mathbf{0}$ else $\mathbf{0}$ is typable under context $x\colon \mathsf{bool}$, yet we consider it an error. But if P is closed (hence typable under the empty context, by Strengthening, lemma 2) then x must be bound by a (νxy) binder. Rule [T-RES] introduces two dual types in the context, $x\colon T, y\colon \overline{T}$, where T is necessarily different from bool, for duality would not be defined otherwise.

Theorem 2. *If $\vdash P$, then P is well formed.*

Proof. The proof is by contradiction. We build the derivation for $\vdash (\nu\tilde{x}\tilde{y})(P_1 \mid P_2 \mid P_3)$; in each of the three cases a simple analysis of the hypothesis shows that P is not typable. □

5 Choice

Choice allows processes to offer a fixed range of alternatives and clients to select among the variety offered. We extend the syntax of our language with support for offering alternatives, called *branching*, and to choose among the alternatives, called *selection*. The details are in Figure 8, where we add to our repertoire another base set—*labels*. Lower case letters l and m are used to denote labels.

New syntactic forms

$$
\begin{array}{rcll}
P & ::= & \ldots & \text{Processes:} \\
 & & x \triangleleft l.P & \text{selection} \\
 & & x \triangleright \{l_i\colon P_i\}_{i\in I} & \text{branching} \\
p & ::= & \ldots & \text{Pretypes:} \\
 & & \oplus\{l_i\colon T_i\}_{i\in I} & \text{select} \\
 & & \&\{l_i\colon T_i\}_{i\in I} & \text{branch}
\end{array}
$$

New duality rules

$$\overline{q \oplus\{l_i\colon T_i\}_{i\in I}} = q\,\&\{l_i\colon \overline{T_i}\}_{i\in I} \qquad \overline{q\,\&\{l_i\colon T_i\}_{i\in I}} = q \oplus \{l_i\colon \overline{T_i}\}_{i\in I}$$

New typing rules

$$\frac{\Gamma_2 \vdash x\colon q \oplus\{l_i\colon T_i\}_{i\in I} \qquad \Gamma_2 \cdot x\colon T_j \vdash P \qquad j \in I}{\Gamma_1 \cdot \Gamma_2 \vdash x \triangleleft l_j.P} \quad \text{[T-SEL]}$$

$$\frac{\Gamma_1 \vdash x\colon q\,\&\{l_i\colon T_i\}_{i\in I} \qquad \Gamma_2 \cdot x\colon T_i \vdash P_i \qquad \forall i \in I}{\Gamma_1 \cdot \Gamma_2 \vdash x \triangleright \{l_i\colon P_i\}_{i\in I}} \quad \text{[T-BRANCH]}$$

New reduction rules

$$\frac{j \in I}{(\nu xy)(x \triangleleft l_j.P \mid y \triangleright \{l_i\colon Q_i\}_{i\in I} \mid R) \to (\nu xy)(P \mid Q_j \mid R)} \quad \text{[R-CASE]}$$

Fig. 8. Choice

A process of the form $x \lhd l.P$ selects one of the options offered by a process prefixed at the co-variable. Conversely, a process $x \rhd \{l_i \colon P_i\}_{i\in I}$ offers a range of options, each labelled with a different label in the set $\{l_i\}_{i\in I}$. Such a process handles a selection at label l_j by executing process P_j.

Imagine a data structure mapping elements from a given type Key to a type Value. Among its various operations one finds *put* and *get*. To *put* key k associated to a value v one writes:

$$\mathit{map} \lhd \mathit{put}.\, \overline{\mathit{map}}\, k.\, \overline{\mathit{map}}\, v$$

To get a value from a map one sends a key and expects a value back, but only if the key is in the data structure. If not then we should be notified of the fact. We use labels *some* and *none* to denote the result of the *get* operation. Further, if the key is in the map, we expect a value as well. Here is a client that runs process P if the key is in the map, and runs Q otherwise.

$$\mathit{map} \lhd \mathit{get}.\, \overline{\mathit{map}}\, k.\, \mathit{map} \rhd \{\mathit{some}\colon \mathit{map}(x).P, \mathit{none}\colon Q\}$$

Types for the new constructors are $\oplus\{l_i \colon T_i\}_{i\in I}$ and $\&\{l_i \colon T_i\}_{i\in I}$, representing channels ready to select or to offer l_i options. In either case type T_j describes the continuation once label l_j has been chosen. Select types are akin to labelled variants in sequential languages, whereas branching types can be compared to labelled records. The new type structures are interpreted as non-ordered records; we do not distinguish $\&\{l\colon T, m\colon U\}$ from $\&\{m\colon U, l\colon T\}$.

The type of the map, as seen from the side of the client, that is the type of variable *map*, is as follows.

$$\oplus\{\mathit{put}\colon \mathrm{!Key.!Value}, \mathit{get}\colon \mathrm{!Key}.\&\{\mathit{some}\colon \mathrm{?Value}.\mathsf{end}, \mathit{none}\colon \mathsf{end}\}\}$$

The two new pretypes are dual to each other. In the third example below x is obviously unrestricted.

$$x_1 \lhd l \mid x_2 \rhd \{l\colon \mathbf{0}\} \qquad \text{:-)}$$
$$x_1 \lhd l \mid x_2 \rhd \{l\colon \mathbf{0}, m\colon \mathbf{0}\} \qquad \text{:-)}$$
$$x_1 \lhd l \mid x_1 \lhd m \mid x_1 \lhd m \mid x_2 \rhd \{l\colon \mathbf{0}, m\colon \mathbf{0}\} \qquad \text{:-)}$$
$$\overline{x_1}\, \mathsf{true} \mid x_2 \rhd \{l\colon \mathbf{0}\} \qquad \text{:-(}$$
$$x_1 \lhd l \mid x_2(z) \qquad \text{:-(}$$
$$x_1 \lhd l \mid x_2 \rhd \{m\colon \mathbf{0}\} \qquad \text{:-(}$$

To type check a branching process prefixed by x at type $\&\{l_i\colon T_i\}_{i\in I}$ we have to check each of the possible continuations P_i at $x\colon T_i$. We use the exact same Γ_2 in all cases for only one of the P_i will be executed, similarly to rule for the conditional process. If rule [T-BRANCH] introduces an external choice type $\&\{l_i\colon T_i\}_{i\in I}$, rule [T-SEL] eliminates the dual, internal choice type $\oplus\{l_i\colon T_i\}_{i\in I}$. To type check a process selecting label l_j at name x at type $\oplus\{l_i\colon T_i\}_{i\in I}$, we have to type check the continuation process at the correspondent type $x\colon T_j$. In both cases, and similarly to the rules for output and input in Figure 5, context splitting $\Gamma \cdot x\colon T$ must be defined.

The operational semantics is extended with rule [R-CASE]. The rule follows the pattern of [R-COM]: the two processes engaging in reduction must be underneath a prefix that puts the two co-variables in correspondence. The selecting party continues with process P, the branching party with the body of the selected choice, P_j.

Exercise 1. Sketch a proof of type preservation for the new language.

Exercise 2. What are the new errors associated with the constructs for branching and selection? Redefine the notion of *well formed* processes. Sketch a proof for the type safety result.

6 Recursive Types

The typing rule for the output process (rule [T-OUT] in Figure 5) does not allow to type check a process $\overline{x}\,v.P$ with x unrestricted, for it requires the continuation T of type $\mathsf{un}!T.U$ to be equal to $\mathsf{un}!T.U$ itself. We would like to consider as a type the regular infinite tree solution to the equation $U = \mathsf{un}!T.U$. A finite notation for such a type uses the μ-notation, as in $\mu a.\mathsf{un}!T.a$.

Figure 9 includes *recursive types* in the syntax of types, where we rely on one more base set, that of *type variables.* Recursive types are required to be *contractive*, i.e., containing no subexpression of the form $\mu a_1 \dots \mu a_n.a_1$. The μ operator is a binder, giving rise, in the standard way, to notions of bound and free variables and alpha-equivalence. We denote by $T[U/a]$ the capture-avoiding substitution of a by U in T. Rather than defining type equivalence directly, we rely on the definition of subtyping discussed in Section 8. In any case, types are understood up to type equivalence, so that, for example, in any mathematical context, types $\mu a.T$ and $T[\mu a.T/a]$ can be used interchangeably, effectively adopting the equi-recursive approach.

The dual function descends a μ-type and leaves type variables unchanged. To check that a given type T is dual of another type U, we first build the type $\overline{T}$ and then use the definition above. For example, to show that $\mu a.?\mathsf{bool}.!\mathsf{bool}.a$

New syntactic forms

$T ::= \dots$		Types:
	a	type variable
	$\mu a.T$	recursive type

New duality rules

$$\overline{\mu a.T} = \mu a.\overline{T} \qquad\qquad \overline{a} = a$$

Fig. 9. Recursive types

is dual of $!\mathsf{bool}.\mu b.?\mathsf{bool}.!\mathsf{bool}.b$, we build $\overline{\mu a.?\mathsf{bool}.!\mathsf{bool}.a} = \mu a.!\mathsf{bool}.?\mathsf{bool}.a$, and then show that $\mu a.!\mathsf{bool}.?\mathsf{bool}.a = !\mathsf{bool}.\mu b.?\mathsf{bool}.!\mathsf{bool}.b$.

The new type constructors are not qualified, instead $\mu a.T$ takes the qualifier of the underneath type T. Contractivity ensures that types can be interpreted as regular infinite trees; it also ensures that we can always find out what the qualifier of a type is. Since not all type constructors are qualified anymore, we have to adjust the un and the lin predicates on types. Predicate q is true of types qp as before; and is now true of type $\mu a.T$ if it is true of type T.

Unlike the linear lambda calculus where unrestricted data structures may not contain linear data structures, unrestricted channels can carry both unrestricted and linear channels. Consider the type $?(\mathsf{lin}!\mathsf{bool}).T$ of an unrestricted channel that receives a linear channel capable of outputting a boolean value. The following sequent is easy to establish,

$$x_2\colon ?(\mathsf{lin}!\mathsf{bool}).T \vdash x_2(z).\overline{z}\,\mathsf{true} \mid x_2(w).\overline{w}\,\mathsf{false} \qquad \text{:-)}$$

but only for an appropriate type T. We have seen that it must be equivalent to $?(\mathsf{lin}!\mathsf{bool}).T$, that is T must be $\mu a.?(\mathsf{lin}!\mathsf{bool}).a$. This form of types is so common that we introduce a short form for them, simply writing $*?(\mathsf{lin}!\mathsf{bool})$.

Our language does not include tuple passing as a primitive construct, rather it can only send or receive a single value at a time. Fortunately, tuple passing is easy to encode. To send a pair of values u, v of types T, U over a linear channel x, we just send the values, one at a time; no interference is possible due to the linear nature of the carrier channel.

$$\overline{x}\,\langle u, v\rangle.P = \overline{x_1}\,u.\overline{x_1}\,v.P$$

If the tuple is to be passed on a unrestricted channel, then we must protect the receiving operations from interference, creating a new lin?T. lin?U channel to carry the values. The standard encoding for the binary sending and the receiving operations are as follows.

$$\overline{x_1}\,\langle u, v\rangle.P = (\nu y_1 y_2)\overline{x_1}\,y_2.\overline{y_1}\,u.\overline{y_1}\,v.P$$
$$x_2(w, t).P = x_2(z).z(w).z(t).P$$

The encodings are typable in our language, if we choose variable y_1 of appropriate linear type, $\mathsf{lin}!T.\mathsf{lin}!U$, and dually for y_2. Variable x_1 is then of type $*!(\mathsf{lin}?T.\mathsf{lin}?U)$, and dually for x_2. We abbreviate the type of channel that sends a pair of values of types T and U to $*!\langle T, U\rangle$, and dually for a channel that receives a pair of values, $*?\langle T, U\rangle$.

Here is another example on passing linear tuples on unrestricted channels. Below is a process that writes two boolean values on a given channel z and then returns the channel (on a given channel w) so that it can be further used.

$$p_1(z, w).\overline{z}\,\mathsf{true}.\overline{z}\,\mathsf{true}.\overline{w}\,z \qquad \text{:-)}$$

A process that calls p_1 to read two boolean values and then writes a third on channel x can be written as

$$\overline{p_2}\,\langle c, x_1\rangle \mid x_2(z).\overline{z}\,\mathsf{false} \qquad \text{:-)}$$

where p_1 is typed at $*?\langle \mathsf{lin!bool.lin!bool.lin?bool}, \mathsf{lin?bool}\rangle$.

A once linear channel can become unrestricted, we just have to get the right types. For example, type $T = \mathsf{lin!bool.*?bool}$ describes a channel that behaves linearly in the first interaction and unrestricted thereafter. Suppose that x_1 is of type T and x_2 of type $\overline{T}$.

$$\overline{x_1}\,\mathsf{true}.(x_1(y) \mid x_1(z)) \mid x_2(x).(\overline{x_2}\,\mathsf{true} \mid \overline{x_2}\,\mathsf{false} \mid \overline{x_2}\,\mathsf{true}) \qquad \text{:-)}$$
$$\overline{x_1}\,\mathsf{true}.x_1(y).x_1(y) \mid x_2(z) \qquad \text{:-)}$$
$$\overline{x_1}\,\mathsf{true}.x_1(y) \mid x_2(y).\overline{x_2}\,\mathsf{true} \mid x_2(w).\overline{x_2}\,\mathsf{true} \qquad \text{:-(}$$

So now we know that a traditional pi calculus channel that can be used an unbounded number of times for outputting boolean values is of type $*!\mathsf{bool}$, that is, $\mu a.!\mathsf{bool}.a$. Conversely, a channel that can be used for reading an unbounded number of boolean values is of type $*!\mathsf{bool} = \mu b.?\mathsf{bool}.b$. What about a channel that can we used both for reading and for writing? There is no such thing in this theory; the channel is in reality a pair of co-variables, one to read, the other to write.

Equipped with the equi-recursive notion of types, typing rules (in Figure 5) remain unchanged. More importantly, the preservation theorem holds as before, and we do not even need to touch the proof.

7 Replication

Up until now our language is strongly normalizing—each reduction step strictly decreases the number of symbols that compose the processes involved. To provide for unbounded behavior we introduce a special form of receptor that remains after reduction, called *replication*. The details are in Figure 10.

The reduction rule [R-REPL] for a replicated process $*x(y).P$ is similar to that of a simple receptor (rule [R-COM] in Figure 7) in all respects except that process $*x(y).P$ persists in the resulting process. The typing rule for replication [T-REPL] is exactly that of a single receptor (rule [T-IN] in Figure 5) except for two things: channel x must be unrestricted, and the context that types the body P of the replicated process is must be unrestricted as well.

As an example, consider an iterator of boolean values—a process that offers operations *hasNext* and *next* repeatedly until *hasNext* returns "no". Further suppose that the iterator accepts requests at x_2. A client that reads and discards every value from the iterator can be written as follows.

$$*\,loop(y).y \triangleleft hasNext.y \triangleright \{yes\colon y \triangleleft next.y(z).\overline{loop}\,y,\ no\colon \mathbf{0}\} \mid \overline{loop}\,x_2 \qquad (1)$$

Clearly, the communication pattern of the iterator, as seen by the client at variable x_2, is of the form

$$\oplus\{hasNext\colon \&\{no\colon \mathsf{end},\ yes\colon \oplus\{next\colon !\mathsf{bool}.\oplus\{hasNext\colon \&\{\ldots\}\}\}\}\}$$

which can be written in finite form as follows.

$$\mu a.\oplus\{hasNext\colon \&\{no\colon \mathsf{end},\ yes\colon \oplus\{next\colon !\mathsf{bool}.a\}\}\} \qquad (2)$$

New syntactic forms

$$P ::= \ldots \qquad \text{Processes:}$$
$$* x(x).P \qquad \text{replication}$$

New typing rules

$$\frac{\Gamma_1 \vdash x\colon \mathsf{un}\,?T.U \qquad (\Gamma_2, y\colon T)\cdot x\colon U \vdash P \qquad \mathsf{un}(\Gamma_2)}{\Gamma_1 \cdot \Gamma_2 \vdash *x(y).P} \quad \text{[T-REPL]}$$

New reduction rules

$$(\nu xy)(\overline{x}\, v.P \mid *y(z).Q \mid R) \to (\nu xy)(P \mid Q[v/z] \mid *y(z).Q \mid R) \quad \text{[R-REPL]}$$

Fig. 10. Replication

Notice that the type in equation 2 is equivalent to the following,

$$\oplus\{\mathit{hasNext}\colon \mu b.\&\{\mathit{no}\colon \mathsf{end}, \mathit{yes}\colon \oplus\{\mathit{next}\colon !\mathsf{bool}. \oplus\{\mathit{hasNext}\colon b\}\}\}\} \quad (3)$$

and that the two types can never be made syntactically equal by finite expansion alone, yet we would not like to distinguish them, for they have the same infinite expansion.

To understand what would happen if we relax the $\mathsf{un}(\Gamma_2)$ restriction in rule [T-REPL], consider the following process

$$*x_2(z).\overline{c}\,\mathsf{true} \mid \overline{x_1}\,\mathsf{true} \mid \overline{x_1}\,\mathsf{false} \qquad \text{:-(}$$

where we would like c to be typed at $\mathsf{lin}!\mathsf{bool}$. The process reduces in two steps to $*x_2(z).\overline{c}\,\mathsf{true} \mid \overline{c}\,\mathsf{true} \mid \overline{c}\,\mathsf{true}$, invalid given the sought linearity for channel c. Instead, procedures that use linear values must receive them as parameters, thus allowing the type system to check possible value duplications. If we pass channel c as parameter,

$$*x_2(z).\overline{z}\,\mathsf{true} \qquad \text{:-)}$$

then the procedure can no longer be used by process $\overline{x_1}\,c \mid \overline{x_1}\,c$, because rule [T-PAR] precludes splitting any context in two parts both containing a channel c of a linear type.

Exercise 3. A general replicated process $*P$, can be simulated by the following process,

$$(\nu x_1 x_2)(\overline{x_1}\,\mathsf{true} \mid *x_2(y).(P \mid \overline{x_1}\,\mathsf{true}))$$

where x_1, x_2 and y do not occur free in P. Devise an admissible rule for the new construct. Why would general replication be uninteresting as a primitive in our language?

Exercise 4. Prove that type preservation still holds for the language with replication.

Exercise 5. In this section we made the input process persistent by using replication. Branching, introduced in Section 5, can be made persistent as well. Devise a typing and a reduction rule for a replicated branching process $*x \triangleright \{l_i\colon P_i\}_{i\in I}$. Sketch the proof of the corresponding case in the type preservation theorem.

8 Subtyping

Subtyping brings extra flexibility to our type system. The insistence that arguments in output processes exactly match input parameters in corresponding receivers leads to the rejection of programs that will never go wrong when executed.

One example can be found in the introduction. For another, the iterator discussed in Section 6 imposes a strict discipline on its clients: they must alternate between operations *hasNext* and *next*, as long as *hasNext* returns *yes*. A more liberal server would allow clients to call, after the first *hasNext*, not only *next* but also and again *hasNext*.

$$\&\{hasNext\colon \mu b. \oplus \{no\colon \mathsf{end}, yes\colon \&\{next\colon !\mathsf{bool}.\&\{hasNext\colon b\}, hasNext\colon b\}\}\} \tag{4}$$

Now imagine the situation where we have typed both the iterator (prefixed at x_1) and its client (at x_2) in context $x_2\colon T, x_1\colon \overline{T}$, where T is the type in equation 2, and we now replace the iterator to conform to the type U in equation 4. Operationally there should be no problem. Below are two snapshots of the system where the client is about to ask *next*, first to the old iterator, and then to the new.

$$(\nu x_2 x_1)(x_2 \triangleleft next.x_2(y).\overline{loop}\, x_2 \mid x_1 \triangleright \{next\colon P\} \mid R) \tag{5}$$

$$(\nu x_2 x_1)(x_2 \triangleleft next.x_2(y).\overline{loop}\, x_2 \mid x_1 \triangleright \{next\colon P, hasNext\colon Q\} \mid R)$$

The types for the client and the server are dual in the first case, but not in the second. The client at x_2 asks $\oplus\{next\colon \dots\}$ whereas the iterator at x_1 offers $\&\{next\colon \dots, hasNext\colon \dots\}$. One solution to the problem allows the server to "forget" options, thus obtaining a type $\&\{next\colon \dots\}$, which is now dual to that of the client.

Subtyping has in our language the generally accepted meaning, where $T <: U$ indicating that any variable of type T can be safely used in a context where a variable of type U is expected, or "every variable described by T is also described by U". The new rule is in Figure 11.

New typing rule

$$\frac{\Gamma \vdash v\colon T \qquad T <: U}{\Gamma \vdash v\colon U} \quad \text{[T-SUB]}$$

Fig. 11. Subtyping

To feel how the subsumption rule works we build a derivation for the parallel composition of the the new iterator and its client. Let

$$
\begin{aligned}
T &= \&\{next\colon T'\} \\
U &= \&\{next\colon T', hasNext\colon U'\} \\
\Gamma_1 &= \Gamma_1', x_1\colon T \\
\Gamma_2 &= \Gamma_2', x_2\colon \overline{T} \\
P_1 &= x_1 \rhd \{next\colon P, hasNext\colon Q\} \\
P_2 &= x_2 \lhd next.x_1(y).\overline{loop}\, x_2
\end{aligned}
$$

in

$$
\dfrac{\dfrac{\dfrac{\dfrac{}{\Gamma_1 \vdash x_1 : T} \quad T <: U}{\Gamma_1 \vdash x_1 : U}\,[\text{T-Sub}] \qquad \dfrac{\vdots}{\Gamma_1, x_1 : T' \vdash P} \qquad \dfrac{\vdots}{\Gamma_1, x_1 : U' \vdash Q}}{\Gamma_1 \vdash P_1} \qquad \dfrac{\vdots}{\Gamma_2 \vdash P_2}}{\Gamma_1 \cdot \Gamma_2 \vdash P_1 \mid P_2}
$$

So here is our first rule of finite subtyping.

$$
\frac{I \subseteq J \qquad T_i <: U_i \qquad \forall i \in I}{\&\{l_i\colon T_i\}_{i\in I} <: \&\{l_j\colon U_j\}_{j\in J}} \qquad [\text{S-BranchFin}]
$$

Conversly, we can fix the mismatch between the new iterator and its client by allowing the client to select more options.

$$
\frac{I \supseteq J \qquad T_j <: U_j \qquad \forall j \in J}{\oplus\{l_i\colon T_i\}_{i\in I} <: \oplus\{l_j\colon U_j\}_{j\in J}} \qquad [\text{S-SelFin}]
$$

To understand why we have $T <: U$ in the hypothesis of rule [S-BranchFin], remember that type S in $\&\{next\colon S\}$ of the iterator above (equation 2) contains multiple (infinite, in fact) nested copies of $\&\{next\colon S\}$ itself, and we want each of them to be a subtype of the larger type $\&\{next\colon \ldots, hasNext\colon \ldots\}$. A similar reason conducts to the exactly same conclusion in the case of [S-SelFin]. For this reason, in all four session-type constructors, continuations are always co-variant.

There remains to study the input and output operations. Suppose the client delegates its variable just before selecting operation *next*. Towards this end, the client uses another channel (another pair of co-variables, y_1, y_2) and sends its variable x_1 on y_1. The receiver gets it in y_2 and calls the pending *next* operation on the iterator. The code for the receiver, the recipient of delegation, is as follows,

$$
y_2(z).z \lhd next
$$

where y_2 is naturally typed at $?(\mathsf{lin} \oplus \{next\colon \ldots\})$. When the new iterator enters operation, the recipient of delegation can call *hasNext* (as well as *next*), and thus rewrites its code to become:

$$
y_2(z).z \lhd hasNext
$$

where y_2 is now typed at $?(\mathsf{lin} \oplus \{next\colon \ldots, hasNext\colon \ldots\})$. We have seen that $\oplus\{next\colon \ldots, hasNext\colon \ldots\} <: \oplus\{next\colon \ldots\}$. If we make

$$?\oplus\{next\colon \ldots, hasNext\colon \ldots\} <: ?\oplus\{next\colon \ldots\}$$

then the piece of code $y_2(z).z \triangleleft hasNext$ typed at the subtype can also be used where the supertype is expected.

The example allows us to conclude that input is co-variant. A similar reasoning on the iterator side would allow to conclude that output is contra-variant.

$$\frac{T' <: T \qquad U <: U'}{!T.U <: !T'.U'} \qquad \frac{T <: T' \qquad U <: U'}{?T.U <: ?T'.U'} \qquad \text{[S-SendFin],[S-RcvFin]}$$

In summary:

- Input operations ($?, \&$) are co-variant; output operations ($!, \oplus$) contra-variant;
- Continuations are always co-variant.

Subtyping in the pi calculus is reversed with respect to that found in the lambda calculus. The notion of co-variable helps in understanding the phenomenon. Our understanding of $T <: U$ is that x_1 of type T can be safely used in a context where a type U is expected. Then it must be the case that the context uses, not x_1, but x_2 the co-channel, hence U must offer more choices, so that it may be used by $x_2\colon \overline{U}$ that selects more choices.

Because of recursive types we use a co-inductive definition, rather than an inductive definition based on the rules we have sketched above.

Definition 1 (Subtyping). *Define the operator $F \in \mathcal{P}(\mathcal{T} \times \mathcal{T}) \to \mathcal{P}(\mathcal{T} \times \mathcal{T})$ as follows.*

$$\begin{aligned}
F(R) = {} & \{(\mathsf{end}, \mathsf{end}), (\mathsf{bool}, \mathsf{bool})\} \\
& \cup \{(?T.U, ?T'.U') \mid (T, T'), (U, U') \in R\} \\
& \cup \{(!T.U, !T'.U') \mid (T', T), (U, U') \in R\} \\
& \cup \{(\&\{l_i\colon T_i\}_{i\in I}, \&\{l_j\colon T'_j\}_{j\in J}) \mid I \subseteq J, (T_i, T'_i) \in R, \forall i \in I\} \\
& \cup \{(\oplus\{l_i\colon T_i\}_{i\in I}, \oplus\{l_j\colon T'_j\}_{j\in J}) \mid I \supseteq J, (T_j, T'_j) \in R, \forall j \in J\} \\
& \cup \{(\mu a.T, T') \mid (T[\mu a.T/a], T') \in R\} \\
& \cup \{(T, \mu a.T') \mid (T, T'[\mu a.T'/a]) \in R\}
\end{aligned}$$

Contractivity ensures that F is monotone. By the Knaster-Tarski theorem, F has least and greatest fixed points; we take the greatest fixed point to be the subtyping relation, writing $T <: U$ if the pair (T, U) is in the relation.

Lemma 6. *Subtyping is a pre-order.*

As mentioned in Section 6 type equivalence is defined on top of subtyping: we say that types T and U are *equivalent* when $T <: U$ and $U <: T$.

The interested reader may have notice that there is already a flavor of subtyping in rule [T-Sel], Figure 8, where given label l_j in a program, we guess the remaining labels in the $\oplus$-type. In fact equipped with subtyping, the rule can be simplified avoiding mentioning extraneous labels.

$$\frac{\Gamma_1 \vdash x\colon q \oplus \{l\colon T\} \qquad \Gamma_2 \cdot x\colon T \vdash P}{\Gamma_1 \cdot \Gamma_2 \vdash x \lhd l.P} \quad \text{[T-SelSimple]}$$

9 Algorithmic Type Checking

The typing rules provided in the previous sections give a concise specification of what we understand by well formed programs. They cannot however be implemented directly for two main reasons. One is the difficulty of implementing the non-deterministic splitting operation, $\Gamma = \Gamma_1 \cdot \Gamma_2$, for we must guess how to split an incoming context Γ in two parts. The other is the problem of guessing the types to include in the context when in presence of scope restriction.

To solve the first problem, we restructure the type checking rules to avoid having to guess context splitting. To address the second difficulty we seek the help of programmers by requiring explicit annotations in the scope restriction constructor. We now write $(\nu xy\colon T)P$, where x is supposed to be of type T and y of type $\overline{T}$ in scope P. Changes are in Figure 12.

We have introduced our language piecewise. To simplify the exposition, we address in this section the language formed by the basics in Figure 5, extended with recursive types in Figure 9 and replication in Figure 10. We assume that type equivalence is decidable. We also need an extra operation on contexts: $\Gamma \backslash x$ removes from Γ the assumption for x, if it exists.

The central idea of the new type checking system is that, rather than splitting the input context into two (or three) parts before checking a complex process, we pass the entire context to the first subprocess and have it return the unused part. This output is then passed to the second subprocess, which in turn returns the unused portion of the context, and so on. The output of the last subprocess is then the output of the process under consideration. Sequents are now of forms $\Gamma_1 \vdash v\colon T; \Gamma_2$ for values and $\Gamma_1 \vdash P\colon \Gamma_2$ for processes, with the understanding that Γ_1 is the input to the algorithm and T and Γ_2 is the output.

The main change in the re-engineered type system is the treatment of linear variables, which as moved from the axioms (and rule[T-Repl]) to the rules that introduce assumptions in the context, [A-Res], [A-In], [A-Repl]. The base cases for variables and constants allow any context to pass through the judgement, even with linear types. Two rules, [A-VarUn] and [A-VarLin], replace the single rule for variables [T-Var] in Figure 5. The former keeps the entry $x\colon T$ in the returned context, the latter removes the entry.

Notation $\mathcal{U}(\Gamma)$ and $\mathcal{L}(\Gamma)$ refers to the set of unrestricted and linear assumptions in Γ respectively. Notation $\operatorname{dom} S$ represents the set of variables in the set of assumptions S. The assumptions for unrestricted types are never consumed, as the following example shows.

$$x\colon *!\mathsf{bool} \vdash \overline{x}\,\mathsf{true}\colon (x\colon *!\mathsf{bool})$$

New syntactic forms

$$P ::= \ldots \qquad \text{Processes:}$$

$$(\nu xy\colon T)P \qquad \text{annotated scope restriction}$$

Context difference

$$\emptyset\backslash x = \emptyset \qquad (\Gamma, x\colon T)\backslash x = \Gamma \qquad \frac{\Gamma\backslash x = \Gamma_1}{(\Gamma, y\colon T)\backslash x = \Gamma_1, y\colon T}$$

Typing rules for values

$$\Gamma \vdash \mathsf{true}, \mathsf{false}\colon \mathsf{bool}; \Gamma \qquad \Gamma_1, x\colon \mathsf{lin}\, p, \Gamma_2 \vdash x\colon \mathsf{lin}\, p; \Gamma_1, \Gamma_2 \qquad \text{[A-Bool] [A-VarLin]}$$

$$\Gamma_1, x\colon \mathsf{un}\, p, \Gamma_2 \vdash x\colon \mathsf{un}\, p; \Gamma_1, x\colon \mathsf{un}\, p, \Gamma_2 \qquad \text{[A-VarUn]}$$

Typing rules for processes

$$\Gamma \vdash \mathbf{0}\colon \Gamma \qquad \frac{\Gamma_1 \vdash v\colon q\,\mathsf{bool}; \Gamma_2 \qquad \Gamma_2 \vdash P\colon \Gamma_3 \qquad \Gamma_2 \vdash Q\colon \Gamma_3}{\Gamma_1 \vdash \mathsf{if}\ v\ \mathsf{then}\ P\ \mathsf{else}\ Q\colon \Gamma_3} \qquad \text{[A-Inact] [A-If]}$$

$$\frac{\Gamma_1 \vdash P\colon \Gamma_2 \qquad \Gamma_2 \setminus (\mathrm{dom}\,\mathcal{U}(\Gamma_2) \setminus \mathrm{dom}\,\mathcal{U}(\Gamma_1)) \vdash Q\colon \Gamma_3}{\Gamma_1 \vdash P \mid Q\colon \Gamma_3} \qquad \text{[A-Par]}$$

$$\frac{\Gamma_1, x_1\colon T, x_2\colon \overline{T} \vdash P\colon \Gamma_2 \qquad x_i\colon U \in \Gamma_2 \Rightarrow \mathsf{un}(U)}{\Gamma_1 \vdash (\nu x_1 x_2\colon T)P\colon \Gamma_2\backslash x_1 x_2} \qquad \text{[A-Res]}$$

$$\frac{\Gamma_1 \vdash x\colon q!T.U; \Gamma_2 \qquad \Gamma_2 \vdash v\colon T; \Gamma_3 \qquad \Gamma_3 \cdot x\colon U \vdash P\colon \Gamma_4}{\Gamma_1 \vdash \overline{x}\, v.P\colon \Gamma_4} \qquad \text{[A-Out]}$$

$$\frac{\Gamma_1 \vdash x\colon q?T.U; \Gamma_2 \qquad (\Gamma_2, y\colon T) \cdot x\colon U \vdash P\colon \Gamma_3 \qquad y\colon V \in \Gamma_3 \Rightarrow \mathsf{un}(V)}{\Gamma_1 \vdash x(y).P\colon \Gamma_3\backslash y} \qquad \text{[A-In]}$$

$$\frac{\Gamma_1 \vdash x\colon \mathsf{un}\,?T.U; \Gamma_2 \qquad (\Gamma_2, y\colon T) \cdot x\colon U \vdash P\colon \Gamma_3 \qquad y\colon V \in \Gamma_3 \Rightarrow \mathsf{un}(V) \qquad \mathsf{un}(\Gamma_2)}{\Gamma_1 \vdash *x(y).P\colon \Gamma_3\backslash y}$$

[A-Repl]

Fig. 12. Algorithmic type checking

For linear assumptions three things can happen: they may remain, they may disappear altogether or they may become unrestricted. But if they remain, then they keep their types.

$$x\colon \mathsf{lin}\,!\mathsf{bool} \vdash \mathbf{0}\colon (x\colon \mathsf{lin}\,!\mathsf{bool})$$

$$x\colon \mathsf{lin}\,!\mathsf{bool}, y\colon *!(\mathsf{lin}\,!\mathsf{bool}) \vdash \overline{y}\, x\colon (y\colon *!(\mathsf{lin}\,!\mathsf{bool}))$$

$$x\colon \mathsf{lin}\,!\mathsf{bool} \vdash \overline{x}\,\mathsf{true}\colon (x\colon \mathsf{end})$$

The above examples motivates rule [A-Par]. The output of the first subprocess P cannot be directly passed to the second subprocess Q; a rule of the form

$$\frac{\Gamma_1 \vdash P\colon \Gamma_2 \qquad \Gamma_2 \vdash Q\colon \Gamma_3}{\Gamma_1 \vdash P \mid Q\colon \Gamma_3}$$

would allow to derive

$$x\colon \mathsf{lin}\,!\mathsf{bool}, y\colon !\mathsf{end} \vdash \overline{x}\,\mathsf{true} \mid \overline{y}\, x\colon (x\colon \mathsf{end}, y\colon !\mathsf{end}) \qquad \text{:-(}$$

but we know that $x\colon \mathsf{lin}\,!\mathsf{bool}, y\colon !\mathsf{end} \not\vdash \overline{x}\,\mathsf{true} \mid \overline{y}x$. In rule [A-Par], operation $\Gamma_2 \setminus (\mathrm{dom}\,\mathcal{U}(\Gamma_2) \setminus \mathrm{dom}\,\mathcal{U}(\Gamma_1))$ removes from Γ_2 the linear assumptions in Γ_1 that where used in P to become unrestricted in Γ_2.

Rule [A-Res] is an example of a rule that introduces assumptions in the context. We read the types for x and y from the process, extend the incoming context Γ_1 with entries $x\colon T, y\colon \overline{T}$, and pass it to subprocess P. If variables x and y are initially linear, then either they are delegated in P or else they remain in Γ_2 but with the initial linear part consumed. The assumptions for x and y, if existent, are then removed from the output context.

The rule [A-Out] process looks in the incoming context Γ_1 for the assumption for variable x. We then use Γ_2, the remaining portion of Γ_1, to type check value v, to obtain a type T (which must match the input part of the type for x) and a context Γ_3. This context is then enriched with a new assumption for x at the continuation type U, and passed to the subprocess P. Similarly to rule [T-Out] in Figure 5, when $q = \mathsf{lin}$ then x is not in Γ_3 and a new assumption for x is introduced in the context; else when $q = \mathsf{un}$ we must have $q!T.U = U$.

Rule [A-In] should be easy to understand based on the description of rules [A-Res] and [A-Out]. Similarly to [A-Out] we look in the input context for the type of x. We then pass to subprocess P the unused portion together with two new assumptions, for x and for y. In the end, if y remains in the context then it must be unrestricted. The rule for replication is similar, but incorporates an extra check on Γ_2 to match that in rule [T-Repl], Figure 5.

Each rule in the algorithm is syntax directed. Furthermore all auxiliary functions, including context membership, context equality, context difference and the context predicates q, are computable. We still need to check that this system is equivalent to the more elegant system introduced in the previous sections.

The proof of equivalence can be broken in two standard parts, *soundness* and *completeness* of the algorithm with respect to the declarative system. Notice however that the two type systems talk about different languages, languages that differ in the annotation in the scope restriction constructor. To obtain a non-annotated process from an annotated one, we use function erase(P) that removes all types from an annotated process P. Function erase is a homomorphism everywhere, except at scope restriction where $\mathrm{erase}((\nu xy\colon T)P) = (\nu xy)\,\mathrm{erase}(P)$.

Lemma 7 (Algorithmic monotonicity). *If $\Gamma_1 \vdash P\colon \Gamma_2$ then $\mathcal{L}(\Gamma_2) \subseteq \mathcal{L}(\Gamma_1)$ and $\mathcal{U}(\Gamma_1) = \mathcal{U}(\Gamma_2) \setminus \mathrm{dom}\,\mathcal{L}(\Gamma_1)$.*

Lemma 8 (Algorithmic weakening). *If $\Gamma_1 \vdash P\colon \Gamma_2$ then $\Gamma_1, x\colon T \vdash P\colon \Gamma_2, x\colon T$.*

Proof. The proofs for the two results follow by induction on the structure of the appropriate derivation. In each case we must establish the corresponding result for values, each of which follows by a simple case analysis. □

Lemma 9 (Algorithmic linear strengthening). *If $\Gamma_1, x\colon T \vdash P\colon \Gamma_2, x\colon T$ and $\mathsf{lin}(T)$ then $\Gamma_1 \vdash P\colon \Gamma_2$.*

Proof. The proof follows by induction on the structure of the derivation. We must establish the corresponding result for values, which follows by a simple case analysis. The inductive cases use Monotonicity, lemma 7. For example, for the parallel composition $P \mid Q$, we have that $\Gamma_2 \vdash Q\colon \Gamma_3, x\colon T$ with $\mathsf{lin}(T)$ and Monotonicity tells us that Γ_2 is of the form $\Gamma_4, x\colon T$, which allows to use induction for $\Gamma_1, x\colon T \vdash P\colon \Gamma_4, x\colon T$. □

Theorem 3 (Algorithmic soundness). *If* $\Gamma_1 \vdash P\colon \Gamma_2$ *and* $\mathsf{un}(\Gamma_2)$ *then* $\Gamma_1 \vdash \text{erase}(P)$.

Proof. The proof follows by induction on the structure of derivation of the hypothesis, using Algorithmic monotonicity and Algorithmic linear strengthening, lemmas 7 and 9. The interesting case is parallel composition. We have $\Gamma_1 \vdash P\colon \Gamma_2$ and $\Gamma_2 \setminus (\operatorname{dom}\mathcal{U}(\Gamma_2) \setminus \operatorname{dom}\mathcal{U}(\Gamma_1)) \vdash Q\colon \Gamma_3$ and $\mathsf{un}(\Gamma_3)$. Using Monotonicity we know that $\Gamma_1 = \Gamma_4, \Gamma_5, \Gamma_6, \Gamma_7$ and that $\Gamma_2 = \Gamma_5, \Gamma_6', \Gamma_7$, where $\Gamma_2 \setminus (\operatorname{dom}\mathcal{U}(\Gamma_2) \setminus \operatorname{dom}\mathcal{U}(\Gamma_1)) = \Gamma_5, \Gamma_7$ and Γ_6', Γ_7 are unrestricted and the remaining gammas linear. We apply Strengthening followed by induction on the hypothesis for P to obtain $\Gamma_4, \Gamma_6, \Gamma_7 \vdash \text{erase}(P)$. On the branch for Q we know that $\Gamma_5, \Gamma_7 \vdash Q\colon \Gamma_3$, and by induction $\Gamma_5, \Gamma_7 \vdash \text{erase}(Q)$. Noticing that $(\Gamma_4, \Gamma_6, \Gamma_7) \cdot (\Gamma_5, \Gamma_7) = \Gamma_1$ we use rule [T-PAR] to conclude the proof. □

Theorem 4 (Algorithmic completeness). *If* $\Gamma_1 \vdash \text{erase}(P)$ *then* $\Gamma_1 \vdash P\colon \Gamma_2$ *and* $\mathsf{un}(\Gamma_2)$.

Proof. The proof follows by induction on the structure of derivation of the hypothesis, using Algorithmic monotonicity and Algorithmic weakening, lemmas 7 and 8. Once again, the interesting case is parallel composition. If $\Gamma_1 = \Gamma_2 \cdot \Gamma_3$, we know by rule [T-PAR] that $\Gamma_2 \vdash \text{erase}(P)$ and $\Gamma_3 \vdash \text{erase}(Q)$. By induction and Monotonicity we have $\Gamma_2 \vdash P\colon \Gamma_4, \Gamma_6$ and $\Gamma_3 \vdash Q\colon \Gamma_4, \Gamma_8$, where $\Gamma_2 = \Gamma_4, \Gamma_5$ and $\Gamma_3 = \Gamma_4, \Gamma_7$ where $\Gamma_4, \Gamma_6, \Gamma_8$ are unrestricted and the remaining gammas linear. Then we use Weakening on P to obtain $\Gamma_1 \vdash P\colon \Gamma_3, \Gamma_6$, and conclude the proof with rule [A-PAR], noticing that $(\Gamma_3, \Gamma_6) \setminus (\operatorname{dom}(\Gamma_4, \Gamma_6) \setminus \operatorname{dom}\Gamma_4) = \Gamma_3$. □

10 Notes

Session types for the pi calculus. Work on session types goes back to Honda and its colleagues at Keio University—Kubo, Takeuchi, and Vasconcelos—first centering on the type structure, then introducing the notion of channel, and finally extending the ideas into a more general setting [18,19,28]. The original work introduces session types, describing chained continuous interactions composed of communication (input and output) and binary choice [18]. The central notion of session types, duality, is also introduced in this work. The subsequent work proposes, at the language level, the concept of *channels* distinct from pi calculus conventional names—channels (linear variables in our terminology) conduct a pattern of interaction between exactly two partners, names (unrestricted variables in this paper) are used by multiple participants to create channels.

The language is constructed around a pair of operations, *accept* and *request*, synchronizing on a common name and establishing a new channel. Channels are endowed with operations to send and receive base values (including names) and to perform choices based on labels, as opposed to the binary choice in [18]. The language in reference [19] takes the idea further, allowing channels to be passed on channels—often called *session delegation*—thus including two more operations on channels: to send and to receive a channel.

In reference [19], channel passing embodies a technique similar to internal mobility [27] whereby the sender and the receiver must agree on the exact channel being handed over, *prior to communication* itself. Using the notation of this paper and forgoing the variable convention, if x and y are linear co-variables, the rule for communicating a linear variable z is of the following form where z is both free in $\overline{x}\, z.P$ and bound $y(z).Q$,

$$\overline{x}\, z.P \mid y(z).Q \rightarrow P \mid Q$$

with the understanding that if the receiving process happens to look like $y(w).Q$ then the bound variable w is renamed as z prior to reduction, *if possible*.

Gay and Hole proposed a variant to this work by introducing two novelties: they work directly on the pi calculus and use free session passing [14]. Their language is similar to the that in this paper, except for two small details: it includes general replication $!P$, as opposed to the more expressive input replication $*x(y).P$ in this work (cf. exercise 3) or to recursion in [19,28], and it annotates variables with polarities $+, -$. The new reduction rule for session passing is a pi calculus conventional communication rule (x and y are co-variables).

$$\overline{x}\, v.P \mid y(z).Q \rightarrow P \mid Q[v/z]$$

Rather than using distinct identifiers x, y that are made co-variables at binding time $(\nu xy)P$, they use one identifier only (x) with polarity annotations (x^+, x^-) that is bound as a single variable in process $(\nu x)P$. The relation that associates x^+ to x^- is left implicit in reduction. In either case, the reason behind the need for syntactically distinguishing the two ends of a same channel comes from free session passing: the same thread may end up possessing the two ends of a channel, as in $\overline{x^+}\, \mathsf{true}.x^-(z)$. After typing $x^-(z)$ we are left with a context where the types for x^+ and x^- are not dual. They will eventually become dual after typing the output process, and should be dual when the derivation reaches scope restriction for x.

Instead we work with two completely unrelated variables x, y that are made co-variables at binding time only. But there is a fundamental difference between the polarity notation and the co-variable technique used in this paper. In [14], polarity annotated variables are associated to channels; names use non-annotated variables. As such, there are two communication rules: for channels, on processes of the form $\overline{x^+}\, v.P \mid x^-(z).Q$, and for names on processes $\overline{x}\, v.P \mid x(z).Q$. We work with co-variables in all cases, using a single communication rule for processes of the form $\overline{x}\, v.P \mid y(z).Q$ where x and y are co-variables. If needed the distinction between channels and names is made by the type qualifiers associated to variables x and y, linear or unrestricted.

Yoshida and Vasconcelos use the polarity technique to endow the language in [19] with free session passing [34]. All the aforementioned works carefully manage the typing context in order to maintain the invariant where each channel is used exactly in one or two threads, with a technique similar to context splitting. Interesting enough, channel polarities were used in [28], then dropped in [19], and finally recovered in [14].

The technique of binding the two ends of a channel together is due to Gay and Vasconcelos [16], working on a buffered semantics where it makes all the sense to distinguish the two ends of a channel, for each has its own queue for incoming messages. The same idea is explored by Giunti el al. [17] to show that the language in [34] equipped with the type system in [19] is type safe even though it does not satisfy type preservation.

Typing and subtyping. Due to delegation [19], types are usually stratified into two categories: one for sessions, the other for names. Types for channels include constructors for input, output, branching, and selection. Those for names include the standard pi calculus types. The separation of the two universes leads to duplication (recursion, input/output) and omissions (there is no choice on names). We take a different approach, starting from *pretypes* comprising all the basic types and required constructors, and then using a linear or unrestricted qualifier depending on the intended usage for the variable, channel or name.

Subtyping as presented in this paper was first introduced by Gay and Hole [14], co-inductively given the presence of recursive types. Rather than using a separate subsumption rule, Gay and Hole distribute the possible occurrences of subtyping by the relevant typing rules. They further present an algorithm for checking the subtyping relation, used for type checking their language. A proof for Lemma 6 in Section 8 can be found in reference [14].

Gay introduces a notion of bounded polymorphism for the pi calculus with session types [13] where polymorphism is associated with labels in branching processes, in such a way that clients selecting a particular branch also instantiate the polymorphic variable with some type. Capecchi, Dezani-Ciancaglini et al. propose a variant of session types for object-oriented languages where choice is provided, based not on labels, but on classes [2,4]. Castagna, Dezani-Ciancaglini et al. propose a set-theoretic semantics for session types based on a labelled transition system and on a coinductively-defined notion of duality [6]. The semantics yields a notion of subtyping and they present an algorithm for deciding the relation. The session types considered in the paper generalize those found in this work by replacing constructors for branching with boolean expressions.

Linear type systems. A linear type system for the pi calculus was studied by Kobayashi, Pierce and Turner [21]. There, as in the lambda calculus, a linear channel is understood as resource that should be used only once. The exactly-once nature of linear values is at odds with the idea of session types capturing continuous sequences of interactions, and therefore naturally occurring more than once in a thread. Instead, a linear channel in this work is understood as occurring in a single thread, possibly multiple times. The machinery used here, linear and unrestricted type qualifiers and context splitting, is inspired by Walker's substructural type systems [33].

Session types in functional languages. Session types emerged in conjunction with process calculi. Gradually, the notion was adapted to other paradigms, including functional languages, object-oriented languages and service-oriented computing. Together, Gay, Ravara, and Vasconcelos proposed the first functional language with session types [16,30,32]. Neubauer and Thiemann [25] took a different approach, embedding session types within the type system of Haskell. Similarly to this chapter, the language in reference [16] works within the standard framework the linear lambda calculus, treating session types as linear in order to guarantee that each co-channel is owned by a unique thread. For example, the type of the receive operation is $?T.U \rightarrow T \otimes U$ so that the channel, with its new type U, is returned together with the received value T.

Session types in object-oriented languages. The area of session types for object-oriented languages has attracted a lot of attention. The work by Vallecillo, Vasconcelos, and Ravara [29] shows how to type the behavior of objects in component models, Corba in particular (the example in the introduction is taken from this work). Starting with the work by Dezani-Ciancaglini, Yoshida et al. [11] that incorporates channel-based communication in a Java-like language, many have followed, including [2,4,7,9,10,20]. A characteristic of these works is that a channel is always created and completely used within a single method call, or else delegated to another method which will have to use the channel to the end. Mostrous and Yoshida [23] add sessions to Abadi and Cardelli's object calculus [1]. Vasconcelos, Gay, et al. use session types to describe the evolving visible interface of an object, according to the object's state [31].

Session types in service-oriented computing. The natural ability of session types to describe protocols have been explored in the realm of service-oriented calculi. Works like [3,5,8,22], to cite a few, use session types to discipline the interaction between service providers and clients.

Buffered semantics for session types. Neubauer and Thiemann first proposed an asynchronous, buffered semantics, allowing two communicating partners to proceed at distinct rates [26]. The idea is to associate to each co-variable a buffer to hold both values and labels—readers (input and branching processes) read from their own buffer; writers (output and selecting processes) write on the co-channel buffer. Gay and Vasconcelos propose a simpler buffered semantics [15,16]; Fähndrich et al. [12] also use buffered communication but have not published a formal semantics.

An interesting application of session types for buffered communication is that buffer size can be predicted from the session type that describes the channel, thus ensuring that well-typed programs do not overflow their buffers. This fact is observed in [12] and proved in [16], where it is shown that static type information can be used to decrease the runtime buffer size and ultimately deallocate the buffer. Another application explores optimisations by exchanging the order by which certain communications are performed, allowing for a large transfer to proceed in front of other lighter transfers [24]. The valid communication exchanges are captured by a subtyping relation.

Multi-party session types. The language of this chapter disciplines the interaction between two threads; sessions types to describe interaction among multiple partners is the object another chapter in this book.

Acknowledgments. The author was partially supported by the EU IST proactive initiative FET-Global Computing (project Sensoria, IST–2005–16004). He thanks Marco Giunti and Francisco Martins for advice and suggestions.

References

1. Abadi, M., Cardelli, L.: A Theory of Objects. Springer, Heidelberg (1996)
2. Bettini, L., Capecchi, S., Dezani-Ciancaglini, M., Giachino, E., Venneri, B.: Session and union types for object oriented programming. In: Degano, P., De Nicola, R., Meseguer, J. (eds.) Concurrency, Graphs and Models. LNCS, vol. 5065, pp. 659–680. Springer, Heidelberg (2008)
3. Boreale, M., Bruni, R., Nicola, R., Loreti, M.: Sessions and pipelines for structured service programming. In: Barthe, G., de Boer, F.S. (eds.) FMOODS 2008. LNCS, vol. 5051, pp. 19–38. Springer, Heidelberg (2008)
4. Capecchi, S., Coppo, M., Dezani-Ciancaglini, M., Drossopoulou, S., Giachino, E.: Amalgamating sessions and methods in object-oriented languages with generics. Theoretical Computer Science 410(2-3), 142–167 (2009)
5. Carbone, M., Honda, K., Yoshida, N.: Structured communication-centred programming for web services. In: De Nicola, R. (ed.) ESOP 2007. LNCS, vol. 4421, pp. 2–17. Springer, Heidelberg (2007)
6. Castagna, G., Dezani-Ciancaglini, M., Giachino, E., Padovani, L.: Foundation of session types (unpublished) (2009)
7. Coppo, M., Dezani-Ciancaglini, M., Yoshida, N.: Asynchronous session types and progress for object-oriented languages. In: Bonsangue, M.M., Johnsen, E.B. (eds.) FMOODS 2007. LNCS, vol. 4468, pp. 1–31. Springer, Heidelberg (2007)
8. Cruz-Filipe, L., Lanese, I., Martins, F., Ravara, A., Vasconcelos, V.T.: Behavioural theory at work: program transformations in a service-centred calculus. In: Barthe, G., de Boer, F.S. (eds.) FMOODS 2008. LNCS, vol. 5051, pp. 59–77. Springer, Heidelberg (2008)
9. Dezani-Ciancaglini, M., Drossopoulou, S., Giachino, E., Yoshida, N.: Bounded session types for object-oriented languages. In: de Boer, F.S., Bonsangue, M.M., Graf, S., de Roever, W.-P. (eds.) FMCO 2006. LNCS, vol. 4709, pp. 207–245. Springer, Heidelberg (2007)
10. Dezani-Ciancaglini, M., Mostrous, D., Yoshida, N., Drossopolou, S.: Session types for object-oriented languages. In: Thomas, D. (ed.) ECOOP 2006. LNCS, vol. 4067, pp. 328–352. Springer, Heidelberg (2006)
11. Dezani-Ciancaglini, M., Yoshida, N., Ahern, A., Drossopolou, S.: A distributed object-oriented language with session types. In: De Nicola, R., Sangiorgi, D. (eds.) TGC 2005. LNCS, vol. 3705, pp. 299–318. Springer, Heidelberg (2005)
12. Fähndrich, M., Aiken, M., Hawblitzel, C., Hodson, O., Hunt, G., Larus, J.R., Levi, S.: Language support for fast and reliable message-based communication in Singularity OS. SIGOPS Operating Systems Review 40(4), 177–190 (2006)
13. Gay, S.J.: Bounded polymorphism in session types. Mathematical Structures in Computer Science 18(5), 895–930 (2008)

14. Gay, S.J., Hole, M.J.: Subtyping for session types in the pi calculus. Acta Informatica 42(2/3), 191–225 (2005)
15. Gay, S.J., Vasconcelos, V.T.: Asynchronous functional session types. TR 2007–251, Department of Computing, University of Glasgow (May 2007)
16. Gay, S.J., Vasconcelos, V.T.: Linear type theory for asynchronous session types (2008) (submitted)
17. Giunti, M., Honda, K., Vasconcelos, V.T., Yoshida, N.: Session-based type discipline for pi calculus with matching. In: PLACES 2009 (2009)
18. Honda, K.: Types for dyadic interaction. In: Best, E. (ed.) CONCUR 1993. LNCS, vol. 715, pp. 509–523. Springer, Heidelberg (1993)
19. Honda, K., Vasconcelos, V.T., Kubo, M.: Language primitives and type discipline for structured communication-based programming. In: Hankin, C. (ed.) ESOP 1998. LNCS, vol. 1381, pp. 122–138. Springer, Heidelberg (1998)
20. Hu, R., Yoshida, N., Honda, K.: Session-based distributed programming in Java. In: Vitek, J. (ed.) ECOOP 2008. LNCS, vol. 5142, pp. 516–541. Springer, Heidelberg (2008)
21. Kobayashi, N., Pierce, B.C., Turner, D.N.: Linearity and the pi-calculus. ACM Transactions on Programming Languages and Systems 21(5), 914–947 (1999)
22. Lanese, I., Vasconcelos, V.T., Martins, F., Ravara, A.: Disciplining orchestration and conversation in service-oriented computing. In: Proceedings of SEFM 2007, pp. 305–314. IEEE Computer Society Press, Los Alamitos (2007)
23. Mostrous, D., Yoshida, N.: A session object calculus for structured communication-based programming (unpublished) (2008)
24. Mostrous, D., Yoshida, N., Honda, K.: Global principal typing in partially commutative asynchronous sessions. In: Castagna, G. (ed.) ESOP 2009. LNCS, vol. 5502, pp. 316–332. Springer, Heidelberg (2009)
25. Neubauer, M., Thiemann, P.: An implementation of session types. In: Jayaraman, B. (ed.) PADL 2004. LNCS, vol. 3057, pp. 56–70. Springer, Heidelberg (2004)
26. Neubauer, M., Thiemann, P.: Session types for asynchronous communication (unpublished) (2004)
27. Sangiorgi, D.: π-calculus, internal mobility and agent-passing calculi. Theoretical Computer Science 167(1,2), 235–274 (1996)
28. Takeuchi, K., Honda, K., Kubo, M.: An interaction-based language and its typing system. In: Halatsis, C., Philokyprou, G., Maritsas, D., Theodoridis, S. (eds.) PARLE 1994. LNCS, vol. 817, pp. 398–413. Springer, Heidelberg (1994)
29. Vallecillo, A., Vasconcelos, V.T., Ravara, A.: Typing the behavior of objects and components using session types. Fundamenta Informaticæ 73(4), 583–598 (2006)
30. Vasconcelos, V.T., Gay, S.J., Ravara, A.: Typechecking a multithreaded functional language with session types. Theoretical Computer Science 368(1–2), 64–87 (2006)
31. Vasconcelos, V.T., Gay, S.J., Ravara, A., Gesbert, N., Caldeira, A.Z.: Dynamic interfaces. In: FOOL 2009 (2009)
32. Vasconcelos, V.T., Ravara, A., Gay, S.J.: Session types for functional multithreading. In: Gardner, P., Yoshida, N. (eds.) CONCUR 2004. LNCS, vol. 3170, pp. 497–511. Springer, Heidelberg (2004)
33. Walker, D.: Substructural Type Systems. In: Advanced Topics in Types and Programming Languages. MIT Press, Cambridge (2005)
34. Yoshida, N., Vasconcelos, V.T.: Language primitives and type discipline for structured communication-based programming revisited: Two systems for higher-order session communication. In: Proceedings of SecReT 2007. ENTCS, vol. 171(4), pp. 73–93. Elsevier Science, Amsterdam (2007)

Asynchronous Session Types: Exceptions and Multiparty Interactions

Marco Carbone[1], Nobuko Yoshida[2], and Kohei Honda[3]

[1] IT University of Copenhagen
[2] Imperial College London
[3] Queen Mary, University of London

Abstract. Session types are a formalism for structuring communication based on the notion of *session*: the structure of a conversation is abstracted as a type which is then used as a basis of validating programs through an associated type discipline. While standard session types have proven to be able to capture many real scenarios, there are cases where they are not powerful enough for describing and validating interactions involving more complex scenarios. In this note, we shall explore two extensions of session types to *interactional exceptions* and *multiparty session* in presence of asynchronous communication.

1 Introduction

Recent years have seen the emergence of a new style of distributed software system, called *web services*, designed to support interoperable machine-to-machine interaction over a network, using the infrastructure of the world-wide web. These interactions can make up a sophisticated application whose major mode of computation is communication among distributed computing entities. The advent of web services, together with other trends such as the emergence of multi-core processors and ubiquitous computing, is contributing to a shift in the software development paradigm, where communication and concurrency are a norm rather than exceptions. This new paradigm however still lacks a mature programming methodology. Programming communication and concurrency is harder than sequential programming, as it exposes programmers and designers to the new level of complexity including composition of communication behaviours, deadlock, livelock, and diverse forms of partial failure. Thus, web services pose major technical challenges in programming methodologies. At one of the most basic level, these challenges may be summarised as follows: i) we should be able to describe communication-centred behaviour clearly, accurately and in a modular way; ii) we should be able to validate and detect critical properties of programs with respect to their communication behaviour; and iii) we should be able to control run-time behaviour of programs including their composition.

Session types [8,16] are types for structuring communication and have been studied over the last decade for a wide range of process calculi and programming languages. In session types, the notion of *session* becomes central: communication-centred applications exhibit a highly structured sequence of interactions involving, for example, branching and recursion, which as a whole form a natural unit of conversation, or

M. Bernardo, L. Padovani, and G. Zavattaro (Eds.): SFM 2009, LNCS 5569, pp. 187–212, 2009.

session. The structure of a conversation is abstracted as a type which is then used as a basis of validating programs through an associated type discipline.

While original session types have proven to be very simple and concise and able to capture many real scenarios, there are cases where they are not powerful enough for describing and validating interactions involving more complex conversation patterns or, they are just too complex to use, making the design stage harder than it should be.

In this lecture note, we shall explore two extensions of the foregoing theories on session types to (1) interactional exceptions [5] and (2) multiparty sessions [1,2,10] in an asynchronous setting which often arise in practical communication-centred applications.

1. Interactional exceptions, an interactional asynchronous generalisation of structured exceptions, allow communicating peers to asynchronously and collaboratively escape from the middle of a dialogue (session) and reach another in a coordinated fashion. New exception types guarantee communication safety and offer a precise type-abstraction of advanced conversation patterns found in practice.
2. Multiparty sessions extend binary sessions to multiparty, asynchronous sessions. In multiparty sessions, interactions involve multiple peers which are directly abstracted, at type level, as a global scenario. Global types retain the friendly type syntax of binary session types while capturing complex causal chains of multiparty asynchronous interactions. The fundamental properties of the session type discipline such as communication safety, progress and session fidelity hold for general n-party asynchronous interactions.

The remainder of this paper is structured as follows: Section 2 gives the common notation for the following sections; Section 3 introduces an extension of standard session types to an exception mechanism similar to the one of imperative programming languages; Section 4 addresses an extension of binary session types to multiparty; and Section 5 contains some concluding remarks.

2 Notation

Works on session types tend to adopt different notation depending on the specific problem modelled. Due to the nature of this lecture note which addresses two extensions of session types to asynchronous interactional exceptions and multiparty sessions, we shall set some common notation, trying not to deviate from the original one used in [8].

Shared channels represent those names/channel that are public i.e. known by any process in the modelled system. Shared channels are also known as *public* or *service* channels and are denoted by $a, b, c, \ldots$.

A session can be seen as a conversation between some parties which share common session identifiers (or channel names) used for communicating values. *Session channels* are denoted by k (as in the original work on session types [8]) or $s, t, r \ldots$.

Session channels can also be polarised (s^+, s^-) i.e. a polarity is assigned to the channel in order to identify the side of the (binary) session [6]. We shall use polarised channels when implementing asynchronous exceptions for telling from/to who an exception has been raised.

Table 1. Notation on Session Types

Term	Symbol	Note
Public channels (or *shared* or *service* channels)	$a, b, \ldots$	
Session channels	$k, s, t, r \ldots$	
Polarised Session channels	κ, λ	$\kappa \in \{s^+, s^-\}$
Variables	x, y, z	
Process Term Variables	X, Y	
Public channel or Variable	$u, u', \ldots$	

Formally, s^p is a *polarised session channel* with p ranging over polarities $\{+, -\}$. We define the dual of a polarised channel s^p as $\overline{s^+} = s^-$ and $\overline{s^-} = s^+$. Polarised channels are denoted by Greek letters κ and λ.

The letters x, y, z denote *variables* while $X, X', \ldots$ are *term variables.*

Table 1 resumes the notation used in this lecture note.

3 Interactional Exceptions in Session Types

3.1 Preview on Interactional Exceptions

According to a Wikipedia entry, an *exception (handler)* is

> *"... a programming language construct [...] designed to handle the occurrence of a condition that changes the normal flow of execution" [18].*

Structured exceptions in modern programming languages such as Java and C♯ allow a thread of control in a block (often designated as "`try` block") to get transferred to another block (exception handler, "`catch` block"), when a system or user raises an exception. Their central merit is to enable a dynamic escape from a block of code to another (like `goto`), but in a controlled and structured way (unlike `goto`). They are useful not only for error-handling but, as suggested by the citation above, also for a flexible control flow while preserving well-structured description and type-safety.

In this section, we address the notion of structured exceptions for distributed, concurrent, asynchronously communicating programs based on session types motivated by collaboration with industry partners in web services [17] and financial protocols [12]. These two application domains contain a wealth of structured conversation patterns arising from practical needs [9], and many of these patterns crucially rely on dynamic escape: a conversation is interrupted by a special communication action, after which all peers move to a different stage. Hence, an exception affects not only a sequential thread but also a collection of parallel processes; and an escape needs to move into another dialogue in a concerted manner. The distinguishing feature of these exceptions in comparison with their traditional counterpart is that they demand not only local but also coordinated actions among communicating peers. We call such exceptions, *interactional exceptions*.

Example 1 (Asynchronous and Nested Escapes). We conclude this preview, with an example scenario based on financial protocols. Suppose a seller Seller wishes to sell a product to a buyer Buyer such that:

1. Seller repeats sending quotes without waiting for an acknowledgement;
2. if Buyer accepts one of the quotes, the loop terminates and the conversation moves to another stage for completing the transaction.

The conversation pattern above contains an asynchronous escape from one part of a conversation to another: after Buyer aborts, both participants should move together to another part of the conversation. The protocol can become more complex, involving other parties e.g. Buyer and Seller negotiate the price through a broker Broker:

1. Buyer initiates a conversation with Broker;
2. as a result, Broker initiates a conversation with Seller, and starts brokering between Buyer and Seller, to reach a successful transaction;
3. if an exceptional situation arises between steps 1 and 2 (e.g. a legal issue), Buyer or Broker aborts and they together move to a quitting dialogue;
4. on the other hand, if there is an exceptional circumstance during 2, then there is an exception dialogue involving all of Broker, Seller and Buyer.

Above, an exception handling at Broker is *nested*, whose later, or inner, exception handling (4, involving all three parties) supersedes the earlier, or outer, one (3, involving only Broker and Seller). As a conversation evolves, more communication peers may be involved, making it necessary to coordinate more parties when an exception is raised.

3.2 The π-Calculus with Asynchronous Sessions and Interactional Exceptions

Syntax. The syntax of (static) processes (denoted by $P, Q, R, \ldots$) written by programmers is given by the following grammar:

$P ::= \; * c(\lambda)[P, Q]$	(accept)	$\mid \overline{c}(\lambda)[\tilde{\kappa}, P, Q]$	(request)
$\mid \kappa?(x).\, P$	(input)	$\mid \kappa!\langle e\rangle.\, P$	(output)
$\mid \kappa \rhd \{l_i \colon P_i\}_{i\in I}$	(branch)	$\mid \kappa \lhd l.\, P$	(select)
$\mid P \mid Q$	(par)	$\mid$ **if** e **then** P **else** P	(cond)
$\mid \mathbf{0}$	(inact)	$\mid (\nu a)\, P$	(resServ)
$\mid X$	(termVar)	$\mid \mu X.\, P$	(recursion)
$\mid$ **throw**	(throw)		

$$e ::= a \mid \mathsf{tt} \mid \mathsf{ff} \mid e \text{ and } e \mid \neg e \mid \ldots \qquad c ::= a \mid x \qquad \kappa, \lambda ::= s^p$$

Above, the accept term $*a(\lambda)[P, Q]$ is a replicated process with shared channel a, polarised session channel κ, *default process* P and *exception handler* Q. The term denotes a service a which, when invoked, establishes a fresh session channel κ and behaves as process P, possibly followed by Q if an exception takes place. Service a is replicated (available in many copies) according to the *Service Channel Principle* (SCP) [4]:

Definition 1 (Service Channel Principle (SCP)). *Invocation channels are always available. Therefore, they can be shared and invoked repeatedly.*

Dually, a request $\overline{c}(\lambda)[\tilde{\kappa}, P, Q]$ interacts with a service via c and establishes a fresh session λ, with its *default process* P and *handler* Q. Because shared channels can be passed, we allow for c to be a variable e.g. it could be bound by a prefixing input.

The session channels $\tilde{\kappa}$, containing already established sessions which the handler Q gets associated with, have a pivotal rôle: in the case P raises an exception, any other handler belonging to an embedding accept $*c'(\lambda')[P', Q']$ or request $\overline{c'}(\lambda')[\tilde{\kappa}', P', Q']$ ($\overline{c}(\lambda)[\tilde{\kappa}, P, Q]$ is in P'), such that $\tilde{t}' \subseteq \tilde{t}$, must be discarded. We call vector $\tilde{t}$ a *refinement* in the sense that channels $\tilde{t}'$ in $\tilde{t}$ are refined i.e. a new handler Q replaces the old Q'. We require λ itself to be included in $\tilde{\kappa}$ which is convenient for typing. As an example, in the process:

$$\overline{a}(\kappa)[\kappa, \quad \overline{b}(\lambda)[(\kappa, \lambda), P, Q] \quad , Q']$$

the term $\overline{b}(\lambda)[(\kappa, \lambda), P, Q]$ is a refinement of κ in the sense that once session b is initiated Q becomes the handler for κ and Q' can be discarded.

Process **throw** denotes the throwing of an exception and it usually occurs inside try-catch blokcs. All other constructs are from [4,8].

Free/bound (term) variables/channels and α-equivalence are standard. $\mathsf{fsc}(P)$, $\mathsf{fn}(P)$ and $\mathsf{fv}(P)$ respectively denote the sets of free session channels, shared channels, and variables in P. We call *program* a process which does not contain free variables or free session channels. We often omit the tailing $\mathbf{0}$.

Syntactic Assumptions. In order to have consistent operational semantics, we stipulate the following syntactic constraints:

1. *(Consistent Refinement)* given $\overline{c}(\lambda)[\tilde{\kappa}, P, Q]$, for each $\overline{c'}(\lambda')[\tilde{\kappa}', P', Q']$ occurring in P and any $\kappa_i \in \tilde{\kappa}$, we have $\kappa_i \in \tilde{\kappa}'$ implies $\tilde{\kappa} \subseteq \tilde{\kappa}'$ (for consistent refinement). Further, such a refinement never occurs inside a handler (otherwise we have ambiguity when launching a handler);
2. recursions is *guarded*, i.e. P in $\mu X.\ P$ is prefixed by an input, output, branch, select or conditional; moreover, a free term variable never occurs free in $\overline{c}(\lambda)[\tilde{\kappa}, P, Q]$;
3. the term (accept) never occurs under an input/output/recursion prefix nor inside a default process or handler thus protecting its availability from exceptions;
4. **throw** never occurs inside a handler hence preventing a handler from throwing a further exception in the same session.

The above restrictions could be enforced with the typing system but have been separated for the sake of presentation.

Example 2 (Asynchronous Escape). We can write the first part of the example in Section 3.1 as:

$$\begin{array}{ll}
\texttt{Buyer} = \overline{\texttt{chSeller}}(s^+)[\ s^+, & \texttt{Seller} = *\texttt{chSeller}(s^-)[\\
\quad \mu X.\ s^+?(y).\ \mathbf{if}\ \mathsf{ok}(y)\ \mathbf{throw\ else}\ X, & \quad \mu X.\ s^-!\langle\texttt{quote}\rangle.\ X\ ,\\
\quad s^+!\langle\texttt{card}\rangle.\ s^+?(z)\ ] & \quad s^-?(y_2).\ s^-!\langle\texttt{time}\rangle\ ]
\end{array}$$

Buyer keeps on reading messages on s^+ until condition $\mathsf{ok}(y)$ is met and then it throws an exception. Seller, instead, is in an infinite loop where it persistently sends a quote over channel s^- (we assume `quote` changes over time). When the exception is raised the handlers are run: Buyer will send the credit card details `card` and Seller will acknowledge on channel s^- with the current time.

Example 3 (Nested Escapes). The second part of Example 1, can be represented in the calculus as (Seller remains unchanged):

$$\begin{array}{ll}
\texttt{Buyer} = \overline{\texttt{chBroker}}(t^+)[\, t^+, & \texttt{Broker} = *\texttt{chBroker}(t^-)[\, t^-, \\
\quad t^+!\langle \texttt{id} \rangle. & \quad t^-?(x).\ \textbf{if}\ \mathsf{bad}(x)\ \textbf{then throw else} \\
 & \quad \overline{\texttt{chSeller}}(s^+)[\,(s^+, t^-), \\
\quad \mu X.\ t^+?(y).\ \textbf{if}\ \mathsf{ok}(y)\ \textbf{throw else}\ X, & \quad \mu X.\ s^+?(x).\ t^-!\langle x + 10\% \rangle.\ X, \\
 & \quad t^- \triangleleft l_1.\ t^-?(y_2).\ s^+!\langle y_2 \rangle. \\
\quad t^+ \triangleright \{\, l_1 : t^+!\langle \texttt{card} \rangle.\ t^+?(z), & \quad s^+?(y_3).\ t^-!\langle y_3 \rangle\ \ ], \\
\quad\quad l_2 : P_{\texttt{abort}} \}\ \ ] & \quad t^- \triangleleft l_2.\ R_{\texttt{abort}}\ \ ]
\end{array}$$

Buyer first sends its identity `id` and then Broker throws an exception or proceeds by invoking Seller based on `bad(id)`. In the first case, process $t^- \triangleleft l_2.\ R_{\texttt{abort}}$ in the outermost handler selects the l_2 branch on Buyer's handler and proceeds with abortion (conversation between $P_{\texttt{abort}}$ and $R_{\texttt{abort}}$). In the other case, Seller is invoked and the protocol proceeds as in Example 2 with Broker forwarding messages and increasing quotes by 10%. When Buyer decides to accept a quote, the innermost handler is run by Broker which selects the l_1 conversation in Buyer's handler and forwards the exception to Seller. Then Broker forwards messages, successfully completing the transaction.

Semantics. We shall now define the semantics of asynchronous sessions [3,5,7,10] with exception handling and exception propagation. Further we ensure that processes always carry out their conversation at properly matching levels (for example when a default process sends a message, a receiving peer may throw an exception before the message arrives, making it no longer relevant), by annotating message queues, hence in effect messages in them, with exception levels.

In order to implement asynchrony of communication (both for messages and exception propagation), we need to extend the grammar of programs with extra syntactic terms called *runtime processes* [3,7,10,5]:

$$\begin{array}{llll}
P ::= \ldots \mid (\nu s)\, P & (\text{resSess}) & \mid \kappa \hookrightarrow_\phi \overline{\kappa} : L & (\text{queue}) \\
\quad\quad \mid \textbf{try}\{\, P \,\}\ \textbf{catch}\ \{\, \tilde{\kappa} : Q \,\} & (\text{try-catch}) & \mid \tilde{\kappa}[\![P]\!] & (\text{wrap}) \\
L ::= \ \epsilon \mid h :: L & & h ::= \ l \mid a \mid \mathsf{tt} \mid \mathsf{ff} \mid \dagger &
\end{array}$$

The *try-catch block* $\textbf{try}\{\, P \,\}\ \textbf{catch}\ \{\, \tilde{\kappa} : Q \,\}$ is the runtime presentation of a default process and a handler: the default process P in the *try-block* is running during which an exception on channels $\tilde{\kappa}$ can be thrown, which terminates P and launches the handler Q in the *catch-block*. When this Q is launched, it becomes a *wrapped process* (or, simply, a *wrap*) $\tilde{\kappa}[\![Q]\!]$, making Q immune to an exception notification at the same or upper levels (note such notifications can come due to asynchrony).

In order to formalise order-preserving asynchronous message passing, we use a directed message queue $\kappa \hookrightarrow_\phi \overline{\kappa} : L$ [3,7,5,10], where κ (source) and $\overline{\kappa}$ (target) are two dual polarised session channels. ϕ ranges over natural numbers, describing the level of the exception at which messages in the queue are to be delivered (e.g. to a try-block or a wrap). This will also be relative to the current position of the queue, which is allowed to

Table 2. Rules for Meta Reduction

$$\text{(MTRY)}\quad P \searrow (P',S) \quad\Rightarrow\quad \mathbf{try}\{P\}\,\mathbf{catch}\,\{\tilde{\kappa} : Q\} \searrow \begin{cases} (P',S) & \text{if } \tilde{\kappa} \subseteq S \\ (\tilde{\kappa}[\![Q]\!] \mid P', S \cup \tilde{\kappa}) & \text{otherwise} \end{cases}$$

$$\text{(MWRAP)}\quad \tilde{\kappa}[\![Q]\!] \searrow (\tilde{\kappa}[\![Q]\!], \emptyset)$$

$$\text{(MPAR)}\quad P \searrow (P',S_1) \text{ and } Q \searrow (Q',S_2) \quad\Rightarrow\quad P \mid Q \searrow (P' \mid Q', S_1 \cup S_2)$$

$$\text{(MNIL)}\quad R \searrow (\mathbf{0},\emptyset) \quad \text{if } R \in \left\{ \begin{array}{l} \text{(inact),(request), (input), (output), (branch),} \\ \text{(select), (cond), (recursion), (throw)} \end{array} \right\}$$

move inside/outside try-catch blocks and wraps. We do not need to consider the level of a sender, since this level is recorded by the number of the exception messages † inside a queue. We often write $\kappa \hookrightarrow \overline{\kappa} : L$ for $\kappa \hookrightarrow_0 \overline{\kappa} : L$. The list $L :: h$ is obtained by extending L with an extra tail element h. Given the list $L = L' :: h'$, we stipulate that inserting a message h in L will result into $h :: L$ while removing an element from L will result into L'.

Session restriction $(\nu s)\,P$ is standard. Free variables and channels are extended to run-time processes.

Meta Reduction. We introduce an extra relation on processes called *meta reduction*, for dearling with sudden termination of try-blocks due to the throwing of an exception. *Meta reduction*

1. erases the remaining activity of the default process in the try-block;
2. propagates exceptions to the try-catch blocks inside the try-block; and
3. leaves wrapped processes as they are.

In traditional structured exceptions as found in Java or C++, an exception completely erases the try-block and lets the handler run in the same state. In our calculus, concurrently running threads inside a try-block may have conversations (sessions) with other agents. Erasing them would make conversations inconsistent, thus an exception is thrown in each of them.

Meta reduction $\searrow$ is the minimum relation satisfying the rules given in Table 2. A reduction $P \searrow (P',S)$ says that the initial process P is transformed into process P', the result of erasing and wrapping; and S denotes session channels via which we should communicate that the exception takes place including the ones of nested try-catch blocks. Rule (MTRY) propagates the exception to a nested try-catch block. If the try-block meta reduces to some P' with some set S then $\mathbf{try}\{P\}\,\mathbf{catch}\,\{\tilde{\kappa} : Q\}$ will reduce either to (i) P' itself or to (ii) the parallel composition of P' and $\tilde{\kappa}[\![Q]\!]$ with the new set $S \cup \tilde{\kappa}$ ensuring that also channels $\tilde{\kappa}$ will be notified with an exception. Case (i) discards handler Q when another handler for $\tilde{\kappa}$ is already in P while case (ii) happens when there is no refinement of $\tilde{\kappa}$ in P. The mechanism is sound because of the assumption that κ_i are always refined together (cf. syntax). Note that, if the try-block is single-threaded, the meta reduction mechanism is identical to the one of standard exception handling.

Table 3. Reduction Semantics

(INIT)
$$*a(s^-)[P,Q] \mid C[\overline{a}(s^+)[\tilde{\kappa}, P', Q']] \longrightarrow$$
$$*a(s^-)[P,Q] \mid (\nu s)\begin{pmatrix} \mathbf{try}\{\,P\,\}\ \mathbf{catch}\ \{\, s^- : Q\,\} & \mid\ s^- \hookrightarrow_0 s^+ : \epsilon \mid \\ C[\mathbf{try}\{\,P'\,\}\ \mathbf{catch}\ \{\,\tilde{\kappa} : Q'\,\}] & \mid\ s^+ \hookrightarrow_0 s^- : \epsilon \end{pmatrix}$$

(OUT)
$$\kappa!\langle e\rangle.\,P \mid \kappa \hookrightarrow_\phi \overline{\kappa} : L \longrightarrow P \mid \kappa \hookrightarrow_\phi \overline{\kappa} : (v :: L) \qquad (e \downarrow v)$$

(IN)
$$\kappa?(x).\,P \mid \overline{\kappa} \hookrightarrow_0 \kappa : (L :: v) \longrightarrow P\{v/x\} \mid \overline{\kappa} \hookrightarrow_0 \kappa : L$$

(SEL)
$$\kappa \lhd l.\,P \mid \kappa \hookrightarrow_\phi \overline{\kappa} : L \longrightarrow P \mid \kappa \hookrightarrow_\phi \overline{\kappa} : (l :: L)$$

(BRA)
$$\kappa \rhd \{l_i : P_i\}_{i\in I} \mid \overline{\kappa} \hookrightarrow_0 \kappa : (L :: l_j) \longrightarrow P_j \mid \overline{\kappa} \hookrightarrow_0 \kappa : L \qquad (j \in I)$$

(CON)
$$P \longrightarrow Q \quad\Rightarrow\quad C[P] \longrightarrow C[Q]$$

(IF)
$$\mathbf{if}\ e\ \mathbf{then}\ P\ \mathbf{else}\ Q \longrightarrow P \quad (e \downarrow \mathrm{tt}) \qquad\qquad \mathbf{if}\ e\ \mathbf{then}\ P\ \mathbf{else}\ Q \longrightarrow Q \quad (e \downarrow \mathrm{ff})$$

(STR)
$$P \equiv P' \text{ and } P' \longrightarrow Q' \text{ and } Q' \equiv Q \quad\Rightarrow\quad P \longrightarrow Q$$

(THR)
$$\mathbf{try}\{\,P\,\}\ \mathbf{catch}\ \{\,\tilde{\kappa} : Q\,\} \searrow (R,S) \quad\Rightarrow$$
$$\mathbf{try}\{\,\mathbf{throw} \mid P\,\}\ \mathbf{catch}\ \{\,\tilde{\kappa} : Q\,\} \mid \Pi_{\kappa\in S}\ \kappa \hookrightarrow_{\phi_\kappa} \overline{\kappa} : L_\kappa \longrightarrow R \mid \Pi_{\kappa\in S}\ \kappa \hookrightarrow_{\phi_\kappa} \overline{\kappa} : (\dagger :: L_\kappa)$$

(RTHR)
$$\mathbf{try}\{\,P\,\}\ \mathbf{catch}\ \{\,\tilde{\kappa} : Q\,\} \searrow (R,S) \quad\Rightarrow$$
$$\mathbf{try}\{\,P\,\}\ \mathbf{catch}\ \{\,\tilde{\kappa} : Q\,\} \mid \overline{\kappa}_j \hookrightarrow_0 \kappa_j : (L :: \dagger) \mid \Pi_{\kappa\in S}\ \kappa \hookrightarrow_{\phi_\kappa} \overline{\kappa} : L_\kappa$$
$$\longrightarrow R \mid \overline{\kappa}_j \hookrightarrow_1 \kappa_j : L \mid \Pi_{\kappa\in S}\ \kappa \hookrightarrow_{\phi_\kappa} \overline{\kappa} : (\dagger :: L_\kappa)$$

(WVAL)
$$\tilde{\kappa}\llbracket Q\rrbracket \mid \overline{\kappa}_i \hookrightarrow_0 \kappa_i : (L :: v) \longrightarrow \tilde{\kappa}\llbracket Q\rrbracket \mid \overline{\kappa}_i \hookrightarrow_0 \kappa_i : L$$

(WTHR)
$$\tilde{\kappa}\llbracket Q\rrbracket \mid \overline{\kappa}_i \hookrightarrow_0 \kappa_i : (L :: \dagger) \longrightarrow \tilde{\kappa}\llbracket Q\rrbracket \mid \overline{\kappa}_i \hookrightarrow_1 \kappa_i : L$$

(CLEAN)
$$P \searrow (R,S),\ (\lambda \in \tilde{\kappa}, \dagger \in L) \Rightarrow$$
$$\mathbf{try}\{\,P \mid \lambda \hookrightarrow_\phi \overline{\lambda} : L\,\}\ \mathbf{catch}\ \{\,\tilde{\kappa} : \tilde{Q}\,\} \mid \Pi_{\kappa\in S}\ \kappa \hookrightarrow_{\phi_\kappa} \overline{\kappa} : L_\kappa$$
$$\longrightarrow R \mid \lambda \hookrightarrow_\phi \overline{\lambda} : L \mid \Pi_{\kappa\in S}\ \kappa \hookrightarrow_{\phi_\kappa} \overline{\kappa} : (\dagger :: L_\kappa)$$

Reduction. We now introduce the main reduction rules. Due to the nesting of wraps and try-catch blocks, the reduction is defined using the following reduction contexts:

$$C ::= \mathbf{try}\{\,C\,\}\ \mathbf{catch}\ \{\,\tilde{\kappa} : Q\,\} \ \mid\ P \mid C \ \mid\ \tilde{\kappa}\llbracket C\rrbracket \ \mid\ (\nu s)\,C \ \mid\ (\nu a)\,C \ \mid\ -$$

Given a context C and a process P, the process $C[P]$ denotes the new process obtained by replacing the whole $-$ in C with P.

The reduction $\longrightarrow$ is the smallest relation generated by the rules in Table 3. (INIT) gives the semantics of session initiation, generating two fresh dual session channels, the associated two empty queues (ϵ denotes the empty string) and the two try-catch blocks **try**{ P } **catch** { s^- : Q } and **try**{ P' } **catch** { $\tilde{\kappa}$: Q' }. Note that $*a(s^-)[P,Q]$ is not in a context. This is because we have assumed that *services never appear nested in a try- or a catch-block* as we do not want them to be terminated (following SCP).

(OUT) and (SEL) enqueue, respectively, a value and a label at the head of the queue for κ. Symmetrically, (IN) and (BRA) dequeue from the tail of the queue. The exception level in the latter two rules is 0, indicating the level of an actual receiver. The exception level of a queue ensures that a message is sent and received at the same level, guaranteeing consistency of communication. This depends on the invariance that the sum of the level of the queue and the number of †'s in the queue before a specific message, determines the depth (the number of wraps) at which the message enqueueing is performed.

These rules say that a sending action is never blocked (asynchrony) and that two messages from the same sender to the same channel arrive in the sending order (order preservation).

In (OUT,IF), $e \downarrow v$ says that expression e evaluates to value v. (CON,STR) are standard. (THR) and (RTHR) represent the firing of an exception. (THR) is when **throw** appears top-level in the try-block, i.e. exception is thrown locally; while (RTHR) is when a remote exception is received as † in the queue. Eventually, all peers will be notified of the exception by sending † via channels in S generated from P as well as $\tilde{\kappa}$.

(WVAL) describes the case when messages at the default level meet a wrapped process and are drained into a sink (i.e. get dequeued but ignored). In (WTHR), † meets a wrap and the exception level of the queue is incremented, allowing the queue to enter the wrap. In (CLEAN), † in the queue reveals the presence of a refinement in P which has now become a wrap due to a local throw. Meta reduction propagates the exception to each parallel process in P and the try-catch block is discarded.

This last step is formally defined by the structural congruence $\equiv$ which plays a key role in treating exceptions and, in particular, moving queues while maintaining their exception levels.

Definition 2 (Structural Congruence). $\equiv$ *is the least congruence relation on processes such that* $(P, |)$ *is a commutative monoid and includes the standard rules for restriction (such as scope extrusion) and recursion and:*

1) $\textbf{try}\{\, P \mid \lambda \hookrightarrow_\phi \overline{\lambda} : L \,\}\, \textbf{catch}\, \{\tilde{\kappa} : Q\} \equiv \textbf{try}\{\, P \,\}\, \textbf{catch}\, \{\tilde{\kappa} : Q\} \mid \lambda \hookrightarrow_\phi \overline{\lambda} : L \quad (\lambda \in \tilde{\kappa} \Rightarrow \dagger \notin L)$
2) $\tilde{\kappa}[\![P \mid \overline{\lambda} \hookrightarrow_\phi \lambda : L]\!] \equiv \tilde{\kappa}[\![P]\!] \mid \overline{\lambda} \hookrightarrow_\phi \lambda : L \quad (\lambda \notin \tilde{\kappa})$
3) $\tilde{\kappa}[\![P]\!] \mid \overline{\kappa}_i \hookrightarrow_\phi \kappa_i : L \equiv \tilde{\kappa}[\![P \mid \overline{\kappa}_i \hookrightarrow_{\phi-1} \kappa_i : L]\!]$
4) $\textbf{try}\{\, (\nu a)\, P \,\}\, \textbf{catch}\, \{\tilde{\kappa} : Q\} \equiv (\nu a)\, \textbf{try}\{\, P \,\}\, \textbf{catch}\, \{\tilde{\kappa} : Q\} \quad (a \notin fn(Q))$
5) $\tilde{\kappa}[\![(\nu a)\, P]\!] \equiv (\nu a)\, \tilde{\kappa}[\![P]\!]$

The first and second rules allow a queue to move into a try-catch block and a wrap respectively. The third rule is applicable when the receiving side of the queue is in $\tilde{\kappa}$: when entering the wrap, ϕ is decreased so that the process inside the wrap can read the value if the level after the decrement is 0. The last two rules open the scope.

Example 4. To illustrate how queue levels work, we consider the following process:

$$\begin{aligned} P = \ & \textbf{try}\{\ \textbf{throw} \mid \kappa!\langle 5\rangle\ \}\ \textbf{catch}\ \{\kappa : \kappa!\langle \texttt{tt}\rangle\} \mid \kappa \hookrightarrow_0 \overline{\kappa} : \epsilon \mid \\ & \textbf{try}\{\ \textbf{throw} \mid \overline{\kappa}?(x)\ \}\ \textbf{catch}\ \{\overline{\kappa} : \overline{\kappa}?(x)\} \mid \overline{\kappa} \hookrightarrow_0 \kappa : \epsilon \end{aligned}$$

Process P can reduce to $P' = \kappa[\![\mathbf{0}]\!] \mid \overline{\kappa}[\![\mathbf{0}]\!] \mid \kappa \hookrightarrow_0 \overline{\kappa} : \epsilon \mid \overline{\kappa} \hookrightarrow_0 \kappa : \epsilon$ in different ways.

$$\begin{aligned} P & \longrightarrow\equiv \kappa[\![\kappa!\langle \texttt{tt}\rangle]\!] \mid \kappa \hookrightarrow_0 \overline{\kappa} : \dagger \mid \textbf{try}\{\ \textbf{throw} \mid \overline{\kappa}?(x)\ \}\ \textbf{catch}\ \{\overline{\kappa} : \overline{\kappa}?(x)\} \mid \overline{\kappa} \hookrightarrow_0 \kappa : \epsilon \\ & \longrightarrow\equiv \kappa[\![\mathbf{0}]\!] \mid \kappa \hookrightarrow_0 \overline{\kappa} : (\texttt{tt} :: \dagger) \mid \textbf{try}\{\ \textbf{throw} \mid \overline{\kappa}?(x)\ \}\ \textbf{catch}\ \{\overline{\kappa} : \overline{\kappa}?(x)\} \mid \overline{\kappa} \hookrightarrow_0 \kappa : \epsilon \\ & \longrightarrow\equiv \kappa[\![\mathbf{0}]\!] \mid \kappa \hookrightarrow_1 \overline{\kappa} : \texttt{tt} \mid \overline{\kappa}[\![\overline{\kappa}?(x)]\!] \mid \overline{\kappa} \hookrightarrow_0 \kappa : \dagger \\ & \longrightarrow\equiv \kappa[\![\mathbf{0}]\!] \mid \overline{\kappa} \hookrightarrow_1 \kappa : \epsilon \mid \kappa \hookrightarrow_1 \overline{\kappa} : \texttt{tt} \mid \overline{\kappa}[\![\overline{\kappa}?(x)]\!] \longrightarrow\equiv P' \end{aligned}$$

In this case, an exception and then tt are sent over κ. Finally the exception is delivered to $\overline{\kappa}$ before delivering tt. But we can also have:

$$\begin{aligned} P & \longrightarrow\longrightarrow\equiv \textbf{try}\{\ \textbf{throw}\ \}\ \textbf{catch}\ \{\kappa : \kappa!\langle \texttt{tt}\rangle\} \mid \kappa \hookrightarrow_0 \overline{\kappa} : 5 \mid \overline{\kappa}[\![\overline{\kappa}?(x)]\!] \mid \overline{\kappa} \hookrightarrow_0 \kappa : \dagger \\ & \longrightarrow\equiv \kappa[\![\kappa!\langle \texttt{tt}\rangle]\!] \mid \kappa \hookrightarrow_0 \overline{\kappa} : (\dagger :: 5) \mid \overline{\kappa}[\![\overline{\kappa}?(x)]\!] \mid \overline{\kappa} \hookrightarrow_1 \kappa : \epsilon \longrightarrow\longrightarrow\longrightarrow\equiv P' \end{aligned}$$

Above, 5 is sent over κ and an exception is thrown on $\overline{\kappa}$. In this situation, the system will ignore 5 (discarded by (WVAL)), and deliver `tt` inside the wrap.

Example 5. The following example shows how refinement of an existing exception is handled:

$$R \; = \; \mathbf{try}\{\; \mathbf{try}\{\mathbf{throw}\}\,\mathbf{catch}\,\{(\kappa,\lambda) : Q_1\}\;\}\,\mathbf{catch}\,\{\kappa : Q_2\} \mid \overline{\kappa} \hookrightarrow_0 \kappa : \dagger \mid \kappa \hookrightarrow_0 \overline{\kappa} : L$$

Process R either throws an exception in the inner try-catch block (by (THR)) or receives a remote exception (by (RTHR)). By applying (THR), (CLEAN) and (WTHR) in the first case or by (RTHR) in the second case, we have (omitting some queues):

$$\begin{array}{l} R \longrightarrow\equiv \mathbf{try}\{\; (\kappa,\lambda)\{\!\{Q_1\}\!\} \mid \kappa \hookrightarrow_0 \overline{\kappa} : \dagger :: L\}\,\mathbf{catch}\,\{\kappa : Q_2\} \mid \overline{\kappa} \hookrightarrow_0 \kappa : \dagger \longrightarrow \\ (\kappa,\lambda)\{\!\{Q_1\}\!\} \mid \kappa \hookrightarrow_0 \overline{\kappa} : \dagger :: L \mid \overline{\kappa} \hookrightarrow_0 \kappa : \dagger \longrightarrow (\kappa,\lambda)\{\!\{Q_1\}\!\} \mid \kappa \hookrightarrow_0 \overline{\kappa} : \dagger :: L \mid \overline{\kappa} \hookrightarrow_1 \kappa : \epsilon \end{array}$$

3.3 Session Types with Interactional Exceptions

In this subsection, we show how to extend the standard type discipline for sessions with interactional exceptions. In comparison with the standard session types, the central difference is the shape of a type itself, which now consists of the abstraction of the default behaviour (the "try" part) and that of the handler behaviour (the "catch" part). This simple extension, combined with the use of levels, allows to establish basic typing properties, guaranteeing that messages are always delivered at proper levels at proper timings in the presence of nested asynchronous escapes, testifying consistency of the operational semantics introduced above.

Type Syntax. The grammar of types extends the standard session types (new parts highlighted with a box $\boxed{}$):

$$\begin{array}{rcl} \alpha,\beta & ::= & \downarrow(\theta).\,\alpha \mid \uparrow(\theta).\,\alpha \mid \oplus\{l_i : \alpha_i\}_{i\in I} \mid \&\{l_i : \alpha_i\}_{i\in I} \mid \boxed{\alpha\{\!\{\beta\}\!\}} \mid \mathbf{end} \mid \mu\mathbf{t}.\,\alpha \mid \mathbf{t} \\ \theta & ::= & \boxed{\langle\alpha\{\!\{\beta\}\!\}\rangle} \mid \mathtt{bool} \mid \ldots \end{array}$$

α and θ are respectively called *session types* and *service types*. The new type $\alpha\{\!\{\beta\}\!\}$ (called *try-catch type*) is an abstraction of a try-catch block: in $\alpha\{\!\{\beta\}\!\}$, α denotes the type of the try-block and β the catch block. A session type α is *plain* if it does not use a try-catch type (except in a service type it carries). We stipulate α and β are both plain in $\alpha\{\!\{\beta\}\!\}$. This is to prevent a try-catch on κ to occur nested in a catch-block of λ if $\kappa = \lambda$.

The *dual* of a type α, written $\overline{\alpha}$, inverts inputs and outputs [8]. The dual of the try-catch type is defined as $\overline{\alpha\{\!\{\beta\}\!\}} = \overline{\alpha}\{\!\{\overline{\beta}\}\!\}$: the other cases are standard. For example, by exchanging input and output, the dual of $\downarrow(\mathtt{string}).\mathbf{end}\{\!\{\uparrow(\mathtt{bool}).\mathbf{end}\}\!\}$ is $\uparrow(\mathtt{string}).\mathbf{end}\{\!\{\downarrow(\mathtt{bool}).\mathbf{end}\}\!\}$.

Environments. *Typing judgements* for processes and expressions have the forms $\Gamma \vdash P \triangleright \Delta$ and $\Gamma \vdash e : \theta$ respectively where Γ is a *service typing*, which typically maps service (public) channels to service types and Δ is a *session typing* which typically maps session channels to session types. For ($n \in \{0, 1\}$ and $\rho \in \{p, u\}$), typings are defined as

$$\begin{array}{lll} \textit{(Session Typing)} & \Delta & ::= \emptyset \mid \Delta,\ \kappa{:}\alpha \mid \Delta,\ (\kappa,\overline{\kappa}){:}\alpha \mid \Delta,\ (\kappa,\overline{\kappa}){:}\bot \\ \textit{(Service Typing)} & \Gamma & ::= \emptyset \mid \Gamma,\ c{:}\langle\alpha\{\!\{\beta\}\!\}\rangle \mid c{:}\mathtt{bool} \mid \Gamma,\ X{:}\Delta \end{array}$$

Table 4. Typing System for Programs

$$(\textsc{Name})\ \Gamma, a : \langle\alpha\rangle \vdash a : \langle\alpha\rangle \qquad (\textsc{Bool})\ \Gamma \vdash \mathsf{tt}, \mathsf{ff} : \mathsf{bool} \qquad (\textsc{Or})\ \frac{\Gamma \vdash e_i : \mathsf{bool}}{\Gamma \vdash e_1\ \mathsf{or}\ e_2 : \mathsf{bool}}$$

$$(\textsc{TReq})\ \frac{\begin{array}{l}\Gamma \vdash P \triangleright \prod_i \kappa_i : \overline{\alpha}_i[\![\overline{\beta}_i]\!] \\ \Gamma' \vdash Q \triangleright \prod_i \kappa_i : \overline{\beta}_i \qquad s^+ = \kappa_j \\ \Gamma \vdash c : \langle \alpha_j [\![\beta_j]\!]\rangle \qquad \Gamma' \subseteq \Gamma,\ \mathsf{fv}(\Gamma') = \emptyset\end{array}}{\Gamma \vdash \overline{c}(s^+)[\tilde{\kappa}, P, Q] \triangleright \prod_{i \neq j} \kappa_i : \overline{\alpha}_i[\![\overline{\beta}_i]\!]} \qquad (\textsc{TServ})\ \frac{\begin{array}{l}\Gamma \vdash P \triangleright s^- : \alpha[\![\beta]\!] \\ \Gamma \vdash Q \triangleright s^- : \beta \qquad \mathsf{fv}(\Gamma) = \emptyset\end{array}}{\Gamma,\ a : \langle \alpha[\![\beta]\!]\rangle \vdash *a(s^-)[P, Q] \rhd \emptyset}$$

$$(\textsc{TThr})\ \frac{\mathsf{fv}(\Gamma) = \emptyset}{\Gamma \vdash \mathbf{throw} \triangleright \prod_i \kappa_i : \alpha_i} \qquad (\textsc{TPar})\ \frac{\Gamma \vdash P_i \triangleright \Delta_i\ (i = 1,2)\ \Delta_1 \asymp \Delta_2}{\Gamma \vdash P_1 \mid P_2 \triangleright \Delta_1 \cup \Delta_2}$$

$$(\textsc{TOut})\ \frac{\Gamma \vdash e : \theta \qquad \Gamma \vdash P \triangleright \Delta \cdot \kappa : \alpha}{\Gamma \vdash \kappa!\langle e\rangle.\, P \triangleright \Delta \cdot \kappa : \uparrow(\theta).\, \alpha} \qquad (\textsc{TIn})\ \frac{\Gamma, x : \theta \vdash P \triangleright \Delta \cdot \kappa : \alpha}{\Gamma \vdash \kappa?(x).\, P \triangleright \Delta \cdot \kappa : \downarrow(\theta).\, \alpha}$$

$$(\textsc{TSel})\ \frac{\Gamma \vdash P \triangleright \Delta \cdot \kappa : \alpha_j}{\Gamma \vdash \kappa \triangleleft l_j.\, P \triangleright \Delta \cdot \kappa : \oplus\{l_i : \alpha_i\}_{i \in I}} \qquad (\textsc{TRes})\ \frac{\Gamma, a : \langle \alpha[\![\beta]\!]\rangle \vdash P \triangleright \Delta}{\Gamma \vdash (\nu a)\, P \triangleright \Delta}$$

$$(\textsc{TBra})\ \frac{\Gamma \vdash P_i \triangleright \Delta \cdot \kappa : \alpha_i \qquad \forall i \in I}{\Gamma \vdash \kappa \rhd \{l_i : P_i\}_{i \in I} \triangleright \Delta \cdot \kappa : \&\{l_i : \alpha_i\}_{i \in I}} \qquad (\textsc{TIf})\ \frac{\begin{array}{l}\Gamma \vdash e : \mathsf{bool} \\ \Gamma \vdash P \triangleright \Delta \quad \Gamma \vdash Q \triangleright \Delta\end{array}}{\Gamma \vdash \mathbf{if}\ e\ \mathbf{then}\ P\ \mathbf{else}\ Q \triangleright \Delta}$$

$$(\textsc{TInact})\ \frac{\mathsf{fv}(\Gamma) = \emptyset \quad \alpha_i \in \{\mathsf{end}, \mathsf{end}[\![\beta_i]\!]\}}{\Gamma \vdash \mathbf{0} \triangleright \prod_i \kappa_i : \alpha_i} \qquad (\textsc{TRec})\ \frac{\Gamma, X : \Delta \vdash P \triangleright \Delta}{\Gamma \vdash \mu X.\, P \triangleright \Delta} \qquad (\textsc{TVar})\ \overline{\Gamma, X : \Delta \vdash X \triangleright \Delta}$$

In session typings, $\kappa : \alpha$ says that: *at a polarised session channel* κ*, there is a session of type* α. In the service typing, c either has type $\alpha[\![\beta]\!]$ (a service using a session channel with default behaviour of type α and with a handler of type β) or an atomic type such as bool. Typing $X : \Delta$ is used for recursion as in [4].

Typing System for Programs. We show the typing system by which the programmer can check whether her program is error free or not, especially w.r.t. its exception usage. A complete list of typing rules is reported in Table 4.

(TReq) types a request on service channel c whose type, according to Γ, is $\alpha_j[\![\beta_j]\!]$. Condition $s^+ = \kappa_j$ makes sure that the fresh name s^+ will also be in the try-catch after reduction. Session s^+ has type $\overline{\alpha}_j[\![\overline{\beta}_j]\!]$, the dual of c's type. This rule checks that each κ_i in Q (exception handler) has type $\overline{\beta}_i$ (note β_i must be plain) whereas in P it has type $\overline{\alpha}_i[\![\overline{\beta}_i]\!]$ where each $\overline{\beta}_i$ may come from a refinement of κ_i in P. Finally, Γ' is a subset of Γ without free variables for service channels (otherwise the queue may store open terms at run-time). In (TServ), because of SCP, services should never be prefixed therefore the only visible (free) session in P and Q should be s^-.

For (TOut), in $\uparrow(\theta).\ \alpha$, the prefixing of a type is read as $(\uparrow(\theta).\ \alpha')[\![\beta]\!]$ whenever α has the form $\alpha'[\![\beta]\!]$. Throwing an exception interrupts any conversation, thus (TThr) allows to type **throw** with any $\kappa : \alpha$. (TInact) allows to start from $\mathsf{end}[\![\beta]\!]$ if we are typing in a try-block, while we may want to start from end in a catch-block.

(TPAR) requires the coherence relation $\asymp$. Formally, we say Δ_1 and Δ_2 are *compatible*, written $\Delta_1 \asymp \Delta_2$, if and only if $\mathsf{fsc}(\Delta_1) \cap \mathsf{fsc}(\Delta_2) = \emptyset$.

Example 6 (Typing Asynchronous and Nested Escapes). The processes in Examples 2 is typable: channel chSeller in both examples has type $\mu\mathbf{t}.\uparrow(\mathtt{int}).\,\mathbf{t}[\![\downarrow(\mathtt{int}).\uparrow(\mathtt{time})]\!]$.

In Example 3, channel chBroker has type $(\downarrow(\mathtt{int}).\,\mu\mathbf{t}.\uparrow(\mathtt{int}).\,\mathbf{t})[\![\oplus\{\mathtt{l}_1 :\downarrow(\mathtt{int}).\uparrow(\mathtt{time}), \mathtt{l}_2 : \alpha\}]\!]$ for some α.

On Run-Time Processes and Subject Reduction. The ultimate goal of the typing system is to show that errors do not occur (type and communication safety). These results are based on subject reduction i.e. typable process remain typable after reductions. However, the typing system introduced above only provides rules for checking (static) programs. In order to have subject reduction, we also need to provide typing rules for run-time processes namely try-catch blocks, wraps, session restriction and queues. Given the purpose of this lecture note, we shall not address the technical details on how to type run-time processes but take an informal approach instead. We redirect the eager reader to [5].

The basic idea for typing try-catch blocks (and wraps) is to assign a try-catch type $\alpha[\![\beta]\!]$ to channels such that α abstracts the channel usage in the try-block and β the usage in the catch-block. The typing of session restriction is standard. However, the treatment of queues is a little peculiar and the following example will give an intuitive explanation. The process

$$\mathbf{try}\{\,\kappa!\langle\text{"}Hi\text{"}\rangle.\,P\,\}\ \mathbf{catch}\ \{\,\kappa : \kappa!\langle 5\rangle\,\} \mid \kappa \hookrightarrow \overline{\kappa} : \epsilon \qquad (1)$$

is such that $\kappa :\uparrow(\mathtt{string})[\![\uparrow(\mathtt{int})]\!]$. Now, after a reduction step to process

$$\mathbf{try}\{\,P\,\}\ \mathbf{catch}\ \{\,\kappa : \kappa!\langle 5\rangle\,\} \mid \kappa \hookrightarrow \overline{\kappa} : \text{"}Hi\text{"} \qquad (2)$$

does the type of κ change? Processes (1) and (2) are identical, except that an output prefix in (1) changes its place to the queue. Thus we can go back from (2) to (1) by placing "*Hi*" on the top of the process. A key idea is to carry out this rollback of a message in typing, using a local type with a hole (a type context) for typing a queue. For example, we type the queue in (2) as the type context $\uparrow(\mathtt{string})[-]$ where $[-]$ indicates a hole. Now, we can cover the type $\mathsf{end}[\![\uparrow(\mathtt{int})]\!]$ with such a type context, obtaining the original type $\uparrow(\mathtt{string})[\![\uparrow(\mathtt{int})]\!]$.

In general, we need to be extra careful when dealing with exception propagation. Queues may contain † which can be preceded and/or followed by other messages. In such cases, all messages sent before the throwing of the exception can be ignored. As an example, if P throws and then outputs 5, (2) reduces to (for some P'):

$$P' \mid \kappa[\![\mathbf{0}]\!] \mid \kappa \hookrightarrow \overline{\kappa} : (5 :: \dagger :: \text{"}Hi\text{"})$$

Above, process $\kappa[\![\mathbf{0}]\!]$ can be typed with the try-catch type $\uparrow(\mathtt{string})[\![\mathsf{end}]\!]$ (in general the try part can be guessed) and, therefore, the composition with the queue type $\uparrow$ (int)[−] will finally yield $\uparrow$ (string)⟦$\uparrow$ (int)⟧. Note that, when applying the queue type to $\uparrow$ (string)⟦end⟧, we must know that it has to cover the catch part: this can be obviously told by the † in the queue.

In the following Theorem, $\longrightarrow^*$ denotes the reflexive and transitive closure of $\longrightarrow$.

Theorem 3 (Subject Reduction). *Let P be a program such that $\Gamma \vdash P \triangleright \emptyset$. If $P \longrightarrow^* Q$ then $\Gamma \vdash Q \triangleright \emptyset$.*

As a corollary, the typing system also satisfies type safety and communication safety including communication-error freedom and linearity [10, Theorem 5.5].

4 Multiparty Asynchronous Session Types

4.1 Preview on Multiparty Interactions

In general, session types do not allow to abstract from inter-session causality which could be useful at a designing stage. As an example, let us consider a simple refinement of the Buyer-Seller protocol [4]: consider two buyers, Buyer1 and Buyer2, wish to buy an expensive product, say a book, from Seller by combining their money:

1. Buyer1 sends the title of the book to Seller;
2. Seller sends to both Buyer1 and Buyer2 its quote;
3. Buyer1 tells Buyer2 how much she can pay, and Buyer2 either *accepts* or *rejects* the quote by notifying Seller.

It is extremely awkward (if logically possible) to decompose this scenario into three binary sessions, between Buyer1 and Seller, between Buyer2 and Seller, and between Buyer1 and Buyer2. Abstracting this protocol as three separate session types also means that our type abstraction loses essential sequencing information in this interaction scenario: for instance, we may want to guarantee that Buyer2 accepts only after Seller has sent a quote to Buyer1. For validating this conversation scenario as a whole, therefore, the conversation structure should be represented as a *single session*.

Many existing business protocols including financial protocols are written as a collaboration of several peers. Typical message-passing parallel algorithms also frequently demand distribution of a request to, and collection of the results from, many peers. All these usecases are most naturally abstracted as a single session. In this section, we adress a generalisation of the foregoing binary session types to multiparty asynchronous sessions [10,1,2,14].

4.2 The π-Calculus with Multiparty Asynchronous Session Types

Syntax. In the sequel, we shall keep the same notation as the one introduced for interactional exceptions. Let e be the set of expression defined as in Section 3. Then *processes* (programs) are given by the following grammar:

$$
\begin{array}{llrlr}
P ::= & a[\mathrm{p}]\,(\tilde{s}).\ P & \text{(accept)} & \mid\ \overline{a}[2..\mathrm{n}]\,(\tilde{s}).\ P & \text{(request)} \\
\mid & s?(\tilde{x}).\ P & \text{(input)} & \mid\ s!\langle\tilde{e}\rangle.\ P & \text{(output)} \\
\mid & s?((\tilde{s})).\ P & \text{(session reception)} & \mid\ s!\langle\langle\tilde{s}\rangle\rangle.\ P & \text{(delegation)} \\
\mid & s \rhd \{l_i : P_i\}_{i\in I} & \text{(branch)} & \mid\ s \lhd l.\ P & \text{(select)} \\
\mid & P \mid Q & \text{(par)} & \mid\ \mathbf{if}\ e\ \mathbf{then}\ P\ \mathbf{else}\ Q & \text{(cond)} \\
\mid & \mathbf{0} & \text{(inact)} & \mid\ (\nu a)\ P & \text{(resServ)} \\
\mid & X & \text{(termVar)} & \mid\ \mu X.\ P & \text{(recursion)}
\end{array}
$$

Most of the primitives above are identical to the ones we saw for interactional exceptions except from (accept), (request), (delegation) and (session reception). The prefix $\overline{a}[2..\mathrm{n}]\,(\tilde{s}).\ P$ initiates a new session through a, by distributing a vector of freshly generated session channels $\tilde{s}$ to the remaining $\mathrm{n}-1$ participants, each of shape $a[\mathrm{p}]\,(\tilde{s}).\ Q_{\mathrm{p}}$ for $2 \leq \mathrm{p} \leq \mathrm{n}$. All receive $\tilde{s}$, over which the actual session communications can now take place among the n parties. p, q,... range over natural numbers called *participants* of a session.

Session communications are performed using the primitives we saw for interactional exceptions but also allowing for session delegation. In delegation, the capability to participate in a session is delegated to the session receiver by passing the whole channels associated with the session. Note that session communication is polyadic (apart from branch/select).

The notions of bound and free identifiers, channels, alpha equivalence $\equiv_\alpha$ and substitution are standardly adapted to the calculus with multuparty sessions.

Example 7 (Two Buyer Protocol). The Two Buyer protocol can be represented by the following diagram:

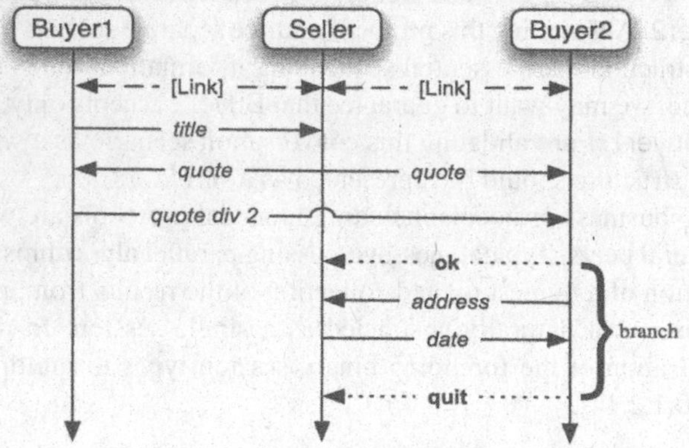

Above, Buyer1 sends a book title to Seller, then Seller sends back a quote to Buyer1/2; Buyer1 now tells Buyer2 how much she can contribute, and Buyer2 notifies Seller if it accepts the quote or not. We now describe the behaviour of Buyer1 as a process:

$$
\begin{array}{rl}
\mathsf{Buyer1} \stackrel{\text{def}}{=} & \overline{a}[2,3]\,(b_1, b_2, b_2', s_1, s_2).\quad s_1!\langle\text{“War and Peace”}\rangle. \\
& b_1?(quote).\ \ b_2'!\langle quote\ \mathsf{div}\ 2\rangle.\ P_1
\end{array}
$$

Channel b_1 is for Buyer1 to receive messages: b_2 and b'_2 for Buyer2 and s_1 and s_2 for Seller. Buyer1 above is willing to contribute to half of the quote. In P_1, Buyer1 may perform the remaining transactions with Seller and Buyer2. The remaining participants follow.

$$\begin{aligned}\text{Buyer2} &\stackrel{\text{def}}{=} a[2]\,(b_1,b_2,b'_2,s_1,s_2).\;\; b_2?(quote).\;\; b'_2?(contrib).\\ &\qquad \textbf{if}\ (quote - contrib \le 99)\\ &\qquad\quad \textbf{then}\quad s_2 \lhd \mathsf{ok}.\ s_2!\langle address\rangle; b_2?(x).\ P_2\\ &\qquad\quad \textbf{else}\quad s_2 \lhd \mathsf{quit}.\ \mathbf{0}\\ \text{Seller} &\stackrel{\text{def}}{=} a[3]\,(b_1,b_2,b'_2,s_1,s_2).\;\; s_1?(title).\;\; b_1,b_2!\langle quote\rangle.\\ &\qquad s_2 \rhd \{\mathsf{ok}\colon s_2?(x).\ b_2!\langle date\rangle; Q,\quad \mathsf{quit}\colon \mathbf{0}\}\end{aligned}$$

Above $b_1,b_2!\langle v\rangle.\ P$ stands for $b_1!\langle v\rangle..\ b_2!\langle v\rangle.\ P$, assuming b_1,b_2 are distinct: due to asynchrony there is in effect no order among the sending actions at b_1,b_2. Note that Buyer2 needs to use two input channels, b_2 and b'_2 while, for Seller, s_1 and s_2 are not necessary. The first input (for *quote*) is from Seller, while the second one (for *contrib*) is from Buyer1. Hence there is no guarantee that they arrive in a fixed order, as can be easily seen by analysing reduction paths (this is Lamport's principle [13]). Thus if we were to use b_2 for both actions, the two messages can be confused, losing linear usage of a channel. Later we shall show our type discipline can avoid such an error.

Example 8 (A Streaming Protocol). We next consider a simple protocol for the standard stream cipher [15].

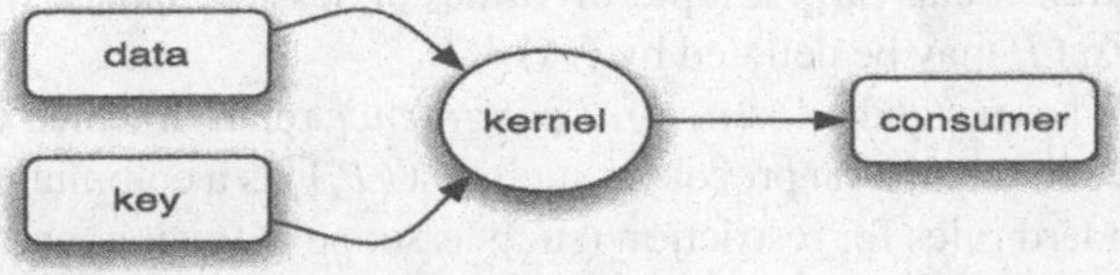

Data Producer and Key Producer continuously send a data stream and a key stream respectively to Kernel. Kernel calculates their XOR and sends the result to Consumer. Assuming streams are sent block by block (say as large arrays), we can realise this protocol as communicating processes. We only focus on communication behaviour. The kernel initiates a session:

$$\text{Kernel} \stackrel{\text{def}}{=} \overline{a}[2,3,4]\,(d,k,c).\ \mu X.\ d?(x).\ k?(y).\ c!\langle x \mathsf{\ xor\ } y\rangle.\ X$$

The channels d and k are used for Kernel to receive data and keys from Data Producer and Key Producer, respectively, while c is used for Consumer to receive the encrypted data from Kernel. Data Producer and Consumer can be given as:

$$\text{DataProducer} \stackrel{\text{def}}{=} a[2]\,(d,k,c).\ \mu Y.\ d!\langle data\rangle.\ Y \qquad \text{Consumer} \stackrel{\text{def}}{=} a[3]\,(d,k,c).\ \mu Z.\ c?(data).\ Z$$

Key Producer is identical to Data Producer except it outputs at k instead of d. When three processes are composed, we can verify that, although processes repeatedly send and receive data using the same channels, messages are always consumed in the order they are produced, an essential requirement for correctness of the protocol. This is because each channel is used by exactly one sender. We shall show how this argument can be cleanly represented and validated through session types.

Table 5. Reduction

(INIT)	$\overline{a}[2..n](\tilde{s}).P_1 \mid a[2](\tilde{s}).P_2 \mid \cdots \mid a[n](\tilde{s}).P_n \rightarrow (\nu\tilde{s})(P_1 \mid P_2 \mid \ldots \mid P_n \mid s_1:\epsilon \mid \cdots \mid s_m:\epsilon)$
(OUT)	$s!\langle\tilde{e}\rangle.P \mid s:L \rightarrow P \mid s:(\tilde{v} :: L) \quad (\tilde{e}\downarrow\tilde{v})$
(DELEG)	$s!\langle\langle\tilde{t}\rangle\rangle.P \mid s:L \rightarrow P \mid s:(\tilde{t} :: L)$
(SEL)	$s \lhd l.P \mid s:L \rightarrow P \mid s:(l :: L)$
(IN)	$s?(\tilde{x}).P \mid s:(L :: \tilde{v}) \rightarrow P[\tilde{v}/\tilde{x}] \mid s:L$
(SREC)	$s?((\tilde{t})).P \mid s:(L :: \tilde{t}) \rightarrow P \mid s:L$
(BRA)	$s \rhd \{l_i : P_i\}_{i\in I} \mid s:(L :: l_j) \rightarrow P_j \mid s:L \quad (j \in I)$
(IF)	$\textbf{if } e \textbf{ then } P \textbf{ else } Q \rightarrow P \quad (e\downarrow \mathsf{tt}) \qquad \textbf{if } e \textbf{ then } P \textbf{ else } Q \rightarrow Q \quad (e\downarrow \mathsf{ff})$
(RES)	$P \rightarrow P' \quad \wedge \quad n \in \{a, s\} \Rightarrow (\nu n)P \rightarrow (\nu n)P'$
(PAR)	$P \rightarrow P' \Rightarrow P \mid Q \rightarrow P' \mid Q$
(STR)	$P \equiv P'$ and $P' \rightarrow Q'$ and $Q' \equiv Q \Rightarrow P \rightarrow Q$

Reduction Semantics. Because of asynchrony, similarly to the case of exceptions, we need to introduce a run-time syntax[1]:

$$P ::= \ldots \mid (\nu s)P \qquad \text{(resSess)} \qquad \mid s:L \qquad \text{(queue)}$$

$$L ::= \epsilon \mid h :: L \qquad h ::= l \mid \tilde{v} \mid \tilde{s} \qquad v ::= a \mid \mathsf{tt} \mid \mathsf{ff}$$

The run-time syntax is almost identical to the interactional exceptions case exept from the queues. In this case, queues are not polarised (we have no polarised channels) and one message in transit can carry a tuple of values or session names. In the sequel, the term $(\nu s_1)\ldots(\nu s_k)P$ may be denoted by $(\nu\tilde{s})P$.

The semantics has a standard *structural congruence* relation which is defined as the smallest congruence relation on processes such that $(P, \mid)$ is a commutative monoid and includes the standard rules for restriction (such as scope extrusion) and recursion.

The reduction semantics is given by the *reduction relation*, defined as the smallest relation on processes generated by the rules in Table 5. (INIT) describes a session initiation among n-parties through synchronisation, generating m fresh session channels and the associated m empty queues. As a result n participants now share the newly generated m channels, hence their queues. Note that, in general, the number of threads (n) can be different from that of session channels (m), giving flexibility in channel usage.

Similarly to Section 3, (OUT), (DELEG) and (SEL) respectively enqueue values, channels and a label in the queue for s. (IN), (SREC) and (BRA) dequeue values, channels and a label. (BRA) further selects the corresponding branch. Other rules are standard.

4.3 Types for Multiparty Sessions

Developing programs for multiparty sessions demands a clear formal design as to how multiple participants communicate and synchronise with each other. To program individual participants without such a design and hope they somehow realise a meaningful and error-free conversation is hardly practical, especially for team programming. In binary session types the type for an endpoint also served as the description of the whole

[1] Note we do not need contexts because there are no nesting operators.

conversation, but this is no longer possible for multiparty sessions. This is why we need the type abstraction which describes global conversation scenarios of multiparty sessions. This is achieved by defining global types, a multiparty session abstraction based on the notion of *choreography* [4]: a type no longer describe the usage of a channel from a one participant viewpoint, but will give a vantage perspective of the whole session (and its session channels). An intuitive example is given by the diagram in the two buyer protocol which gives us a global view, or choreography, of how the session would run. However, having a global description may be useful at designing stage, but needs a correspondent description of the local behaviour of each participant in the session. The process of generating each participant local behaviour (or local session type) is called end-point projection (EPP) or, simply, *projection* [4]. For instance, the EPP of Buyer1's behaviour from the diagram in the two buyer protocol would be a sequence of an output (book title), an input (quote) and, finally, an output (quote halved).

Once we are capable of projecting global descriptions into end-point behaviour, we can consider the following development steps for programs with multiparty sessions:

1. A programmer describes an intended interaction scenario as a global type G;
2. she develops code, one for each participant, incrementally validating its conformance to the projection of G onto each participant by efficient type-checking.

When programs are executed, their interactions are guaranteed to follow the stipulated scenario. The type specification also serves as a basis for maintenance and upgrade.

Global Types. A *global session type*, or *global type*, denoted $G, G', \ldots$, is given by the following grammar:

$$
\begin{array}{rcll}
G & ::= & \mathsf{p} \to \mathsf{p}' : k\,\langle\theta\rangle.G' & \text{(values)} \\
 & \mid & \mathsf{p} \to \mathsf{p}' : k\,\{l_j : G_j\}_{j\in J} & \text{(branching)} \\
 & \mid & G, G' & \text{(parallel)} \\
 & \mid & \mu\mathbf{t}.G & \text{(recursive)} \\
 & \mid & \mathbf{t} & \text{(variable)} \\
 & \mid & \mathsf{end} & \text{(end)}
\end{array}
$$

$$\theta \ ::= \ \tilde{S} \mid \alpha@\mathsf{p} \qquad S \ ::= \ \mathsf{bool} \mid \mathsf{nat} \mid \ldots \mid \langle G\rangle$$

Type $\mathsf{p} \to \mathsf{p}' : k\,\langle\theta\rangle.G'$ says that participant p sends a message of type θ to channel k (represented as a finite natural number) received by participant p′ and interactions described in G' take place. We assume that in each prefix from p to p′ we have $\mathsf{p} \neq \mathsf{p}'$, i.e. we prohibit reflexive interaction. θ ranges over *value types* $\tilde{S}$ or *local types* α paired with participant names. Each value type is a vector of types for shared names called *sorts*. A local type α, whose details will be addressed in the next subsection, may hereby used for delegation of session channels. Type $\mathsf{p} \to \mathsf{p}' : k\,\{l_j : G_j\}_{j\in J}$ says participant p sends one of the labels to channel k which is then received by participant p′. If l_j is sent, interactions described in G_j take place.

Type G, G' represents concurrent run of interactions specified by G and G'. Type $\mu\mathbf{t}.G$ is a recursive type for recurring conversation structures, assuming type variables $(\mathbf{t}, \mathbf{t}', \ldots)$ are guarded in the standard way, i.e. type variables only appear under the prefixes. As in standard session types, we take an *equi-recursive* view, not distinguishing between $\mu\mathbf{t}.G$ and its unfolding $G[\mu\mathbf{t}.G/\mathbf{t}]$. We assume that $\langle G\rangle$ in the grammar of sorts is closed, i.e. without type variables. Type end represents the termination of the session. We identify "G, end" and "end, G" with G.

We stipulate that, in a global type G, each channel can only be used, one or more times, among two fixed parties, one party using it for input/session reception/branching while the other party for output/delegation/selection. This condition is not restrictive and dispenses with the need for linearity check to ensure well-formedness of global types found in [10] (see [2] for details).

Example 9 (A Global Type for the Two Buyer Protocol). We write principals and channels with legible symbols though they are actually numbers: $\mathtt{Bi} = i$, $\mathtt{S} = 3$, $b_1 = 1$, $b_2 = 2$, $b_2' = 3$, $s_1 = 4$ and $s_2 = 5$. The following is a global type for the two buyer protocol:

$$\mathtt{B1} \to \mathtt{S} : s_1\langle\mathsf{string}\rangle. \quad \mathtt{S} \to \mathtt{B1} : b_1\langle\mathsf{int}\rangle. \quad \mathtt{S} \to \mathtt{B2} : b_2\langle\mathsf{int}\rangle. \quad \mathtt{B1} \to \mathtt{B2} : b_2'\langle\mathsf{int}\rangle.$$
$$\mathtt{B2} \to \mathtt{S} : s_2 \begin{Bmatrix} \mathsf{ok} : \mathtt{B2} \to \mathtt{S} : s_2\,\langle\mathsf{string}\rangle.\mathtt{S} \to \mathtt{B2} : b_2\,\langle\mathsf{date}\rangle.\mathsf{end}, \\ \mathsf{quit} : \mathsf{end} \end{Bmatrix}$$

The type gives a vantage view of the whole conversation scenario.

Example 10 (A Global Type for the Streaming Protocol). In this example, we present the global type of the simple streaming protocol. Below we unfold its recursion once, and set: $d = 1$, $k = 2$, $c = 3$, $\mathtt{K} = 1$, $\mathtt{DP} = 2$, $\mathtt{C} = 3$ and $\mathtt{KP} = 4$.

$$\mu\mathbf{t}.\ \mathtt{DP} \to \mathtt{K}\colon d\,\langle\mathsf{bool}\rangle.\ \ \mathtt{KP} \to \mathtt{K}\colon k\,\langle\mathsf{bool}\rangle.\ \ \mathtt{K} \to \mathtt{C}\colon c\,\langle\mathsf{bool}\rangle.$$
$$\mathtt{DP} \to \mathtt{K}\colon d\,\langle\mathsf{bool}\rangle.\ \ \mathtt{KP} \to \mathtt{K}\colon k\,\langle\mathsf{bool}\rangle.\ \ \mathtt{K} \to \mathtt{C}\colon c\,\langle\mathsf{bool}\rangle.\mathbf{t}$$

Local Types. *Local session types* or *local types*, ranged over by $\alpha, \beta, ..$, are types for local behaviour of processes in a multiparty session, acting as a link between global types and processes (they have many analogies to standard session types) and are defined by the following grammar:

$$\alpha \ ::= \quad k!\,\langle\theta\rangle.\,\alpha \ \mid\ k?\,\langle\theta\rangle.\,\alpha \ \mid\ k \oplus \{l_i\colon \alpha_i\}_{i\in I} \ \mid\ k\,\&\,\{l_i\colon \alpha_i\}_{i\in I} \ \mid\ \mu\mathbf{t}.\,\alpha \ \mid\ \mathbf{t} \ \mid\ \mathsf{end}$$

All constructs come from standard binary session types except from the following major changes for multiparty interactions:

- Since a session now uses multiple channels, a session type needs to record the identity (number) of a session channel it uses at each action type as found in [4].
- Since a type is inferred for each participant, we use the notation $\alpha@\mathtt{p}$ (*located type*) representing a local type α assigned to participant p. A located type is also used for delegation.

Type $k?\,\langle\theta\rangle.\,\alpha$ represents the behaviour of inputting values of type θ while $k!\,\langle\theta\rangle.\,\alpha$ is for sending. Types $k\,\&\,\{l_i\colon \alpha_i\}_{i\in I}$ and $k \oplus \{l_i\colon \alpha_i\}_{i\in I}$ are respectively for branching and select at k. The rest is the same as the global types, demanding type variables occur guarded by a prefix and taking an equi-recursive approach for recursive types. Note local types α do not contain parallel composition like in [4].

Projection. In the introduction to this section, we have discussed the need for a projection of global types into local behaviour. The following is the formal definition of such a projection:

Definition 4 (Projection). Let G be linear. Then the *projection of G onto* p, written $G \upharpoonright \mathrm{p}$, is inductively given as:

$$(\mathrm{p}_1 \to \mathrm{p}_2 : k\,\langle\theta\rangle.G') \upharpoonright \mathrm{p} = \begin{cases} k!\,\langle\theta\rangle.(G' \upharpoonright \mathrm{p}) & \text{if } \mathrm{p} = \mathrm{p}_1 \neq \mathrm{p}_2 \\ k?\,\langle\theta\rangle.(G' \upharpoonright \mathrm{p}) & \text{if } \mathrm{p} = \mathrm{p}_2 \neq \mathrm{p}_1 \\ (G' \upharpoonright \mathrm{p}) & \text{if } \mathrm{p} \neq \mathrm{p}_2 \wedge \mathrm{p} \neq \mathrm{p}_1 \end{cases}$$

$$(\mathrm{p}_1 \to \mathrm{p}_2 : k\,\{l_j : G_j\}_{j\in J}) \upharpoonright \mathrm{p} = \begin{cases} k \oplus \{l_j : (G_j \upharpoonright \mathrm{p})\}_{j\in J} & \text{if } \mathrm{p} = \mathrm{p}_1 \neq \mathrm{p}_2 \\ k\&\{l_j : (G_j \upharpoonright \mathrm{p})\}_{j\in J} & \text{if } \mathrm{p} = \mathrm{p}_2 \neq \mathrm{p}_1 \\ (\bigsqcup_{i\in I} G_i \upharpoonright \mathrm{p}) & \text{if } \mathrm{p} \neq \mathrm{p}_2 \wedge \mathrm{p} \neq \mathrm{p}_1 \\ & \text{and } \forall i, j \in I. G_i \upharpoonright \mathrm{p} \bowtie G_j \upharpoonright \mathrm{p} \end{cases}$$

$$(G_1, G_2) \upharpoonright \mathrm{p} = \begin{cases} G_i \upharpoonright \mathrm{p} & \text{if } \mathrm{p} \in G_i \text{ and } \mathrm{p} \notin G_j,\ i \neq j \in \{1,2\} \\ \mathsf{end} & \text{if } \mathrm{p} \notin G_1 \text{ and } \mathrm{p} \notin G_2 \end{cases}$$

$$(\mu \mathbf{t}.G) \upharpoonright \mathrm{p} = \mu \mathbf{t}.(G \upharpoonright \mathrm{p}) \qquad \mathbf{t} \upharpoonright \mathrm{p} = \mathbf{t} \qquad \mathsf{end} \upharpoonright \mathrm{p} = \mathsf{end}$$

Whenever the projection is defined, G is said to be *projectable*.

The mapping is intuitive. We regard the map to act on the syntax of global types. In parallel composition, p should be contained in at most a single type, ensuring each type is single-threaded. In the branching, all projections should generate an identical local type (otherwise undefined) up to mergeability $\bowtie$. Mergeability [4], not present in the original work on multiparty session types [10], is the smallest equivalence over local types closed under all type contexts and the rule:

$$\frac{\forall i \in (I \cap J).\ \alpha_i \bowtie \beta_i \qquad \forall i \in I\backslash J.\ \forall j \in J\backslash I.\ l_i \neq l_j}{k\ \&\ \{l_i : \alpha_i\}_{i\in I} \bowtie k\ \&\ \{l_j : \beta_j\}_{j\in J}}$$

Intuitively, the mergeability condition requires two local types to be identical except from branches &, where branches with different labels may be different.

The projection of branching is then defined as the merging $\sqcup$ of the projections of the branches. Formally, $\alpha \sqcup \beta$ is a partial commutative operator over local types which is well-defined iff $\alpha \bowtie \beta$ and is an isomorphism except from the following case:

$$k\ \&\ \{l_i : \alpha_i\}_{i\in I} \sqcup k\ \&\ \{l_j : \beta_j\}_{j\in J} \;=\; k\&(\{l_i : \alpha_i \sqcup \beta_i\}_{i\in I\cap J} \cup \{l_i : \alpha_i\}_{i\in I} \cup \{l_j : \beta_j\}_{j\in J})$$

Using the merging operator above allows for more global types to have a projection. In fact, we can also write global types where, for instance, in a binary branching from p_1 to p_2, a third participant p_3 can behave differently depending on the selection made by p_1. This is *only* allowed when p_3 can be projected with branching local type: each branch corresponds to a branch in the global type and may be selected by p_2 (or some other causally notified participant) according to p_1's selection. The following is an example of projection and clarifies the usefulness of merging.

Example 11. Consider the following global type:

$$\begin{array}{l} \mathsf{p}_1 \to \mathsf{p}_2 : k\,\{ \\ \quad \mathsf{ok} : \mathsf{p}_2 \to \mathsf{p}_3 : k'\,\{\mathsf{paymore} : \ldots\}, \\ \quad \mathsf{quit} : \mathsf{p}_2 \to \mathsf{p}_3 : k'\,\{\mathsf{refund} : \ldots\} \\ \} \end{array}$$

Above, p_1 selects, over k, ok or quit. Based on this selection p_2 will either select paymore or refund. The projection of p_1 is the local type $k \oplus \{\mathsf{ok}: \ \ldots, \mathsf{quit}: \ \ldots,\}$ while p_2 is projected as:

$$k\&\{ \quad \mathsf{ok}\colon k' \oplus \{\mathsf{paymore}\colon \ \ldots\}, \quad \mathsf{quit}\colon k' \oplus \{\mathsf{reject}\colon \ \ldots\} \quad \}$$

However, the projection of p_3 on the ok branch is $k'\&\{\mathsf{paymore}\colon \ \ldots\}$ whereas, on the quit branch, it is $k'\&\{\mathsf{refund}\colon \ \ldots\}$. Such a projection is not allowed in [10], however, we can easily merge the two local types, yielding:

$$k'\&\{\ \mathsf{paymore}\colon \ \ldots, \ \mathsf{refund}\colon \ \ldots\ \}$$

Example 12. The following global type is *not* projectable:

$$\mathtt{A} \to \mathtt{B} : k\{\mathsf{ok} : \mathtt{C} \to \mathtt{D} : k'\langle\mathsf{bool}\rangle, \ \mathsf{quit} : \mathtt{C} \to \mathtt{D} : k'\langle\mathsf{nat}\rangle\}$$

Intuitively, when we project this type onto C or D, regardless of the choice made by A, they should behave in the same way: participants C and D should be independent threads. If we change the above nat to bool as: $\mathtt{A} \to \mathtt{B} : k\{\mathsf{ok} : \mathtt{C} \to \mathtt{D} : k'\langle\mathsf{bool}\rangle, \mathsf{quit} : \mathtt{C} \to \mathtt{D} : k'\langle\mathsf{bool}\rangle\}$, we can define the coherent projection as follows:

$$\{\ k \oplus \{\mathsf{ok} : \mathsf{end}, \ \mathsf{quit} : \mathsf{end}\}@\mathtt{A}, \ k\&\{\mathsf{ok} : \mathsf{end}, \ \mathsf{quit} : \mathsf{end}\}@\mathtt{B}, \ k'!\langle\mathsf{bool}\rangle@\mathtt{C}, \ k'?\langle\mathsf{bool}\rangle@\mathtt{D}\ \}$$

Environments. Assuming global types are projectable, judgements are shaped like the ones for interactional exception:

$$\begin{array}{lcl} \Gamma & ::= & \emptyset \mid \Gamma, u : S \mid \Gamma, X : \Delta \\ \Delta & ::= & \emptyset \mid \Delta \cdot \tilde{s} : \{\alpha@\mathsf{p}\}_{\mathsf{p}\in I} \end{array}$$

The *service environment* (also called *sorting*) Γ is a finite map from names to sorts and from process variables to session environment. A *session environment* Δ records linear usage of session channels. In the binary sessions, it assigned a type to a single channel; now it assigns a family of located types to a vector of session channels. We write $\tilde{s} : \alpha@\mathsf{p}$ for a singleton typing $\tilde{s} : \{\alpha@\mathsf{p}\}$.

Therefore, judgements have the shape $\Gamma \vdash P \triangleright \Delta$ which reads: "under the environment Γ, process P has typing Δ".

Typing System for Programs. The type system for programs is given in Table 6. Note that if we set $|\tilde{s}| = 1$ and $\mathtt{n} = 2$, and delete p from located type, the shape of rules is essentially identical with the original binary session typing [19].

We shall now comment the rules that differ from standard binary session typing.

In (TReq), the rule for the session request, the type for $\tilde{s}$ is the *first* projection of the declared global type for a in Γ. Similarly, when typing session accept with (TAcc), we take the p-th projection. The local type $(G \upharpoonright \mathsf{p})@\mathsf{p}$ means that the participant p has $G \upharpoonright \mathsf{p}$,

Table 6. Typing System for Expressions and Processes

$$(\text{NAME})\ \Gamma, a:S \vdash a:S \qquad (\text{BOOL})\ \Gamma \vdash \mathsf{true}, \mathsf{false}: \mathsf{bool} \qquad (\text{OR})\ \frac{\Gamma \vdash e_i \triangleright \mathsf{bool}}{\Gamma \vdash e_1 \mathsf{or}\ e_2 : \mathsf{bool}}$$

$$(\text{TREQ})\ \frac{\Gamma \vdash a:\langle G\rangle \quad \Gamma \vdash P \triangleright \Delta, \tilde{s}:(G \upharpoonright 1)@1 \quad |\tilde{s}| = \max(\mathsf{sid}(G))}{\Gamma \vdash \overline{a}[2..\mathrm{n}]\,(\tilde{s}).\,P \triangleright \Delta}$$

$$(\text{TACC})\ \frac{\Gamma \vdash a:\langle G\rangle \quad \Gamma \vdash P \triangleright \Delta, \tilde{s}:(G \upharpoonright \mathrm{p})@\mathrm{p} \quad |\tilde{s}| = \max(\mathsf{sid}(G))}{\Gamma \vdash a[\mathrm{p}]\,(\tilde{s}).\,P \triangleright \Delta}$$

$$(\text{TOUT})\ \frac{\forall j.\ \Gamma \vdash e_j : S_j \quad \Gamma \vdash P \triangleright \Delta \cdot \tilde{s}:\alpha@\mathrm{p}}{\Gamma \vdash s_k!\langle\tilde{e}\rangle.\,P \triangleright \Delta \cdot \tilde{s}:k!\langle\tilde{S}\rangle.\,\alpha@\mathrm{p}} \qquad (\text{TIN})\ \frac{\Gamma, x:\tilde{S} \vdash P \triangleright \Delta \cdot \tilde{s}:\alpha@\mathrm{p}}{\Gamma \vdash s_k?(\tilde{x}).\,P \triangleright \Delta \cdot \tilde{s}:k?\langle\tilde{S}\rangle.\,\alpha@\mathrm{p}}$$

$$(\text{TDELEG})\ \frac{\Gamma \vdash P \triangleright \Delta \cdot \tilde{s}:\alpha@\mathrm{p}}{\Gamma \vdash s_k!\langle\!\langle\tilde{t}\rangle\!\rangle.\,P \triangleright \Delta \cdot \tilde{s}:k!\langle\alpha'@\mathrm{p}'\rangle.\,\alpha@\mathrm{p} \cdot \tilde{t}:\alpha'@\mathrm{p}'}$$

$$(\text{TSREC})\ \frac{\Gamma \vdash P \triangleright \Delta \cdot \tilde{s}:\alpha@\mathrm{p} \cdot \tilde{t}:\alpha'@\mathrm{p}'}{\Gamma \vdash s_k\,?((\tilde{t})).\,P \triangleright \Delta \cdot \tilde{s}:k?\langle\alpha'@\mathrm{p}'\rangle.\,\alpha@\mathrm{p}}$$

$$(\text{TSEL})\ \frac{\Gamma \vdash P \triangleright \Delta \cdot \tilde{s}:\alpha_j@\mathrm{p} \quad j \in I}{\Gamma \vdash s_k \lhd l_j.\,P \triangleright \Delta \cdot \tilde{s} : k \oplus \{l_i:\alpha_i\}_{i\in I}@\mathrm{p}} \qquad (\text{TBRA})\ \frac{\Gamma \vdash P_j \triangleright \Delta \cdot \tilde{s}:\alpha_j@\mathrm{p} \quad \forall j \in J \quad I \subseteq J}{\Gamma \vdash s_k \rhd \{l_j:P_j\}_{j\in J} \triangleright \Delta \cdot \tilde{s}:k\,\&\,\{l_i:\alpha_i\}_{i\in I}@\mathrm{p}}$$

$$(\text{TPAR})\ \frac{\Gamma \vdash P \triangleright \Delta \quad \Gamma \vdash Q \triangleright \Delta' \quad \Delta \sim \Delta'}{\Gamma \vdash P \mid Q \triangleright \Delta \circ \Delta'} \qquad (\text{TIF})\ \frac{\Gamma \vdash e \triangleright \mathsf{bool} \quad \Gamma \vdash P \triangleright \Delta \quad \Gamma \vdash Q \triangleright \Delta}{\Gamma \vdash \mathbf{if}\ e\ \mathbf{then}\ P\ \mathbf{else}\ Q \triangleright \Delta}$$

$$(\text{TINACT})\ \frac{\Delta\ \mathsf{end\ only}}{\Gamma \vdash \mathbf{0} \triangleright \Delta} \quad (\text{TRES})\ \frac{\Gamma, a:\langle G\rangle \vdash P \triangleright \Delta}{\Gamma \vdash (\nu a)\,P \triangleright \Delta} \quad (\text{TVAR})\ \Gamma, X:\Delta \vdash X \triangleright \Delta \quad (\text{TREC})\ \frac{\Gamma, X:\Delta \vdash P \triangleright \Delta}{\Gamma \vdash \mu X.\,P \triangleright \Delta}$$

which is the projection of G onto p, as its local type. The condition $|\tilde{s}| = \max(\mathsf{sid}(G))$ ensures the number of session channels meets those in G. The typing $\tilde{s} : \alpha@\mathrm{p}$ (which stands for $\tilde{s} : \{\alpha@\mathrm{p}\}$) ensures each prefix does not contain parallel threads sharing $\tilde{s}$. Both rules, (TREQ) and (TAcc), are applicable whenever G is projectable.

(TOUT) and (TIN) are the rules for sending and receiving values. Since the k-th name s_k of $\tilde{s}$ is used as the subject, we record the number k. In both rules, "p" in $\alpha@\mathrm{p}$ ensures that P is (being inferred as) the behaviour for participant p, and its domain should be $\tilde{s}$. Then the relevant type prefixes ($k!\langle\tilde{S}\rangle$ for the output and $k?\langle\tilde{S}\rangle$ for the input) are composed in the conclusion's session environment.

(TDELEG) and (TSREC) are the rules for delegation of a session and its dual (not present in Section 3). Delegation of a multiparty session passes the whole capability to participate in a multiparty session: thus operationally we send the whole vector of session channels. The carried type α' is located, making sure that the behaviour by the receiver at the passed channels takes the role of a specific participant (here p′) in the delegated multiparty session. The rest follows the standard delegation rule [19], observing (TDELEG) says that $\tilde{t}: \alpha'@\mathrm{p}'$ does not appear in P symmetrically to (TSREC) which uses the channels in P.

(TSEL) is the rule for selection, and identical with the one used for interactional exceptions. In (TBRANCH), the type may have less branches than the actual ones occurring in the process: this still ensures that a selection is never made on a branch that does not exist [4]. This change in the rule was made to allow merging. The original work on multiparty session types [10] adopts a rule like the one we used for exceptions.

(TPAR) uses $\asymp$ to ensure well-formedness of the session typing, taking a the disjoint union of each local type. The partial operator $\circ$ is defined as:

$$\{\alpha_{\mathtt{p}}@\mathtt{p}\}_{\mathtt{p}\in I} \circ \{\alpha'_{\mathtt{p}'}@\mathtt{p}'\}_{\mathtt{p}'\in J} = \{\alpha_{\mathtt{p}}@\mathtt{p}\}_{\mathtt{p}\in I} \cup \{\alpha'_{\mathtt{p}'}@\mathtt{p}'\}_{\mathtt{p}'\in J}$$

if $I \cap J = \emptyset$. Then we say Δ_1 and Δ_2 are *compatible*, written $\Delta_1 \sim \Delta_2$, if for all $\tilde{s}_i \in \mathsf{dom}(\Delta_i)$ such that $\tilde{s}_1 \cap \tilde{s}_2 \neq \emptyset$, $\tilde{s} = \tilde{s}_1 = \tilde{s}_2$ and $\Delta_1(\tilde{s}) \circ \Delta_2(\tilde{s})$ is defined. When $\Delta_1 \sim \Delta_2$, the *composition of* Δ_1 *and* Δ_2, written $\Delta_1 \circ \Delta_2$, is given as:

$$\Delta_1 \circ \Delta_2 = \{\Delta_1(\tilde{s}) \circ \Delta_2(\tilde{s}) \mid \tilde{s} \in \mathsf{dom}(\Delta_1) \cap \mathsf{dom}(\Delta_2)\}$$
$$\cup \Delta_1 \setminus \mathsf{dom}(\Delta_2) \cup \Delta_2 \setminus \mathsf{dom}(\Delta_1)$$

In (TINACT) and (TVAR), "end only" means Δ only contains end as session types.

Example 13 (Two Buyer Protocol). In the two buyer protocol, write Buyer1 as process $\overline{a}_{[2,3]}(b_1, b_2, b'_2, s_1, s_2).\ Q_1$ and Buyer2 as $a_{[2]}(b_1, b_2, b'_2, s_1, s_2).\ Q_2$. Then Q_1 and Q_2 have the following typing under $\Gamma = \{a : \langle G\rangle\}$ where G is given in the corresponding example in pag. 204, letting $\mathtt{Bi} = i$, $\mathtt{S} = 3$, $b_1 = 1$, $b_2 = 2$, $b'_2 = 3$, $s_1 = 4$ and $s_2 = 5$ and assuming P_1, P_2, Q are $\mathbf{0}$:

$$\Gamma \vdash Q_1 \triangleright \tilde{s} : s_1!\langle\mathsf{string}\rangle.\ b_1?\langle\mathsf{int}\rangle.\ b'_2!\langle\mathsf{int}\rangle@\mathtt{B1}$$
$$\Gamma \vdash Q_2 \triangleright \tilde{s} : b_2?\langle\mathsf{int}\rangle.\ b'_2?\langle\mathsf{int}\rangle.\ s_2 \oplus \{\mathsf{ok} : s_2!\langle\mathsf{string}\rangle.\ b_2?\langle\mathsf{date}\rangle.\ \mathsf{end},\ \mathsf{quit} : \mathsf{end}\}@\mathtt{B2}$$

Similarly for Seller. After prefixing at a, we can compose all three by (TPAR).

Example 14 (The Streaming Protocol). We let $\Gamma = \{a : \langle G'\rangle\}$ where G' is given in Example 9. Let $d = 1$, $k = 2$, $c = 3$, $\mathtt{K} = 1$, $\mathtt{DP} = 2$, $\mathtt{C} = 3$ and $\mathtt{KP} = 4$. Write R_1, R_2, R_3 and R_4 for the processes which are under the initial prefix (at the shared name) of Kernel, DataProducer, Consumer and KeyProducer, respectively. Then we can type each agent as:

$$\Gamma \vdash R_1 \triangleright dkc : \mu\mathbf{t}.d?\langle\mathsf{bool}\rangle; k?\langle\mathsf{bool}\rangle; c!\langle\mathsf{bool}\rangle; \mathbf{t}@\mathtt{K}$$
$$\Gamma \vdash R_2 \triangleright dkc : \mu\mathbf{t}.d!\langle\mathsf{bool}\rangle; \mathbf{t}@\mathtt{DP} \qquad \Gamma \vdash R_4 \triangleright dkc : \mu\mathbf{t}.c?\langle\mathsf{bool}\rangle; \mathbf{t}@\mathtt{C}$$

(R_4 is similar as R_2). Note these types correspond to the projection of G' onto respective participants: thus Kernel, DataProducer, Consumer and KeyProducer are typable programs, which can be composed to make the initial configuration.

Example 15 (An Example of Delegation). One source of the expressiveness of the session types comes from a facility of *delegation* (often called *higher-order session passing*). We will type and see the relationship with global and local types. Consider the following three participants:

$$\mathsf{Alice} \stackrel{\text{def}}{=} \overline{a}_{[2]}(t_1, t_2).\ \overline{b}_{[2,3]}(s_1, s_2).\ t_1!\langle\!\langle s_1, s_2\rangle\!\rangle.\ \mathbf{0}$$
$$\mathsf{Bob} \stackrel{\text{def}}{=} a_{[2]}(t_1, t_2).\ b_{[1]}(s_1, s_2).\ t_1?(\!(s_1, s_2)\!).\ s_1!\langle 1\rangle; \mathbf{0}$$
$$\mathsf{Carol} \stackrel{\text{def}}{=} b_{[2]}(s_1, s_2).\ s_1?(x); P$$

where Alice delegates its capability to Bob. Since there are two multicasting, there are two global specifications, one for a and another for b as follows:

$$G_a = \mathtt{A} \to \mathtt{B}\colon t_1 \langle s_1 ! \langle \mathsf{int} \rangle @\mathtt{A} \rangle.\mathsf{end}$$
$$G_b = \mathtt{A} \to \mathtt{C}\colon s_1 \langle \mathsf{int} \rangle.\mathsf{end}$$

where the type $s_1 ! \langle \mathsf{int} \rangle @\mathtt{A}$ means the capability to send an integer from participant A via channel s_1. This capability is passed to B so that B behaves as A. However, since two specifications are independent, C does not have to know who would pass the capability.

Example 16 (Addition Protocol [1]). In this protocol, a client Client sends two natural numbers n and m to a server Addition and waits for a reply containing the sum $n + m$. Addition reacts to Client's messages as follows: if the second operand is 0 then it sends the first operand n back to Client as a result, otherwise it sends n and m to a third participant called SuccPred which will reply with $n + 1$ and $m - 1$ and then send a looping message to Client. This behaviour is repeated until the second operand becomes 0. Starting from the global type G, we have:

$$\mathtt{Client} \to \mathtt{Addition}\colon k_1 \langle int \rangle.\quad \mathtt{Client} \to \mathtt{Addition}\colon k_1 \langle int \rangle.$$
$$\mu \mathbf{t}.\ \mathtt{Addition} \to \mathtt{SuccPred}: k_2$$
$$\left\{\begin{array}{l} \mathsf{tt}: \mathtt{Addition} \to \mathtt{Client}\colon k_3\ \{\mathsf{ok}\colon \mathtt{Addition} \to \mathtt{Client}\colon k_3 \langle int \rangle.\mathsf{end}\} \\ \mathsf{ff}: \mathtt{Addition} \to \mathtt{SuccPred}\colon k_2 \langle int, int \rangle.\mathtt{SuccPred} \to \mathtt{Addition}\colon k_4 \langle int, int \rangle. \\ \quad\ \mathtt{Addition} \to \mathtt{Client}\colon k_3\ \{\mathsf{wait}\colon \mathbf{t}\} \end{array}\right\}$$

The projection of G generates the following local types:

$$G \upharpoonright \mathtt{Client} \quad = k_1 ! \langle int \rangle.\ k_1 ! \langle int \rangle.\ \mu \mathbf{t}.\ k_3 \& \{\mathsf{ok}: k_3 ? \langle int \rangle.\ \mathsf{end},\ \mathsf{wait}: \mathbf{t}\}$$
$$G \upharpoonright \mathtt{Addition} \ = k_1 ? \langle int \rangle.\ k_1 ? \langle int \rangle.\ \mu \mathbf{t}.\ k_2 \oplus \left\{\begin{array}{l} \mathsf{tt}: k_3 \oplus \{\mathsf{ok}: k_3 ! \langle int \rangle.\mathsf{end}\}, \\ \mathsf{ff}: k_2 ! \langle int, int \rangle.k_4 ? \langle int, int \rangle.k_3 \oplus \{\mathsf{wait}: \mathbf{t}\} \end{array}\right\}$$
$$G \upharpoonright \mathtt{SuccPred} \ = \mu \mathbf{t}.\ k_2 \& \{\mathsf{tt}: \mathsf{end},\ \mathsf{ff}: k_2 ? \langle int, int \rangle.k_4 ! \langle int, int \rangle.\mathbf{t}\}$$

and, finally, the protocol can be implemented as:

$$\mathsf{Client} \quad = \overline{a}[2,3]\,(k_1, k_2, k_3, k_4).\ k_1 ! \langle n \rangle.\ k_1 ! \langle m \rangle.\ \mu X.\ k_3 \triangleright \{\mathsf{ok}: k_3 ?(x),\ \mathsf{wait}: X\}$$

$$\begin{array}{l} \mathsf{Addition} \quad = a[2]\,(k_1, k_2, k_3, k_4).\ k_1 ?(x_1).\ k_1 ?(x_2). \\ \qquad \mu X.\ \mathbf{if}\ x_2 = 0 \\ \qquad\quad \mathbf{then}\ k_2 \triangleleft \mathsf{tt}.\ k_3 \triangleleft \mathsf{ok}.\ k_3 ! \langle x_1 \rangle \\ \qquad\quad \mathbf{else}\ \ k_2 \triangleleft \mathsf{ff}.\ k_2 ! \langle x_1, x_2 \rangle.\ k_4 ?(x_1, x_2).\ k_3 \triangleleft \mathsf{wait}.\ X \end{array}$$

$$\mathsf{SuccPred} = a[3]\,(k_1, k_2, k_3, k_4).\ \mu X.\ k_2 \triangleright \{\mathsf{tt}: \mathbf{0},\ \mathsf{ff}: k_2 ?(x, y).\ k_4 ! \langle x + 1, y - 1 \rangle\}$$

where a is the shared name for the protocol, Client = 1, Addition = 2 and SuccPred = 3. Note that we had to introduce a synchronisation between Addition and Client at each iteration. This avoids the case when Client waits forever in case of negative m hence violating safety (in such case the global type would not be projectable).

On Run-Time Processes and Subject Reduction. Similarly to what we have discussed for asynchronous exceptions, also multiparty session types enjoy a subject reduction property.

Informally, we need to extend the typing rules to include those for runtime processes which involve message queues in a fashion similar to what discussed for asynchronous interactional exceptions. .

Theorem 5 (Subject Reduction). *$\Gamma \vdash P \triangleright \emptyset$ and $P \rightarrow P'$ imply $\Gamma \vdash P' \triangleright \emptyset$.*

By the correspondence between local types and global types, these results guarantee that interactions between typed processes exactly follow the conversation scenario specified in a global type. Also in this case, *safety* and *session fidelity* follow. Also, under a certain condition we can also have *progress* [10].

5 Discussion

5.1 Interactional Exceptions

Comparing to the original work in [5], we have omitted the typing of run-time processes which, although important, is only used as a technique for proving type safety. The original work also addresses the problem of termination for try-catch blocks. For instance, suppose there are two (and only two) processes in a configuration, which are try-catch blocks and which are communicating in a session. If each party's default process becomes the inaction process, it is natural to reduce each try-catch block to the inaction, freeing up the resources for its handler. This garbage collection is essential when we consider integration of interactional exceptions into the standard imperative programming languages with sequential composition since in this case launching a handler depends on whether a process reduces to the inaction or not. In [5], it is shown that a well-typed process satisfies a liveness condition with such a garbage collector.

As discussed in [5], programs can be extended such that in the session initialisation processes $*c(\lambda)[P, Q]$ and $\overline{c}(\lambda)[\tilde{k}, P, Q]$, the handler Q may contain another try-catch at the same λ (currently, try-catch is only used at run-time). Such an extension of the formalism would allow a process to "try" again after an exception has been thrown (cascading exceptions). For this purpose, try-catch types should be extended such that in $\alpha\{\!|\beta|\!\}$ the type α is always plain while β can be either plain or a try-catch type. With essentially the same operational semantics, this generalised calculus satisfies the subject reduction and liveness properties.

The key idea of the presented operational semantics is the use of exception levels in queues and their interplay with wrapped processes. In implementation, the queue level can be recorded in a header of each message which its receiver can check efficiently. The wrapping level can be a part of a process state, recording its exception depth. Various optimisations are possible, for example dispensing with most coordination protocols when the handler type is trivial, obtaining essentially the same level of efficiency as local exception.

Session delegations are not allowed in [5] but can be formulated by storing frozen processes in queues. The type soundness holds by extending the typing rules with those in [8].

A further generalisation to multiparty session types for flexible multicast exception propagation is currently being investigated.

5.2 Multiparty Session Types

Multiparty session types have been further investigated since the original work in [10]. The theory presented in this lecture note mainly differs from [10] in two points: (i) session channels can only be used between two fixed parties (in one direction), first discovered in [2] and (ii) the introduction of the merging operator for allowing a broader set of projectable global types (first proposed here).

Bejleri and Yoshida [1] have studied multiparty *synchronous* session types, a variant where communication is synchronous (no queues) as in [8]. They introduce multicasting, higher-order communication via multi-polarity labels and an alternative definition of delegation in global types. The work in [2] develops a type system (built up on the original one) for global progress in multiparty sessions: well typed terms guarantee the absence of deadlock. A very recent work, [14], introduces communication subtyping, which allows for partial commutativity of actions, providing flexibility and safe optimisation. The authors propose an algorithm for the subtyping relation, which can calculate conformance of end-point processes to an agreed global specification. Moreover, they introduce an algorithm for abstracting a global specification from end-point processes allowing programmer to choose between a top-down and a bottom-up style of communication programming.

There are several significant future topics on the theory and applications of multiparty session types. This generalised session type structure is currently being used as one of the formal foundations of the next version of a web service description language, WS-CDL from W3C [17] and a message scheme for financial protocols, UNIFI from ISO [12]. Another topic is the use of this theory as a basis of communication-centred extensions of general purpose programming languages [11]. Others include tools assistance for the design and elaboration of global types; and integration of the type discipline with diverse specification concerns including security and assertional methods.

References

1. Bejleri, A., Yoshida, N.: Synchronous multiparty session types. In: Proceedings of Programming Languages Approaches to Concurrency and Communication-Centric Software, PLACES 2008 (2008)
2. Bettini, L., Coppo, M., D'Antoni, L., Luca, M.D., Dezani-Ciancaglini, M., Yoshida, N.: Global progress in dynamically interleaved multiparty sessions. In: van Breugel, F., Chechik, M. (eds.) CONCUR 2008. LNCS, vol. 5201, pp. 418–433. Springer, Heidelberg (2008)
3. Bonelli, E., Compagnoni, A.: Multipoint Session Types for a Distributed Calculus. In: Barthe, G., Fournet, C. (eds.) TGC 2007 and FODO 2008. LNCS, vol. 4912, pp. 240–256. Springer, Heidelberg (2008)
4. Carbone, M., Honda, K., Yoshida, N.: Structured Communication-Centred Programming for Web Services. In: De Nicola, R. (ed.) ESOP 2007. LNCS, vol. 4421, pp. 2–17. Springer, Heidelberg (2007)
5. Carbone, M., Honda, K., Yoshida, N.: Structured interactional exceptions for session types. In: van Breugel, F., Chechik, M. (eds.) CONCUR 2008. LNCS, vol. 5201, pp. 402–417. Springer, Heidelberg (2008)

6. Gay, S., Hole, M.: Subtyping for Session Types in the Pi-Calculus. Acta Informatica 42(2/3), 191–225 (2005)
7. Gay, S., Vasconcelos, V.T.: Asynchronous functional session types. TR 2007–251, University of Glasgow (May 2007)
8. Honda, K., Vasconcelos, V.T., Kubo, M.: Language Primitives and Type Disciplines for Structured Communication-based Programming. In: Hankin, C. (ed.) ESOP 1998. LNCS, vol. 1381, pp. 122–138. Springer, Heidelberg (1998)
9. Honda, K., Yoshida, N., Carbone, M.: Web Services, Mobile Processes and Types. The Bulletin of the European Association for Theoretical Computer Science 91, 165–185 (2007)
10. Honda, K., Yoshida, N., Carbone, M.: Multiparty Asynchronous Session Types. In: POPL 2008, pp. 273–284. ACM, New York (2008)
11. Hu, R., Yoshida, N., Honda, K.: Session-Based Distributed Programming in Java. In: Vitek, J. (ed.) ECOOP 2008. LNCS, vol. 5142, pp. 516–541. Springer, Heidelberg (2008)
12. International Organization for Standardization ISO 20022 UNIversal Financial Industry message scheme, http://www.iso20022.org/index.cfm?item_id=56664#interest
13. Lamport, L.: Time, clocks and the ordering of events in a distributed system. Communications of the ACM 21(7), 558–564 (1978)
14. Mostrous, D., Yoshida, N., Honda, K.: Global Principal Typing in Partially Commutative Asynchronous Sessions. In: Castagna, G. (ed.) ESOP 2009. LNCS, vol. 5502, pp. 316–332. Springer, Heidelberg (2009)
15. Schneier, B.: Applied Cryptography: Protocols, Algorithms, and Source Code in C. John Wiley & Sons, Inc., Chichester (1993)
16. Takeuchi, K., Honda, K., Kubo, M.: An Interaction-based Language and its Typing System. In: Halatsis, C., Philokyprou, G., Maritsas, D., Theodoridis, S. (eds.) PARLE 1994. LNCS, vol. 817, pp. 398–413. Springer, Heidelberg (1994)
17. Web Services Choreography Working Group, http://www.w3.org/2002/ws/chor/
18. Wikipedia. Exception handling (2009), http://en.wikipedia.org/wiki/Exception_handling
19. Yoshida, N., Vasconcelos, V.T.: Language primitives and type disciplines for structured communication-based programming revisit. ENTCS 171(4), 73–93 (2007)

Contract-Based Discovery and Adaptation of Web Services

Luca Padovani

Istituto di Scienze e Tecnologie dell'Informazione – Università di Urbino
padovani@sti.uniurb.it

Abstract. A *contract* describes the observable behavior of a Web service. When looking for Web services providing specific capabilities, the contract can be used as an important search key. This calls for a notion of contract equivalence that goes beyond nominal or structural equivalence.

In this paper we define a simple, yet expressive formal language for describing Web service contracts. We provide a natural, set-theoretic semantics of contracts and we use it for defining a family of equivalence relations that can be effectively used for discovering and adapting Web services implementing a specific contract.

1 Introduction

Web services are distributed processes equipped with a public description of their interface. Such description typically includes the type – or *schema* – of messages exchanged with the service, the *operations* provided by the service [12], and also the behavior – or *contract* – supported by the service [1,3].

As an example, Figure 1 shows (a streamlined fragment of) the WS-BPEL document describing the behavior of a Web service that waits for purchase orders from a client, verifies that the client has enough credit for the purchase, and arranges the delivery of the ordered items with the deposit if the ordered item is available. The `receive` operation (line 3) waits for the order from the client, and stores the order information into a local variable `Request`. The `flow` activity (lines 4–9) invokes the credit and deposit services in parallel, and waits for the answer from both invocations. Then, the `switch` activity (lines 10–23) checks the responses from the credit and deposit services. If both responses are positive, namely if the client has enough credit and if the ordered item is available from the deposit (lines 11–12), the service sends a shipment notification to the deposit (line 13) and a confirmation to the client (line 14). If the item is not available, but the client does have enough credit (line 16), then the service issues a refund to the client (line 17) and notifies the client that the order was unsuccessful (line 18). In the remaining cases (lines 20–22) the service simply notifies the client of the unsuccessful transaction (line 21).

A service is advertised by registering its description in one or more Web service repositories [4,6,13,31] that can be queried for discovering services satisfying a particular client. This calls for a formalization of the contract language and of a notion of client satisfaction.

M. Bernardo, L. Padovani, and G. Zavattaro (Eds.): SFM 2009, LNCS 5569, pp. 213–260, 2009.

```
1  <process>
2    <sequence>
3      <receive operation="Order" variable="Request"/>
4      <flow>
5        <invoke operation="Deposit" inputVariable="Request"
6                outputVariable="Deposit"/>
7        <invoke operation="Credit" inputVariable="Request"
8                outputVariable="Credit"/>
9      </flow>
10     <switch>
11       <case condition="getVariableData(Deposit) == true
12               && getVariableData(Credit) == true)">
13         <invoke operation="Ship" inputVariable="Request"/>
14         <reply operation="Order" value="OK"/>
15       </case>
16       <case condition="getVariableData(Credit) == true)">
17         <invoke operation="Refund" inputVariable="Request"/>
18         <reply operation="Order" value="NO"/>
19       </case>
20       <otherwise>
21         <reply operation="Order" value="NO"/>
22       </otherwise>
23     </switch>
24   </sequence>
25 </process>
```

Fig. 1. WS-BPEL description of ordering service

The contract language. As regards the formalization of the contract language, we will focus on the *observable behavior* of services by abstracting every detail that is specific to a particular implementation. For example, by looking at Figure 1, we realize that one possible abstraction is given by the actions `O`, `D`, `C`, `S`, and `R` (which we use for the sake of brevity in place of the more verbose `Order`, `Deposit`, `Credit`, `Ship`, and `Refund` in Figure 1) that are performed by the service. The fact, for example, that the service declares a local variable `Request` is not interesting, as far as the observable behavior is concerned. However, this abstraction of the service behavior is too weak, because it does not say anything about the *order* in which those actions are (or can be) executed by the service. A more precise abstraction of the service behavior is to consider the set of *traces* of actions that can be performed by the service. In the example of Figure 1 we have 6 possible traces, namely

$$\{\texttt{ODCSO}, \texttt{OCDSO}, \texttt{ODCRO}, \texttt{OCDRO}, \texttt{ODCO}, \texttt{OCDO}\}$$

which are obtained by considering the 3 outcomes of the transaction (successful, unsuccessful because the item is not available, all the remaining cases) times the possible interleaving of the actions `D` and `C` in the `flow` activity (lines 5–10). In practice, we are approximating the behavior of two activities occurring in parallel with all the possible permutations of these actions (interleaving semantics).

This is without doubt a more precise description of the service, but still it has a major shortcoming in that it confuses two very different choices. On one hand, the simultaneous presence of traces of the form $\mathtt{OD}s$ and traces of the form $\mathtt{OC}s$ must be interpreted as the fact that the service does not mandate which of the two actions D and C should occur first. More technically, this is an *external choice* between the actions D and C. It is the environment in which the service operates, and not the service itself, that decides which of the two actions to perform. On the other hand, the simultaneous presence of traces such as $s\mathtt{SO}$, $s\mathtt{RO}$, and $s\mathtt{O}$ must be interpreted as the fact that the service decides whether the order is successful, in which case an S action is performed followed by the notification to the client, or unsuccessful because the item is unavailable, in which case a R action is performed followed by the notification to the client, or only a notification is sent. More technically, this is an *internal choice* between the actions S, R, and O, each one followed by a corresponding continuation. It is the service that autonomously decides, depending on its internal state, which of these actions to perform.

In summary, the contract of a service is a structured term that describes the actions performed, the order in which these actions are performed, and the branching points (corresponding to external and internal choices) in the service behavior. Additionally, we will distinguish actions denoting *incoming messages* received by the service, from actions denoting *outgoing messages* that correspond to invocations to other services or to responses to the client of the service. This distinction will be essential for determining possible causal dependencies between actions, as we will see in a later section. More technically, we express contracts using a fragment of CCS [16] with two choice operators ($+$ for external choice and $\oplus$ for internal choice) without relabeling, restriction, and parallel composition. For example, the service in Figure 1 can be described by the term

$$\mathtt{O}.(\overline{\mathtt{D}}.\overline{\mathtt{C}}.\mathtt{D}.\mathtt{C}.(\overline{\mathtt{S}}.\overline{\mathtt{O}} \oplus \overline{\mathtt{R}}.\overline{\mathtt{O}} \oplus \overline{\mathtt{O}}) + \overline{\mathtt{C}}.\overline{\mathtt{D}}.\mathtt{D}.\mathtt{C}.(\overline{\mathtt{S}}.\overline{\mathtt{O}} \oplus \overline{\mathtt{R}}.\overline{\mathtt{O}} \oplus \overline{\mathtt{O}}))$$

where we have distinguished the requests $\overline{\mathtt{D}}$ and $\overline{\mathtt{C}}$ from the corresponding responses D and C.[1]

The subcontract relation. As regards the formalization of the satisfaction relation between a client and a service, the intuition is that a client is *compliant with* (or *satisfied by*) a service if every possible interaction between the client and the service leads the client into a successful state. If we represent the behavior of the client by means of a contract ρ and σ is the contract of the service, we denote this fact by writing $\rho \dashv \sigma$. The definition of compliance calls for two more notions: that of interaction between client and service, and that of successful state for a client. We will postpone the exact definition of these two notions to a later section. For the time being, we observe that a formal notions of compliance may be used for implementing contract-based query engines. The query for services that satisfy ρ is answered with the set $\mathscr{Q}(\rho) = \{\sigma \mid \rho \dashv \sigma\}$.

A major drawback of this approach is that the complexity of running a query grows with the number of services registered in the repository, independently of the fact that many registered services may actually be equivalent, in terms of the clients they satisfy.

[1] We have deliberately chosen to read the response from the deposit service first, followed by the response from the credit service. This is not restrictive since the service cannot proceed until both responses are received.

In fact, it makes sense to relax this equivalence relation into a *subcontract relation*: we say that σ is a subcontract of τ, notation $\sigma \preceq \tau$, if every client satisfied by σ is also satisfied by τ. In this sense, any service with contract τ (or greater, according to $\preceq$) can appear in the answer of a query for a service σ if $\sigma \preceq \tau$. Now, if we are able to compute the *canonical service* that satisfies ρ, namely the smallest (according to $\preceq$) contract $\rho^\perp$ such that $\rho \dashv \rho^\perp$, then we can answer the above query with the set $\mathscr{Q}(\rho) = \{\sigma \mid \rho^\perp \preceq \sigma\}$. The advantage of this approach is that the $\preceq$ relation between services can be precomputed as services are registered in the repository, and the query engine needs only scan through the $\preceq$-minimal contracts. Furthermore, the definition of a formal theory of contracts and of a notion of contract equivalence finds useful applications also outside the scope of Web service discovery: it may help and drive the development of new Web services, as well as supporting maintenance and refactoring of existing ones.

Technical issues aside, it is possible to argue about some of the properties that we expect from the subcontract relation. For example, it is reasonable to expect that $\sigma \oplus \tau \preceq \sigma$, namely that it is possible to use a service with contract σ in place of a service that internally decides to behave according to either σ or τ. The larger service is more deterministic than the smaller one. In general, we expect $\preceq$ to *reduce nondeterminism*. In a dual manner, it is also reasonable to expect that $\sigma \preceq \sigma + \tau$, namely that it is possible to use a service that externally offers more possible behaviors in place of a service that offers a subset of them. Unfortunately, this relation is much more subtle, and it does not hold in general because the additional behavior τ may cause interferences with σ and also with clients of the smaller service. We will see that it is possible to partially guarantee this desirable property if we assume that the interaction between the client and a service is mediated by a suitable orchestrator. In a context where a third process, the orchestrator, helps client and service to interact smoothly, other relations become feasible. For example, it would be reasonable to expect that $a.b.\sigma \preceq b.a.\sigma$, namely that the order in which subsequent input actions are performed by the service should be irrelevant and similarly for sequences of output actions. In general, it should be possible to replace a service with contract $a.\overline{b}.\sigma$ with another one with contract $\overline{b}.a.\sigma$, since the latter is able to send the b message without needing an a message from the client. Conversely, it should not be possible to replace a service with contract $\overline{a}.b.\sigma$ with another one with contract $b.\overline{a}.\sigma$, since a client of the first service may need the content of the a message before being able to send b to the service.

The aim of this tutorial is the definition of a subcontract relation that can be effectively used for the discovery of *all* and *only* those Web services that *can* satisfy a given client. Here, "only" means that Web services whose contracts are deemed equivalent should be compatible, namely they should satisfy the same clients; "all" means that the equivalence relation should be as coarse as possible, so a to maximize the search space and favor Web service reuse; "can" means that we should tolerate a certain amount of incompatibility between Web services whose contracts are deemed equivalent, provided that there is a sufficiently simple (i.e. automatic) way of avoiding such incompatibilities.

Structure of the paper. In §2 we define syntax and semantics of the contract language and we define strong variants of the compliance and subcontract relations. We will see that these relations enjoy nice properties, but are too strict for the purposes of Web service discovery. In §3 we define weak variants of compliance and subcontract relation, corresponding to the scenario where client and services interact while being mediated by a simple orchestrator that blocks some actions and permits others. We proceed by studying simple orchestrators and the fundamental properties of the weak relations they induce, including their connection with the corresponding strong variants and a sound and complete deduction system for the weak subcontract relation. In §4 we give orchestrators the ability of buffering messages from the client of from the service, and of delivering them at later stages in the interaction. We will go through a similar round of properties and results as we did for the simple orchestrators in §3. §5 shows how to compute the principal dual contract $\rho^\perp$ of a client contract ρ. In §6 we argue that all the definitions and results from previous sections can be naturally extended to the case of potentially infinite behaviors. We will do so by departing from standard process-algebraic techniques and by adopting a more basic, yet elegant approach. In §7 we devise an algorithm for the subcontract relation defined in §4, which includes the ones in §2 and in §3. The algorithm is proved to be sound and complete. §8 provides a somewhat more extensive example of application of the theory to an adaptation of the dining philosophers problem in the Web service setting. §9 concludes the paper with a survey of some closely related work and a sketch of possible tracks of future research. Long proofs and auxiliary results have been moved to the appendix for improving readability.

2 A Theory of Contracts

2.1 Contracts: Syntax and Semantics

Let us begin by fixing some notation. The syntax of contracts makes use of a denumerable set $\mathscr{N}$ of *names* ranged over by $a, b, \ldots$; we write $\overline{\mathscr{N}}$ for the set of *co-names* $\overline{a}$, where $a \in \mathscr{N}$. Names represent input actions, while co-names represent output actions; we let $\alpha, \beta, \ldots$ range over actions, namely elements of $\mathscr{N} \cup \overline{\mathscr{N}}$; we let $\varphi, \varphi', \ldots$ range over strings of actions, ε being the empty string as usual; we let $\mathtt{R}, \mathtt{S}, \ldots$ range over finite sets of actions; we let $\overline{\overline{\alpha}} = \alpha$ and $\overline{\mathtt{R}} = \{\overline{\alpha} \mid \alpha \in \mathtt{R}\}$ and $\overline{\varphi}$ be the sequence obtained by changing every action α in φ with its corresponding co-action $\overline{\alpha}$. The meaning of names is left unspecified: they can stand for ports, operations, message types, and so forth.

Definition 1 (contract syntax). *Contracts are ranged over by $\rho, \sigma, \tau, \ldots$ and their syntax is given by the following grammar:*

$\sigma ::=$		***contract***	$\alpha ::=$		***action***
	0	*(null)*		a	*(input)*
$\mid$	$\alpha.\sigma$	*(action prefix)*	$\mid$	$\overline{a}$	*(output)*
$\mid$	$\sigma + \sigma$	*(external choice)*			
$\mid$	$\sigma \oplus \sigma$	*(internal choice)*			

The null contract 0 describes the idle process that offers no action; the contract $\alpha.\sigma$ describes a process that offers the action α and then behaves as σ; the contract $\sigma + \tau$ is the *external choice* of σ and τ and describes a process that can either behave as σ or as τ depending on the party it is interacting with; the contract $\sigma \oplus \tau$ is the *internal choice* of σ and τ and describes a process that autonomously decides to behave as either σ or τ. For the sake of brevity we will omit trailing 0's, so for instance we will write $a.b$ in place of $a.b.0$.

We proceed by giving contracts an operational semantics that describes how they evolve over time and which actions they offer. In this chapter, we will blur the distinction between processes and contracts so that whenever we speak of a contract that emits or offers an action or exhibits a certain behavior, what we really mean is that the process respecting the contract emits or offers the same action or exhibits the same behavior.

Definition 2 (operational semantics of contracts). *The operational semantics of contracts is described by the rules below*

$$\alpha.\sigma \xrightarrow{\alpha} \sigma \qquad \sigma \oplus \tau \longrightarrow \sigma \qquad \frac{\sigma \xrightarrow{\alpha} \sigma'}{\sigma + \tau \xrightarrow{\alpha} \sigma'} \qquad \frac{\sigma \longrightarrow \sigma'}{\sigma + \tau \longrightarrow \sigma' + \tau}$$

plus the symmetric of the last three rules.

The relation $\longrightarrow$ denotes internal, invisible transitions, while $\xrightarrow{\alpha}$ denotes visible transitions labeled with an action α. The first rule states that a contract $\alpha.\sigma$ may offer an action α and evolve to the residual contract σ. The second rule states that a contract $\sigma \oplus \tau$ may evolve to σ (or to τ) by means of an invisible, internal transition. The third rule states that a contract $\sigma + \tau$ offers all the actions that are offered by either σ or τ. Finally, the last rule states that $+$ is a truly external choice: the internal transition $\sigma \longrightarrow \sigma'$ does not preempt the τ branch.[2] We write $\Longrightarrow$ for the reflexive, transitive closure of $\longrightarrow$; let $\stackrel{\alpha}{\Longrightarrow}$ be $\Longrightarrow\xrightarrow{\alpha}\Longrightarrow$; we write $\sigma \xrightarrow{\alpha}$ if there exists σ' such that $\sigma \xrightarrow{\alpha} \sigma'$, and similarly for $\sigma \stackrel{\alpha}{\Longrightarrow}$; let $\mathsf{init}(\sigma) \stackrel{\text{def}}{=} \{\alpha \mid \sigma \stackrel{\alpha}{\Longrightarrow}\}$.

We now have all the technical instruments for defining how a client and a service interact and what it means for a client to be in a successful state. As regards the latter notion, we reserve a special action e (for "end") that we assume to occur in client contracts only and we say that a client ρ is satisfied if $\rho \xrightarrow{\mathsf{e}}$, namely if it has the immediate possibility of offering an e action. Observe that, by the last rule in Definition 2, if $\rho \xrightarrow{\mathsf{e}}$, then $\rho' \xrightarrow{\mathsf{e}}$ for every residual ρ' such that $\rho \Longrightarrow \rho'$. In general, once an action is offered *externally* by a contract, it cannot be revoked by means of internal moves of the same contract.

Definition 3 (strong compliance). *A* system *is a pair $\rho \parallel \sigma$ of a (client) contract ρ and a (service) contract σ interacting with each other. Let $\longrightarrow$ be the least relation between systems inductively defined as follows:*

$$\frac{\rho \longrightarrow \rho'}{\rho \parallel \sigma \longrightarrow \rho' \parallel \sigma} \qquad \frac{\sigma \longrightarrow \sigma'}{\rho \parallel \sigma \longrightarrow \rho \parallel \sigma'} \qquad \frac{\rho \xrightarrow{\overline{\alpha}} \rho' \quad \sigma \xrightarrow{\alpha} \sigma'}{\rho \parallel \sigma \longrightarrow \rho' \parallel \sigma'}$$

[2] The transition relation of contracts is the same as that of CCS without τ's [16].

We write $\Longrightarrow$ for the reflexive, transitive closure of $\longrightarrow$; we write $\rho \parallel \sigma \not\longrightarrow$ if there exist no ρ' and σ' such that $\rho \parallel \sigma \longrightarrow \rho' \parallel \sigma'$. We say that (the client contract) ρ is strongly compliant with *(the service contract) σ, notation $\rho \dashv \sigma$, if $\rho \parallel \sigma \Longrightarrow \rho' \parallel \sigma' \not\longrightarrow$ implies $\rho' \stackrel{\mathsf{e}}{\longrightarrow}$.*

The first two rules in the definition of $\longrightarrow$ for systems indicate that client and service may evolve autonomously by means of internal moves. The last rule describes a synchronization between client and service performing complementary actions. A client ρ is strongly compliant with a service σ if *every* computation of the system $\rho \parallel \sigma$ reaching a stable state $\rho' \parallel \sigma'$ is such that $\rho' \stackrel{\mathsf{e}}{\longrightarrow}$, which denotes the satisfaction of the client. For instance $a.\mathsf{e} + b.\mathsf{e} \dashv \overline{a} \oplus \overline{b}$ and $a.\mathsf{e} \oplus b.\mathsf{e} \dashv \overline{a} + \overline{b}$, but $a.\mathsf{e} \oplus b.\mathsf{e} \not\dashv \overline{a} \oplus \overline{b}$ because of the computation $a.\mathsf{e} \oplus b.\mathsf{e} \parallel \overline{a} \oplus \overline{b} \Longrightarrow a.\mathsf{e} \parallel \overline{b} \not\longrightarrow$.

Observe that compliance is an asymmetric relation as it only concerns the client's satisfaction. Also, compliance is preserved by system reduction. Namely, if $\rho \dashv \sigma$ and $\rho \parallel \sigma \Longrightarrow \rho' \parallel \sigma'$, then $\rho' \dashv \sigma'$.

The (strong) compliance relation provides us with the most natural equivalence for comparing services: the (service) contract σ is "smaller than" the (service) contract τ if every client that is compliant with σ is also compliant with τ.

Definition 4 (strong subcontract relation). *Let $[\![\sigma]\!]^{\mathsf{s}} \stackrel{\text{def}}{=} \{\rho \mid \rho \dashv \sigma\}$. We say that σ is a* subcontract *of τ, notation $\sigma \sqsubseteq \tau$, if $[\![\sigma]\!]^{\mathsf{s}} \subseteq [\![\tau]\!]^{\mathsf{s}}$. We write $\simeq$ for the equivalence relation induced by $\sqsubseteq$, namely $\simeq \, = \, \sqsubseteq \cap \sqsupseteq$.*

For instance, we have $a \oplus b \sqsubseteq a$ because every client that is satisfied by a service that may decide to offer either a or b is also satisfied by a service that systematically offers a. On the other hand $a.(\overline{b} + \overline{d}) \not\sqsubseteq a.\overline{b} + a.\overline{d}$ since $\overline{a}.b.\mathsf{e} \dashv a.(\overline{b} + \overline{d})$ but $\overline{a}.b.\mathsf{e} \not\dashv a.\overline{b} + a.\overline{d}$ because of the computation $\overline{a}.b.\mathsf{e} \parallel a.\overline{b} + a.\overline{d} \longrightarrow b.\mathsf{e} \parallel \overline{d} \not\longrightarrow$. In the last example a client of $a.(\overline{b} + \overline{d})$ can decide whether to receive $\overline{b}$ or $\overline{d}$ after sending $\overline{a}$, whereas in $a.\overline{b} + a.\overline{d}$ only one of these actions is available, according to the branch taken by the service. In fact it is possible to prove that $a.\overline{b} + a.\overline{d} \simeq a.(\overline{b} \oplus \overline{d})$.

2.2 Alternative Characterization

The set-theoretic definition of the subcontract relation above embeds the notion of safe-substitutability by its own definition, but gives little insight on the properties of $\sqsubseteq$ and is also hard to use in proofs. For these reasons it is desirable to define an alternative characterization of $\sqsubseteq$, which is also propedeutic to the alternative characterizations of the weak subcontract relations in §3 and in §4. In order to define it we need two auxiliary notions, that of contract continuation and of ready set.

The transition relation of contracts describes the evolution of a contract from the point of view of the process exposing, or implementing, the contract. The notion of *contract continuation*, which we are to define next, considers the point of view of the process it is interacting with.

Definition 5 (contract continuation). *Let $\sigma \stackrel{\alpha}{\Longrightarrow}$. The* continuation *of σ with respect to α, notation $\sigma(\alpha)$, is defined as $\sigma(\alpha) \stackrel{\text{def}}{=} \bigoplus_{\sigma \Longrightarrow \stackrel{\alpha}{\longrightarrow} \sigma'} \sigma'$. We generalize the notion of continuation to finite sequences of actions so that $\sigma(\varepsilon) = \sigma$ and $\sigma(\alpha\varphi) = \sigma(\alpha)(\varphi)$.*

For example, $a.\overline{b}+a.\overline{d} \xrightarrow{a} \overline{b}$ (the process knows which branch has been taken after an action a) but $(a.\overline{b}+a.\overline{d})(a) = \overline{b} \oplus \overline{d}$ (the party interacting with $a.\overline{b}+a.\overline{d}$ does not know which branch has been taken after seeing an a action, hence it considers both).

The *ready sets* of a contract tell us about its internal nondeterminism.

Definition 6 (ready set). *We say that σ has* ready set R, *written $\sigma \Downarrow \mathrm{R}$, if $\sigma \Longrightarrow \sigma' \not\longrightarrow$ and $\mathrm{R} = \mathsf{init}(\sigma')$.*

Intuitively, $\sigma \Downarrow \mathrm{R}$ means that σ can independently evolve, by means of internal transitions, to a stable contract σ' which only offers the actions in R. For example, $\{a,b\}$ is the only ready set of $a+b$ (both a and b are always available), whereas the ready sets of $a \oplus b$ are $\{a\}$ and $\{b\}$ (the contract $a \oplus b$ may evolve into a state where only a is available, or into a state where only b is available). Similarly, $a+(b \oplus c)$ has two ready sets $\{a,b\}$ and $\{a,c\}$. Namely, the availability of action a is always guaranteed (it can be chosen externally, see "+" in the contract), but only one of b or c will be available (the choice of which is made internally, see "$\oplus$" in the contract).

We are now ready to define an alternative characterization of $\sqsubseteq$.

Definition 7 (coinductive strong subcontract). *We say that $\mathscr{S}$ is a* coinductive strong subcontract relation *if $(\sigma, \tau) \in \mathscr{S}$ implies*

1. *$\tau \Downarrow \mathrm{S}$ implies $\sigma \Downarrow \mathrm{R}$ and $\mathrm{R} \subseteq \mathrm{S}$ for some* R, *and*
2. *$\tau \stackrel{\alpha}{\Longrightarrow}$ implies $\sigma \stackrel{\alpha}{\Longrightarrow}$ and $(\sigma(\alpha), \tau(\alpha)) \in \mathscr{S}$.*

Condition (1) requires τ to be more deterministic than σ (every ready set of τ has a corresponding one of σ that offers fewer actions). Condition (2) requires τ to offer no more actions than those offered by σ, and every continuation after an action offered by both σ and τ to be in the subcontract relation.

The next results proves that Definition 7 is indeed a sound and complete characterization of $\sqsubseteq$.

Theorem 1. *$\sqsubseteq$ is the largest coinductive subcontract relation.*

2.3 Properties of the Strong Subcontract Relation

The alternative characterization of $\sqsubseteq$ allows us to prove some interesting properties of the strong subcontract relation. First of all, we have now formal evidence that $\sigma \oplus \tau \sqsubseteq \sigma$ holds for every σ and τ. Indeed, the ready sets of σ are a subset of the ready sets of $\sigma \oplus \tau$, hence both conditions in Definition 7 are trivially satisfied. However, $\sqsubseteq$ turns out to be rather restrictive, at least if compared to the hypothetical subcontract relation $\preceq$ we have informally used in the introduction. In particular, we have $a \not\sqsubseteq a+b$, because $a+b$ can offer a b action that is not offered by a, thus violating condition (2). For example, the client $\rho \stackrel{\text{def}}{=} \overline{a}.\mathsf{e} + \overline{b}$ is such that $\rho \dashv a$, but $\rho \not\dashv a+b$. Obviously, permutation of actions is also unsupported by $\sqsubseteq$. Nonetheless, $\sqsubseteq$ enjoys other fundamental properties, and it is at the core of the weak subcontract relations we will define in later sections.

Proposition 1. *The following properties hold:*

1. *$\sqsubseteq$ coincides with the* must *preorder [16,15,21] for strongly convergent processes;*
2. *$\sqsubseteq$ is a precongruence with respect to all the operators of the contract language.*

Property (1) connects $\sqsubseteq$ with the well-known *must* testing preorder. This result is not entirely obvious because the notion of "satisfied client" we use for comparing services differs from that of "passing a test" used for comparing processes in the standard testing framework (see [24] for more details).

Property (2) states that $\sqsubseteq$ is well behaved and that it can be used for modular refinement. Namely, we can refine parts of a contract separately, with the guarantee that the resulting contract is a refinement of the original one. The weak variants of the subcontract relation that we will define in the following sections do not enjoy this property in general, but not without reason as we will see.

Further insight on $\sqsubseteq$ can be gained by giving a sound and complete axiomatization of the subcontract relation. This consists of a finite set of *laws* that express the fundamental properties of $\preceq$ and that can be used for proving every relation $\sigma \sqsubseteq \tau$.

Table 1. Axiomatization for $\sqsubseteq$

(E1)	$\sigma + \sigma = \sigma$	(D1)	$\sigma + (\sigma' \oplus \sigma'') = (\sigma + \sigma') \oplus (\sigma + \sigma'')$
(E2)	$\sigma + \tau = \tau + \sigma$	(D2)	$\sigma \oplus (\sigma' + \sigma'') = (\sigma \oplus \sigma') + (\sigma \oplus \sigma'')$
(E3)	$\sigma + (\sigma' + \sigma'') = (\sigma + \sigma') + \sigma''$	(D3)	$\alpha.\sigma + \alpha.\tau = \alpha.(\sigma \oplus \tau)$
(E4)	$\sigma + 0 = \sigma$	(D4)	$\alpha.\sigma \oplus \alpha.\tau = \alpha.(\sigma \oplus \tau)$
(I1)	$\sigma \oplus \sigma = \sigma$	(RED)	$\sigma \oplus \tau \leq \sigma$
(I2)	$\sigma \oplus \tau = \tau \oplus \sigma$		
(I3)	$\sigma \oplus (\sigma' \oplus \sigma'') = (\sigma \oplus \sigma') \oplus \sigma''$		

Table 1 defines an axiomatization for the relation $\leq$, which coincides with $\sqsubseteq$ as we will see shortly. In the table we use a single axiom $\sigma = \tau$ in place of two axioms $\sigma \leq \tau$ and $\tau \leq \sigma$. Rules (E1–E4) state that the external choice is an idempotent, commutative, and associative operator with neutral element 0. Rules (I1–I3) state that internal choice is idempotent, commutative, and associative. Rules (D1–D2) state that the two choices distribute over each other, while rules (D3–D4) state the distributivity laws of prefix over choices. Rules (D3) and (D4) together state a particularly important fact: an external choice $\alpha.\sigma + \alpha.\tau$ where both branches are guarded by the *same* action is actually an internal choice $\alpha.\sigma \oplus \alpha.\tau$ in disguise. This is one of the reasons why $\sigma \leq \sigma + \tau$ does *not* hold in general, the other being that τ can introduce interferences as we have seen in an earlier example. Rule (RED) is perhaps the most important one in that it characterizes the essence of $\sqsubseteq$ as a relation that reduces nondeterminism.

The axiomatization in Table 2 is sound and complete with respect to $\sqsubseteq$.

Theorem 2. $\sqsubseteq = \leq$.

The proof of this result is omitted since in §3 we are going to prove soundness and completeness of the deduction system for a weaker subcontract relation that includes $\sqsubseteq$ at its core.

3 Towards a Weaker Subcontract Relation

3.1 Synchronous Orchestrators

We have seen that the strong subcontract relation (Definition 4) is quite restrictive in the contracts that it deems comparable and the reason lies, not surprisingly, in the compliance relation (Definition 3) from which it is defined. Thus, we need to re-consider the compliance relation and in particular we have to investigate in more details the *reasons why* some clients are not satisfied by some services. Let us start by considering the interaction

$$\overline{a}.\mathsf{e} \oplus \overline{b}.\mathsf{e} \parallel a \longrightarrow \overline{b}.\mathsf{e} \parallel a \tag{1}$$

which tells us that the client $\overline{a}.\mathsf{e} \oplus \overline{b}.\mathsf{e}$ is not compliant with the service a. In this example we could say that the client is the one to blame, since it may autonomously decide to send a message b that the service is not willing to receive. We could also say that the service is the one to blame, since it is not flexible enough to receive every message that the client is willing to send. In a dual manner, we can consider the interaction

$$\overline{a}.\mathsf{e} \parallel a \oplus b \longrightarrow \overline{a}.\mathsf{e} \parallel a \tag{2}$$

which tells us that the client $\overline{a}.\mathsf{e}$ is not compliant with the service $a \oplus b$. In this case too we can put the blame on either the client or the service, but the point we want to make here is that in both examples the missed compliance is a consequence of some *internal* behavior of either (or both) parties, and that there is no way to mend the situation, since we assume that clients and services are black boxes whose internal behavior cannot be constrained from the outside.

Consider now the interaction

$$\overline{a}.\mathsf{e} + \overline{b}.c.\mathsf{e} \parallel a + b.\overline{d} \longrightarrow c.\mathsf{e} \parallel \overline{d}$$

which proves that $\overline{a}.\mathsf{e} + \overline{b}.c.\mathsf{e}$ is not compliant with $a + b.\overline{d}$. If we were to describe contracts using English words, it is as if the client says: "here are a message a and a message b, please pick one. If you choose the message b, send me back a message c". On the other side, the service says: "I'm willing to receive a message a or a message b, please choose what you want. If you choose the message b, I will send you back a message d". We realize that this example of failed compliance differs significantly from the previous ones, because the failure is due to a choice that is *external* from both the client and the service. None of them mandates a particular synchronization, on a or on b, to occur, but the strong compliance takes into account *every possible synchronization*, and in the interaction above the bad one has been chosen. Had client and service synchronized on a, which was a perfectly feasible option for both the client and the service, the client would have been satisfied.

The last example provides us with the necessary enlightenment for relaxing the definition of compliance: if there is a third party that controls the interaction between the client and the service, in the sense that it may prevent certain synchronizations from happening, then $\overline{a}.\mathsf{e} + \overline{b}.c.\mathsf{e}$ *can be made* compliant with $a + b.\overline{d}$. In the Web service domain, this centralized control of several interacting processes is called orchestration, and the controller is itself a process called orchestrator. Here we consider a simpler scenario in which we have only two interacting processes, the client and the service, and where the orchestrator can only prevent some synchronizations from occurring. We will relax this latter assumption in §4. For the time being, we will use the term *synchronous orchestrator* to indicate an orchestrator that is only capable of enabling or disabling some synchronizations.

It is worth to remark that in no way an orchestrator can affect the internal choices of a process. For example, there is no orchestrator that can make the clients of the interactions (1) and (2) compliant with the corresponding services.

Having realized that we might need an orchestrator to enforce the compliance relation, we now proceed into formalizing the language of synchronous orchestrators. It turns out that the orchestrators required for fixing the kind of problems depicted above are made of orchestration actions having one of the following two forms:

$$\langle a,\overline{a}\rangle \qquad \text{or} \qquad \langle \overline{a},a\rangle$$

An orchestration action of the form $\langle a,\overline{a}\rangle$ permits a synchronization between client and service provided that the client is ready to send a message on a and the service is ready to receive it. An orchestration action of the form $\langle \overline{a},a\rangle$ permits the dual synchronization, in which the client is ready to receive a message on a and the service is ready to send it. It is as if the orchestrator is a process with two distinct interfaces, one that connects with the client, the other that connects with the service. Orchestration actions $\langle \alpha,\overline{\alpha}\rangle$ show which actions the orchestrator simultaneously offers on both interfaces. These orchestration actions are called *synchronous* because they permit client and service to synchronize when *both* parties are ready to perform an action and the corresponding co-action. We will extend filters to asynchronous actions in §4.

Definition 8 (synchronous orchestrators). Synchronous orchestrators, *ranged over by $f,g,\ldots$, are described by the following grammar:*

$f ::=$		***orchestrator***	$\mu ::=$	***action***
	0	*(null)*	$\langle a,\overline{a}\rangle$	*(input/output)*
$\mid$	$\mu.f$	*(action prefix)*	$\mid\ \langle \overline{a},a\rangle$	*(output/input)*
$\mid$	$f\vee f$	*(disjunction)*		

The null orchestrator 0 is the one that does not permit any synchronization between client and service. The orchestrator $\mu.f$ allows the orchestration action μ. If this action is performed, it continues as the orchestrator f. The orchestrator $f\vee g$ is the *disjunction* of the orchestrators f and g: it permits all orchestration actions that are permitted by either f or by g. As for contracts we will omit trailing 0's in orchestrators.

In our development orchestrators do not exhibit internal nondeterminism. This calls for a operational semantics merely expressing which orchestration actions are available.

Definition 9 (operational semantics of orchestrators). *The operational semantics of orchestrators is inductively defined by the rules below*

$$\mu.f \xrightarrow{\mu} f \qquad \frac{f \xrightarrow{\mu} f'}{f\vee g \xrightarrow{\mu} f'} \qquad \frac{g \xrightarrow{\mu} g'}{f\vee g \xrightarrow{\mu} g'}$$

In practice we will identify orchestrators with the set $[\![f]\!]$ of strings of orchestration actions they offer, namely

$$[\![f]\!] \stackrel{\text{def}}{=} \{\mu_1 \cdots \mu_n \mid \exists g : f \stackrel{\mu_1}{\longmapsto} \cdots \stackrel{\mu_n}{\longmapsto} g\}$$

Observe that $[\![f]\!]$ is a non-empty, prefix-closed, set of strings over the alphabet of orchestration actions and that $\vee$ corresponds to a union operator on the traces of orchestrators, namely $[\![f \vee g]\!] = [\![f]\!] \cup [\![g]\!]$. We write $f \stackrel{\mu}{\longmapsto} g$ if $[\![g]\!] = \{\mu_1 \cdots \mu_n \mid \mu\mu_1 \cdots \mu_n \in [\![f]\!]\}$, namely g is the residual of f after the action μ. Note that $f \stackrel{\mu}{\longmapsto} f'$ and $f \stackrel{\mu}{\longmapsto} f''$ implies $[\![f']\!] = [\![f'']\!]$. We write $f \stackrel{\mu_1 \cdots \mu_n}{\longmapsto}$ if $\mu_1 \cdots \mu_n \in [\![f]\!]$; we write $f \stackrel{\mu}{\not\longmapsto}$ if $\mu \notin [\![f]\!]$; let $\mathsf{init}(f) \stackrel{\text{def}}{=} \{\mu \mid f \stackrel{\mu}{\longmapsto}\}$.

A better intuition of the semantics of orchestrator can be given by inspecting directly the weak variant of the compliance relation, where client and service interact under the supervision of an orchestrator.

Definition 10 (weak compliance relation). *An* orchestrated system *is a triple* $\rho \parallel_f \sigma$ *of a (client) contract* ρ *and a (service) contract* σ *interacting with each other while being supervised by an orchestrator* f. *Let* $\longrightarrow$ *be the least relation between orchestrated systems inductively defined as follows:*

$$\frac{\rho \longrightarrow \rho'}{\rho \parallel_f \sigma \longrightarrow \rho' \parallel_f \sigma} \qquad \frac{\sigma \longrightarrow \sigma'}{\rho \parallel_f \sigma \longrightarrow \rho \parallel_f \sigma'} \qquad \frac{\rho \stackrel{\overline{\alpha}}{\longrightarrow} \rho' \quad f \stackrel{\langle \alpha, \overline{\alpha} \rangle}{\longmapsto} f' \quad \sigma \stackrel{\alpha}{\longrightarrow} \sigma'}{\rho \parallel_f \sigma \longrightarrow \rho' \parallel_{f'} \sigma'}$$

We write $\Longrightarrow$ *for the reflexive, transitive closure of* $\longrightarrow$*; we write* $\rho \parallel_f \sigma \not\longrightarrow$ *if there exist no* ρ', f', *and* σ' *such that* $\rho \parallel_f \sigma \longrightarrow \rho' \parallel_{f'} \sigma'$. *We write* $f : \rho \dashv\!\!\mid \sigma$ *if* $\rho \parallel_f \sigma \Longrightarrow \rho' \parallel_{f'} \sigma' \not\longrightarrow$ *implies* $\rho' \stackrel{\mathsf{e}}{\longrightarrow}$. *We say that* ρ *is* weakly compliant with σ, *notation* $\rho \dashv\!\!\mid \sigma$, *if there exists an orchestrator* f *such that* $f : \rho \dashv\!\!\mid \sigma$.

The first two rules in the definition of $\longrightarrow$ for orchestrated systems are basically the same as for the strong compliance relation. In particular the orchestrator has no way to affect the internal moves of client and service. The third rule expresses the fact that client and service can synchronize with each other, but only if the orchestrator permits it (the action $\langle \alpha, \overline{\alpha} \rangle$ "connects" the action $\overline{\alpha}$ performed by the client with the action α performed by the service). For example, we have $\langle a, \overline{a} \rangle : \overline{a}.\mathsf{e} + \overline{b}.c.\mathsf{e} \dashv\!\!\mid a + b.\overline{d}$ because the orchestrator $\langle a, \overline{a} \rangle$ disallows the synchronization on b at the first step while permitting the synchronization on a. At the same time $\overline{a}.\mathsf{e} \oplus \overline{b}.\mathsf{e} \not\dashv\!\!\mid a$ because no orchestrator can prevent the client from autonomously evolving to $\overline{b}.\mathsf{e}$.

Weak compliance induces the weak subcontract relation as follows:

Definition 11 (weak subcontract). *Let* $[\![\sigma]\!]^{\mathsf{w}} \stackrel{\text{def}}{=} \{\rho \mid \rho \dashv\!\!\mid \sigma\}$. *We say that* σ *is a* weak subcontract *of* τ, *notation* $\sigma \preceq \tau$, *if* $[\![\sigma]\!]^{\mathsf{s}} \subseteq [\![\tau]\!]^{\mathsf{w}}$.

According to this definition, $\sigma \preceq \tau$ holds whenever every client satisfied by σ (that is $\rho \dashv \sigma$) can also be satisfied by τ (that is $\rho \dashv\!\!\mid \tau$) by means of some orchestrator f. So, it is safe to replace σ with τ, provided that f mediates the interaction between the client and τ.

Whether or not $\preceq$ is the subcontract relation we are looking for is hard to tell from Definition 11. In part this is because it is very reasonable to expect that the orchestrator f may depend on the particular client ρ that we are considering. In addition, it is not even obvious that $\preceq$ is transitive, which is required if we plan to use $\preceq$ as stated in the introduction. We will thus devote the following subsection to the study of $\preceq$ and of its main properties.

3.2 Basic Properties of the Weak Subcontract Relation

Among all the orchestrators involved in a relation $\sigma \preceq \tau$, we can restrict our interest to a relatively small class of *relevant* ones. In order to define relevant orchestrators, we need three auxiliary notions. The first one is the *identity orchestrator* $I(\sigma)$ for a contract σ, which is the orchestrator that enables all the traces of actions in σ:

$$I(\sigma) \stackrel{\text{def}}{=} \bigvee_{\sigma \stackrel{\alpha}{\Longrightarrow}} \langle \alpha, \overline{\alpha} \rangle . I(\sigma(\alpha)) \tag{3}$$

The second notion we need is a derived operator $\wedge$ over orchestrators that is dual of $\vee$. We define

$$f \wedge g \stackrel{\text{def}}{=} \bigvee_{f \stackrel{\mu}{\longmapsto} f', g \stackrel{\mu}{\longmapsto} g'} \mu.(f' \wedge g')$$

It is trivial to see that $[\![f \wedge g]\!] = [\![f]\!] \cap [\![g]\!]$. The third and last notion is an ordering that allows us to compare orchestrators. We define

$$f \leqslant g \stackrel{\text{def}}{\iff} [\![f]\!] \subseteq [\![g]\!]$$

namely $f \leqslant g$ holds if every sequence of orchestration actions offered by f is also offered by g. Using this ordering, we see that $f \vee g$ and $f \wedge g$ respectively correspond to the least upper bound and to the greatest lower bound of f and g.

Definition 12 (relevant orchestrator). *Let $\sigma \preceq \tau$ and f be an orchestrator. We say that f is* relevant *for $\sigma \preceq \tau$ if $f \leqslant I(\sigma) \wedge I(\tau)$.*

An orchestrator that is relevant for $\sigma \preceq \tau$ never offers orchestration actions that do not correspond to actions offered by σ or that would never be enabled by τ. It is easy to see that, given an orchestrator f such that $f : \rho \dashv\mid \tau$, then $f \wedge I(\sigma) \wedge I(\tau) : \rho \dashv\mid \tau$ where $f \wedge I(\sigma) \wedge I(\tau)$ is relevant for $\sigma \preceq \tau$.

The relation $\sigma \preceq \tau$ means that every client ρ satisfied by σ is weakly compliant with τ by means of *some* orchestrator which, in principle, may depend on ρ. The next result shows that it is always possible to find an orchestrator that makes τ work seamlessly with *every* client satisfied by σ. We call such orchestrator "universal", since it is independent of a particular client.

Definition 13 (universal orchestrator). *We say that f is a* universal orchestrator *proving $\sigma \preceq \tau$, notation $f : \sigma \preceq \tau$, if $\rho \dashv \sigma$ implies $f : \rho \dashv\mid \tau$ for every ρ.*

On the theoretical side, the existence of the universal orchestrator allows us to study the properties of $\preceq$ independently of specific clients. On the practical side, it makes it possible to precompute not only the subcontract relation $\preceq$ but also the orchestrator that proves it, regardless of the client performing the query. The next result assures us that if $\sigma \preceq \tau$, then a universal orchestrator proving the relation always exists.

Proposition 2. *$\sigma \preceq \tau$ if and only if $f : \sigma \preceq \tau$ for some orchestrator f.*

Orchestrators as morphisms. When $f : \sigma \preceq \tau$ *every* client that is strongly compliant with σ is also weakly compliant with τ by means of the orchestrator f. In a sense, if we think of contracts as of (behavioral) types, the orchestrator f is an *explicit coercion* [8,11,29] that maps the service with contract τ into a service with contract σ. The function determined by an orchestrator can be effectively computed as by the following definition.

Definition 14 (orchestrator application). *The* application *of the orchestrator f to the contract σ, notation $f(\sigma)$, is defined as*

$$f(\sigma) \stackrel{\text{def}}{=} \bigoplus_{\sigma \Downarrow \mathrm{R}} \sum_{f \xrightarrow{\langle \alpha, \overline{\alpha} \rangle} f', \alpha \in \mathrm{R}} \alpha . f'(\sigma(\alpha))$$

The next result proves that $f(\sigma)$ is indeed the contract of the orchestrated service, namely it satisfies the same clients that are weakly compliant with σ by means of f:

Theorem 3. *$f : \rho \dashv\!\!| \sigma$ if and only if $\rho \dashv f(\sigma)$.*

We are now able to connect the strong and weak subcontract relations.

Corollary 1. *$f : \sigma \preceq \tau$ if and only if $\sigma \sqsubseteq f(\tau)$.*

Proof. By Theorem 3 $f : \sigma \preceq \tau$ if and only if $\rho \dashv \sigma$ implies $f : \rho \dashv\!\!| \tau$ if and only if $\rho \dashv \sigma$ implies $\rho \dashv f(\sigma)$ if and only if $\sigma \sqsubseteq f(\tau)$. □

Corollary 1 also provides us with a handy tool for studying the properties of $\preceq$ since we can reduce the weak subcontract relation $\preceq$ to the more familiar strong subcontract relation $\sqsubseteq$. For example, we can reduce checking $f : \sigma \preceq \tau$ to checking $\sigma \sqsubseteq f(\tau)$ by computing $f(\tau)$. The next few examples show that $\preceq$ includes $\sqsubseteq$ and that $\preceq$ permits width and depth extensions:

- $a \oplus b \preceq a$ since $a \oplus b \sqsubseteq a = \langle a, \overline{a} \rangle (a)$;
- $a \preceq a + b$ since $a = \langle a, \overline{a} \rangle (a + b)$;
- $a \preceq a.b$ since $a = \langle a, \overline{a} \rangle (a.b)$.

The morphism induced by an orchestrator f is monotone with respect to the strong subcontract relation and is well behaved with respect to the choice operators.

Proposition 3. *The following properties hold:*

1. *$\sigma \sqsubseteq \tau$ implies $f(\sigma) \sqsubseteq f(\tau)$;*
2. *$f(\sigma) + f(\tau) \simeq f(\sigma + \tau)$;*
3. *$f(\sigma) \oplus f(\tau) \simeq f(\sigma \oplus \tau)$.*

Composition of synchronous orchestrators. Transitivity of the weak subcontract relation is not granted by Definition 11, because $\sigma \preceq \tau$ means that every client that is *strongly* compliant with σ is also *weakly* compliant with τ. So it is not clear whether

$\sigma \preceq \tau$ and $\tau \preceq \sigma'$ implies $\sigma \preceq \sigma'$. Observe that transitivity of $\preceq$ is necessary in order to enhance Web service discovery as described in §1.

Let us start from the hypotheses $f : \sigma \preceq \tau$ and $g : \tau \preceq \sigma'$. By Corollary 1 we know that $\sigma \sqsubseteq f(\tau)$ and $\tau \sqsubseteq g(\sigma')$. Furthermore, by Proposition 3(1) and transitivity of $\sqsubseteq$ we deduce that $\sigma \sqsubseteq f(\tau) \sqsubseteq f(g(\sigma'))$. Thus we can conclude $\sigma \preceq \sigma'$ provided that for any two orchestrators f and g their functional composition $f \circ g$ is still an orchestrator. The next result, whose proof is left as an easy exercise, confirms that this is indeed the case and that $\wedge$ corresponds to the functional composition operator between synchronous orchestrators.

Proposition 4. $f(g(\sigma)) \simeq (f \wedge g)(\sigma)$.

3.3 Alternative Characterization of the Weak Subcontract Relation

We now proceed to define an alternative, coinductive characterization of $\preceq$, as we have done for $\sqsubseteq$. Observe that, when an orchestrator mediates the interaction between a client and a service, it proposes at each interaction step a set of orchestration actions A whose effect is to filter out some actions offered by either the client or by the service. Since a synchronization occurs only if both client and service are willing to interact on corresponding co-actions, it is sufficient to consider the effect of the orchestrator on only one of the two interacting parties, which we take to be the service.

If S is a service ready set, then $\mathrm{A} \circ \mathrm{S}$ denotes the ready set filtered by the orchestrator, as perceived by the client:

$$\mathrm{A} \circ \mathrm{S} \stackrel{\text{def}}{=} \{\alpha \in \mathrm{S} \mid \langle \alpha, \overline{\alpha} \rangle \in \mathrm{A}\}$$

Namely, the client sees an action α only if that action is provided by the service ($\alpha \in \mathrm{S}$) *and* the orchestrator does not hide it ($\langle \alpha, \overline{\alpha} \rangle \in \mathrm{A}$).

With this notion we can now define the coinductive characterization of weak subcontract relation, in a similar manner as for the strong variant.

Definition 15 (coinductive weak subcontract). *We say that* $\mathscr{W}$ *is a* coinductive weak subcontract relation *if* $(\sigma, \tau) \in \mathscr{W}$ *implies that there exists a set of orchestration actions* A *such that*

1. $\tau \Downarrow \mathrm{S}$ *implies* $\sigma \Downarrow \mathrm{R}$ *and* $\mathrm{R} \subseteq \mathrm{A} \circ \mathrm{S}$ *for some* R, *and*
2. $\tau \stackrel{\alpha}{\Longrightarrow}$ *and* $\langle \alpha, \overline{\alpha} \rangle \in \mathrm{A}$ *implies* $\sigma \stackrel{\alpha}{\Longrightarrow}$ *and* $(\sigma(\alpha), \tau(\alpha)) \in \mathscr{W}$.

Condition (1) requires that τ must look like a more deterministic version of σ when filtered by the orchestrator (the ready set $\mathrm{A} \circ \mathrm{S}$ of the orchestrated service has a corresponding one of σ that offers fewer actions). Condition (2) poses the usual requirement that the continuations must be in the subcontract relation, but only for those actions that are permitted by the orchestrator. Observe that the set A of orchestration actions must be defined independently of the internal state of the larger contract: the implicit universal quantifier over the ready sets S of τ in condition (1) falls within the scope of the existential quantifier that binds A. This enforces the fact that the orchestrator treats τ as a black box, and that it is not able to sense its internal state.

The two definitions of weak subcontract are equivalent:

Theorem 4. $\preceq$ *is the largest coinductive weak subcontract relation.*

3.4 Deduction System for the Weak Subcontract Relation

Unlike the strong subcontract relation, $\preceq$ is *not* a precongruence with respect to the external choice. For example, we have

$$0 : 0 \preceq a.c \qquad \text{and} \qquad \langle a,\overline{a}\rangle.\langle b,\overline{b}\rangle : a.b \preceq a.b$$

but $a.b + 0 \not\preceq a.b + a.c$ since $a.b + a.c \simeq a.(b \oplus c)$. However, there is actually a good reason why $\preceq$ is not a precongruence in general. The relation $0 \preceq a.c$ holds because the 0 orchestrator turns a service with contract $a.c$ into a service with contract 0, and the identity $a.b \preceq a.b$ holds because of the orchestrator $I(a.b)$. When we combine $a.b$ and 0 into $a.b + 0$ we are creating a new service that externally offers either the $a.b$ behavior or the null one. When this service interacts with a client, it must do so by means of an orchestrator, but which one? The problem is that we need two different orchestrators for relating the two branches of the external choice, and there is no single orchestrator that works equally well for both branches, in particular $0 \wedge I(a.b) : a.b \not\preceq a.b$ and $0 \vee I(a.b) : 0 \not\preceq a.c$.

As a direct consequence of the lack of the precongruence property for $\preceq$, we have that the axiomatization of $\preceq$ is more challenging than that of $\sqsubseteq$. Since $\preceq$ is not a precongruence, we cannot "substitute equals for equals" when applying the rewriting rules. This means that we have to look for the conditions under which substitution in a context is safe, and to explicitly provide precongruence deduction rules that enforce these conditions. Luckily, all the additional information we need is stored in the orchestrator that proves a relation $\sigma \preceq \tau$. This allows us to design a deduction system for judgments of the form

$$f : \sigma \leq \tau$$

where f is the orchestrator that "proves" the relation $\sigma \leq \tau$.

Table 2. Deduction system for the weak subcontract relation

(RED) $\quad I(\sigma) : \sigma \oplus \tau \leq \sigma$	(PREFIX) $\quad \dfrac{f : \sigma \leq \tau}{\langle \alpha, \overline{\alpha}\rangle.f : \alpha.\sigma \leq \alpha.\tau}$
(DEPTH) $\quad 0 : 0 \leq \sigma$	(INT) $\quad \dfrac{f : \sigma \leq \sigma' \quad f : \tau \leq \tau'}{f : \sigma \oplus \tau \leq \sigma' \oplus \tau'}$
(WEAK) $\quad \dfrac{f : \sigma \leq \tau \quad g \wedge I(\tau) \leqslant f}{f \vee g : \sigma \leq \tau}$	(EXT) $\quad \dfrac{f : \sigma \leq \sigma' \quad f : \tau \leq \tau'}{f : \sigma + \tau \leq \sigma' + \tau'}$
(TRANS) $\quad \dfrac{f : \sigma \leq \sigma' \quad g : \sigma' \leq \sigma''}{f \wedge g : \sigma \leq \sigma''}$	

The deduction system for $\preceq$ is defined by the equalities in Table 1 and the axioms and rules in Table 2. Every equality $\sigma = \tau$ inherited from Table 1 is meant to be a shorthand for two axioms $I(\tau) : \sigma \leq \tau$ and $I(\sigma) : \tau \leq \sigma$. Let us comment the remaining deduction rules. Rule (RED) is the same as in Table 1, except that the relation is now witnessed by the orchestrator $I(\sigma)$. In fact, this relation holds without the need of filtering any action, hence the orchestrator $I(\sigma \oplus \tau)$ would work as well. However, the rule as is stated has the advantage that $I(\sigma)$ is relevant for $\sigma \oplus \tau \leq \sigma$, and the judgment with orchestrator $I(\sigma \oplus \tau)$ is derivable by means of (WEAK), which we are to describe shortly. Rule (DEPTH) expresses the fact that the weak subcontract relation always supports depth extensions of contracts, by means of the null orchestrator which prevents any interference caused by the larger σ contract. Thus, 0 is the least element for $\preceq$. Rule (WEAK) is a sort of weakening rule that allows less restrictive orchestrators to be used without compromising safety. The rule says that if f proves $\sigma \leq \tau$, then $f \vee g$ also proves the same relation provided that $f \vee g$ does not enable any action from τ that must be kept hidden in order for $\sigma \leq \tau$ to hold. This is guaranteed if the projection of g on the traces of τ ($g \wedge I(\tau)$) is a subset of the traces of actions that are already enabled by f. Rule (TRANS) is the standard transitivity rule, where the resulting orchestrator is the composition of the two orchestrators in the premises of the rule (see Proposition 4). On the right hand side of Table 2 we have three rules of (restricted) precongruence. Rule (PREFIX) shows that $\leq$ is a precongruence with respect to prefixes. Rules (INT) and (EXT) state restricted precongruence of $\leq$ with respect to the two choices. In both cases the requirement is that both branches of a choice must be orchestrated in the same way.

The rest of this subsection is devoted to proving that the deduction system is sound and complete. Observe that soundness and completeness of the deduction system now have a stronger meaning since they must take into account the fact that judgments $f : \sigma \leq \tau$ include an orchestrator f. Hence, "soundness" means not only that if $f : \sigma \leq \tau$, then $\sigma \preceq \tau$, but also that f is an orchestrator that proves the relation. At the same time, "completeness" means that if f is an orchestrator proving $\sigma \preceq \tau$, then f can be obtained by means of the rules in the deduction system.

Theorem 5 (soundness). *If $f : \sigma \leq \tau$, then $f : \sigma \preceq \tau$.*

As usual soundness of the deduction system is relatively straightforward, whereas completeness is much harder to prove. The completeness proof relies on the ability to rewrite a contract, by means of the axioms in Table 1, in a so-called *normal form*, which is a syntactic, canonical representation of the contract's semantics. Once two contracts are in normal-form, checking that they are related is a much simpler matter. Much of the development that follows is an adaptation of the completeness proof of the must testing preorder found in [21].

The normal form of a contract arises by observing that the set of ready sets of a contract can be saturated without changing the semantics of a contract, according to the strong subcontract relation. More precisely, we close ready sets by union and by convex closure. For example, we have $a \oplus b \simeq a \oplus b \oplus (a+b)$, where we have added the ready set $\{a,b\}$ as the union of the ready sets $\{a\}$ and $\{b\}$ of the contract on the l.h.s. of $\simeq$. As another example, we have $a \oplus (a+b+c) \simeq a \oplus (a+b) \oplus (a+c) \oplus (a+b+c)$, where we have added the ready sets $\{a,b\}$ and $\{a,c\}$ which include $\{a\}$ and are included in $\{a,b,c\}$. The usefulness of saturation comes from the fact that once two contracts have been saturated, condition (1) of Definition (7) reduces to verifying that every ready set of the larger contract is also a ready set of the smaller contract. This makes the application of rule (RED) in the completeness proof (almost) straightforward.

Definition 16 (contract normal form [21]). *The* saturated set of ready sets *of a contract σ, notation $\mathscr{R}(\sigma)$, is defined as* $\mathscr{R}(\sigma) \stackrel{\text{def}}{=} \{\mathrm{R} \subseteq \mathsf{init}(\sigma) \mid \exists \mathrm{S} : \sigma \Downarrow \mathrm{S} \wedge \mathrm{S} \subseteq \mathrm{R}\}$. *We say that a contract σ is in* normal form *if* $\sigma \equiv \bigoplus_{\mathrm{R} \in \mathscr{R}(\sigma)} \sum_{\alpha \in \mathrm{R}} \alpha.\sigma_\alpha$ *where every continuation σ_α is itself in normal form and $\equiv$ denotes syntactic equality up to associativity and commutativity of the choice operators.*

Observe that if a contract σ is in normal form, the residual of the contract after a visible action is unique, namely $\sigma \Longrightarrow\xrightarrow{\alpha} \sigma'$ and $\sigma \Longrightarrow\xrightarrow{\alpha} \sigma''$ implies $\sigma' \equiv \sigma''$.

Following [21], we derive a bunch of handy axioms and rules (Table 3). Axioms (S1) and (S2) implement the saturation of ready set as described above. Axiom (CO) is used to combine the residual of a contract with respect to some given action α. Rules (E-PREFIX), (E-INT), and (E-EXT) respectively specialize rules (PREFIX), (INT), and (EXT) so as to make it possible the substitution of equals for equals in arbitrary contexts. Finally, rule (WIDTH) embeds width extensions of contracts, provided that the additional capabilities (in τ) do not interfere with the old ones (in σ). This is implied by the fact that the identity orchestrator for σ shares no common trace with the identity orchestrator for τ, except for ε ($I(\sigma) \wedge I(\tau) \leqslant 0$).

Table 3. Derived rules

(S1)	$\sigma \oplus \tau = \sigma \oplus \tau \oplus (\sigma + \tau)$	(E-PREFIX)	$\dfrac{\sigma = \sigma'}{\alpha.\sigma = \alpha.\sigma'}$
(S2)	$\sigma \oplus (\sigma + \tau + \rho) = \sigma \oplus (\sigma + \tau) \oplus (\sigma + \tau + \rho)$		
(CO)	$(\alpha.\sigma' + \tau') \oplus (\alpha.\sigma'' + \tau'') = (\alpha.(\sigma' \oplus \sigma'') + \tau') \oplus (\alpha.(\sigma' \oplus \sigma'') + \tau'')$	(E-EXT)	$\dfrac{\sigma = \sigma' \quad \tau = \tau'}{\sigma + \tau = \sigma' + \tau'}$
(WIDTH)	$\dfrac{I(\sigma) \wedge I(\tau) \leqslant 0}{I(\sigma) : \sigma \leq \sigma + \tau}$	(E-INT)	$\dfrac{\sigma = \sigma' \quad \tau = \tau'}{\sigma \oplus \tau = \sigma' \oplus \tau'}$

Lemma 1. *The axioms and rules in Table 3 can be derived from those in Tables 1 and 2.*

The last auxiliary result is the one assuring us that every contract can be rewritten into a $\simeq$-equivalent one that is in normal form.

Lemma 2 (normal form). *For every contract σ there exists σ' in normal form such that $\sigma = \sigma'$.*

The deduction system for $\preceq$ defined by Tables 1 and 2 is complete for $\preceq$ and the sets of filters that prove it.

Theorem 6 (completeness). *If $f : \sigma \preceq \tau$, then $f : \sigma \leq \tau$.*

3.5 Interpretations of Synchronous Orchestrators

At the beginning of this section we have introduced orchestrators as centralized control points mediating the interaction between clients and services. Orchestrators are limited in that they can only affect the way client and service try to interact with each other, but they cannot affect in any way the internal moves of clients and services. This is clearly reflected in the transition relation for orchestrated systems (Definition 10) and more technically in the coinductive characterization of the weak subcontract relation (Definition 15).

Corollary 1 provides us with another interpretation of orchestrators: they are morphisms that transform services into services with a (slightly) different contract. In this interpretation an orchestrator is like an explicit behavioral coercion that is applied to (wrapped around) a process so as to change its contract. Along the section we have made the implicit assumption that the coercion is applied to the service, because this view has allowed us to develop a theory of synchronous orchestrators that is oblivious to the specific client that we are considering. In practice, it is perhaps more reasonable to expect that the morphism is applied to the client, which is the one that must be satisfied.

When interpreting orchestrators as mediators or as morphisms, the query to a registry of Web service should return not only the services that satisfy the client with contract ρ, but also the orchestrator that ensures the successful interaction. Namely, the query looks like this:

$$\mathscr{Q}(\rho) = \{(f,\sigma) \mid f : \rho^{\perp} \preceq \sigma\}$$

There is a further interpretation of orchestrators as abstract specifications of those clients that can interact successfully with a given service. Consider for example a relation $f : \sigma \preceq \tau$ that is proved by an orchestrator f that never hides any action from τ. Any further action that the orchestrator may allow is practically useless, hence by replacing σ with τ the orchestrator is never actually preventing any synchronization between the client and the service with contract τ. This is formalized by the following proposition, which gives a sufficient (and also necessary, for that matters) condition when the weak subcontract relation reduces to the strong one:

Proposition 5. *If $f : \sigma \preceq \tau$ and $I(\tau) \leqslant f$, then $\sigma \sqsubseteq \tau$.*

A finer control can be implemented if the contract of the client performing the query is known. Suppose for example that the client contract is ρ and that the Web service repository contains a registered service whose contract is σ, where $f : \rho^{\perp} \preceq \sigma$. In principle, the client is satisfied by the service provided that the orchestrator f mediates the interaction between the two parties. However, suppose in addition that the orchestrator never hides any action that the client is offering to the service. This can be expressed as $I(\rho^{\perp}) \leqslant f$. Then, the particular client with contract ρ is also *strongly compliant* with the service with contract σ, and no orchestration is actually necessary. This is formalized by the following proposition:

Proposition 6. *If $f : \rho^{\perp} \preceq \sigma$ and $I(\rho^{\perp}) \leqslant f$, then $\rho \dashv \sigma$.*

For example, consider a client with contract $\rho \stackrel{\text{def}}{=} \overline{a}.b.\mathsf{e}$ and suppose that the registry contains a Web service with contract $a.\overline{b} + c.\overline{d}$. Although we have not seen how to compute the dual of the client's contract yet, in this case it is intuitively obtained by simply swapping inputs and outputs. Namely, $\rho^{\perp} = a.\overline{b}$ (the e action disappears as it is only used for denoting client's satisfaction). We observe that $I(\rho^{\perp}) = \langle a,\overline{a}\rangle.\langle\overline{b},b\rangle$, and that $I(\rho^{\perp}) : \rho^{\perp} \preceq a.\overline{b}+c.\overline{d}$, hence by Proposition 6 we can conclude that $\rho \dashv a.\overline{b}+c.\overline{d}$, without the intervention of any orchestrator at all. Observe however that $\rho^{\perp} \not\sqsubseteq a.\overline{b}+c.\overline{d}$, so the service with contract $a.\overline{b}+c.\overline{d}$ would not be retrieved if the strong subcontract relation were used instead of the weak one.

4 Asynchronous Orchestrators

In the previous section we have resorted to the use of an orchestrator that guarantees the successful termination of the client. It is then natural to investigate whether, by augmenting the capabilities of the orchestrator, it is possible to further enlarge the spectrum of services that can satisfy a given client. We observe that both the strong and the weak compliance relations (Definitions 3 and 10) are based on interactions where at each synchronization progress is always guaranteed for *both* client and service. In this section we relax this requirement and assume that the orchestrator that mediates the interaction of a client and a service ensures that at each synchronization progress is guaranteed for *at least one* of the interacting parties. The orchestrator must be *fair*, in the sense that client and service must have equal opportunities to make progress. In other words, the orchestrator should not indefinitely guarantee progress to only one of the two parties. Also, the orchestrator must not disrupt the communication flow between client and service: it cannot bounce a message back to the same party that sent it, nor it can pretend to send a message to a party if that message has not been previously received from the other party.

4.1 Buffered Compliance and Subcontract Relations

We extend orchestration actions so that they are described by the following grammar:

$$\mu ::= \langle \alpha, \varepsilon \rangle \mid \langle \varepsilon, \alpha \rangle \mid \langle a, \overline{a} \rangle \mid \langle \overline{a}, a \rangle$$

The action $\langle \alpha, \varepsilon \rangle$ means that the orchestrator offers α to the client; the action $\langle \varepsilon, \alpha \rangle$ means that the orchestrator offers α to the service. Actions $\langle \alpha, \varepsilon \rangle$ and $\langle \varepsilon, \alpha \rangle$ are called *asynchronous* orchestration actions because, if executed, they guarantee progress to only one party among client and service. On the other hand, $\langle \alpha, \overline{\alpha} \rangle$ are *synchronous* orchestration actions because, if executed, they guarantee simultaneous progress to both client and service.

A *directional buffer* is a map $\{\circ, \bullet\} \times \overline{\mathscr{N}} \to \mathbb{Z}$ associating pairs $(r, \overline{a})$ with the number of $\overline{a}$ messages stored in the buffer and available for delivery to the role r, where r can be $\circ$ for "client" or $\bullet$ for "service"; we let $\mathbb{B}, \mathbb{B}', \ldots$ range over buffers. Directionality is ensured by distinguishing messages to be delivered to the client from messages to be delivered to the service. For technical reasons we allow $\mathsf{cod}(\mathbb{B})$ – the codomain of $\mathbb{B}$ – to range over $\mathbb{Z}$, although every well-formed buffer will always contain a nonnegative number of messages. We write $\tilde{\emptyset}$ for the empty buffer, the one having $\{0\}$ as codomain; we write $\mathbb{B}[(r, \overline{a}) \mapsto n]$ for the buffer $\mathbb{B}'$ which is the same as $\mathbb{B}$ except that $(r, \overline{a})$ is associated with n; we write $\mathbb{B}\mu$ for the buffer $\mathbb{B}$ updated after the orchestration action μ:

$$
\begin{array}{ll}
\mathbb{B}\langle a,\varepsilon\rangle = \mathbb{B}[(\bullet,\overline{a}) \mapsto \mathbb{B}(\bullet,\overline{a})+1] & \text{(accept } \overline{a} \text{ from the client)} \\
\mathbb{B}\langle \overline{a},\varepsilon\rangle = \mathbb{B}[(\circ,\overline{a}) \mapsto \mathbb{B}(\circ,\overline{a})-1] & \text{(send } \overline{a} \text{ to the client)} \\
\mathbb{B}\langle \varepsilon,a\rangle = \mathbb{B}[(\circ,\overline{a}) \mapsto \mathbb{B}(\circ,\overline{a})+1] & \text{(accept } \overline{a} \text{ from the service)} \\
\mathbb{B}\langle \varepsilon,\overline{a}\rangle = \mathbb{B}[(\bullet,\overline{a}) \mapsto \mathbb{B}(\bullet,\overline{a})-1] & \text{(send } \overline{a} \text{ to the service)} \\
\mathbb{B}\langle \alpha,\overline{\alpha}\rangle = \mathbb{B} & \text{(synchronize client and service)}
\end{array}
$$

We say that $\mathbb{B}$ has rank k, or is a k-buffer, if $\mathsf{cod}(\mathbb{B}) \subseteq [0,k]$; we say that the k-buffer $\mathbb{B}$ *enables* the orchestration action μ, notation $\mathbb{B} \vdash_k \mu$, if $\mathbb{B}\mu$ is still a k-buffer. For instance $\tilde{\mathbf{0}} \vdash_1 \langle a,\varepsilon\rangle$ but $\tilde{\mathbf{0}} \nvdash_k \langle \overline{a},\varepsilon\rangle$ because $-1 \in \mathsf{cod}(\tilde{\mathbf{0}}\langle \overline{a},\varepsilon\rangle)$. We extend the notion to sets of actions so that $\mathbb{B} \vdash_k \mathrm{A}$ if $\mathbb{B}$ enables every action in A. Synchronization actions are enabled regardless of the rank of the buffer, because they leave the buffer unchanged.

The language of simple orchestrators remains unchanged, except that now μ ranges over synchronous as well as asynchronous orchestration actions. The operational and denotation semantics of orchestrators with asynchronous orchestration actions are simple extensions of those with only synchronous orchestration actions and will not be repeated here.

We say that f is a *valid orchestrator of rank k*, or is a k-orchestrator, if $f \overset{\mu_1\cdots\mu_n}{\longmapsto}$ implies that $\tilde{\mathbf{0}}\mu_1\cdots\mu_n$ is a k-buffer. Not every term f denotes a valid orchestrator of finite rank. For instance $\langle a,\varepsilon\rangle.\langle a,\varepsilon\rangle$ is not a valid orchestrator of rank 1 because it accepts two a messages from the client without delivering them to the service; it is, however, a valid orchestrator of rank 2; $\langle \overline{a},\varepsilon\rangle$ is invalid because it tries to deliver to the client a message that it has not received from the service; symmetrically, $\langle \varepsilon,\overline{a}\rangle$ is invalid because it tries to deliver to the service a message that it has not received from the client; finally, $\langle \varepsilon,a\rangle.\langle \overline{a},\varepsilon\rangle$ is a valid orchestrator of rank 1 (or greater). In the following we will always work with valid orchestrators of finite rank.

We now proceed to extending weak compliance (Definition 10) to asynchronous orchestrators.

Definition 17 (weak k-compliance relation). *A k-orchestrated system is a triple $\rho \parallel_f \sigma$ of a (client) contract ρ and a (service) contract σ interacting with each other while being supervised by a k-orchestrator f. Let $\longrightarrow$ be the least relation between orchestrated systems inductively defined as follows:*

$$
\frac{\rho \longrightarrow \rho'}{\rho \parallel_f \sigma \longrightarrow \rho' \parallel_f \sigma}
\qquad
\frac{\sigma \longrightarrow \sigma'}{\rho \parallel_f \sigma \longrightarrow \rho \parallel_f \sigma'}
\qquad
\frac{\rho \overset{\overline{\alpha}}{\longrightarrow} \rho' \quad f \overset{\langle \alpha,\overline{\alpha}\rangle}{\longmapsto} f' \quad \sigma \overset{\alpha}{\longrightarrow} \sigma'}{\rho \parallel_f \sigma \longrightarrow \rho' \parallel_{f'} \sigma'}
$$

$$
\frac{\rho \overset{\overline{\alpha}}{\longrightarrow} \rho' \quad f \overset{\langle \alpha,\varepsilon\rangle}{\longmapsto} f'}{\rho \parallel_f \sigma \longrightarrow \rho' \parallel_{f'} \sigma}
\qquad
\frac{f \overset{\langle \varepsilon,\overline{\alpha}\rangle}{\longmapsto} f' \quad \sigma \overset{\alpha}{\longrightarrow} \sigma'}{\rho \parallel_f \sigma \longrightarrow \rho \parallel_{f'} \sigma'}
$$

The transitive closure of $\Longrightarrow$ as well as the usual notation built on top of $\longrightarrow$ is the same as in Definition 10. We say that ρ is weakly k-compliant with σ, *notation $\rho \dashv\!|_k\, \sigma$, if there exists a k-orchestrator f such that $f : \rho \dashv\!| \sigma$.*

The first three rules in the definition of $\longrightarrow$ for orchestrated systems are exactly the same as for the weak compliance relation (Definition 10) and deserve no further comment. The last two rules express the fact that client and service may interact with the orchestrator, independently of the other partner, if the orchestrator provides suitable asynchronous actions. Observe that in each rule progress is guaranteed for at least one of the interacting parties, and that weak compliance and weak 0-compliance do coincide.

As an example of weak k-compliance we have $\overline{a}.\overline{c}.b.\mathsf{e} \dashv\!|_1 c.a.\overline{b}$, by means of the orchestrator $\langle a,\varepsilon\rangle.\langle c,\varepsilon\rangle.\langle\varepsilon,\overline{c}\rangle.\langle\varepsilon,\overline{a}\rangle.\langle\overline{b},b\rangle$ which accepts the messages in the order required by the client, but delivers them in the order expected by the service. However, we have $a.\overline{c}.\mathsf{e} \not\dashv\!|_k c.\overline{a}$ for every k, since no k-orchestrator is capable of creating the a message that the client is waiting for, before delivering c to the service.

Weak k-compliance induces the weak k-subcontract relation in a similar way as weak compliance induces weak subcontract:

Definition 18 (weak k-subcontract). *Let* $[\![\sigma]\!]^{\mathsf{w}}_k \stackrel{\text{def}}{=} \{\rho \mid \rho \dashv\!|_k \sigma\}$. *We say that* σ *is a* weak k-subcontract *of* τ, *notation* $\sigma \preceq_k \tau$, *if* $[\![\sigma]\!]^{\mathsf{s}} \subseteq [\![\tau]\!]^{\mathsf{w}}_k$.

As for the weak subcontract, this definition says little about the properties of $\preceq_k$, hence we will go through a similar sequence of preliminary results. Luckily, all the properties enjoyed by $\preceq$ are also valid, in their essence, for $\preceq_k$. However, the proofs of the results are sometimes more involved because of buffering.

4.2 Basic Properties of the Weak k-Subcontract Relation

Among all the orchestrators involved in a relation $\sigma \preceq \tau$, we can restrict our interest to a relatively small class of *relevant* ones.

Definition 19 (relevant k-orchestrator). *Let* $\sigma \preceq_k \tau$ *and* f *be a* k*-orchestrator. We say that* f *is* relevant *for* $\sigma \preceq_k \tau$ *if* $\sigma \stackrel{\varphi_1\cdots\varphi_n}{\Longrightarrow}$ *and* $f \stackrel{\langle\varphi_1,\overline{\varphi}'_1\rangle\cdots\langle\varphi_n,\overline{\varphi}'_n\rangle\langle\varphi,\overline{\varphi}'\rangle}{\longmapsto}$ *and* $\tau \stackrel{\varphi'_1\cdots\varphi'_n}{\Longrightarrow}$ *imply* $\sigma(\varphi_1\cdots\varphi_n) \stackrel{\varphi}{\Longrightarrow}$ *and* $\tau(\varphi'_1\cdots\varphi'_n) \stackrel{\varphi'}{\Longrightarrow}$.

A k-orchestrator that is relevant for $\sigma \preceq_k \tau$ never offers orchestration actions that do not correspond to actions offered by σ and that would never be enabled by τ. However, the existence of a relevant orchestrator is much less obvious than in the synchronous case. Indeed, it is clear that actions of the form $\langle\alpha,\overline{\alpha}\rangle$ and $\langle\varepsilon,\overline{\alpha}\rangle$ can be safely removed if τ does not offer corresponding co-actions. However, asynchronous actions of the form $\langle\alpha,\varepsilon\rangle$ may actually be necessary for the orchestrator to satisfy the client, even if σ never offers α actions. For instance, $\overline{a}.\mathsf{e}+\overline{b}.\mathsf{e}+\overline{c}.\overline{a}.\mathsf{e} \dashv a \oplus b$ and $a \oplus b \preceq a$ and $\langle c,\varepsilon\rangle.\langle a,\overline{a}\rangle : \overline{a}.\mathsf{e}+\overline{b}.\mathsf{e}+\overline{c}.\overline{a}.\mathsf{e} \dashv\!| a$. Simply removing the $\langle c,\varepsilon\rangle$ action (and the corresponding continuation) would produce the null orchestrator, which clearly cannot satisfy the client.

Proposition 7. *Let* $\sigma \preceq_k \tau$ *and* $\rho \dashv \sigma$. *Then there exists a* k*-orchestrator* g *relevant for* $\sigma \preceq_k \tau$ *such that* $g : \rho \dashv\!| \tau$.

As for the synchronous case, when $\sigma \preceq_k \tau$ holds it is possible to find a universal k-orchestrator that makes every client that is strongly compliant with σ also weakly k-compliant with τ.

Proposition 8. $\sigma \preceq_k \tau$ *if and only if there exists a* k*-orchestrator* f *such that* $\rho \dashv \sigma$ *implies* $f : \rho \dashv\!| \tau$ *for every* ρ.

Orchestrators as morphisms. Like synchronous orchestrators, asynchronous k-orchestrators can be seen as morphisms transforming service contracts. The exact definition of orchestration application is much more involved due to the fact that the orchestrator may synchronize with the service regardless of the behavior of the client.

Definition 20 (orchestrator application). *The* application *of the orchestrator f to the (service) contract σ, notation $f(\sigma)$, is defined as*

$$f(\sigma) \stackrel{\text{def}}{=} \bigoplus_{\sigma \Downarrow \mathrm{R}} \begin{cases} \sum_{f \xrightarrow{\langle \alpha,\varepsilon \rangle} f'} \alpha.f'(\sigma) + \sum_{f \xrightarrow{\langle \alpha,\overline{\alpha} \rangle} f', \alpha \in \mathrm{R}} \alpha.f'(\sigma(\alpha)) & \\ \qquad\qquad\qquad \textit{if } \{\alpha \mid \langle \varepsilon, \alpha \rangle \in \mathsf{init}(f)\} \cap \overline{\mathrm{R}} = \emptyset \\ ((\sum_{f \xrightarrow{\langle \alpha,\varepsilon \rangle} f'} \alpha.f'(\sigma) + \sum_{f \xrightarrow{\langle \alpha,\overline{\alpha} \rangle} f', \alpha \in \mathrm{R}} \alpha.f'(\sigma(\alpha))) \oplus 0) & \\ \quad + \bigoplus_{f \xrightarrow{\langle \varepsilon,\overline{\alpha} \rangle} f', \alpha \in \mathrm{R}} f'(\sigma(\alpha)) & \textit{otherwise} \end{cases}$$

The equation reminds of the *expansion law* for the parallel operator in full CCS [21], but describing the interaction of the orchestrator and the service. The first line defines the behavior of the orchestrated service when no synchronization between orchestrator and service occurs ($\{\alpha \mid \langle \varepsilon, \alpha \rangle \in \mathsf{init}(f)\} \cap \overline{\mathrm{R}} = \emptyset$): all the asynchronous orchestration actions are available, in addition to all the synchronous orchestration actions that are enabled by the service contract when in state R. In the second line there is at least one asynchronous orchestration action that can synchronize with the service in state R ($\{\alpha \mid \langle \varepsilon, \alpha \rangle \in \mathsf{init}(f)\} \cap \overline{\mathrm{R}} \neq \emptyset$). In this case the client perceives an appropriate combination of actions among those that are available before and after the synchronization occurs. The internal choice with the null summand indicates that actions available before the synchronization are not guaranteed (if the synchronization does actually occur), whereas all the actions after the synchronization are (the client can just wait for the orchestrator and the service to reach a stable state). As an example consider $f \stackrel{\text{def}}{=} \langle a, \varepsilon \rangle.\langle c, \varepsilon \rangle.(\langle \varepsilon, \overline{a} \rangle.\langle \overline{b}, b \rangle \vee \langle \varepsilon, \overline{c} \rangle.\langle \overline{d}, d \rangle)$. Then:

- $f(a.\overline{b}) = a.c.\overline{b}$;
- $f(a.\overline{b} + c.\overline{d}) = a.c.(\overline{b} \oplus \overline{d})$;
- $f(a.\overline{b} \oplus c.\overline{d}) = a.c.(0 \oplus \overline{b} \oplus \overline{d})$.

In general we have $\langle \alpha, \overline{\alpha} \rangle.f(\alpha.\sigma) = \alpha.f(\sigma)$ and $\langle \alpha, \varepsilon \rangle.f(\sigma) = \alpha.f(\sigma)$ and $\langle \varepsilon, \overline{\alpha} \rangle.f(\alpha.\sigma) = f(\sigma)$.

The next result proves that $f(\sigma)$ is indeed the contract of the orchestrated service, namely it satisfies the same clients that are weakly compliant with σ by means of f:

Theorem 7. $f : \rho \dashv\!|_k \sigma$ *if and only if* $\rho \dashv f(\sigma)$.

We are now able to connect the strong and weak k-subcontract relations as we did for the weak subcontract relation. The proof is identical to that of Corollary 1, except that Theorem 7 is used instead.

Corollary 2. $f : \sigma \preceq_k \tau$ *if and only if* $\sigma \sqsubseteq f(\tau)$.

The next few examples show that $\preceq_k$ extends $\preceq$ by permitting some permutation of actions:

- $\overline{a}.\overline{c}.b \preceq_1 \overline{c}.\overline{a}.b$ since $\overline{a}.\overline{c}.b = \langle \varepsilon, c\rangle.\langle \overline{a}, a\rangle.\langle \overline{c}, \varepsilon\rangle.\langle \overline{b}, b\rangle(\overline{c}.\overline{a}.b)$;
- $a.c.\overline{b} \preceq_1 c.a.\overline{b}$ since $a.c.\overline{b} = \langle a, \varepsilon\rangle.\langle c, \overline{c}\rangle.\langle \varepsilon, \overline{a}\rangle.\langle b, \overline{b}\rangle(c.a.\overline{b})$;
- $a.\overline{c}.\overline{b} \preceq_1 \overline{c}.a.\overline{b}$ since $a.\overline{c}.\overline{b} = \langle a, \varepsilon\rangle.\langle \overline{c}, c\rangle.\langle \varepsilon, \overline{a}\rangle.\langle b, \overline{b}\rangle(\overline{c}.a.\overline{b})$.

It is possible in general to postpone input actions. For instance we have $a.\beta.\sigma \preceq_k \beta.a.\sigma$ where the service on the r.h.s. of $\preceq_k$ is able to perform the β action without having performed a first. On the other hand, we have $\overline{a}.b.\sigma \not\preceq_k b.\overline{a}.\sigma$ for every k because no valid orchestrator is capable of sending an $\overline{a}$ message to the client, without having received it in advance from the service. The fact that this relation does not hold is reasonable since a client of the service on the l.h.s. may need the information contained in the $\overline{a}$ message before sending the b message back to the service.

The morphism induced by an orchestrator f is monotone with respect to the strong subcontract relation and is well behaved with respect to the choice operators.

Proposition 9. *The following properties hold:*

1. $\sigma \sqsubseteq \tau$ *implies* $f(\sigma) \sqsubseteq f(\tau)$;
2. $f(\sigma) + f(\tau) \sqsubseteq f(\sigma + \tau)$;
3. $f(\sigma) \oplus f(\tau) \simeq f(\sigma \oplus \tau)$.

Observe that, unlike the purely synchronous case, $f(\sigma) + f(\tau) \simeq f(\sigma + \tau)$ does not hold in general, because of the asynchronous actions that f may offer to the client side. Consider for example $f \stackrel{\text{def}}{=} \langle a, \varepsilon\rangle.(\langle \overline{b}, b\rangle + \langle \overline{d}, d\rangle)$. Then $f(\overline{b}) + f(\overline{d}) = a.\overline{b} + a.\overline{d} \simeq a.(\overline{b} \oplus \overline{d}) \sqsubseteq a.(\overline{b} + \overline{d}) = f(\overline{b} + \overline{d})$ but $f(\overline{b} + \overline{d}) \not\sqsubseteq f(\overline{b}) + f(\overline{d})$. Nonetheless Proposition 9 is still sufficient for proving that if $\sigma \sqsubseteq f(\sigma')$ and $\tau \sqsubseteq f(\tau')$, then $\sigma + \tau \sqsubseteq f(\sigma' + \tau')$ and $\sigma \oplus \tau \sqsubseteq f(\sigma' \oplus \tau')$.

Composing asynchronous orchestrators. As we have seen for synchronous orchestrators, monotonicity of orchestrator composition (Proposition 9) plays a central role in proving that $\preceq_k$ is a pre-order. Unfortunately, a nasty consequence of buffering is that the functional composition of two orchestrator is not an orchestrator in general. To see why, consider for example

$$f \stackrel{\text{def}}{=} \langle a, \varepsilon\rangle.\langle c, \varepsilon\rangle.(\langle \varepsilon, \overline{a}\rangle.\langle \overline{b}, b\rangle \vee \langle \varepsilon, \overline{c}\rangle.\langle \overline{d}, d\rangle) \quad \text{and} \quad g \stackrel{\text{def}}{=} \langle a, \varepsilon\rangle.\langle \overline{b}, b\rangle \vee \langle c, \varepsilon\rangle.\langle \overline{d}, d\rangle$$

and apply them to the contract $\sigma \stackrel{\text{def}}{=} \overline{b} + \overline{d}$. We obtain

$$f(g(\sigma)) \simeq f(a.\overline{b} + c.\overline{d}) \simeq a.c.(\overline{b} \oplus \overline{d})$$

The subsequent applications of g first and then f introduce some nondeterminism due to the uncertainty as to which synchronization (on a or on c) will occur. This uncertainty yields the internal choice $\overline{b} \oplus \overline{d}$ in the resulting contract. No single orchestrator can turn $\overline{b} + \overline{d}$ into $a.c.(\overline{b} \oplus \overline{d})$ for orchestrators do not manifest internal nondeterminism. The problem could be addressed by adding internal nondeterminism to the orchestration language, but this seems quite artificial and, as a matter of facts, is unnecessary. If we are able to find an orchestrator $f \cdot g$ such that $(f \circ g)(\sigma') \sqsubseteq (f \cdot g)(\sigma')$, then $\sigma \sqsubseteq (f \cdot g)(\sigma')$ follows by transitivity of $\sqsubseteq$.

The orchestrator composition operator $\cdot$ is a generalization of $\wedge$ that considers asynchronous orchestration actions:

Definition 21 (orchestrator composition). *The* composition *of two orchestrators f and g, notation $f \cdot g$, is defined as:*

$$f \cdot g \stackrel{\text{def}}{=} \bigvee_{f \stackrel{\langle\alpha,\varepsilon\rangle}{\longmapsto} f'} \langle\alpha,\varepsilon\rangle.(f' \cdot g) \vee \bigvee_{g \stackrel{\langle\varepsilon,\overline{\alpha}\rangle}{\longmapsto} g'} \langle\varepsilon,\overline{\alpha}\rangle.(f \cdot g') \vee \bigvee_{f \stackrel{\langle\varphi,\overline{\alpha}\rangle}{\longmapsto} f', g \stackrel{\langle\alpha,\varphi'\rangle}{\longmapsto} g', \varphi\varphi' \neq \varepsilon} \langle\varphi,\varphi'\rangle.(f' \cdot g') \vee \bigvee_{f \stackrel{\langle\varepsilon,\overline{\alpha}\rangle}{\longmapsto} f', g \stackrel{\langle\alpha,\varepsilon\rangle}{\longmapsto} g'} (f' \cdot g')$$

The first two subterms in the definition of $f \cdot g$ indicate that all the asynchronous actions offered by f (respectively, g) to the client (respectively, service) are available. The third subterm turns synchronous actions into asynchronous ones: for example, $\langle\alpha,\overline{\alpha}\rangle \cdot \langle\alpha,\varepsilon\rangle = \langle\alpha,\varepsilon\rangle$ and $\langle\varepsilon,\overline{\alpha}\rangle \cdot \langle\alpha,\overline{\alpha}\rangle = \langle\varepsilon,\alpha\rangle$. The last subterm accounts for the "synchronizations" occurring within the orchestrator, when f and g exchange a message and the two actions annihilate each other. If we consider the orchestrators f and g defined above, we obtain $f \cdot g = \langle a,\varepsilon\rangle.\langle c,\varepsilon\rangle.(\langle\overline{b},b\rangle \vee \langle\overline{d},d\rangle)$ and we observe $(f \cdot g)(\overline{b} + \overline{d}) = a.c.(\overline{b} + \overline{d})$.

The next result proves that $f \cdot g$ is correct and consequently that $\preceq_k$ is a preorder:

Theorem 8. $f(g(\sigma)) \sqsubseteq (f \cdot g)(\sigma)$.

It may be argued that $f \cdot g$ is somewhat "more powerful" than $f \circ g$, because $(f \circ g)(\sigma) \sqsubseteq (f \cdot g)(\sigma)$ but $(f \circ g)(\sigma) \not\simeq (f \cdot g)(\sigma)$ in general. Against this objection it is sufficient to observe that if f and g are k-orchestrators, then $f \cdot g$ is a $2k$-orchestrator. Thus, $f \cdot g$ is really nothing more than some proper combination of f and g, as expected.

4.3 Alternative Characterization of the Weak k-Subcontract Relation

We now provide an alternative characterization of $\preceq_k$, which will also guide us in defining the algorithm for deciding $\preceq_k$ in §7.[3] As for synchronous orchestrators, asynchronous orchestrators modify the ready sets of the service as they are perceived by the client. The converse is also true, because of asynchronous orchestration actions. Assume A is a set of orchestration actions proposed by an asynchronous orchestrator. If R is a client ready set and S is a service ready set, then we write $\mathrm{A} \circ \mathrm{S}$ for the service ready set perceived by the client and we write $\mathrm{R} \bullet \mathrm{A}$ for the client ready set perceived by the service. These two modified ready sets can be defined thus:

$$\mathrm{A} \circ \mathrm{S} \stackrel{\text{def}}{=} \{\alpha \mid \langle\alpha,\varepsilon\rangle \in \mathrm{A}\} \cup \{\alpha \in \mathrm{S} \mid \langle\alpha,\overline{\alpha}\rangle \in \mathrm{A}\}$$
$$\mathrm{R} \bullet \mathrm{A} \stackrel{\text{def}}{=} \{\overline{\alpha} \mid \langle\varepsilon,\overline{\alpha}\rangle \in \mathrm{A}\} \cup \{\overline{\alpha} \in \mathrm{R} \mid \langle\alpha,\overline{\alpha}\rangle \in \mathrm{A}\}$$

[3] Unlike the strong and weak subcontract relations, a sound and complete deduction system for the weak k-subcontract relation is not known at the time of this writing.

Namely, the client sees an action α if either that action is provided asynchronously by the orchestrator ($\langle\alpha,\varepsilon\rangle \in \mathrm{A}$), or if it is provided by the service ($\alpha \in \mathrm{S}$) and the orchestrator does not hide it ($\langle\alpha,\overline{\alpha}\rangle \in \mathrm{A}$); symmetrically for the service.

With these notions we can now define the coinductive characterization of weak subcontract relation, in a similar manner as for the weak variant.

Definition 22 (coinductive weak k-subcontract). *We say that* $\mathscr{W}_k$ *is a* coinductive weak k-subcontract relation *if* $(\mathbb{B},\sigma,\tau) \in \mathscr{W}_k$ *implies that* $\mathbb{B}$ *is a k-buffer and there exists a set of orchestration actions* A *such that* $\mathbb{B} \vdash_k \mathrm{A}$ *and*

1. $\tau \Downarrow \mathrm{S}$ *implies either* ($\sigma \Downarrow \mathrm{R}$ *and* $\mathrm{R} \subseteq \mathrm{A} \circ \mathrm{S}$ *for some* R) *or* $(\emptyset \bullet \mathrm{A}) \cap \overline{\mathrm{S}} \neq \emptyset$, *and*
2. $\tau \stackrel{\varphi'}{\Longrightarrow}$ *and* $\langle\varphi,\overline{\varphi}'\rangle \in \mathrm{A}$ *implies* $\sigma \stackrel{\varphi}{\Longrightarrow}$ *and* $(\mathbb{B}\langle\varphi,\overline{\varphi}'\rangle,\sigma(\varphi),\tau(\varphi')) \in \mathscr{W}_k$.

Condition (1) requires that either τ can be made more deterministic than σ by means of the orchestrator (the ready set $\mathrm{A} \circ \mathrm{S}$ of the orchestrated service has a corresponding one of σ that offers fewer actions), or that τ can be satisfied by the orchestrator without any help from the client ($(\emptyset \bullet \mathrm{A}) \cap \overline{\mathrm{S}} \neq \emptyset$ implies that $\langle\varepsilon,\overline{\alpha}\rangle \in \mathrm{A}$ and $\alpha \in \mathrm{S}$ for some α). Condition (2) poses the usual requirement that the continuations must be in the subcontract relation.

The two definitions of weak subcontract are equivalent:

Theorem 9. $\preceq_k$ *is the largest coinductive weak k-subcontract relation.*

5 Contract Duality with Orchestration

We tackle the problem of finding the dual contract $\rho^{\perp}$ of a given client contract ρ. Recall that $\rho^{\perp}$ should be the smallest (according to $\preceq_k$) contract such that ρ is compliant with $\rho^{\perp}$.

Before proceeding, we must face the fact that some clients cannot by satisfied by any service. For instance, there is no service that satisfies (the client) 0; similarly, there is no service that satisfies $\overline{a}.(0 \oplus b.\mathsf{e})$ since this client, after sending $\overline{a}$, may internally evolve into the state 0. We thus need a characterization of those (client) contracts that can be satisfied:

Definition 23 (viable contract). *A (client) contract* ρ *is* viable, *notation* $\mathsf{viable}(\rho)$, *if there exists* σ *such that* $\rho \dashv \sigma$.

It is quite easy to provide an alternative, coinductive characterization of viable contracts.

Definition 24 (coinductive viability). *We say that the predicate* $\mathscr{V}$ *is a* coinductive viability *if* $\rho \in \mathscr{V}$ *and* $\rho \Downarrow \mathrm{R}$ *implies either* $\mathsf{e} \in \mathrm{R}$ *or* $\rho(\alpha) \in \mathscr{V}$ *for some* $\alpha \in \mathrm{R}$.

This characterization mandates that no viable client contract can expose an empty ready set: every ready set must contain either the special action e denoting the client's ability to terminate successfully, or *at least* one action α whose continuation is itself a viable contract. So e is the simplest viable client contract, whereas $(a+b.\mathsf{e}) \oplus a.\overline{c}$ is not viable because its continuation after a is $0 \oplus \overline{c}$ that has an empty ready set.

Proposition 10. $\mathsf{viable}(\cdot)$ *is the largest coinductive viability.*

Now that we have a notion of viability, we are ready to define the dual contract.

Definition 25 (dual contract). *Let* ρ *be a viable client contract. The* dual contract *of* ρ*, denoted by* $\rho^\perp$*, is defined as:*

$$\rho^\perp \stackrel{\text{def}}{=} \sum_{\rho \Downarrow \mathsf{R}, \mathsf{e} \notin \mathsf{R}} \bigoplus_{\alpha \in \mathsf{R}, \mathsf{viable}(\rho(\alpha))} \overline{\alpha}.\rho(\alpha)^\perp$$

The idea of the dual operator is to consider every state R of the client in which the client cannot terminate successfully ($\mathsf{e} \notin \mathsf{R}$). For every such state the service must provide at least one way for the client to proceed, and the least service that guarantees this is given by the internal choice of all the co-actions in $\overline{\mathsf{R}}$ that have viable continuations (note that there must be at least one of such actions because the client is viable by hypothesis). A few examples of dual contracts follow:

- $(a.\mathsf{e})^\perp = (a.\mathsf{e} \oplus \mathsf{e})^\perp = \overline{a}$ (the service must provide $\overline{a}$);
- $(a.\mathsf{e} + \mathsf{e})^\perp = 0$ (the service need not provide anything because the client can terminate immediately);
- $(a.\mathsf{e} + b.\mathsf{e})^\perp = \overline{a} \oplus \overline{b}$ (the service can decide whether to provide $\overline{a}$ or $\overline{b}$);
- $(a.\mathsf{e} \oplus b.\mathsf{e})^\perp = \overline{a} + \overline{b}$ (the service must provide both $\overline{a}$ and $\overline{b}$).

Theorem 10 (duality). *Let* ρ *be a viable client contract. Then*

1. $\rho \dashv \rho^\perp$;
2. $\rho \dashv \sigma$ *implies* $\rho^\perp \preceq \sigma$.

The assumption of using orchestrators is essential as far as duality is concerned: $(a.\mathsf{e} + \mathsf{e})^\perp = 0$ but 0 is *not* the smallest (according to $\sqsubseteq$) contract satisfying $a.\mathsf{e} + \mathsf{e}$. For example, $0 \oplus b \sqsubseteq 0$ and $a.\mathsf{e} + \mathsf{e} \dashv 0 \oplus b$. On the contrary, 0 is the least element of $\preceq_k$ and it can be used in place of any service contract that exposes an empty ready set. A notion a duality without orchestrators can only be achieved if the subcontract relation being considered provides a least element. This is possible for $\sqsubseteq$ if we extend the theory with diverging processes, as done in [24].

6 Contracts for Infinite Behaviors

Until now we have been working with *finite* contracts, namely with contracts that provide a maximum number of nested prefixes. This means that we can only model client and service behaviors corresponding to *finite* interactions, but we cannot model, for example, a client and a service that interact infinitely often if the client performs an unbounded number of requests and the service is able to satisfy them all.

There are three well-known ways of dealing with repeated (or recursive) behavior. In regular expressions, for example, the algebra includes a $*$ operator (the so-called Kleene star) so that, for example, a^* denotes the set of arbitrarily long, but finite, sequences of a symbols. In process algebra, it is more frequent the use of *definitions* or of *recursion* *terms*. In the former case, the syntax is extended to include variables X, and a global environment defines a finite set of equations of the form

$$X \stackrel{\text{def}}{=} \sigma$$

giving the meaning to variables. In the latter case, the syntax is extended with two constructs: recursion is expressed by a term $\mathsf{rec}\, x.\sigma$ which binds the recursion variable x within σ; every occurrence of the variable x within σ stands for an occurrence of the whole term $\mathsf{rec}\, x.\sigma$. In other words, the contracts $\mathsf{rec}\, x.\sigma$ and its *unfolding* $\sigma\{^{\mathsf{rec}\, x.\sigma}/_{x}\}$ (the latter being the same as σ except that every free occurrence of x has been replaced by $\mathsf{rec}\, x.\sigma$) are equivalent.

Observe that all the three approaches require an extension of the syntax of contracts (Definition 1) as well as corresponding extensions in their operational semantics (Definition 2). In addition, it is not obvious how to apply the approach using the Kleene star in our scenario since it is well known [2,17] that, in a nondeterministic setting, there are behaviors that cannot be expressed using that syntax.

Instead, we resort to the theory of regular trees [14]. This approach is more commonly used in type theory and has the remarkable advantage that it virtually requires no change at all to the whole theory we have developed so far. The basic idea is extremely simple: infinite contracts are represented as infinite terms generated by the grammar in Definition 1. In practice, this amounts to working directly with the solutions of the equations $X \stackrel{\text{def}}{=} \sigma$ or with the infinite unfoldings of recursive terms $\mathsf{rec}\, x.\sigma$. However, saying that we use "infinite terms" is not enough to ensure that such terms do actually make sense or that the theory remains decidable. To guarantee these facts we must enforce two additional constraints, hence the precise definition of the infinite terms we consider is the following:

Definition 26 (contracts). *The set of contracts is the set of possibly infinite, regular trees generated by the grammar in Definition 1 such that every infinite branch of a tree contains infinitely many occurrences of "." (the prefix constructor).*

This definition imposes two fundamental requirements on the infinite terms we have mentioned earlier. First of all, we require that the term must be a *regular tree*. A regular tree contains finitely many different subtrees (observe that every finite term is a regular tree). Second, we impose a *contractivity condition*[4] by requiring that if a contract term is infinite, it is because it proposes an unbound sequence of actions. For example, we exclude regular terms that are solutions of the equations $X = X + X$ or $X = X \oplus X$. As a side effect of the contractivity condition, we enforce the fact that the behaviors we consider are *everywhere convergent*. Namely, contracts can never exhibit an infinite number of internal transitions, hence we are not able to describe the behavior of clients and services that may diverge. This is in practice the only limitation of our approach, if compared to the more traditional approaches that deal with infinite behaviors. The reader interested in one possible way of dealing with divergent contracts can refer to [24].

The definition of orchestrators can be extended to infinite behaviors in a similar way, by imposing regularity and contractivity of the orchestrator.

[4] The term "contractivity" has nothing to do with the fact that we talk about "contracts", see [14].

We now revisit the definitions and results we have developed for the theory of finite contracts and see now they change when we consider contracts as by Definition 26.

The strong compliance relation (Definition 3) now takes into account the possibility that client and service interact infinitely often. Observe that, since contracts are everywhere convergent, every infinite computation starting from $\rho \parallel \sigma$ involves an infinite number of synchronizations between client and service. For example, we have $\overline{a}.\overline{a}.\overline{a}.\cdots \dashv a.a.a.\cdots$.

As regards contract continuations (Definition 5), observe that $\sigma(\alpha)$ is still well defined because contracts are everywhere convergent: there is always a finite number of residuals σ' such that $\sigma \Longrightarrow\xrightarrow{\alpha} \sigma'$. In fact we can state an even stronger property which is fundamental for asserting the well-foundedness of several definitions.

Proposition 11. *Let* $D(\sigma) \stackrel{\text{def}}{=} \{\sigma(\varphi) \mid \sigma \stackrel{\varphi}{\Longrightarrow}\}$. *Then* $D(\sigma)$ *is finite for every* σ.

Proof. It is sufficient to observe that $\sigma(\varphi)$ is the internal choice of some subtrees σ. Since a regular tree has finite different subtrees, there is a finite number of terms $\sigma(\varphi)$. An alternative, direct proof can be found in [25]. □

A similar result can be proved for orchestrators and the corresponding $\stackrel{\mu}{\longmapsto}$ relation. Because of these results, it is easy to see that all the inductive definitions given in the paper are well founded, not in the sense that a base case is eventually reached, but that they yield regular and contractive contracts and orchestrators. Consider for example the definition of the identity orchestrator $I(\sigma)$ for a contract σ. According to equation 3 on page 225 we see that $I(\sigma)$ depends on $I(\sigma(\alpha))$ for a finite set of actions α. In turn, each $I(\sigma(\alpha))$ will depend upon a finite set of $I(\sigma(\alpha)(\beta))$. Now observe that $\sigma(\alpha)(\beta) = \sigma(\alpha\beta)$. Hence, if we think of $I(\sigma(\varphi))$ as of a label, Proposition 11 let us conclude that $I(\sigma)$ depends on a finite number of labels $I(\sigma(\varphi))$, hence it can be represented as a regular orchestrator. A similar reasoning can be applied for deducing that the definitions of orchestrator composition, orchestrator application (Definition 14), asynchronous orchestrator application (Definition 20), and other inductive definitions are all well founded.

As regards the deduction system presented in §3.4 for the weak subcontract relation, it is still complete, provided that we admit infinite (but regular and contractive) proofs, where a contractive proof is one where every infinite branch of the derivation tree contains infinite occurrences of the (PREFIX) rule. Details can be found in the full version of [10]. Observe that if divergence is added to the contract language, the deduction system must be suitably extended with new axioms [21].

As regards asynchronous orchestrators, the validity constraint and the finiteness of the rank have fundamental consequences: a valid orchestrator of finite rank cannot read an unbound number of messages from just one of the two interacting parties. Thus, finiteness of the orchestrator's rank guarantees that the orchestrator is *fair*: it still holds, as in the case of synchronous orchestrators, that every infinite interaction between a client and a service is such that both client and service interact infinitely often.

Finally, the proofs of all the results presented are all still valid, since none of them, except for the completeness proof of the deduction system, proceed by induction on the depth of contracts or orchestrators (as a matter of facts, most proofs are based on coinduction).

7 Automatic Synthesis of Orchestrators

In this section we devise an algorithm for computing the k-orchestrator witnessing $\sigma \preceq_k \tau$, provided there is one. Actually, we have already seen that there can be more than one orchestrator proving a relation $\sigma \preceq_k \tau$, so when devising the algorithm we need a criterion for choosing a particular orchestrator as the "right" one. We know that orchestrators are closed under union, namely if $f : \sigma \preceq_k \tau$ and $g : \sigma \preceq_k \tau$, then $f \vee g : \sigma \preceq_k \tau$. So we may naively attempt to define an algorithm that synthesizes the *largest* orchestrator, according to their trace semantics. This approach is not effective since the largest orchestrator proving $\sigma \preceq_k \tau$ involves an infinite number of different names, and thus is not representable as a proper orchestrator. The idea is that, by means of Proposition 7, we may restrict our interest to the subclass of the orchestrators that are relevant for $\sigma \preceq_k \tau$.

Definition 27 (best relevant orchestrator). *We say that f is the* best relevant k-orchestrator *such that $f : \sigma \preceq_k \tau$ if $g : \sigma \preceq_k \tau$ and g is a relevant k-orchestrator implies $g \leqslant f$.*

The algorithm that synthesizes the best relevant orchestrator proving $\sigma \preceq_k \tau$, provided there is one, is defined inductively by the rule:

$$\frac{\begin{array}{c} \mathrm{A}_r = \{\langle \varphi, \overline{\varphi}' \rangle \mid \sigma \stackrel{\varphi}{\Longrightarrow}, \tau \stackrel{\varphi'}{\Longrightarrow}, \mathbb{B} \vdash_k \langle \varphi, \overline{\varphi}' \rangle\} \\ \mathrm{A} = \{\langle \varphi, \overline{\varphi}' \rangle \in \mathrm{A}_r \mid \mathbb{B}\langle \varphi, \overline{\varphi}' \rangle \vdash_k f_{\langle \varphi, \overline{\varphi}' \rangle} : \sigma(\varphi) \trianglelefteq \tau(\varphi')\} \\ \tau \Downarrow \mathrm{S} \Rightarrow (\exists \mathrm{R} : \sigma \Downarrow \mathrm{R} \wedge \mathrm{R} \subseteq \mathrm{A} \circ \mathrm{S}) \vee (\emptyset \bullet \mathrm{A}) \cap \overline{\mathrm{S}} \neq \emptyset \end{array}}{\mathbb{B} \vdash_k \bigvee_{\mu \in \mathrm{A}} \mu . f_\mu : \sigma \trianglelefteq \tau}$$

A judgment of the form $\mathbb{B} \vdash_k f : \sigma \trianglelefteq \tau$ means that f is a k-orchestrator proving that $\sigma \preceq_k \tau$ when the buffer of the orchestrator is in state $\mathbb{B}$. The k-buffer $\mathbb{B}$ keeps track of the past history of the orchestrator (which messages the orchestrator has accepted and not yet delivered). We write $f : \sigma \trianglelefteq_k \tau$ if $\tilde{\emptyset} \vdash_k f : \sigma \trianglelefteq \tau$.

Although the algorithm looks formidable, it embeds the conditions in Definition 7 in a straightforward way. Recall that the purpose of the algorithm is to find the best relevant orchestrator f such that every client strongly compliant with σ is weakly compliant with τ when this service is orchestrated by f, assuming that the buffer of the orchestrator is $\mathbb{B}$. Since $\mathbb{B}$ is a k-buffer, the number of enabled asynchronous orchestration actions is finite: an action $\langle \overline{a}, \varepsilon \rangle$ is enabled only if $\mathbb{B}(\circ, \overline{a}) > 0$; an action $\langle a, \varepsilon \rangle$ is enabled only if the buffer has not reached its capacity, namely if $\mathbb{B}(\bullet, \overline{a}) < k$; symmetrically for asynchronous service actions. Also, it is pointless to consider any orchestration action that would not cause any synchronization to occur. Hence, the set A_r of relevant, enabled orchestration actions in the first premise of the rule is finite. Of all the actions in this set, the algorithm considers only those in some subset A such that the execution of any orchestration action in A does not lead to a deadlock later on during the interaction. This is guaranteed if for every $\langle \varphi, \overline{\varphi}' \rangle \in \mathrm{A}$ we are able to find an orchestrator $f_{\langle \varphi, \overline{\varphi}' \rangle}$ that proves $\tau(\varphi') \preceq_k \sigma(\varphi)$ (second premise of the rule). When checking the continuations, the buffer is updated to account for the orchestration action just occurred. If the set A is large enough so as to satisfy the third premise of the rule, which is exactly condition (1) of Definition 15, then σ and τ can be related. The orchestrator computed in the conclusion of rule (A1) offers the union of all the relevant, enabled orchestration actions μ, each one followed by the corresponding continuation f_μ.

Observe that the algorithm hides a base case, when the set A_r is empty. This case is eventually reached when σ and τ are *finite* contracts, since each application of the rule in the algorithm decreases the *depth* of either σ or τ, or both.[5] The algorithm can also be extended for dealing with possibly infinite (but regular) contracts, as by Definition 26, using standard memoization techniques. The reader interested in the details can refer to [27].

The algorithm described above is correct and complete and it always terminates.

Theorem 11. *The following properties hold:*

1. *(termination) it is decidable to check whether there exists f such that $f : \sigma \trianglelefteq_k \tau$;*
2. *(correctness) $f : \sigma \trianglelefteq_k \tau$ implies that f has rank k and $f : \sigma \preceq_k \tau$;*
3. *(completeness) $f : \sigma \preceq_k \tau$ and f is relevant for $\sigma \preceq_k \tau$ implies $g : \sigma \trianglelefteq_k \tau$ for some g such that $f \leqslant g$.*

8 Application Example

Consider a variant of the problem of the dining philosophers in which service providers hire philosophers for generating philosophical thoughts to those clients that provide two forks. Each philosopher is modeled by the following contract:

$$P_i \stackrel{\mathrm{def}}{=} \mathit{fork}_i.\mathit{fork}_i.\overline{\mathit{thought}}.\overline{\mathit{fork}}.\overline{\mathit{fork}}$$

where the fork_i actions model the philosopher's request of two forks, $\overline{\mathit{thought}}$ models the generation of a thought, and the $\overline{\mathit{fork}}$ actions model the fact that the philosophers return both forks after having generated a thought. We decorate fork_i actions with an index i for distinguishing fork requests coming from different philosophers.

We consider two potential clients of such services, a "sloppy" client C and a "diligent" client D which are defined as follows:

$$C \stackrel{\mathrm{def}}{=} \Sigma_{i=1..2}\overline{\mathit{fork}_i}.\Sigma_{i=1..2}\overline{\mathit{fork}_i}.\mathit{thought}.\mathit{fork}.\mathit{fork}$$
$$D \stackrel{\mathrm{def}}{=} \Sigma_{i=1..2}\overline{\mathit{fork}_i}.\overline{\mathit{fork}_i}.\mathit{thought}.\mathit{fork}.\mathit{fork}$$

The difference between the two clients is that the sloppy one provides two forks, but it does not care that the two forks it provides end up to the same philosopher. In a system with two philosophers this may cause the system to deadlock. The diligent client provides two forks and it does not care which philosopher gets the forks, but it does care that the two forks end up to the same philosopher.

In order to see which services can satisfy these clients, we compute the corresponding dual contracts and we obtain:

$$C^\perp \stackrel{\mathrm{def}}{=} \bigoplus_{i=1..2}\mathit{fork}_i.\bigoplus_{i=1..2}\mathit{fork}_i.\overline{\mathit{thought}}.\overline{\mathit{fork}}.\overline{\mathit{fork}}$$
$$D^\perp \stackrel{\mathrm{def}}{=} \bigoplus_{i=1..2}\mathit{fork}_i.\mathit{fork}_i.\overline{\mathit{thought}}.\overline{\mathit{fork}}.\overline{\mathit{fork}}$$

---
[5] The depth of a finite contract is the maximum number of nested prefixes in it.

We observe that $C^\perp \sqsubseteq P_i$ and $D^\perp \sqsubseteq P_i$ for $i = 1..2$, hence we conclude that $C \dashv P_i$ and $D \dashv P_i$. Namely, both clients are satisfied by any service that hires one of the two philosophers for generating thoughts. Consider now a richer service provider who can afford two hire *both* philosophers. Intuitively, this service has contract $P_1 \mid P_2$, which denotes the *parallel composition* of P_1 and P_2. Even though our contract language is not equipped with a parallel composition operator, we can faithfully capture its semantics using just the operators provided by our contract language. Assuming that σ and τ are the contracts of two services that never synchronize with each other, which is the case in this example, we can express $\sigma \mid \tau$ using a simplified form of *expansion law* [21]:

$$\sigma \mid \tau \stackrel{\text{def}}{=} \bigoplus_{\sigma \Downarrow \mathrm{R}, \tau \Downarrow \mathrm{S}} \left(\Sigma_{\alpha \in \mathrm{R}} \, \alpha.(\sigma(\alpha) \mid \tau) + \Sigma_{\alpha \in \mathrm{S}} \, \alpha.(\sigma \mid \tau(\alpha)) \right)$$

With this definition, we can now see that $C^\perp \not\sqsubseteq P_1 \mid P_2$ and $D^\perp \not\sqsubseteq P_1 \mid P_2$, hence the richer service with contract $P_1 \mid P_2$ cannot be used as is to satisfy either client. Let us now run the algorithm to see whether $C^\perp \preceq_0 P_1 \mid P_2$. If we consider the sequence of actions $\overline{fork_1}\,\overline{fork_2}$ we reduce to checking

$$\overline{thought}.\overline{fork}.\overline{fork} \preceq_0 P_1(fork_1) \mid P_2(fork_2)$$

The contract $P_1(fork_1) \mid P_2(fork_2)$ has only the ready set $\{fork_1, fork_2\}$, while the residual of the client's dual contract has only the ready set $\{\overline{thought}\}$. A similar situation occurs when considering the sequence of actions $\overline{fork_2}\,\overline{fork_1}$. There is no orchestration action that can let the algorithm make some progress from these states. In a sense the algorithm finds out that the two forks sent by the client must be delivered to the same philosopher, and this is testified by the resulting orchestrator

$$f \stackrel{\text{def}}{=} \bigvee_{i=1..2} \langle fork_i, \overline{fork_i} \rangle . \langle fork_i, \overline{fork_i} \rangle . \langle thought, \overline{thought} \rangle . \langle fork, \overline{fork} \rangle . \langle fork, \overline{fork} \rangle$$

which allows us to prove $f : C^\perp \preceq_0 P_1 \mid P_2$.

In this particular example, the same orchestrator f also allows us to prove $f : D^\perp \preceq_0 P_1 \mid P_2$. However, there is an important difference with the case of $C^\perp$ because we have $I(D^\perp) \leqslant f$. This means that $D^\perp$ never exposes any action that must be filtered out by f. Since $D^\perp$ is the dual of D, this in turn means that D never tries to perform any action that is not filtered by f. In conclusion, while $D^\perp \not\sqsubseteq P_1 \mid P_2$, hence there are clients of $D^\perp$ that are not satisfied by $P_1 \mid P_2$ if not by means of some orchestrator, it is the case that $D \dashv P_1 \mid P_2$ and we are able to conclude this fact from $f : D^\perp \preceq_0 P_1 \mid P_2$ and $I(D^\perp) \leqslant f$.

Suppose now that the rich service provider is forced to update the service with two new philosophers who, according to their habit, produce their thoughts only after having returned the forks. Their behavior can be described by the contract

$$Q_i \stackrel{\text{def}}{=} fork_i.fork_i.\overline{fork}.\overline{fork}.\overline{thought}$$

The service provider may wonder whether the clients of the old service will still be satisfied by the new one. The problem can be formulated as checking whether $P_1 \mid P_2 \preceq_k Q_1 \mid Q_2$ for some k and the interesting step is when the algorithm eventually checks $P_1(fork_1 fork_1) \mid P_2 \preceq_k Q_1(fork_1 fork_1) \mid Q_2$ (symmetrically for P_2 and the sequence of actions $fork_2 fork_2$). At this stage $P_1(fork_1 fork_1) \mid P_2$ has just the ready set $\{\overline{thought}, fork_2\}$, whereas the contract $Q_1(fork_1\overline{fork_1}) \mid Q_2$ has just the ready set $\{\overline{fork}, fork_2\}$. By accepting the two $\overline{fork}$ messages asynchronously we reduce to checking whether $P_1(fork_1\overline{fork_1}) \mid P_2 \preceq_k \overline{thought}.Q_1 \mid Q_2$, which holds by allowing the $\overline{thought}$ action to occur, followed by the asynchronous sending of the two buffered $\overline{fork}$ messages. Overall the relation is proved by the orchestrator

$$g \stackrel{\text{def}}{=} \bigvee_{i=1..2}\langle fork_i, \overline{fork_i}\rangle . \bigvee_{i=1..2}\langle fork_i, \overline{fork_i}\rangle . \langle \varepsilon, fork\rangle . \langle \varepsilon, fork\rangle . \langle thought, \overline{thought}\rangle . \langle \overline{fork}, \varepsilon\rangle . \langle \overline{fork}, \varepsilon\rangle$$

and now the sloppy client C will be satisfied by the service $Q_1 \mid Q_2$ by means of the orchestrator

$$f \cdot g = \bigvee_{i=1..2}\langle fork_i, \overline{fork_i}\rangle . \langle fork_i, \overline{fork_i}\rangle . \langle \varepsilon, fork\rangle . \langle \varepsilon, fork\rangle . \langle thought, \overline{thought}\rangle . \langle \overline{fork}, \varepsilon\rangle$$

9 Related and Future Work

This work originated by revisiting CCS without τ's [16] in the context of Web services. Contracts are in fact just a concrete representation of *acceptance trees* [20,21]. Early attempts to define a reasonable subcontract relation [9] have eventually led to the conclusion that some control over actions is necessary: [24] proposes a static form of control that makes use of explicit contract interfaces whereas [10] proposes a dynamic form of control by means of so-called *filters* and [27] elaborates on the idea of [10] by adding asynchrony and buffering to filters: this apparently simple addition significantly increases the technicalities of the resulting theory, both because of the very nature of asynchrony and also because orchestrator composition and conjunction no longer coincide.

[18] provides a very clear and interesting comparison of several refinement relations among which *reduction* refinement, which corresponds to the *must* preorder and to our notion of strong subcontract (see §2), and *implementation* refinement, which roughly corresponds to the subcontract relation defined in [9] and that can be traced back to the LOTOS language [7]. The authors of [18] emphasize the importance of implementation refinement, which enables *width* and *depth* extensions of partial specifications, but also its lack of transitivity, which hinders its application in practice. Thus, the work done in [10,27] can be seen as a solution to the lack of transitivity of this (and similar) refinement relations, by the introduction of suitable coercions/orchestrators/connectors.

WS-BPEL [1] is often presented as an orchestration language for Web services. Remarkably WS-BPEL features boil down to storing incoming messages into variables (buffering) and controlling the interactions of other parties. Our orchestrators can be seen as streamlined WS-BPEL orchestrators in which all the internal nondeterminism of the orchestrator itself is abstracted away. ORC [26] is perhaps the most notable example of orchestration-oriented, algebraic language. The peculiar operators $\gg$ and **where** of ORC represent different forms of *pipelining* and can be seen as orchestration actions in conjunction with the composition operator · of simple orchestrators (§4).

There has been extensive research on the automatic synthesis of connectors both in the domain of software architectures (see for example [23]) and also in the more specific domain of Web services [5,19,22,28,30]. In these contexts the problem consists in finding a connector component (if there is one) which coordinates n given components (associated with corresponding behaviors) so as to accomplish a specific goal (for example, adhering to a target behavior). There is a clear analogy with the present work in that a component of the system (which we call orchestrator) is synthesized so as to make other components interact in some restricted way. We can highlight four main differences between the two scenarios: (1) there is a conceptual difference in that we focus on *finding* an existing service with a desired behavior, whereas Web service composition tries to synthesize a desired behavior starting from n given services. (2) The nature of simple orchestrators is driven by a notion of safe replacement for Web services (the subcontract relation). Although they play an essential role, simple orchestrators are just a tool for reasoning on service equivalence, which is the real main concern in this work. (3) The connector resulting from the automatic composition of Web services is *ad hoc* for the particular set of services that have been composed. In our case, it is possible to synthesize a *universal orchestrator* that satisfies all the clients of a desired service. The tight relationship between the subcontract relation and orchestrators provides us with an efficient way of composing connectors, which is not possible in the more complex scenario of Web service composition. (4) The automatic composition of Web services can only generate stub connectors whose low-level details must still be filled in by programmers. This is due to the fact that in most cases the behavioral description of the Web services is not detailed enough (or is too complex) to fully automate the code generating process. In our restricted scenario, the orchestrators are simple enough to admit a fully automatic code generation.

Future work. The presented theory of contracts is based on (a variant of) the CCS language, whose terms describe interactions without any information on the content of the exchanged messages. Consequently, this theory is adequate as long as the topology of the interaction network and the roles (client/service) of the participants to an interaction are fixed. In more complex scenarios, one can be interested in modelling systems with multiple participants that interact by opening private sessions and by exchanging (delegating) opened sessions between them. In this scenario, the crisp distinction between client and service is lost, and the exchange of communication channels during interaction cannot be adequately captured by a CCS-based contract language. Consequently, the theory presented in this paper is currently being extended to a π-calculus based contract language, which enables the description of processes creating and exchanging communication channels.

Acknowledgments. Parts of the work presented in this paper have been developed in collaboration with Samuele Carpineti, Giuseppe Castagna, Nils Gesbert, and Cosimo Laneve. The sound and complete deduction system in §3 is an adaptation of the one in the full version of [10] which, in turn, closely follows the one for the must preorder presented in [21].

References

1. Alves, A., Arkin, A., Askary, S., Barreto, C., et al.: Web Services Business Process Execution Language Version 2.0 (2007)
2. Baeten, J.C.M., Corradini, F., Grabmayer, C.A.: A characterization of regular expressions under bisimulation. J. ACM 54(2), 6 (2007)

3. Banerji, A., Bartolini, C., Beringer, D., Chopella, V., et al.: Web Services Conversation Language (WSCL) 1.0 (2002)
4. Bellwood, T., Capell, S., Clement, L., Colgrave, J., et al.: UDDI Version 3.0.2. OASIS Standard (2005), http://uddi.org/pubs/uddi-v3.0.2-20041019.htm
5. Berardi, D., Calvanese, D., De Giacomo, G., Lenzerini, M., Mecella, M.: Automatic composition of e-services that export their behavior. In: Orlowska, M.E., Weerawarana, S., Papazoglou, M.P., Yang, J. (eds.) ICSOC 2003. LNCS, vol. 2910, pp. 43–58. Springer, Heidelberg (2003)
6. Beringer, D., Kuno, H., Lemon, M.: Using WSCLin a UDDIRegistry 1.0 (2001)
7. Brinksma, E., Scollo, G., Steenbergen, C.: LOTOS specifications, their implementations and their tests. IEEE Computer Society Press, Los Alamitos (1995)
8. Bruce, K.B., Longo, G.: A modest model of records, inheritance and bounded quantification. Information and Computation 87(1/2), 196–240 (1990)
9. Carpineti, S., Castagna, G., Laneve, C., Padovani, L.: A formal account of contracts for Web Services. In: Bravetti, M., Núñez, M., Zavattaro, G. (eds.) WS-FM 2006. LNCS, vol. 4184, pp. 148–162. Springer, Heidelberg (2006)
10. Castagna, G., Gesbert, N., Padovani, L.: A theory of contracts for Web services. In: Proceedings of POPL 2008, pp. 261–272. ACM, New York (2008)
11. Chen, G.: Soundness of coercion in the calculus of constructions. Journal of Logic and Computation 14(3), 405–427 (2004)
12. Chinnici, R., Moreau, J.-J., Ryman, A., Weerawarana, S.: Web Services Description Language (WSDL) Version 2.0 Part 1: Core Language (2007)
13. Colgrave, J., Januszewski, K.: Using WSDL in a UDDI registry, version 2.0.2. Technical note, OASIS (2004)
14. Courcelle, B.: Fundamental properties of infinite trees. Theoretical Computer Science 25, 95–169 (1983)
15. De Nicola, R., Hennessy, M.: Testing equivalences for processes. Theoretical Computer Science 34, 83–133 (1984)
16. De Nicola, R., Hennessy, M.: CCS without τ's. In: Ehrig, H., Levi, G., Montanari, U. (eds.) CAAP 1987 and TAPSOFT 1987. LNCS, vol. 249, pp. 138–152. Springer, Heidelberg (1987)
17. De Nicola, R., Labella, A.: Nondeterministic regular expressions as solutions of equational systems. Theor. Comput. Sci. 302(1-3), 179–189 (2003)
18. Eshuis, R., Fokkinga, M.M.: Comparing refinements for failure and bisimulation semantics. Fundamenta Informaticae 52(4), 297–321 (2002)
19. De Giacomo, G., Sardiña, S.: Automatic synthesis of new behaviors from a library of available behaviors. In: IJCAI, pp. 1866–1871 (2007)
20. Hennessy, M.: Acceptance trees. JACM: Journal of the ACM 32(4), 896–928 (1985)
21. Hennessy, M.: Algebraic Theory of Processes. Foundation of Computing. MIT Press, Cambridge (1988)
22. Hull, R., Benedikt, M., Christophides, V., Su, J.: E-services: a look behind the curtain. In: PODS 2003: Proceedings of the twenty-second ACM SIGMOD-SIGACT-SIGART symposium on Principles of database systems, pp. 1–14. ACM, New York (2003)
23. Inverardi, P., Tivoli, M.: Software architecture for correct components assembly. In: Bernardo, M., Inverardi, P. (eds.) SFM 2003. LNCS, vol. 2804, pp. 92–121. Springer, Heidelberg (2003)
24. Laneve, C., Padovani, L.: The *must* preorder revisited – an algebraic theory for web services contracts. In: Caires, L., Vasconcelos, V.T. (eds.) CONCUR 2007. LNCS, vol. 4703, pp. 212–225. Springer, Heidelberg (2007)
25. Laneve, C., Padovani, L.: The pairing of contracts and session types. In: Degano, P., De Nicola, R., Meseguer, J. (eds.) Concurrency, Graphs and Models. LNCS, vol. 5065, pp. 681–700. Springer, Heidelberg (2008)

26. Misra, J., Cook, W.R.: Computation orchestration – a basis for wide-area computing. Software and Systems Modeling 6(1), 83–110 (2007)
27. Padovani, L.: Contract-directed synthesis of simple orchestrators. In: van Breugel, F., Chechik, M. (eds.) CONCUR 2008. LNCS, vol. 5201, pp. 131–146. Springer, Heidelberg (2008)
28. Pistore, M., Traverso, P., Bertoli, P., Marconi, A.: Automated synthesis of composite BPEL4WS web services. In: ICWS 2005: Proceedings of the IEEE International Conference on Web Services, Washington, DC, USA, pp. 293–301. IEEE Computer Society, Los Alamitos (2005)
29. Soloviev, S., Jones, A., Luo, Z.: Some Algorithmic and Proof-Theoretical Aspects of Coercive Subtyping. In: Giménez, E. (ed.) TYPES 1996. LNCS, vol. 1512, pp. 173–196. Springer, Heidelberg (1998)
30. Traverso, P., Pistore, M.: Automated composition of semantic web services into executable processes. In: McIlraith, S.A., Plexousakis, D., van Harmelen, F. (eds.) ISWC 2004. LNCS, vol. 3298, pp. 380–394. Springer, Heidelberg (2004)
31. von Riegen, C., Trickovic, I.: Using BPEL4WS in a UDDI registry. Technical note, OASIS (2004)

A Proofs

A.1 Proofs of §2

Proof (of Theorem 1). First of all we prove that $\sqsubseteq$ is a coinductive strong subcontract relation. Let $\sigma \sqsubseteq \tau$. As regards condition (1) in Definition 7, let $\{\mathtt{R}_1, \dots, \mathtt{R}_n\}$ be the ready sets of σ and assume by contradiction that there exists $\mathtt{S}$ such that $\tau \Downarrow \mathtt{S}$ and $\mathtt{R}_i \not\subseteq \mathtt{S}$ for every $1 \leq i \leq n$. Namely, for every $1 \leq i \leq n$ there exists $\alpha_i \in \mathtt{R}_i \setminus \mathtt{S}$. Consider $\rho \stackrel{\text{def}}{=} \sum_{1 \leq i \leq n} \overline{\alpha}_i.\mathtt{e}$. Then $\rho \dashv \sigma$ but $\rho \not\dashv \tau$, which is absurd by hypothesis. As regards condition (2), let $\tau \stackrel{\alpha}{\Longrightarrow}$ and assume by contradiction that $\sigma \stackrel{\alpha}{\not\Longrightarrow}$. Consider $\rho \stackrel{\text{def}}{=} \mathtt{e} + \overline{\alpha}$. Then $\rho \dashv \sigma$ but $\rho \not\dashv \tau$, which is absurd by hypothesis. Let ρ' be a client contract such that $\rho' \dashv \sigma(\alpha)$ and consider $\rho \stackrel{\text{def}}{=} \mathtt{e} + \overline{\alpha}.\rho'$. Then $\rho \dashv \sigma$, from which we derive $\rho \dashv \tau$, hence $\rho' \dashv \tau(\alpha)$. We conclude $\sigma(\alpha) \sqsubseteq \tau(\alpha)$ because ρ' is arbitrary.

Then we prove that $\sqsubseteq$ is the largest among all the coinductive strong subcontract relations. To this aim it is sufficient to show that any coinductive strong subcontract relation $\mathscr{S}$ is included in $\sqsubseteq$. Let $(\sigma, \tau) \in \mathscr{S}$ and assume $\rho \dashv \sigma$. Consider now a maximal computation $\rho \mid \tau \Longrightarrow \rho' \mid \tau' \longrightarrow\!\!\!\!\!\!/\;\;$. We can "unzip" this derivation into two derivations $\rho \stackrel{\overline{\varphi}}{\Longrightarrow} \rho' \longrightarrow\!\!\!\!\!\!/\;\;$ and $\tau \stackrel{\varphi}{\Longrightarrow} \tau' \longrightarrow\!\!\!\!\!\!/\;\;$ for some string φ of actions. From condition (2) of Definition 7 and by induction on φ we derive that $\sigma \stackrel{\varphi}{\Longrightarrow}$ and $(\sigma(\varphi), \tau(\varphi)) \in \mathscr{S}$. From $\tau(\varphi) \Downarrow \mathsf{init}(\tau')$ and condition (1) of Definition 7 we derive that there exists $\mathtt{R} \subseteq \mathsf{init}(\tau')$ such that $\sigma(\varphi) \Downarrow \mathtt{R}$. By definition of ready set we obtain that there exists σ' such that $\sigma \stackrel{\varphi}{\Longrightarrow} \sigma' \longrightarrow\!\!\!\!\!\!/\;\;$ and $\mathsf{init}(\sigma') \subseteq \mathsf{init}(\tau')$. We can now "zip" the two derivations starting from ρ and σ and obtain a derivation $\rho \mid \sigma \Longrightarrow \rho' \mid \sigma'$. We observe that $\rho' \mid \sigma' \longrightarrow\!\!\!\!\!\!/\;\;$ since $\rho' \longrightarrow\!\!\!\!\!\!/\;\;$ and $\sigma' \longrightarrow\!\!\!\!\!\!/\;\;$ and $\mathsf{init}(\sigma') \subseteq \mathsf{init}(\tau')$. From $\rho \dashv \sigma$ we conclude $\rho' \stackrel{\mathtt{e}}{\longrightarrow}$. □

The proof of Proposition 1 is omitted. A proof of property (1) can be found in [24], while a proof that $\sqsubseteq$ is a precongruence with respect to the operators of the contract language is included in [21].

A.2 Proofs of §3

Proof (of Proposition 2). The "if" part is trivial. As regards the "only if" part, the intuition is that if we are able to find the "most demanding" client satisfied by σ, then its corresponding orchestrator is universal. The most demanding client satisfied by σ, denoted by $\sigma^\top$, can be defined thus:

$$\sigma^\top \stackrel{\text{def}}{=} \sum_{\sigma \Downarrow \mathrm{R}} \begin{cases} \mathsf{e} & \text{if } \mathrm{R} = \emptyset \\ \bigoplus_{\alpha \in \mathrm{R}} \overline{\alpha}.\sigma(\alpha)^\top & \text{otherwise} \end{cases}$$

It is trivial to verify that $\sigma^\top \dashv \sigma$. Let f be an orchestrator such that $f : \sigma^\top \dashv\mid \tau$ and assume, without loss of generality, that f is relevant for $\sigma \preceq \tau$. We prove that $f : \sigma \preceq \tau$ by contradiction. Assume that there exists ρ such that $\rho \dashv \sigma$ and $f : \rho \not\dashv\mid \tau$. Then there exists a derivation $\rho \parallel_f \tau \Longrightarrow \rho' \parallel_{f'} \tau' \not\longrightarrow$ such that $\rho' \stackrel{\mathsf{e}}{\not\longrightarrow}$. Consequently there exist $\alpha_1, \dots, \alpha_n$ and such that $\rho \stackrel{\overline{\alpha}_1 \cdots \overline{\alpha}_n}{\Longrightarrow} \rho' \not\longrightarrow$ and $\tau \stackrel{\alpha_1 \cdots \alpha_n}{\Longrightarrow} \tau' \not\longrightarrow$ and $f \xmapsto{\langle \alpha_1, \overline{\alpha}_1 \rangle \cdots \langle \alpha_n, \overline{\alpha}_n \rangle} f'$. Since f is relevant, it is easy to deduce, by induction on n, that $\sigma \stackrel{\alpha_1 \cdots \alpha_n}{\Longrightarrow}$. From $\rho' \parallel_{f'} \tau' \not\longrightarrow$ we deduce that $\rho' \stackrel{\overline{\alpha}}{\longrightarrow}$ and $f' \stackrel{\langle \alpha, \overline{\alpha} \rangle}{\longmapsto}$ imply $\tau' \stackrel{\alpha}{\not\longrightarrow}$. Let $\mathrm{R}_1, \dots, \mathrm{R}_m$ be the ready sets of $\sigma(\alpha_1 \cdots \alpha_n)$. From $\rho \dashv \sigma$ and $\rho' \stackrel{\mathsf{e}}{\not\longrightarrow}$ we deduce that for every $1 \leq i \leq n$ there exists $\beta_i \in \mathrm{R}_i$ and $\rho' \stackrel{\overline{\beta}_i}{\longrightarrow}$. By definition of most demanding client we have $\sigma(\alpha_1 \cdots \alpha_n)^\top \Downarrow \{\overline{\beta}_1, \dots, \overline{\beta}_m\}$, because each ready set of $\sigma(\alpha_1 \cdots \alpha_n)^\top$ is obtained by taking one action from every non-empty ready set of $\sigma(\alpha_1 \cdots \alpha_n)$. Hence there exists ρ'' such that $\sigma^\top \stackrel{\overline{\alpha}_1 \cdots \overline{\alpha}_n}{\Longrightarrow} \rho'' \not\longrightarrow$ and $\mathsf{init}(\rho'') = \{\overline{\beta}_1, \dots, \overline{\beta}_m\} \subseteq \mathsf{init}(\rho')$. By zipping the derivations starting from $\sigma^\top$, f, and τ we obtain a derivation $\sigma^\top \parallel_f \tau \Longrightarrow \rho'' \parallel_{f'} \tau' \not\longrightarrow$ where $\rho'' \stackrel{\mathsf{e}}{\not\longrightarrow}$. This is absurd, for $f : \sigma^\top \dashv\mid \tau$ by hypothesis. □

Proof (of Theorem 3). ($\Rightarrow$) Assume $f : \rho \dashv\mid \sigma$ and consider a derivation $\rho \parallel f(\sigma) \Longrightarrow \rho' \parallel \tau \not\longrightarrow$. Then there exist φ and f' such that $\rho \stackrel{\overline{\varphi}}{\Longrightarrow} \rho' \not\longrightarrow$ and $f(\sigma) \stackrel{\varphi}{\Longrightarrow} f'(\sigma(\varphi)) \Longrightarrow \tau \not\longrightarrow$. By definition of $f(\sigma)$ there exist $\alpha_1, \dots, \alpha_n$ and such that $\varphi = \alpha_1 \cdots \alpha_n$ and $f \xmapsto{\langle \alpha_1, \overline{\alpha}_1 \rangle \cdots \langle \alpha_n, \overline{\alpha}_n \rangle} f'$. From $\rho' \parallel \tau \not\longrightarrow$ we deduce $\overline{\mathsf{init}(\rho')} \cap \mathsf{init}(\tau) = \emptyset$. From $f'(\sigma(\varphi)) \Longrightarrow \tau \not\longrightarrow$ and by definition of $f'(\sigma(\varphi))$ we deduce that there exists σ' such that $\sigma \stackrel{\varphi}{\Longrightarrow} \sigma' \not\longrightarrow$ and $\mathsf{init}(f'(\sigma')) = \mathsf{init}(\tau)$. By zipping the derivations starting from ρ, f, and σ we obtain $\rho \parallel_f \sigma \Longrightarrow \rho' \parallel_{f'} \sigma'$. Furthermore $\rho' \parallel_{f'} \sigma' \not\longrightarrow$ because $\rho' \not\longrightarrow$ and $\sigma' \not\longrightarrow$. From the hypothesis $f : \rho \dashv\mid \sigma$ we conclude $\rho' \stackrel{\mathsf{e}}{\longrightarrow}$.

($\Leftarrow$) Assume $\rho \dashv f(\sigma)$ and consider a derivation $\rho \parallel_f \sigma \Longrightarrow \rho' \parallel_{f'} \sigma' \not\longrightarrow$. By "unzipping" this derivation we have that there exist $\alpha_1, \dots, \alpha_n$ such that $\rho \stackrel{\overline{\alpha}_1 \cdots \overline{\alpha}_n}{\Longrightarrow} \rho' \not\longrightarrow$ and $f \xmapsto{\langle \alpha_1, \overline{\alpha}_1 \rangle \cdots \langle \alpha_n, \overline{\alpha}_n \rangle} f'$ and $\sigma \stackrel{\alpha_1 \cdots \alpha_n}{\Longrightarrow} \sigma' \not\longrightarrow$. Furthermore from $\rho' \parallel_{f'} \sigma' \not\longrightarrow$ we derive $\overline{\mathsf{init}(\rho')} \cap \mathsf{init}(f'(\sigma')) = \emptyset$. By definition of $f(\sigma)$ there exists τ such that $f(\sigma) \stackrel{\alpha_1 \cdots \alpha_n}{\Longrightarrow} \tau \not\longrightarrow$ and $\mathsf{init}(\tau) = \mathsf{init}(f'(\sigma'))$. By zipping the derivations starting from ρ and $f(\sigma)$ we obtain $\rho \parallel f(\sigma) \Longrightarrow \rho' \parallel \tau$. Furthermore $\rho' \parallel \tau \not\longrightarrow$ because $\rho' \not\longrightarrow$, $\tau \not\longrightarrow$, and $\overline{\mathsf{init}(\rho')} \cap \mathsf{init}(\tau) = \overline{\mathsf{init}(\rho')} \cap \mathsf{init}(f'(\sigma')) = \emptyset$. From $\rho \dashv f(\sigma)$ we conclude $\rho' \stackrel{\mathsf{e}}{\longrightarrow}$. □

Proof (of Proposition 3). We prove item (1); items (2) and (3) are similar. By Theorem 3 it is sufficient to prove that $f : \rho \dashv\mid \sigma$ implies $f : \rho \dashv\mid \tau$ for every ρ, under the hypothesis $\sigma \sqsubseteq \tau$. Consider a derivation $\rho \parallel_f \tau \Longrightarrow \rho' \parallel_{f'} \tau' \not\longrightarrow$. Then there exist $\alpha_1,\dots,\alpha_n$ such that $\rho \stackrel{\overline{\alpha}_1\cdots\overline{\alpha}_n}{\Longrightarrow} \rho' \not\longrightarrow$ and $f \xmapsto{\langle\alpha_1,\overline{\alpha}_1\rangle\cdots\langle\alpha_n,\overline{\alpha}_n\rangle} f'$ and $\tau \stackrel{\alpha_1\cdots\alpha_n}{\Longrightarrow} \tau' \not\longrightarrow$. Furthermore, from $\rho' \parallel_{f'} \tau' \not\longrightarrow$ we deduce $\overline{\mathsf{init}(\rho')} \cap \mathsf{init}(f'(\tau')) = \emptyset$. From $\sigma \sqsubseteq \tau$ we derive that there exists σ' such that $\sigma \stackrel{\alpha_1\cdots\alpha_n}{\Longrightarrow} \sigma' \not\longrightarrow$ and $\mathsf{init}(\sigma') \subseteq \mathsf{init}(\tau')$. By zipping the derivations starting from ρ, f, and σ we obtain $\rho \parallel_f \sigma \Longrightarrow \rho' \parallel_{f'} \sigma'$. Furthermore, $\overline{\mathsf{init}(\rho')} \cap \mathsf{init}(f'(\sigma')) \subseteq \overline{\mathsf{init}(\rho')} \cap \mathsf{init}(f'(\tau')) = \emptyset$, hence $\rho' \parallel_{f'} \sigma' \not\longrightarrow$. From $f : \rho \dashv\mid \sigma$ we conclude $\rho' \stackrel{\mathsf{e}}{\longrightarrow}$. □

Proof (of Theorem 4). First we show that $\preceq$ is a coinductive weak subcontract relation. Let $f : \sigma \preceq \tau$ and assume, without loss of generality, that f is relevant for $\sigma \preceq \tau$. It is sufficient to prove that

$$\mathscr{W} \stackrel{\text{def}}{=} \{(\sigma(\alpha_1\cdots\alpha_n), \tau(\alpha_1\cdots\alpha_n)) \mid f \xmapsto{\langle\alpha_1,\overline{\alpha}_1\rangle\cdots\langle\alpha_n,\overline{\alpha}_n\rangle}\}$$

is a coinductive weak subcontract relation. Let $(\sigma',\tau') \in \mathscr{W}$. Then there exist $\alpha_1,\dots,\alpha_n$ and $\alpha_1,\dots,\alpha_n$ and f' such that $f \xmapsto{\langle\alpha_1,\overline{\alpha}_1\rangle\cdots\langle\alpha_n,\overline{\alpha}_n\rangle} f'$, $\sigma' = \sigma(\alpha_1\cdots\alpha_n)$, and $\tau' = \tau(\alpha_1\cdots\alpha_n)$. Let $\mathrm{A} \stackrel{\text{def}}{=} \mathsf{init}(f')$. As regards condition (1) of Definition 15, let $\mathrm{R}_1,\dots,\mathrm{R}_m$ be the ready sets of σ'. Assume by contradiction that there exists S such that $\tau' \Downarrow \mathrm{S}$ and $\mathrm{R}_i \not\subseteq \mathrm{A} \circ \mathrm{S}$ for every $1 \leq i \leq m$. Then there exists $\alpha_i \in \mathrm{R}_i \setminus \mathrm{A} \circ \mathrm{S}$ for every $1 \leq i \leq m$. Let $\rho \stackrel{\text{def}}{=} \sum_{1\leq i\leq m} \overline{\alpha}_i.\mathsf{e}$. We have $\rho \dashv \sigma'$ but $f' : \rho \not\dashv\mid \tau'$, which is absurd. As regards condition (2) of Definition 15, assume $\tau' \stackrel{\alpha}{\Longrightarrow}$ and $\langle\alpha,\overline{\alpha}\rangle \in \mathrm{A}$. Since f is relevant for $\sigma \preceq \tau$ we have $\sigma' \stackrel{\alpha}{\Longrightarrow}$. We conclude $(\sigma'(\alpha), \tau'(\alpha)) \in \mathscr{W}$ by definition of $\mathscr{W}$.

Now we prove that $\preceq$ is the largest coinductive weak subcontract, by showing that every coinductive weak subcontract is included in it. Let $\mathscr{W}$ be a coinductive weak subcontract relation such that $(\sigma,\tau) \in \mathscr{W}$ and assume $\rho \dashv \sigma$. Let $\mathrm{A}(\sigma',\tau')$ stand for the set A of orchestration actions satisfying conditions (1) and (2) of Definition 15 whenever $(\sigma',\tau') \in \mathscr{W}$. Let

$$f(\sigma',\tau') \stackrel{\text{def}}{=} \bigvee_{\langle\alpha,\overline{\alpha}\rangle \in \mathrm{A}(\sigma',\tau')} \langle\alpha,\overline{\alpha}\rangle.f(\sigma'(\alpha),\tau'(\alpha)) \tag{4}$$

and let $f \stackrel{\text{def}}{=} f(\sigma,\tau)$. We prove $f : \rho \dashv\mid \tau$. Consider a derivation $\rho \parallel_f \tau \Longrightarrow \rho' \parallel_{f'} \tau' \not\longrightarrow$. By "unzipping" this derivation we obtain that there exist $\alpha_1,\dots,\alpha_n$ such that $\rho \stackrel{\overline{\alpha}_1\cdots\overline{\alpha}_n}{\Longrightarrow} \rho' \not\longrightarrow$ and $f \xmapsto{\langle\alpha_1,\overline{\alpha}_1\rangle\cdots\langle\alpha_n,\overline{\alpha}_n\rangle} f'$ and $\tau \stackrel{\alpha_1\cdots\alpha_n}{\Longrightarrow} \tau' \not\longrightarrow$. By condition (2) of Definition 15 and by induction on n we derive that $\sigma \stackrel{\alpha_1\cdots\alpha_n}{\Longrightarrow}$ and $(\sigma(\alpha_1\cdots\alpha_n), \tau(\alpha_1\cdots\alpha_n)) \in \mathscr{W}$. Observe that $\tau(\alpha_1\cdots\alpha_n) \Downarrow \mathsf{init}(\tau')$. By condition (1) of Definition 15 we have that there exists R such that $\sigma(\alpha_1\cdots\alpha_n) \Downarrow \mathrm{R}$ and $\mathrm{R} \subseteq \mathsf{init}(f') \circ \mathsf{init}(\tau')$, hence there exists σ' such that $\sigma \stackrel{\alpha_1\cdots\alpha_n}{\Longrightarrow} \sigma' \not\longrightarrow$ and $\mathsf{init}(\sigma') \subseteq \mathsf{init}(f') \circ \mathsf{init}(\tau')$. By "zipping" the derivations starting from ρ and σ we obtain $\rho \parallel \sigma \Longrightarrow \rho' \parallel \sigma'$. Furthermore $\rho' \parallel \sigma' \not\longrightarrow$ because $\mathsf{init}(\sigma') \subseteq \mathsf{init}(f') \circ \mathsf{init}(\tau')$. From $\rho \dashv \sigma$ we conclude $\rho' \stackrel{\mathsf{e}}{\longrightarrow}$. □

Proof (of Theorem 5). Let $\mathscr{W} \stackrel{\text{def}}{=} \{(\sigma,\tau) \mid \exists f : f : \sigma \leq \tau\}$. We prove that $\mathscr{W}$ is a coinductive weak subcontract relation by showing that $f : \sigma \leq \tau$ implies

1. $\tau \Downarrow \mathrm{S}$ implies $\sigma \Downarrow \mathrm{R}$ and $\mathrm{R} \subseteq \mathsf{init}(f) \circ \mathrm{S}$, and
2. $\tau \stackrel{\alpha}{\Longrightarrow}$ and $\langle \alpha, \overline{\alpha} \rangle \in \mathsf{init}(f)$ implies $\sigma \stackrel{\alpha}{\Longrightarrow}$ and $f' : \sigma(\alpha) \leq \tau(\alpha)$ where $f \stackrel{\langle \alpha, \overline{\alpha} \rangle}{\longmapsto} f'$.

We proceed by induction on the maximum depth of an axiom or of an unnested instance of rule (PREFIX) in the derivation tree of $f : \sigma \leq \tau$ and by cases on the last rule applied.

Assume the last rule was (PREFIX). Then $f = \langle \alpha, \overline{\alpha} \rangle . f'$, $\sigma \equiv \alpha.\sigma'$, $\tau \equiv \alpha.\tau'$, and $f' : \sigma' \leq \tau'$ is derivable (we use $\equiv$ to denote syntactic equality up to associativity and commutativity of $\oplus$). Suppose $\tau \Downarrow \mathrm{S}$. Then $\mathrm{S} = \{\alpha\}$ and we notice that $\sigma \Downarrow \{\alpha\}$ and $\mathsf{init}(f) \circ \mathrm{S} = \{\alpha\}$. We also notice that $\tau \stackrel{\alpha}{\Longrightarrow}$ and $\langle \alpha, \overline{\alpha} \rangle \in \mathsf{init}(f)$ and $\sigma \stackrel{\alpha}{\Longrightarrow}$ and that this is the only possible transition for σ and τ. We conclude by observing that $\sigma(\alpha) \equiv \sigma'$ and $\tau(\alpha) \equiv \tau'$ and that $f' : \sigma' \leq \tau'$ is derivable by hypothesis.

Assume the last rule was (RED). Then $\sigma \equiv \sigma' \oplus \tau$ and $f = I(\tau)$. Suppose $\tau \Downarrow \mathrm{S}$. Then $\mathsf{init}(f) \circ \mathrm{S} = \mathrm{S}$ and $\sigma \Downarrow \mathrm{S}$. Suppose $\tau \stackrel{\alpha}{\Longrightarrow}$ and $\langle \alpha, \overline{\alpha} \rangle \in \mathsf{init}(f)$. We distinguish two subcases: if $\sigma' \stackrel{\alpha}{\Longrightarrow}$, then $\sigma(\alpha) \equiv \sigma'(\alpha) \oplus \tau(\alpha)$ and we conclude $f' : \sigma'(\alpha) \oplus \tau(\alpha) \leq \tau(\alpha)$ by (RED) since $f' = I(\tau(\alpha))$. If $\sigma' \stackrel{\alpha}{\not\Longrightarrow}$, then $\sigma(\alpha) \equiv \tau(\alpha)$, hence we conclude by reflexivity of $\leq$ (indeed $\sigma = \sigma \oplus \sigma$ and $I(\sigma) : \sigma \oplus \sigma \leq \sigma$).

Assume the last rule was (DEPTH). Then $\sigma \equiv 0$ and $f = 0$. The condition on ready sets of τ trivially holds because $\sigma \Downarrow \emptyset$ and there is nothing left to prove since $\mathsf{init}(f) = \emptyset$.

Assume the last rule was (WEAK). Then $f = f_1 \vee f_2$, $f_1 : \sigma \leq \tau$, and $f_2 \wedge I(\tau) \leqslant f_1$. Suppose $\tau \Downarrow \mathrm{S}$. By induction hypothesis we have $\sigma \Downarrow \mathrm{R}$ where $\mathrm{R} \subseteq \mathsf{init}(f_1) \circ \mathrm{S}$. We conclude $\mathrm{R} \subseteq \mathsf{init}(f) \circ \mathrm{S}$ by observing that $\mathsf{init}(f_1) \subseteq \mathsf{init}(f)$. Suppose $\tau \stackrel{\alpha}{\Longrightarrow}$ and $\langle \alpha, \overline{\alpha} \rangle \in \mathsf{init}(f)$. Then $\langle \alpha, \overline{\alpha} \rangle \in \mathsf{init}(f \wedge I(\tau)) = \mathsf{init}((f_1 \vee f_2) \wedge I(\tau)) = \mathsf{init}((f_1 \wedge I(\tau)) \vee (f_2 \wedge I(\tau))) \subseteq \mathsf{init}(f_1)$ since $f_2 \wedge I(\tau) \leqslant f_1$. By induction hypothesis we have $\sigma \stackrel{\alpha}{\Longrightarrow}$ and $f_1' : \sigma(\alpha) \leq \tau(\alpha)$ where $f_1 \stackrel{\langle \alpha, \overline{\alpha} \rangle}{\longmapsto} f_1'$. We distinguish two subcases. If $f_2 \stackrel{\langle \alpha, \overline{\alpha} \rangle}{\longmapsto}$, then $f' = f_1' \vee f_2'$ where $f_2 \stackrel{\langle \alpha, \overline{\alpha} \rangle}{\longmapsto} f_2'$. From $f_2 \wedge I(\tau) \leqslant f_1$ we deduce $f_2' \wedge I(\tau(\alpha)) \leqslant f_1'$, hence we conclude $f_1' \vee f_2' : \sigma(\alpha) \leq \tau(\alpha)$ by rule (WEAK). If $f_2 \stackrel{\langle \alpha, \overline{\alpha} \rangle}{\not\longmapsto}$, then $f' = f_1'$ and there is nothing left to prove.

Assume the last rule was (TRANS). Then $f = f_1 \wedge f_2$, $f_1 : \sigma \leq \sigma'$, $f_2 : \sigma' \leq \tau$ for some σ'. Suppose $\tau \Downarrow \mathrm{S}$. By induction hypothesis $\sigma' \Downarrow \mathrm{R}'$ for some $\mathrm{R}' \subseteq \mathsf{init}(f_2) \circ \mathrm{S}$. Again by induction hypothesis $\sigma \Downarrow \mathrm{R}$ for some $\mathrm{R} \subseteq \mathsf{init}(f_1) \circ \mathrm{R}' \subseteq \mathsf{init}(f_1) \circ \mathsf{init}(f_2) \circ \mathrm{S} = \mathsf{init}(f) \circ \mathrm{S}$. Suppose $\tau \stackrel{\alpha}{\Longrightarrow}$ and $\langle \alpha, \overline{\alpha} \rangle \in \mathsf{init}(f)$. Then $\langle \alpha, \overline{\alpha} \rangle \in \mathsf{init}(f_1) \cap \mathsf{init}(f_2)$. By induction hypothesis $\sigma' \stackrel{\alpha}{\Longrightarrow}$ and $f_2' : \sigma'(\alpha) \leq \tau(\alpha)$ where $f_2 \stackrel{\langle \alpha, \overline{\alpha} \rangle}{\longmapsto} f_2'$. Again by induction hypothesis $f_1' : \sigma(\alpha) \leq \sigma'(\alpha)$. By (TRANS) we have that $f_1' \wedge f_2' : \sigma(\alpha) \leq \tau(\alpha)$ is derivable and we conclude by observing that $f' = f_1' \wedge f_2'$.

Assume the last rule was (INT). Then $\sigma \equiv \sigma_1 \oplus \sigma_2$, $\tau \equiv \tau_1 \oplus \tau_2$, $f : \sigma_1 \leq \tau_1$, and $f : \sigma_1 \leq \tau_2$. Suppose $\tau \Downarrow \mathrm{S}$. Then $\tau_i \Downarrow \mathrm{S}$ for some $i \in \{1,2\}$. By induction hypothesis we deduce $\sigma_i \Downarrow \mathrm{R}$ for some $\mathrm{R} \subseteq \mathsf{init}(f) \circ \mathrm{S}$ and we conclude by observing that $\sigma \Downarrow \mathrm{R}$. Suppose $\tau \stackrel{\alpha}{\Longrightarrow}$ and $\langle \alpha, \overline{\alpha} \rangle \in \mathsf{init}(f)$. We distinguish three interesting subcases, depending on which contracts admit α-successors. Assume $\tau_1 \stackrel{\alpha}{\Longrightarrow}$ and $\tau_2 \stackrel{\alpha}{\Longrightarrow}$. By induction hypothesis we deduce $\sigma_1 \stackrel{\alpha}{\Longrightarrow}$ and $\sigma_2 \stackrel{\alpha}{\Longrightarrow}$ and $f' : \sigma_i(\alpha) \leq \tau_i(\alpha)$ for every $i \in \{1,2\}$. By rule (INT) we deduce $f' : \sigma_1(\alpha) \oplus \sigma_2(\alpha) \leq \tau_1(\alpha) \oplus \tau_2(\alpha)$ and we conclude $f' : \sigma(\alpha) \leq \tau(\alpha)$ by observing that $\sigma(\alpha) \equiv \sigma_1(\alpha) \oplus \sigma_2(\alpha)$ and $\tau(\alpha) \equiv \tau_1(\alpha) \oplus \tau_2(\alpha)$.

Assume $\tau_1 \overset{\alpha}{\Longrightarrow}$ and $\sigma_2 \overset{\alpha}{\not\Longrightarrow}$. Then $\tau_2 \overset{\alpha}{\not\Longrightarrow}$. By induction hypothesis we deduce $\sigma_1 \overset{\alpha}{\Longrightarrow}$ and $f' : \sigma_1(\alpha) \leq \tau_1(\alpha)$. We conclude by observing that $\sigma(\alpha) \equiv \sigma_1(\alpha)$ and $\tau(\alpha) \equiv \tau_1(\alpha)$. Assume $\tau_1 \overset{\alpha}{\Longrightarrow}$ and $\tau_2 \overset{\alpha}{\not\Longrightarrow}$ and $\sigma_2 \overset{\alpha}{\Longrightarrow}$. By induction hypothesis we deduce $\sigma_1 \overset{\alpha}{\Longrightarrow}$ and $f' : \sigma_1(\alpha) \leq \tau_1(\alpha)$. By rule (RED) we have $I(\sigma_1(\alpha)) : \sigma_1(\alpha) \oplus \sigma_2(\alpha) \leq \sigma_1(\alpha)$. From $f' \wedge I(\sigma_1(\alpha)) \leq I(\sigma_1(\alpha))$ and by rule (WEAK) we obtain $I(\sigma_1(\alpha)) \vee f' : \sigma_1(\alpha) \oplus \sigma_2(\alpha) \leq \sigma_1(\alpha)$. By rule (TRANS) we deduce $f' : \sigma_1(\alpha) \oplus \sigma_2(\alpha) \leq \tau_1(\alpha)$. We conclude by observing that $\sigma(\alpha) \equiv \sigma_1(\alpha) \oplus \sigma_2(\alpha)$ and $\tau(\alpha) \equiv \tau_1(\alpha) \oplus \tau_2(\alpha)$.

Assume the last rule was (EXT). Then we can proceed as for the previous case, the only thing that changes being the reasoning on ready sets. The details are left to the reader. □

Proof (of Lemma 1). In the rewritings that follow we indicate only the most relevant laws that are applied. As regards (S1):

$$\begin{aligned} \sigma \oplus \tau &= (\sigma \oplus \tau) + (\sigma \oplus \tau) && (1) \\ &= \sigma \oplus \tau \oplus (\sigma + \tau) && (2) \end{aligned}$$

where (1) is justified by (E1) and (2) is justified by (D1).

As regards (S2):

$$\begin{aligned} \sigma \oplus (\sigma + \tau + \rho) &= \sigma + (\sigma \oplus \tau) + (\sigma \oplus \rho) && (1) \\ &= \sigma + (\sigma \oplus (\sigma + \tau) \oplus (\sigma + \rho) \oplus (\tau + \rho)) && (2) \\ &= \sigma \oplus (\sigma + \tau) \oplus (\sigma + \rho) \oplus (\sigma + \tau + \rho) && (3) \\ &= \sigma \oplus (\sigma + \tau) \oplus (\sigma + \tau) \oplus (\sigma + \rho) \oplus (\sigma + \tau + \rho) && (4) \\ &= \sigma \oplus (\sigma + \tau) \oplus (\sigma + \tau + \rho) && (5) \end{aligned}$$

where (1) is justified by (D2), (2) is justified by (D1), (3) is justified by (D2), (4) is justified by (I1) and finally (5) is justified by rewriting the subterm of step (3) with the original one.

As regards (CO):

$$\begin{aligned} &(\alpha.\sigma + \tau) \oplus (\alpha.\sigma' + \tau') \\ &\quad = (\alpha.\sigma + \tau) \oplus (\alpha.\sigma' + \tau') \oplus (\alpha.\sigma + \alpha.\sigma' + \tau + \tau') && (1) \\ &\quad = (\alpha.\sigma + \tau) \oplus (\alpha.\sigma' + \tau') \oplus (\alpha.\sigma + \alpha.\sigma' + \tau + \tau') \\ &\qquad \oplus (\alpha.\sigma + \alpha.\sigma' + \tau) \oplus (\alpha.\sigma + \alpha.\sigma' + \tau') && (2) \\ &\quad = (\alpha.\sigma + \tau) \oplus (\alpha.\sigma' + \tau') \oplus (\alpha.\sigma + \alpha.\sigma' + \tau + \tau') \\ &\qquad \oplus (\alpha.(\sigma \oplus \sigma') + \tau) \oplus (\alpha.(\sigma \oplus \sigma') + \tau') && (3) \\ &\quad = (\alpha.\sigma + \tau) \oplus (\alpha.\sigma' + \tau') \oplus (\alpha.(\sigma \oplus \sigma') + \tau) \oplus (\alpha.(\sigma \oplus \sigma') + \tau') && (4) \\ &\quad = ((\alpha.\sigma \oplus \alpha.(\sigma \oplus \sigma')) + \tau) \oplus ((\alpha.\sigma' \oplus \alpha.(\sigma \oplus \sigma')) + \tau') && (5) \\ &\quad = (\alpha.(\sigma \oplus \sigma') + \tau) \oplus (\alpha.(\sigma \oplus \sigma') + \tau') && (6) \end{aligned}$$

where (1) is justified by (S1), (2) is justified by (S2), (3) is justified by (D3), (4) is justified by (S1), (5) is justified by (D1), and (6) is justified by (D4) and (I1).

Proving (E-PREFIX) is trivial. As regards (E-EXT), observe that from $I(\sigma') : \sigma \leq \sigma'$ and $I(\tau') \wedge I(\sigma') \leqslant I(\sigma')$ we derive $I(\sigma') \vee I(\tau') : \sigma \leq \sigma'$ by an application of (WEAK). Similarly we can derive $I(\sigma') \vee I(\tau') : \tau \leq \tau'$, hence we can apply (EXT) and derive $I(\sigma') \vee I(\tau') : \sigma + \tau \leq \sigma' + \tau'$. By a similar argument we can also derive $I(\sigma) \vee I(\tau) : \sigma' + \tau' \leq \sigma + \tau$, hence $\sigma + \tau = \sigma' + \tau'$. Rule (E-INT) is analogous.

As regards (WIDTH), from the axiom $0 : 0 \leq \tau$ and the hypothesis $I(\sigma) \wedge I(\tau) \leqslant 0$ we derive $I(\sigma) : 0 \leq \tau$. From $I(\sigma) : \sigma \leq \sigma$ and applying (EXT) we conclude $I(\sigma) : \sigma + 0 \leq \sigma + \tau$, hence $I(\sigma) : \sigma \leq \sigma + \tau$. □

Proof (of Lemma 2). We define the *head normal form* of σ as

$$\mathsf{hnf}(\sigma) \stackrel{\text{def}}{=} \bigoplus_{\mathtt{R} \in \mathscr{R}(\sigma)} \sum_{\alpha \in \mathtt{R}} \alpha.\sigma(\alpha)$$

It is sufficient to prove that $\sigma = \mathsf{hnf}(\sigma)$ is derivable. The statement of the Lemma then follows by a simple induction on the maximum number of nested prefixes in σ. We prove $\sigma = \mathsf{hnf}(\sigma)$ by induction on the maximum depth of a topmost prefix in σ and by cases on the structure of σ. If $\sigma \equiv 0$, then σ is already in head normal form.

If $\sigma \equiv \alpha.\sigma'$, then σ is already in head normal form because $\sigma(\alpha)$ is σ'.

If $\sigma \equiv \sigma_1 + \sigma_2$, then

$$\begin{aligned}
\sigma &= (\textstyle\bigoplus_{\mathtt{R}_1 \in \mathscr{R}(\sigma_1)} \sum_{\alpha \in \mathtt{R}_1} \alpha.\sigma_1(\alpha)) + (\bigoplus_{\mathtt{R}_2 \in \mathscr{R}(\sigma_2)} \sum_{\beta \in \mathtt{R}_2} \beta.\sigma_2(\beta)) && (1)\\
&= \textstyle\bigoplus_{\mathtt{R}_1 \in \mathscr{R}(\sigma_1), \mathtt{R}_2 \in \mathscr{R}(\sigma_2)} (\sum_{\alpha \in \mathtt{R}_1} \alpha.\sigma_1(\alpha) + \sum_{\beta \in \mathtt{R}_2} \beta.\sigma_2(\beta)) && (2)\\
&= \textstyle\bigoplus_{\mathtt{R}_1 \in \mathscr{R}(\sigma_1), \mathtt{R}_2 \in \mathscr{R}(\sigma_2)} \sum_{\alpha \in \mathtt{R}_1 \cup \mathtt{R}_2} \alpha.\sigma(\alpha) && (3)\\
&= \textstyle\bigoplus_{\mathtt{R} \in \mathscr{R}(\sigma)} \sum_{\alpha \in \mathtt{R}} \alpha.\sigma(\alpha) && (4)
\end{aligned}$$

where (1) is justified by the induction hypothesis and congruence rules, (2) is justified by the repeated use of (D1), (3) is justified by (CO), and (4) follows from $\mathscr{R}(\sigma) = \{\mathtt{R}_1 \cup \mathtt{R}_2 \mid \mathtt{R}_1 \in \mathscr{R}(\sigma_1), \mathtt{R}_2 \in \mathscr{R}(\sigma_2)\}$. Indeed, if $\mathtt{R} \in \mathscr{R}(\sigma)$, then there exist $\mathtt{R}_1'$ and $\mathtt{R}_2'$ such that $\sigma_1 \Downarrow \mathtt{R}_1'$ and $\sigma_2 \Downarrow \mathtt{R}_2'$ and $\mathtt{R}_1' \cup \mathtt{R}_2' \subseteq \mathtt{R}$. Now $\mathtt{R}_1' \subseteq \mathtt{R} \cap \mathsf{init}(\sigma_1) \subseteq \mathsf{init}(\sigma_1)$ and $\mathtt{R}_2' \subseteq \mathtt{R} \cap \mathsf{init}(\sigma_2) \subseteq \mathsf{init}(\sigma_2)$, hence $\mathtt{R} \cap \mathsf{init}(\sigma_1) \in \mathscr{R}(\sigma_1)$ and $\mathtt{R} \cap \mathsf{init}(\sigma_2) \in \mathscr{R}(\sigma_2)$. We conclude by observing that $(\mathtt{R} \cap \mathsf{init}(\sigma_1)) \cup (\mathtt{R} \cap \mathsf{init}(\sigma_2)) = \mathtt{R}$ because $\mathtt{R} \subseteq \mathsf{init}(\sigma_1) \cup \mathsf{init}(\sigma_2)$. On the other hand, let $\mathtt{R}_1 \in \mathscr{R}(\sigma_1)$ and $\mathtt{R}_2 \in \mathscr{R}(\sigma_2)$. Then there exist ready sets $\mathtt{R}_1'$ and $\mathtt{R}_2'$ of respectively σ_1 and σ_2 such that $\mathtt{R}_1' \subseteq \mathtt{R}_1 \subseteq \mathsf{init}(\sigma_1)$ and $\mathtt{R}_2' \subseteq \mathtt{R}_2 \subseteq \mathsf{init}(\sigma_2)$. Hence $\mathtt{R}_1' \cup \mathtt{R}_2' \subseteq \mathtt{R}_1 \cup \mathtt{R}_2 \subseteq \mathsf{init}(\sigma_1) \cup \mathsf{init}(\sigma_2)$ and we conclude $\mathtt{R}_1 \cup \mathtt{R}_2 \in \mathscr{R}(\sigma)$ by observing that $\sigma \Downarrow \mathtt{R}_1' \cup \mathtt{R}_2'$ and $\mathsf{init}(\sigma) = \mathsf{init}(\sigma_1) \cup \mathsf{init}(\sigma_2)$.

Finally, if $\sigma \equiv \sigma_1 \oplus \sigma_2$, then

$$\begin{aligned}
\sigma &= (\textstyle\bigoplus_{\mathtt{R}_1 \in \mathscr{R}(\sigma_1)} \sum_{\alpha \in \mathtt{R}_1} \alpha.\sigma_1(\alpha)) \oplus (\bigoplus_{\mathtt{R}_2 \in \mathscr{R}(\sigma_2)} \sum_{\beta \in \mathtt{R}_2} \beta.\sigma_2(\beta)) && (1)\\
&= (\textstyle\bigoplus_{\mathtt{R}_1 \in \mathscr{R}(\sigma_1)} \sum_{\alpha \in \mathtt{R}_1} \alpha.\sigma(\alpha)) \oplus (\bigoplus_{\mathtt{R}_2 \in \mathscr{R}(\sigma_2)} \sum_{\beta \in \mathtt{R}_2} \beta.\sigma(\beta)) && (2)\\
&= \textstyle\bigoplus_{\mathtt{R} \in \mathscr{R}(\sigma)} \sum_{\alpha \in \mathtt{R}} \alpha.\sigma(\alpha) && (3)
\end{aligned}$$

where (1) is justified by the induction hypothesis and congruence rules, (2) is justified by (CO), and (3) is justified by the repeated use of (S1) and (S2). □

Proof (of Theorem 6). By Lemma 2 we can assume that σ and τ are in normal form. We reason by induction on the depth of σ and τ.

If $\tau \equiv 0$, then σ must have an empty ready set hence by (MUST) we have $0 : \sigma \leq 0$ and we conclude $f : \sigma \leq \tau$ by (WEAK) because $f \wedge I(0) \leqslant 0$.

For the remaining cases, assume

$$\sigma \equiv \textstyle\bigoplus_{\mathtt{R} \in \mathscr{R}(\sigma)} \sum_{\alpha \in \mathtt{R}} \alpha.\sigma_\alpha \qquad \text{and} \qquad \tau \equiv \bigoplus_{\mathtt{S} \in \mathscr{R}(\tau)} \sum_{\alpha \in \mathtt{S}} \alpha.\tau_\alpha$$

and assume $\tau \stackrel{\alpha}{\Longrightarrow}$ and $f \stackrel{\langle\alpha,\overline{\alpha}\rangle}{\longmapsto}$. From $f : \sigma \preceq \tau$ we deduce $\sigma \stackrel{\alpha}{\Longrightarrow}$ and by induction hypothesis we derive

$$f' : \sigma_\alpha \leq \tau_\alpha$$

where $f \stackrel{\langle\alpha,\overline{\alpha}\rangle}{\longmapsto} f'$. Then, by (PREFIX),

$$\langle\alpha,\overline{\alpha}\rangle.f' : \alpha.\sigma_\alpha \leq \alpha.\tau_\alpha\,.$$

Now assume $\tau \Downarrow \mathrm{R}$. From $f : \sigma \preceq \tau$ and the fact that σ and τ are in head normal form we have $\sigma \Downarrow \mathsf{init}(f) \circ \mathrm{R}$. Let $f_{\mathrm{R}} \stackrel{\text{def}}{=} \bigvee_{f \stackrel{\langle\alpha,\overline{\alpha}\rangle}{\longmapsto} f'', \alpha\in\mathrm{R}} \langle\alpha,\overline{\alpha}\rangle.f''$ and notice that $f_{\mathrm{R}} \wedge \langle\alpha,\overline{\alpha}\rangle.I(\tau_\alpha) \leqslant \langle\alpha,\overline{\alpha}\rangle.f'$. Hence, by (WEAK),

$$f_{\mathrm{R}} : \alpha.\sigma_\alpha \leq \alpha.\tau_\alpha$$

and, by (EXT),

$$f_{\mathrm{R}} : \sum_{\alpha\in\mathrm{R}, f \stackrel{\langle\alpha,\overline{\alpha}\rangle}{\longmapsto}} \alpha.\sigma_\alpha \leq \sum_{\alpha\in\mathrm{R}, f \stackrel{\langle\alpha,\overline{\alpha}\rangle}{\longmapsto}} \alpha.\tau_\alpha\,.$$

From $\mathsf{init}(f) \circ \mathrm{R} \subseteq \mathrm{R}$ and by applying (WIDTH),

$$f_{\mathrm{R}} : \sum_{\alpha\in\mathrm{R}, f \stackrel{\langle\alpha,\overline{\alpha}\rangle}{\longmapsto}} \alpha.\sigma_\alpha \leq \sum_{\alpha\in\mathrm{R}} \alpha.\tau_\alpha\,.$$

Let $f' \stackrel{\text{def}}{=} \bigvee_{\tau\Downarrow\mathrm{R}'} f_{\mathrm{R}'}$. From $(\bigcup_{\tau\Downarrow\mathrm{R}'} \mathsf{init}(f) \circ \mathrm{R}') \cap \mathrm{R} = (\mathsf{init}(f) \circ \bigcup_{\tau\Downarrow\mathrm{R}'} \mathrm{R}') \cap \mathrm{R} \subseteq \mathsf{init}(f) \circ \mathrm{R}$ we observe that $f' \wedge \bigvee_{\alpha\in\mathrm{R}} \langle\alpha,\overline{\alpha}\rangle.I(\tau_\alpha) \leqslant f_{\mathrm{R}}$. Hence, by (WEAK), by iterating over all the ready sets of τ, and by (INT), we obtain

$$f' : \bigoplus_{\tau\Downarrow\mathrm{R}} \sum_{\alpha\in\mathrm{R}, f \stackrel{\langle\alpha,\overline{\alpha}\rangle}{\longmapsto}} \alpha.\sigma_\alpha \leq \tau\,.$$

Now

$$f' : \sigma \leq \bigoplus_{\tau\Downarrow\mathrm{R}} \sum_{\alpha\in\mathrm{R}, f \stackrel{\alpha}{\longmapsto}} \alpha.\sigma_\alpha$$

by possibly applying (RED) for removing all the ready sets of σ that are not in $\{\mathsf{init}(f) \circ \mathrm{S} \mid \tau \Downarrow \mathrm{S}\}$ hence, by (TRANS), we conclude $f' : \sigma \leq \tau$. In order to prove $f : \sigma \leq \tau$ it is sufficient to apply (WEAK). This is possible because $f \wedge I(\tau) \leqslant f'$. Indeed, assume $\tau \stackrel{\alpha}{\Longrightarrow}$ and $\langle\alpha,\overline{\alpha}\rangle \in \mathsf{init}(f)$. Then $\alpha \in \mathrm{R}$ for some $\tau \Downarrow \mathrm{R}$, hence $\sigma \Downarrow \mathsf{init}(f) \circ \mathrm{R}$ and now $\alpha \in \mathsf{init}(f) \circ \mathrm{R}$. So, it must be $f_{\mathrm{R}} \stackrel{\langle\alpha,\overline{\alpha}\rangle}{\longmapsto}$ from which we conclude $f' \stackrel{\langle\alpha,\overline{\alpha}\rangle}{\longmapsto}$. □

A.3 Proofs of §4

Proof (of Proposition 7). We say that a subterm $\overline{\alpha}.\rho'$ of ρ is useless if $\rho \stackrel{\overline{\varphi}}{\Longrightarrow}\stackrel{\overline{\alpha}}{\longrightarrow} \rho'$ and $\sigma \stackrel{\varphi}{\Longrightarrow}$ implies $\sigma(\varphi) \stackrel{\alpha}{\not\Longrightarrow}$. Let ρ_r be the (client) contract obtained from ρ by replacing every useless subterm $\overline{\alpha}.\rho'$ with $\overline{\alpha}.0$. Clearly $\rho_r \dashv \sigma$ since no synchronization will ever occur on those $\overline{\alpha}$ actions that guard useless subterms of ρ. From the hypothesis $\sigma \preceq_k \tau$ there exists a k-orchestrator g such that $g : \rho_r \dashv\!\mid \tau$. Let

$$R(g,\sigma,\tau) \stackrel{\text{def}}{=} \bigvee_{g \stackrel{\langle\varphi,\overline{\varphi}'\rangle}{\longmapsto} g', \sigma \stackrel{\varphi}{\Longrightarrow}, \tau \stackrel{\varphi'}{\Longrightarrow}} \langle\varphi,\overline{\varphi}'\rangle.R(g',\sigma(\varphi),\tau(\varphi'))$$

and let $g_r \stackrel{\text{def}}{=} R(g,\sigma,\tau)$. Observe that g_r is relevant for $\sigma \preceq_k \tau$ by its own definition and $g_r : \rho_r \dashv\!\vdash \tau$ because every derivation starting from $\rho_r \parallel_{g_r} \tau$ is also a possible derivation starting from $\rho_r \parallel_g \tau$. We prove that $g_r : \rho \dashv\!\vdash \tau$. Consider a derivation $\rho \parallel_{g_r} \tau \Longrightarrow \rho' \parallel_{g_r'} \tau' \not\longrightarrow$. Then there exist $\varphi_1,\dots,\varphi_n$ and $\varphi_1',\dots,\varphi_n'$ such that $\rho \stackrel{\overline{\varphi}_1\cdots\overline{\varphi}_n}{\Longrightarrow} \rho' \not\longrightarrow$ and $g_r \xmapsto{\langle\varphi_1,\overline{\varphi}_1'\rangle\cdots\langle\varphi_n,\overline{\varphi}_n'\rangle} g_r'$ and $\tau \stackrel{\varphi_1'\cdots\varphi_n'}{\Longrightarrow} \tau' \not\longrightarrow$. None of the φ_i can be an α guarding a useless subterm of ρ, by construction of g_r. By definition of ρ_r, there exists ρ_r' such that $\rho_r \stackrel{\overline{\varphi}_1\cdots\overline{\varphi}_n}{\Longrightarrow} \rho_r'$ and $\mathsf{init}(\rho_r') = \mathsf{init}(\rho')$ (in fact it is possible to find a ρ_r' that is the same as ρ' except that useless subterms $\overline{\alpha}.\rho''$ have been replaced by $\overline{\alpha}.0$). By zipping the derivations starting from ρ_r, g_r, and τ we obtain $\rho_r \parallel_{g_r} \tau \Longrightarrow \rho_r' \parallel_{g_r'} \tau'$ and we notice that $\rho_r' \parallel_{g_r'} \tau' \not\longrightarrow$ since $\mathsf{init}(\rho_r') = \mathsf{init}(\rho')$. From $g_r : \rho_r \dashv\!\vdash \tau$ we deduce $\rho_r' \stackrel{\mathsf{e}}{\longrightarrow}$, hence we conclude $\rho' \stackrel{\mathsf{e}}{\longrightarrow}$. □

Proof (of Proposition 8). The "if" part is trivial. As regards the "only if" part, we use the same intuition as for the synchronous case, by considering the most demanding client $\sigma^\top$ that is satisfied by σ. Let f be a k-orchestrator such that $f : \sigma^\top \dashv\!\vdash \tau$ and assume, without loss of generality, that f is relevant for $\sigma \preceq_k \tau$. We prove that $f : \sigma \preceq_k \tau$ by contradiction. Assume that there exists ρ such that $\rho \dashv \sigma$ and $f : \rho \not\dashv\!\vdash \tau$. Then there exists a derivation $\rho \parallel_f \tau \Longrightarrow \rho' \parallel_{f'} \tau' \not\longrightarrow$ such that $\rho' \stackrel{\mathsf{e}}{\not\longrightarrow}$. Consequently there exist $\varphi_1,\dots,\varphi_n$ and $\varphi_1',\dots,\varphi_n'$ such that $\rho \stackrel{\overline{\varphi}_1\cdots\overline{\varphi}_n}{\Longrightarrow} \rho' \not\longrightarrow$ and $\tau \stackrel{\varphi_1'\cdots\varphi_n'}{\Longrightarrow} \tau' \not\longrightarrow$ and $f \xmapsto{\langle\varphi_1,\overline{\varphi}_1'\rangle\cdots\langle\varphi_n,\overline{\varphi}_n'\rangle} f'$. Since f is relevant, it is easy to deduce, by induction on n, that $\sigma \stackrel{\varphi_1\cdots\varphi_n}{\Longrightarrow}$. From $\rho' \parallel_{f'} \tau' \not\longrightarrow$ we deduce that $\rho' \stackrel{\overline{\alpha}}{\longrightarrow}$ implies $f' \stackrel{\langle\alpha,\varepsilon\rangle}{\not\longmapsto}$ and $f' \stackrel{\langle\alpha,\overline{\alpha}\rangle}{\longmapsto}$ implies $\tau' \stackrel{\alpha}{\not\longrightarrow}$. Let $\mathrm{R}_1,\dots,\mathrm{R}_m$ be the ready sets of $\sigma(\varphi_1\cdots\varphi_n)$. From $\rho \dashv \sigma$ and $\rho' \stackrel{\mathsf{e}}{\not\longrightarrow}$ we deduce that for every $1 \le i \le n$ there exists $\alpha_i \in \mathrm{R}_i$ and $\rho' \stackrel{\overline{\alpha}_i}{\longrightarrow}$. By definition of most demanding client we have $\sigma(\varphi_1\cdots\varphi_n)^\top \Downarrow \{\overline{\alpha}_1,\dots,\overline{\alpha}_m\}$, because each ready set of $\sigma(\varphi_1\cdots\varphi_n)^\top$ is obtained by taking one action from every non-empty ready set of $\sigma(\varphi_1\cdots\varphi_n)$. Hence there exists ρ'' such that $\sigma^\top \stackrel{\overline{\varphi}_1\cdots\overline{\varphi}_n}{\Longrightarrow} \rho'' \not\longrightarrow$ and $\mathsf{init}(\rho'') = \{\overline{\alpha}_1,\dots,\overline{\alpha}_m\} \subseteq \mathsf{init}(\rho')$. By zipping the derivations starting from $\sigma^\top$, f, and τ we obtain a derivation $\sigma^\top \parallel_f \tau \Longrightarrow \rho'' \parallel_{f'} \tau' \not\longrightarrow$ where $\rho'' \stackrel{\mathsf{e}}{\not\longrightarrow}$. This is absurd, for $f : \sigma^\top \dashv\!\vdash \tau$ by hypothesis. □

Proof (of Theorem 7). ($\Rightarrow$) Assume $f : \rho \dashv\!\vdash_k \sigma$ and consider a derivation $\rho \parallel f(\sigma) \Longrightarrow \rho' \parallel \tau \not\longrightarrow$. Then there exist φ, φ', and f' such that $\rho \stackrel{\overline{\varphi}}{\Longrightarrow} \rho' \not\longrightarrow$ and $f(\sigma) \stackrel{\varphi}{\Longrightarrow} f'(\sigma(\varphi')) \Longrightarrow \tau \not\longrightarrow$. By definition of $f(\sigma)$ there exist $\varphi_1,\dots,\varphi_n$ and $\varphi_1',\dots,\varphi_n'$ such that $\varphi = \varphi_1\cdots\varphi_n$ and $\varphi' = \varphi_1'\cdots\varphi_n'$ and $f \xmapsto{\langle\varphi_1,\overline{\varphi}_1'\rangle\cdots\langle\varphi_n,\overline{\varphi}_n'\rangle} f'$. From $\rho' \parallel \tau \not\longrightarrow$ we deduce $\overline{\mathsf{init}(\rho')} \cap \mathsf{init}(\tau) = \emptyset$. From $f'(\sigma(\varphi')) \Longrightarrow \tau \not\longrightarrow$ and by definition of $f'(\sigma(\varphi'))$ we deduce that there exist $\alpha_1,\dots,\alpha_m$ and σ' and f'' such that $\sigma \stackrel{\varphi'\alpha_1\cdots\alpha_m}{\Longrightarrow} \sigma' \not\longrightarrow$ and $f' \xmapsto{\langle\varepsilon,\overline{\alpha}_1\rangle\cdots\langle\varepsilon,\overline{\alpha}_m\rangle} f''$ and $(\emptyset \bullet \mathsf{init}(f'')) \cap \overline{\mathsf{init}(\sigma')} = \emptyset$ and $\mathsf{init}(f'') \bullet \mathsf{init}(\sigma') \subseteq \mathsf{init}(\tau)$. By zipping the derivations starting from ρ, f, and σ we obtain $\rho \parallel_f \sigma \Longrightarrow \rho' \parallel_{f''} \sigma'$. Furthermore $\rho' \parallel_{f''} \sigma' \not\longrightarrow$ because $\rho' \not\longrightarrow$ and $\sigma' \not\longrightarrow$ and $\overline{\mathsf{init}(\rho')} \cap (\mathsf{init}(f'') \bullet \mathsf{init}(\sigma')) \subseteq \overline{\mathsf{init}(\rho')} \cap \mathsf{init}(\tau) = \emptyset$. From $f : \rho \dashv\!\vdash_k \sigma$ we conclude $\rho' \stackrel{\mathsf{e}}{\longrightarrow}$.

($\Leftarrow$) Assume $\rho \dashv f(\sigma)$ and consider a derivation $\rho \parallel_f \sigma \Longrightarrow \rho' \parallel_{f'} \sigma' \not\longrightarrow$. By "unzipping" this derivation we have that there exist $\varphi_1,\dots,\varphi_n$ and $\varphi'_1,\dots,\varphi'_n$ such that $\rho \xRightarrow{\overline{\varphi}_1\cdots\overline{\varphi}_n} \rho' \not\longrightarrow$ and $f \xmapsto{\langle\varphi_1,\overline{\varphi}'_1\rangle\cdots\langle\varphi_n,\overline{\varphi}'_n\rangle} f'$ and $\sigma \xRightarrow{\varphi'_1\cdots\varphi'_n} \sigma' \not\longrightarrow$. Furthermore from $\rho' \parallel_{f'} \sigma' \not\longrightarrow$ we derive $\overline{\mathsf{init}(\rho')} \cap (\mathsf{init}(f') \bullet \mathsf{init}(\sigma')) = \emptyset$. By definition of $f(\sigma)$ there exists τ such that $f(\sigma) \xRightarrow{\varphi_1\cdots\varphi_n} \tau \not\longrightarrow$ and $\mathsf{init}(\tau) = \mathsf{init}(f') \bullet \mathsf{init}(\sigma')$. By zipping the derivations starting from ρ and $f(\sigma)$ we obtain $\rho \parallel f(\sigma) \Longrightarrow \rho' \parallel \tau$. Furthermore $\rho' \parallel \tau \not\longrightarrow$ because $\rho' \not\longrightarrow$, $\tau \not\longrightarrow$, and $\overline{\mathsf{init}(\rho')} \cap \mathsf{init}(\tau) = \overline{\mathsf{init}(\rho')} \cap (\mathsf{init}(f') \bullet \mathsf{init}(\sigma')) = \emptyset$. From $\rho \dashv f(\sigma)$ we conclude $\rho' \xrightarrow{\mathsf{e}}$. □

Proof (of Proposition 9). We prove item (1); items (2) and (3) are similar. By Theorem 7 it is sufficient to prove that $f : \rho \dashv\!\vert\, \sigma$ implies $f : \rho \dashv\!\vert\, \tau$ for every ρ, under the hypothesis $\sigma \sqsubseteq \tau$. Consider a derivation $\rho \parallel_f \tau \Longrightarrow \rho' \parallel_{f'} \tau' \not\longrightarrow$. Then there exist $\varphi_1,\dots,\varphi_n$ and $\varphi'_1,\dots,\varphi'_n$ such that $\rho \xRightarrow{\overline{\varphi}_1\cdots\overline{\varphi}_n} \rho' \not\longrightarrow$ and $f \xmapsto{\langle\varphi_1,\overline{\varphi}'_1\rangle\cdots\langle\varphi_n,\overline{\varphi}'_n\rangle} f'$ and $\tau \xRightarrow{\varphi'_1\cdots\varphi'_n} \tau' \not\longrightarrow$. Furthermore, from $\rho' \parallel_{f'} \tau' \not\longrightarrow$ we deduce $\overline{\mathsf{init}(\rho')} \cap (\mathsf{init}(f') \bullet \mathsf{init}(\tau')) = \emptyset$. From $\sigma \sqsubseteq \tau$ we derive that there exists σ' such that $\sigma \xRightarrow{\varphi'_1\cdots\varphi'_n} \sigma' \not\longrightarrow$ and $\mathsf{init}(\sigma') \subseteq \mathsf{init}(\tau')$. By zipping the derivations starting from ρ, f, and σ we obtain $\rho \parallel_f \sigma \Longrightarrow \rho' \parallel_{f'} \sigma'$. Furthermore, $\overline{\mathsf{init}(\rho')} \cap (\mathsf{init}(f') \bullet \mathsf{init}(\sigma')) \subseteq \overline{\mathsf{init}(\rho')} \cap (\mathsf{init}(f') \bullet \mathsf{init}(\tau')) = \emptyset$, hence $\rho' \parallel_{f'} \sigma' \not\longrightarrow$. From $f : \rho \dashv\!\vert\, \sigma$ we conclude $\rho' \xrightarrow{\mathsf{e}}$. □

The proof that $f \cdot g$ is the orchestrator we are looking for needs the following technical result, which tells us about the "unzipping" of compound orchestrators.

Lemma 3. *$f \cdot g \xmapsto{\langle\psi_1,\overline{\psi}'_1\rangle\cdots\langle\psi_m,\overline{\psi}'_m\rangle} h$ implies that there exist $\varphi_1,\dots,\varphi_n$ and $\varphi'_1,\dots,\varphi'_n$ and $\varphi''_1,\dots,\varphi''_n$ such that $f \xmapsto{\langle\varphi_1,\overline{\varphi}'_1\rangle\cdots\langle\varphi_n,\overline{\varphi}'_n\rangle} f'$ and $g \xmapsto{\langle\varphi'_1,\overline{\varphi}''_1\rangle\cdots\langle\varphi'_n,\overline{\varphi}''_n\rangle} g'$ and $\psi_1\cdots\psi_m = \varphi_1\cdots\varphi_n$ and $\psi'_1\cdots\psi'_m = \varphi''_1\cdots\varphi''_n$ and $\mathsf{init}(f' \cdot g') \subseteq \mathsf{init}(h)$.*

Proof. In this proof we adopt the following notation: we write $f \xhookrightarrow{\langle\alpha_1\cdots\alpha_n,\varepsilon\rangle} f'$ if $f \xmapsto{\langle\alpha_1,\varepsilon\rangle\cdots\langle\alpha_n,\varepsilon\rangle} f'$ and $f \xhookrightarrow{\langle\varepsilon,\alpha_1\cdots\alpha_n\rangle} f'$ if $f \xmapsto{\langle\varepsilon,\alpha_1\rangle\cdots\langle\varepsilon,\alpha_n\rangle} f'$. We admit $n = 0$, in which case we have $f \xhookrightarrow{\langle\varepsilon,\varepsilon\rangle} f$. We prove the result for $m = 1$. The general statement follows by a simple induction on m. Assume $f \cdot g \xmapsto{\langle\psi,\overline{\psi}'\rangle} h$. Then

$$h = \bigvee_{\substack{f \xhookrightarrow{\langle\varepsilon,\overline{\varphi}\rangle} f' \\ g \xhookrightarrow{\langle\varphi,\varepsilon\rangle} g'}} \left(\bigvee_{\substack{f' \xmapsto{\langle\psi,\varepsilon\rangle} f'' \\ \psi'=\varepsilon}} f'' \cdot g' \vee \bigvee_{\substack{g' \xmapsto{\langle\varepsilon,\overline{\psi}'\rangle} g'' \\ \psi=\varepsilon}} f' \cdot g'' \vee \bigvee_{\substack{f' \xmapsto{\langle\psi,\overline{\alpha}\rangle} f'' \\ g' \xmapsto{\langle\alpha,\overline{\psi}'\rangle} g''}} f'' \cdot g'' \right)$$

namely h accounts for all the possible continuations of the action $\langle\psi,\overline{\psi}'\rangle$ considering all the possible "synchronizations" occurring within $f \cdot g$. All these synchronizations are captured by iterating over all φ such that $f \xhookrightarrow{\langle\varepsilon,\overline{\varphi}\rangle} f'$ and $g \xhookrightarrow{\langle\varphi,\varepsilon\rangle} g'$. There is a finite number of them because f and g are valid orchestrators of finite rank. We deduce that there exist $\varphi'_1,\dots,\varphi'_n$ such that

$$f \xmapsto{\langle\varepsilon,\overline{\varphi}'_1\rangle\cdots\langle\varepsilon,\overline{\varphi}'_{n-1}\rangle\langle\psi,\overline{\varphi}'_n\rangle} f' \qquad \text{and} \qquad g \xmapsto{\langle\varphi'_1,\varepsilon\rangle\cdots\langle\varphi'_{n-1},\varepsilon\rangle\langle\varphi'_n,\psi'\rangle} g'$$

and we conclude by taking $\varphi_1 = \cdots = \varphi_{n-1} = \varphi''_1 = \cdots = \varphi''_{n-1} = \varepsilon$ and $\varphi_n = \psi$ and $\varphi''_n = \psi'$. The fact that $\mathsf{init}(f' \cdot g') \subseteq \mathsf{init}(h)$ is an immediate consequence of the fact that $f' \cdot g'$ is a summand occurring in h. □

Proof (of Theorem 8). Let $\rho \dashv f(g(\sigma))$. By Theorem 7 it is sufficient to show that $f \cdot g : \rho \dashv\mid \sigma$, so consider a derivation $\rho \parallel_{f\cdot g} \sigma \Longrightarrow \rho' \parallel_h \sigma' \not\longrightarrow$. By unzipping this derivation we deduce that there exist $\psi_1, \dots, \psi_m$ and $\psi'_1, \dots, \psi'_m$ such that $\rho \stackrel{\overline{\psi}_1\cdots\overline{\psi}_m}{\Longrightarrow} \rho' \not\longrightarrow$ and $f \cdot g \xmapsto{\langle\psi_1,\overline{\psi}'_1\rangle\cdots\langle\psi_m,\overline{\psi}'_m\rangle} h$ and $\sigma \stackrel{\psi'_1\cdots\psi'_m}{\Longrightarrow} \sigma' \not\longrightarrow$. From $\rho' \parallel_h \sigma' \not\longrightarrow$ we deduce $\overline{\mathsf{init}(\rho')} \cap (\mathsf{init}(h) \bullet \mathsf{init}(\sigma')) = \emptyset$. By Lemma 3 we derive that there exist $\varphi_1, \dots, \varphi_n$, $\varphi'_1, \dots, \varphi'_n$, and $\varphi''_1, \dots, \varphi''_n$ such that $f \xmapsto{\langle\varphi_1,\overline{\varphi}'_1\rangle\cdots\langle\varphi_n,\overline{\varphi}'_n\rangle} f'$ and $g \xmapsto{\langle\varphi'_1,\overline{\varphi}''_1\rangle\cdots\langle\varphi'_n,\overline{\varphi}''_n\rangle} g'$ and $\psi_1 \cdots \psi_m = \varphi_1 \cdots \varphi_n$ and $\psi'_1 \cdots \psi'_m = \varphi''_1 \cdots \varphi''_n$ and $\mathsf{init}(f' \cdot g') \subseteq \mathsf{init}(h)$. Since f and g are valid orchestrators of finite rank, there exist f'', g'', and φ such that $f' \xhookrightarrow{\langle\varepsilon,\overline{\varphi}\rangle} f''$ and $g' \xhookrightarrow{\langle\varphi,\varepsilon\rangle} g''$ and $f'' \xmapsto{\langle\varepsilon,\overline{\alpha}\rangle}$ implies $g'' \not\xmapsto{\langle\alpha,\varepsilon\rangle}$. Namely f'' and g'' are two residual orchestrators that do not "synchronize" with each other. By definition of orchestrator composition, observe that $\mathsf{init}(f'' \cdot g'') \subseteq \mathsf{init}(f' \cdot g')$ because $f'' \cdot g''$ is a summand within $f' \cdot g'$. By definition of orchestrator application we have $g(\sigma) \stackrel{\varphi'_1\cdots\varphi'_n}{\Longrightarrow} g'(\sigma(\varphi''_1 \cdots \varphi''_n)) \Longrightarrow g'(\sigma') \stackrel{\varphi}{\Longrightarrow} g''(\sigma')$. Furthermore $\emptyset \circ \mathsf{init}(g'') \subseteq \emptyset \circ \mathsf{init}(f'' \cdot g'') \subseteq \emptyset \circ \mathsf{init}(f' \cdot g') \subseteq \emptyset \circ \mathsf{init}(h)$ hence $(\emptyset \circ \mathsf{init}(g'')) \cap \overline{\mathsf{init}(\sigma')} = \emptyset$ and $g''(\sigma') \not\longrightarrow$ and $\mathsf{init}(g''(\sigma)) = \mathsf{init}(g'') \bullet \mathsf{init}(\sigma')$. By definition of orchestrator application we have $f(g(\sigma)) \stackrel{\varphi_1\cdots\varphi_n}{\Longrightarrow} f'(g(\sigma)(\varphi'_1 \cdots \varphi'_n)) = f'(g'(\sigma(\varphi''_1 \cdots \varphi''_n))) \Longrightarrow f'(g'(\sigma')) \Longrightarrow f''(g''(\sigma'))$. Now we want to show that $(\emptyset \circ \mathsf{init}(f'')) \cap \overline{\mathsf{init}(g''(\sigma'))} = \emptyset$. From $\mathsf{init}(g''(\sigma')) = \mathsf{init}(g'') \bullet \mathsf{init}(\sigma')$ we derive that $(\emptyset \circ \mathsf{init}(f'')) \cap \overline{\mathsf{init}(g''(\sigma'))} \neq \emptyset$ if and only if there exists α such that $f'' \xmapsto{\langle\varepsilon,\overline{\alpha}\rangle}$ and either $g'' \xmapsto{\langle\alpha,\varepsilon\rangle}$ or ($g'' \xmapsto{\langle\alpha,\overline{\alpha}\rangle}$ and $\sigma' \xrightarrow{\alpha}$). However, by the way f'' and g'' have been chosen we have that $f'' \xmapsto{\langle\varepsilon,\overline{\alpha}\rangle}$ implies $g'' \not\xmapsto{\langle\alpha,\varepsilon\rangle}$. Furthermore, if $f'' \xmapsto{\langle\varepsilon,\overline{\alpha}\rangle}$ and $g'' \xmapsto{\langle\alpha,\overline{\alpha}\rangle}$, then $\langle\varepsilon,\overline{\alpha}\rangle \in \mathsf{init}(f'' \cdot g'') \subseteq \mathsf{init}(h)$. Then $\sigma' \not\xrightarrow{\alpha}$ because $\rho' \parallel_h \sigma' \not\longrightarrow$. Hence $(\emptyset \circ \mathsf{init}(f'')) \cap \overline{\mathsf{init}(g''(\sigma'))} = \emptyset$, so $f''(g''(\sigma')) \not\longrightarrow$ and $\mathsf{init}(f''(g''(\sigma'))) = \mathsf{init}(f'') \bullet \mathsf{init}(g''(\sigma')) = \mathsf{init}(f'') \bullet \mathsf{init}(g'') \bullet \mathsf{init}(\sigma') = \mathsf{init}(f'' \cdot g'') \bullet \mathsf{init}(\sigma') \subseteq \mathsf{init}(h) \bullet \mathsf{init}(\sigma')$. By zipping the derivations starting from ρ and $f(g(\sigma))$ we obtain $\rho \parallel f(g(\sigma)) \Longrightarrow \rho' \parallel f''(g''(\sigma')) \not\longrightarrow$, hence we conclude $\rho' \xrightarrow{\mathsf{e}}$. □

Proof (of Theorem 9). We prove that $\preceq_k$ is a coinductive weak k-subcontract relation. Let $f : \sigma \preceq_k \tau$ and assume, without loss of generality, that f is relevant for $\sigma \preceq_k \tau$. It is sufficient to prove that

$$\mathscr{W}_k \stackrel{\text{def}}{=} \{(\tilde{\emptyset}\langle\varphi_1,\overline{\varphi}'_1\rangle \cdots \langle\varphi_n,\overline{\varphi}'_n\rangle, \sigma(\varphi_1 \cdots \varphi_n), \tau(\varphi'_1 \cdots \varphi'_n)) \mid f \xmapsto{\langle\varphi_1,\overline{\varphi}'_1\rangle\cdots\langle\varphi_n,\overline{\varphi}'_n\rangle}\}$$

is a coinductive k-subcontract relation. Let $(\mathbb{B}, \sigma', \tau') \in \mathscr{W}_k$. Then there exist $\varphi_1, \dots, \varphi_n$ and $\varphi'_1, \dots, \varphi'_n$ and f' such that $f \xmapsto{\langle\varphi_1,\overline{\varphi}'_1\rangle\cdots\langle\varphi_n,\overline{\varphi}'_n\rangle} f'$, $\mathbb{B} = \tilde{\emptyset}\langle\varphi_1,\overline{\varphi}'_1\rangle \cdots \langle\varphi_n,\overline{\varphi}'_n\rangle$, $\sigma' = \sigma(\varphi_1 \cdots \varphi_n)$, and $\tau' = \tau(\varphi'_1 \cdots \varphi'_n)$. Since f is a k-orchestrator we have that $\mathbb{B}$ is a k-buffer. Let $\mathrm{A} \stackrel{\text{def}}{=} \mathsf{init}(f')$. As regards condition (1) of Definition 22, let $\mathrm{R}_1, \dots, \mathrm{R}_m$ be the ready sets of σ'. Assume by contradiction that there exists S such that $\tau' \Downarrow \mathrm{S}$ and

$\mathrm{R}_i \not\subseteq \mathrm{A} \circ \mathrm{S}$ for every $1 \le i \le m$ and $(\mathbf{0} \bullet \mathrm{A}) \cap \overline{\mathrm{S}} = \mathbf{0}$. Then there exists $\alpha_i \in \mathrm{R}_i \setminus \mathrm{A} \circ \mathrm{S}$ for every $1 \le i \le m$. Let $\rho \stackrel{\text{def}}{=} \sum_{1 \le i \le m} \overline{\alpha}_i.\mathsf{e}$. We have $\rho \dashv \sigma'$ but $f' : \rho \not\dashv\!\mid \tau'$, which is absurd. As regards condition (2) of Definition 22, assume $\tau' \stackrel{\varphi'}{\Longrightarrow}$ and $\langle \varphi, \overline{\varphi}' \rangle \in \mathrm{A}$. Since f is relevant we have $\sigma' \stackrel{\varphi}{\Longrightarrow}$. We conclude $(\mathbb{B}\langle \varphi, \overline{\varphi}' \rangle, \sigma'(\varphi), \tau'(\varphi')) \in \mathscr{W}_k$ by definition of $\mathscr{W}_k$.

Now we prove that $\preceq_k$ is the largest coinductive weak k-subcontract relation, by showing as usual that every coinductive weak k-subcontract relation is included in it. Let $\mathscr{W}_k$ be a coinductive weak k-subcontract relation such that $(\tilde{\mathbf{0}}, \sigma, \tau) \in \mathscr{W}_k$ and assume $\rho \dashv \sigma$. Let $\mathrm{A}(\mathbb{B}, \sigma', \tau')$ stand for the set A of orchestration actions satisfying conditions (1) and (2) of Definition 22 whenever $(\mathbb{B}, \sigma', \tau') \in \mathscr{W}_k$. Let

$$f(\mathbb{B}, \sigma', \tau') \stackrel{\text{def}}{=} \bigvee_{\langle \varphi, \varphi' \rangle \in \mathrm{A}(\mathbb{B}, \sigma', \tau')} \langle \varphi, \varphi' \rangle . f(\mathbb{B}\langle \varphi, \overline{\varphi}' \rangle, \sigma'(\varphi), \tau'(\varphi'))$$

and let $f \stackrel{\text{def}}{=} f(\tilde{\mathbf{0}}, \sigma, \tau)$. Observe that f is well defined by regularity of σ and τ and that it is a k-orchestrator. We prove $f : \rho \dashv\!\mid \tau$. Consider a derivation $\rho \parallel_f \tau \Longrightarrow \rho' \parallel_{f'} \tau' \not\longrightarrow$. By "unzipping" this derivation we obtain that there exist $\varphi_1, \dots, \varphi_n$ and $\varphi_1', \dots, \varphi_n'$ such that $\rho \stackrel{\overline{\varphi}_1 \cdots \overline{\varphi}_n}{\Longrightarrow} \rho' \not\longrightarrow$ and $f \stackrel{\langle \varphi_1, \overline{\varphi}_1' \rangle \cdots \langle \varphi_n, \overline{\varphi}_n' \rangle}{\longmapsto} f'$ and $\tau \stackrel{\varphi_1' \cdots \varphi_n'}{\Longrightarrow} \tau' \not\longrightarrow$. By condition (2) of Definition 22 and by induction on n we derive that $\sigma \stackrel{\varphi_1 \cdots \varphi_n}{\Longrightarrow}$ and $(\tilde{\mathbf{0}}\langle \varphi_1, \overline{\varphi}_1' \rangle \cdots \langle \varphi_n, \overline{\varphi}_n' \rangle, \sigma(\varphi_1 \cdots \varphi_n), \tau(\varphi_1' \cdots \varphi_n')) \in \mathscr{W}_k$. Observe that $\tau(\varphi_1' \cdots \varphi_n') \Downarrow \mathsf{init}(\tau')$. By condition (1) of Definition 22 we have that either there exists R such that $\sigma(\varphi_1 \cdots \varphi_n) \Downarrow \mathrm{R}$ and $\mathrm{R} \subseteq \mathsf{init}(f') \circ \mathsf{init}(\tau')$ or $(\mathbf{0} \bullet \mathsf{init}(f')) \cap \overline{\mathsf{init}(\tau')} \neq \mathbf{0}$. However from $\rho' \parallel_{f'} \tau' \not\longrightarrow$ we derive $(\mathbf{0} \bullet \mathsf{init}(f')) \cap \overline{\mathsf{init}(\tau')} = \mathbf{0}$, hence there exists σ' such that $\sigma \stackrel{\varphi_1 \cdots \varphi_n}{\Longrightarrow} \sigma'$ and $\mathsf{init}(\sigma') \subseteq \mathsf{init}(f') \circ \mathsf{init}(\tau')$. By "zipping" the derivations starting from ρ and σ we obtain $\rho \parallel \sigma \Longrightarrow \rho' \parallel \sigma'$. Furthermore $\rho' \parallel \sigma' \not\longrightarrow$ because $\mathsf{init}(\sigma') \subseteq \mathsf{init}(f') \circ \mathsf{init}(\tau')$. From $\rho \dashv \sigma$ we conclude $\rho' \stackrel{\mathsf{e}}{\longrightarrow}$. □

A.4 Proofs of §5

Proof (of Proposition 10). First we prove that $\mathsf{viable}(\cdot)$ is a coinductive viability. Let $\mathsf{viable}(\rho)$ and $\rho \Downarrow \mathrm{R}$. Then there exists σ such that $\rho \dashv \sigma$ and ρ' such that $\rho \Longrightarrow \rho' \not\longrightarrow$ and $\mathrm{R} = \mathsf{init}(\rho')$. If $\rho' \stackrel{\mathsf{e}}{\longrightarrow}$ there is nothing to prove, so assume $\rho' \stackrel{\mathsf{e}}{\not\longrightarrow}$ and $\sigma \Longrightarrow \sigma' \not\longrightarrow$. We have $\rho \parallel \sigma \Longrightarrow \rho' \parallel \sigma'$ and from $\rho \dashv \sigma$ we deduce that $\rho' \parallel \sigma' \longrightarrow \rho'' \parallel \sigma''$ for some ρ'' and σ''. Hence there exists α such that $\rho \Longrightarrow \rho' \stackrel{\overline{\alpha}}{\longrightarrow} \rho''$ and $\sigma \Longrightarrow \sigma' \stackrel{\alpha}{\longrightarrow} \sigma''$. It is trivial to see that from $\rho \dashv \sigma$ and $\rho \stackrel{\overline{\alpha}}{\Longrightarrow}$ and $\sigma \stackrel{\alpha}{\longrightarrow}$ we have $\rho(\overline{\alpha}) \dashv \sigma(\alpha)$, hence we conclude $\mathsf{viable}(\rho(\overline{\alpha}))$.

To show that $\mathsf{viable}(\cdot)$ is indeed the largest coinductive viability, we show that any coinductive viability is included in $\mathsf{viable}(\cdot)$. To do this, assume that $\rho \in \mathscr{V}$ for some coinductive viability $\mathscr{V}$. We must be able to find a service $S(\rho)$ such that $\rho \dashv S(\rho)$. We define $S(\rho)$ thus

$$S(\rho) \stackrel{\text{def}}{=} \sum_{\rho \Downarrow \mathrm{R}, \alpha \in \mathrm{R} \setminus \{\mathsf{e}\}, \rho(\alpha) \in \mathscr{V}} \overline{\alpha}.S(\rho(\alpha))$$

and we leave the easy proof that $\rho \dashv S(\rho)$ to the reader. □

Proof (of Theorem 10). As regards item (1), consider a derivation $\rho \parallel \rho^\perp \Longrightarrow \rho' \parallel \sigma \not\longrightarrow$ and assume by contradiction that $\rho' \stackrel{\mathsf{e}}{\not\longrightarrow}$. By unzipping this derivation we obtain that there exists φ such that $\rho \stackrel{\varphi}{\Longrightarrow} \rho' \not\longrightarrow$ and $\rho^\perp \stackrel{\overline{\varphi}}{\Longrightarrow} \sigma \not\longrightarrow$. In particular, by definition of $\rho^\perp$ we can rewrite this latter derivation as $\rho^\perp \stackrel{\overline{\varphi}}{\Longrightarrow} \rho(\varphi)^\perp \Longrightarrow \sigma \not\longrightarrow$. From $\rho' \parallel \sigma \not\longrightarrow$ we deduce $\overline{\mathsf{init}(\rho')} \cap \mathsf{init}(\sigma) = \emptyset$. Let $\mathrm{R}_1, \ldots, \mathrm{R}_n$ be the ready sets of $\rho(\varphi)$ not containing e (there must be at least one since $\rho' \stackrel{\mathsf{e}}{\not\longrightarrow}$). From the fact that ρ is viable and by definition of $\rho^\perp$ we know that every ready set of $\rho(\varphi)^\perp$ contains one co-action from every ready set of $\rho(\varphi)$ that does not contain e and whose continuation is viable. Hence, $\mathsf{init}(\sigma) = \{\overline{\alpha}_1, \ldots, \overline{\alpha}_n\}$ where $\alpha_i \in \mathrm{R}_i$ and $\rho(\varphi\alpha_i)$ is viable. From $\rho(\varphi) \Longrightarrow \rho' \not\longrightarrow$ we deduce that $\mathsf{init}(\rho') = \mathrm{R}_k$ for some $k \in \{1, \ldots, n\}$. Now $\rho' \stackrel{\alpha_k}{\longrightarrow}$ and $\sigma \stackrel{\overline{\alpha}_k}{\longrightarrow}$, which contradicts $\overline{\mathsf{init}(\rho')} \cap \mathsf{init}(\sigma) = \emptyset$.

As regards item (2), it is sufficient to prove that $\mathscr{W} \stackrel{\text{def}}{=} \{(\tilde{\emptyset}, \rho(\overline{\varphi})^\perp, \sigma(\varphi)) \mid \rho \stackrel{\overline{\varphi}}{\Longrightarrow}, \sigma \stackrel{\varphi}{\Longrightarrow}\}$ is a coinductive weak 0-subcontract relation, because $(\tilde{\emptyset}, \rho^\perp, \sigma) \in \mathscr{W}$. Let $(\tilde{\emptyset}, \rho', \sigma') \in \mathscr{W}$. Then there exists φ such that $\rho' = \rho(\overline{\varphi})^\perp$ and $\sigma' = \sigma(\varphi)$. Consider $\mathrm{A} \stackrel{\text{def}}{=} \{\langle \alpha, \overline{\alpha} \rangle \mid \rho' \stackrel{\overline{\alpha}}{\Longrightarrow}\}$ and observe that $\tilde{\emptyset} \vdash_0 \mathrm{A}$. As regards condition (1) in Definition 18, let $\{\mathrm{R}_1, \ldots, \mathrm{R}_n\} = \{\mathrm{R} \mid \rho \Downarrow \mathrm{R}, \mathsf{e} \notin \mathrm{R}\}$ be the ready sets of $\rho(\overline{\varphi})$ not containing e. From the hypothesis $\rho \dashv \sigma$ we derive $\rho(\overline{\varphi}) \dashv \sigma(\varphi)$, hence $\overline{\mathrm{R}_i} \cap \mathrm{S} \neq \emptyset$ for every $1 \leq i \leq n$. Namely, for every $1 \leq i \leq n$ there exists $\overline{\alpha}_i \in \overline{\mathrm{R}_i} \cap \mathrm{S}$. By definition of dual contract we have $\rho(\overline{\varphi})^\perp \Downarrow \{\overline{\alpha}_1, \ldots, \overline{\alpha}_n\}$. We conclude $\{\overline{\alpha}_1, \ldots, \overline{\alpha}_n\} \subseteq \mathrm{A} \circ \mathrm{S}$. As regards condition (2), assume $\sigma(\varphi) \stackrel{\alpha}{\Longrightarrow}$ and $\langle \alpha, \overline{\alpha} \rangle \in \mathrm{A}$. Then $\sigma \stackrel{\varphi\alpha}{\Longrightarrow}$ and $\rho(\overline{\varphi})^\perp \stackrel{\alpha}{\Longrightarrow}$ hence $\rho \stackrel{\overline{\varphi\alpha}}{\Longrightarrow}$. By definition of $\mathscr{W}$ we conclude that $(\tilde{\emptyset}, \rho(\overline{\varphi})^\perp(\alpha), \sigma(\varphi)(\alpha)) \in \mathscr{W}$ because $\rho(\overline{\varphi})^\perp(\alpha) = \rho(\overline{\varphi\alpha})^\perp$ and $\sigma(\varphi)(\alpha) = \sigma(\varphi\alpha)$. □

A.5 Proofs of §7

Proof (Proof of Theorem 11). Item (1) is trivial for finite contracts. The extension of the algorithm to infinite contracts is done in a standard way using a memoziation context. The details can be found in the full version of [27].

As regards item (2), by a simple structural induction it is easy to establish that, given a derivation for $\mathbb{B} \vdash_k f : \sigma \trianglelefteq \tau$ where $\mathbb{B}$ is a k-buffer, every buffer $\mathbb{B}'$ in every judgment occurring in the derivation is also a k-buffer. It is sufficient to show that $\mathscr{W} \stackrel{\text{def}}{=} \{(\mathbb{B}, \sigma, \tau) \mid \mathbb{B} \vdash_k f : \sigma \trianglelefteq \tau\}$ is a coinductive weak k-subcontract relation. Let $(\mathbb{B}, \sigma, \tau) \in \mathscr{W}$. Then $\mathbb{B} \vdash_k f : \sigma \trianglelefteq \tau$ is derivable. Let $\mathrm{A} \stackrel{\text{def}}{=} \mathsf{init}(f)$ and observe that $\mathbb{B} \vdash_k \mathrm{A}$. As regards condition (1) in Definition 11, there is nothing to prove because it exactly coincides with the third premise in rule (A1). As regards condition (2), assume $\tau \stackrel{\varphi'}{\Longrightarrow}$ and $\langle \varphi, \overline{\varphi}' \rangle \in \mathrm{A}$. From the first premise of rule (A1) we derive $\sigma \stackrel{\varphi}{\Longrightarrow}$. From the second premise we know that $\mathbb{B}\langle \varphi, \overline{\varphi}' \rangle \vdash_k f_{\langle \varphi, \overline{\varphi}' \rangle} : \sigma(\varphi) \trianglelefteq \tau(\varphi')$ is derivable. We conclude $(\mathbb{B}\langle \varphi, \overline{\varphi}' \rangle, \sigma(\varphi), \tau(\varphi')) \in \mathscr{W}$ by definition of $\mathscr{W}$.

As regards item (3), from $g : \sigma \preceq \tau$ we derive that

$$\mathscr{W}_k \stackrel{\text{def}}{=} \{(\tilde{\emptyset}\langle \varphi_1, \overline{\varphi}_1' \rangle \cdots \langle \varphi_n, \overline{\varphi}_n' \rangle, \sigma(\varphi_1 \cdots \varphi_n), \tau(\varphi_1' \cdots \varphi_n')) \mid g \xmapsto{\langle \varphi_1, \overline{\varphi}_1' \rangle \cdots \langle \varphi_n, \overline{\varphi}_n' \rangle}\}$$

is a weak k-subcontract relation. Note that since g is relevant, we have that $g \xmapsto{\langle\varphi_1,\overline{\varphi}'_1\rangle\cdots\langle\varphi_n,\overline{\varphi}'_n\rangle}$ implies $\sigma \stackrel{\varphi_1\cdots\varphi_n}{\Longrightarrow}$ and $\tau \stackrel{\varphi'_1\cdots\varphi'_n}{\Longrightarrow}$. We prove that, if $(\mathbb{B},\sigma,\tau) \in \mathscr{W}_k$, then $\mathbb{B} \vdash_k f : \sigma \trianglelefteq \tau$ is derivable by induction on the depth of σ and τ.

The base case is when both σ and τ have null depth. In this case, $\mathrm{A}_r = \mathrm{A} = \emptyset$ and the premises of the algorithm are trivially satisfied, since both σ and τ have just the empty ready set. In the inductive case, from $(\mathbb{B},\sigma',\tau') \in \mathscr{W}_k$ and by definition of $\mathscr{W}_k$ we deduce that there exist $\varphi_1,\ldots,\varphi_n$, $\varphi'_1,\ldots,\varphi'_n$ such that $g \xmapsto{\langle\varphi_1,\overline{\varphi}'_1\rangle\cdots\langle\varphi_n,\overline{\varphi}'_n\rangle} g'$ and $\mathbb{B} = \tilde{\emptyset}\langle\varphi_1,\overline{\varphi}'_1\rangle\cdots\langle\varphi_n,\overline{\varphi}'_n\rangle$ and $\sigma' = \sigma(\varphi_1\cdots\varphi_n)$ and $\tau' = \tau(\varphi'_1\cdots\varphi'_n)$. Since g is relevant for $\sigma \preceq \tau$ and has rank k, we deduce that $\mathsf{init}(g') \subseteq \mathrm{A}_r$ in the first premise of the algorithm. Let $\langle\varphi,\overline{\varphi}'\rangle \in \mathsf{init}(g')$. By definition of coinductive weak k-subcontract relation and from the fact that g is relevant we know that $(\mathbb{B}\langle\varphi,\overline{\varphi}'\rangle,\sigma'(\varphi),\tau'(\varphi')) \in \mathscr{W}_k$. Since $\varphi\varphi' \neq \varepsilon$, by induction hypothesis we obtain that there exists $f_{\langle\varphi,\overline{\varphi}'\rangle}$ such that $\mathbb{B}\langle\varphi,\overline{\varphi}'\rangle \vdash_k f_{\langle\varphi,\overline{\varphi}'\rangle} : \sigma'(\varphi) \trianglelefteq \tau'(\varphi')$. Hence $\mathsf{init}(g') \subseteq \mathrm{A}$ in the second premise of the algorithm. Since g proves $\sigma \preceq \tau$, we have that $\mathsf{init}(g')$ satisfies condition (1) of Definition 15, which coincides with the third premise of the algorithm. From $\mathsf{init}(g') \subseteq \mathrm{A}$ we deduce that A also satisfies the third premise of the algorithm. Hence we can apply the rule and conclude $\mathbb{B} \vdash_k \bigvee_{\mu\in\mathrm{A}} f_\mu : \sigma' \trianglelefteq \tau'$. The fact that the algorithm computes the best relevant orchestrator proving $\sigma \preceq \tau$ is an immediate consequence of $\mathsf{init}(g') \subseteq \mathrm{A}$, as shown earlier. □

Contract-Based Discovery and Composition of Web Services*

Mario Bravetti and Gianluigi Zavattaro

Department of Computer Science, University of Bologna, Italy

Abstract. In the context of Service Oriented Computing behavioural contracts are descriptions of the observable message-passing behaviour of services. In other terms, contracts are behavioural interfaces that can be used, for instance, to check whether a group of services can be safely combined avoiding, e.g., undesired deadlocks. In this paper we consider the problem of discovering available services that can be used to implement a given service system. The idea is to first design a service system by describing the overall behaviour of each of its participant, and then instantiate such participants retrieving services exposing a behavioural contract which is conformant with the corresponding given behaviour.

1 Introduction

Service Oriented Computing (SOC) is a paradigm for distributed computing based on services intended as autonomous and heterogeneous components that can be published and discovered via standard interface languages and publish/discovery protocols. Web Services are the most prominent service oriented technology: Web Services publish their interface expressed in WSDL, they are discovered through the UDDI protocol, and they are invoked using SOAP.

Even if one of the declared goal of Web Services is to support the automatic discovery of services, this is not yet practically achieved. Two main problems are still to be satisfactorily solved. The first one, investigated by the semantic web research community, is concerned with the lack of semantic information in the description of services. The second problem, addressed in this paper, is concerned with the problem of guaranteeing that the interacting services are compliant in the sense that their behaviours are complementary. In particular, it is important to check whether in a set of services, combined in order to collaborate, no service deadlocks waiting indefinitely for a message that never arrives.

In order to be able to check the compliance of the composed services, it is necessary that the services expose in their interface also the description of their expected behaviour. In the service oriented computing literature, this kind of information is referred to as the behavioural *service contract* [15]. More precisely, the service contract describes the sequence of input/output operations that the service intends to execute within a session of interaction with other services.

* Research partially funded by EU Integrated Project Sensoria, contract n. 016004.

M. Bernardo, L. Padovani, and G. Zavattaro (Eds.): SFM 2009, LNCS 5569, pp. 261–295, 2009.

Compliance checking based on the behavioural descriptions of the composed entities has been already considered, for instance, in the context of component-based systems (see e.g. [9,2,23]) or for client-service interaction [14]. In this paper, we consider a different scenario with respect to both approaches.

As far as component-based systems are concerned, the commonly adopted approach is to synthesize either *wrappers* or *adaptors* that respectively block (the non compatible) part of the behaviour of one component or deal with possible mismatchings between the combined components. The approach adopted in this paper is different because we address the problem of composition without the introduction of any additional wrapper or adaptor. In other terms, we consider the problem of retrieving some already available services in order to implement a correct composition without the introduction of any additional element. In the service oriented computing literature, the approach we consider is known with the name of *choreography* [27], which contrasts with the *orchestrated* approach [25] according to which all services communicate only with a central orchestrator. It is worth mentioning the fact that we could define our theory having in mind components instead of services. Nevertheless, our assumption about the choreographic approach makes all our theory more related to the current vision of service oriented computing.

As far as client-service interaction is concerned, we assume a more general context in which an arbitrary number of interacting services communicate directly without the presence of any central coordinator. We call this different context *multi-party* composition. Moving from a simpler client-service to a more complex multi-party scenario introduces several interesting new problems such as independent refinement. By independent refinement we mean the possibility to replace several services in a composition with other services that are selected one independently from the other ones.

More precisely, the aim of this paper is to exploit the notion of behavioural service contracts in order to define a theory that, on the one hand, permits to formally verify whether they are compliant (thus giving rise to a correct composition) and, on the other hand, permits to replace a service with another one without affecting the correctness of the overall system. In this case we say that the initially expected contract is replaced with one of its *subcontracts*.

We intend to formalize a notion of subcontract to be exploited in the *service discovery* phase. Consider, for instance, a service system defined in terms of the behavioural contracts to be fulfilled by each of the service components. The actual services to be combined could be retrieved independently one from the other (e.g. querying contemporaneously different service registries) collecting services that either expose the expected contract, or one of its subcontracts. Another application that we foresee for our notion of subcontract is for *service updates*, as a mean to ensure backward compatibility. Consider, e.g., a service that should be updated in order to provide new functionalities; if the new version exposes a subcontract of the previous service, our theory ensures that the new service is a correct substitute for the previous one.

1.1 Technical Contribution

The main contribution of this paper is to generalize results that we have presented in [3,7], where we have presented for the first time our approach for the definition of a subcontract relation: we first assume that this relation should be a pre-order, then we formalize the property that we want a "good" subcontract pre-order should preserve, and finally we define our relation as the maximum of such pre-orders (i.e. the union of all pre-orders satisfying the considered property). This is similar to the co-inductive approach considered, e.g., in the definition of the bisimulation relation for CCS [24]. More precisely, in [3,7] we have presented a theory, developed following this approach, considering two specific languages, one for contracts and one for service systems. In this paper we generalize such theory in two ways. On the one hand, we do not consider any specific contract language thus presenting a version of our theory that can be applied to any contract language satisfying a property, called *output persistence*, that we will discuss in the following. On the other hand, we do not make any specific assumption on the way service systems are specified (in [3,7] we defined a subcontract relation assuming a precise form of service system specifications in which the restriction operator is applied directly to contracts and not to parallel compositions of contracts).

More formally, we consider a generic language for behavioural contracts essentially consisting of a process algebraic representation of labeled transition systems defined on internal, input and output actions, and an additional action representing successful completion. Then, we define a language for service system specification that simply allows for the composition of contracts with the parallel and restriction operators. We use this latter language to formalize the notion of compliance: n services/contracts are compliant if their composition is guaranteed to successfully complete without deadlocks or livelocks. After having formalized compliance, we are able to formalize the property that each refinement should satisfy: a refinement is a subcontract pre-order if it preserves service compliance, namely, given n compliant services, and substituting each of them with one of its refinements, the achieved n services are still compliant. Then we define the *subcontract relation* as the union of all subcontract pre-orders. One of the main results proved in this paper is that for the class of behavioural contracts that we consider, the subcontract relation achieved according to this approach is actually the largest subcontract pre-order thus allowing for the independent replacement/retrieval of contracts. In fact, in other theories of contracts recently proposed in the literature (details are reported in the next subsection), independent replacement is not allowed.

This difference with respect to other contract theories relies on the *output persistence* property that we impose on behavioural contracts: a contract is output persistent if once a contract reaches a state in which it can perform an output operation, this operation must be eventually executed from the contract before successful completion. This property is usually satisfied by languages for composing services, such as WS-BPEL [25], in which output operations cannot be guard in external choices. In these languages, once an output action is executable by a process, this output must be executed before the process successfully completes.

Another important technical achievement of [3,7] that we report in this paper is a characterization of the subcontract relation in a testing-like scenario [18]: we can prove that a contract C' is a subcontract of C if, after some appropriate transformations applied to both C' and C, the former is guaranteed to satisfy at least all the tests satisfied by the latter. In particular, we show how to use the theory of *should-testing* [26] to prove that one contract is a subcontract of another one. An important consequence of this characterization is a precise localization of our refinement with respect to traditional refinements such as failure refinement, or simulation (i.e. half-bisimulation): the refinement that we achieve as the largest one preserving compliance is coarser than both failure refinement and simulation.

1.2 Related Work

As stated above, we resort to the theory of testing, in particular, to the must-testing pre-order. There are some significant differences between our form of testing and the traditional one proposed by De Nicola-Hennessy [18]. The most significant difference is that, besides requiring the success of the test, we impose also that the tested process should successfully complete its execution. This further requirement has important consequences; for instance, we do not distinguish between the always unsuccessful process $\mathbf{0}$ and other processes, such as $a.\mathbf{1} + a.b.\mathbf{1}$,[1] for which there are no guarantees of successful completion in any possible context. Another significant difference is in the treatment of divergence: we do not follow the traditional catastrophic approach, but the fair approach introduced by the theory of should-testing of Rensink-Vogler [26]. In fact, we do not impose that all computations must succeed, but that all computations can always be extended in order to reach success.

It is well known that the De Nicola-Hennessy must testing pre-order and the CSP failure refinement [20] coincide (at least for finitely branching processes without divergences [17]). It is interesting to say that the failure refinement has been already exploited for checking component compatibility by Allen and Garlan in [1]. Similarly to our theory, the failure refinement is used to prove that a component can be replaced by one of its refinements in a component composition. Differently from our theory, a composition of several components is obtained adding a *Glue* component which behaves as a mediator for every component interaction. This *Glue* component permits to cut the additional actions that the refined components may include. The main difference with our theory is that, in our context, we have no mediator that allows us to cut additional behaviours of refined services. Nevertheless, the output persistence property that we consider allows us to replace a service with another one having additional behaviour.

Behavioural contracts have been initially introduced in the context of process calculi by Fournet et al. [19]. As far as service oriented computing is concerned,

[1] We use $\mathbf{0}$ to denote unsuccessful termination, $\mathbf{1}$ for successful completion and $\_ + \_$ for choice composition.

an initial theory of contracts for client-service interaction has been proposed by Carpineti et al. [14] and then independently extended along different directions by Bravetti and Zavattaro (see e.g. [3,4,5]) by Laneve and Padovani [22], and by Castagna et al. [16]

In [19] contracts are CCS-like processes; a generic process P is defined as compliant to a contract C if, for every tuple of names $\tilde{a}$ and process Q, whenever $(\nu\tilde{a})(C|Q)$ is stuck-free then also $(\nu\tilde{a})(P|Q)$ is. Our notion of contract refinement differs from stuck-free conformance mainly because we consider a different notion of stuck process state. In [19] a process state is stuck (on a tuple of channel names $\tilde{a}$) if it has no internal moves (but it can execute at least one action on one of the channels in $\tilde{a}$). In our approach, an end-state different from successful termination is stuck (independently of any tuple $\tilde{a}$). Thus, we distinguish between internal deadlock and successful completion while this is not the case in [19]. Another difference follows from the exploitation of the restriction $(\nu\tilde{a})$; this is used in [19] to explicitly indicate the local channels of communication used between the contract C and the process Q. In our context we can make a stronger *closed-world* assumption (corresponding to a restriction on all channel names) because service contracts do not describe the entire behaviour of a service, but the flow of execution of its operations inside one session of communication.

The closed-world assumption is considered also in [14] where, as in our case, a service oriented scenario is considered. In particular, in [14] a theory of contracts is defined for investigating the compatibility between one client and one service. Our paper considers multi-party composition where several services are composed in a peer-to-peer manner. Moreover, we impose service substitutability as a mandatory property for our notion of refinement; this does not hold in [14] where it is not in general possible to substitute a service exposing one contract with another one exposing a subcontract. Another significant difference is that the contracts in [14] comprise also external mixed choices that do not satisfy the output persistence property.

The preliminary versions of this paper [3,7] introduces several interesting new aspects not considered in the initial approach of Carpineti et al. For instance, we consider also contracts with an infinite behaviour admitting the recursive operator in contracts, we consider multi-party compositions, and we present how to resort to the theory of testing pre-orders. Moreover, in another paper [4] we also investigate a new stronger notion of correctness for contract systems in which we assume that output operations cannot wait indefinitely. This problem naturally arises when also unlimited contract behaviours are permitted. For instance, the three contracts

$$\overline{a}.\overline{b} \qquad a.recX.(\overline{c}.d.X) \qquad recX.(c.\overline{d}.X) + b$$

($recX.\_$ denotes the classical recursive definition operator) are typically assumed to be compliant as their composition is stuck-free. Nevertheless, the second output of the first contract can wait indefinitely due to the possible unlimited interaction between the second and the third contract. In [4] we address this problem: we propose a new stronger notion of compliance, called *strong compliance*, and we present a new theory of contracts which is consistent with strong compliance.

In [5] we discuss how contracts can be exploited in a more general theory for choreography conformance. Choreography languages, used to describe from a global point of view the peer-to-peer interactions among services in a composition, have been already investigated in a process algebraic setting by Busi et al. [10,11] and by Carbone et al. [12]. The notion of choreography conformance is in general used to check whether a service can play a specific role within a given choreography. In [5] we present a basic choreography language, and we define conformance between that language and a contract language as follows: we check conformance by projecting a choreography on the considered role, and then exploiting contract refinement.

The work of Carpineti et al. [14] discussed above has been extended by (some of) the original authors in two ways, in [22] by explicitly associating to a contract the considered input/output alphabet, in [16] by associating to services a dynamic filter which eliminates from the service behaviour those interactions that are not admitted by the considered contract.

The explicit information about the input/output alphabet used in [22] allows the corresponding theory of contracts to be applied also to multi-party compositions. Nevertheless, the complete symmetry between inputs and outputs in the contract language considered in [22], does not permit to achieve one of the most interesting property we prove in this paper, that is, independent contract refinement. In fact, according to [22] the contracts in a multi-party composition cannot be independently refined, because if a refinement includes more inputs or outputs with respect to the corresponding contract, these additional names cannot be part of the input/output alphabets of other refinements. As the refinement cannot be applied independently the theory of contracts in [22] does not admit parallel discovery of services in multi-party service systems.

The dynamic filters of [16], on the contrary, allow for independent refinement, at the price of synthesizing a specific filter used to eliminate the additional behaviours of refinements. Even if very interesting from a theoretical point of view, the practical application of filters is not yet clear. In fact, it is not possible to assume the possibility to associate a filter to a remote service. This problem can be solved in client-service systems, assuming that a co-filter is applied to the local client, but it is not clear how to solve this problem in multi-party systems composed of services running on different hosts.

Finally, also the work based on types (e.g. that in [21] and [13]) gives rise to notions of refinement in terms of subtyping. For instance, the work in [21] allows subsystems like $a.(P|b.Q)$ to be replaced by $a.P|b.Q$ under the knowledge that the context is of the kind $\bar{a}.P'|\bar{b}.Q'$, while in the work of [13] a subterm can be replaced by another one where inputs can be syntactically added in external choices and outputs can be syntactically added in internal choices. The latter approach leads to a notion of refinement which is included in the one obtained in this paper. In our approach, however, features like input external choice extension and internal choice reduction are inferred and not taken by syntactical definition. The former approach is incomparable because it deals with very special cases: in fact, following our approach we have that $a|b$ does not refine $a.b$ because the latter is compliant with the pair of contracts $\overline{b}$ and $b.\overline{a}.\overline{b}$, while this is not the case for the former.

1.3 Structure of the Paper

In Section 2 we introduce our notation for behavioural contracts. In Section 3 we introduce the model for the representation of service systems in terms of contract compositions. Section 4 presents our theory for contract refinement. Finally, Section 5 reports some conclusive remarks.

This paper is a generalised version of [7] where we consider a language independent modeling of contracts (here a contract is any output persistent labeled transition system while in [7] a specific contract language is considered) and we do not impose any constraint on the way contracts can be composed (in [7] only service systems with restriction directly applied to contracts are considered).

2 Behavioural Contracts

Contracts are defined as transition systems labeled over internal, input, and output action names. We first define the class of labeled transition systems of interest for this paper.

Definition 1. *A finite connected labeled transition system (LTS) with termination transitions is a tuple* $\mathcal{T} = (S, \mathcal{L}, \longrightarrow, s_h, s_0)$ *where* S *is a finite set of states, L is a set of labels, the transition relation* $\longrightarrow$ *is a finite subset of* $(S - \{s_h\}) \times (\mathcal{L} \cup \{\surd\}) \times S$ *such that* $(s, \surd, s') \in\longrightarrow$ *implies* $s' = s_h$, $s_h \in S$ *represents a halt state,* $s_0 \in S$ *represents the initial state, and it holds that every state in* S *is reachable (according to* $\longrightarrow$*) from* s_0.

In a finite connected LTS with termination transitions we use $\surd$ transitions (leading to the halt state s_h) to represent successful termination. On the contrary, if we get (via a transition different from $\surd$) into a state with no outgoing transitions (like, e.g., s_h) then we represent an internal failure or a deadlock.

We assume a denumerable set of action names $\mathcal{N}$, ranged over by $a, b, c, \ldots$. We use $\tau \notin \mathcal{N}$ to denote an internal (unsynchronizable) computation. In contracts the possible transition labels are the typical internal τ action and the input/output actions $a, \overline{a}$.

Definition 2. *A contract is a finite connected LTS with termination transitions, that is a tuple* $(S, \mathcal{L}, \longrightarrow, s_h, s_0)$*, where* $\mathcal{L} = \{a, \overline{a}, \tau \mid a \in \mathcal{N}\}$*, i.e. labels are either a receive (input) on some operation* $a \in \mathcal{N}$ *or an invoke (output) directed to some operation* $a \in \mathcal{N}$ *at some location* l.

In the following we introduce a process algebraic representation for contracts by using a basic process algebra (a simple extension of basic CCS [24] with successful termination) with prefixes over $\{a, \overline{a}, \tau \mid a \in \mathcal{N}\}$ and we show that from the LTS denoting a contract we can derive a process algebraic term whose behaviour is the same as that of the LTS. In the algebra syntax, we use $\mathbf{0}$ and $\mathbf{1}$ to denote unsuccessful and successful termination, respectively.

Definition 3. *We consider a denumerable set of contract variables Var ranged over by X, Y, ⋯. The syntax of contracts is defined by the following grammar*

$$C ::= \mathbf{0} \mid \mathbf{1} \mid \alpha.C \mid C{+}C \mid X \mid recX.C$$
$$\alpha ::= \tau \mid a \mid \overline{a}$$

*where $recX.\_$ is a binder for the process variable X. The set of the contracts C in which all process variables are bound, i.e. C is a closed term, is denoted by $\mathcal{P}_{con}$. In the following we will often omit trailing "**1**" when writing contracts.*

The structured operational semantics of contracts is defined in terms of a transition system labeled by $\mathcal{L} = \{a, \overline{a}, \tau, \mid a \in \mathcal{N}\}$ obtained by the rules in Table 1 (plus symmetric rule for choice), where we take λ to range over $\mathcal{L} \cup \{\surd\}$. In particular the semantics of a contract $C \in \mathcal{P}_{con}$ gives rise to a finite connected LTS with termination transitions $(S, \mathcal{L}, \longrightarrow, \mathbf{0}, C)$ where S is the set of states reachable from C and $\longrightarrow$ includes only transitions between states of S. Note that the fact that such a LTS is finite (i.e. finite-state and finitely branching) is a well-known fact for basic CCS [24] (and obviously the additional presence of successful termination does not change this fact).

Table 1. Semantic rules for contracts (symmetric rules omitted)

$$\mathbf{1} \xrightarrow{\surd} \mathbf{0} \qquad\qquad \alpha.C \xrightarrow{\alpha} C$$

$$\frac{C \xrightarrow{\lambda} C'}{C{+}D \xrightarrow{\lambda} C'} \qquad\qquad \frac{C\{recX.C/X\} \xrightarrow{\lambda} C'}{recX.C \xrightarrow{\lambda} C'}$$

In Appendix A we formalize the correspondence between contracts and terms of $\mathcal{P}_{con}$ by showing how to obtain from a contract $\mathcal{T} = (S, \mathcal{L}, \longrightarrow, s_h, s_0)$ a corresponding $C \in \mathcal{P}_{con}$ such that there exists a (surjective) homomorphism from the operational semantics of $\mathcal{C}$ to $\mathcal{T}$ itself. In the light of this correspondence result, we can safely consider the introduced process algebra to develop general theories for behavioural contracts.

In the remainder of the paper we use the following notations: $C \xrightarrow{\lambda}$ to mean that there exists C' such that $C \xrightarrow{\lambda} C'$ and, given a string of labels $w \in \mathcal{L}^*$, that is $w = \lambda_1\lambda_2 \cdots \lambda_{n-1}\lambda_n$ (possibly empty, i.e., $w = \varepsilon$), we use $C \xrightarrow{w} C'$ to denote the sequence of transitions $C \xrightarrow{\lambda_1} C_1 \xrightarrow{\lambda_2} \cdots \xrightarrow{\lambda_{n-1}} C_{n-1} \xrightarrow{\lambda_n} C'$ (in case of $w = \varepsilon$ we have $C' = C$, i.e., $C \xrightarrow{\varepsilon} C$).

2.1 Output Persistence

We now introduce a property for behavioural contracts that we call *output persistence*. We first present the formal definition.

Definition 4 (Output persistence). *Let $C \in \mathcal{P}_{con}$ be a contract. It is output persistent if given $C \xrightarrow{w} C'$ with $C' \xrightarrow{\overline{a}}$ then: $C' \stackrel{\surd}{\not\longrightarrow}$ and if $C' \xrightarrow{\alpha} C''$ with $\alpha \neq \overline{a}$ then also $C'' \xrightarrow{\overline{a}}$.*

The output persistence property states that once a contract decides to execute an output, its actual execution is mandatory in order to successfully complete the execution of the contract. This property typically hold in languages for the description of service behaviours or for service orchestrations (see e.g. WS-BPEL) in which output actions cannot be used as guards in external choices (see e.g. the `pick` operator of WS-BPEL which is an external choice guarded on input actions). In these languages, when a process instance or an internal thread decides to execute an output actions, it will have to complete such action before successful completion.

In the context of process algebra with parallel composition a syntactical characterization that guarantees output persistence can be found in [3]. The idea is to require that every output prefix (i.e. the term $\overline{a}.P$) is preceded by an internal τ prefix (i.e. the above term always occurs in the larger term $\tau.\overline{a}.P$).

As we also anticipated in the introduction, the actual impact of output persistence (in turn coming from the asymmetric treatment of inputs and outputs) in our theory is the existence of maximal independent refinement. This statement will be made precise by means of a counter-example that we are going to present after the Definition 9 –we postpone the presentation of this example because we first need to formalize contract compositions as well as the notion of correct composition– and by the results presented in Section 4.

We now formalize a direct consequence of output persistence that we will use in the following.

Proposition 1. *Let $C \in \mathcal{P}_{con}$ be an output persistent contract such that $C \xrightarrow{w} C' \xrightarrow{\overline{a}}$. If $C' \xrightarrow{w'} C''$ and $C'' \xrightarrow{\surd}$ then the string w' must include $\overline{a}$.*

Proof. We proceed by contradiction assuming that the premise in the statement of the Proposition holds even for a sequence of actions w' that does not include $\xrightarrow{\overline{a}}$. As $C' \xrightarrow{\overline{a}}$, due to output persistence, if w' does not include $\overline{a}$ then also $C'' \xrightarrow{\overline{a}}$. Output persistence then guarantees that $C'' \stackrel{\surd}{\not\longrightarrow}$, thus contradicting the premise $C'' \xrightarrow{\surd}$. □

In the remainder of the paper we restrict to output persistent contracts, namely, $\mathcal{P}_{con}$ denotes the set of output persistent contracts from now on. Note that, it is meaningful to do this because: any derivative of an output persistent contract is again an output persistent contract (as it can be immediately inferred from Definition 4) and homomorphism preserves output persistence (two homomorphic contracts are either both output persistent or no one is).

3 Service Systems

We now introduce the calculus for modeling systems of composed contracts. This is an extension of the previous calculus; the basic terms are contracts under execution denoted with $[C]$. Such a notation is inspired by process algebras with locations in which brackets "[","]" are used to denote a located process.

Besides the parallel composition operator $\|$, we consider also restriction $\setminus\!\!\setminus$ in order to model the possibility to open local channels of interaction among contracts. The restriction operator that we consider is non-standard because it distinguishes between input and output operations. For instance, in the system $[C]\setminus\!\!\setminus\{a,\overline{b}\}$ we have that C cannot perform inputs on a and cannot perform outputs on b. This operator is useful for the modeling of private directed channels. For instance, if we want to model the fact that the service $[C_1]$ is the unique receptor on a particular channel a, we can simply restrict all the other services on action a (and $[C_1]$ on $\overline{a}$):

$$[C_1]\setminus\!\!\setminus\overline{a} \;\|\; [C_2]\setminus\!\!\setminus a \;\|\; [C_3]\setminus\!\!\setminus a \;\|\cdots\|\; [C_n]\setminus\!\!\setminus a$$

As another example, consider a system composed of two contracts C_1 and C_2 such that channel a is used for communications from C_1 to C_2 and channel b is used for communications along the opposite directions. We can model such system as follows:

$$([C_1]\setminus\!\!\setminus\{a,\overline{b}\}) \;\|\; ([C_2]\setminus\!\!\setminus\{\overline{a},b\})$$

As a final example of the flexibility of the restriction operator $\setminus\!\!\setminus$ we consider the system

$$(([C]\|[C'])\setminus\!\!\setminus a) \;\|\; [D]$$

where we have that C, C' and D can execute input actions on the name a, but the inputs of C and C' cannot synchronize with output actions performed by D, while the inputs of D can synchronize with outputs performed by C and C'.

Definition 5 (Contract composition). *The syntax of contract compositions is defined by the following grammar*

$$P \;::=\; [C] \;\mid\; P\|P \;\mid\; P\setminus\!\!\setminus L$$

where $C\in\mathcal{P}_{con}$ *and* $L\subseteq\{a,\overline{a}\mid a\in\mathcal{N}\}$.

We use P, P', $\cdots$, Q, Q', $\cdots$ to range over terms representing contract compositions, also called *systems.* The set of systems is denoted by $\mathcal{P}_{sys}$. Moreover, given a set of action names L we denote with $\overline{L}$ the set of complementary actions: $\overline{L}=\{\overline{a}|a\in L\}\cup\{a|\overline{a}\in L\}$.

In the following we will sometimes omit parenthesis "[ ]" when writing contract compositions.

The operational semantics of systems is defined by the rules in Table 2 (plus the omitted symmetric rules).

Note that given $[C]\setminus\!\!\setminus L$, we obtain a transition system homomorphic to that of the contract $C\{\mathbf{0}/\alpha.D|\alpha\in L\}$ or, equivalently, to that of $[C\{\mathbf{0}/\alpha.D|\alpha\in L\}]$, where $C\{\mathbf{0}/\alpha.D|\alpha\in L\}$ represents the syntactical substitution of $\mathbf{0}$ for every occurrence of any subterm $\alpha.D$ such that $\alpha\in L$. In the light of this equivalence result, we will overload the restriction operator applying it also to contracts:

Table 2. Semantic rules for contract compositions (symmetric rules omitted)

$$\frac{C \xrightarrow{\lambda} C'}{[C] \xrightarrow{\lambda} [C']} \qquad \frac{P \xrightarrow{\lambda} P' \quad \lambda \neq \surd}{P\|Q \xrightarrow{\lambda} P'\|Q}$$

$$\frac{P \xrightarrow{a} P' \quad Q \xrightarrow{\overline{a}} Q'}{P\|Q \xrightarrow{\tau} P'\|Q'} \qquad \frac{P \xrightarrow{\surd} P' \quad Q \xrightarrow{\surd} Q'}{P\|Q \xrightarrow{\surd} P'\|Q'} \qquad \frac{P \xrightarrow{\lambda} P' \quad \lambda \notin L}{P \backslash\!\backslash L \xrightarrow{\lambda} P' \backslash\!\backslash L}$$

$C \backslash\!\backslash L = C\{\mathbf{0}/\alpha.D | \alpha \in L\}$. It is immediate to verify (by just applying definition 4) that, for any set L, the restriction of an output persistent contract is again an output persistent contract.

We are now ready to define our notion of correct composition of contracts. Intuitively, a system composed of contracts is *correct* if all possible computations may guarantee completion; this means that the system is both deadlock and, under the fairness assumption[2], livelock free (there could be an infinite computation, but given any possible prefix of this infinite computation, it can be extended to reach a successfully completed computation). Note that our notion of correctness simply checks the compliance of the composed services without verifying whether the replies computed by the services actually corresponds to some desired functionalities. Henceforth, our notion of correct service composition should not be confused with the classical notion of program correctness.

Definition 6 (Correct contract composition). *A system P is a correct contract composition, denoted $P\downarrow$, if for every P' such that $P \xrightarrow{\tau}{}^{*} P'$ there exists P'' such that $P' \xrightarrow{\tau}{}^{*} P'' \xrightarrow{\surd}$.*

As examples of correct contract compositions, you can consider $C_1 \| C_2$ with

$$\begin{array}{ll}
C_1 = a + b & C_2 = \tau.\overline{a} + \tau.\overline{b} \\
C_1 = a.b & C_2 = \overline{a}.\overline{b} \\
C_1 = a + b + c & C_2 = \tau.\overline{a} + \tau.\overline{b} \\
C_1 = (a.b) + (b.a) & C_2 = \overline{a}.\overline{b} + \overline{b}.\overline{a} \\
C_1 = recX.(a.\overline{b}.(X + \mathbf{1})) & C_2 = recX.(\tau.\overline{a}.b.(X + \mathbf{1}))
\end{array}$$

As an example of contract composition which is not correct we can consider $[\overline{a}.b] \| [a]$ in which the first service deadlocks after executing the first output action (thus successful completion cannot be reached). Another interesting example is $[recX.(\tau.\overline{a}.b.(X + \mathbf{1}))] \| [a.recX(\tau.\overline{b}.a(X + \mathbf{1}))]$, in which only an infinite computation (livelock) is executed (also in this case successful completion cannot be reached). We can also consider an additional example in which we combine both deadlock and livelock: $[recX.(\tau.\overline{a}.b.X + \tau.\overline{c}.d)] \| [recX.(\tau.\overline{b}.a.X + c)]$.

The design choice of requiring livelock freedom under the fairness assumption is related to considering the following aspects.

[2] The notion of fairness that we consider is the following: when a state is traversed infinitely often each of its outgoing transitions is not discarded infinitely often.

– it is unsatisfactory to just require deadlock freedom (accepting too many systems as correct ones as, e.g., the system with livelock discussed above $[recX.(\tau.\overline{a}.b.(X+\mathbf{1}))]\|[a.recX(\tau.\overline{b}.a(X+\mathbf{1}))]$) as often multi-party conversations of services are executed inside sessions and it seems natural to ask for the ability of all the party involved to successfully terminate for the session to finish;
– it is too demanding to require livelock freedom without the fairness assumption (discarding too many systems that intuitively should be correct in the presence of infinite computations as, e.g., the last pair of contracts C_1 C_2 presented in the example above).

4 Service Discovery

In this Section we introduce our theory of contracts. The basic idea is to have a notion of refinement of contracts such that, given a system composed of the contracts $C_1, \cdots, C_n$, we can replace each contract C_i by one of its refinements C'_i without breaking the correctness of the system.

This notion of refinement is useful when considering the problem of service discovery. Given the specification of a contract composition (composed of the so called "initial contracts"), the actual services to be composed are discovered independently sending queries to registries. It could be the case that services with a contract which exactly correspond to the "initial contracts" are not available; in this case, it is fundamental to accept also different contracts that could be replaced without affecting the overall correctness of the system.

One of the peculiarities of our theory of refinement, is that we consider the possibility of relying on some knowledge about the "initial contracts", in particular, the input and output actions that occur in them. A very important consequence of this knowledge, is that we have the guarantee that a contract can be refined by another one that performs additional external input actions on names that do not occur in the initial contracts. For instance, the contract a can be refined by $a+b$ if we know that b is not among the possible outputs of the other initial contracts.

Some additional simple examples of refinement follow. Consider the correct system $C_1\|C_2$ with

$$C_1 = a + b \qquad C_2 = \tau.\overline{a} + \tau.\overline{b}$$

We can replace C_1 with $C'_1 = a + b + c$ or C_2 with $C'_2 = \overline{a}$ without breaking the correctness of the system. This example shows a first important intuition: a contract could be replaced with another one that has more external nondeterminism and/or less internal nondeterminism.

Consider now

$$D_1 = a + b + c \qquad D_2 = \tau.\overline{a} + \tau.\overline{b}$$

where we can refine D_1 with $D'_1 = a + b + d$. Clearly, this refinement does not hold in general because we could have another correct system

$$D_1 = a + b + c \qquad D'_2 = \tau.\overline{a} + \tau.\overline{b} + \tau.\overline{c}$$

where such a refinement does not hold. This second example shows that refinement is influenced by the potential actions that could be executed by the other contracts in the system. Indeed, D_1' is not a correct substitute for D_1 because D_2' has the possibility to produce $\overline{c}$.

Based on this intuition, we parameterize our notion of subcontract relation $C' \leq_{I,O} C$ on the set I of inputs, and the set O of outputs, that could be potentially executed by the other contracts in the system. We will see that $D_1' \leq_{\mathcal{N},\mathcal{N}-\{c,d\}} D_1$ but $D_1' \not\leq_{\mathcal{N},\mathcal{N}} D_1$.

4.1 Subcontract Pre-orders as Correctness Preserving Refinements

We first introduce the notion of context: a context is a system in which some contract is left unspecified and abstractly represented by a contract variable. In this way we can use contexts to represent architectures of systems in which we use contract variables to represent placeholders for contracts.

Definition 7 (Contexts). *Contexts $\mathcal{C}$ are terms over the same syntax as contract compositions P with the addition of the term $[\mathcal{X}]$:*

$$P \ ::= \ [\mathcal{X}] \ | \ [C] \ | \ P\|P \ | \ P\backslash\!\backslash L$$

where $\mathcal{X}$ is a contract variable belonging to a totally ordered set $CVar$, ranged over by $\mathcal{X}, \mathcal{Y}, \ldots$. In the following we assume contexts $\mathcal{C}$ not to include multiple occurrences of the same variable $\mathcal{X}$.

Given a set of terms W_i, with $1 \leq i \leq n$, where either $W_i \in \mathcal{P}_{con}$ (i.e. W_i is a contract) or $W_i \in CVar$ and a context $\mathcal{C}$ such that n is the number of term variables included in $\mathcal{C}$, we use $\mathcal{C}(W_1, \ldots, W_n)$ to stand for $\mathcal{C}\{W_i/\mathcal{X}_i | 1 \leq i \leq n\}$, where $\mathcal{X}_1, \ldots, \mathcal{X}_n$ are the term variables included $\mathcal{C}$ ordered according to the order on the set $CVar$.

As the notion of refinement that we define is parametrized on the sets of input and output actions that can be performed by the other contracts in the system, we need to formally define these sets.

Definition 8 (Input and Output sets). *Given the contract $C \in \mathcal{P}_{con}$, we define $I(C)$ (resp. $O(C)$) as the subset of $\mathcal{N}$ of the potential input (resp. ouput) actions of C. Formally, we define $I(C)$ as follows:*

$$I(\mathbf{0}) = I(\mathbf{1}) = I(X) = \emptyset \qquad I(\tau.C) = I(\overline{a}.C) = I(recX.C) = I(C)$$
$$I(a.C) = \{a\} \cup I(C) \qquad I(C{+}C') = I(C) \cup I(C')$$

and $O(C)$ as follows:

$$O(\mathbf{0}) = O(\mathbf{1}) = O(X) = \emptyset \qquad O(\tau.C) = O(a.C) = O(recX.C) = O(C)$$
$$O(\overline{a}.C) = \{a\} \cup O(C) \qquad O(C{+}C') = O(C) \cup O(C')$$

Given the system P, we define $I(P)$ (resp. $O(P)$) as the subset of $\mathcal{N}$ of the potential input (resp. output) actions of P. Formally, we define $I(P)$ as follows:

$$I([C]) = I(C) \qquad I(P\|P') = I(P) \cup I(P') \qquad I(P\backslash\!\backslash L) = I(P) - \{a \mid a \in L\}$$

and $O(P)$ *as follows:*

$$O([C]) = O(C) \qquad O(P\|P') = O(P) \cup O(P') \qquad O(P\backslash L) = O(P) - \{a \mid \overline{a} \in L\}$$

Given a context $\mathcal{C}$ *containing exactly one contract variable* $\mathcal{X}$*, we define* $I(\mathcal{C})$ *(resp.* $O(\mathcal{C})$*) as the subset of* $\mathcal{N}$ *of the potential input (resp. output) actions of contracts in the context that can possibly synchronize with actions executed by any contract replacing* $\mathcal{X}$ *in the context. Formally, assuming that* $\mathcal{C}$ *contains exactly one variable* $\mathcal{X}$ *we define* $I(\mathcal{C})$ *as follows:*

$$I([\mathcal{X}]) = \emptyset \qquad I(\mathcal{C}\|P) = I(P\|\mathcal{C}) = I(\mathcal{C}) \cup (I(P) - outr(\mathcal{C})) \qquad I(\mathcal{C}\backslash L) = I(\mathcal{C})$$

and

$$O([\mathcal{X}]) = \emptyset \qquad O(\mathcal{C}\|P) = O(P\|\mathcal{C}) = O(\mathcal{C}) \cup (O(P) - inr(\mathcal{C})) \qquad O(\mathcal{C}\backslash L) = O(\mathcal{C})$$

where $inr(\mathcal{C})$ *(resp.* $out(\mathcal{C})$*) are the input (resp. output) actions on which the variable* $\mathcal{X}$ *occurring in* $\mathcal{C}$ *is restricted defined as follows:*

$$\begin{array}{ll} inr([\mathcal{X}]) = \emptyset & inr(\mathcal{C}\|P) = inr(P\|\mathcal{C}) = inr(\mathcal{C}) \\ inr(\mathcal{C}\backslash L) = inr(\mathcal{C}) \cup \{a \mid a \in L\} & \end{array}$$

and

$$\begin{array}{ll} outr([\mathcal{X}]) = \emptyset & outr(\mathcal{C}\|P) = outr(P\|\mathcal{C}) = outr(\mathcal{C}) \\ outr(\mathcal{C}\backslash L) = outr(\mathcal{C}) \cup \{a \mid \overline{a} \in L\} & \end{array}$$

We are now ready to define the notion of subcontract pre-order $C'_i \leq_{I,O} C_i$ in which the substitutability of contract C_i with C'_i is parameterized in the possible input and output actions I and O of the other contracts in the considered system.

More precisely, we consider a correct system $\mathcal{C}(C_1, \ldots, C_n)$, and we require that the system is still correct even if we replace each C_i with any C'_i such that $C'_i \leq_{I(\mathcal{C}'), O(\mathcal{C}')} C_i$ where $\mathcal{C}' = \mathcal{C}(C_1, \ldots, C_{i-1}, \mathcal{X}, C_{i+1}, \ldots, C_n)$.

Definition 9 (Subcontract pre-order family). *A family* $\{\leq_{I,O} \mid I, O \subseteq \mathcal{N}\}$ *of pre-orders over* $\mathcal{P}_{con}$ *is a subcontract pre-order family if, for any context* $\mathcal{C}$ *with n contract variables and including no contracts, contracts* $C_1, \ldots, C_n \in \mathcal{P}_{con}$ *and* $C'_1, \ldots, C'_n \in \mathcal{P}_{con}$*, and* $\mathcal{C}_i = \mathcal{C}(C_1, \ldots, C_{i-1}, \mathcal{X}, C_{i+1}, \ldots, C_n)$*, we have*

$$\begin{array}{l} \mathcal{C}(C_1, \ldots, C_n)\downarrow \;\wedge\; \forall i.\, (C'_i \leq_{I_i, O_i} C_i \;\wedge\; I(\mathcal{C}_i) \subseteq I_i \;\wedge\; O(\mathcal{C}_i) \subseteq O_i) \\ \qquad \Rightarrow \qquad \mathcal{C}(C'_1, \ldots, C'_n)\downarrow \end{array}$$

In the next subsection we will prove that there exists a maximal subcontract pre-order family; this is a direct consequence of the output persistence property. In fact, if we consider possible outputs that can disappear without being actually executed (as in an external choice among outputs $\overline{a} + \overline{b}$ or in a mixed choice $a + \overline{b}$ in which, e.g., the possible $\overline{b}$ is no longer executable after the output or input on a) it is easy to prove that there exists no maximal subcontract pre-order family.

Now consider, e.g., the trivially correct system $C_1 \| C_2$ with $C_1 = a$ and $C_2 = \overline{a}$; we could have two subcontract pre-order families $\leq^1$ and $\leq^2$ such that

$$a + c.\mathbf{0} \leq^1_{\mathcal{N}-c,\mathcal{N}-c} a \text{ and } \overline{a} + c.\mathbf{0} \leq^1_{\mathcal{N}-c,\mathcal{N}-c} \overline{a}$$

and

$$a + \overline{c}.\mathbf{0} \leq^2_{\mathcal{N}-c,\mathcal{N}-c} a \text{ and } \overline{a} + \overline{c}.\mathbf{0} \leq^2_{\mathcal{N}-c,\mathcal{N}-c} \overline{a}$$

but no subcontract pre-order family $\leq$ could have

$$a + c.\mathbf{0} \leq_{\mathcal{N}-c,\mathcal{N}-c} a \text{ and } \overline{a} + \overline{c}.\mathbf{0} \leq_{\mathcal{N}-c,\mathcal{N}-c} \overline{a}$$

because if we refine C_1 with $a+c.\mathbf{0}$ and C_2 with $\overline{a}+\overline{c}.\mathbf{0}$ we achieve the incorrect system $a + c.\mathbf{0} \| \overline{a} + \overline{c}.\mathbf{0}$ that can deadlock after synchronization on channel c. Note that, if we instead assume output persistence of contracts, as we do in this paper, subcontracts cannot add reachable outputs on new types. For instance an output persistent contract $a + \tau.\overline{c}$ adding a new output on c with respect to a, similarly to the pre-order $\leq^2$ in the example above, would not be a correct subcontract because when composed in parallel with the other initial contract $\overline{a}$ would lead to a deadlock.

The existence of the maximal subcontract pre-order family permits to define co-inductively a subcontract relation achieved as union of all subcontract pre-orders. The co-inductive definition allows us to prove that two contracts are in subcontract relation, simply showing the existence of a subcontract pre-order which relates them. Moreover, we can use different subcontract pre-orders to refine independently several contracts in a multi-party composition, without affecting the correctness of the overall system.

4.2 Input-Output Subcontract Relation as the Maximal Subcontract Pre-order

We will show that (over output persistent contracts) the maximal subcontract pre-order family exists, and we will characterize it with a relation on contracts called the *input-output subcontract relation*. Differently from the subcontract pre-orders, that permit to refine contemporaneously several contracts in a composition, this new relation allows for the refinement of one contract only. Besides giving the possibility to prove the existence of the maximal subcontract pre-order family, this relation will allow us to resort to the theory of testing in the next subsection.

Before presenting the definition of the input-output subcontract relation, we present a coarser form of subcontract pre-order, called the *singular subcontract pre-order*, according to which, given any system composed of a set of contracts, refinement is applied to one contract only (thus leaving the other unchanged). This new pre-order will allow us to prove that the input-output subcontract relation is coarser than any subcontract pre-order.

Definition 10 (Singular subcontract pre-order family). *A family* $\{\leq_{I,O} | I, O \subseteq \mathcal{N}\}$ *of pre-orders over* $\mathcal{P}_{con}$ *is a singular subcontract pre-order family if, for any context* $\mathcal{C}$ *with a single contract variable (and possibly some contracts) and* $C, C' \in \mathcal{P}_{con}$ *we have*

$$\mathcal{C}(C)\downarrow \ \wedge\ C' \leq_{I,O} C \ \wedge\ I(\mathcal{C}) \subseteq I \ \wedge\ O(\mathcal{C}) \subseteq O \qquad \Rightarrow \qquad \mathcal{C}(C')\downarrow$$

The following Proposition shows that a subcontract pre-order family is also a singular subcontract pre-order family. Intuitively, this means that if we can refine several contracts in a system without affecting its correctness, we can also refine only one of those contracts, leaving the others unchanged.

Proposition 2. *If a family of pre-orders* $\{\leq_{I,O} | I, O \subseteq \mathcal{N}\}$ *is a subcontract pre-order family then it is also a singular subcontract pre-order family.*

Proof. Suppose that $\{\leq_{I,O} | I, O \subseteq \mathcal{N}\}$ is a subcontract pre-order family. Consider a context $\mathcal{C}$ with one contract variable $\mathcal{X}_1$ and $n-1$ contracts. Let $C \in \mathcal{P}_{con}$ be a contract such that $\mathcal{C}(C)\downarrow$. Consider now $C' \in \mathcal{P}_{con}$ such that $C' \leq_{I,O} C$ for I, O such that $I(\mathcal{C}) \subseteq I$ and $O(\mathcal{C}) \subseteq O$. We now prove that also $\mathcal{C}(C')\downarrow$. Let $\mathcal{C}'$ be the context obtained from $\mathcal{C}$ replacing all contracts $C_2, \ldots, C_n$ with the contract variables $\mathcal{X}_2, \ldots, \mathcal{X}_n$. We have that $\mathcal{C}(C) = \mathcal{C}'(C, C_2, \ldots, C_n)$. By $\mathcal{C}(C)\downarrow$ we have that also $\mathcal{C}'(C, C_2, \ldots, C_n)\downarrow$. As $I(\mathcal{C}) = I(\mathcal{C}'(\mathcal{X}, C_2, \ldots, C_n))$ and $O(\mathcal{C}) = O(\mathcal{C}'(\mathcal{X}, C_2, \ldots, C_n))$ we can replace C with C', and by reflexivity of pre-orders we can replace all other contracts C_i with themselves (in fact, we have that $D \leq_{I,O} D$ for every I, O and D). Thus, also $\mathcal{C}'(C', C_2, \ldots, C_n)\downarrow$. The proof is completed by observing that $\mathcal{C}'(C', C_2, \ldots, C_n) = \mathcal{C}(C')$ thus also $\mathcal{C}(C')\downarrow$. □

We now have to prove that the singular subcontract pre-order families have maximum. This result is obtained in two steps: we first observe that we can restrict the set of contexts of interest in the definition of the singular subcontract pre-order families to contexts of the form $[\mathcal{X}] \| P$, then we define the maximum of the singular subcontract pre-order families considering this restricted set of contexts (this new relation is called *input-output subcontract relation*).

The first observation is formalized by the following Proposition.

Proposition 3. *Let* $\mathcal{C}$ *be a context with a single contract variable. There exists* $P \in \mathcal{P}_{sys}$ *such that:* $I(P) = I(\mathcal{C})$, $O(P) = O(\mathcal{C})$, *and for every contract* $C \in \mathcal{P}_{con}$ *we have that* $\mathcal{C}(C)\downarrow$ *if and only if* $C \| P\downarrow$.

Proof. The proof is in Appendix B. □

In the light of the above proposition we can conclude that we could restrict the contexts in the Definition 10 only to contexts of the form $[\mathcal{X}] \| P$. We now define the maximum of the singular subcontract pre-order families considering this restricted set of contexts. In this definition (and in the remainder of the paper) we use $\mathcal{P}_{sys,I,O}$ to denote the subset of processes of $\mathcal{P}_{sys}$ such that $I(P) \subseteq I$ and $O(P) \subseteq O$.

Definition 11 (Input-Output Subcontract relation). *A contract C' is a subcontract of a contract C with respect to a set of input channel names $I \subseteq \mathcal{N}$ and output channel names $O \subseteq \mathcal{N}$, denoted $C' \preceq_{I,O} C$, if*

$$\forall P \in \mathcal{P}_{sys,I,O}. \quad (C \| P)\downarrow \quad \Rightarrow \quad (C' \| P)\downarrow$$

The main difference between the Definition 10 and the Definition 11 is that in the former we describe a property that every singular subcontract pre-order should satisfy, while in the latter we define a new relation (the input-output subcontract relation) that relates all those pairs of contracts C' and C that satisfy the same property. For instance, the identity relation is a singular subcontract pre-order because it satisfies the property, but it does not coincide with the input-output subcontract relation because it does not relate all those pairs of contracts C' and C that satisfy the property even if C' is not syntactically equal to C. In the following we will consider only the input-output subcontract relation (Definition 11), but we have presented both definitions because this simplify the proof of the following Theorem (stating that the input-output subcontract relation includes all subcontract pre-order families) that, indeed, is a simple corollary of the Proposition 2 in which we made use of the Definition 10.

Theorem 1. *Given a subcontract pre-order family $\{\leq_{I,O} | \ I, O \subseteq \mathcal{N}\ \}$, we have that it is* included *in the family of pre-orders $\{\preceq_{I,O} | \ I, O \subseteq \mathcal{N}\ \}$, that is*

$$C' \leq_{I,O} C \ \Rightarrow \ C' \preceq_{I,O} C$$

Proof. From Proposition 2 we know that each subcontract pre-order family $\{\leq_{I,O} | \ I, O \subseteq \mathcal{N}\ \}$ is also a singular subcontract pre-order family. The thesis directly follows from the observation that the input-output subcontract relation $\preceq_{I,O}$ is the maximum of all singular subcontract pre-orders $\leq_{I,O}$, due to Proposition 3. □

In the light of this last Theorem, the existence of the maximal subcontract pre-order family can be proved simply showing that $\{\preceq_{I,O} | \ I, O \subseteq \mathcal{N}\ \}$ is itself a subcontract pre-order family (thus it is the maximum among all subcontract pre-order families). The proof of this result (Theorem 2) is rather complex and requires several preliminary results.

The following proposition states an intuitive contravariant property: given $\preceq_{I',O'}$, and the greater sets I and O (i.e. $I' \subseteq I$ and $O' \subseteq O$) we obtain a smaller pre-order $\preceq_{I,O}$ (i.e. $\preceq_{I,O} \subseteq \preceq_{I',O'}$).

Proposition 4. *Let $C, C' \in \mathcal{P}_{con}$ be two contracts, $I, I' \subseteq \mathcal{N}$ be two sets of input channel names and $O, O' \subseteq \mathcal{N}$ be two sets of output channel names. We have:*

$$C' \preceq_{I,O} C \ \wedge \ I' \subseteq I \ \wedge \ O' \subseteq O \quad \Rightarrow \quad C' \preceq_{I',O'} C$$

Proof. The thesis follows from the fact that extending the sets of input and output actions means considering a greater set of discriminating contexts. □

The following proposition states that a subcontract is still a subcontract even if we restrict its actions in order to consider only the inputs and outputs already available in the supercontract. The result about the possibility to restrict the outputs will be extensively used in the proof of Theorem 2.

Proposition 5. *Let $C, C' \in \mathcal{P}_{con}$ be contracts and $I, O \subseteq \mathcal{N}$ be sets of input and output names. We have*

$$C' \preceq_{I,O} C \quad \Rightarrow \quad C' \backslash \overline{(I(C') - I(C))} \preceq_{I,O} C$$
$$C' \preceq_{I,O} C \quad \Rightarrow \quad C' \backslash \overline{(O(C') - O(C))} \preceq_{I,O} C$$

Proof. We discuss the result concerned with restriction of outputs (the proof for the restriction of inputs is symmetrical). Let $C' \preceq_{I,O} C$. Given any $P \in \mathcal{P}_{sys,I,O}$ such that $(C \| P)\downarrow$, we will show that $(C' \backslash \overline{(O(C') - O(C))} \parallel P)\downarrow$. We first observe that $(C \parallel P \backslash \overline{(O(C') - O(C))})\downarrow$. Since $C' \preceq_{I,O} C$, we derive $(C' \parallel P \backslash \overline{(O(C') - O(C))})\downarrow$. As a consequence $(C' \backslash \overline{(O(C') - O(C))} \parallel P \backslash \overline{(O(C') - O(C))})\downarrow$. We can conclude $(C' \backslash \overline{(O(C') - O(C))} \parallel P)\downarrow$. □

All the results discussed so far do not depend on the output persistence property. The first significant result depending on this peculiarity of the considered contracts is reported in the following proposition. It states that if we substitute a contract with one of its subcontract, the latter cannot activate outputs that were not included in the potential outputs of the supercontract.

Proposition 6. *Let $C, C' \in \mathcal{P}_{con}$ be contracts and $I, O \subseteq \mathcal{N}$ be sets of input and output names. If $C' \preceq_{I,O} C$ we have that, for every $P \in \mathcal{P}_{sys,I,O}$ such that $(C \| P)\downarrow$,*

$$(C' \| P) \xrightarrow{\tau}{}^{*} (C'_{der} \| P_{der}) \quad \Rightarrow \quad \forall\, a \in O(C') - O(C).\, C'_{der} \overset{\overline{a}}{\not\longrightarrow}$$

Proof. We proceed by contradiction. Suppose that there exist C'_{der}, P_{der} such that $(C' \| P) \xrightarrow{\tau}{}^{*} (C'_{der} \| P_{der})$ and $C'_{der} \xrightarrow{\overline{a}}$ for some $a \in O(C') - O(C)$. We further suppose (without loss of generality) that such a path is minimal, i.e. no intermediate state $(C'_{der2} \| P_{der2})$ is traversed, such that $C'_{der2} \xrightarrow{\overline{a}}$ for some $a \in O(C') - O(C)$. This implies that the same path must be performable by $(C' \backslash \overline{(O(C') - O(C))} \parallel P)$, thus reaching the state $(C'_{der} \backslash \overline{(O(C') - O(C))} \| P_{der})$. However, since in the state C'_{der} of contract C' we have $C'_{der} \xrightarrow{\overline{a}}$ for some $a \in O(C') - O(C)$ and the execution of $\overline{a}$ is disallowed by restriction, due to output persistence, the contract will never be able to reach success (no matter what contracts in P will do). Therefore $(C' \backslash \overline{(O(C') - O(C))} \parallel P)\not\downarrow$ and (due to Proposition 5) we reached a contradiction. □

The following proposition permits to conclude that the set of potential inputs of the other contracts in the system is an information that does not influence the subcontract relation.

Proposition 7. *Let $C \in \mathcal{P}_{con}$ be contracts, $O \subseteq \mathcal{N}$ be a set of output names and $I, I' \subseteq \mathcal{N}$ be two sets of input names such that $O(C) \subseteq I, I'$. We have that for every contract $C' \in \mathcal{P}_{con}$,*

$$C' \preceq_{I,O} C \iff C' \preceq_{I',O} C$$

Proof. Let us suppose $C' \preceq_{I',O} C$ (the opposite direction is symmetric). Given any $P \in \mathcal{P}_{sys,I,O}$ such that $(C \| P) \downarrow$, we will show that $(C' \| P) \downarrow$. We first observe that $(C \parallel P \backslash\!\backslash (I - O(C))) \downarrow$. Since $C' \preceq_{I',O} C$ and $O(C) \subseteq I'$, we derive $(C' \parallel P \backslash\!\backslash (I - O(C))) \downarrow$. Due to Proposition 6 we have that $(C' \parallel P \backslash\!\backslash (I - O(C)))$ can never reach by τ transitions a state where outputs in $O(C') - O(C)$ are executable by some derivative of C', so we conclude $(C' \parallel P) \downarrow$. □

It is worth noting that a similar result does not hold for the output set, that is, if $O \subseteq O'$ we can have $C' \preceq_{I,O} C$ but $C' \not\preceq_{I,O'} C$ even under the assumption $I(C) \subseteq O, O'$. As an example, you can consider $\tau.\overline{a} + b \preceq_{\mathcal{N},\mathcal{N}-b} \overline{a}$. This holds in general because the addition of an input on b is admitted in a subcontract if we know that no outputs on that channel can be executed by the other initial contracts in the system. On the contrary, we have that $\tau.\overline{a} + b \not\preceq_{\mathcal{N},\mathcal{N}} \overline{a}$ because

$$[\overline{a}] \parallel [a.b] \parallel [\overline{b}]$$

is a correct composition while

$$[\tau.\overline{a} + b] \parallel [a.b] \parallel [\overline{b}]$$

is not, because the first and the second contracts are now in competition to consume the unique output on b produced by the third contract.

We are now in place to prove one of the main results of this paper, i.e., that the input-output subcontract relation defined in the Definition 11 is also a subcontract pre-order family.

Theorem 2. *The family of pre-orders $\{\preceq_{I,O} \mid I, O \subseteq \mathcal{N}\}$ is a subcontract pre-order family.*

Proof. Consider a context $\mathcal{C}$ containing n contract variables and no contracts. Let $C_1, \ldots, C_n \in \mathcal{P}_{con}$ be contracts such that $\mathcal{C}(C_1, \ldots, C_n) \downarrow$. We consider contracts $C'_1, \ldots, C'_n \in \mathcal{P}_{con}$ such that, for every i from 1 to n, $C'_i \preceq_{I_i,O_i} C_i$ for $I(\mathcal{C}_i) \subseteq I_i$ and $O(\mathcal{C}_i) \subseteq O_i$ with $\mathcal{C}_i = \mathcal{C}(C_1, \ldots, C_{i-1}, \mathcal{X}, C_{i+1}, \ldots, C_n)$.

We now derive that also $\mathcal{C}(C'_1, \ldots, C'_n) \downarrow$.

We first observe that, for every i from 1 to n, we have that:

$$\mathcal{C}(C'_1 \backslash\!\backslash \overline{(O(C'_1) - O(C_1))}, \ldots, C_i, \ldots, C'_n \backslash\!\backslash \overline{(O(C'_n) - O(C_n))}) \downarrow$$

In fact, as the input-output subcontract relation is also a singular subcontract pre-order family, we can apply it $n-1$ times to replace the contracts C_j with $j \neq i$ with their subcontract $C_j \backslash\!\backslash \overline{(O(C'_j) - O(C_j))}$ (the latter is a subcontract of the former due to Proposition 5).

For any i, since $C'_i \preceq_{I_i,O_i} C_i$, by Proposition 6 we have that

$$\mathcal{C}(C'_1\backslash\overline{(O(C'_1)-O(C_1))},\ldots,C'_i,\ldots,C'_n\backslash\overline{(O(C'_n)-O(C_n))})$$

can never reach by τ transitions a state where outputs in $O(C'_i)-O(C_i)$ are executable by the derivative $C'_{i,der}$ of C'_i. If now we consider the behaviour of $\mathcal{C}(C'_1\backslash\overline{(O(C'_1)-O(C_1))},\ldots,C'_n\backslash\overline{(O(C'_n)-O(C_n))})$ we derive that, for any i, we cannot reach by τ transitions a state

$$\mathcal{C}(C'_{1,der}\backslash\overline{(O(C'_1)-O(C_1))},\ldots,C'_{i,der}\backslash\overline{(O(C'_i)-O(C_i))},\ldots,\\ \|C'_{n,der}\backslash\overline{(O(C'_n)-O(C_n))})$$

where $C'_{i,der}$ can execute outputs in $O(C'_i)-O(C_i)$. Hence the presence of the restriction operators does not affect the internal behaviour of

$$\mathcal{C}(C'_1\backslash\overline{(O(C'_1)-O(C_1))},\ldots,C'_n\backslash\overline{(O(C'_n)-O(C_n))})$$

with respect to $\mathcal{C}(C'_1,\ldots,C'_n)$. Therefore, we can finally derive $\mathcal{C}(C'_1,\ldots,C'_n)\downarrow$ from

$$\mathcal{C}(C'_1\backslash\overline{(O(C'_1)-O(C_1))},\ldots,C'_n\backslash\overline{(O(C'_n)-O(C_n))})\downarrow$$

that is obtained by further applying the definition of singular subcontract pre-order to refine C_i in any of the i-indexed statements at the beginning of the proof. □

In Theorem 1 we proved that all subcontract pre-order families are included in $\{\preceq_{I,O} | I,O\subseteq\mathcal{N}\}$; this last Theorem proves that this family of relations is also a subcontract pre-order family, thus it is the maximal one.

4.3 Subcontract Relation

In the previous subsection we have introduced the input-output subcontract relation $\preceq_{I,O}$, and we have proved that it is the maximal subcontract pre-order family. Moreover, the Proposition 7 permits to abstract away from the index I of $\preceq_{I,O}$ assuming always $I=\mathcal{N}$. In this way we achieve a simpler relation $\preceq_O$, corresponding to $\preceq_{\mathcal{N},O}$, that we simply call *subcontract relation*, which has only one parameter indicating the set of names on which the expected contexts can perform outputs. In the definition of the subcontract relation we use $\mathcal{P}_{sys,O}$ to denote the set of processes $\mathcal{P}_{sys,\mathcal{N},O}$.

Definition 12 (Subcontract relation). *A contract C' is a subcontract of a contract C with respect to a set of output channel names $O\subseteq\mathcal{N}$, denoted $C'\preceq_O C$, if*

$$\forall P\in\mathcal{P}_{sys,O}.\quad (C\|P)\downarrow \;\Rightarrow\; (C'\|P)\downarrow$$

In order to prove that one contract C' is a subcontract of C, the Definition 12 is not exploitable due to the universal quantification on all possible parallel process P. The remainder of this subsection is devoted to the definition of an actual way for proving that two contracts are in subcontract relation. This is achieved resorting to the theory of *should-testing* [26]. The main difference of should-testing with respect to the standard must-testing [18] is that fairness is taken into account; an (unfair) infinite computation that never gives rise to success is observed in the standard must-testing scenario, while this is not the case in the should-testing scenario. The formal definition of should-testing is reported in the proof of Theorem 3.

We need a preliminary result that essentially proves that $C' \preceq_O C$ if and only if $C' \backslash\!\!\backslash \mathcal{N}-O \preceq_{\mathcal{N}} C \backslash\!\!\backslash \mathcal{N}-O$.

Lemma 1. *Let C, C' be two contracts and $O \subseteq \mathcal{N}$ be a set of output names. We have*

$$C' \preceq_O C \quad \Leftrightarrow \quad (\forall P \in \mathcal{P}_{sys}.\, (C \backslash\!\!\backslash \mathcal{N}-O \,\|\, P)\!\downarrow \;\Rightarrow\; (C' \backslash\!\!\backslash \mathcal{N}-O \,\|\, P)\!\downarrow)$$

Proof. Given $P \in \mathcal{P}_{sys}$, we have $(C \backslash\!\!\backslash \mathcal{N}-O \,\|\, P)\!\downarrow \iff (C \backslash\!\!\backslash \mathcal{N}-O \,\|\, P \backslash\!\!\backslash \overline{\mathcal{N}-O})\!\downarrow \iff (C \,\|\, P \backslash\!\!\backslash \overline{\mathcal{N}-O})\!\downarrow$. The same holds also for C', i.e., $(C' \backslash\!\!\backslash \mathcal{N}-O \,\|\, P)\!\downarrow \iff (C' \backslash\!\!\backslash \mathcal{N}-O \,\|\, P \backslash\!\!\backslash \overline{\mathcal{N}-O})\!\downarrow \iff (C' \,\|\, P \backslash\!\!\backslash \overline{\mathcal{N}-O})\!\downarrow$. In the particular case of $P \in \mathcal{P}_{sys,O}$, the processes of interest in the definition of $\preceq_O$, we have that $P \backslash\!\!\backslash \overline{\mathcal{N}-O}$ is isomorphic to P, thus $(C \,\|\, P \backslash\!\!\backslash \overline{\mathcal{N}-O})\!\downarrow \iff (C \,\|\, P)\!\downarrow$ and $(C' \,\|\, P \backslash\!\!\backslash \overline{\mathcal{N}-O})\!\downarrow \iff (C' \,\|\, P)\!\downarrow$.

In the following we denote with $\preceq_{test}$ the *should-testing* pre-order defined in [26] as follows. Intuitively, two processes P' and P are related by testing pre-order, namely $P' \preceq_{test} P$, if P' satisfies at least the same *tests* as P. A test t is any process including a special action representing success (denoted with $\surd$ in [26], but denoted with $\surd'$ to avoid confusion with the action $\surd$ used in this paper to denote successful completion). Before presenting the formal definition we need to introduce the set of actions Λ as being $\Lambda = \{a, \overline{a} | a \in \mathcal{N}\} \cup \{\surd\}$ (i.e. we consider input and output actions and $\surd$: the latter is included in the set of actions of terms being tested as any other action). Similarly as in [26] we use and Λ_τ to denote $\Lambda \cup \{\tau\}$.

Formally, we write $P' \preceq_{test} P$, if P **shd** t implies P' **shd** t, where Q **shd** t means that

$$\forall w \in \Lambda_\tau^*, Q'. \qquad Q\|_\Lambda t \xrightarrow{w} Q' \qquad \Rightarrow \qquad \exists v \in \Lambda_\tau^*, Q'' : Q' \xrightarrow{v} Q'' \xrightarrow{\surd'}$$

where $\|_\Lambda$ is the CSP parallel composition operator: in $R\|_\Lambda R'$ transitions of R and R' con be executed only if they are labeled with τ, $\surd'$ or some $\lambda \in \Lambda$, but in this last case both R and R' must perform an action λ and their synchronization yields a transition still with label λ.

In order to resort to the setting used in [26], we define a normal form representation with terms of the process algebra considered in [26] of the finite labeled transition system (LTS) of a system P. In the following we use quadruples $(S, Lab, \longrightarrow, s_{init})$ to represent LTSes, where S is the set of states of the LTS, Lab the set of transition labels, $\longrightarrow$ the set of transitions with $\longrightarrow \subseteq S \times Lab \times S$ and $s_{init} \in S$ the initial state. We have that the semantics $[\![P]\!]$ of a system P is defined as being the LTS $[\![P]\!] = (S, \Lambda_\tau, \longrightarrow, P)$, where S is the set of terms P'

reachable from P according to the transition relation defined by the operational rules for systems in Tables 1 and 2, i.e. such that $P \xrightarrow{w} P'$ for some (possibly empty) sequence of labels w, and $\longrightarrow$ is the subset of such a transition relation obtained by just considering transitions between states in S.

The normal form for a system P (denoted with $\mathcal{NF}(P)$) is derived from its semantics $[\![P]\!] = (S, \Lambda_\tau, \longrightarrow, P)$ as follows, by using the operator $rec_X \theta$ (defined in [26]) that represents the value of X in the solution of the minimum fixpoint of the finite set of equations θ,

$$\mathcal{NF}(P) = rec_{X_P}\theta \qquad \text{where } \theta \text{ is the set of } S\text{-indexed equations}$$
$$X_{P'} = \sum\nolimits_{(\lambda, P''):P' \xrightarrow{\lambda} P''} \lambda; X_{P''}$$

where we assume empty sums to be equal to $\mathbf{0}$, i.e. if there are no outgoing transitions from $X_{P'}$, we have $X_{P'} = \mathbf{0}$. Note that differently from our syntax, in [26] the CSP sequential composition operator ; is considered instead of the prefix operator we consider in this paper, thus the process $\alpha.P$ is written $\alpha; P$.

According to the definitions in [26], the semantics $[\![\mathcal{NF}(P)]\!]$ of the normal form $\mathcal{NF}(P) \equiv rec_{X_P}\theta$ is, as expected, the labeled transition system $[\![\mathcal{NF}(P)]\!] = (S', \Lambda_\tau, \longrightarrow', \mathcal{NF}(P))$, where:

- $S' = \{\mathcal{NF}(P') \equiv rec_{X_{P'}}\theta \mid P' \in S\}$
- $\longrightarrow' = \{(\mathcal{NF}(P'), \lambda, \mathcal{NF}(P'')) \mid P' \xrightarrow{\lambda}{}' P''\}$

In the following, given a contract C, we will use $\mathcal{NF}(C)$ to stand for $\mathcal{NF}([C])$. We are now in a position to define the sound characterization of the subcontract relation in terms of testing.

Theorem 3. *Let C, C' be two contracts and $O \subseteq \mathcal{N}$ be a set of output names. We have*

$$\mathcal{NF}(C' \backslash\!\backslash (\mathcal{N}-O)) \preceq_{test} \mathcal{NF}(C \backslash\!\backslash (\mathcal{N}-O)) \quad \Rightarrow \quad C' \preceq_O C$$

Proof. The proof is in Appendix C.

Note that the opposite implication

$$C' \preceq_O C \;\Rightarrow\; \mathcal{NF}(C' \backslash\!\backslash (\mathcal{N}-O)) \preceq_{test} \mathcal{NF}(C \backslash\!\backslash (\mathcal{N}-O))$$

does not hold in general. For example if we take contracts $C = a + a.c$ and $C' = b + b.c$ we have that $C' \preceq_O C$ (and $C \preceq_O C'$) for any O (there is no contract P such that $(C \| P)\!\downarrow$ or $(C' \| P)\!\downarrow$), but obviously $\mathcal{NF}(C' \backslash\!\backslash (\mathcal{N}-O)) \preceq_{test} \mathcal{NF}(C \backslash\!\backslash (\mathcal{N}-O))$ (and $\mathcal{NF}(C \backslash\!\backslash (\mathcal{N}-O)) \preceq_{test} \mathcal{NF}(C' \backslash\!\backslash (\mathcal{N}-O))$) does not hold for any O that includes $\{a, b, c\}$. As another example, consider contracts $C = \tau.\mathbf{0} + a$ and $C' = \tau.\mathbf{0} + b$. We have that $C' \preceq_O C$ (and $C \preceq_O C'$) for any O (there is no contract P such that $(C \| P)\downarrow$ or $(C' \| P)\downarrow$), but $\mathcal{NF}(C' \backslash\!\backslash (\mathcal{N}-O)) \preceq_{test} \mathcal{NF}(C \backslash\!\backslash (\mathcal{N}-O))$ (and $\mathcal{NF}(C \backslash\!\backslash (\mathcal{N}-O)) \preceq_{test} \mathcal{NF}(C' \backslash\!\backslash (\mathcal{N}-O))$) does not hold for any O that includes $\{a, b\}$: this can be seen by considering the test $t = \surd' + b; \mathbf{0}$ (and $t = \surd' + a; \mathbf{0}$).

Finally, we observe that as the labeled transition system of each contract C is finite state by definition (see Definition 2), also $\mathcal{NF}(C\backslash\mathcal{N} - O)$ is finite state for any O. In [26] it is proved that for finite state terms *should-testing* pre-order is decidable and an actual verification algorithm is presented. This algorithm, in the light of our Theorem 3, can be used in our setting to prove whether a contract C' is a subcontract of C (for some set of output names O). As the characterization we give in Theorem 3 is sound but not complete, it could be the case that C' is a subcontract of C even if the algorithm answers negatively thus leading to a *false negative* result. Nevertheless, all the cases of false negative we have experienced so far are related to extreme cases as those reported above, that is contracts that cannot be used in any correct system. We leave as an open problem the definition of a sound and complete characterization of the subcontract relation.

5 Conclusion

We have introduced a notion of subcontract relation useful for service oriented computing, where services are to be composed in such a way that deadlocks and livelocks are avoided. In order to be as much flexible as possible, we want to relate with our subcontract relation all those services that could safely replace their supercontracts. In the Introduction we have already discussed the practical impact of our notion of subcontract and we have compared our theory with the related literature.

Here, we add some comments about the work we have done in our previous papers, that, with respect to this paper, is also concerned with choreographic descriptions of service systems. In particular, we first perform a conceptual summary of our results (encompassing both this paper and previous papers), then we consider more detailed technical differences of this paper with respect to our previous papers.

5.1 Summary of Results

Besides the problem of contract-based service retrieval that we have faced in this paper, often the design and functioning of service oriented systems, is based on high level languages called *choreography* languages in the SOC literature. Choreography languages are intended as notations for representing multi-party service compositions, that is, descriptions of the global behaviour of service-based applications in which several services reciprocally communicate in order to complete a predefined task. One of the most popular choreography languages has been developed by W3C and is called Web Services Choreography Description Language WS-CDL [27]. In WS-CDL, the basic activities in a service choreography are interactions, that is, the atomic execution of a send and a receive operations performed by two communicating partners, called *roles*. For this reason, WS-CDL is said to follow an *interaction-oriented* approach.

When implementing an interaction-oriented choreography by assembling already available services, several mechanisms and notions need to be introduced.

Often the possibility is considered of extracting, from the global specification, the behaviour of each of the involved processes in the form of a contract or of an abstract workflow. Such an extraction is often called "projection of the choreography on the roles" (see, e.g. [5]). The idea is that, based on such a projection, services are retrieved that expose a behaviour which is compatible with the extracted processes (based, e.g., on a contract refinement theory like the one presented in this paper).

We now summarize the results that we have obtained in [3,5,4,6,7,8] about contract refinement in different scenarios.

The first mean of classification of possible scenarios is based on the *amount of knowledge* about the (initial) behavioural description of the other roles the conformance relation may depend on. We considered: knowledge about the whole choreography (full knowledge about the behaviour of other roles) or knowledge restricted to input types (receive operations) and/or output types (invoke operations) that the other roles may use. Note that in this paper we used knowledge of the latter kind. The second mean of classification of possible scenarios is based on the *kind of service compliance* assumed (i.e. of the principle assumed for assessing when multiple services work well together and form a correct system). We considered: "normal" compliance, as reported in this paper, where service interaction via invoke and receive primitives is based on synchronous handshake communication and both receive and invoke primitives may wait indefinitely (with no exception occurring) for a communication to happen (the standard CCS synchronization); "strong compliance", where we additionally require that, whenever a service may perform an invoke on some operation, the invoked service must be already in the receive state for that operation; "queue-based compliance", where service interaction via invoke and receive primitives is based on asynchronous communication: the receiving service puts invoke requests in an unbounded queue. Concerning service compliance we considered in all cases the fair termination property, i.e. for any finite behavioural path of the system there exists a finite path from the reached state that leads all services to successful termination. This guarantees that the system is both deadlock and, under the fairness assumption (i.e. whenever a choice is traversed infinitely often every possible outcome is chosen infinitely often), live-lock free.

Our results are summarized in the following.

- Knowledge about the whole choreography (direct conformance relation with respect to a choreography for a certain role): the maximal independent conformance relation does not exist, no matter which kind of service compliance (among those mentioned above) is considered.
- Knowledge about other initial contracts limited to input/output types they use (conformance by means of refinement of a single contract parameterized on the I/O knowledge about the others, as in this paper):
  - In the case of "normal compliance" we have that: for unconstrained contracts the maximal independent conformance relation does not exist; for contracts such that the output persistence property holds, as in the case of this paper, the maximal independent conformance relation exists

and knowledge about input types is not significant; for output persistent contracts where locations expressing a unique address for every system contract are introduced and outputs are directed to a location, the maximal relation exists and knowledge about both input and output types is not significant.
- In the case of "strong compliance" we have that: for unconstrained contracts (where outputs are directed to a location identifying a unique system contract) the maximal relation exists and knowledge about both input and output types is not significant.
- In the case of "queue-based compliance" we have that: for unconstrained contracts (where outputs are directed to a location identifying a unique system contract) the maximal relation exists and knowledge about both input and output types is not significant.

For every maximal refinement relation above (apart from the queue-based one), we provide a sound characterization that is decidable, by resorting to an encoding into should-testing [26], a fair version of must testing. As a consequence we obtain:

– An algorithm (based on that in [26]) to check refinement.
– A classification of the maximal refinement relations with respect to existing pre-orders as, e.g., (half) bisimulation, (fair/must) testing, trace inclusion. In particular we show that the maximal refinement relations are coarser with respect to bisimulation and must testing preorders (up to some adequate encoding and treatment of fairness) in that, e.g., they allow external nondeterminism on inputs to be added in refinements.

5.2 Detailed Comparison with Our Previous Work

Here, we add some comments about significant technical differences between this paper and our previous papers [5,4,8]. The first technical difference is that in this paper we prove the coincidence between multiple contemporaneous refinement and singular refinement, for any combination of input and output sets I, O. On the contrary, in the other papers we more simply consider the maximal sets for inputs and outputs $\mathcal{N}$, $\mathcal{N}$. This more specific result, on the one hand, required a significant technical effort (see Theorem 2 and all its preliminary results), on the other hand, allow us to achieve a more general refinement that permits also to reduce external nondeterminism. According to the theory in this paper we have, for instance, that $a+b \preceq_{\mathcal{N}-c} a+b+c$, similarly to the examples reported at the beginning of Section 4. This kind of refinement that removes internal nondeterminism is not permitted in the other papers. Another interesting technical difference is that in this paper we use restriction in order to model the possibility to have channels that can be written by some processes and read by some other ones. In [5,4,8] we consider a more specific channel policy according to which channels are located, meaning that they can be read only by the processes running on the channel location. This additional constraint has an important consequence: if C' is a subcontract of C assuming a set O of possible outputs for the other contracts in the system, then C' is a subcontract of C even if we consider a larger set of outputs O' (knowledge about output types is not significant). This result does not hold in this paper as proved by the counterexample reported after Proposition 7. A final remark, is concerned with the paper [4,8] where we present a stronger notion of compliance according to which when an output operation is ready to be executed, than the corresponding input should be already available. The interesting result is that the strong subcontract relation achieved in that paper starting from strong compliance is incomparable with the subcontract relation presented in this paper considering (standard) compliance. In fact, it is possible to show the existence of C' and C in subcontract relation according to one notion of subcontract, but not according to the other one. For instance, in this paper we have $\tau.a \preceq_{\mathcal{N}} a$, while $\tau.a$ is not strongly compliant with $\overline{a}$ which can send an invocation on a even if the server is not yet ready to serve it. On the contrary, using the characterization of the strong subcontract relation in [4,8], it is easy to prove that $\tau.\overline{a}.\overline{b} + \tau.\overline{b}.\overline{a}$ is a strong subcontract of $\overline{a}.\overline{b} + \overline{b}.\overline{a}$, while the former is not (standard) compliant with the contract $a.b$ which is compliant with the latter.

References

1. Allen, R., Garlan, D.: Formalizing Architectural Connection. In: Proc. ICSE 1994, pp. 71–80. IEEE Computer Society Press, Los Alamitos (1994)
2. Autili, M., Inverardi, P., Navarra, A., Tivoli, M.: SYNTHESIS: a tool for automatically assembling correct and distributed component-based systems. In: Proc. ICSE 2007, pp. 784–787. IEEE Computer Society Press, Los Alamitos (2007)
3. Bravetti, M., Zavattaro, G.: Contract based Multi-party Service Composition. In: Arbab, F., Sirjani, M. (eds.) FSEN 2007. LNCS, vol. 4767, pp. 207–222. Springer, Heidelberg (2007)
4. Bravetti, M., Zavattaro, G.: A Theory for Strong Service Compliance. In: Murphy, A.L., Vitek, J. (eds.) COORDINATION 2007. LNCS, vol. 4467, pp. 96–112. Springer, Heidelberg (2007)
5. Bravetti, M., Zavattaro, G.: Towards a Unifying Theory for Choreography Conformance and Contract Compliance. In: Lumpe, M., Vanderperren, W. (eds.) SC 2007. LNCS, vol. 4829, pp. 34–50. Springer, Heidelberg (2007)
6. Bravetti, M., Zavattaro, G.: Contract Compliance and Choreography Conformance in the Presence of Message Queues. In: Proc. WS-FM 2008. LNCS. Springer, Heidelberg (2008) (to appear)
7. Bravetti, M., Zavattaro, G.: A Foundational Theory of Contracts for Multi-party Service Composition. Fundamenta Informaticae 89(4), 451–478 (2008)
8. Bravetti, M., Zavattaro, G.: A Theory of Contracts for Strong Service Compliance. In: Mathematical Structure in Computer Science. Cambridge University Press, Cambridge (2009) (in publication)
9. Brogi, A., Canal, C., Pimentel, E.: Component adaptation through flexible subservicing. Science of Computer Programming 63, 39–56 (2006)
10. Busi, N., Gorrieri, R., Guidi, C., Lucchi, R., Zavattaro, G.: Choreography and orchestration: A synergic approach for system design. In: Benatallah, B., Casati, F., Traverso, P. (eds.) ICSOC 2005. LNCS, vol. 3826, pp. 228–240. Springer, Heidelberg (2005)

11. Busi, N., Gorrieri, R., Guidi, C., Lucchi, R., Zavattaro, G.: Choreography and orchestration conformance for system design. In: Ciancarini, P., Wiklicky, H. (eds.) COORDINATION 2006. LNCS, vol. 4038, pp. 63–81. Springer, Heidelberg (2006)
12. Carbone, M., Honda, K., Yoshida, N.: Structured Communication-Centred Programming for Web Services. In: De Nicola, R. (ed.) ESOP 2007. LNCS, vol. 4421, pp. 2–17. Springer, Heidelberg (2007)
13. Carbone, M., Honda, K., Yoshida, N., Milner, R., Brown, G., Ross-Talbot, S.: A Theoretical Basis of Communication-Centred Concurrent Programming, WCD-Working Note (2006), `http://www.dcs.qmul.ac.uk/~carbonem/cdlpaper/workingnote.pdf`
14. Carpineti, S., Castagna, G., Laneve, C., Padovani, L.: A Formal Account of Contracts for Web Services. In: Bravetti, M., Núñez, M., Zavattaro, G. (eds.) WS-FM 2006. LNCS, vol. 4184, pp. 148–162. Springer, Heidelberg (2006)
15. Carpineti, S., Laneve, C.: A Basic Contract Language for Web Services. In: Sestoft, P. (ed.) ESOP 2006. LNCS, vol. 3924, pp. 197–213. Springer, Heidelberg (2006)
16. Castagna, G., Gesbert, N., Padovani, L.: A Theory of Contracts for Web Services. In: Proc. POPL 2008, pp. 261–272. ACM Press, New York (2008)
17. De Nicola, R.: Extensional equivalences for transition systems. Acta Informatica 24(2), 211–237 (1987)
18. De Nicola, R., Hennessy, M.: Testing Equivalences for Processes. Theoretical Computer Science 34, 83–133 (1984)
19. Fournet, C., Hoare, C.A.R., Rajamani, S.K., Rehof, J.: Stuck-Free Conformance. In: Alur, R., Peled, D.A. (eds.) CAV 2004. LNCS, vol. 3114, pp. 242–254. Springer, Heidelberg (2004)
20. Hoare, C.A.R.: Communicating Sequential Processes. Prentice-Hall, Englewood Cliffs (1985)
21. Kobayashi, N.: Type Systems for Concurrent Processes: From Deadlock-Freedom to Livelock-Freedom, Time-Boundedness. In: Watanabe, O., Hagiya, M., Ito, T., van Leeuwen, J., Mosses, P.D. (eds.) TCS 2000. LNCS, vol. 1872, pp. 365–389. Springer, Heidelberg (2000)
22. Laneve, C., Padovani, L.: The must preorder revisited - An algebraic theory for web services contracts. In: Caires, L., Vasconcelos, V.T. (eds.) CONCUR 2007. LNCS, vol. 4703, pp. 212–225. Springer, Heidelberg (2007)
23. Mateescu, R., Poizat, P., Salaün, G.: Behavioral adaptation of component compositions based on process algebra encodings. In: Proc. ASE 2007, pp. 385–388. ACM Press, New York (2007)
24. Milner, R.: Communication and Concurrency. Prentice-Hall, Englewood Cliffs (1989)
25. OASIS: WS-BPEL: Web Services Business Process Execution Language Version 2.0, Technical Report, OASIS (2003)
26. Rensink, A., Vogler, W.: Fair testing. Information and Computation 205, 125–198 (2007)
27. W3C: WS-CDL: Web Services Choreography Description Language, Technical Report, W3C (2004)

A Process Algebraic Representation of Contracts

In this appendix we formalize the correspondence result between contracts and terms of the language $\mathcal{P}_{con}$ by showing how to obtain from a contract

$\mathcal{T} = (S, \mathcal{L}, \longrightarrow, s_h, s_0)$ a corresponding $C \in \mathcal{P}_{con}$ such that there exists a (surjective) homomorphism from the operational semantics of $\mathcal{C}$ to $\mathcal{T}$ itself.

Definition 13. *A set of process algebraic equations is denoted by $\theta = \{X_i = C_i \mid 0 \leq i \leq n-1\}$, where n is the number of equation in the set, X_i are process variables, C_i are contract terms (possibly including free process variables). A set of process algebraic equations $\theta = \{X_i = C_i \mid 0 \leq i \leq n-1\}$ is closed if only process variables X_i, with $0 \leq i \leq n-1$, occur free in the bodies C_j, with $0 \leq j \leq n-1$, of the equations in the set.*

Definition 14. *Let $\mathcal{T} = (S, \mathcal{L}, \longrightarrow, s_h, s_0)$ be a contract. A contract term $C \in \mathcal{P}_{con}$ is obtained from $\mathcal{T}$ as follows.*

- *Supposed $S = \{s_0, \ldots, s_{n-1}\}$ (i.e. any given numbering on the states S), we first obtain from $\mathcal{T}$ a finite closed set of equations $\theta = \{X_i = C_i \mid 0 \leq i \leq n-1\}$ as follows. Denoted by m_i the number of transitions outgoing from s_i, by α^i_j the label of the $j-th$ transition outgoing from s_i (for any given numbering on the transitions outgoing from s_i), with $j \leq m_i$, and by $s_{succ^i_j}$ its target state, we take $C_i = \sum_{j \leq m_i} \alpha^i_j.X_{succ^i_j} + \{\mathbf{1}\}$, where $\mathbf{1}$ is present only if $s_i \stackrel{\surd}{\longrightarrow} s_h$ and an empty sum is assumed to yield $\mathbf{0}$.*
- *We then obtain, from the closed set of equations $\theta = \{X_i = C_i \mid 0 \leq i \leq n-1\}$, a closed contract term C by induction on the number of equations. The base case is $n = 1$: in this case we have that C is $recX_0.C_0$. In the inductive case we have that C is inductively defined as the term obtained from the equation set $\{X_i = C'_i \mid 0 \leq i \leq n-2\}$, where $C'_i = C_i\{recX_{n-1}.C_{n-1}/X_{n-1}\}$.*

Definition 15. *A homomorphism from a finite connected LTS with termination transitions $\mathcal{T} = (S, \mathcal{L}, \longrightarrow, s_h, s_0)$ to a finite connected LTS with termination transitions $\mathcal{T}' = (S', \mathcal{L}, \longrightarrow', s'_h, s'_0)$ is a function f from S to S' such that: $f(s_0) = s'_0$, $f(s_h) = s'_h$, and for all $s \in S$ we have $\{(\lambda, s') \mid f(s) \stackrel{\lambda}{\longrightarrow}' s'\} = \{(\lambda, f(s')) \mid s \stackrel{\lambda}{\longrightarrow} s'\}$, i.e. the set of transitions performable by $f(s)$ is the same as the set of transitions performable by s when f-images of the target states are considered.*

Note that, if f is a homomorphism between finite connected LTSs with finite states then f is surjective: this because all states reachable by $f(s_0)$ must be f-images of states reachable from s_0.

Proposition 8. *Let $\mathcal{T} = (S, \mathcal{L}, \longrightarrow, s_h, s_0)$ be a contract and $C \in \mathcal{P}_{con}$ be a contract term obtained from $\mathcal{T}$. There exists a (surjective) homomorphism from the semantics of C to $\mathcal{T}$ itself.*

Proof. Let us consider the ordering $S = \{s_0, \ldots, s_{n-1}\}$ on states of S used to derive C from $\mathcal{T}$. We first show that every state C' in the semantics of C is such that

1) $C' = \mathbf{0}$ or C' is of the form $recX_i.C''$, for some $0 \leq i \leq n-1, C'' \in \mathcal{P}_{con}$
2) Every subterm of C' of the form $recX_k.C''$, for any k, C'', is such that: $C'' = \sum_{0 \leq j \leq m} \alpha_j.C_j + \{\mathbf{1}\}$ where C_j is either of the form $recX_{succ_j}.C'_j$, for some $0 \leq succ_j \leq n-1, C'_j$, or of the form X_{succ_j}, for some $0 \leq succ_j \leq n-1$; and the following holds: $\{(\alpha, s') \mid s_k \xrightarrow{\lambda} s'\} = \{(\alpha_j, s_{succ_j}) \mid 0 \leq j \leq m\}$ and $\mathbf{1}$ is present in C'' if and only if $s_k \xrightarrow{\surd} s_h$.

Once proved this fact, the assert of the proposition is then simply derived as follows. We consider the function f from closed terms of the semantics of C to states of $\mathcal{T}$ defined as: $f(\mathbf{0}) = s_h$ and $f(recX_i.C') = s_i$ for any i such that $0 \leq i \leq n-1$ and term C'. From property 2) above we conclude that f is an homomorphism from the semantics of C to $\mathcal{T}$.

The assert above on states $C' \in \mathcal{P}_{con}$ in the semantics of C is proved as follows. First we prove it to hold for C itself and we then prove that, given a contract $C_1 \in \mathcal{P}_{con}$ that satisfies it, any contract $C_2 \in \mathcal{P}_{con}$ reached by a transition from C_1 (according to the operational semantics) satisfies it.

Concerning C, we prove the assert above by showing that all equation sets θ considered when inductively obtaining C from the LTS $\mathcal{T}$ are such that, for every term C' in the body of θ it holds:

1) $C' = \sum_{0 \leq j \leq m} \alpha_j.C_j + \{\mathbf{1}\}$ where C_j is either of the form $recX_{succ_j}.C'_j$, for some $0 \leq succ_j \leq n-1, C'_j$, or of the form X_{succ_j}, for some $0 \leq succ_j \leq n-1$; and the following holds: $\{(\alpha, s') \mid s_k \xrightarrow{\lambda} s'\} = \{(\alpha_j, s_{succ_j}) \mid 0 \leq j \leq m\}$ and $\mathbf{1}$ is present in C' if and only if $s_k \xrightarrow{\surd} s_h$.
2) Every subterm of C' of the form $recX_k.C''$, for any k, C'', is such that: $C'' = \sum_{0 \leq j \leq m} \alpha_j.C_j + \{\mathbf{1}\}$ where C_j is either of the form $recX_{succ_j}.C'_j$, for some $0 \leq succ_j \leq n-1, C'_j$, or of the form X_{succ_j}, for some $0 \leq succ_j \leq n-1$; and the following holds: $\{(\alpha, s') \mid s_k \xrightarrow{\lambda} s'\} = \{(\alpha_j, s_{succ_j}) \mid 0 \leq j \leq m\}$ and $\mathbf{1}$ is present in C'' if and only if $s_k \xrightarrow{\surd} s_h$.

This can be easily verified by "reversed" induction on the number of equations in equation sets θ. It obviously holds for the initial equation set with n equations directly derived from $\mathcal{T}$: 1) directly holds by construction and 2) trivially holds because no $recX_k.C''$ subterm is present in the body of any equation. If we suppose it to hold for the equation set θ with m equations, it holds for the equation set θ' with $m-1$ equations as it can be immediately verified by considering the construction procedure of θ' from θ in the second item of Definition 14. From this we can conclude that the assert above holds for C in that C is obtained from the equation set with the single equation $X_0 = C'$ by just taking it to be $recX_0.C'$.

We finally deal with preservation of the assert above when going from a contract $C_1 \in \mathcal{P}_{con}$ to a contract $C_2 \in \mathcal{P}_{con}$. In order to prove this fact, we show, by induction on the length of the inference of transitions from C_1 to C_2, for any $C_1, C_2 \in \mathcal{P}_{con}$, that if C_1 satisfies

1) C_1 is either of the form $recX_i.C''$, for some $0 \leq i \leq n-1, C'' \in \mathcal{P}_{con}$ or is such that: $C_1 = \sum_{0\leq j\leq m} \alpha_j.recX_{succ_j}.C_j + \{\mathbf{1}\}$ for some $0 \leq succ_j \leq n-1, C_j$ and $m \geq 0$.
2) Every subterm of C_1 of the form $recX_k.C''$, for any k, C'', is such that: $C'' = \sum_{0\leq j\leq m} \alpha_j.C_j + \{\mathbf{1}\}$ where C_j is either of the form $recX_{succ_j}.C'_j$, for some $0 \leq succ_j \leq n-1, C'_j$, or of the form X_{succ_j}, for some $0 \leq succ_j \leq n-1$; and the following holds: $\{(\alpha, s') \mid s_k \xrightarrow{\lambda} s'\} = \{(\alpha_j, s_{succ_j}) \mid 0 \leq j \leq m\}$ and $\mathbf{1}$ is present in C'' if and only if $s_k \xrightarrow{\checkmark} s_h$,

then C_2 satisfies the assert above. This can be easily verified by cases on the operational rule applied at the inductive step and on the operational rules with no premises, corresponding to the base case of the induction. □

B Proof of Proposition 3

In this appendix we provide the proof of Proposition 3 that shows that a context with a single contract variable $\mathcal{X}$ can be turned into a context of the form $[\mathcal{X}]\|P$. After giving some preliminary definitions we prove Lemma 2 which formalizes a result which is more general than the one stated in Proposition 3 (thus, from which Proposition 3 trivially derives).

Given a system $P \in \mathcal{P}_{sys}$ we call "reduction behaviour" of P the finite connected LTS with termination transitions $(S, \{\tau\}, \longrightarrow, s_h, P)$ defined as follows. S is the finite subset of $\mathcal{P}_{sys}$ of systems reachable from P via (possibly empty sequences of) τ transitions, $\longrightarrow$ are τ transitions between states of S, and s_h is the system obtained from the system P by replacing each contract with the $\mathbf{0}$ contract. We say that the reduction behaviour of a system P is homomorphic to that of a system P' if there exists an homomorphism from the reduction behaviour of P to the reduction behaviour of P' according to Definition 15.

Lemma 2. *Let $\mathcal{C}$ be a context with a single contract variable. There exists $P \in \mathcal{P}_{sys}$ such that $I(P) = I(\mathcal{C})$, $O(P) = O(\mathcal{C})$ and, for every $C \in \mathcal{P}_{con}$, the reduction behaviour of $\mathcal{C}(C)$ is homomorphic to that of $C\|P$ and.*

Proof. We first observe that the reduction behaviours of two systems such that one is obtained from the other one by just exploiting commutativity and associativity of parallel composition "$\|$" are obviously homomorphic. Similarly the inputs and outputs offered by contexts (see Definition 8) such that one is obtained from the other one by just exploiting commutativity and associativity of parallel composition are the same. Moreover the composition of two homomorphisms yields an homomorphism.

We call $\mathcal{X}$ the unique contract variable included in $\mathcal{C}$. We can assume that the topmost operator of $\mathcal{C}$ is parallel composition. If it is a restriction we can just exploit the fact that, for every $C \in \mathcal{P}_{con}$, the reduction behaviour of $\mathcal{C}(C) = (\mathcal{C}'\backslash\!\backslash L)(C)$ is homomorphic to that of $\mathcal{C}'(C)$ and the inputs and outputs offered by the contexts $\mathcal{C}'\backslash\!\backslash L$ and $\mathcal{C}'$ (according to Definition 8) are the same. If $\mathcal{C}$ is directly in the form $[\mathcal{X}]$, then the assert trivially holds true for $P = [\mathbf{1}]$.

We can also assume that the contract variable $\mathcal{X}$ occurs in $\mathcal{C}$ in the scope of a restriction operator, otherwise the assert trivially holds by commutativity and associativity of parallel composition.

Therefore there exists a context $\mathcal{C}'$, a system R and a set L such that, for every $C \in \mathcal{P}_{con}$, $\mathcal{C}(C)$ can be turned into $\big((\mathcal{C}' \backslash L) \| Q\big)(C)$ by commutativity and associativity of parallel composition.

Moreover, we have that, for every $C \in \mathcal{P}_{con}$, the reduction behaviour of $\big((\mathcal{C}' \backslash L) \| Q\big)(C)$ is homomorphic to the reduction behaviour of $\big(\mathcal{C}' \| (Q \backslash \overline{L})\big)(C)$ and the inputs and outputs offered by the contexts $(\mathcal{C}' \backslash L) \| Q$ and $\mathcal{C}' \| (Q \backslash \overline{L})$ (according to Definition 8) are the same.

Now, if $\mathcal{X}$ does not occur in $\mathcal{C}'$ in the scope of a restriction operator then we are done, otherwise we consider the following function $f_{\mathcal{X}}$.

Given a context $\mathcal{C}''$, such that $\mathcal{X}$ occurs in $\mathcal{C}''$ in the scope of a restriction operator and a system R, $f_{\mathcal{X}}(\mathcal{C}'', R)$ is inductively defined by means of the following two cases (depending on whether $\mathcal{C}''$ is in the form $\mathcal{C}''' \backslash L$ or $(\mathcal{C}''' \backslash L) \| S$):

$$f_{\mathcal{X}}(\mathcal{C}''' \backslash L, R) = \begin{cases} \mathcal{C}''' \| (R \backslash \overline{L}) & \text{if } \mathcal{X} \text{ is not inside a restriction in } \mathcal{C}''' \\ f_{\mathcal{X}}(\mathcal{C}''', R \backslash \overline{L}) & \text{otherwise} \end{cases}$$

$$f_{\mathcal{X}}((\mathcal{C}''' \backslash L) \| S, R) = \begin{cases} \mathcal{C}''' \| ((S \| R) \backslash \overline{L}) & \text{if } \mathcal{X} \text{ is not inside a restriction in } \mathcal{C}''' \\ f_{\mathcal{X}}(\mathcal{C}''', (S \| R) \backslash \overline{L}) & \text{otherwise} \end{cases}$$

In the following we show that, for any context $\mathcal{C}''$ such that $\mathcal{X}$ occurs in $\mathcal{C}''$ in the scope of a restriction operator and system R, $f_{\mathcal{X}}(\mathcal{C}'', R)$ is such that, for every $C \in \mathcal{P}_{con}$, the reduction behaviour of the system $\big(\mathcal{C}'' \| R\big)(C)$ is homomorphic to that of $\big(f_{\mathcal{X}}(\mathcal{C}'', R)\big)(C)$; the inputs and outputs offered by the contexts $\mathcal{C}'' \| R$ and $f_{\mathcal{X}}(\mathcal{C}'', R)$ (according to Definition 8) are the same; and $\big(f_{\mathcal{X}}(\mathcal{C}'', R)\big)(C)$ can be turned by using commutativity and associativity of parallel composition into the form $C \| P$, for some $P \in \mathcal{P}_{sys}$.

This result yields the thesis by taking $\mathcal{C}''$ to be $\mathcal{C}'$ and R to be $Q \backslash \overline{L}$.

The result above can be shown by induction on depth of the inductive definition of function $f_{\mathcal{X}}$.

The base case is either $\mathcal{C}'' = \mathcal{C}''' \backslash L$ or $\mathcal{C}'' = (\mathcal{C}''' \backslash L) \| S$ with (in both cases) $\mathcal{X}$ not occurring in $\mathcal{C}'''$ in the scope of a restriction. In such cases the result obviously holds true because, for every $C \in \mathcal{P}_{con}$, the reduction behaviour of the system $\big((\mathcal{C}''' \backslash L) \| R\big)(C)$ is homomorphic to that of $\big(\mathcal{C}''' \| (R \backslash \overline{L})\big)(C)$ and the reduction behaviour of the system $\big((\mathcal{C}''' \backslash L) \| S \| R\big)(C)$ is homomorphic to that of $\big(\mathcal{C}''' \| ((S \| R) \backslash \overline{L})\big)(C)$. Moreover the inputs and outputs offered by the contexts $(\mathcal{C}''' \backslash L) \| R$ and $\mathcal{C}''' \| (R \backslash \overline{L})$ are the same and the inputs and outputs offered by the contexts $(\mathcal{C}''' \backslash L) \| S \| R$ and $\mathcal{C}''' \| ((S \| R) \backslash \overline{L})$ are the same.

In the inductive case the result is derived directly from the induction hypothesis and, again, from the fact that the reduction behaviour of the system $\big((\mathcal{C}''' \backslash L) \| R\big)(C)$ is homomorphic to that of $\big(\mathcal{C}''' \| (R \backslash \overline{L})\big)(C)$ and the reduction behaviour of the system $\big((\mathcal{C}''' \backslash L) \| S \| R\big)(C)$ is homomorphic to that of the system $(\mathcal{C}'''\|((S\|R)\setminus\!\setminus\overline{L}))(C)$ and the inputs and outputs offered by the respective contexts are (pairwise) the same. □

C Proof of Theorem 3

In this appendix we provide the proof of Theorem 3 stating a sound characterization of the subcontract relation in terms of the should-testing pre-order of [26]. Before reporting the proof of the theorem, we first introduce some technical machinery.

In order to build a test for the transformation $\mathcal{NF}(C\setminus\!\setminus(\mathcal{N}-O))$ of a contract C we have to consider a similar transformation for a system P that is executed in parallel with the contract. First of all, we consider the normal form $\mathcal{NF}(P)$ as defined above. Then, we perform the following two additional transformations that, respectively, add the $\surd'$ success label to the test and perform an input/output inversion so to deal with the CSP-like synchronization (where equal actions are synchronized) considered in the testing scenario of [26].

We first consider $\mathcal{NF}'(P) \equiv \mathcal{NF}(P)\{\surd;\surd';X_{P'}/\surd;X_{P'} \mid P' \in \mathcal{P}_{sys}\}$, i.e. $\mathcal{NF}'(P)$ is the term $rec_{X_P}\theta'$ where θ' is obtained from θ in $\mathcal{NF}(P) \equiv rec_{X_P}\theta$ by replacing every subterm $\surd;X_{P'}$ occurring in θ, for any P', with the subterm $\surd;\surd';X_{P'}$. The LTS $[\![\mathcal{NF}'(P)]\!] = (S'', \Lambda_\tau, \longrightarrow'', \mathcal{NF}'(P))$ turns out to be, according to the definitions in [26], as follows

- $S'' = \{\mathcal{NF}'(P') \equiv rec_{X_{P'}}\theta' \mid P' \in S\} \cup \{\mathcal{NF}'_{\surd}(P'') \equiv \surd'.rec_{X_{P''}}\theta' \mid \exists P' \in S : P' \xrightarrow{\surd} P''\}$
- $\longrightarrow'' = \{(\mathcal{NF}'(P'), \lambda, \mathcal{NF}'(P'')) \mid P' \xrightarrow{\lambda} P'' \wedge \lambda \neq \surd\}$
  $\cup\{(\mathcal{NF}'(P'), \surd, \mathcal{NF}'_{\surd}(P'')) \mid P' \xrightarrow{\surd} P''\}$
  $\cup\{(\mathcal{NF}'_{\surd}(P''), \surd', \mathcal{NF}'(P'')) \mid \mathcal{NF}'_{\surd}(P'') \in S''\}$

where we assume $(S, \Lambda_\tau, \longrightarrow, P)$ to denote the LTS $[\![P]\!]$.

We then consider $\overline{\mathcal{NF}'(P)}$, i.e. the term $rec_{X_P}\theta''$ where θ'' is obtained from θ' in $\mathcal{NF}'(P) \equiv rec_{X_P}\theta'$ by turning every a occurring in θ', for any $a \in \mathcal{N}$, into $\overline{a}$ and every $\overline{a}$ occurring in θ', for any $a \in \mathcal{N}$, into a. The LTS $[\![\overline{\mathcal{NF}'(P)}]\!] = (S''', \Lambda_\tau, \longrightarrow''', \overline{\mathcal{NF}'(P)})$ turns out to be a transformation of $[\![\mathcal{NF}'(P)]\!]$ where θ'' instead of θ' is considered inside states (the state obtained in this way from a state $\mathcal{NF}'(P')$ is denoted by $\overline{\mathcal{NF}'(P')}$ and similarly a state $\mathcal{NF}'_{\surd}(P')$ is turned into $\overline{\mathcal{NF}'_{\surd}(P')}$) and whose transition labels are transformed by inverting input/output actions as described above.

We now introduce mapping of traces of $[\![[C]]\!]$ into $[\![\mathcal{NF}(C)]\!]$ and mapping of traces of $[\![P]\!]$ into $[\![\mathcal{NF}'(P)]\!]$. First of all we define a n-length trace $tr \in Tr_n^{\mathcal{T}}$, with $n \geq 0$, of a LTS $\mathcal{T} = (S, Lab, \longrightarrow, s_{init})$ to be a pair (s, λ), where s is a function from the interval of integers $[0, n]$ to states in S (we will use s_i to stand for $s(i)$) and λ is a function from the interval of integers $[1, n]$ to labels in Lab (we will use λ_i to stand for $\lambda(i)$) such that $s_{i-1} \xrightarrow{\lambda_i} s_i$, for $1 \leq i \leq n$. A n-length initial trace $tr \in ITr_n^{\mathcal{T}}$ is defined in the same way with the additional constraint that $s_0 = s_{init}$. We let $Tr^{\mathcal{T}}$ to stand for $\bigcup_{n \geq 0} Tr_n^{\mathcal{T}}$. In the following we will also denote a n-length trace tr simply by writing the sequence of its transitions, i.e. $tr = s_0 \xrightarrow{\lambda_1} s_1 \xrightarrow{\lambda_2} \dots \xrightarrow{\lambda_{n-1}} s_{n-1} \xrightarrow{\lambda_n} s_n$. We denote concatenation of two traces $tr' \in Tr_n^{\mathcal{T}}$ and $tr'' \in Tr_m^{\mathcal{T}}$ such that $s'_n = s''_0$ by $tr' \frown tr''$ defined as the trace $tr \in Tr_{n+m}^{\mathcal{T}}$ with $s_i = s'_i$ for $0 \leq i \leq n$, $\lambda_i = \lambda'_i$ for $1 \leq i \leq n$, $s_{n+i} = s''_i$ for $1 \leq i \leq m$ and $\lambda_{n+i} = \lambda''_i$ for $1 \leq i \leq m$. We also use $less_i(tr)$ to stand for the shortened trace $tr' \in Tr_{n-i}^{\mathcal{T}}$ obtained from the trace $tr \in Tr_n^{\mathcal{T}}$ by simply letting $s'_i = s_i$ for $0 \leq i \leq n-i$ and $\lambda'_i = \lambda_i$ for $1 \leq i \leq n-i$. We use $less(tr)$ to stand for $less_1(tr)$. Finally we denote with $vis(tr)$ the sequence of visible labels of the trace tr, i.e., the string $w \in (\mathcal{L} - \{\tau\})^*$ defined by induction on the length $n \geq 0$ of trace tr as follows. If $n = 0$ then $vis(tr) = \varepsilon$. If $n \geq 1$ then: $vis(tr) = vis(less(tr))$ if $\lambda_n = \tau$, $vis(tr) = vis(less(tr)) \frown \lambda_n$ otherwise (where we use $w' \frown w''$ to denote string concatenation).

Let us consider a transition $s \xrightarrow{\lambda} s'$ of $[\![[C]]\!]$. We can take $tr = s \xrightarrow{\lambda} s'$ with $tr \in Tr_1^{[\![[C]]\!]}$ and we define $map(tr) = \mathcal{NF}(s) \xrightarrow{\lambda} \mathcal{NF}(s')$. We then define the mapping $map(tr)$ of a whatever transition $tr = (s, \lambda) \in Tr_n^{[\![[C]]\!]}$ to be the transition $tr' = (s', \lambda') \in Tr_n^{[\![\mathcal{NF}(C)]\!]}$ with $s'_0 = \mathcal{NF}(s_0)$ and $s'_n = \mathcal{NF}(s_n)$ achieved by induction on $n \geq 0$ as follows. If $n = 0$ then $map(tr)$ is the trace $tr' \in Tr_0^{[\![\mathcal{NF}(C)]\!]}$ such that $s'_0 = \mathcal{NF}(s_0)$. If $n \geq 1$ then $map(tr) = map(less(tr)) \frown map(s_{n-1} \xrightarrow{\lambda_n} s_n)$. It is immediate to verify that for any $tr \in Tr^{[\![[C]]\!]}$, $vis(map(tr)) = vis(tr)$. Moreover we have that $map : Tr^{[\![[C]]\!]} \rightarrow Tr^{[\![\mathcal{NF}(C)]\!]}$ is obviously injective and surjective.

Let us consider a transition $s \xrightarrow{\lambda} s'$ of $[\![P]\!]$. We can take $tr = s \xrightarrow{\lambda} s'$ with $tr \in Tr_1^{[\![P]\!]}$. We define $map_{\surd}(tr)$ as follows. If $\lambda \neq \surd$ then $map_{\surd}(tr) = \mathcal{NF}'(s) \xrightarrow{\lambda} \mathcal{NF}'(s')$. Otherwise, if $\lambda = \surd$ then $map_{\surd}(tr) = \mathcal{NF}'(s) \xrightarrow{\surd} \mathcal{NF}'_{\surd}(s')$. We then define the mapping $map_{\surd}(tr)$ of a whatever transition $tr = (s, \lambda) \in Tr_n^{[\![P]\!]}$ (tr may include $\surd$ only as the final transition because target states of $\surd$ transitions have no outgoing transitions in the semantics of systems) to be the transition $tr' = (s', \lambda') \in Tr_n^{[\![\mathcal{NF}(P)]\!]}$ with $s'_0 = \mathcal{NF}'(s_0)$ and, in the case $n \geq 1$, $s'_n = \mathcal{NF}'(s_n)$ if $\lambda_n \neq \surd$, $s'_n = \mathcal{NF}'_{\surd}(s_n)$ otherwise, achieved by induction on $n \geq 0$ as follows. If $n = 0$ then $map_{\surd}(tr)$ is the trace $tr' \in Tr_0^{[\![\mathcal{NF}'(P)]\!]}$ such that $s'_0 = \mathcal{NF}'(s_0)$. If $n \geq 1$ then $map_{\surd}(tr) = map_{\surd}(less(tr)) \frown map_{\surd}(s_{n-1} \xrightarrow{\lambda_n} s_n)$. It is immediate to verify that for any $tr \in Tr^{[\![P]\!]}$, $vis(map_{\surd}(tr)) = vis(tr)$. Moreover we have that $map_{\surd} : Tr^{[\![P]\!]} \rightarrow Tr^{[\![\mathcal{NF}'(P)]\!]}$ is injective (because the last transition of the trace singles out at each inductive step a unique mapping that can produce it) and is surjective over the codomain of traces that begin with a state of the form $\mathcal{NF}'(s)$ with $s \in [\![P]\!]$ and do not include $\surd'$ transitions.

We finally define some other auxiliary functions that will be used in the proof. Given a trace $tr \in Tr^{[\![\mathcal{NF}'(P)]\!]}$ or $tr \in Tr^{[\![\overline{\mathcal{NF}'(P)}]\!]}$, we define $\overline{tr}$ to be $tr' = (s', \lambda')$ defined as: $s'_i = \overline{s_i}$ and $\lambda'_i = \overline{\lambda_i}$ for any i (where the application of the overbar to states or labels that have it already causes its removal and it has no effect when applied to τ and $\surd$ labels). Notice that $vis(\overline{tr}) = \overline{vis(tr)}$ denoting the application of the overbar to any label occurring in the sequence of visible labels.

Proof of Theorem 3

According to the definition of should-testing of [26], since

$$\mathcal{NF}(C' \backslash\!\backslash (\mathcal{N}-O)) \preceq_{test} \mathcal{NF}(C \backslash\!\backslash (\mathcal{N}-O))$$

we have that, for every test t, if $\mathcal{NF}(C \backslash\!\backslash (\mathcal{N}-O))$ **shd** t, then also $\mathcal{NF}(C' \backslash\!\backslash (\mathcal{N}-O))$ **shd** t, where Q **shd** t iff

$$\forall w \in \Lambda_\tau^*, Q'. \qquad Q \|_\Lambda t \xrightarrow{w} Q' \qquad \Rightarrow \qquad \exists v \in \Lambda_\tau^*, Q'' : Q' \xrightarrow{v} Q'' \xrightarrow{\surd'}$$

where $\|_\Lambda$ is the CSP parallel operator.

Let us now consider $P \in P_{sys}$ with $(C \backslash\!\backslash \mathcal{N}-O \| P)\!\downarrow$. In the following we will provide a first subproof that this implies $\mathcal{NF}(C \backslash\!\backslash (\mathcal{N}-O))$ **shd** $\overline{\mathcal{NF}'(P)}$. Since $\mathcal{NF}(C' \backslash\!\backslash (\mathcal{N}-O)) \preceq_{test} \mathcal{NF}(C \backslash\!\backslash (\mathcal{N}-O))$, from this we can derive $\mathcal{NF}(C' \backslash\!\backslash (\mathcal{N}-O))$ **shd** $\overline{\mathcal{NF}'(P)}$. In the following we will provide a second subproof that this implies $(C' \backslash\!\backslash \mathcal{N}-O \| P)\!\downarrow$. The thesis, then, directly follows from Lemma 1.

First subproof: $(\tilde{C} \| P)\!\downarrow \Rightarrow \mathcal{NF}(\tilde{C})$ **shd** $\overline{\mathcal{NF}'(P)}$, with $\tilde{C} = C \backslash\!\backslash (\mathcal{N}-O)$.

We consider the trace $tr = (s, \lambda) \in ITr_r^{[\![\mathcal{NF}(\tilde{C}) \|_\Lambda \overline{\mathcal{NF}'(P)}]\!]}$ such that $\lambda_i \neq \surd'$ for any i. There exist $\dot{tr} \in ITr_n^{[\![\mathcal{NF}(\tilde{C})]\!]}$ and $\ddot{tr} \in ITr_m^{[\![\overline{\mathcal{NF}'(P)}]\!]}$, corresponding to the local moves performed by the two parallel processes when doing trace tr, such that $vis(\dot{tr}) = vis(\ddot{tr})$.

We have two cases for the structure of the last state of trace $\ddot{tr}$:

1. $\ddot{s}_m \equiv \overline{\mathcal{NF}'(s)}$ for some $s \in [\![P]\!]$
2. $\ddot{s}_m \equiv \overline{\mathcal{NF}'_\surd(s)}$ for some $s \in [\![P]\!]$

Let us start by taking $\ddot{tr}$ to be as in the simpler case (2). Since, by def. of $\mathcal{NF}'(P)$, $\ddot{s}_m = \overline{\mathcal{NF}'_\surd(s)} \Rightarrow \ddot{s}_m \xrightarrow{\surd'}$, we have $s_r = \dot{s}_n \|_\Lambda \ddot{s}_m \xrightarrow{\surd'}$ and we are done.

We now move to the non-trivial case (1) for $\ddot{tr}$. Consider $\ddot{tr}' = map_\surd^{-1}(\overline{\ddot{tr}}) \in ITr_m^{[\![P]\!]}$. We have $\ddot{s}_m = \overline{\mathcal{NF}'(\ddot{s}'_m)}$. Let us also consider $\dot{tr}' = map^{-1}(\dot{tr}) \in ITr_n^{[\![[\tilde{C}]]\!]}$. We have $\dot{s}_n = \mathcal{NF}(\dot{s}'_n)$. Moreover, $vis(\ddot{tr}') = \overline{vis(\ddot{tr})} = \overline{vis(\dot{tr})} = \overline{vis(\dot{tr}')}$.

Therefore, there exists $tr' \in ITr_r^{[\![\tilde{C} \| P]\!]}$, with $\lambda'_i = \tau$ for any i, such that $s'_r = \dot{s}'_n \| \ddot{s}'_m$.

Since $(\tilde{C} \| P)\!\downarrow$ we have that there exists $tr'' \in Tr_{r''}^{[\![\tilde{C} \| P]\!]}$ with $s''_0 = s'_r$, $\lambda''_i = \tau$ for $1 \leq i \leq r'' - 1$ and $\lambda''_{r''} = \surd$. Therefore, there exist $\dot{tr}'' \in Tr_{n''}^{[\![[\tilde{C}]]\!]}$ with $\dot{s}''_0 = \dot{s}'_n$ and $\ddot{tr}'' \in Tr_{m''}^{[\![P]\!]}$, with $\ddot{s}''_0 = \ddot{s}'_m$ corresponding to the local moves performed by the two parallel processes when doing trace tr'', such that $vis(\dot{tr}'') = \overline{vis(\ddot{tr}'')}$.

Let us now consider $\dot{tr}''' = map(\dot{tr}'') \in Tr_{n''}^{[\![\mathcal{NF}(\tilde{C})]\!]}$. We have $\dot{s}'''_0 = \mathcal{NF}(\dot{s}''_0) = \mathcal{NF}(\dot{s}'_n)$ and $\dot{\lambda}'''_{n''} = \surd$. Let us also consider $\ddot{tr}''' = map_{\surd}(\ddot{tr}'') \in Tr_{m''}^{[\![\overline{\mathcal{NF}'(P)}]\!]}$. We have $\ddot{s}'''_0 = \overline{\mathcal{NF}'(\ddot{s}''_0)} = \overline{\mathcal{NF}'(\ddot{s}'_m)}$ and $\ddot{\lambda}'''_{m''} = \surd$. Moreover, $vis(\dot{tr}''') = vis(\dot{tr}'') = vis(\ddot{tr}'') = vis(\ddot{tr}''')$.

Therefore, there exists $tr''' \in Tr_{r''}^{[\![\mathcal{NF}(\tilde{C}) \|_A \overline{\mathcal{NF}'(P)}]\!]}$. Such trace has initial state $s'''_0 = \mathcal{NF}(\dot{s}'_n) \|_A \overline{\mathcal{NF}'(\ddot{s}'_m)} = \dot{s}_n \|_A \ddot{s}_m = s_r$, and $s'''_{r''} = \dot{s}'''_{n''} \|_A \ddot{s}'''_{m''}$. Moreover, since, by def. of $\mathcal{NF}'(P)$, $\ddot{\lambda}'''_{m''} = \surd \Rightarrow \ddot{s}'''_{m''} \xrightarrow{\surd'}$, we have $s'''_{r''} \xrightarrow{\surd'}$.

Second subproof: $\mathcal{NF}(\tilde{C}')$ **shd** $\overline{\mathcal{NF}'(P)} \Rightarrow (\tilde{C}' \| P) \downarrow$, with $\tilde{C}' = C' \backslash\!\backslash (\mathcal{N} - O)$. We consider the trace $tr = (s, \lambda) \in ITr_r^{[\![\tilde{C}' \| P]\!]}$ such that $\lambda_i = \tau$ for any i. There exist $\dot{tr} \in ITr_n^{[\![[\tilde{C}']]\!]}$ and $\ddot{tr} \in ITr_m^{[\![P]\!]}$ corresponding to the local moves performed by the two parallel processes when doing trace tr, such that $vis(\dot{tr}) = \overline{vis(\ddot{tr})}$.

Let us now consider $\dot{tr}' = map(\dot{tr}) \in ITr_n^{[\![\mathcal{NF}(\tilde{C}')]\!]}$. We have $\dot{s}'_n = \mathcal{NF}(\dot{s}_n)$. Let us also consider $\ddot{tr}' = \overline{map_{\surd}(\ddot{tr})} \in ITr_m^{[\![\overline{\mathcal{NF}'(P)}]\!]}$. We have $\ddot{s}'_m = \overline{\mathcal{NF}'(\ddot{s}_m)}$ because $\ddot{tr}$ does not include a $\surd$ transition. Moreover, $vis(\dot{tr}') = vis(\dot{tr}) = \overline{vis(\ddot{tr})} = vis(\ddot{tr}')$. Therefore, there exists $tr' \in ITr_r^{[\![\mathcal{NF}(\tilde{C}') \|_A \overline{\mathcal{NF}'(P)}]\!]}$ with $s'_r = \dot{s}'_n \|_A \ddot{s}'_m = \mathcal{NF}(\dot{s}_n) \|_A \overline{\mathcal{NF}'(\ddot{s}_m)}$.

Since $\mathcal{NF}(\tilde{C}')$ **shd** $\overline{\mathcal{NF}'(P)}$ we have that there exists $tr'' \in Tr_{r''}^{[\![\mathcal{NF}(\tilde{C}') \|_A \overline{\mathcal{NF}'(P)}]\!]}$ with $s''_0 = s'_r$, such that $\lambda''_i \neq \surd'$ for $1 \leq i \leq r'' - 1$ and $\lambda''_{r''} = \surd'$.

There exist $\dot{tr}'' \in Tr_{n''}^{[\![\mathcal{NF}(\tilde{C}')]\!]}$ with $\dot{s}''_0 = \dot{s}'_n$ and $\ddot{tr}'' \in Tr_{m''}^{[\![\overline{\mathcal{NF}'(P)}]\!]}$, with $\ddot{s}''_0 = \ddot{s}'_m$ corresponding to the local moves performed by the two parallel processes when doing trace tr''. We must have $\ddot{\lambda}''_{m''} = \surd'$ and, since $\ddot{s}''_0 = \ddot{s}'_m$ is in the form $\overline{\mathcal{NF}'(\ddot{s}_m)}$, by def. of $\mathcal{NF}'(P)$ we have ($r'' \geq 2$ and) $\ddot{\lambda}''_{m''-1} = \surd$. Moreover we must have $vis(\dot{tr}'') = vis(less(\ddot{tr}''))$, hence in particular $\dot{\lambda}''_{n''} = \surd$: the $\surd$ transition must be the last one in such a trace (i.e. there are no τ transitions afterward) because target states of $\surd$ transition have no outgoing transitions in the semantics of contracts and the transformation $\mathcal{NF}(\tilde{C}')$ cannot add outgoing τ transitions to such states.

Let us now consider $\dot{tr}''' = map^{-1}(\dot{tr}'') \in Tr_{n''}^{[\![[\tilde{C}']]\!]}$. We have $\dot{s}''_0 = \dot{s}'_n = \mathcal{NF}(\dot{s}'''_0)$ and $\dot{\lambda}'''_{n''} = \surd$. Let us also consider $\ddot{tr}''' = map_{\surd}^{-1}(less(\ddot{tr}'')) \in Tr_{m''-1}^{[\![P]\!]}$. We have $\ddot{s}''_0 = \ddot{s}'_m = \overline{\mathcal{NF}'(\ddot{s}'''_0)}$ and $\ddot{\lambda}'''_{m''-1} = \surd$. Moreover, $vis(\ddot{tr}''') = \overline{vis(less(\ddot{tr}''))} = \overline{vis(\dot{tr}'')} = \overline{vis(\dot{tr}''')}$.

Therefore, there exists $tr''' \in Tr_{r''}^{[\![\tilde{C}' \| P]\!]}$ such that $\lambda'''_i = \tau$ for $1 \leq i \leq r'' - 1$, with $s'''_0 = \dot{s}'''_0 \|_A \ddot{s}'''_0 = \dot{s}_n \|_A \ddot{s}_m = s_r$ and $\lambda'''_{r''} = \surd$. □

Quantitative Analysis of Web Services Using SRMC

Allan Clark, Stephen Gilmore, and Mirco Tribastone

Laboratory for Foundations of Computer Science
The University of Edinburgh, Scotland

Abstract. In this tutorial paper we present quantitative methods for analysing Web Services with the goal of understanding how they will perform under increased demand, or when asked to serve a larger pool of service subscribers. We use a process calculus called SRMC to model the service. We apply efficient analysis techniques to numerically evaluate our model. The process calculus and the numerical analysis are supported by a set of software tools which relieve the modeller of the burden of generating and evaluating a large family of related models. The methods are illustrated on a classical example of Web Service usage in a business-to-business scenario.

1 Introduction

Web Services are a popular and effective method of component-based development of distributed systems. Using widely-agreed standards service providers are able to quickly develop flexible assemblies of components to respond to new business demands. Legacy systems can be incorporated using application servers as intermediates which expose the functionality of the legacy system on the network, allowing it to be invoked by a remote service. This might itself have been invoked by another service, allowing these components to be built into complex workflows and managed as either an orchestration or a choreography.

Service providers publish their services in a public registry. Service consumers discover services at run-time and bind to them dynamically, choosing from the available service instances according to the criteria which are of most importance to them. This architecture provides robust service in difficult operational conditions. If one instance of a service is temporarily unavailable then another one is there to take its place.

It is likely though that this replacement is not fully functionally identical. It might have some missing functionality, or it might even offer additional functionality not found in the temporarily unavailable service instance. One reason why differences such as this arise is that new versions of services are released in order to correct errors or add new features. These updates are applied at different times at different sites and therefore it is quite common for different hosts to be running different versions of the software services. Some will be running an older version, others the latest. Even if they are hosting the same version

M. Bernardo, L. Padovani, and G. Zavattaro (Eds.): SFM 2009, LNCS 5569, pp. 296–339, 2009.

of the software then because of different security policies at different sites some hosts will have disabled certain features, whereas others will not have done this because their security policy is more permissive.

Even in the rare case of finding a functionally-identical replacement matters are still not straightforward when non-functional criteria such as availability and performance are brought into the picture. It is very unusual indeed for all of the hosts which offer instances of a service to have identical performance profiles. In contrast, the best practice in virtualisation argues that the hosts should intentionally be heterogeneous (using different processors, memory, caches or disks) in order that not all of them can be affected by a single flaw in a hardware component. Seemingly small modifications such as this can have a vast impact on performance which affects essentially all of the performance measures which one would think to evaluate over the system configuration.

In practice it is very frequently the case that the functionally-equivalent replacement for the temporarily unavailable service will exhibit different performance characteristics. Ultimately this is because it hosts a copy of the service on another hardware platform which has either been intentionally made different for reasons such as virtualisation practice, or unintentionally because it has been commissioned at a different time when other hardware components were the most cost-effective purchase.

Analytical or numerical performance evaluation provides valuable insights into the timed behaviour of systems over the short or long run. Important methods used in the field include the numerical evaluation of continuous-time Markov chains (CTMCs) (see, for example, [1]) and the use of fluid-flow approximation using systems of ordinary differential equations (ODEs) (see, for example, [2]). In the present paper we work with a timed process calculus, the Sensoria Reference Markovian Calculus (SRMC) [3,4] which builds on Performance Evaluation Process Algebra (PEPA) [1]. PEPA has both a discrete-state Markovian semantics and a continuous-state differential equation semantics. We make use of both kinds of analysis here.

Mathematical modelling formalisms such as CTMCs and ODEs are often applied to study fixed, static system configurations with known subcomponents with known rate parameters. This is far from the operating conditions of service-oriented computing where for critical service components a set of replacements with perhaps vastly different performance qualities stand ready to substitute for components which are either unavailable, or the consumer just simply chooses not to bind to them.

We seek to address this issue with SRMC by building into the calculus a mechanism for the formal expression of uncertainty about binding and parameters (in addition to the other dimension of uncertainty about durations modelled in the Markovian setting through the use of exponentially-distributed random variables). We put forward a method of numerical evaluation for this calculus which scales well with increasing problem size to allow precise comparisons to be made across all of the possible service bindings and levels of availability considered.

Numerical evaluation is supported inside a modelling environment for the calculus. In addition to comparing the results of particular service configurations we can combine the results to provide overall performance characteristics such as are required for service level agreements.

Structure of this paper. SRMC allows three levels of uncertainty; uncertainty as to the configuration of the system, uncertainty as to the rate parameters of some system components and finally uncertainty as to the duration of events. After an introduction to the calculus in Section 2 we build up to the full SRMC language in reverse order of these levels of uncertainty. In Section 2.2 we review the PEPA process algebra, a stochastic process algebra with support for compositional construction of an underlying Markov chain. Thus we can reason about the performance of a known system with unknown duration of events. We continue in this section to show how we can augment this process algebra with the ability to specify a range of rate parameters such that not only is the duration of a particular event unknown but its average duration is specified as a set of possible values. Because of this a single model in the SRMC calculus gives rise to a related family of models in the PEPA stochastic process algebra. In Section 4 we explain how this family of models is derived. Our intention is to perform analysis on these models. In Section 5 we present a high-level query language for models, eXtended Stochastic Probes (XSP). We show how this language is used to query models to determine whether or not they satisfy precise service-level agreements on their quality of service. In Section 6 we apply Markovian analysis techniques to all of the models in this related family. In Section 7 we address the challenge of large-scale modelling and recast the modelling problem in the continuous world where we can apply Hillston's fluid-flow approximation method [2] to obtain a system of ordinary differential equations which allow us to efficiently analyse large-scale versions of our models. In Section 8 we consider the suite of software tools which are available to support the SRMC and PEPA process calculi. Section 9 surveys related work and we present our conclusions after this.

2 Background

In order to introduce the concepts of SRMC we build up a generic example of a Web Service. We will provide a specific example later.

2.1 SRMC

In this example we have a service which remains idle until it receives a request from a client. The service does not specify the rate at which requests arrive, this is specified elsewhere (in the definition of the client). Once a request comes in the service computes (at rate `r_c`) and then returns the response (at rate `r_r`) before becoming idle again.

Listing 1.1. SRMC model of a Web Service

```
WS_A::{
  r_c = 10.0;  r_r = 1.0;
  Idle       = (request, _).Computing;
  Computing  = (compute, r_c).Responding;
  Responding = (response, r_r).Idle;
};
```

This high-level model of the service describes only three states, `Idle`, `Computing` and `Responding`, abstracting from many details of the service. These three related definitions are collected into the namespace for the component `WS_A` together with the values of the rates for the activities `compute` and `response`.

This definition gives rise to a small transition system with only three states and three transitions. The transition system corresponding to the component `WS_A` is shown in Figure 1. Note that component names and rate names have been replaced by their fully qualified versions. Activity type names (such as `request`, `compute` and `response`) are not subject to this expansion because these names are used to define synchronisation points with other components (and therefore cannot be renamed).

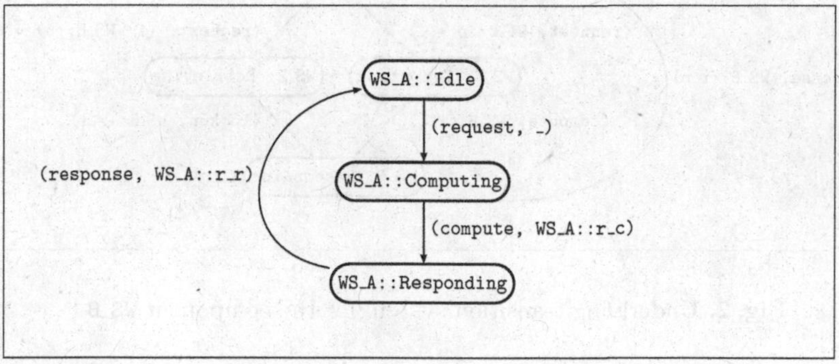

Fig. 1. Underlying transition system for the component `WS_A`

We now consider an optimised version of this service where some computation is avoided because the service can retrieve a previously computed result. Looking up a result is ten times faster than re-calculating it. Only 30% of incoming requests can be answered in this way, the remaining 70% of requests lead to the result being computed as before.

Model components with similar names can be distinguished because they are collected under a different namespace `WS_B`. Thus here we have the definition of a process term whose fully qualified name is `WS_B::Idle` whereas the fully qualified name of the previous process term is `WS_A::Idle`.

Listing 1.2. SRMC model of an optimised Web Service

```
WS_B::{
  r_l = 100.0;  p = 0.7;  r_c = 10.0;
  r_r = { 1.0, 0.6, 0.2 };
  Idle        = (request, p * _).Computing;
              + (request, (1 - p) * _).Retrieving;
  Computing   = (compute, r_c).Responding;
  Retrieving  = (lookup, r_l).Responding;
  Responding  = (response, r_r).Idle;
};
```

The advantage of using this optimised version of the service is reduced slightly because connectivity to the service is very variable and responses coming back from the service may be delayed (even though the service generated them quickly by looking up a previously-calculated result). The transition system corresponding to the component WS_B is shown in Figure 2.

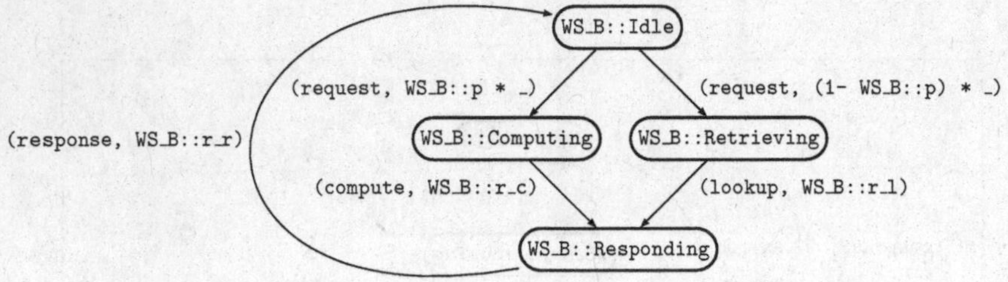

Fig. 2. Underlying transition system for the component WS_B

In SRMC we can characterise this kind of variability by recording different possible parameter values for the `response` activity. We denote these by listing a set of possible values for the rate parameter ($\{ 1.0, 0.6, 0.2 \}$ above). Uncertainty about a rate parameter is represented in SRMC in this way (by listing a set of possibilities) and uncertainty about a service binding is represented in a very similar way.

Listing 1.3. Specifying binding uncertainty in SRMC

```
WS ::= { WS_A, WS_B };
Service = WS::Idle;
```

These definitions record that the Web Service which we use will either be A (the unoptimised version) or B (the optimised version) and that the service is initially in its idle state.

Now we are able to complete our model by providing the definition of a client who thinks for some time before requesting the service and waiting for the response.

Listing 1.4. SRMC model of a Client

```
Client::{
  r_t = 0.002;  r_r = 0.5;
  Idle        = (think, r_t).Requesting;
  Requesting = (request, r_r).Waiting;
  Waiting     = (response, _).Idle;
};
```

The namespace mechanism is helpful here also because there is no clash between the name of the rate identifier used here for requests (whose fully qualified name is `Client::r_r`) and rate identifiers used earlier for responses (whose fully qualified names are respectively `WS_A::r_r` and `WS_B::r_r`). The transition system corresponding to the client is shown in Figure 3.

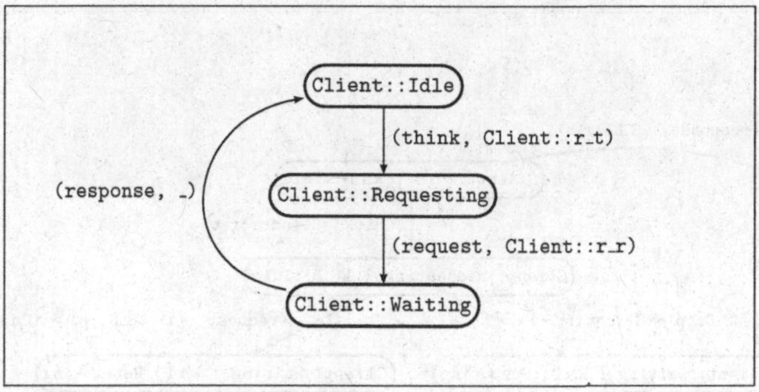

Fig. 3. Underlying transition system for the client

Finally, we complete the model by requiring the Client and the Web Service (whichever one it is) to cooperate on the `request` and `response` activities. All other activities are performed by a single component independently from the others.

Listing 1.5. SRMC model composition

```
Client::Idle <request, response> Service
```

In the case where the binding is resolved in favour of WS_A then the overall model has the transition system corresponding to the client paired with WS_A as shown in Figure 4. All of the definitions which relate to the WS_B namespace are removed from this model and have no impact on the underlying transition system.

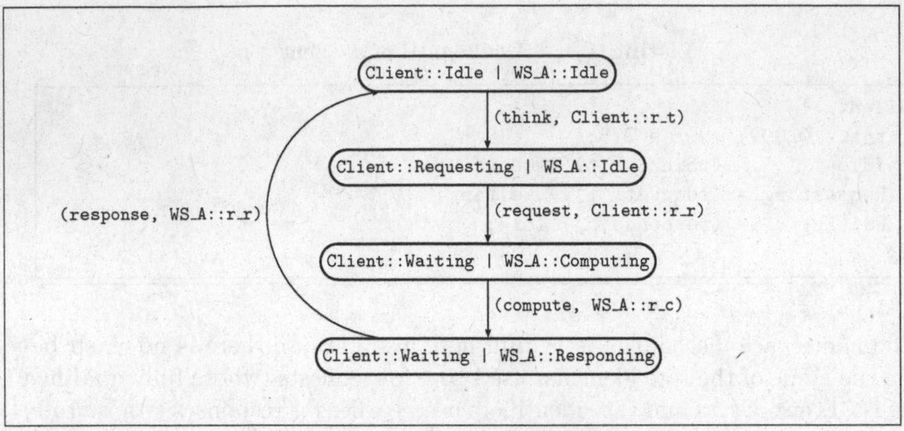

Fig. 4. Underlying transition system for the client paired with WS_A

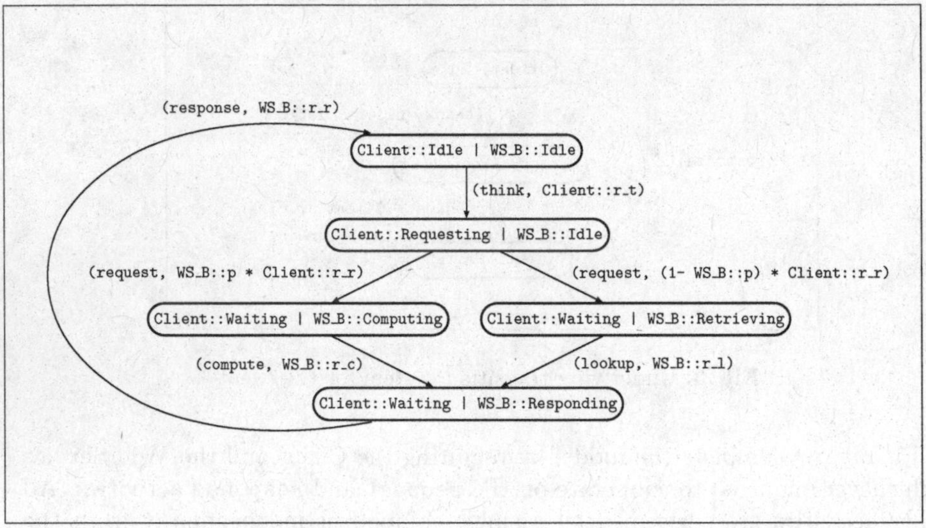

Fig. 5. Underlying transition system for the client paired with WS_B

If, on the other hand, the binding is resolved in favour of WS_B then the overall model has the transition system corresponding to the client paired with WS_B as shown in Figure 5. All of the definitions which relate to the WS_A namespace are removed from this model.

2.2 PEPA

The starting point for the new calculus was the stochastic process algebra PEPA [1]. The PEPA language has the following combinators:

$$P ::= (a, \lambda).P \mid P + P \mid P \underset{L}{\bowtie} P \mid P/L$$

A $(a, \lambda).P$ describes a process which may perform the action a at rate λ to become the process P. The rate may be a numerical rate or the special rate $\top$ (written as _ in SRMC) which means the operation is performed passively by this process which must be subsequently synchronised with over this activity. The other process involved in the synchronisation determines the rate of the activity. The process $P_1 + P_2$ depicts competitive choice between the processes P_1 and P_2 and therefore may perform any of activity which P_1 may perform or any which P_2 may perform. The operator $\underset{L}{\bowtie}$ is cooperation/synchronisation between two components over the given set of actions L. The process P/L behaves exactly as P except that the activities in the set L are no longer observable and hence it is not possible for another process to cooperate on these activities. This is referred to as *hiding*, and we will not make use of hiding in this tutorial.

A model is represented by a series of definitions which describe the sequential behaviour of named components. These named components are then combined together in a main system equation which represents the interaction between the various components in a model. This description of a model has an underlying Markov chain representation though the user is hidden from the details of the underlying states. Each defined sequential component is a description of a small stateful process and each such is combined using the cooperation combinator with the restriction that the two must synchronise over the specified action labels. This may mean that some states are unreachable so composition does not always increase the state space but in general the state-space size does increase rapidly. Full details of the PEPA stochastic process algebra can be found in [1].

3 Case Study

In this tutorial the SRMC language is illustrated by means of a case study of a Web-service orchestration. Our case study is adapted from the example proposed in the specification of WS-BPEL 2.0, the OASIS standard for the description of business process behaviour of Web services [5]. Figure 6 depicts an informal outline of the business process of a sample order management system. Boxes with straight corners represent the invocation of Web services. Dotted lines impose sequentiality between invocations, and solid lines indicate data dependency. For example, the invocation of *Complete Price Calculation* does not start until *Decide On Shipper* returns. Similarly, *Complete Production Scheduling* needs the output of *Arrange Logistics* before being called. The box with rounded corners indicates the execution of parallel flows. After *Receive Purchase Order* is executed, the executions of *Initiate Price Calculation*, *Decide On Shipper*, and *Initiate Production Scheduling* may start in parallel. Finally, after all these activities terminate *Invoice Processing* may be invoked.

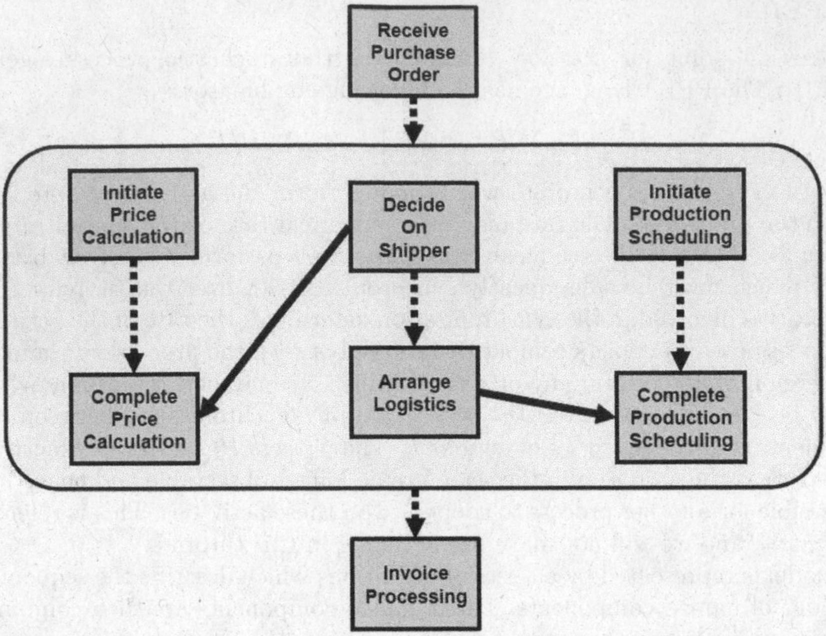

Fig. 6. Sketch of the order management system case study used in this tutorial

The aim of this tutorial is not to provide an algorithmic procedure to automatically translate BPEL processes into SRMC models, rather we show how the features of the language may be exploited to model web service orchestration. Nevertheless, the tutorial will also give directions on how to capture other, more fine-grained behaviours which are not strictly in the domain of web service description languages albeit they may affect the system's performance. The construction of the performance model of the case study will be carried out incrementally — from the components which exhibit sequential behaviour to their arrangement through the cooperation operator to impose synchronisation and ordering. The initial SRMC model will be kept intentionally simple — it will not capture dynamic binding or rate uncertainty, in effect making it fall within the realm of PEPA. This initial model will primarily serve the purpose of guiding the reader through the most basic constituents of the language. Nevertheless, we will show how it may give a coarse-grained understanding of the system's performance characteristics.

3.1 Initial Performance Model

Figure 6 clearly shows that the BPEL process is composed of four distinct components with sequential behaviour. The first component, which describes the main flow of execution, is responsible for the reception of a purchase order and the final issue of an invoice. Between these two actions, three sequential components perform some activities in parallel, as discussed above. To generate the performance model, it is necessary to associate each activity of the business process with a rate, which uniquely describes the exponentially distributed variable which indicates the duration of the activity. Listing 1.6 shows the PEPA sequential component corresponding to the main flow of execution. The operator prefix is used to describe the execution of an activity. Throughout this paper we adopt the convention that the activity name is the initials of the associated process name in Figure 6, and its rate of execution is indicated by `r_<name>`. (For example, the rate of *Receive Purchase Order* is `r_rpo`). The sequential component is cyclic so as to model the behaviour that the system is capable of processing a new order after the previous one has completed. The sequential components involved in price calculation, shipping management and production scheduling may be derived in a similar fashion. Their underlying performance models are shown in Listings 1.7, 1.8, and 1.9, respectively.

Listing 1.6. PEPA model of the main flow of execution of the BPEL process in Figure 6

```
ReceivePurchaseOrder = (rpo, r_rpo).InvoiceProcessing;
InvoiceProcessing = (ip, r_ip).ReceivePurchaseOrder;
```

Listing 1.7. PEPA model for price calculation

```
InitiatePriceCalculation = (ipc, r_ipc).CompletePriceCalculation;
CompletePriceCalculation = (cpc, r_cpc).InitiatePriceCalculation;
```

Listing 1.8. PEPA model for shipping management

```
DecideOnShipper = (dos, r_dos).ArrangeLogistics;
ArrangeLogistics = (al, r_al).DecideOnShipper;
```

Listing 1.9. PEPA model for production scheduling

```
InitiateProductionScheduling = (ips, r_ips).CompleteProductionScheduling;
CompleteProductionScheduling = (cps, r_cps).InitiateProductionScheduling;
```

In order to capture the business logic of the orchestration, these sequential components need to be augmented with further behaviour. Price calculation, shipping management, and production scheduling can only start after an order is received. Moreover, these activities may run in parallel. In SRMC this can be modelled by preceding their descriptions with a local state which synchronises over some action `fork`. Similarly, the invoice processing activity can be executed after all the parallel flows are completed. To express this, a local state is added to the descriptions, which synchronises over the action ip. Thus, Listings 1.7, 1.8, and 1.9 are revised as shown in Listings 1.10, 1.11, and 1.12, respectively. In all descriptions, the names of the synchronising components are prefixed by the words Fork and Join and their activities are executed passively.

Listing 1.10. Revised PEPA model for price calculation

```
ForkPriceCalculation = (fork, _).InitiatePriceCalculation;
InitiatePriceCalculation = (ipc, r_ipc).CompletePriceCalculation;
CompletePriceCalculation = (cpc, r_cpc).JoinPriceCalculation;
JoinPriceCalculation = (ip, _).ForkPriceCalculation;
```

Listing 1.11. Revised PEPA model for shipping management

```
ForkShipper = (fork, _).DecideOnShipper;
DecideOnShipper = (dos, r_dos).ArrangeLogistics;
ArrangeLogistics = (al, r_al).JoinShipper;
JoinShipper = (ip, _).ForkShipper;
```

Listing 1.12. Revised PEPA model for production scheduling

```
ForkProductionScheduling = (fork, _).InitiateProductionScheduling;
InitiateProductionScheduling = (ips, r_ips).CompleteProductionScheduling;
CompleteProductionScheduling = (cps, r_cps).JoinProductionScheduling;
JoinProductionScheduling = (ip, _).ForkProductionScheduling;
```

Other sequential components are added to the system to observe the causality rules of the orchestration:

1. The fork action must be performed after rpo is executed.
2. The cpc action must be performed after dos is executed.
3. The cps action must be performed after al is executed.

Each rule is implemented by a cyclic two-state sequential component which observes the related actions in the order in which they must be executed. The component in Listing 1.13 models the first rule. An excerpt of the system equation (which will be fully shown later in this section) is presented in Listing 1.14. After a purchase order is received the component Fork1 behaves as Fork2. This will in turn enable the activity fork, which will start the price calculation process.

Listing 1.13. Implementation of the causality rule for the execution of the parallel flows

```
Fork1 = (rpo, _).Fork2;
Fork2 = (fork, r_fork).Fork1;
```

Listing 1.14. Excerpt of the model's system equation showing the cooperation between the main flow and the price calculation component

```
(ReceivePurchaseOrder <rpo> Fork1) <fork> ForkPriceCalculation
```

Rules 2 and 3 are handled in a similar way: A cyclic two-state sequential component enforces the order of execution of the activities by enabling them passively. The corresponding sequential components used in this example are shown in Listings 1.15 and 1.16. Finally, the complete system equation for this model is shown in Listing 1.17.

Listing 1.15. Implementation of the causality rule between price calculation and shipping management

```
PriceShipping1 = (dos, _).PriceShipping2;
PriceShipping2 = (cpc, _).PriceShipping1;
```

Listing 1.16. Implementation of the causality rule between shipping management and production scheduling

```
ShippingProduction1 = (al, _).ShippingProduction2;
ShippingProduction2 = (cps, _).ShippingProduction1;
```

Listing 1.17. Complete system equation of the PEPA model

```
Sys = (ReceivePurchaseOrder <rpo> Fork1)
          <fork,ip>
          (
              (ForkPriceCalculation <cpc> PriceShipping1)
                  <fork,dos,ip> ForkShipper
          )
          <fork,al,ip>
          (ForkProductionScheduling <cps> ShippingProduction1)
```

Model of user workload. The system equation is combined with the model of user workload, which represents the external agents that invoke the service. Although various kinds of workload can be modelled, in this tutorial we shall consider the case of *closed workload*, i.e., a collection of users which cyclically execute the orchestration, interposing some think time between successive requests. The model of a user is shown in Listing 1.18. It describes a typical request/response scenario in which the activity `rpo` triggers the execution of the orchestration and the activity `ip` indicates the response of the system. The composition with the model of the orchestration is shown in Listing 1.19. Here, we made use of the array operator `[N_U]` to indicate N_U distinct users of the system.

Listing 1.18. Model of a user of a closed workload

```
Think = (think, r_think).Execute;
Execute = (rpo, r_rpo).Wait;
Wait = (ip, _).Think;
```

Listing 1.19. Complete model with user workload

```
Model = Think[N_U] <rpo,ip> Sys
```

System concurrency level. Similarly to the user workload, the concurrency levels of the system should be specified. The model in Listing 1.17 features one copy for each sequential component of the system. Thus, if the number of users is greater than one, then there is contention amongst these users to access the orchestration. After a user executes the shared action `rpo`, all the remaining users are *blocked* because the action cannot be enabled by the system. Indeed, the sequential component `ReceivePurchaseOrder` will behave as `InvoiceProcessing`, hence `rpo` is enabled again only after the current request has been completely processed.

In this scenario, one sequential component can be thought of as a single flow of execution which can handle only one request at all times. If multiple requests are to be handled simultaneously, then multiple copies of the sequential components need to be deployed. Again, SRMC makes use of the array operator to model this situation. The concurrency level has a clear impact on the performance of the system — it increases the system's throughput, or equivalently, reduces the response time. The concurrency level has also a clear counterpart in the actual system that the SRMC description is modelling. For instance it may refer to the number of threads or processes which are allocated to a given web service.

However, the modelling approach adopted in this case study poses an additional difficulty: although some sequential components clearly correspond to real units of execution, others have been introduced only to serve the auxiliary purpose of guaranteeing the intended order of execution of the business logic.

For this reason, the deployment of the latter kind of components will be dependent upon the concurrency levels of the sequential components which they are supporting.

One such example is the sequential component in Listing 1.15. To determine its concurrency level, we first observe that its initial local state `PriceShipping1` enables an action (i.e., `dos`) which must be executed in cooperation with the component `DecideOnShipper`, a local state of Listing 1.11. Let N_{FS} be the concurrency level of `ForkShipper` and N_{PS} be the concurrency level of `PriceShipping1`. If $N_{FS} > N_{PS}$ a reachable state of the system may have N_{FS} components in state `DecideOnShipper` and N_{PS} components in state `PriceShipping1`. Therefore, $N_{FS} - N_{PS}$ `DecideOnShipper` components cannot engage in the `dos` action. This introduces a form of blocking in the SRMC model which does not correspond to the real behaviour of the system, because `dos` is in fact an independent activity. Thus, it must hold that $N_{PS} = N_{FS}$ in order to avoid this undesired delay. On the other hand, the local state `PriceShipping2` enables a shared action which is carried out in cooperation with `CompletePriceCalculation`, a local state of the component in Listing 1.10. If the concurrency level of this component, denoted by N_{PC}, is lower than N_{PS}, then the activity `cpc` will be subject to delay. Conversely, if the concurrency level is higher, then some of the flows of `ForkPriceCalculation` will be under-utilised because there are not be enough requests to be served. In either case, the behaviour reflects that of the real system, thus the concurrency level of `ForkPriceCalculation` does not affect the calculation of the concurrency level of the auxiliary component `PriceShipping1`.

It is worthwhile pointing out that setting $N_{PS} > N_{FS}$ does not alter the performance results of the system. To understand this, observe that with such a setting there are more auxiliary components than the number of flows which can enable the `dos` action. The $N_{PS} - N_{FS}$ surplus components will be idle across the entire state space of the system. This is confirmed by the result that the state spaces of the models with $N_{PS} \geq N_{FS}$ are *lumpably equivalent* [1,6], which guarantees the equivalence of the derived performance measures.

Listing 1.20. Revised system equation of the PEPA model with concurrency levels

```
Sys = (ReceivePurchaseOrder[N_RP] <rpo> Fork1[N_RP])
        <fork,ip>
        (
        (ForkPriceCalculation[N_PC] <cpc> PriceShipping1[N_FS])
          <fork,dos,ip> ForkShipper[N_FS]
        )
        <fork,al,ip>
        (
            ForkProductionScheduling[N_PS]
            <cps>
             ShippingProduction1[N_FS]
          )
```

The concurrency levels of `ShippingProduction1` and `Fork1` can be determined with similar arguments. The revised system equation is shown in Listing 1.20.

3.2 Uncertainty about Parameters

The model described in the previous section may be subjected to quantitative analysis to extract performance indices. By interpreting it against the operational semantics of PEPA, a CTMC is built and transient as well as steady-state measures can be computed. However, one single analysis run often provides only a partial understanding of the system under study. More often, one is interested in the sensitivity of the performance to the variation of some of the system's parameters. For instance, one would like to ask questions such as: How is the system's performance affected by an increase in concurrency levels or an increase in the rate of execution of an action?

These questions arise at all stages of a modelling study. For example, performance analysis serves as a useful predictive tool which helps size the initial capacity of the system; further along the system's lifetime, it constitutes valuable support for planning system upgrades. With PEPA, answering these questions requires building a family of similar models, which maintain the same syntactic structure expect for one of more parameters which change in value. For instance, *sensitivity analysis* of the concurrency levels requires the construction of different models as in Listing 1.20 with distinct values for the parameters `N_RP`, `N_PC`, `N_FS`, or `N_PS`. If carried out manually, this process would be tedious and error prone. Fortunately, software tools for PEPA automate this form of analysis, requiring minimal user intervention [7,8].

If, on the one hand, this process is transparent to language, on the other hand the information about parameter uncertainty must be stored separately from the model. SRMC supports the declaration of *array of parameters*, which takes the form `param = { 1.0, 2.0, ... }`. This gives rise to distinct performance models in which the parameter `param` takes the different values in the set. (The syntax is not limited to numerical literals, but arbitrary expressions are also allowed.) This construct can be used for rate as well as concurrency level uncertainty. In the latter case, the elements of the set are restricted to be positive integers and expressions thereof.

Figure 7 shows the results of two sensitivity analysis studies conducted on the model in Listing 1.20. In both cases the performance metric of interest is the system's steady-state throughput, indicated by the throughput of the action `ip`. Figure 7(a) studies its sensitivity with respect to the rate `r_dos`, specified in the SRMC model with the definition

```
r_dos = {0.1,0.2,...,5.0}.
```

These results enable the insight that the system benefits from increases in the rate of the `dos` activity, albeit the relative gain diminishes significantly in the region $[2.0, 5.0]$. For instance, doubling the rate from 0.5 to 1.0 gives a system's throughput improvement of about 30% while doubling the rate again from 2.0 to

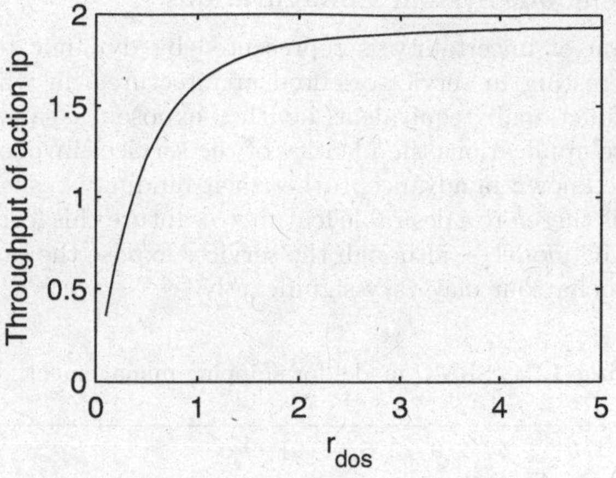

(a)

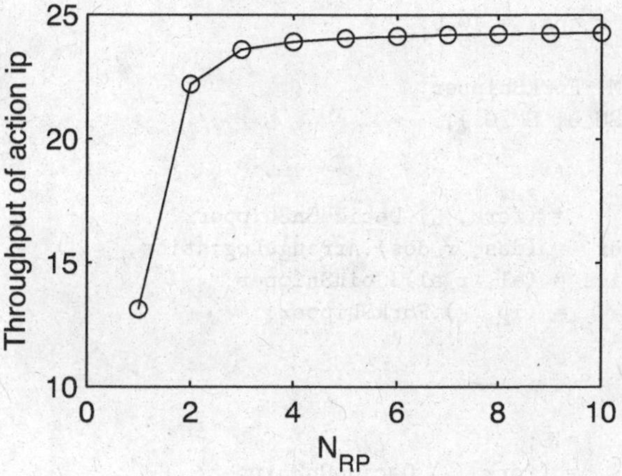

(b)

Fig. 7. Examples of parameter sweep for the model in Listing 1.20. Sensitivity analyses are conducted with (a) rate `r_dos` and (b) concurrency level `N_RP`. In (a), `N_RP = 4` and in (b) `r_dos = 5`. In both cases the other parameters were set as follows: `N_U = 4`,`N_PC = 3`, `N_FS = 3`, `N_PS = 2`, `r_think = 1.0`; all other rates were set to 10.0.

4.0 provides only an improvement of about 4%. A similar qualitative behaviour is shown in Figure 7(b), which studies the sensitivity analysis with respect to the concurrency level of `ReceivePurchaseOrder`, by using the definition

```
N_RP = {1,2,...,10}.
```

Unlike the former, the latter analysis gives rise to structurally different underlying CTMCs because the values of `N_RP` alter the number of sequential components in the model and therefore the state space size.

3.3 Uncertainty about System Configurations

A further dimension of uncertainty is represented by dynamic binding. This is particularly interesting in service-oriented architectures, in which different providers may be functionally equivalent, i.e. they expose the same interface of the service. In these applications the identity of the services invoked by a client does not need to be known in advance, rather their binding is usually mediated by registries [9]. It is therefore a desirable feature to capture this form of dynamic binding in the SRMC model — although the services expose the same interface, their performance behaviour may vary significantly.

Listing 1.21. SRMC model for shipping management

```
r_rpo   = {0.5, 1.0, 1.5, 2.0, 2.5, 3.0};
r_think = {1, 2, 3, 4};
r_ip    = 10.0; r_fork = 10.0; r_ipc = 10.0;
r_cpc   = 10.0; r_dos  = 5.0;  r_al  = 10.0;
r_ips   = 10.0; r_cps  = 10.0;

ForkShipper = SM::ForkShipper;
SM ::= { SM_A, SM_B, SM_C };

SM_A::{
  ForkShipper       = (fork, _).DecideOnShipper;
  DecideOnShipper   = (dos, r_dos).ArrangeLogistics;
  ArrangeLogistics  = (al, r_al).JoinShipper;
  JoinShipper       = (ip, _).ForkShipper;
};

SM_B::{
  r_delay          = 5;
  ForkShipper      = (fork, _).DecideOnShipper;
  DecideOnShipper  = (dos, r_dos).Delay;
  Delay            = (delay, r_delay).ArrangeLogistics;
  ArrangeLogistics = (al, r_al).JoinShipper;
  JoinShipper = (ip, _).ForkShipper;
};

SM_C::{
  r_fail            = 5;
  r_repair          = {1, 2};
  ForkShipper       = (fork, _).DecideOnShipper;
  DecideOnShipper   = (dos, r_dos).ArrangeLogistics
                    + (failure, r_fail).Failure;
  Failure           = (repair, r_repair).DecideOnShipper;
  ArrangeLogistics  = (al, r_al).JoinShipper;
  JoinShipper       = (ip, _).ForkShipper;
};
```

Our language incorporates dynamic binding by means of *namespace* definitions. A namespace is used to isolate the definitions that are needed to fully define an individual component of the system under study. Functional equivalence among namespaces is then imposed through an array operator syntactically and semantically similar to the rate array operator introduced in Section 3.2. These features are now introduced by means of our running example. Let us suppose that the shipping management activities are outsourced and that they are accessed via web-service invocations. An interesting matter is to determine the impact on the overall orchestration of the shipping management services which can be bound. In order to answer this question, let us suppose that the dynamic behaviour of three of these services is known to the performance modeller. Each implementation of this service is assigned a namespace, `SM_A`, `SM_B`, and `SM_C`. The model of shipping management in Listing 1.11 is revised as shown in Listing 1.21. The namespace array `SM` indicates the set of possible bindings. Each element is a process definition within a namespace, accessed using the format `<namespace>::<process>`. Process and rate definitions are uniquely identified by their name as well as the namespace in which they are defined, thus the same definition can appear within distinct namespaces. This property has been exploited in our case study in order to stress the functional uniformity across the possible bindings. The implementation `SM_A` encapsulates the original definition of the process; `SM_B` interposes some external delay between the actions `dos` and `al`; finally, `SM_C` models a less reliable service which may fail. After failure occurs, some delay is introduced to reset the server to a fully working state. Additionally, `SM_C` has a rate array which indicates uncertainty about the rate of failure `r_f`.

This SRMC model gives rise to four underlying PEPA models, organised in a tree as shown in Figure 8. Each node represents a binding to a specific namespace or the selection of a rate of an array. Here, the nodes of the first level denote the binding to the three implementations of the shipping management component. The leaves indicate the parameter sweep across the rate of failure `r_f`. This

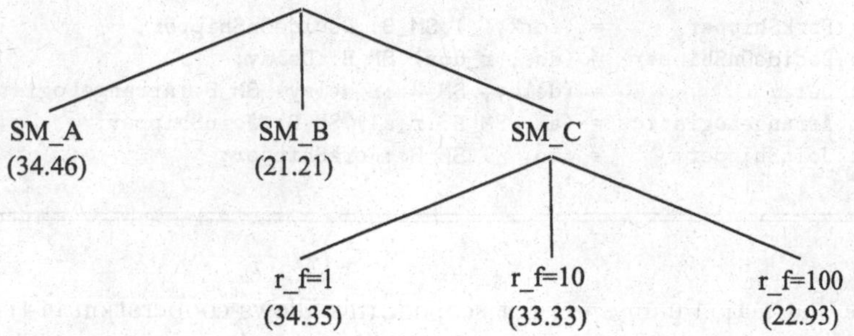

Fig. 8. The four PEPA models which underlie the SRMC description in Listing 1.21, represented as leaves of a tree. The nodes along the path from the root indicate the bindings to namespaces and the choice of rates for each PEPA model. In parentheses is the steady-state system throughput for each configuration.

analysis is not performed with SM_A and SM_B because these namespaces do not define a rate array. Each leaf is also labelled with the steady-state system throughput (action ip, in parentheses). The results show that the extra delay in SM_B has a negative effect on the performance. Conversely, the throughput does not deteriorate significantly when the rate of failure is relatively small, i.e. r_f = {1,10}. On the other hand, the perceived performance for r_f = 100 is comparable to that of the system which binds to SM_B.

4 Deriving Experiments

In this section we explain precisely how all individual experiments are derived from a single SRMC model file. We will continue to use our running example for illustration. The aim is to derive a number of separate PEPA models corresponding to the number of distinct system configurations. We then analyse each PEPA model once for each configuration of the appropriate variable rates.

4.1 Namespace Scoping

The first part of our algorithm is to scope the identifiers used within namespaces. This is a straightforward translation which makes sure that each defined identifier is prefixed with the list of namespaces in which it occurs. There may be more than one if it occurs within a nested namespace. Additionally each reference to an identifier must be similarly prefixed in the same way as the definition was scoped. Shown below is the scoping as applied to the SM_B namespace:

Listing 1.22. Scoped SM_B

```
SM_B::{
  SM_B::r_delay          = 5;

  SM_B::ForkShipper      = (fork, _).SM_B::DecideOnShipper;
  SM_B::DecideOnShipper  = (dos, r_dos).SM_B::Delay;
  SM_B::Delay            = (delay, SM_B::r_delay).SM_B::ArrangeLogistics;
  SM_B::ArrangeLogistics = (al, SM_B::r_al).SM_B::JoinShipper;
  SM_B::JoinShipper      = (ip, _).SM_B::ForkShipper;
};
```

Notice that action names are not scoped, this allows cooperation in the final system equation between components defined in separate namespaces. The globally defined rate r_dos is also not prefixed with any namespace since this rate is defined at the top level.

4.2 Namespace Selections

The key component in distinguishing system configurations in SRMC models is the namespace selection definitions. In our example this is the line:

```
SM ::= { SM_A, SM_B, SM_C };
```

We do a depth first search of all namespace selections because some namespace selections will entail further namespace choices. This occurs when we have a namespace selection nested within a namespace which is itself a choice. In our example this does not occur and in fact we have only one choice leading to three system configurations. Once a namespace has been chosen there are two tasks left to do; the first is to promote the definitions made within the given namespace into the top level and remove the now empty namespace definition. The second task is to substitute references to the selection definition (in this case `SM`) for references to the selected namespace. In this example we have been quite frugal in our use of the abstract namespace `SM`, so there is only one line to change other than the promoted definitions, namely the line:

```
ForkShipper = SM::ForkShipper;
```

Because we made this definition and then used the name `ForkShipper` the system equation is the same for all three models. However in general the system equation is modified according to the namespace selections. So that references to `SM::ForkShipper` and `SM::DecideOnShipper` would be replaced with references to `SM_A::ForkShipper` and `SM_A::DecideOnShipper` and respectively so for the other definitions and the other derived models.

The completion of these two tasks results in what is an almost valid PEPA model for each possible configuration. The remaining non-valid PEPA definitions are those rate definitions with uncertainty; these are removed in the next section. The (almost valid) PEPA model given in Listing 1.23 corresponds to choosing `SM_A` and the Listings 1.24 and 1.25 show the differences between that model and the derived instances resulting from choosing `SM_B` and `SM_C` respectively.

Listing 1.23. Scoped PEPA model example

```
r_rpo   = {0.5, 1.0, 1.5, 2.0, 2.5, 3.0};
r_think = {1, 2, 3, 4};
r_ip    = 10.0; r_fork = 10.0; r_ipc = 10.0;
r_cpc   = 10.0; r_dos  = 5.0;  r_al  = 10.0;
r_ips   = 10.0; r_cps  = 10.0;
```

```
ReceivePurchaseOrder = (rpo, r_rpo).InvoiceProcessing;
InvoiceProcessing = (ip, r_ip).ReceivePurchaseOrder;

Fork1 = (rpo, _).Fork2;
Fork2 = (fork, r_fork).Fork1;

ForkPriceCalculation = (fork, _).InitiatePriceCalculation;
InitiatePriceCalculation = (ipc, r_ipc).CompletePriceCalculation;
CompletePriceCalculation = (cpc, r_cpc).JoinPriceCalculation;
JoinPriceCalculation = (ip, _).ForkPriceCalculation;

PriceShipping1 = (dos, _).PriceShipping2;
PriceShipping2 = (cpc, _).PriceShipping1;

ForkShipper = SM_A::ForkShipper;
SM_A::ForkShipper        = (fork, _).SM_A::DecideOnShipper;
SM_A::DecideOnShipper    = (dos, r_dos).SM_A::ArrangeLogistics;
SM_A::ArrangeLogistics = (al, r_al).SM_A::JoinShipper;
SM_A::JoinShipper        = (ip, _).SM_A::ForkShipper;
SM_A::Deciding           = [ SM_A::DecideOnShipper ];

ShippingProduction1 = (al, _).ShippingProduction2;
ShippingProduction2 = (cpc, _).ShippingProduction1;

ForkProductionScheduling = (fork, _).InitiateScheduling;
InitiateScheduling = (ips, r_ips).CompleteProduction;
CompleteProduction = (cps, r_cps).JoinProductionScheduling;
JoinProductionScheduling = (ip, _).ForkProductionScheduling;

User    = (think, r_think).Execute;
Execute = (rpo, _).Wait;
Wait    = (ip, _) .User;

Waiting = [ Wait ];

n_u   = {7000, 8000, 9000};
n_rp  = 800;
n_pc  = {500, 600, 700};
n_fs  = {500, 600, 700};
n_ps  = 400;

User[n_u] <rpo, ip>
  (  (ReceivePurchaseOrder[n_rp] <rpo> Fork1[n_rp])
      <ip,fork>
     (  (ForkPriceCalculation[n_pc] <cpc> PriceShipping1[n_fs])
         <dos,fork,ip>
         ForkShipper[n_fs]
     )
```

```
    <fork,al,ip>
   ( ForkProductionScheduling[n_ps] <cps>
     ShippingProduction1[n_fs]
   )
 )
```

Listing 1.24. Scoped PEPA model example

```
// Same as in the other model

ForkShipper = SM_B::ForkShipper;
SM_B::r_delay           = 20;

SM_B::ForkShipper       = (fork, _).SM_B::DecideOnShipper;
SM_B::DecideOnShipper   = (dos, r_dos).SM_B::Delay;
SM_B::Delay             = (delay, SM_B::r_delay).SM_B::ArrangeLogistics;
SM_B::ArrangeLogistics = (al, SM_B::r_al).SM_B::JoinShipper;
SM_B::JoinShipper       = (ip, _).SM_B::ForkShipper;
SM_B::Deciding          = [ SM_B::DecideOnShipper ];
// The rest is also the same including the system equation
```

Listing 1.25. Scoped PEPA model example

```
// Same as in the other model

ForkShipper = SM_C::ForkShipper;
SM_C::r_fail = 5;
SM_C::r_repair = {1, 2};
SM_C::ForkShipper      = (fork, _).SM_C::DecideOnShipper;
SM_C::DecideOnShipper = (dos, r_dos).SM_C::ArrangeLogistics
                      + (failure, SM_C::r_fail).SM_C::Failure;
SM_C::Failure = (repair, SM_C::r_repair).SM_C::DecideOnShipper;
SM_C::ArrangeLogistics = (al, r_al).SM_C::JoinShipper;
SM_C::JoinShipper = (ip, _).SM_C::ForkShipper;
SM_C::Deciding = [ SM_C::DecideOnShipper + SM_C::Failure ];

// The rest is also the same including the system equation
```

4.3 Rate Parameter Experiments

The rate parameter selections are removed simply by creating a standard PEPA rate specification using the first of the possible selections for the rate. This gives us three PEPA models which are written out to three files: SM_A.pepa and SM_B.pepa and SM_C.pepa. It remains only to perform sensitivity analysis over these PEPA models. We create an experiment for each which ranges over all possible combinations of the rate selections, we use these to override the definitions given in the standard PEPA model using substitution. The first two PEPA models corresponding to the choices `SM_A` and `SM_B` use only globally defined rate choices while the choice of `SM_C` uses a rate choice which need not be ranged over for the other models. So the number of experiments will be larger for the configuration in which `SM_C` is chosen. Where the ... stand for the rest of the arguments given to compute the specified measure, the experimentation for the first configuration begins with:

```
ipc --rate r_po=1,r_think=1,n_u=7000,n_pc=500,n_pc=500 ...
ipc --rate r_po=2,r_think=1,n_u=7000,n_pc=500,n_pc=500 ...

ipc --rate r_po=1,r_think=2,n_u=7000,n_pc=500,n_pc=500 ...
ipc --rate r_po=2,r_think=2,n_u=7000,n_pc=500,n_pc=500 ...

ipc --rate r_po=1,r_think=3,n_u=7000,n_pc=500,n_pc=500 ...
ipc --rate r_po=2,r_think=3,n_u=7000,n_pc=500,n_pc=500 ...
...
```

In this way we range over all possible rate configurations appropriate for the `SM_A` system configuration. We are not ranging over the rate `SM_C::r_repair` because this rate is not used in the first (or second) configuration. The experiment for the second configuration looks much the same, for the third we must range over the extra rate `SM_C::r_repair` and our experiment looks like:

```
ipc --rate r_po=1,r_think=1,n_u=7000,n_pc=500,n_pc=500,r_repair=1
ipc --rate r_po=2,r_think=1,n_u=7000,n_pc=500,n_pc=500,r_repair=1

ipc --rate r_po=1,r_think=2,n_u=7000,n_pc=500,n_pc=500,r_repair=1
ipc --rate r_po=2,r_think=2,n_u=7000,n_pc=500,n_pc=500,r_repair=1

ipc --rate r_po=1,r_think=3,n_u=7000,n_pc=500,n_pc=500,r_repair=1
ipc --rate r_po=2,r_think=3,n_u=7000,n_pc=500,n_pc=500,r_repair=1
...
```

The number of experiments produced for each of the derived PEPA models is equal to the product of the lengths of all the appropriate rate selections. For the `SM_A` PEPA model this is $6 \times 4 \times 3 \times 3 \times 3 = 648$ and the same is true for the second (`SM_B`) configuration. For the `SM_C` configuration it is this number multiplied by the extra uncertainty of the rate `r_repair` which is $2 \times 648 = 1296$ adding these all together we get the total number of experiments to be 2592.

5 Query Specification

When performing analysis over a SRMC model we generate many — perhaps several thousand — PEPA model instances which must all be analysed separately. Clearly we do not wish to analyse each of these PEPA model instances by hand but automatically. We therefore require a query specification technique that is portable across many similar models. Our query specification language is that of eXtended Stochastic Probes [10]. We enhance this by allowing *virtual components.*

When specifying a measurement we are often concerned with specifying a set or sets of states. In the Markovian world these states are the states of the CTMC which underlies the PEPA model in question. Even when analysing a single PEPA model one does not wish to specify the states of the Markov chain directly since these are automatically derived from the PEPA model. We wish to specify such states compositionally just as we have compositionally described the model. One method of doing this is with a state specification where the full state space of the model is filtered with respect to the population sizes of the sequential states of the individual components. Figure 9 reports the grammar of state specifications.

expr	:=	*Process*	population
	|	*int*	constant
	|	*expr relop expr*	comparison
	|	*expr binop expr*	arithmetic
relop	:=	$= \mid \neq \mid > \mid <$	
	|	$\geq \mid \leq$	relational operators
binop	:=	$+ \mid - \mid \times \mid \div$	binary operators
pred	:=	$\neg$*pred*	not
	|	true | false	boolean
	|	if *pred* then *pred* else *pred*	conditional
	|	*pred* && *pred*	disjunction
	|	*pred* || *pred*	conjunction
	|	*expr*	expression

Fig. 9. The full grammar of the state specifications

State specifications can work well for measurements of steady-state condition probabilities but are not so appropriate for passage-time measurements. This is because for passage-time analysis we are concerned with events which happen and the states which result from those events. This means that slight changes to the model can affect the passage-time specification greatly because there are more or fewer states along the passage. In SRMC we mitigate this to some extent with our use of virtual components. A virtual component is one which has no representation within the CTMC but takes its population value as a function of the populations of other related components. For example using the following definition it is possible to define a component whose population is a measure of the number of components which are in either the `Broken` state or the `Offline` state:

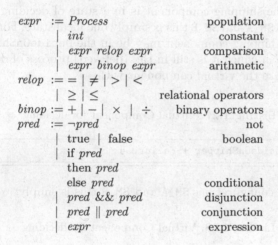

Listing 1.26. Virtual Component for an unavailable service

```
Unavailable = [ Broken + Offline ] ;
```

When we wish to measure the states of a component that correspond to some abstract state, such as being unavailable or being within a passage to be measured, we can use a virtual component to ensure that the query specification may be the same across several configurations. When modelling with a single PEPA model this can be useful in that the states along the passage are defined in the same place as the behaviour of the component(s) involved in the passage — such as a user component which is in an abstract state of *Waiting* in order to analyse reponse-time. This is especially useful in SRMC when the definitions for a service component can change based on the system configuration in use for a specific derived PEPA model. In our running example we use virtual components to specify when the shipping component is in a state of deciding on a shipper. For configurations `SM_A` and `SM_B` this is simply one local state. For configuration `SM_C` though the shipping component may be in the `DecideOnShipper` state or the `Failure` state in which it is still in the (delayed) process of deciding on the shipper. So we make the virtual component with:

Listing 1.27. Virtual Component for deciding

```
Deciding = [ DecideOnShipper + Failure ];
```

For each of the configurations `SM_A` and `SM_B` this is simply:

Listing 1.28. Virtual Component for deciding

```
Deciding = [ DecideOnShipper ];
```

Now when we make the selection we can simply refer to `SM::Deciding` in this way we have a measure of the number of components in the abstract state of 'Deciding' which is portable across all of the derived PEPA models.

Activity probes can allow a more intuitive query specification when the states we are interested in are the results of a sequence of event observations. This is the common case when the query is a passage-time query. In `xsp` the modeller specifies a series of activities to be observed and the compiler automatically translates this into a PEPA sequential component which can then be queried as a filter on the entire state space of the model. For passage-time measurements the user can label activities of the probe as either `start` activities which begin the passage or `stop` activities which end the passage. The probe states which are source, target or passage states are then mechanically derived and given to the analyser. The user therefore need not specify the states they are interested in at all, only the events/observations. A very common passage-time query which measures the response-time is given by the probe specification:

Listing 1.29. Response-time probe specification

```
request:start, response:stop
```

In our example the request is started with the completion of a `think` activity and is terminated with the completion of a `ip` activity. So the equivalent probe for our example model is:

Listing 1.30. Response-time probe specification

```
think:start, ip:stop
```

However often we are concerned with the response-time as observed by a single client, rather than that observed by the system above. The above probe will measure the passage between the occurrence of a `request` activity performed by any component in the model (usually a synchronisation between one client and the service being modelled) and an occurrence of a `response` activity again performed by any component. To observe only those `request` and `response` activities which originate from a single 'tagged' client we can attach the probe to a single `Client` component rather than the whole model. The following probe using the double colon syntax achieves this for our example:

Listing 1.31. Response-time probe specification

```
User::(think:start, ip:stop)
```

Sometimes events are not powerful enough to express the queries that we are interested in. This is often the case when we are interested in the response-time when the service is in a particular state. For example we may have made one passage-time measurement already using the above probe and found that the general response-time is adequate, but that we wish to know more about how this general response-time profile is made up. One possibility is to split up the query into several analysing response-times when the service is in different states. The following two probes analyse the response-time for all requests that are initially made when the service is entirely available or (at least) partially unavailable.

Listing 1.32. Response-time probe specification

```
User::({Unavailable == 0}think:start, ip:stop)
User::({Unavailable > 0}think:start, ip:stop)
```

The guards on the first activity observation (of the `think` activity) are state specifications. Note that these may refer to virtual components as well as to regular component populations. Guards need not always be used to make a distinction as to when a passage is begun, they may also be used to terminate the passage. The following two probes analyse the time it takes for a system to become fully repaired after the initial breakdown of one of its components/servers.

Listing 1.33. Response-time probe specification

```
break:start, {Broken == 1}repair:stop
break:start, {Broken == 0}:stop
```

Here we do not assume that there is a single server which may be broken or not, but several servers each of which may be broken independently. So the probe must begin the passage on observation of the first breakage and only terminate the passage when a `repair` activity fixes the only broken server (other servers may have broken since the first one did). The first probe achieves this by only observing a `repair` activity if there is exactly one server in the `Broken` state. However this may still not be robust enough since we may change the model such that a `repair` does not necessarily fix the broken server, for example there may

P_{def}	$:=$	$name :: R$	locally attached probe
	$\mid$	R	globally attached probe
R	$:=$	$activity$	observe action
	$\mid$	R_1, R_2	sequence
	$\mid$	$R_1 \mid R_2$	choice
	$\mid$	R:label	labelled
	$\mid$	$R/activity$	resetting
	$\mid$	(R)	bracketed
	$\mid$	$R\ n$	iterate
	$\mid$	$R\{m, n\}$	iterate
	$\mid$	R^+	one or more
	$\mid$	R^*	zero or more
	$\mid$	$R^?$	zero or one
R	$:=$	$\ldots \mid \{pred\}R$	guarded

Fig. 10. The full grammar of the eXtended Stochastic Probes query specification language

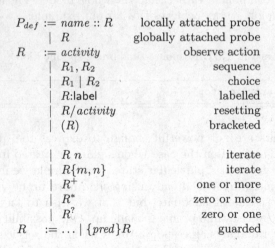

be more than one thing broken within the server. The second probe by contrast has the guard placed on the :stop label itself. This means that the probe will consider itself to have terminated the passage precisely when we first move into a state in which there are no servers in the Broken state. Figure 10 provides the full grammar for the xsp language.

6 Markovian Modelling with Many Models

In the Markovian world in which we generate a CTMC from a PEPA model we suffer from the well-known state-space explosion problem. Small increases in the size of the PEPA model or the population size of a component or components within the model can cause the number of distinct states of the generated CTMC to increase dramatically. We mitigate this to some extent with our use of aggregation [6] but this can provide only so much relief — this is described in [11]. When the model state space becomes large we cannot simply allow more time for the numerical solver because at some point the state space is simply too large to even generate or hold in memory. From our single SRMC model we generate a large number of PEPA models each of which can be solved independently. Because we do not model uncertainty by increasing the complexity of a single large PEPA model then provided each derived PEPA model is not itself too large we avoid state space explosion. In other words we can solve many small models better than we can solve one very large model. Indeed each of the generated PEPA models may be solved in parallel on many machines using a grid or cluster computing environment. The task of separately solving each of these models falls into the class of problems which are known in the parallel computing community as "embarrassingly parallelisable". That is to say, they are essentially a large number of independent processes without synchronisation points and therefore they deliver impressive speedups when executed on a compute cluster.

Even with this the model sizes which can be solved using the CTMC technology is still low. Although in our example model presented so far we have several thousand users and several hundred server processes. Unfortunately this would result in an unmanageably large CTMC with a state-space size described in astronomical terms. Given this, instead of analysing the whole system we are obliged to analyse a portion of it, such as the performance of one set of server processes. To this end we modified our SRMC model to have one for each kind of server process — this means we set the values N_{RP}, N_{PC}, N_{FS} and N_{PS} all to one. We are therefore able to reduce the number of clients since some clients will be served by other server processes. In this example we ranged over the number of users N_U with the SRMC definition:

Listing 1.34. Number of users specification

```
N_U = { 2, 3, 4, 5, 6};
```

This also meant that we are not ranging over the values N_{PC} and N_{FS} and hence there were not as many experiments to run. We ran 750 experiments each of which took between 30 seconds and one 1 minute to complete on an ordinary desktop computer.

Prior to solving each of the models we must specify some query with which to analyse each model. This is because some queries require us to automatically add components to the model in order to distinguish states. For our model of the web service we are interested in the response-time as observed by a single user. Often we are interested in average response-time but compiling the PEPA models to CTMCs allows a finer grained analysis known as passage-time quantile analysis [12,13]. This allows the prediction of not just the average response-time but the response-time profile, such that we know the probability of receiving a response at or within any given time t after the request was made. This allows us to answer such service-level agreements as: "90 percent of all requests will be serviced within 10 seconds" something which is not possible to answer with only the average response-time. Having specified this as our performance query once for the SRMC model, this is then translated into the equivalent query for each of the generated PEPA models. Thus, for each of the generated PEPA models we calculate a cumulative distribution function which plots the time t for a specified range (in this case 0 to 10) against the probability that a specific user observes the `ip` event t time units after performing a `think` action.

Having calculated this function for each of the generated PEPA models we now have a database mapping process instantions and rate parameters to response-time profiles. We can extract information from this database as we wish. The graph on the left of Figure 11 shows for one specific set of process instantiations (or system configuration) the response-time profile as we vary the number of users. All the other rates are held constant — by this we mean that we have selected results from runs which have the same parameters other than the number of users. This graph indicates that the number of users has a quite dramatic effect on the response-time of the system, where there is a low number of users the probability of passage completion rises very quickly with time. As the number of users is increased the rise of the probability of completion against time is more languid. The graph on the right hand side of the same figure does the same kind of analysis except here we have kept constant the number of users and the parameter that we are varying — whereby again 'varying' means selecting the already computed results which correspond to a varying — rate of `rpo` the rate at which the service can receive orders. From this graph we learn that at least for the parameter range chosen the rate of `rpo` does not drastically affect the response-time as observed by a single user. This is a perhaps surprising result because the activity performed at this rate is included within the analysed passage.

Figure 12 shows a similar kind of surface plot except in these graphs we are holding only the system configuration as constant and ranging over the whole rate configuration space for each derived PEPA model. What you see is the depths of probabilities at each time for the given system configuration. Where

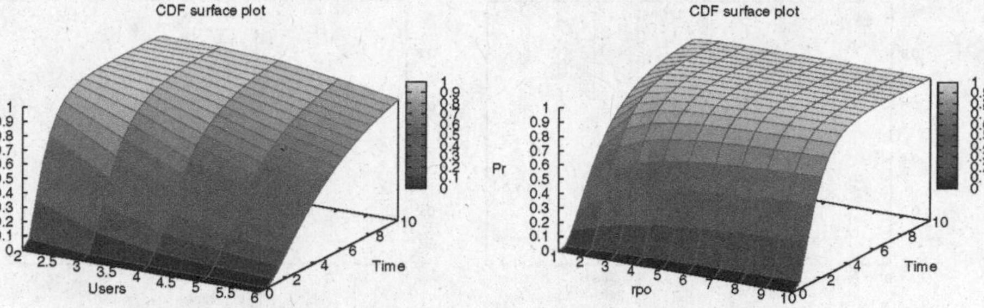

Fig. 11. A surface plot showing how the number of users affects the response-time profile

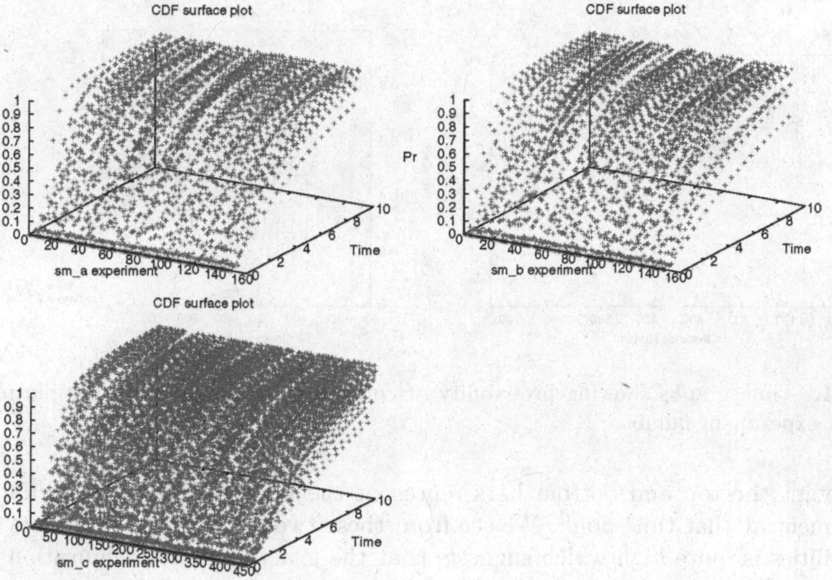

Fig. 12. Surface plots depicting the cumulative distribution functions for each system configuration across all rate configurations

this depth is long there is great variability in the probability of completing the passage at that time. In other words at that time the rates have a large affect on the probability of completing the passage. Where the depth is low the rates do not affect so much the probability of completion, this may be because there is either always low or always high proability at that time or it may be because there is some bottleneck in the passage and therefore altering other rates has less effect.

Figure 13 depicts the candle-stick graphs of completion of the passage for all the experiments performed automatically from the SRMC model. At each

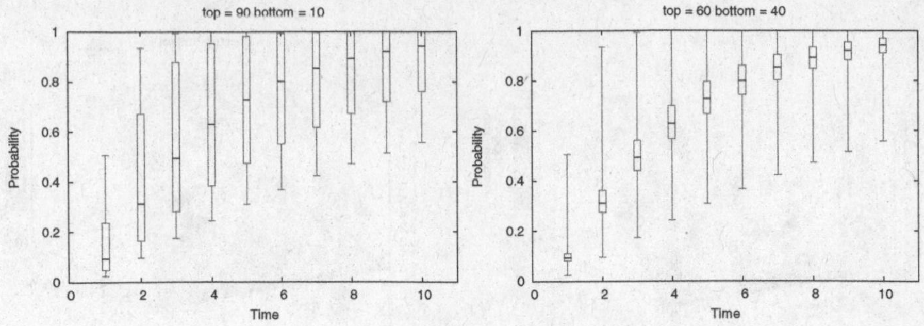

Fig. 13. Candlestick graphs showing the probability of completion ranging over all of the experiments performed automatically from the SRMC model

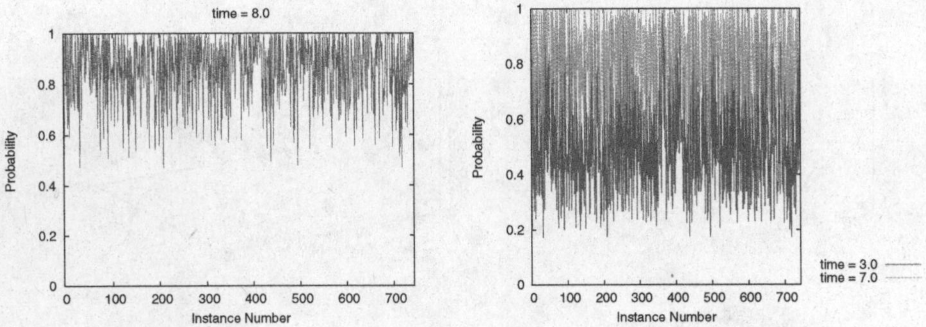

Fig. 14. Time graphs showing probability of completion at the given times plotted against experiment number

time point the top and bottom bars represent the best and worst performing experiment at that time point. We see from these two graphs that the range of possibilities is quite high which suggests that the exact system configuration is important for the modelled system. The thick bar along each line represents a particular middle-percentage range for that time — in other words we remove some percentage of best performing experiments and some percentage of the worst performing experiments. The graph on the left plots between 10 and 90 percent while the graph on the right plots between 40 and 60 percent. In general this can highlight the possibility that the best or worst performing experiment is really an outlier and the wide variability of the experiments is not a true reflection of the variability of the system as a whole. It can also allow the modeller to zero in on experiments which are causing particularly good or poor results and determine whether or not the system/model can be improved as a whole.

Another kind of graph which we plot are called simply *time graphs*. These plot the probability of completing the passage within the given times against all the experiment numbers of all the system and rate parameter configurations ranged over within the SRMC model. On the left of Figure 14 we see only the single time

8.0 being plotted. From this graph we can see that with few exceptions there is at least a sixty percent chance that the passage will be completed and in some configurations it is close to a certainty. On the graph of the right of the same figure we plot more than one time, indeed our software ranges over sets of times although more than two is not very useful when the graphs are in black and white. From these two times we can see that there are some configurations that are more likely to complete the passage within time 3.0 than other poorer performing configurations are at time 7.0. Again this demonstrates wide variability in the system we are modelling.

7 Large-Scale Modelling with Differential Equations

Our use of SRMC to model uncertainty by splitting up the possible system configurations has ensured that our model does not inflate to an unmanageable size through the modelling of uncertainty. However there are many models which are inherently large, in particular models of web services often hope to have many thousands of users. Therefore even when modelling one single configuration the state-space size is simply too massive. Recently it has become possible to analyse such systems with a fluid-flow approach. In this case the PEPA model is translated into a system of ordinary differential equations. These are solved until the model has reached a steady-state in which the population levels of each kind of component are stationary. This gives us the same kind of steady-state measurements that are possible with the CTMC analysis. Systems in which the limit of user components for CTMC analysis was of the order of a few tens can now be analysed with a more realistic number of users in the many thousands. Unfortunately the price paid for this extraordinary rise in model size capacity is a reduced set of analyses which are appropriate. In particular our passage-time analysis used on the CTMC models of the Section 6 in as of yet unavailable.

In our example model we can instead calculate a measure of the average response-time by looking at the number of users who are typically in a state of waiting for their response. For each derived PEPA model instance and rate configuration we solve the assocated ODEs to provide a time-series analysis. These plot the population of the specified component types against time. Three such graphs are shown in Figure 15 one for each of the three system configurations. Note that after some time each of these time-series becomes stable in that the population of each component type is not changing. This allows us to infer the steady-state or long-term average poplulation of each component type. By analysing the long-term population level of the number of waiting users we can gain a measure of the response-time of the system. The graph in Figure 16 plots the steady-state population of waiting users for all of the experiments (that is all system configurations at all rate configurations). We did the same for the number of deciding shippers (recall from Section 5 that 'Deciding' was a virtual component) and the results are plotted in Figure 17. Overall we ran 2592 experiments each of which took between 1 and 3 seconds to complete. We invoked these in serial on an ordinary desktop PC and achieved results within 2 hours.

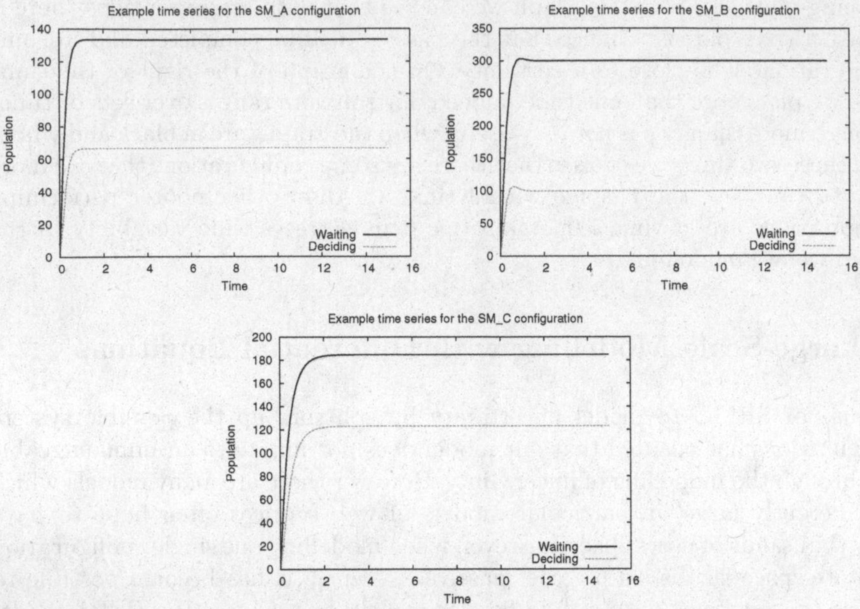

Fig. 15. Example time-series showing how the population of a subset of the component types in specific model instances change with time

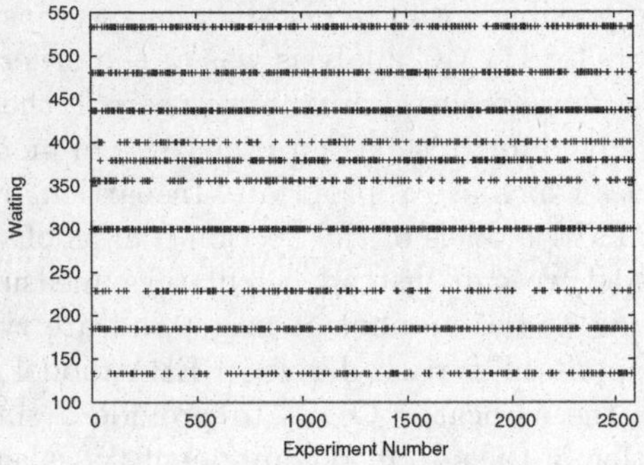

Fig. 16. Graphs showing how configurations affect the number of waiting users

For some models the time taken to produce one result is longer, alternatively we may have a larger uncertainty space resulting in many more experiments. In these cases it is worth considering farming out the solving of each experiment (or a set of experiments) using a parallel computing cluster such as Condor as we have done before [14].

The results show that the population levels tend to concentrate on a very small number of values, as can be intuitively appreciated by the presence of horizontal lines in the graphs. An explanation of this behaviour is that there are dominant elements in the parameter space considered in this case study. Particularly, the rate `r_rpo` and the instance of `SM` have a strong impact on

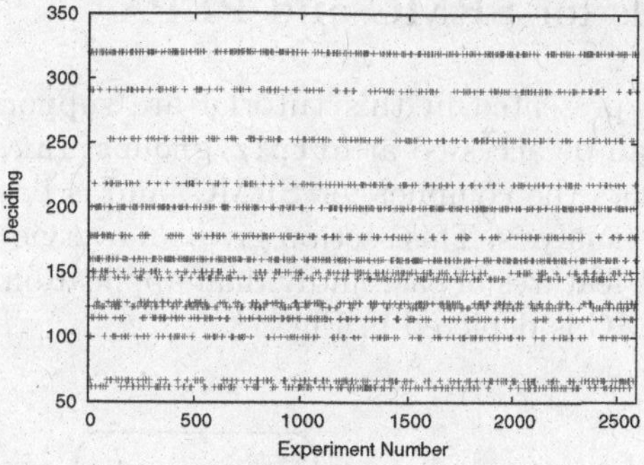

Fig. 17. Graphs showing how configurations affect the number of deciding shippers

Table 1. Results of Figure 16 grouped by `SM` and `r_rpo`. The third column shows the average population level across all the experiments with the same configuration.

SM	r_rpo	Average Value
SM_A	0.5	66.65
SM_A	1.0	114.25
SM_A	1.5	149.94
SM_A	2.0	177.70
SM_A	2.5	199.90
SM_A	3.0	218.07
SM_B	0.5	61.52
SM_B	1.0	99.97
SM_B	1.5	126.28
SM_B	2.0	145.40
SM_B	2.5	159.85
SM_B	3.0	159.85
SM_C	0.5	123.05
SM_C	1.0	199.95
SM_C	1.5	252.56
SM_C	2.0	290.91
SM_C	2.5	319.69
SM_C	3.0	319.69

the population levels considered. Table 1 gives the results of Figure 16 in an aggregated form by grouping the experiments according to these two parameters. It shows the average population level across all the experiments with the same values of `r_rpo` and `SM`. Each group of experiments exhibits a negligible standard deviation, confirming the strong influence of the two parameters on the performance measure.

The specific instance of `SM` seems to have a stronger impact in some cases. For instance, the groups of experiments (`SM_B`, 2.5) and (`SM_B`, 3.0) have the same average population level, suggesting a low sensitivity of result with respect to the change in the value of the rate `r_rpo`. The same situation is observer for the groups (`SM_C`, 2.5) and (`SM_B`, 3.0).

8 Software Tools for SRMC and PEPA

The kinds of analysis presented in this tutorial are supported by a suite of software tools which can be accessed at `http://groups.inf.ed.ac.uk/srmc/`. The tool smc implements the compiler for SRMC, and is based on Pepato and ipc for the quantitative analysis. This section gives an overview of the tool-chain and discusses the main features of each individual application. The architecture of the software for SRMC is depicted in Fig. 18.

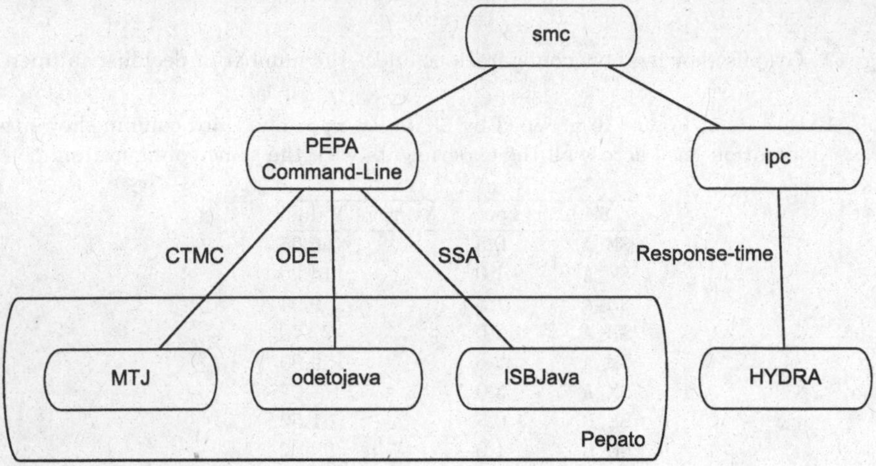

Fig. 18. Architecture of the software tools for SRMC

8.1 Pepato

Pepato is a Java Application Programming Interface (API) which provides core services for the execution of PEPA-related tasks. The API is centred around an abstract syntax tree representation of a PEPA model which can be created programmatically or via the parsing of a file with the concrete syntax presented throughout this tutorial. This in-memory representation gives access to functionality for Markovian analysis and fluid-flow approximation through ODEs.

The modules for Markovian analysis include a *state-space explorer*, which infers the labelled transition system according to the semantics rules of PEPA. The generated state space is the input to the *steady-state analyser* which constructs the underlying Markov chain and solves it for the equilibrium distribution using the external library MTJ (Matrix Toolkit for Java) [15]. The solution can be used for the calculation of a predefined set of performance indices, indicated as reward structures over the Markov chain: the *throughput* is calculated for each action type, and the mean population level is given for each sequential process in the system. An alternative form of Markovian analysis is *stochastic simulation*, which is offered by Pepato with the implementation of a semantics for PEPA [16] which maps onto efficient methods such as Gillespie's direct method [17] and Gibson-Bruck's algorithms [18]. This module, which relies on the stochastic simulation algorithms implemented by the Java library ISBjava [19], permits the tuning of the most common parameters of a simulation study, including number of replications, time horizon, confidence intervals, and output variables of interest.

The module for fluid-flow analysis transforms a PEPA model into a system of first-order ODEs according to the semantics described in [20]. The differential equation model can be analysed with a range of numerical solvers and the output provides the evolution of the population levels of the system's components over time. The module uses the odetojava package by Patterson and Spiteri [21], available in the ISBjava library.

Pepato is exposed through a command-line interface for the purpose of communication with the other non-Java elements of the SRMC tool-chain.

8.2 ipc

The ipc tool is written in Haskell and supports the analysis of response-time quantiles for PEPA [13]. The tool permits the definition of performance measures (called *probes*) by using a regular-expression like specification language called xsp which we described in Section 5. The tool converts a PEPA model and its measurement specification into an equivalent PEPA model for the numerical analysis. In its latest incarnation, backed by the library ipclib [7], the solvers are implemented natively. Optionally, the user can invoke the original tool-chain, which translates the model into the input format accepted by Hydra [22], implemented in C++, which has been designed to cope efficiently with large-sized models (i.e. up to 10^7 states).

8.3 smc

The SRMC Model Compiler (smc) is our software support for translating from the SRMC language into multiple PEPA models. The tool is written in Haskell alongside the ipc library and hence uses the same parsing for the PEPA specific portions of the SRMC syntax. The user provides both a SRMC model together with a query specification. From this, one PEPA model per system configuration is produced. The query specification is robust enough to be used over all the PEPA models. Note that we do not produce one PEPA model for each experiment. Each experiment consists of a system configuration (or equivalently a derived PEPA model) and a set of rate parameter instantiations. So our smc compiler produces for each derived PEPA model a list of rate parameter instantiations relevant to that particular model instance. For each experiment the ipc tool is invoked with the particular PEPA model, the particular rate parameter instantiations and the globally appropriate query specification. The ipc tool may then produce the result itself for a Markovian response-time quantile query or pass the instantiated model onto Pepato to solve using ordinary differential equations.

9 Related Work

This tutorial paper is concerned with using process calculi to model Web Services with a particular focus on quantitative evaluation. As others have before us, we used a process calculus to express our model. The process calculus SRMC builds on the simpler process algebra PEPA which has been used for numerous studies of stochastically-timed systems (for a recent overview of modelling with PEPA see [23] and [24]).

SRMC can be seen as an extension of PEPA. Formally, it is a superset of the PEPA language in the sense that every PEPA model is immediately an SRMC model which gives rise to a singleton set of PEPA model instances. Another extension of PEPA which had *mobility* (rather than *binding*) as its motivation was the language of PEPA nets [25,26]. PEPA nets are stochastic Petri nets whose tokens are PEPA terms. We find this language applied to modelling Web Services in [27].

PEPA nets and the stochastic π-calculus are applied to modelling a Web Service in [28]. Of note with regard to this paper is that properties of interest to the PEPA net model are specified using PML_ν, an extension of Larsen and Skou's Probabilistic Modal Logic (PML). This is a distinctive approach to characterising sets of states which are of interest in the specification of performance measures. Modal logics are rarely used for this purpose and temporal logics such as CSL are more commonly applied here.

However, the style of modelling pursued in the above work is discrete-state Markovian modelling. With the advent of the theory presented in [2] and the algorithm presented in [29] it was possible to map process algebra models to systems of ordinary differential equations for solution. The relationship between these two kinds of models is explored from a theoretical perspective in [30] and by example in [31] and [11].

One of the earliest published papers to include a PEPA modelling case study which is carried out using this evaluation method is [32]. In this paper a large-scale model of the BitTorrent distribution protocol is developed in PEPA and solved using the fluid-flow approximation. Previous models of Web Services considered in this style include the distributed e-learning and course management system considered in [33] in PEPA and the same system considered in the untimed process calculus SOCK and in PEPA in [34].

10 Conclusion and Future Perspectives

In this paper we have addressed an inherent difficulty of modelling studies, namely that we lack certainty about details of the system which we are modelling. Very often this problem can be due to a lack of knowledge about rate parameters but it is also possible that we lack certainty about the function of some components of the system. This can be because we are undertaking a prospective modelling study of a still-to-be-constructed system. At this point decisions about the specification have not yet been finalised (and a quantitative modelling study can guide us in making the right decisions).

There are principally two ways to address these kinds of problems within a model. The first is to try to abstract away from the details of the components about which we are uncertain but such an approach risks missing too much detail and then our models will be unconvincing and their results will be inaccurate. The second is to try to include all of the detail of each possible component, presenting these as internal choices made by the model. Unfortunately, if we have included too much detail then we encounter the well-known state-space explosion problem where we simply do not have enough memory available to represent the detailed model or not enough time to compute the desired results. The model might be useful, if it helped us to think clearly, but we will always feel uncertain about it because we will be unable to test it or make predictions based on it.

The alternative which we have pursued here is to accept that we have *more than one model* to consider and that we need to apply our analysis to a related family of models. There are two attendant difficulties here. The first is that if we are to consider a large family of models then we surely want to generate these models automatically via a repeatable transformation. The `smc` compiler performs this function for the SRMC language, generating many PEPA models for a single input SRMC model. The second difficulty which we encounter here is that we have a daunting number of model evaluations to perform. For this approach to be feasible we need an evaluation mechanism which has low unitary cost. Fortunately the cost of solving initial value problems for systems of differential equations can extremely low.

We have applied these methods here to modelling Web Services and it seems that they suit this domain well because of its inherent uncertainty about binding sites and the attendant level of performance which we can expect to receive. However, we hope that our methods will also be useful beyond the domain of Web Services and that we may find many possible applications of the SRMC language in the future.

Acknowledgements. The authors are supported by the EU FET-IST Global Computing 2 project SENSORIA ("Software Engineering for Service-Oriented Overlay Computers" (IST-3-016004-IP-09)).

References

1. Hillston, J.: A Compositional Approach to Performance Modelling. Cambridge University Press, Cambridge (1996)
2. Hillston, J.: Fluid flow approximation of PEPA models. In: Proceedings of the Second International Conference on the Quantitative Evaluation of Systems, Torino, Italy, September 2005, pp. 33–43. IEEE Computer Society Press, Los Alamitos (2005)
3. Clark, A., Gilmore, S., Tribastone, M.: Service-level agreements for service-oriented computing. In: Proceedings of the 19th International Workshop on Algebraic Development Techniques (WADT 2008), Pisa, Italy (June 2008) (to appear)

4. Clark, A., Gilmore, S., Tribastone, M.: Scalable analysis of scalable systems. In: Proceedings of Fundamental Approaches to Software Engineering (FASE 2009), New York, England (March 2009) (to appear)
5. OASIS Web Services Business Process Execution Language (WSBPEL) Technical Commitee. Web Services Business Process Execution Language Version 2.0 (April 2007)
6. Gilmore, S., Hillston, J., Ribaudo, M.: An efficient algorithm for aggregating PEPA models. IEEE Transactions on Software Engineering 27(5), 449–464 (2001)
7. Clark, A.: The ipclib PEPA Library. In: QEST [35], pp. 55–56
8. Tribastone, M.: The PEPA Plug-in Project. In: QEST [35], pp. 53–54
9. OASIS UDDI Specifications Technical Committee. Universal Description Discovery and Integration (UDDI), `http://www.oasis-open.org/committees/uddi-spec/doc/tcspecs.htm`
10. Clark, A., Gilmore, S.: State-aware performance analysis with eXtended Stochastic Probes. In: Thomas, N., Juiz, C. (eds.) EPEW 2008. LNCS, vol. 5261, pp. 125–140. Springer, Heidelberg (2008)
11. Clark, A., Duguid, A., Gilmore, S., Tribastone, M.: Partial evaluation of PEPA models for fluid-flow analysis. In: Thomas, N., Juiz, C. (eds.) EPEW 2008. LNCS, vol. 5261, pp. 2–16. Springer, Heidelberg (2008)
12. Bradley, J.T., Dingle, N.J., Gilmore, S.T., Knottenbelt, W.J.: Derivation of passage-time densities in PEPA models using IPC: The Imperial PEPA Compiler. In: Kotsis, G. (ed.) Proceedings of the 11th IEEE/ACM International Symposium on Modeling, Analysis and Simulation of Computer and Telecommunications Systems, University of Central Florida, October 2003, pp. 344–351. IEEE Computer Society Press, Los Alamitos (2003)
13. Bradley, J., Dingle, N., Gilmore, S., Knottenbelt, W.: Extracting passage times from PEPA models with the HYDRA tool: A case study. In: Jarvis, S. (ed.) Proceedings of the Nineteenth annual UK Performance Engineering Workshop, July 2003, pp. 79–90. University of Warwick (2003)
14. Clark, A., Gilmore, S.: Evaluating quality of service for service level agreements. In: Brim, L., Leucker, M. (eds.) Proceedings of the 11th International Workshop on Formal Methods for Industrial Critical Systems, Bonn, Germany, August 2006, pp. 172–185 (2006)
15. Heimsund, B.-O.: MTJ: Matrix Toolkit for Java, `http://ressim.berlios.de/`
16. Bradley, J., Gilmore, S.: Stochastic simulation methods applied to a secure electronic voting model. Electr. Notes Theor. Comput. Sci. 151(3), 5–25 (2006)
17. Gillespie, D.T.: Exact stochastic simulation of coupled chemical reactions. Journal of Physical Chemistry 81(25), 2340–2361 (1977)
18. Gibson, M.A., Bruck, J.: Efficient exact stochastic simulation of chemical systems with many species and many channels. Journal of Physical Chemistry 104, 1876–1889 (2000)
19. CompBio Group, Institute for Systems Biology. ISBJava, `http://magnet.systemsbiology.net/software/ISBJava/`
20. Hillston, J.: Fluid flow approximation of PEPA models. In: Proceedings of the Second International Conference on the Quantitative Evaluation of Systems, Torino, Italy, September 2005, pp. 33–43. IEEE Computer Society Press, Los Alamitos (2005)
21. odeToJava library, `http://www.netlib.org/ode/odeToJava.tgz`
22. Dingle, N.J., Harrison, P.G., Knottenbelt, W.J.: HYDRA: HYpergraph-Based Distributed Response-Time Analyzer. In: Arabnia, H.R., Mun, Y. (eds.) PDPTA, pp. 215–219. CSREA Press (2003)

23. Hillston, J.: Tuning systems: From composition to performance. The Computer Journal 48(4), 385–400 (2005); The Needham Lecture paper
24. Hillston, J.: Process algebras for quantitative analysis. In: Proceedings of the 20th Annual IEEE Symposium on Logic in Computer Science (LICS 2005), Chicago, June 2005, pp. 239–248. IEEE Computer Society Press, Los Alamitos (2005)
25. Gilmore, S., Hillston, J., Ribaudo, M., Kloul, L.: PEPA nets: A structured performance modelling formalism. Performance Evaluation 54(2), 79–104 (2003)
26. Hillston, J., Ribaudo, M.: Modelling mobility with PEPA nets. In: Aykanat, C., Dayar, T., Körpeoğlu, İ. (eds.) ISCIS 2004. LNCS, vol. 3280, pp. 513–522. Springer, Heidelberg (2004)
27. Gilmore, S., Hillston, J., Kloul, L., Ribaudo, M.: Software performance modelling using PEPA nets. In: Proceedings of the Fourth International Workshop on Software and Performance, Redwood Shores, California, USA, January 2004, pp. 13–24. ACM Press, New York (2004)
28. Brodo, L., Degano, P., Gilmore, S., Hillston, J., Priami, C.: Performance evaluation for global computation. In: Priami, C. (ed.) GC 2003. LNCS, vol. 2874, pp. 229–253. Springer, Heidelberg (2003)
29. Calder, M., Gilmore, S., Hillston, J.: Automatically deriving ODEs from process algebra models of signalling pathways. In: Plotkin, G. (ed.) Proceedings of Computational Methods in Systems Biology (CMSB 2005), Edinburgh, Scotland, April 2005, pp. 204–215 (2005)
30. Geisweiller, N., Hillston, J., Stenico, M.: Relating continuous and discrete PEPA models of signalling pathways. Theor. Comput. Sci. 404(1-2), 97–111 (2008)
31. Zhao, Y., Thomas, N.: Approximate solution of a PEPA model of a key distribution centre. In: Kounev, S., Gorton, I., Sachs, K. (eds.) SIPEW 2008. LNCS, vol. 5119, pp. 44–57. Springer, Heidelberg (2008)
32. Duguid, A.: Coping with the parallelism of BitTorrent: Conversion of PEPA to ODEs in dealing with state space explosion. In: Asarin, E., Bouyer, P. (eds.) FORMATS 2006. LNCS, vol. 4202, pp. 156–170. Springer, Heidelberg (2006)
33. Gilmore, S., Tribastone, M.: Evaluating the scalability of a web service-based distributed e-learning and course management system. In: Bravetti, M., Núñez, M.T., Zavattaro, G. (eds.) WS-FM 2006. LNCS, vol. 4184, pp. 214–226. Springer, Heidelberg (2006)
34. Bravetti, M., Gilmore, S., Guidi, C., Tribastone, M.: Replicating web services for scalability. In: Barthe, G., Fournet, C. (eds.) TGC 2007 and FODO 2008. LNCS, vol. 4912, pp. 204–221. Springer, Heidelberg (2008)
35. Fourth International Conference on the Quantitative Evaluation of Systems (QEST 2007), Edinburgh, Scotland, UK, September 2007. IEEE Computer Society, Los Alamitos (2007)

A Detailed Results

In this section we depict some of the graphs that we have produced from our example models which have not been shown in the main text. We include these here for completeness because it is sometimes the case that one can see the significance of one graph only in comparison to others.

Figure 19 shows some more of the candle stick graph possibilities which were not shown in Section 6. Figures 20 and 21 and shows all of the *time graphs* which plot probability of completion within the given time against experiment number.

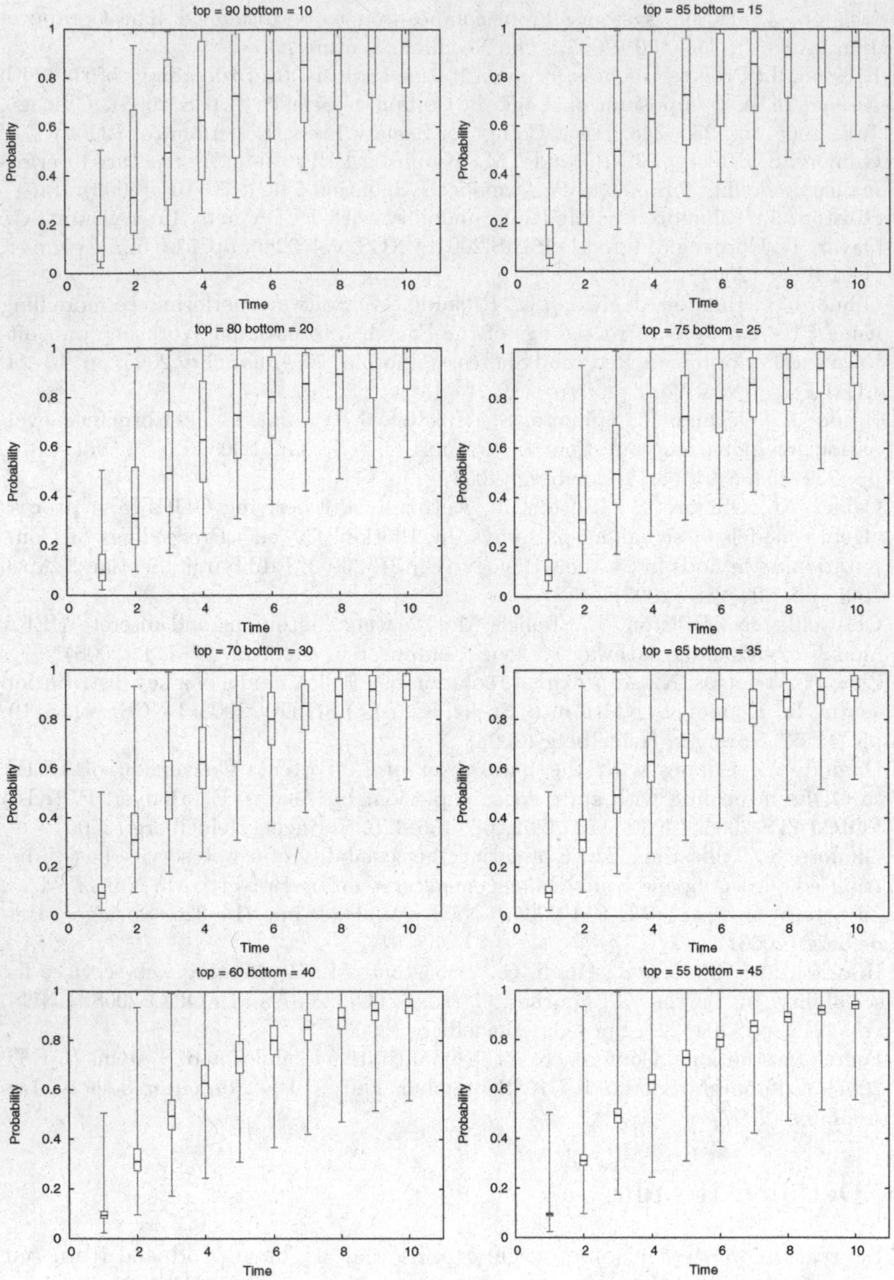

Fig. 19. Candlestick graphs showing the probability of completion ranging over all of the experiments performed automatically from the SRMC model

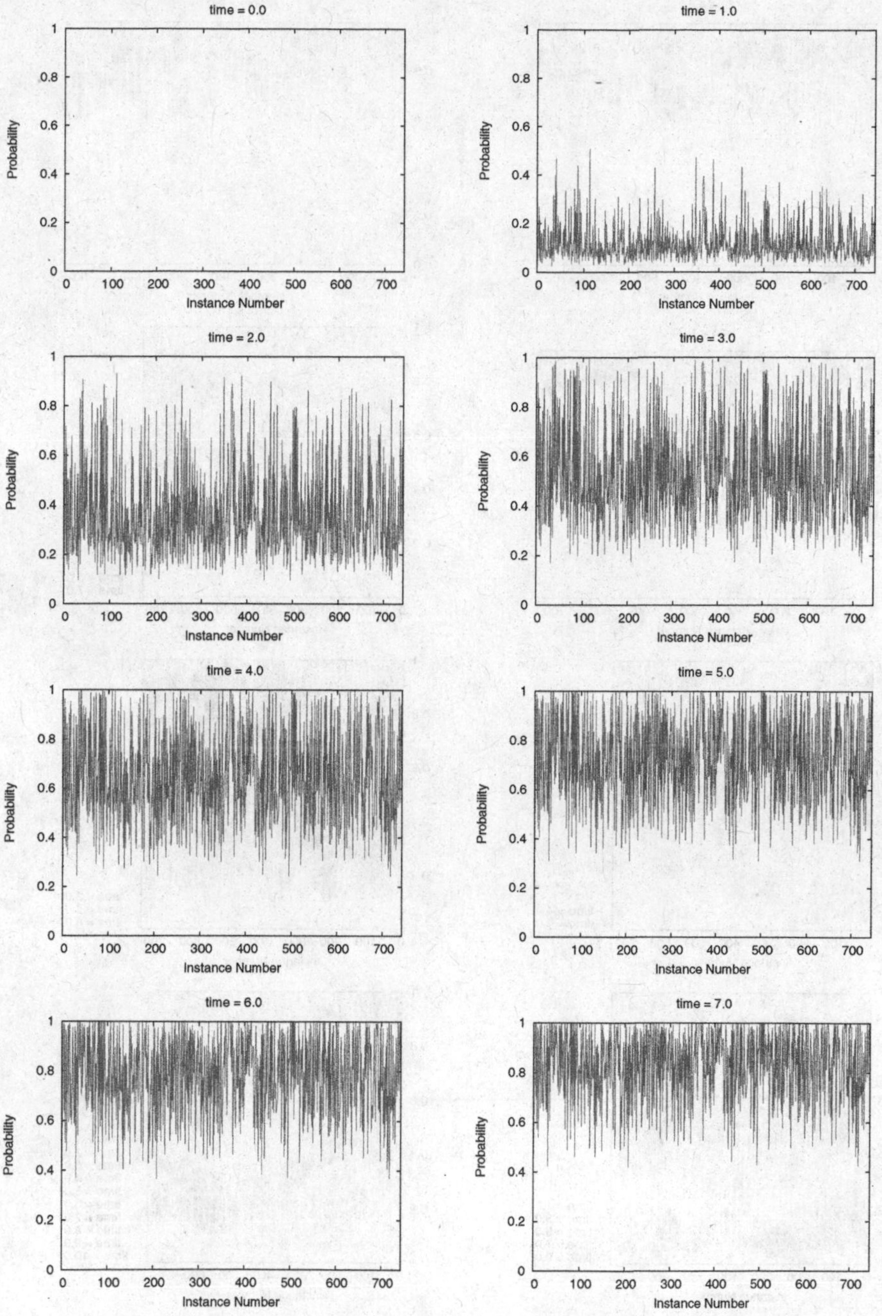

Fig. 20. Time graphs showing the probability of completion within the given times ranging over all of the experiments performed automatically from the SRMC model

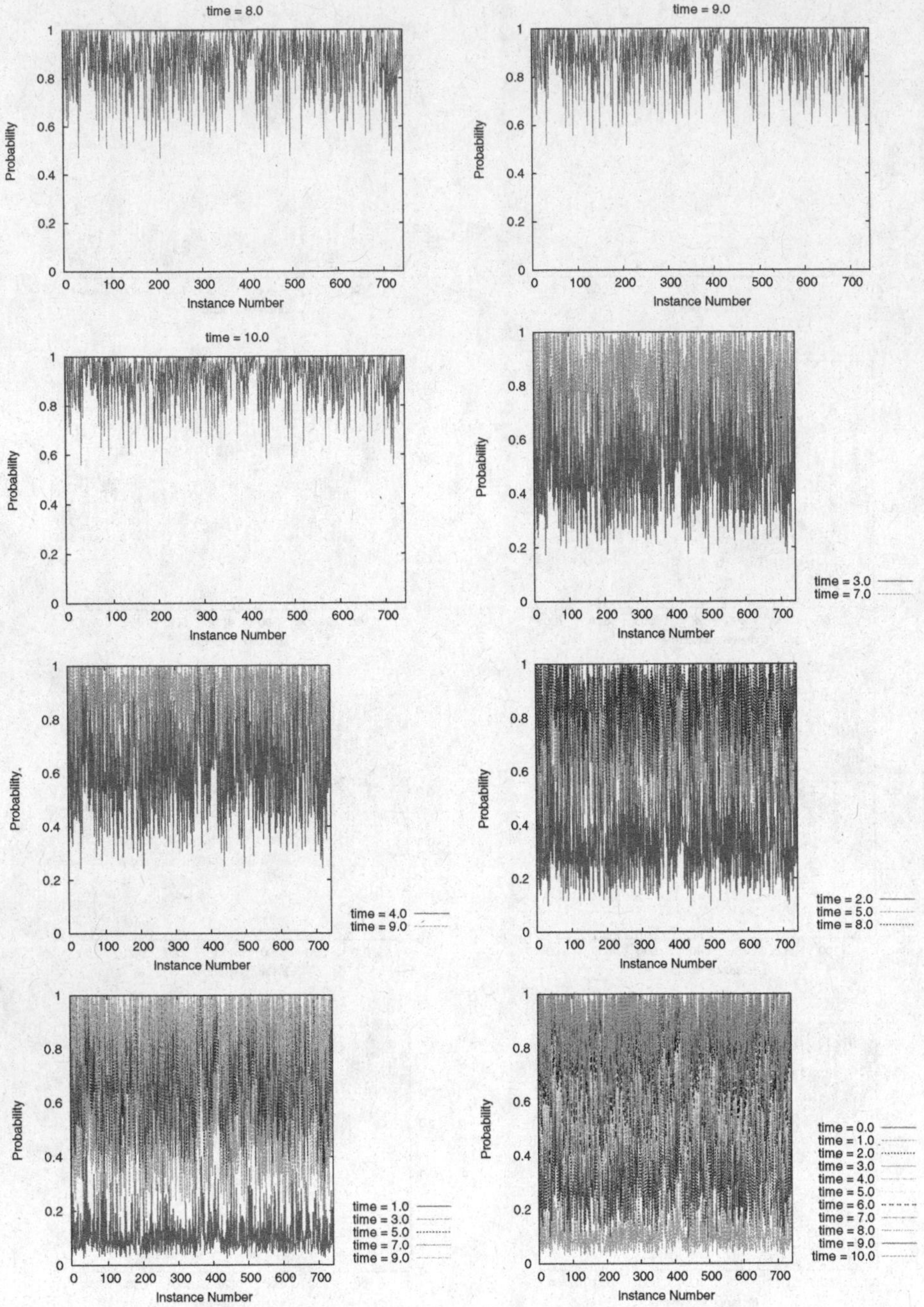

Fig. 21. Time graphs showing the probability of completion within the given times ranging over all of the experiments performed automatically from the SRMC model

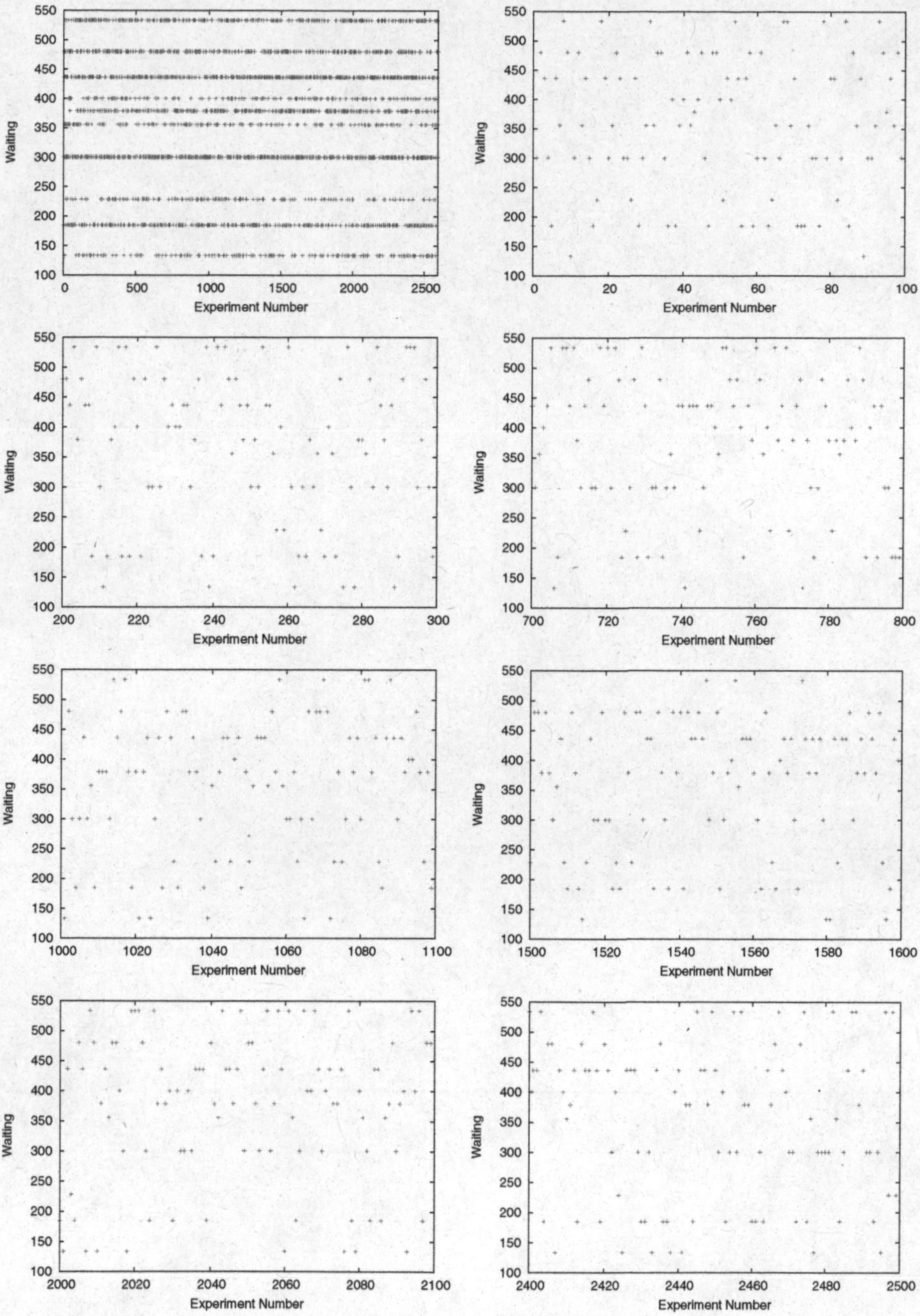

Fig. 22. Selected experiment number interval graphs for the SRMC model ODEs

Author Index